Linux: Powerful Server Administration

Recipes for CentOS 7, RHEL 7, and Ubuntu Server Administration

A course in three modules

BIRMINGHAM - MUMBAI

Linux: Powerful Server Administration

Published on: April 2017

Production reference: 1080517

Published by Packt Publishing Ltd.
Livery Place
35 Livery Street
Birmingham B3 2PB, UK.

ISBN 978-1-78829-377-8

www.packtpub.com

Credits

Authors

Uday R. Sawant

Oliver Pelz

Jonathan Hobson

William Leemans

Reviewers

Dominik Jakub Szynk

Mitja Resman

Kyung Huh

Marcus Young

Content Development Editor

Devika Battike

Graphics

Jason Monterio

Production Coordinator

Aparna Bhagat

Preface

Linux servers are frequently selected over other server operating systems for their stability, security and flexibility advantages. This Learning Path will teach you how to get up and running with three of the most popular Linux server distros: Ubuntu Server, CentOS 7 Server, and RHEL 7 Server.

Ubuntu is an open source operating system and is based on Debian, a well-established Linux distribution. Since Debian is kind of limited to geeks, Ubuntu added an easy user interface named Unity that made it popular with various desktop users. Ubuntu carefully selects the best things from Debian and adds its own flavors to make it easy and more enjoyable for the end users. In addition to desktop systems, Ubuntu provides separate editions for various server platforms, cloud systems, mobile devices and tablets. With its easy-to-use package management tools and availability of well-known packages, we can quickly set up our own services such as web servers and database servers using Ubuntu.

CentOS is a community-based enterprise class operating system. It is available free of charge, and as a fully compatible derivative of Red Hat Enterprise Linux (RHEL), it represents the first choice operating system for organizations, companies, professionals, and home users all over the world who intend to run a server. It's widely respected as a very powerful and flexible Linux distribution.

Dominating the server market, the Red Hat Enterprise Linux operating system gives you the support you need to modernize your infrastructure and boost your organization's efficiency. Combining both stability and flexibility, RHEL helps you meet the challenges of today and adapt to the demands of tomorrow.

This Learning Path begins with the Ubuntu Server and shows you how to make the most of Ubuntu's advanced functionalities. Moving on, we will provide you with all the knowledge that will give you access to the inner workings of the latest CentOS version 7. Finally, touching RHEL 7, we will provide you with solutions to common RHEL 7 Server challenges.

What this learning path covers

Module 1, Ubuntu Server Cookbook, will help you develop the skills required to set up high performance and secure services with open source tools. Starting from user management and an in-depth look at networking, we then move on to cover the installation and management of web servers and database servers, as well as load balancing various services. You will quickly learn to set up your own cloud and minimize costs and efforts with application containers. Next, you will get to grips with setting up a secure real-time communication system. Finally, we'll explore source code hosting and various collaboration tools. By the end of this module, you will be able to make the most of Ubuntu's advanced functionalities.

Module 2, CentOS 7 Linux Server Cookbook- Second Edition, will provide you with a comprehensive series of starting points that will give you direct access to the inner workings of the latest CentOS version 7 and help you trim the learning curve to master your server. You will begin with the installation and basic configuration of CentOS 7, followed by learning how to manage your system, services and software packages. You will then gain an understanding of how to administer the file system, secure access to your server and configure various resource sharing services such as file, printer and DHCP servers across your network. Further on, we cover advanced topics such as FTP services, building your own DNS server, running database servers, and providing mail and web services. Finally, you will get a deep understanding of SELinux and you will learn how to work with Docker operating-system virtualization and how to monitor your IT infrastructure with Nagios. By the end of this module, you will have a fair understanding of all the aspects of configuring, implementing and administering CentOS 7 Linux server and how to put it in control.

Module 3, Red Hat Enterprise Linux Server Cookbook , will help you get to grips with RHEL 7 Server and automating its installation. Designed to provide targeted assistance through hands-on recipe guidance, it will introduce you to everything you need to know about KVM guests and deploying multiple standardized RHEL systems effortlessly. Get practical reference advice that will make complex network setups look like child's play, and dive into in-depth coverage of configuring a RHEL system. Including full recipe coverage of how to set up, configure and troubleshoot SELinux, you'll also discover how to secure your operating system, as well as how to monitor it.

What you need for this learning path

The primary requirements are as follows:

- Ubuntu server 16.04
- A minimum hardware configuration of 512 MB memory with single CPU
- CentOS operating system
- Red Hat Enterprise Linux 7 Installation DVD

Who this learning path is for

This Learning Path is intended for system administrators with a basic understanding of Linux operating systems and written with the novice-to-intermediate Linux user in mind. To get the most of this Learning Path, you should have a working knowledge of basic system administration and management tools.

Reader feedback

Feedback from our readers is always welcome. Let us know what you think about this course—what you liked or disliked. Reader feedback is important for us as it helps us develop titles that you will really get the most out of.

To send us general feedback, simply e-mail feedback@packtpub.com, and mention the course's title in the subject of your message.

If there is a topic that you have expertise in and you are interested in either writing or contributing to a book, see our author guide at www.packtpub.com/authors.

Customer support

Now that you are the proud owner of a Packt course, we have a number of things to help you to get the most from your purchase.

Downloading the example code

You can download the example code files for this course from your account at http://www.packtpub.com. If you purchased this course elsewhere, you can visit http://www.packtpub.com/support and register to have the files e-mailed directly to you.

You can download the code files by following these steps:

1. Log in or register to our website using your e-mail address and password.
2. Hover the mouse pointer on the **SUPPORT** tab at the top.
3. Click on **Code Downloads & Errata**.
4. Enter the name of the course in the **Search** box.
5. Select the course for which you're looking to download the code files.
6. Choose from the drop-down menu where you purchased this course from.
7. Click on **Code Download**.

You can also download the code files by clicking on the **Code Files** button on the course's webpage at the Packt Publishing website. This page can be accessed by entering the course's name in the **Search** box. Please note that you need to be logged in to your Packt account.

Once the file is downloaded, please make sure that you unzip or extract the folder using the latest version of:

- WinRAR / 7-Zip for Windows
- Zipeg / iZip / UnRarX for Mac
- 7-Zip / PeaZip for Linux

The code bundle for the course is also hosted on GitHub at `https://github.com/PacktPublishing/Linux-Powerful-Server-Administration`. We also have other code bundles from our rich catalog of books, videos, and courses available at `https://github.com/PacktPublishing/`. Check them out!

Errata

Although we have taken every care to ensure the accuracy of our content, mistakes do happen. If you find a mistake in one of our courses — maybe a mistake in the text or the code — we would be grateful if you could report this to us. By doing so, you can save other readers from frustration and help us improve subsequent versions of this course. If you find any errata, please report them by visiting `http://www.packtpub.com/submit-errata`, selecting your course, clicking on the **Errata Submission Form** link, and entering the details of your errata. Once your errata are verified, your submission will be accepted and the errata will be uploaded to our website or added to any list of existing errata under the Errata section of that title.

To view the previously submitted errata, go to `https://www.packtpub.com/books/content/support` and enter the name of the course in the search field. The required information will appear under the **Errata** section.

Piracy

Piracy of copyrighted material on the Internet is an ongoing problem across all media. At Packt, we take the protection of our copyright and licenses very seriously. If you come across any illegal copies of our works in any form on the Internet, please provide us with the location address or website name immediately so that we can pursue a remedy.

Please contact us at copyright@packtpub.com with a link to the suspected pirated material.

We appreciate your help in protecting our authors and our ability to bring you valuable content.

Questions

If you have a problem with any aspect of this course, you can contact us at questions@packtpub.com, and we will do our best to address the problem.

Module 1: Ubuntu Server Cookbook

Chapter 1: Managing Users and Groups	**3**
Introduction	3
Creating a user account	4
Creating user accounts in batch mode	8
Creating a group	9
Adding group members	10
Deleting a user account	11
Managing file permissions	13
Getting root privileges with sudo	17
Setting resource limits with limits.conf	19
Setting up public key authentication	21
Securing user accounts	24
Chapter 2: Networking	**29**
Introduction	29
Connecting to a network with a static IP	30
Installing the DHCP server	34
Installing the DNS server	36
Hiding behind the proxy with squid	44
Being on time with NTP	47
Discussing load balancing with HAProxy	50
Tuning the TCP stack	53
Troubleshooting network connectivity	56
Securing remote access with OpenVPN	62
Securing a network with uncomplicated firewall	67
Securing against brute force attacks	71
Discussing Ubuntu security best practices	75

Chapter 3: Working with Web Servers   79

Introduction   79
Installing and configuring the Apache web server   81
Serving dynamic contents with PHP   86
Hosting multiple websites with a virtual domain   90
Securing web traffic with HTTPS   94
Installing Nginx with PHP_FPM   99
Setting Nginx as a reverse proxy   104
Load balancing with Nginx   108
Setting HTTPs on Nginx   112
Benchmarking and performance tuning of Apache   115
Securing the web server   117
Troubleshooting the web server   121

Chapter 4: Working with Mail Servers   125

Introduction   125
Sending e-mails with Postfix   125
Enabling IMAP and POP3 with Dovecot   129
Adding e-mail accounts   132
Mail filtering with spam-assassin   135
Troubleshooting the mail server   137
Installing the Zimbra mail server   140

Chapter 5: Handling Databases   145

Introduction   145
Installing relational databases with MySQL   146
Storing and retrieving data with MySQL   149
Importing and exporting bulk data   152
Adding users and assigning access rights   154
Installing web access for MySQL   156
Setting backups   160
Optimizing MySQL performance – queries   161
Optimizing MySQL performance – configuration   166
Creating MySQL replicas for scaling and high availability   169
Troubleshooting MySQL   173
Installing MongoDB   175
Storing and retrieving data with MongoDB   176

Chapter 6: Network Storage   181

Introduction   181
Installing the Samba server   182
Adding users to the Samba server   185

Installing the secure FTP server | 189
Synchronizing files with Rsync | 191
Performance tuning the Samba server | 195
Troubleshooting the Samba server | 197
Installing the Network File System | 201

Chapter 7: Cloud Computing | 205

Introduction | 205
Creating virtual machine with KVM | 206
Managing virtual machines with virsh | 210
Setting up your own cloud with OpenStack | 215
Adding a cloud image to OpenStack | 219
Launching a virtual instance with OpenStack | 224
Installing Juju a service orchestration framework | 228
Managing services with Juju | 232

Chapter 8: Working with Containers | 235

Introduction | 236
Installing LXD, the Linux container daemon | 237
Deploying your first container with LXD | 240
Managing LXD containers | 244
Managing LXD containers – advanced options | 247
Setting resource limits on LXD containers | 248
Networking with LXD | 252
Installing Docker | 256
Starting and managing Docker containers | 260
Creating images with a Dockerfile | 264
Understanding Docker volumes | 270
Deploying WordPress using a Docker network | 273
Monitoring Docker containers | 277
Securing Docker containers | 279

Chapter 9: Streaming with Ampache | 283

Introduction | 283
Installing the Ampache server | 283
Uploading contents and creating catalogs | 290
Setting on-the-fly transcoding | 292
Enabling API access for remote streaming | 294
Streaming music with Ampache | 296

Chapter 10: Communication Server with XMPP | 299

Introduction | 299
Installing Ejabberd | 300

Creating users and connecting with the XMPP client   303
Configuring the Ejabberd installation   310
Creating web client with Strophe.js   315
Enabling group chat   320
Chat server with Node.js   324

Chapter 11: Git Hosting   **329**
Introduction   329
Installing Git   330
Creating a local repository with Git CLI   333
Storing file revisions with Git commit   335
Synchronizing the repository with a remote server   339
Receiving updates with Git pull   343
Creating repository clones   346
Installing GitLab, your own Git hosting   348
Adding users to the GitLab server   350
Creating a repository with GitLab   352
Automating common tasks with Git hooks   354

Chapter 12: Collaboration Tools   **359**
Introduction   359
Installing the VNC server   360
Installing Hackpad, a collaborative document editor   365
Installing Mattermost – a self-hosted slack alternative   371
Installing OwnCloud, self-hosted cloud storage   377

Chapter 13: Performance Monitoring   **383**
Introduction   383
Monitoring the CPU   384
Monitoring memory and swap   390
Monitoring the network   396
Monitoring storage   402
Setting performance benchmarks   406

Chapter 14: Centralized Authentication Service   **413**
Introduction   413
Installing OpenLDAP   414
Installing phpLDAPadmin   418
Ubuntu server logins with LDAP   422
Authenticating Ejabberd users with LDAP   425

Module 2: CentOS 7 Linux Server Cookbook, Second Edition

Chapter 1: Installing CentOS   **431**

Introduction   431
Downloading CentOS and confirming the checksum on Windows or OS X   432
Creating USB installation media on Windows or OS X   434
Performing an installation of CentOS using the graphical installer   437
Running a netinstall over HTTP   439
Installing CentOS 7 using a kickstart file   441
Getting started and customising the boot loader   445
Troubleshooting the system in rescue mode   446
Updating the installation and enhancing   450
the minimal install with additional administration and development tools   450

Chapter 2: Configuring the System   **453**

Introduction   453
Navigating text files with less   454
Introduction to Vim   454
Speaking the right language   455
Synchronizing the system clock with NTP and the chrony suite   459
Setting your hostname and resolving the network   462
Building a static network connection   466
Becoming a superuser   468
Customizing your system banners and messages   471
Priming the kernel   473

Chapter 3: Managing the System   **477**

Introduction   477
Knowing and managing your background services   478
Troubleshooting background services   482
Tracking system resources with journald   484
Configuring journald to make it persistent   486
Managing users and their groups   487
Scheduling tasks with cron   489
Synchronizing files and doing more with rsync   492
Maintaining backups and taking snapshots   494
Monitoring important server infrastructure   496
Taking control with GIT and Subversion   497

Chapter 4: Managing Packages with YUM — 503

Introduction — 503
Using YUM to update the system — 503
Using YUM to search for packages — 505
Using YUM to install packages — 507
Using YUM to remove packages — 509
Keeping YUM clean and tidy — 510
Knowing your priorities — 512
Using a third-party repository — 515
Creating a YUM repository — 517
Working with the RPM package manager — 521

Chapter 5: Administering the Filesystem — 525

Introduction — 525
Creating a virtual block device — 526
Formatting and mounting a filesystem — 528
Using disk quotas — 532
Maintaining a filesystem — 537
Extending the capacity of the filesystem — 539

Chapter 6: Providing Security — 545

Introduction — 545
Locking down remote access and hardening SSH — 546
Installing and configuring fail2ban — 549
Working with a firewall — 551
Forging the firewall rules by example — 555
Generating self-signed certificates — 558
Using secure alternatives to FTP — 561

Chapter 7: Building a Network — 567

Introduction — 567
Printing with CUPS — 568
Running a DHCP server — 573
Using WebDAV for file sharing — 576
Installing and configuring NFS — 579
Working with NFS — 582
Securely sharing resources with Samba — 584

Chapter 8: Working with FTP — 589

Introduction — 589
Installing and configuring the FTP service — 589
Working with virtual FTP users — 593

Customizing the FTP service   596
Troubleshooting users and file transfers   598

Chapter 9: Working with Domains   601

Introduction   601
Installing and configuring a caching-only nameserver   602
Setting up an authoritative-only DNS server   606
Creating an integrated nameserver solution   615
Populating the domain   618
Building a secondary (slave) DNS server   620

Chapter 10: Working with Databases   625

Introduction   625
Installing a MariaDB database server   626
Managing a MariaDB database   628
Allowing remote access to a MariaDB server   632
Installing a PostgreSQL server and managing a database   633
Configuring remote access to PostgreSQL   637
Installing phpMyAdmin and phpPgAdmin   639

Chapter 11: Providing Mail Services   643

Introduction   643
Configuring a domain-wide mail service with Postfix   643
Working with Postfix   651
Delivering the mail with Dovecot   653
Using Fetchmail   659

Chapter 12: Providing Web Services   667

Introduction   667
Installing Apache and serving web pages   667
Enabling system users and building publishing directories   671
Implementing name-based hosting   674
Implementing CGI with Perl and Ruby   677
Installing, configuring, and testing PHP   681
Securing Apache   683
Setting up HTTPS with Secure Sockets Layer (SSL)   687

Chapter 13: Operating System-Level Virtualization   691

Introduction   691
Installing and configuring Docker   691
Downloading an image and running a container   693
Creating your own images from Dockerfiles and uploading to Docker Hub 697
Setting up and working with a private Docker registry   700

Chapter 14: Working with SELinux   **705**
  Introduction   705
  Installing and configuring important SELinux tools   705
  Working with SELinux security contexts   708
  Working with policies   711
  Troubleshooting SELinux   714

Chapter 15: Monitoring IT Infrastructure   **717**
  Introduction   717
  Installing and configuring Nagios Core   717
  Setting up NRPE on remote client hosts   719
  Monitoring important remote system metrics   721

Module 3: Red Hat Enterprise Linux Server Cookbook

Chapter 1: Working with KVM Guests   **729**
  Introduction   729
  Installing and configuring a KVM   730
  Configuring resources   735
  Building guests   741
  Adding CPUs on the fly   744
  Adding RAM on the fly   746
  Adding disks on the fly   747
  Moving disks to another storage   749
  Moving VMs   751
  Backing up your VM metadata   753

Chapter 2: Deploying RHEL "En Masse"   **755**
  Introduction   755
  Creating a kickstart file   755
  Publishing your kickstart file using httpd   766
  Deploying a system using PXE   768
  Deploying a system using a custom boot ISO file   771

Chapter 3: Configuring Your Network   **777**
  Introduction   777
  Creating a VLAN interface   778
  Creating a teamed interface   783
  Creating a bridge   790
  Configuring IPv4 settings   795
  Configuring your DNS resolvers   798
  Configuring static network routes   801

Chapter 4: Configuring Your New System — 805

Introduction — 805
The systemd service and setting runlevels — 806
Starting and stopping systemd services — 808
Configuring the systemd journal for persistence — 814
Monitoring services using journalctl — 815
Configuring logrotate — 818
Managing time — 822
Configuring your boot environment — 824
Configuring smtp — 827

Chapter 5: Using SELinux — 831

Introduction — 831
Changing file contexts — 832
Configuring SELinux booleans — 837
Configuring SELinux port definitions — 839
Troubleshooting SELinux — 840
Creating SELinux policies — 847
Applying SELinux policies — 850

Chapter 6: Orchestrating with Ansible — 853

Introduction — 853
Install Ansible — 854
Configuring the Ansible inventory — 857
Creating a template for a kickstart file — 861
Creating a playbook to deploy a new VM with kickstart — 864
Creating a playbook to perform system configuration tasks — 867
Troubleshooting Ansible — 875

Chapter 7: Puppet Configuration Management — 881

Introduction — 881
Installing and configuring Puppet Master — 882
Installing and configuring the Puppet agent — 886
Defining a simple module to configure time — 888
Defining nodes and node grouping — 891
Deploying modules to single nodes and node groups — 892

Chapter 8: Yum and Repositories — 895

Introduction — 895
Managing yum history — 896
Creating a copy of an RHN repository — 902
Configuring additional repositories — 905
Setting up yum to automatically update — 907

Configuring logrotate for yum	**909**
Recovering from a corrupted RPM database	**910**
Chapter 9: Securing RHEL 7	**913**
Introduction	**913**
Installing and configuring IPA	**914**
Securing the system login	**917**
Configuring privilege escalation with sudo	**919**
Secure the network with firewalld	**921**
Using kdump and SysRq	**923**
Using ABRT	**929**
Auditing the system	**931**
Chapter 10: Monitoring and Performance Tuning	**935**
Introduction	**935**
Tuning your system's performance	**936**
Setting up PCP – Performance Co-Pilot	**937**
Monitoring basic system performance	**939**
Monitoring CPU performance	**943**
Monitoring RAM performance	**945**
Monitoring storage performance	**947**
Monitoring network performance	**949**
Bibliography	**953**
Index	**955**

Module 1

Ubuntu Server Cookbook

Arm yourself to make the most of the versatile, powerful Ubuntu Server with over 100 hands-on recipes

1
Managing Users and Groups

In this chapter, we will cover the following recipes:

- ▶ Creating a user account
- ▶ Creating user accounts in batch mode
- ▶ Creating a group
- ▶ Adding group members
- ▶ Deleting a user account
- ▶ Managing file permissions
- ▶ Getting root privileges with sudo
- ▶ Setting resource limits with limits.conf
- ▶ Setting up public key authentication
- ▶ Securing user accounts

Introduction

In this chapter, you will see how to add new users to the Ubuntu server, update existing users, and set permissions for users. You will get to know the default setting for new users and how to change them. Also, you will take a look at secure shell (SSH) access and securing user profiles.

Creating a user account

While installing Ubuntu, we add a primary user account on the server; if you are using the cloud image, it comes preinstalled with the default user. This single user is enough to get all tasks done in Ubuntu. There are times when you need to create more restrictive user accounts. This recipe shows how to add a new user to the Ubuntu server.

Getting ready

You will need super user or root privileges to add a new user to the Ubuntu server.

How to do it...

Follow these steps to create the new user account:

1. To add a new user in Ubuntu, enter following command in your shell:

   ```
   $ sudo adduser bob
   ```

2. Enter your password to complete the command with `sudo` privileges:

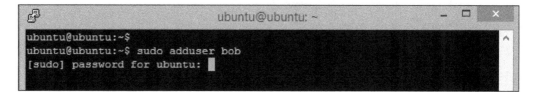

3. Now enter a password for the new user:

```
ubuntu@ubuntu:~$
ubuntu@ubuntu:~$ sudo adduser bob
[sudo] password for ubuntu:
Adding user `bob' ...
Adding new group `bob' (1009) ...
Adding new user `bob' (1006) with group `bob' ...
Creating home directory `/home/bob' ...
Copying files from `/etc/skel' ...
Enter new UNIX password:
```

4. Confirm the password for the new user:

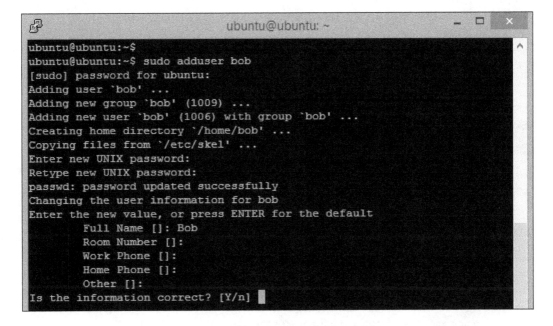

5. Enter the full name and other information about the new user; you can skip this part by pressing the *Enter* key.

6. Enter Y to confirm that information is correct:

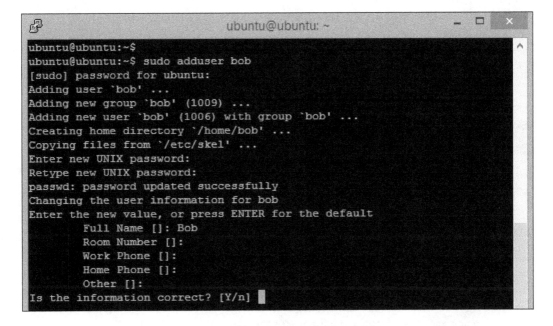

7. This should have added new user to the system. You can confirm this by viewing the file /etc/passwd:

```
ubuntu@ubuntu:~$ tail -n 2 /etc/passwd
user2:x:1005:1007:user2,,,:/home/user2:/bin/bash
bob:x:1006:1009:Bob,,,:/home/bob:/bin/bash
ubuntu@ubuntu:~$
```

How it works...

In Linux systems, the adduser command is higher level command to quickly add a new user to the system. Since adduser requires root privileges, we need to use sudo along with the command, adduser completes following operations:

1. Adds a new user.
2. Adds a new default group with the same name as the user.
3. Chooses **UID** (**user ID**) and **GID** (**group ID**) conforming to the Debian policy.
4. Creates a home directory with skeletal configuration (template) from /etc/skel.
5. Creates a password for the new user.
6. Runs the user script, if any.

If you want to skip the password prompt and finger information while adding the new user, use the following command:

$ **sudo adduser --disabled-password --gecos "" username**

Alternatively, you can use the useradd command as follows:

$ **sudo useradd -s <SHELL> -m -d <HomeDir> -g <Group> UserName**

Where:

▶ -s specifies default login shell for the user
▶ -d sets the home directory for the user
▶ -m creates a home directory if one does not already exist
▶ -g specifies the default group name for the user

Creating a user with the command useradd does not set password for the user account. You can set or change the user password with the following command:

$ **sudo passwd bob**

This will change the password for the user account `bob`.

 Note that if you skip the username part from the above command you will end up changing the password of the root account.

There's more...

With `adduser`, you can do five different tasks:

- Add a normal user
- Add a system user with system option
- Add user group with the `--group` option and without the `--system` option
- Add a system group when called with the `--system` option
- Add an existing user to existing group when called with two non-option arguments

Check out the manual page `man adduser` to get more details.

You can also configure various default settings for the `adduser` command. A configuration file `/etc/adduser.conf` can be used to set the default values to be used by the `adduser`, `addgroup`, and `deluser` commands. A key value pair of configuration can set various default values, including the `home` directory location, directory structure `skel` to be used, default groups for new users, and so on. Check the manual page for more details on `adduser.conf` with following command:

```
$ man adduser.conf
```

See also

- Check out the command `useradd`, a low level command to add new user to system
- Check out the command `usermod`, a command to modify a user account
- See why every user has his own group at `http://unix.stackexchange.com/questions/153390/why-does-every-user-have-his-own-group`

Creating user accounts in batch mode

In this recipe, you will see how to create multiple user accounts in batch mode without using any external tool.

Getting ready

You will need a user account with root or root privileges.

How to do it...

Follow these steps to create a user account in batch mode:

1. Create a new text file `users.txt` with the following command:

    ```
    $ touch users.txt
    ```

2. Change file permissions with the following command:

    ```
    $ chmod 600 users.txt
    ```

3. Open `users.txt` with **GNU nano** and add user account details:

    ```
    $ nano users.txt
    ```

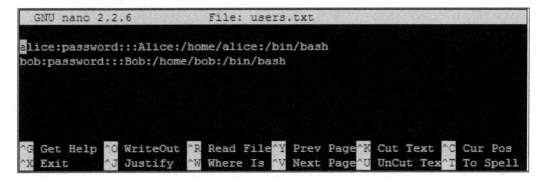

4. Press *Ctrl + O* to save the changes.
5. Press *Ctrl + X* to exit **GNU nano**.
6. Enter `$ sudo newusers users.txt` to import all users listed in `users.txt` file.
7. Check `/etc/passwd` to confirm that users are created:

```
ubuntu@ubuntu:~$ tail -n 4 /etc/passwd
user1:x:1004:1006:user1,,,:/home/user1:/bin/bash
user2:x:1005:1007:user2,,,:/home/user2:/bin/bash
alice:x:1006:1009:Alice:/home/alice:/bin/bash
bob:x:1007:1010:Bob:/home/bob:/bin/bash
ubuntu@ubuntu:~$ 
```

How it works...

We created a database of user details listed in same format as the `passwd` file. The default format for each row is as follows:

```
username:passwd:uid:gid:full name:home_dir:shell
```

Where:

- ► `username`: This is the login name of the user. If a user exists, information for user will be changed; otherwise, a new user will be created.
- ► `password`: This is the password of the user.
- ► `uid`: This is the `uid` of the user. If empty, a new `uid` will be assigned to this user.
- ► `gid`: This is the `gid` for the default group of user. If empty, a new group will be created with the same name as the username.
- ► `full name`: This information will be copied to the `gecos` field.
- ► `home_dir`: This defines the `home` directory of the user. If empty, a new `home` directory will be created with ownership set to new or existing user.
- ► `shell`: This is the default login `shell` for the user.

The new user command reads each row and updates the user information if the user already exists, or it creates a new user.

We made the `users.txt` file accessible to owner only. This is to protect this file, as it contains the user's login name and password in unencrypted format.

Creating a group

Group is a way to organize and administer user accounts in Linux. Groups are used to collectively assign rights and permissions to multiple user accounts.

Getting ready

You will need super user or root privileges to add a group to the Ubuntu server.

How to do it...

Follow these steps to create a group:

1. Enter the following command to add a new group:

    ```
    $ sudo addgroup guest
    ```

2. Enter your password to complete `addgroup` with root privileges.

How it works...

Here, we are simply adding a new group `guest` to the server. As `addgroup` needs root privileges, we need to use `sudo` along with the command. After creating a new group, `addgroup` displays the GID of the new group.

There's more...

Similar to `adduser`, you can use `addgroup` in different modes:

▶ Add a normal group when used without any options

▶ Add a system group with the `--system` option

▶ Add an existing user to an existing group when called with two non-option arguments

Check out the manual page for the `addgroup(man addgroup)` to get more details.

See also

▶ Check out `groupadd`, a low level utility to add new group to the server

Adding group members

Once you have groups in place, you can add existing users as well as new users to that group. All access rights and permissions assigned to the group will be automatically available to all the members of the group.

Getting ready

You will need super user or root privileges to add a group member to the Ubuntu server.

How to do it...

Follow these steps to add group members:

1. Here, you can use `adduser` command with two non-option arguments:

   ```
   $ sudo adduser john guest
   ```

2. Enter your password to complete `addgroup` with root privileges.

How it works...

As mentioned previously, you can use the `adduser` command to add an existing user to an existing group. Here, we have passed two non-option arguments:

- `john`: This is the name of the user to be added to the group
- `guest`: This is the name of the group

There's more...

Alternatively, you can use the command `usermod` to modify the group assigned to the user:

```
$ sudo usermod -g <group> <username>
```

To add a user to multiple groups, use the following command:

```
$ sudo usermod -a -G <group1>,<group2>,<group3> <username>
```

This will add `<username>` to `<group1>`, `<group2>`, and `<group3>`. Without `flag -a`, any previously assigned groups will be replaced with new groups.

Deleting a user account

If you no longer need a user account, it is good idea to delete that account.

Getting ready

You will need super user or root privileges to delete a group from the Ubuntu server.

How to do it...

Follow these steps to delete the user account:

1. Enter the following command to delete a user account:

    ```
    $ sudo deluser --remove-home john
    ```

2. Enter your password to complete addgroup with root privileges:

```
ubuntu@ubuntu:~$ sudo deluser --remove-home bob
[sudo] password for ubuntu:
Looking for files to backup/remove ...
Removing files ...
Removing user `bob' ...
Warning: group `bob' has no more members.
Done.
ubuntu@ubuntu:~$
```

How it works...

Here, we used the deluser command with the option --remove-home. This will delete the user account named john and also remove the home and mail spool directories associated with john. By default, the deluser command will delete the user without deleting the home directory.

It is a good idea to keep a backup of user files before removing the home directory and any other files. This can be done with an additional flag along with the deluser command:

```
$ deluser --backup --remove-home john
```

This will create a backup file with the name john.tar.gz in the current working directory, and then the user account and the home directory will removed.

There's more...

When called with the --group option, the deluser command will remove the group. Similarly, when called with two non-option arguments, the deluser command will try to remove a user from a specific group:

```
$ deluser john guest # this will remove user john from group guest
$ deluser --group guest # this will remove a group
```

If you want to disable the user account rather than delete it, you can do it with the following commands:

```
$ sudo usermod --expiredate 1 john # disable the user account john
$ sudo usermod --expiredate "" john # re-enable user account john
$ sudo usermod -e YYYY-MM-DD john # specify expiry date
```

See also

▶ Refer to the manual page for `deluser` with `man deluser`

Managing file permissions

We have created users and groups. In this recipe, you will work with default file permissions for users and groups, as well as see how to modify those permissions.

Getting ready

Create two users, `user1` and `user2`. Create new group `editor` and add `user1` and `user2` as members.

How to do it...

Follow these steps to manage file permissions, follow these steps:

1. To change groups for files and directories:

    1. Log in with `user1`.

    2. Create a new directory `documents` under `home`:
       ```
       user1@ubuntu:~$ mkdir documents
       ```

    3. Create a text file under `documents`:
       ```
       user1@ubuntu:~$ echo "hello world"> documents/file.txt
       ```

    4. Now log in with `user2`:
       ```
       user1@ubuntu:~$ su user2
       ```

5. Try to edit the same text file. It should say `Permission denied`:

   user2@ubuntu:/home/user1$ echo "hello again"> documents/file.txt

```
user2@ubuntu:/home/user1$
user2@ubuntu:/home/user1$ echo "hello again" > documents/file.txt
bash: documents/file.txt: Permission denied
user2@ubuntu:/home/user1$ █
```

6. log in as `user1` and change the group of `documents` to `editor`:

   user1@ubuntu:~$ chgrp -R editor documents

```
user1@ubuntu:~$ chgrp -R editor documents/
user1@ubuntu:~$ ls -l
total 4
drwxrwxr-x 2 user1 editor 4096 Jun 26 15:36 documents
user1@ubuntu:~$ █
```

7. Switch to `user2` and try editing the same file. Now it should work:

```
user1@ubuntu:~$ su user2
Password:
user2@ubuntu:/home/user1$ echo "hello again" > documents/file.txt
user2@ubuntu:/home/user1$ █
```

2. To set permissions with `chmod`, follow these steps:

   1. Create simple shell script with the following command:

      $ echo 'echo "Hello World!!"'> hello.sh

   2. Execute a shell script with the following command:

      $ ./hello.sh

```
user1@ubuntu:~$ echo 'echo "hello world!!!"' > hello.sh
user1@ubuntu:~$ ls -l
total 8
drwxrwxr-x 2 user1 editor 4096 Jun 26 15:36 documents
-rw-rw-r-- 1 user1 user1    22 Jun 26 15:59 hello.sh
user1@ubuntu:~$ ./hello.sh
bash: ./hello.sh: Permission denied
```

   3. Set executable permission to `hello.sh` with the following command:

      $ chmod u+x hello.sh

4. Check new permission with the following command:

   `$ ls -l`

```
user1@ubuntu:~$ chmod u+x hello.sh
user1@ubuntu:~$ ls -l
total 8
drwxrwxr-x 2 user1 editor 4096 Jun 26 15:36 documents
-rwxrw-r-- 1 user1 user1    23 Jun 26 15:54 hello.sh
user1@ubuntu:~$
```

5. Execute `hello.sh` again:

```
user1@ubuntu:~$ ./hello.sh
hello world!!!
user1@ubuntu:~$
```

3. To protect shared files with sticky bit, follow these steps:

   1. Log in as `user1` and set sticky bit for directory `documents`:

      user1@ubuntu:~$ chmod +t documents

   2. Log in as `user2` and create a new file.

   3. Try to delete any file under `documents`. It should fail:

```
user1@ubuntu:~$ chmod +t documents/
user1@ubuntu:~$ ls -l
total 4
drwxrwxr-t 2 user1 editor 4096 Jun 26 15:36 documents
user1@ubuntu:~$ su user2
Password:
user2@ubuntu:/home/user1$ rm documents/file.txt
rm: cannot remove 'documents/file.txt': Operation not permitted
user2@ubuntu:/home/user1$
```

How it works...

When you create a new file or directory in Ubuntu, the default permissions for files are read and write access to owner and owner's private group, along with read, write, and execute access for directories. You can check the default setting with `umask -S`.

In our example, we have `user1` and `user2`. Both of them are members of the `editor` group. When `user1` creates a file, the default permissions are limited to `user1` and its private group (`user1`) named after the user account. This is the reason `user2` sees `Permission denied` on editing file. By changing the group of `documents` to `editor` we allow all members of `editor` to read and write to files in `documents`.

With the `chmod` command, we can set permissions at a more granular level. In our example of `hello.sh`, we have set the executable permission for `hello.sh`. Similarly, we can set read permission as follows:

```
$chmod +r filename
```

To set write permission, use the following command:

```
$chmod +w filename
```

You can set more selective permissions with additional parameters before mode expression as follows:

```
$chmod ugo+x filename
```

Here, u sets the permission for user, g for group, and o for all others.

To remove permissions, replace + with -. For example, `$chmod o-w filename`. Alternatively, you can use the Octal format to specify permissions:

```
$chmod 777 filename
```

This gives read, write, and execute permission to user group and others, whereas the command `$chmod 600 filename` gives set, read, and write permissions for owner and no permission to groups and others. In Octal format [777], the first bit is used for the user or owner of the file, the second bit is for group, and the third bit is for everyone else. Check out the following table for more information:

Notation	Octal value	Permissions
-|---|---|---	0|000|000|000	Regular files, no permissions
d|r--|r--|r--	d|400|400|400	Directory, read permission to owner, group, and others
-|rw-|r--|r--	-|644|644|644	Regular file, read and write permission to owner and read permission to group or others
-|rwx|rwx|rwx	-|777|777|777	Regular file, all permissions to everyone

Finally, when you share files within a group of users, there are chances that someone deletes the file that is required by other users. Sticky bit can protect these file from deletion. When sticky bit is set, only the owner or a user with root privileges can delete a file.

You can set sticky bit with the command `chmod` as `$chmod +t directoryName`. Sticky bit is shown in long listing (`ls -l`) with symbol t or T. Additionally, sticky bit works only with directories and is ignored on ordinary files.

There's more...

Many times when working as a root user, all files and directories created are owned by root. A non-root user can't write to these directories or files. You can use the command `chown` to change the ownership of such files and assign them to respective users.

To change ownership of a file, use the following command:

```
$chown newuser filename
```

To change the owner as well as the group of file, use the following command:

```
$chown newuser:newgroup filename
```

You can skip changing owner and change only the group with the following command:

```
$chown :newgroup filename
```

Note that the `chown` command can only be used by users with root privileges.

Getting root privileges with sudo

When you create a new Ubuntu server in the cloud, by default you get the root account. This account has full system access with no restrictions at all and should only be used for administrative tasks. You can always create a new user account with fewer privileges. But there are times when you need extra root privileges to add a new user or change some system setting. You can use the `sudo` command to temporarily get extra privileges for a single command. In this recipe, you will see how to grant `sudo` privileges to a newly created user.

Getting ready

You will need a root account or an account with root privileges.

How to do it...

Follow these steps to get the root privileges with `sudo`:

1. Add new user if required:

    ```
    $sudo adduser john
    ```

2. Make `john` a member of `sudo` group with the following command:

    ```
    $sudo adduser username sudo
    ```

How it works...

All `sudo` access rules are configured in a file located at `/etc/sudoers`. This file contains a list of users and groups that are allowed to use the `sudo` command:

```
alan ALL=(ALL:ALL)ALL // allow sudo access to user alan
%sudo  ALL=(ALL)  ALL // allow sudo access to members of sudo
```

The line `alan  ALL=(ALL:ALL)  ALL` specifies that the user `alan` can run any command as any user and optionally set any group (taken from `man` pages for sudoers: `man sudoers`).

The entry `%sudo ALL=(ALL)  ALL` specifies that any member of system group `sudo` can run any command as any user.

All we have to do is add a new user to the group `sudo` and that user will automatically get `sudo` privileges. After getting the membership of the `sudo` group, user needs to log out and log back in for the changes to take effect. Basically, the user shell needs to be restarted with new privileges. Optionally, you can always go and change the `sudoers` file for a specific condition.

> Make sure that you use the `visudo` tool to make any changes to sudoers file.

There's more...

Here, we will discuss how to set a password-less `sudo` and some additional benefits of `sudo`.

Setting password less sudo

`sudo` is a useful and handy tool for temporary root privileges, but you need to enter your password every time. This creates problems especially for users with no password set. This problem can be solved by setting the `NOPASSWD` flag in the `sudoers` file. Make sure you use the `visudo` tool to edit the `sudoers` file:

1. Open the `sudoers` file with the `visudo` command:

    `$sudo visudo`

2. Select the line for user or group you want to allow password-less `sudo` access.

3. Add `NOPASSWD` after closing the bracket:

    `%sudo    ALL=(ALL:ALL) NOPASSWD: ALL`

4. Press *Ctrl* + *O* and then confirm with the *Enter* key to save the changes.

5. Press *Ctrl* + *X* to exit `visudo`.

Now, the users of the group `sudo` should be able to use the `sudo` command without providing a password. Alternatively, you can add a separate entry to limit password-less access to a specific user.

Note that the `sudoers` program performs cache authentication for a small time (default is 15 minutes). When repeated within timeout, you may notice password-less `sudo` without setting the `NOPASSWD` flag.

Other uses of sudo

In addition to running a single command with `sudo`, you might want to execute a list of commands with the `sudo` privileges. Then, you can open a shell with root access (`# prompt`) with the command `$sudo -s`. The shell environment remains same as original user, but now you can execute commands as a root user.

Alternatively, you can switch user to root with the command `$sudo su -`. This command will open a new shell as a root user.

See also

- ▸ Check manual pages for `sudo` with `$man sudo`
- ▸ For more details on `adduser`, check the *Creating user account* recipe

Setting resource limits with limits.conf

Ubuntu is a multiuser and multi-process operating system. If a single user or process is consuming too many resources, other processes might not be able to use the system. In this recipe, you will see how to set resource limits to avoid such problems.

Getting ready

User account with root privileges is required.

How to do it...

Following are the steps to set the resource limits:

1. Check the CPU use limit with `$ulimit -t`.
2. To set new limit, open `limits.conf` with the following command:

   ```
   $sudo nano /etc/security/limits.conf
   ```

3. Scroll to the end of the file and add following lines:

```
username  soft  cpu  0    # max cpu time in minutes
username  hard  cpu  1000 # max cpu time in minutes
```

4. Enter *Ctrl + O* to save the changes.

5. Enter *Ctrl + X* to exit **GNU nano** editor.

How it works...

PAM stands for pluggable authentication module. The PAM module `pam_limits.so` provides functionality to set a cap on resource utilization. The command `ulimit` can be used to view current limits as well as set new limits for a session. The default values used by `pam_limits.so` can be set in `/etc/security/limits.conf`.

In this recipe, we are updating `limits.conf` to set a limit on CPU uses by user `username`. Limits set by the `ulimit` command are limited to that session. To set the limits permanently, we need to set them in the `limits.conf` file.

The syntax of the `limits.conf` file is as follows:

```
<domain> <type> <item> <value>
```

Here, `<domain>` can be a username, a group name, or a wildcard entry.

`<type>` denotes the type of the limit and it can have the following values:

- ▸ `soft`: This is a soft limit which can be changed by user
- ▸ `hard`: This is a cap on soft limit set by super user and enforced by kernel

`<item>` is the resource to set the limit for. You can get a list of all items with `$ulimit -a`:

```
user2@ubuntu:/home/user1$ ulimit -a
core file size          (blocks, -c) 0
data seg size           (kbytes, -d) unlimited
scheduling priority             (-e) 0
file size               (blocks, -f) unlimited
pending signals                 (-i) 3887
max locked memory       (kbytes, -l) 64
max memory size         (kbytes, -m) unlimited
open files                      (-n) 1024
pipe size            (512 bytes, -p) 8
POSIX message queues     (bytes, -q) 819200
real-time priority              (-r) 0
stack size              (kbytes, -s) 8192
cpu time               (seconds, -t) unlimited
max user processes              (-u) 3887
virtual memory          (kbytes, -v) unlimited
file locks                      (-x) unlimited
```

In our example, we have set `soft` limit on CPU uses to `0` minutes and `hard` limit to `1000` minutes. You can changes soft limit values with the `ulimit` command. To view existing limits on open files, use the command `$ulimit -n`. To change limits on open files, pass the new limit as follows:

```
$ulimit -n 4096
```

An unprivileged process can only set its `soft` limit value between `0` and `hard` limit, and it can irreversibly lower `hard` limit. A privileged process can change either limit values.

There's more...

The command `ulimit` can be used to set limits on per process basis. You can't use the `ulimit` command to limit resources at the user level. You can use `cgroups` to set a cap on resource use.

Setting up public key authentication

In this recipe, you will see how to set up secure public key authentication.

Getting ready

You might need root privileges for certain tasks.

How to do it...

Follow these steps to set up public key authentication:

1. Add a new user. You can skip this step if you have already created a user:
   ```
   $sudo adduser john
   ```

2. Log in as `john` and change to the home directory with `cd ~/`:

3. Create a `.ssh` directory if it doesn't already exist:
   ```
   $ mkdir .ssh
   ```

4. Create a file named `authorized_keys` under the `.ssh` directory:
   ```
   $ touch .ssh/authorized_keys
   ```

5. Set permissions on the `.ssh` directory to `700`:
   ```
   $chmod 700 .ssh
   ```

6. Set permissions for `authorized_keys` to `600`:

   `$ chmod 600 .ssh/authorized_keys`

7. Generate public key pair on your local system with the following command:

   `$ ssh-keygen`

8. Copy the generated public key from the `.ssh/id_rsa.pub` file to the `authorized_keys` file on the server.

9. Now, open an `ssh` connection from local to server with the following command:

   `$ ssh john@server`

10. If asked for confirmation, type `yes` and press the *Enter* key to continue:

```
user1@ubuntu:~$ ssh localhost
The authenticity of host 'localhost (::1)' can't be established.
ECDSA key fingerprint is c7:1c:46:a4:1a:9f:4a:3b:81:df:a8:3c:ef:89:a1:59.
Are you sure you want to continue connecting (yes/no)?
```

How it works...

Logging in with SSH supports different authentication methods. Public key authentication and password-based authentication are two common methods. To log in with public key authentication, we need a public private key pair. We generate this key pair with the `ssh-keygen` command. This command creates two files under the `.ssh` directory in the user's home:

▶ `id_rsa`: This is the private key file

▶ `id_rsa.pub`: This is the public key file

You can view the contents of the files with `$cat id_rsa.pub`. It should start with something like `ssh-rsa AAAA...` (except for the trailing dots).

```
ubuntu@ubuntu:~$ cat .ssh/id_rsa.pub
ssh-rsa AAAAB3NzaC1yc2EAAAADAQABAAABAQDJEA0wVaTOmhE+PTjE0N1YAs3QG0UdyKdT8vNwMhVT
3fAHYwq5ka3Lo5dS9tHcio6kWINrbyjD3cBoAnCwcvGOY3YDB1Lf4IAm3Re10g/MvJECcd99WuAvNCk0
knnqJ/LVJk6W7YSOHAV1X+Q8HaVbLijWYBjNnZNdSYAFM4Hh91PMCn4FpuqfLW+EzXO3xDoiGdqcHGuc
stuSkpaej+ZDteVX4s4hMr/XlDf38y7rDzdy9EzI2iDA9AMohxWEKM2rpcLhP3YAuNi4m+Ueef+wzlCx
YJMfOsQuP1B95/1931Ne/UnOESHINqlHadmaPbreVGF9JSJv4Fj0btUBPEAH ubuntu@ubuntu
```

We then copy the contents of public key to the server's `authorized_keys` file. Ensure that all contents are listed on single line in the `authorized_keys` file.

Also, ensure the permissions are properly set for the `.ssh` directory, and ensure that the `authorized_keys` file and directory are owned by the user. The permissions for the `.ssh` directory limits read, write, and execute permissions to the owner of the file. Similarly, for `authorized_keys` file, permissions are limited to read and write for owner only. This ensures that no other user can modify the data in the `.ssh` directory. If these permissions are not properly set, the SSH daemon will raise the warning `Permission denied?`.

Working of SSH authentication

When the SSH client initiates a connection with the server, the server sends public key identification of server to client. If a client is connecting to the server for the first time, it shows a warning and asks for user confirmation to store the server key in the `known_hosts` file under the `.shh` directory. After receiving the identity, the client authenticates server to ensure that it is really the intended server.

After server authentication, the server sends a list of possible authentication methods. The client selects the authentication method and selection to the server. After receiving the authentication method, the server sends a challenge string encrypted with client's private key. The client has to decrypt this string and send it back to server along with previously shared session key. If the response from the client matches the response generated by the server, then client authentication succeeds.

There's more...

You might be searching for a secure option to install key on server. Here's one way!

If your local system has the `ssh-copy-id` tool installed, you can directly add your public key to the server's `authorized_keys` file with a single command:

```
$ ssh-copy-id john@serverdomain
```

After providing the password, your local public key will be added to the `authorized_keys` file under the `.ssh` directory of the user `john`.

Troubleshooting SSH connections

Most of the connection issues are related with configuration problems. If you happen to face any such issue, read the error message in detail. It is descriptive enough to understand the mistake. You can also go through following checklist:

- ▸ Check if the SSH daemon is running. Check the port in use and port conflicts, if any
- ▸ Check whether the firewall configuration allows SSH ports
- ▸ Check the list of configuration methods that are enabled

- ▶ Check permissions for your private keys on your local system
- ▶ Check `authorized_keys` file for your public key on the server
- ▶ Check for any entry with the old address of the server in `known_hosts` on the local system

Additionally, you can use the verbose flag (`-v` or `-vvv`) with the `ssh` command to get details of every step taken by the SSH client. Also, check SSH daemon logs on server.

SSH tools for the Windows platform

If your local system runs Windows, then you can use tools provided by puTTYto generate new keys and connect to the server:

- ▶ `putty.exe`: This is the SSH client on Windows
- ▶ `puttygen.exe`: This tool generates public or private keys
- ▶ `pscp.exe`: This is the SCP client for secure file transfer

When using public key generated by the `puttygen.exe` tool, make sure that you convert the key to OpenSSH key format. Remove all comments and prepend `ssh-rsa`. Additionally, the entire key should be listed on a single line.

Another easy option is to use `puttygen.exe`. Load your private key in PuTTYgen and then copy the public key from the **Key** section of the PuTTYgen window.

See also

- ▶ For more information on the full working of SSH authentication, visit `http://www.slashroot.in/secure-shell-how-does-ssh-work`

Securing user accounts

In this recipe, we will look at ways to make user profiles more secure.

How to do it...

Follow these steps to secure the user account:

1. Set a strong password policy with the following steps:
   - ❑ Open the `/etc/pam.d/common-password` file with **GNU nano**:

     ```
     $ sudo nano /etc/pam.d/common-password
     ```

   - ❑ Find the line similar to this:

     ```
     password    [success=1 default=ignore]   pam_unix.so obscure
     sha512
     ```

- ❑ Add `minlen` to the end of this line:

  ```
  password    [success=1 default=ignore]  pam_unix.so obscure
  sha512 minlen=8
  ```

- ❑ Add this line to enforce alphanumeric passwords:

  `password requisite pam_cracklib.so ucredit=-1 lcredit=-1 dcredit=-1  ocredit=-1`

- ❑ Save changes and exit **GNU nano** editor.
- ❑ Press *Ctrl* + *O* to save changes.
- ❑ Press *Ctrl* + *X* to exit **GNU nano** editor.

2. Secure the `home` directory with the following steps:

   - ❑ Check `home` directory permissions with the following command:

     `$ ls -ld /home/username`

   - ❑ Restrict permissions to user and group with the following command:

     `$ chmod 750 /home/username`

   - ❑ Change `adduser` default permissions by editing `/etc/adduser.conf`. Find `DIR_MODE=0755` and change it to `DIR_MODE=0750`.

3. Disable SSH access to root user with the following step:

   - ❑ Open `/etc/ssh/sshd_config` and add or edit `PermitRootLogin` to `PermitRootLogin no`

4. Disable password authentication with the following step:

   - ❑ Open `/etc/ssh/sshd_config` and add or edit `PasswordAuthentication no`

5. Install `fail2ban` with `sudo apt-get install fail2ban`.

How it works...

This recipe discussed a few important steps to make user accounts more secure.

A password is the most important aspect in securing user accounts. A weak password can be easily broken with brute force attacks and dictionary attacks. It is always a good idea to avoid password-based authentication, but if you are still using it, then make sure you enforce a strong password policy.

Password authentication is controlled by the PAM module `pam_unix`, and all settings associated with login are listed at `/etc/pam.d/login`. An additional configuration file `/etc/pam.d/common-password` includes values that control password checks.

The following line in the primary block of `common-password` file defines the rules for password complexity:

```
password [success=1 default=ignore] pam_unix.so obscure sha512
```

The default setting already defines some basic rules on passwords. The parameter `obscure` defines some extra checks on password strength. It includes the following:

- ▸ Palindrome check
- ▸ Case change only
- ▸ Similar check
- ▸ Rotated check

The other parameter, `sha512`, states that the new password will be encrypted with the `sha512` algorithm. We have set another option, `minlen=8`, on the same line, adding minimum length complexity to passwords.

 For all settings of the `pam_unix` module, refer to the manual pages with the command `man pam_unix`.

Additionally, we have set alphanumeric checks for new passwords with the PAM module `pam_cracklib`:

```
password requisite pam_cracklib.so ucredit=-1 lcredit=-1 dcredit=-
1  ocredit=-1
```

The preceding line adds requirement of one uppercase letter, one lowercase letter, one digit (`dcredit`), and one special character (`ocredit`)

There are other PAM modules available, and you can search them with the following command:

$ apt-cache search limpam-

You might also want to secure the `home` directory of users. The default permissions on Ubuntu allow read and execute access to everyone. You can limit the access on the `home` directory by changing permission on the `home` directory as required. In the preceding example, we changed permissions to `750`. This allows full access to the user, and allows read and execute access to the user's primary group.

You can also change the default permissions on the user's `home` directory by changing settings for the `adduser` command. These values are located at `/etc/adduser.conf`. We have changed default permissions to `750`, which limits access to the user and the group only.

Additionally, you can disable remote login for the root account as well as disable password-based authentication. Public key authentication is always more secure than passwords, unless you can secure your private keys. Before disabling password authentication, ensure that you have properly enabled public key authentication and you are able to log in with your keys. Otherwise, you will lock yourself out of the server.

You might want to install a tool like `fail2ban` to watch and block repeated failed actions. It scans through access logs and automatically blocks repeated failed login attempts. This can be a handy tool to provide a security against brute force attacks.

2
Networking

In this chapter, we will cover the following recipes:

- ▶ Connecting to a network with a static IP
- ▶ Installing the DHCP server
- ▶ Installing the DNS server
- ▶ Hiding behind the proxy with squid
- ▶ Being on time with NTP
- ▶ Discussing load balancing with HAProxy
- ▶ Tuning the TCP stack
- ▶ Troubleshooting network connectivity
- ▶ Securing remote access with OpenVPN
- ▶ Securing a network with uncomplicated firewall
- ▶ Securing against brute force attacks
- ▶ Discussing Ubuntu security best practices

Introduction

When we are talking about server systems, networking is the first and most important factor. If you are using an Ubuntu server in a cloud or virtual machine, you generally don't notice the network settings, as they are already configured with various network protocols. However, as your infrastructure grows, managing and securing the network becomes the priority.

Networking can be thought of as an umbrella term for various activities that include network configurations, file sharing and network time management, firewall settings and network proxies, and many others. In this chapter, we will take a closer look at the various networking services that help us set up and effectively manage our networks, be it in the cloud or a local network in your office.

Connecting to a network with a static IP

When you install Ubuntu server, its network setting defaults to dynamic IP addressing, that is, the network management daemon in Ubuntu searches for a DHCP server on the connected network and configures the network with the IP address assigned by DHCP. Even when you start an instance in the cloud, the network is configured with dynamic addressing using the DHCP server setup by the cloud service provider. In this chapter, you will learn how to configure the network interface with static IP assignment.

Getting ready

You will need an Ubuntu server with access to the root account or an account with `sudo` privileges. If network configuration is a new thing for you, then it is recommended to try this on a local or virtual machine.

How to do it...

Follow these steps to connect to the network with a static IP:

1. Get a list of available Ethernet interfaces using the following command:

    ```
    $ ifconfig -a | grep eth
    ```

2. Open /etc/network/interfaces and find the following lines:

   auto eth0

   iface eth0 inet dhcp

```
# The loopback network interface
auto lo
iface lo inet loopback

# The primary network interface
auto eth0
iface eth0 inet dhcp
```

3. Change the preceding lines to add an IP address, net mask, and default gateway (replace samples with the respective values):

   auto eth0

   iface eth0 inet static

       address 192.168.1.100

       netmask 255.255.255.0

       gateway 192.168.1.1

       dns-nameservers 192.168.1.45 192.168.1.46

4. Restart the network service for the changes to take effect:

   $ sudo /etc/init.d/networking restart

5. Try to ping a remote host to test the network connection:

   $ ping www.google.com

```
                            ubuntu@ubuntu: ~                        _  □  ×
ubuntu@ubuntu:~$ ping -c 3 www.google.com
PING www.google.com (216.58.220.4) 56(84) bytes of data.
64 bytes from bom05s05-in-f4.1e100.net (216.58.220.4): icmp_seq=1 ttl=56 time=12.3 ms
64 bytes from bom05s05-in-f4.1e100.net (216.58.220.4): icmp_seq=2 ttl=56 time=5.59 ms
64 bytes from bom05s05-in-f4.1e100.net (216.58.220.4): icmp_seq=3 ttl=56 time=5.75 ms

--- www.google.com ping statistics ---
3 packets transmitted, 3 received, 0% packet loss, time 2004ms
rtt min/avg/max/mdev = 5.597/7.912/12.386/3.164 ms
ubuntu@ubuntu:~$ []
```

How it works...

In this recipe, we have modified the network configuration from dynamic IP assignment to static assignment.

First, we got a list of all the available network interfaces with `ifconfig -a`. The -a option of `ifconfig` returns all the available network interfaces, even if they are disabled. With the help of the pipe (|) symbol, we have directed the output of `ifconfig` to the `grep` command. For now, we are interested with Ethernet ports only. The `grep` command will filter the received data and return only the lines that contain the `eth` character sequence:

```
ubuntu@ubuntu:~$ ifconfig -a | grep eth
eth0      Link encap:Ethernet   HWaddr 08:00:27:bb:a6:03
```

Here, `eth0` means first Ethernet interface available on the server. After getting the name of the interface to configure, we will change the network settings for `eth0` in interfaces file at `/etc/network/interfaces`. By default, `eth0` is configured to query the DHCP server for an IP assignment. The `eth0` line `auto` is used to automatically configure the `eth0` interface at server startup. Without this line, you will need to enable the network interface after each reboot. You can enable the `eth0` interface with the following command:

```
$ sudo ifup eth0
```

Similarly, to disable a network interface, use the following command:

```
$ sudo ifdown eth0
```

The second `iface eth0 inet static` line sets the network configuration to static assignment. After this line, we will add network settings, such as IP address, netmask, default gateway, and DNS servers.

After saving the changes, we need to restart the networking service for the changes to take effect. Alternatively, you can simply disable the network interface and enable it with `ifdown` and `ifup` commands.

There's more...

The steps in this recipe are used to configure the network changes permanently. If you need to change your network parameters temporarily, you can use the `ifconfig` and `route` commands as follows:

1. Change the IP address and netmask, as follows:
   ```
   $ sudo ifconfig eth0 192.168.1.100 netmask 255.255.255.0
   ```

2. Set the default gateway:

    ```
    $ sudo route add default gw 192.168.1.1 eth0
    ```

3. Edit /etc/resolv.conf to add temporary name servers (DNS):

    ```
    nameserver 192.168.1.45
    nameserver 192.168.1.46
    ```

4. To verify the changes, use the following command:

    ```
    $ ifconfig eth0
    $ route -n
    ```

5. When you no longer need this configuration, you can easily reset it with the following command:

    ```
    $ ip addr flush eth0
    ```

6. Alternatively, you can reboot your server to reset the temporary configuration.

IPv6 configuration

You may need to configure your Ubuntu server for IPv6 IP address. Version six IP addresses use a 128-bit address space and include hexadecimal characters. They are different from simple version four IP addresses that use a 32-bit addressing space. Ubuntu supports IPv6 addressing and can be easily configured with either DHCP or a static address. The following is an example of static configuration for IPv6:

```
iface eth0 inet6 static
address 2001:db8::xxxx:yyyy
gateway your_ipv6_gateway
```

See also

You can find more details about network configuration in the Ubuntu server guide:

*   https://help.ubuntu.com/lts/serverguide/network-configuration.html
*   Checkout the Ubuntu wiki page on IP version 6 - https://wiki.ubuntu.com/IPv6

Installing the DHCP server

DHCP is a service used to automatically assign network configuration to client systems. DHCP can be used as a handy tool when you have a large pool of systems that needs to be configured for network settings. Plus, when you need to change the network configuration, say to update a DNS server, all you need to do is update the DHCP server and all the connected hosts will be reconfigured with new settings. Also, you get reliable IP address configuration that minimizes configuration errors and address conflicts. You can easily add a new host to the network without spending time on network planning.

DHCP is most commonly used to provide IP configuration settings, such as IP address, net mask, default gateway, and DNS servers. However, it can also be set to configure the time server and hostname on the client.

DHCP can be configured to use the following configuration methods:

> ▶ **Manual allocation**: Here, the configuration settings are tied with the MAC address of the client's network card. The same settings are supplied each time the client makes a request with the same network card.

> ▶ **Dynamic allocation**: This method specifies a range of IP addresses to be assigned to the clients. The server can dynamically assign IP configuration to the client on first come, first served basis. These settings are allocated for a specified time period called **lease**; after this period, the client needs to renegotiate with the server to keep using the same address. If the client leaves the network for a specified time, the configuration gets expired and returns to pool where it can be assigned to other clients. Lease time is a configurable option and it can be set to infinite.

Ubuntu comes pre-installed with the DHCP client, `dhclient`. The DHCP `dhcpd` server daemon can be installed while setting up an Ubuntu server or separately with the `apt-get` command.

Getting ready

Make sure that your DHCP host is configured with static IP address.

You will need an access to the root account or an account with `sudo` privileges.

How to do it...

Follow these steps to install a DHCP server:

1. Install a DHCP server:

```
$ sudo apt-get install isc-dhcp-server
```

2. Open the DHCP configuration file:

```
$ sudo nano -w /etc/dhcp/dhcpd.conf
```

3. Change the default and max lease time if necessary:

```
default-lease-time 600;

max-lease-time 7200;
```

4. Add the following lines at the end of the file (replace the IP address to match your network):

```
subnet 192.168.1.0 netmask 255.255.255.0 {

   range 192.168.1.150 192.168.1.200;

   option routers 192.168.1.1;

   option domain-name-servers 192.168.1.2, 192.168.1.3;

   option domain-name "example.com";

}
```

5. Save the configuration file and exit with *Ctrl + O* and *Ctrl + X*.

6. After changing the configuration file, restart dhcpd:

```
$ sudo service isc-dhcp-server restart
```

How it works...

Here, we have installed the DHCP server with the isc-dhcp-server package. It is open source software that implements the DHCP protocol. **ISC-DHCP** supports both IPv4 and IPv6.

After the installation, we need to set the basic configuration to match our network settings. All dhcpd settings are listed in the /etc/dhcp/dhcpd.conf configuration file. In the sample settings listed earlier, we have configured a new network, 192.168.1.0. This will result in IP addresses ranging from 192.168.1.150 to 192.168.1.200 to be assigned to clients. The default lease time is set to 600 seconds with maximum bound of 7200 seconds. A client can ask for a specific time to a maximum lease period of 7200 seconds. Additionally, the DHCP server will provide a default gateway (routers) as well as default DNS servers.

If you have multiple network interfaces, you may need to change the interface that dhcpd should listen to. These settings are listed in /etc/default/isc-dhcp-server. You can set multiple interfaces to listen to; just specify the interface names, separated by a space, for example, INTERFACES="wlan0 eth0".

There's more...

You can reserve an IP address to be assigned to a specific device on network. Reservation ensures that a specified device is always assigned to the same IP address. To create a reservation, add the following lines to dhcpd.conf. It will assign IP 192.168.1.201 to the client with the 08:D2:1F:50:F0:6F MAC ID:

```
host Server1 {
  hardware ethernet 08:D2:1F:50:F0:6F;
  fixed-address 192.168.1.201;
}
```

Installing the DNS server

DNS, also known as name server, is a service on the Internet that provides mapping between IP addresses and domain names and vice versa. DNS maintains a database of names and related IP addresses. When an application queries with a domain name, DNS responds with a mapped IP address. Applications can also ask for a domain name by providing an IP address.

DNS is quite a big topic, and an entire chapter can be written just on the DNS setup. This recipe assumes some basic understanding of the working of the DNS protocol. We will cover the installation of BIND, installation of DNS server application, configuration of BIND as a caching DNS, and setup of Primary Master and Secondary Master. We will also cover some best practices to secure your DNS server.

Getting ready

In this recipe, I will be using four servers. You can create virtual machines if you want to simply test the setup:

1. ns1: Name server one/Primary Master
2. ns2: Name server two/Secondary Master
3. host1: Host system one
4. host2: Host system two, optional

    ❑ All servers should be configured in a private network. I have used the 10.0.2.0/24 network
    ❑ We need root privileges on all servers

How to do it...

Install BIND and set up a caching name server through the following steps:

1. On ns1, install BIND and `dnsutils` with the following command:

   ```
   $ sudo apt-get update
   $ sudo apt-get install bind9 dnsutils
   ```

2. Open `/etc/bind/named.conf.optoins`, enable the `forwarders` section, and add your preferred DNS servers:

   ```
   forwarders {
        8.8.8.8;
        8.8.4.4;
   };
   ```

3. Now restart BIND to apply a new configuration:

   ```
   $ sudo service bind9 restart
   ```

4. Check whether the BIND server is up and running:

   ```
   $ dig -x 127.0.0.1
   ```

5. You should get an output similar to the following code:

   ```
   ;; Query time: 1 msec
   ;; SERVER: 10.0.2.53#53(10.0.2.53)
   ```

6. Use `dig` to external domain and check the query time:

   ```
   ;; Query time: 268 msec
   ;; SERVER: 10.0.2.53#53(10.0.2.53)
   ;; WHEN: Tue Jul 28 10:17:10 IST 2015
   ;; MSG SIZE  rcvd: 270
   ```

7. Dig the same domain again and cross check the query time. It should be less than the first query:

   ```
   ;; Query time: 29 msec
   ;; SERVER: 10.0.2.53#53(10.0.2.53)
   ;; WHEN: Tue Jul 28 10:20:11 IST 2015
   ;; MSG SIZE  rcvd: 270
   ```

Set up Primary Master through the following steps:

1. On the ns1 server, edit `/etc/bind/named.conf.options` and add the `acl` block above the `options` block:

```
acl "local" {
    10.0.2.0/24;  # local network
};
```

2. Add the following lines under the `options` block:

```
recursion yes;
allow-recursion { local; };
listen-on { 10.0.2.53; };  # ns1 IP address
allow-transfer { none; };
```

3. Open the `/etc/bind/named.conf.local` file to add forward and reverse zones:

```
$ sudo nano /etc/bind/named.conf.local
```

4. Add the forward `zone`:

```
zone "example.com" {
    type master;
    file "/etc/bind/zones/db.example.com";
};
```

5. Add the reverse `zone`:

```
zone "2.0.10.in-addr.arpa" {
    type master;
    file "/etc/bind/zones/db.10";
};
```

6. Create the `zones` directory under `/etc/bind/`:

```
$ sudo mkdir /etc/bind/zones
```

7. Create the forward `zone` file using the existing zone file, `db.local`, as a template:

```
$ cd /etc/bind/
$ sudo cp db.local  zones/db.example.com
```

8. The default file should look similar to the following image:

```
ubuntu@ns1:~$ cat /etc/bind/db.local
;
; BIND data file for local loopback interface
;
$TTL    604800
@       IN      SOA     localhost. root.localhost. (
                              2         ; Serial
                         604800         ; Refresh
                          86400         ; Retry
                        2419200         ; Expire
                         604800 )       ; Negative Cache TTL
;
@       IN      NS      localhost.
@       IN      A       127.0.0.1
@       IN      AAAA    ::1
```

9. Edit the SOA entry and replace localhost with FQDN of your server.

10. Increment the serial number (you can use the current date time as the serial number, 201507071100)

11. Remove entries for localhost, 127.0.0.1 and ::1.

12. Add new records:

```
; name server - NS records
@   IN   NS   ns.exmple.com
; name server A records
ns   IN   A 10.0.2.53
; local - A records
host1   IN A   10.0.2.58
```

13. Save the changes and exit the nano editor. The final file should look similar to the following image:

```
ubuntu@ns1:~$ cat /etc/bind/zones/db.example.com
;
; BIND data file for local loopback interface
;
$TTL    604800
@       IN      SOA     example.com. root.example.com. (
                              3         ; Serial
                         604800         ; Refresh
                          86400         ; Retry
                        2419200         ; Expire
                         604800 )       ; Negative Cache TTL
;
@       IN      NS      ns.example.com.
@       IN      A       10.0.2.53
@       IN      AAAA    ::1
NS      IN      A       10.0.2.53
host1   IN      A       10.0.2.58
host2   IN      A       10.0.2.55
```

14. Now create the reverse `zone` file using `/etc/bind/db.127` as a template:

    ```
    $ sudo cp db.127 zones/db.10
    ```

15. The default file should look similar to the following screenshot:

```
ubuntu@ns1:~$ cat /etc/bind/db.127
;
; BIND reverse data file for local loopback interface
;
$TTL    604800
@       IN      SOA     localhost. root.localhost. (
                              1         ; Serial
                         604800         ; Refresh
                          86400         ; Retry
                        2419200         ; Expire
                         604800 )       ; Negative Cache TTL
;
@       IN      NS      localhost.
1.0.0   IN      PTR     localhost.
```

16. Change the `SOA` record and increment the serial number.

17. Remove `NS` and `PTR` records for `localhost`.

18. Add `NS`, `PTR`, and `host` records:

    ```
    ; NS records
    @  IN  NS  ns.example.com
    ; PTR records
    53  IN  PTR  ns.example.com
    ; host records
    58  IN  PTR  host1.example.com
    ```

19. Save the changes. The final file should look similar to the following image:

```
ubuntu@ns1:~$ cat /etc/bind/zones/db.10
;
; BIND reverse data file for local loopback interface
;
$TTL    604800
@       IN      SOA     ns.example.com. root.ns.example.com. (
                              2         ; Serial
                         604800         ; Refresh
                          86400         ; Retry
                        2419200         ; Expire
                         604800 )       ; Negative Cache TTL
;
@       IN      NS      ns.
53      IN      PTR     ns.example.com.
58      IN      PTR     host1.example.com.
55      IN      PTR     host2.example.com.
```

20. Check the configuration files for syntax errors. It should end with no output:

```
$ sudo named-checkconf
```

21. Check `zone` files for syntax errors:

```
$ sudo named-checkzone example.com
/etc/bind/zones/db.example.com
```

22. If there are no errors, you should see an output similar to the following:

```
zone example.com/IN: loaded serial 3
OK
```

23. Check the reverse `zone` file, `zones/db.10`:

```
$ sudo named-checkzone example.com /etc/bind/zones/db.10
```

24. If there are no errors, you should see output similar to the following:

```
zone example.com/IN: loaded serial 3
OK
```

25. Now restart the DNS server bind:

```
$ sudo service bind9 restart
```

26. Log in to host2 and configure it to use `ns.example.com` as a DNS server. Add `ns.example.com` to `/etc/resolve.conf` on host2.

27. Test forward lookup with the `nslookup` command:

```
$ nslookup host1.example.com
```

28. You should see an output similar to following:

```
$ nslookup host1.example.com
Server:  10.0.2.53
Address: 10.0.2.53#53
Name: host1.example.com
Address: 10.0.2.58
```

29. Now test the reverse lookup:

```
$ nslookup 10.0.2.58
```

30. It should output something similar to the following:

```
$ nslookup 10.0.2.58
Server:  10.0.2.53
Address: 10.0.2.53#53
58.2.0.10.in-addr.arpa    name = host1.example.com
```

Set up Secondary Master through the following steps:

1. First, allow zone transfer on Primary Master by setting the `allow-transfer` option in `/etc/bind/named.conf.local`:

```
zone "example.com" {
    type master;
    file "/etc/bind/zones/db.example.com";
    allow-transfer { 10.0.2.54; };
};
zone "2.0.10.in-addr.arpa" {
    type master;
    file "/etc/bind/zones/db.10";
    allow-transfer { 10.0.2.54; };
};
```

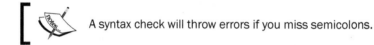 A syntax check will throw errors if you miss semicolons.

2. Restart BIND9 on Primary Master:

```
$ sudo service bind9 restart
```

3. On Secondary Master (ns2), install the BIND package.

4. Edit `/etc/bind/named.conf.local` to add `zone` declarations as follows:

```
zone "example.com" {
    type slave;
    file "db.example.com";
    masters { 10.0.2.53; };
};
zone "2.0.10.in-addr.arpa" {
    type slave;
    file "db.10";
    masters { 10.0.2.53; };
};
```

5. Save the changes made to `named.conf.local`.

6. Restart the BIND server on Secondary Master:

```
$ sudo service bind9 restart
```

7. This will initiate the transfer of all zones configured on Primary Master. You can check the logs on Secondary Master at `/var/log/syslog` to verify the zone transfer.

 A zone is transferred only if the serial number under the `SOA` section on Primary Master is greater than that of Secondary Master. Make sure that you increment the serial number after every change to the zone file.

How it works...

In the first section, we have installed the BIND server and enabled a simple caching DNS server. A caching server helps to reduce bandwidth and latency in name resolution. The server will try to resolve queries locally from the cache. If the entry is not available in the cache, the query will be forwarded to external DNS servers and the result will be cached.

In the second and third sections, we have set Primary Master and Secondary Master respectively. Primary Master is the first DNS server. Secondary Master will be used as an alternate server in case the Primary server becomes unavailable.

Under Primary Master, we have declared a forward zone and reverse zone for the `example.com` domain. The forward zone is declared with domain name as the identifier and contains the type and filename for the database file. On Primary Master, we have set `type` to `master`. The reverse zone is declared with similar attributes and uses part of an IP address as an identifier. As we are using a 24-bit network address (`10.0.2.0/24`), we have included the first three octets of the IP address in reverse order (`2.0.10`) for the reverse zone name.

Lastly, we have created zone files by using existing files as templates. Zone files are the actual database that contains records of the IP address mapped to FQDN and vice versa. It contains SOA record, A records, and NS records. An SOA record defines the domain for this zone; A records and AAAA records are used to map the hostname to the IP address.

When the DNS server receives a query for the `example.com` domain, it checks for zone files for that domain. After finding the zone file, the host part from the query will be used to find the actual IP address to be returned as a result for query. Similarly, when a query with an IP address is received, the DNS server will look for a reverse zone file matching with the queried IP address.

See also

▶ Checkout the DNS configuration guide in the Ubuntu server guide at `https://help.ubuntu.com/lts/serverguide/dns-configuration.html`

▶ For an introduction to DNS concepts, check out this tutorial by the DigitalOcean community at `https://www.digitalocean.com/community/tutorials/an-introduction-to-dns-terminology-components-and-concepts`

- ▶ Get manual pages for BIND9 at `http://www.bind9.net/manuals`
- ▶ Find manual pages for named with the following command:

  ```
  $ man named
  ```

Hiding behind the proxy with squid

In this recipe, we will install and configure the squid proxy and caching server. The term **proxy** is generally combined with two different terms: one is forward proxy and the other is reverse proxy.

When we say proxy, it generally refers to forward proxy. A forward proxy acts as a gateway between a client's browser and the Internet, requesting the content on behalf of the client. This protects intranet clients by exposing the proxy as the only requester. A proxy can also be used as a filtering agent, imposing organizational policies. As all Internet requests go through the proxy server, the proxy can cache the response and return cached content when a similar request is found, thus saving bandwidth and time.

A reverse proxy is the exact opposite of a forward proxy. It protects internal servers from the outside world. A reverse proxy accepts requests from external clients and routes them to servers behind the proxy. External clients can see a single entity serving requests, but internally, it can be multiple servers working behind the proxy and sharing the load. More details about reverse proxies are covered in *Chapter 3, Working with Web Servers*.

In this recipe, we will discuss how to install a squid server. Squid is a well-known application in the forward proxy world and works well as a caching proxy. It supports HTTP, HTTPS, FTP, and other popular network protocols.

Getting ready

As always, you will need access to a root account or an account with `sudo` privileges.

How to do it...

Following are the steps to setup and configure Squid proxy:

1. Squid is quite an old, mature, and commonly used piece of software. It is generally shipped as a default package with various Linux distributions. The Ubuntu package repository contains the necessary pre-compiled binaries, so the installation is as easy as two commands.

2. First, update the `apt` cache and then install squid as follows:

   ```
   $ sudo apt-get update
   $ sudo apt-get install squid3
   ```

3. Edit the `/etc/squid3/squid.conf` file:

   $ sudo nano /etc/squid3/squid.conf

4. Ensure that the `cache_dir` directive is not commented out:

   cache_dir ufs /var/spool/squid3 100 16 256

5. Optionally, change the `http_port` directive to your desired TCP port:

   http_port 8080

6. Optionally, change the squid hostname:

   visible_hostname proxy1

7. Save changes with *Ctrl + O* and exit with *Ctrl + X*.

8. Restart the squid server:

   $ sudo service squid3 restart

9. Make sure that you have allowed the selected `http_port` on firewall.

10. Next, configure your browser using the squid server as the `http/https` proxy.

How it works...

Squid is available as a package in the Ubuntu repository, so you can directly install it with the `apt-get install squid` command. After installing squid, we need to edit the `squid.conf` file for some basic settings. The `squid.conf` file is quite a big file and you can find a large number of directives listed with their explanation. It is recommended to create a copy of the original configuration file as a reference before you do any modifications.

In our example, we are changing the port squid listens on. The default port is `3128`. This is just a security precaution and it's fine if you want to run squid on the default port. Secondly, we have changed the hostname for squid.

Other important directive to look at is `cache_dir`. Make sure that this directive is enabled, and also set the cache size. The following example sets `cache_dir` to `/var/spool/suid3` with the size set to `100MB`:

cache_dir ufs /var/spool/squid3 100   16   256

To check the cache utilization, use the following command:

$ sudo du /var/spool/squid3

There's more...

Squid provides lot more features than a simple proxy server. Following is a quick list of some important features:

Access control list

With squid ACLs, you can set the list of IP addresses allowed to use squid. Add the following line at the bottom of the `acl` section of `/etc/squid3/squid.conf`:

```
acl developers  src 192.168.2.0/24
```

Then, add the following line at the top of the `http_access` section in the same file:

```
http_access allow developers
```

Set cache refresh rules

You can change squid's caching behavior depending on the file types. Add the following line to cache all image files to be cached—the minimum time is an hour and the maximum is a day:

```
refresh_pattern -i \.(gif|png|jpg|jpeg|ico)$  3600    90%    86400
```

This line uses a regular expression to find the file names that end with any of the listed file extensions (`gif`, `png`, and `etc`)

Sarg – tool to analyze squid logs

Squid Analysis Report Generator is an open source tool to monitor the squid server usages. It parses the logs generated by Squid and converts them to easy-to-digest HTML-based reports. You can track various metrics such as bandwidth used per user, top sites, downloads, and so on. Sarg can be quickly installed with the following command:

```
$ sudo apt-get install sarg
```

The configuration file for Sarg is located at `/etc/squid/sarg.conf`. Once installed, set the `output_dir` path and run `sarg`. You can also set cron jobs to execute `sarg` periodically. The generated reports are stored in `output_dir` and can be accessed with the help of a web server.

Squid guard

Squid guard is another useful plugin for squid server. It is generally used to block a list of websites so that these sites are inaccessible from the internal network. As always, it can also be installed with a single command, as follows:

```
$ sudo apt-get install squidguard
```

The configuration file is located at `/etc/squid/squidGuard.conf`.

See also

- ▸ Check out the squid manual pages with the `man squid` command
- ▸ Check out the Ubuntu community page for squid guard at `https://help.ubuntu.com/community/SquidGuard`

Being on time with NTP

Network Time Protocol (**NTP**) is a TCP/IP protocol for synchronizing time over a network. Although Ubuntu has a built-in clock that is helpful for keeping track of local events, it may create issues when the server is connected over a network and provides time-critical services to the clients. This problem can be solved with the help of NTP time synchronization. NTP works by synchronizing time across all servers on the Internet.

NTP uses hierarchies of servers with top-level servers synchronizing time with atomic clocks. This hierarchy levels are known as **stratum**, and the level can range between 1 and 15, both inclusive. The highest stratum level is 1 and is determined by the accuracy of the clock the server synchronizes with. If a server synchronizes with other NTP server with stratum level 3, then the stratum level for this server is automatically set to 4.

Another time synchronization tool provided by Ubuntu is `ntpdate`, which comes preinstalled with Ubuntu. It executes once at boot time and synchronizes the local time with Ubuntu's NTP servers. The problem with `ntpdate` is that it matches server time with central time without considering the big drifts in local time, whereas the NTP daemon `ntpd` continuously adjusts the server time to match it with the reference clock. As mentioned in the `ntpdate` manual pages (`man ntpdate`), you can use `ntpdate` multiple times throughout a day to keep time drifts low and get more accurate results, but it does not match the accuracy and reliability provided by ntpd.

In this recipe, we will set up a standalone time server for an internal network. Our time server will synchronize its time with public time servers and provide a time service to internal NTP clients.

How to do it...

Following are the steps to install and configure NTP daemon:

1. First, synchronize the server's time with any Internet time server using the `ntpdate` command:

   ```
   $ ntpdate -s ntp.ubuntu.com
   ```

2. To install ntpd, enter the following command in the terminal:

   ```
   $ sudo apt-get install ntp
   ```

3. Edit the `/etc/ntp.conf` NTP configuration file to add/remove external NTP servers:

   `$ sudo nano /etc/ntp.conf`

4. Set a fallback NTP server:

   `server ntp.ubuntu.com`

5. Block any external access to the server, comment the first `restrict` line, and add the following command:

   `restrict default noquery notrust nomodify`

6. Allow the clients on local network to use the NTP service:

   `restrict 192.168.1.0 mask 255.255.255.0`

7. Save changes with *Ctrl + O* and exit nano with *Ctrl + X*.

8. Reload the NTP daemon with the following command:

   `$ sudo service ntp restart`

How it works...

Sometimes, the NTP daemon refuses to work if the time difference between local time and central time is too big. To avoid this problem, we have synchronized the local time and central time before installing ntpd. As ntpd and ntpdate both use the same UDP port, 123, the `ntpdate` command will not work when the ntpd service is in use.

 Make sure that you have opened UDP port 123 on the firewall.

After installing the NTP server, you may want to set time servers to be used. The default configuration file contains time servers provided by Ubuntu. You can use the same default servers or simply comment the lines by adding # at the start of each line and add the servers of your choice. You can dig into `http://www.pool.ntp.org` to find time servers for your specific region. It is a good idea to provide multiple reference servers, as NTP can provide more accurate results after querying each of them.

You can control polling intervals for each server with the `minpoll` and `maxpoll` parameters. The value is set in seconds to the power of two. `minpoll` defaults to 6 (2^6 = 64 sec) and `maxpoll` defaults to 10 (2^10 = 1024 sec).

Additionally, we have set a fallback server that can be used in case of network outage or any other problems when our server cannot communicate with external reference servers. You can also use a system clock as a fallback, which can be accessed at `127.127.1.0`. Simply replace the fallback server with the following line to use a system clock as a fallback:

```
server 127.127.0.1
```

Lastly, we have set access control parameters to protect our server from external access. The default configuration is to allow anyone to use the time service from this server. By changing the first `restrict` line, we blocked all external access to the server. The configuration already contains the exception to local NTP service indicated by the following:

```
restrict 127.0.0.1
```

We created another exception by adding a separate line to allow access to the clients on local network (remember to replace the IP range with your network details):

```
restrict 192.168.1.0 mask 255.255.255.0
```

There's more...

A central DHCP server can be configured to provide NTP settings to all DHCP clients. For this to work, your clients should also be configured to query NTP details from DHCP. A DHCP client configuration on Ubuntu already contains the query for network time servers.

Add the following line to your DHCP configuration to provide NTP details to the clients:

```
subnet 192.168.1.0 netmask 255.255.255.0 {

    ...

    option ntp-servers  your_ntp_host;
}
```

On the clientside, make sure that your `dhclient.conf` contains `ntp-servers` in its default `request`:

```
request subnet-mask, broadcast-address, time-offset, routers,

        ...

        rfc3442-classless-static-routes, ntp-servers,
```

See also

▶ Check the default `/etc/ntp.conf` configuration file. It contains a short explanation for each setting.

▶ Check the manual pages for ntpd with `man ntpd`.

Discussing load balancing with HAProxy

When an application becomes popular, it sends an increased number of requests to the application server. A single application server may not be able to handle the entire load alone. We can always scale up the underlying hardware, that is, add more memory and more powerful CUPs to increase the server capacity; but these improvements do not always scale linearly. To solve this problem, multiple replicas of the application server are created and the load is distributed among these replicas. Load balancing can be implemented at OSI Layer 4, that is, at TCP or UDP protocol levels, or at Layer 7, that is, application level with HTTP, SMTP, and DNS protocols.

In this recipe, we will install a popular load balancing or load distributing service, HAProxy. HAProxy receives all the requests from clients and directs them to the actual application server for processing. Application server directly returns the final results to the client. We will be setting HAProxy to load balance TCP connections.

Getting ready

You will need two or more application servers and one server for HAProxy:

> You will need the root access on the server where you want to install HAProxy

> It is assumed that your application servers are properly installed and working

How to do it...

Follow these steps to discus load balancing with HAProxy:

1. Install HAProxy:

   ```
   $ sudo apt-get update
   $ sudo apt-get install haproxy
   ```

2. Enable the HAProxy `init` script to automatically start HAProxy on system boot. Open `/etc/default/haproxy` and set `ENABLE` to 1:

```
ubuntu: ~ $ cat /etc/default/haproxy
# Set ENABLED to 1 if you want the init script to start haproxy.
ENABLED=1
# Add extra flags here.
#EXTRAOPTS="-de -m 16"
ubuntu: ~ $
```

3. Now, edit the HAProxy `/etc/haproxy/haproxy.cfg` configuration file. You may want to create a copy of this file before editing:

   ```
   $ cd /etc/haproxy
   $ sudo cp haproxy.cfg haproxy.cfg.copy
   $ sudo nano haproxy.cfg
   ```

4. Find the `defaults` section and change the `mode` and `option` parameters to match the following:

   ```
   mode    tcp
   option    tcplog
   ```

   ```
   defaults
           log     global
           mode    tcp
           option  tcplog
           option  dontlognull
           contimeout 5000
   ```

5. Next, define `frontend`, which will receive all requests:

   ```
   frontend www
       bind 57.105.2.204:80     # haproxy public IP
       default_backend as-backend     # backend used
   ```

6. Define `backend` application servers:

   ```
   backend as-backend
       balance leastconn
       mode tcp
       server as1 10.0.2.71:80 check     # application srv 1
       server as2 10.0.2.72:80 check     # application srv 2
   ```

7. Save and quit the HAProxy configuration file.

8. We need to set `rsyslog` to accept HAProxy logs. Open the `rsyslog.conf` file, `/etc/rsyslog.conf`, and uncomment following parameters:

   ```
   $ModLoad imudp
   $UDPServerRun 514
   ```

   ```
   # provides UDP syslog reception
   $ModLoad imudp
   $UDPServerRun 514
   ```

9. Next, create a new file under `/etc/rsyslog.d` to specify the HAProxy log location:

    ```
    $ sudo nano /etc/rsyslog.d/haproxy.conf
    ```

10. Add the following line to the newly created file:

    ```
    local2.*   /var/log/haproxy.log
    ```

11. Save the changes and exit the new file.

12. Restart the `rsyslog` service:

    ```
    $ sudo service rsyslog restart
    ```

13. Restart HAProxy:

    ```
    $ sudo service haproxy restart
    ```

14. Now, you should be able to access your backend with the HAProxy IP address.

How it works...

Here, we have configured HAProxy as a frontend for a cluster of application servers. Under the `frontend` section, we have configured HAProxy to listen on the public IP of the HAProxy server. We also specified a backend for this frontend. Under the `backend` section, we have set a private IP address of the application servers. HAProxy will communicate with the application servers through a private network interface. This will help to keep the internal network latency to a minimum.

HAProxy supports various load balancing algorithms. Some of them are as follows:

- **Round-robin** distributes the load in a round robin fashion. This is the default algorithm used.
- **leastconn** selects the backend server with fewest connections.
- **source** uses the hash of the client's IP address and maps it to the backend. This ensures that requests from a single user are served by the same backend server.

We have selected the **leastconn** algorithm, which is mentioned under the `backend` section with the `balance leastconn` line. The selection of a load balancing algorithm will depend on the type of application and length of connections.

Lastly, we configured `rsyslog` to accept logs over UDP. HAProxy does not provide separate logging system and passes logs to the system log daemon, `rsyslog`, over the UDP stream.

There's more ...

Depending on your Ubuntu version, you may not get the latest version of HAProxy from the default `apt` repository. Use the following repository to install the latest release:

```
$ sudo apt-get install software-properties-common
```

```
$ sudo add-apt-repository ppa:vbernat/haproxy-1.6  # replace 1.6 with
required version
```

```
$ sudo apt-get update && apt-get install haproxy
```

See also

▸ An introduction to load balancing the HAProxy concepts at `https://www.digitalocean.com/community/tutorials/an-introduction-to-haproxy-and-load-balancing-concepts`

Tuning the TCP stack

Transmission Control Protocol and **Internet Protocol** (**TCP/IP**) is a standard set of protocols used by every network-enabled device. TCP/IP defines the standards to communicate over a network. TCP/IP is a set of protocols and is divided in two parts: TCP and IP. IP defines the rules for IP addressing and routing packets over network and provides an identity IP address to each host on the network. TCP deals with the interconnection between two hosts and enables them to exchange data over network. TCP is a connection-oriented protocol and controls the ordering of packets, retransmission, error detection, and other reliability tasks.

TCP stack is designed to be very general in nature so that it can be used by anyone for any network conditions. Servers use the same TCP/IP stack as used by their clients. For this reason, the default values are configured for general uses and not optimized for high-load server environments. New Linux kernel provides a tool called `sysctl` that can be used to modify kernel parameters at runtime without recompiling the entire kernel. We can use `sysctl` to modify and TCP/IP parameters to match our needs.

In this recipe, we will look at various kernel parameters that control the network. It is not required to modify all parameters listed here. You can choose ones that are required and suitable for your system and network environment.

It is advisable to test these modifications on local systems before doing any changes on live environment. A lot of these parameters directly deal with network connections and related CPU and memory uses. This can result in connection drops and/or sudden increases in resource use. Make sure that you have read the documentation for the parameter before you change anything.

Also, it is a good idea to set benchmarks before and after making any changes to `sysctl` parameters. This will give you a base to compare improvements, if any. Again, benchmarks may not reveal all the effects of parameter changes. Make sure that you have read the respective documentation.

Getting ready...

You will need root access.

Note down basic performance metrics with the tool of your choice.

How to do it...

Follow these steps to tune the TCP stack:

1. Set the maximum open files limit:

    ```
    $ ulimit -n    # check existing limits for logged in user
    # ulimit -n 65535    # root change values above hard limits
    ```

2. To permanently set limits for a user, open `/etc/security/limits.conf` and add the following lines at end of the file. Make sure to replace values in brackets, `<>`:

    ```
    <username>  soft  nofile  <value>    # soft limits
    <username>  hard  nofile  <value>    # hard limits
    ```

3. Save `limits.conf` and exit. Then restart the user session.

4. View all available parameters:

    ```
    # sysctl -a
    ```

5. Set the TCP default read-write buffer:

    ```
    # echo 'net.core.rmem_default=65536' >> /etc/sysctl.conf
    # echo 'net.core.wmem_default=65536' >> /etc/sysctl.conf
    ```

6. Set the TCP read and write buffers to 8 MB:

    ```
    # echo 'net.core.rmem_max=8388608' >> /etc/sysctl.conf
    # echo 'net.core.wmem_max=8388608' >> /etc/sysctl.conf
    ```

7. Increase the maximum TCP orphans:

    ```
    # echo 'net.ipv4.tcp_max_orphans=4096' >> /etc/sysctl.conf
    ```

8. Disable slow start after being idle:

    ```
    # echo 'net.ipv4.tcp_slow_start_after_idle=0' >>
    /etc/sysctl.conf
    ```

9. Minimize TCP connection retries:

    ```
    # echo 'net.ipv4.tcp_synack_retries=3' >> /etc/sysctl.conf

    # echo 'net.ipv4.tcp_syn_retries =3' >> /etc/sysctl.conf
    ```

10. Set the TCP window scaling:

```
# echo 'net.ipv4.tcp_window_scaling=1' >> /etc/sysctl.conf
```

11. Enable timestamps:

```
# echo 'net.ipv4.tcp_timestamp=1' >> /etc/sysctl.conf
```

12. Enable selective acknowledgements:

```
# echo 'net.ipv4.tcp_sack=0' >> /etc/sysctl.conf
```

13. Set the maximum number of times the IPV4 packet can be reordered in the TCP packet stream:

```
# echo 'net.ipv4.tcp_reordering=3' >> /etc/sysctl.conf
```

14. Send data in the opening SYN packet:

```
# echo 'net.ipv4.tcp_fastopen=1'  >> /etc/sysctl.conf
```

15. Set the number of opened connections to be remembered before receiving acknowledgement:

```
# echo 'tcp_max_syn_backlog=1500' >> /etc/sysctl.conf
```

16. Set the number of TCP keep-alive probes to send before deciding the connection is broken:

```
# echo 'tcp_keepalive_probes=5' >> /etc/sysctl.conf
```

17. Set the keep-alive time, which is a timeout value after the broken connection is killed:

```
# echo 'tcp_keepalive_time=1800' >> /etc/sysctl.conf
```

18. Set intervals to send keep-alive packets:

```
# echo 'tcp_keepalive_intvl=60' >> /etc/sysctl.conf
```

19. Set to reuse or recycle connections in the wait state:

```
# echo 'net.ipv4.tcp_tw_reuse=1' >> /etc/sysctl.conf
# echo 'net.ipv4.tcp_tw_recycle=1' >> /etc/sysctl.conf
```

20. Increase the maximum number of connections:

```
# echo 'net.ipv4.ip_local_port_range=32768 65535' >>
/etc/sysctl.conf
```

21. Set TCP FIN timeout:

```
# echo 'tcp_fin_timeout=60' >> /etc/sysctl.conf
```

How it works...

The behavior of Linux kernel can be fine tuned with the help of various Linux kernel parameters. These are the options passed to the kernel in order to control various aspects of the system. These parameters can be passed while compiling the kernel, at boot time, or at runtime using the /proc filesystem and tools such as sysctl.

In this recipe, we have used sysctl to configure network-related kernel parameters to fine tune network settings. Again, you need to cross check each configuration to see if it's working as expected.

Along with network parameters, tons of other kernel parameters can be configured with the sysctl command. The -a flag to sysctl will list all the available parameters:

```
$ sysctl -a
```

All these configurations are stored in a filesystem at the /proc directory, grouped in their respective categories. You can directly read/write these files or use the sysctl command:

```
ubuntu@ubuntu:~$ sysctl fs.file-max
fs.file-max = 98869
ubuntu@ubuntu:~$ cat /proc/sys/fs/file-max
98869
```

See also

Find the explanation of various kernel parameters at the following websites:

▶ http://www.cyberciti.biz/files/linux-kernel/Documentation/networking/ip-sysctl.txt

▶ https://www.kernel.org/doc/Documentation/networking/ip-sysctl.txt

Troubleshooting network connectivity

Networking consists of various components and services working together to enable systems to communicate with each other. A lot of times it happens that everything seems good, but we are not able to access other servers or the Internet. In this recipe, we will look at some tools provided by Ubuntu to troubleshoot the network connectivity issues.

Getting ready

As you are reading this recipe, I am assuming that you are facing a networking issue. Also, I am assuming that the problems are with a primary network adapter, eth0.

You may need access to root account or account with similar privileges.

How to do it...

Follow these steps to troubleshoot network connectivity:

1. Let's start with checking the network card. If it is working properly and is detected by Ubuntu. Check boot time logs and search for lines related to Ethernet, `eth`:

    ```
    $ dmesg | grep eth
    ```

    ```
    ubuntu@ubuntu:~$ dmesg | grep eth
    [    2.667415] e1000 0000:00:03.0 eth0: (PCI:33MHz:32-bit) 08:00:27:bb:a6:03
    [    2.672249] e1000 0000:00:03.0 eth0: Intel(R) PRO/1000 Network Connection
    [   12.592892] IPv6: ADDRCONF(NETDEV_UP): eth0: link is not ready
    [   12.593695] e1000: eth0 NIC Link is Up 1000 Mbps Full Duplex, Flow Control: R
    X
    [   12.605255] IPv6: ADDRCONF(NETDEV_CHANGE): eth0: link becomes ready
    ```

2. If you don't find anything in the boot logs, then most probably, your network hardware is faulty or unsupported by Ubuntu.

3. Next, check whether the network cable is plugged in and is working properly. You can simply check the LED indicators on the network card or use the following command:

    ```
    $ sudo mii-tool
    ```

    ```
    ubuntu@ubuntu:~$ sudo mii-tool
    [sudo] password for ubuntu:
    eth0: no autonegotiation, 1000baseT-FD flow-control, link ok
    ubuntu@ubuntu:~$
    ```

4. If you can see a line with `link ok`, then you have a working Ethernet connection.

5. Next, check whether a proper IP address is assigned to the `eth0` Ethernet port:

    ```
    $ ifconfig eth0
    ```

    ```
    ubuntu@ubuntu:~$ ifconfig eth0
    eth0      Link encap:Ethernet  HWaddr 08:00:27:bb:a6:03
              inet addr:10.0.2.15  Bcast:10.0.2.255  Mask:255.255.255.0
              inet6 addr: fe80::a00:27ff:febb:a603/64 Scope:Link
              UP BROADCAST RUNNING MULTICAST  MTU:1500  Metric:1
    ```

6. Check whether you can find a line that starts with `inet addr`. If you cannot find this line or it is listed as inet addr 169.254, then you don't have an IP address assigned.

7. Even if you see a line stating the IP address, make sure that it is valid for network that you are connected to.

8. Now assuming that you have not assigned an IP address, let's try to get dynamic IP address from the DHCP server. Make sure that `eth0` is set for dynamic configuration. You should see line similar to `iface eth0 inet dhcp`:

   ```
   $ cat /etc/network/interfaces
   ```

   ```
   ubuntu@ubuntu:~$ cat /etc/network/interfaces
   # The loopback network interface
   auto lo
   iface lo inet loopback

   # The primary network interface
   auto eth0
   iface eth0 inet dhcp
   ```

9. Execute the `dhclient` command to query the local DHCP server:

   ```
   $ sudo dhclient -v
   ```

   ```
   ubuntu@ubuntu:~$ sudo dhclient -v
   Internet Systems Consortium DHCP Client 4.2.4
   Copyright 2004-2012 Internet Systems Consortium.
   All rights reserved.
   For info, please visit https://www.isc.org/software/dhcp/

   Listening on LPF/eth0/08:00:27:bb:a6:03
   Sending on   LPF/eth0/08:00:27:bb:a6:03
   Sending on   Socket/fallback
   DHCPDISCOVER on eth0 to 255.255.255.255 port 67 interval 3 (xid=0x408c0d92)
   DHCPREQUEST of 10.0.2.15 on eth0 to 255.255.255.255 port 67 (xid=0x408c0d92)
   DHCPOFFER of 10.0.2.15 from 10.0.2.2
   DHCPACK of 10.0.2.15 from 10.0.2.2
   RTNETLINK answers: File exists
   bound to 10.0.2.15 -- renewal in 40826 seconds.
   ```

10. If you can see a line similar to bound to 10.0.2.15, then you are assigned with a new IP address. If you keep getting DHCPDISCOVER messages, this means that your DHCP server is not accessible or not assigning an IP address to this client.

11. Now, if you check the IP address again, you should see a newly IP address listed:

    ```
    $ ifconfig eth0
    ```

12. Assuming that you have received a proper IP address, let's move on to the default gateway:

    ```
    $ ip route
    ```

```
ubuntu@ubuntu:~$ route -n
Kernel IP routing table
Destination     Gateway         Genmask         Flags Metric Ref    Use Iface
0.0.0.0         10.0.2.2        0.0.0.0         UG    0      0        0 eth0
10.0.2.0        0.0.0.0         255.255.255.0   U     0      0        0 eth0
```

13. The preceding command lists our default route. In my case, it is 10.0.2.2. Let's try to ping the default gateway:

    ```
    $ ping -c 5 10.0.2.2
    ```

14. If you get a response from the gateway, this means that your local network is working properly. If you do not get a response from gateway, you may want to check your local firewall.

15. Check the firewall status:

    ```
    $ sudo ufw status
    ```

16. Check the rules or temporarily disable the firewall and retry reaching your gateway:

    ```
    $ sudo ufw disable
    ```

17. Next, check whether we can go beyond our gateway. Try to ping an external server. I am trying to ping a public DNS server by Google:

    ```
    $ ping -c 5 8.8.8.8
    ```

18. If you successfully receive a response, then you have a working network connection. If this does not work, then you can check the problem with the `mtr` command. This command will display each router between your server and the destination server:

```
$ mtr -r -c 1 8.8.8.8
```

```
ubuntu@ubuntu:~$ mtr -r -c 1 8.8.8.8
Start: Tue Jul 28 11:57:48 2015
HOST: ubuntu                        Loss%   Snt   Last    Avg   Best   Wrst StDev
  1.|-- 10.0.2.2                    0.0%     1    0.6    0.6    0.6    0.6   0.0
  2.|-- 192.168.0.1                 0.0%     1   10.0   10.0   10.0   10.0   0.0
  3.|-- 78-212-119-111.mysipl.com   0.0%     1    5.0    5.0    5.0    5.0   0.0
  4.|-- 77-212-119-111.mysipl.com   0.0%     1    6.4    6.4    6.4    6.4   0.0
  5.|-- 157-134.87.183.mysipl.com   0.0%     1    7.9    7.9    7.9    7.9   0.0
  6.|-- 72.14.196.213               0.0%     1    5.7    5.7    5.7    5.7   0.0
  7.|-- 209.85.142.228              0.0%     1    6.1    6.1    6.1    6.1   0.0
  8.|-- 66.249.94.39                0.0%     1   34.1   34.1   34.1   34.1   0.0
  9.|-- 216.239.48.227              0.0%     1   58.7   58.7   58.7   58.7   0.0
 10.|-- 209.85.246.37               0.0%     1   67.5   67.5   67.5   67.5   0.0
 11.|-- ???                       100.0      1    0.0    0.0    0.0    0.0   0.0
 12.|-- google-public-dns-a.googl   0.0%     1   60.4   60.4   60.4   60.4   0.0
```

19. Next, we need to check DNS servers:

```
$ nslookup www.ubuntu.com
```

```
ubuntu@ubuntu:~$ nslookup www.ubuntu.com
Server:         192.168.0.1
Address:        192.168.0.1#53

Non-authoritative answer:
Name:   www.ubuntu.com
Address: 91.189.89.103
```

20. If you received an IP address for Ubuntu servers, then the DNS connection is working properly. If it's not, you can try changing the DNS servers temporarily. Add the `nameserver` entry to `/etc/resolve.conf` above other `nameserver`, if any:

`nameserver 8.8.8.8`

21. At this point, you should be able to access the Internet. Try to ping an external server by its name:

```
$ ping -c 3 www.ubuntu.com
```

```
ubuntu@ubuntu:~$ ping -c 2 www.ubuntu.com
PING www.ubuntu.com (91.189.89.103) 56(84) bytes of data.
64 bytes from www-ubuntu-com.privet.canonical.com (91.189.89.103): icmp_seq=1 tt
l=47 time=125 ms
64 bytes from www-ubuntu-com.privet.canonical.com (91.189.89.103): icmp_seq=2 tt
l=47 time=128 ms

--- www.ubuntu.com ping statistics ---
2 packets transmitted, 2 received, 0% packet loss, time 1003ms
rtt min/avg/max/mdev = 125.001/126.741/128.481/1.740 ms
```

There's more...

The following are some additional commands that may come handy while working with a network:

- lspci lists all pci devices. Combine it with grep to search for specific device.

- Lsmod shows the status of modules in Linux kernels.

- ip link lists all the available network devices with status and configuration parameters.

- ip addr shows the IP addresses assigned for each device.

- ip route displays routing table entries.

- tracepath/traceroute lists all the routers (path) between local and remote hosts.

- iptables is an administration tool for packet filtering and NAT.

- dig is a DNS lookup utility.

- ethtool queries and controls network drivers and hardware settings.

- route views or edits the IP routing table.

- telnet was the interface for telnet protocol. Now it is a simple tool to quickly check remote working ports.

- Nmap is a powerful network mapping tool.

- netstat displays network connections, routing tables, interface stats, and more.

- ifdown and ifup start or stop the network interface. They are similar to ifconfig down or ifconfig up.

Securing remote access with OpenVPN

VPN enables two or more systems to communicate privately and securely over the public network or Internet. The network traffic is routed through the Internet, but is encrypted. You can use VPN to set up a secure connection between two datacenters or to access office resources from the leisure of your home. The VPN service is also used to protect your online activities, access location restricted contents, and bypass restrictions imposed by your ISP.

VPN services are implemented with a number of different protocols, such as **Point-to-Point Tunneling Protocol** (**PPTP**), **Layer two tunneling protocol** (**L2TP**), IPSec, and SSL. In this recipe, we will set up a free VPN server, OpenVPN. OpenVPN is an open source SSL VPN solution and provides a wide range of configurations. OpenVPN can be configured to use either TCP or UDP protocols. In this recipe, we will set up OpenVPN with its default UDP port 1194.

Getting ready...

You will need one server and one client system and root or equivalent access to both systems.

How to do it...

1. Install OpenVPN with the following command:

    ```
    $ sudo apt-get update
    $ sudo apt-get install openvpn easy-rsa
    ```

2. Now, set up your own certification authority and generate certificate and keys for the OpenVPN server.

3. Next, we need to edit the OpenVPN files that are owned by the root user, and the build-ca script needs root access while writing new keys. Temporarily, change to root account using sudo su:

    ```
    $ sudo su
    ```

    Copy the Easy-RSA directory to /etc/openvpn:

    ```
    # cp -r /usr/share/easy-rsa  /etc/openvpn/
    ```

4. Now edit /etc/openvpn/easy-rsa/vars and change the variables to match your environment:

    ```
    export KEY_COUNTRY="US"
    export KEY_PROVINCE="ca"
    export KEY_CITY="your city"
    export KEY_ORG="your Company"
    ```

```
export KEY_EMAIL="you@company.com"
export KEY_CN="MyVPN"
export KEY_NAME="MyVPN"
export KEY_OU="MyVPN"
```

5. Generate a Master certificate with the following commands:

```
# cd /etc/openvpn/easy-vars
# source vars
# ./clean-all
# ./build-ca
```

6. Next, generate a certificate and private key for the server. Replace the server name with the name of your server:

```
# ./build-key-server servername
```

7. Press the *Enter* key when prompted for the password and company name.

8. When asked for signing the certificate, enter y and then press the *Enter* key.

9. Build **Diffie Hellman** parameters for the OpenVPN server:

```
# ./build-dh
```

10. Copy all the generated keys and certificates to /etc/openvpn:

```
# cp /etc/openvpn/easy-rsa/keys/{servername.crt,
servername.key, ca.crt, dh2048.pem}  /etc/openvpn
```

11. Next, generate a certificate for the client with the following commands:

```
# cd /etc/openvpn/easy-rsa
# source vars
# ./build-key clientname
```

12. Copy the generated key, certificate, and server certificate to the client system. Use a secure transfer mechanism such as SCP:

```
/etc/openvpn/ca.crt
/etc/openvpn/easy-rsa/keys/clientname.crt
/etc/openvpn/easy-rsa/keys/clientname.key
```

13. Now, configure the OpenVPN server. Use the sample configuration files provided by OpenVPN:

```
$ gunzip -c /usr/share/doc/openvpn/examples/sample-config-
files/server.conf.gz > /etc/openvpn/server.conf
```

14. Open `server.conf` in your favorite editor:

    ```
    # nano /etc/openvpn/server.conf
    ```

15. Make sure that the certificate and key path are properly set:

    ```
    ca ca.crt
    cert servername.crt
    key servername.key
    dh dh2048.pen
    ```

16. Enable clients to redirect their web traffic through a VPN server. Uncomment the following line:

    ```
    push "redirect-gateway def1 bypass-dhcp"
    ```

17. To protect against DNS leaks, push DNS settings to VPN clients and uncomment the following lines:

    ```
    push "dhcp-option DNS 208.67.222.222"
    push "dhcp-option DNS 208.67.220.220"
    ```

18. The preceding lines point to OpenDNS servers. You can set them to any DNS server of your choice.

19. Lastly, set OpenVPN to run with unprivileged `user` and `group` and uncomment the following lines:

    ```
    user nobody
    group nogroup
    ```

20. Optionally, you can enable compression on the VPN link. Search and uncomment the following line:

    ```
    comp-lzo
    ```

21. Save the changes and exit the editor.

22. Next, edit `/etc/sysctl` to enable IP forwarding. Find and uncomment the following line by removing the hash, #, in front of it:

    ```
    #net.ipv4.ip_forward=1
    ```

23. Update `sysctl` settings with the following command:

    ```
    # sysctl -p
    ```

24. Now start the server. You should see an output similar to the following:

    ```
    # service openvpn start
     * Starting virtual private network daemon(s)
     *    Autostarting VPN 'server'
    ```

25. When it starts successfully, OpenVPN creates a new network interface named `tun0`. This can be checked with the `ifconfig` command:

```
# ifconfig tun0

tun0      Link encap:UNSPEC  HWaddr 00-00-00-00-00-00-00-
00-00-00-00-00-00-00-00-00
          inet addr:10.8.0.1  P-t-P:10.8.0.2
Mask:255.255.255.255
```

26. If the server does not start normally, you can check the logs at `/var/log/syslog`. It should list all the steps completed by the OpenVPN service.

How it works...

OpenVPN is the open source VPN solution. It is a traffic-tunneling protocol that works in client-server mode. You might already know that VPN is widely used to create a private and secure network connection between two endpoints. It is generally used to access your servers or access office systems from your home. The other popular use of VPN servers is to protect your privacy by routing your traffic through a VPN server. OpenVPN needs two primary components, namely a server and a client. The preceding recipe installs the server component. When the OpenVPN service is started on the OpenVPN host, it creates a new virtual network interface, a tun device named `tun0`. On the client side, OpenVPN provides the client with tools that configure the client with a similar setup by creating a tap device on the client's system.

Once the client is configured with a server hostname or IP address, a server certificate, and client keys, the client initiates a virtual network connection using a tap device on client to a tun device on the server. The provided keys and certificate are used to cross-check server authenticity and then authenticate itself. As the session is established, all network traffic on the client system is routed or tunneled via a tap network interface. All the external services that are accessed by the OpenVPN client, and you get to see the requests as if they are originated from the OpenVPN server and not from the client. Additionally, the traffic between the server and client is encrypted to provide additional security.

There's more...

In this recipe we have installed and configured OpenVPN server. To use the VPN service from your local system you will need a VPN client tool.

Following are the steps to install and configure VPN client on Ubuntu systems:

1. Install the **OpenVPN** client with a similar command the one we used to install the server:

```
$ sudo apt-get update

$ sudo apt-get install openvpn
```

2. Copy the sample `client.conf` configuration file:

```
$ sudo cp /usr/share/doc/openvpn/examples/sample-config-
files/client.conf /etc/openvpn/
```

3. Copy the certificates and keys generated for this client:

```
$ scp user@yourvpnserver:/etc/openvpn/easy-
rsa/keys/client1.key /etc/openvpn
```

4. You can use other tools such as **SFTP** or **WinSCP** on the Windows systems.

5. Now edit `client.conf`, enable client mode, and specify the server name or address:

```
client
```

```
remote your.vpnserver.com 1194
```

6. Make sure that you have set the correct path for keys copied from the server.

7. Now save the configuration file and start the OpenVPN server:

```
$ service openvpn start
```

8. This should create the `tun0` network interface:

```
$ ifconfig tun0
```

9. Check the new routes created by VPN:

```
$ netstat -rn
```

10. You can test your VPN connection with any What's My IP service. You can also take a DNS leak test with online DNS leak tests.

For Windows and Mac OS systems, OpenVPN provides respective client tools. You need an OpenVPN profile with the `.ovpn` extension. A template can be found with the OpenVPN client you are using or on the server under OpenVPN examples. The following is the complete path:

```
/usr/share/doc/openvpn/examples/sample-config-
files/client.conf
```

Note that OpenVPN provides a web-based admin interface to manage VPN clients. This is a commercial offering that provides an easy-to-use admin interface to manage OpenVPN settings and client certificates.

Securing a network with uncomplicated firewall

It is said that the best way to improve server security is to reduce the attack surface. Network communication in any system happens with the help of logical network ports, be it TCP ports or UDP ports. One part of the attack surface is the number of open ports that are waiting for connection to be established. It is always a good idea to block all unrequired ports. Any traffic coming to these ports can be filtered, that is, allowed or blocked with the help of a filtering system.

The Linux kernel provides a built-in packet filtering mechanism called **netfilter**, which is used to filter the traffic coming in or going out of the system. All modern Linux firewall systems use netfilter under the hood. Iptables is a well-known and popular user interface to set up and manage filtering rules for netfilter. It is a complete firewall solution that is highly configurable and highly flexible. However, iptables need effort on the user's part to master the firewall setup. Various frontend tools have been developed to simplify the configuration of iptables. UFW is among the most popular frontend solutions to manage iptables.

Uncomplicated firewall (**UFW**) provides easy-to-use interface for people unfamiliar with firewall concepts. It provides a framework for managing netfilter as well as the command-line interface to manipulate the firewall. With its small command set and plain English parameters, UFW makes it quick and easy to understand and set up firewall rules. At the same time, you can use UFW to configure most of the rules possible with iptables. UFW comes preinstalled with all Ubuntu installations after version 8.04 LTS.

In this recipe, we will secure our Ubuntu server with the help of UFW and also look at some advance configurations possible with UFW.

Getting ready

You will need an access to a root account or an account with root privileges.

How to do it...

Follow these steps to secure network with uncomplicated firewall:

1. UFW comes preinstalled on Ubuntu systems. If it's not, you can install it with the following commands:

```
$ sudo apt-get udpate
$ sudo apt-get install UFW
```

2. Check the status of UFW:

```
$ sudo ufw status
```

```
ubuntu@ubuntu:~$ sudo ufw status
Status: inactive
ubuntu@ubuntu:~$ _
```

3. Add a new rule to allow SSH:

```
$ sudo ufw allow ssh
```

4. Alternatively, you can use a port number to open a particular port:

```
$ sudo ufw allow 22
```

5. Allow only TCP traffic over HTTP (port 80):

```
$ sudo ufw allow http/tcp
```

```
ubuntu@ubuntu:~$ sudo ufw allow http/tcp
Rules updated
Rules updated (v6)
ubuntu@ubuntu:~$ _
```

6. Deny incoming FTP traffic:

```
$ sudo ufw deny ftp
```

7. Check all added rules before starting the firewall:

```
$ sudo ufw show added
```

```
ubuntu@ubuntu:~$ sudo ufw show added
Added user rules (see 'ufw status' for running firewall):
ufw allow 22/tcp
ufw deny 21/tcp
ufw allow 80/tcp
ubuntu@ubuntu:~$ _
```

8. Now enable the firewall:

```
$ sudo ufw enable
```

```
ubuntu@ubuntu:~$ sudo ufw enable
Firewall is active and enabled on system startup
ubuntu@ubuntu:~$ _
```

9. Check the `ufw` status, the `verbose` parameter is optional:

   ```
   $ sudo ufw status verbose
   ```

```
ubuntu@ubuntu:~$ sudo ufw status verbose
Status: active
Logging: on (low)
Default: deny (incoming), allow (outgoing), disabled (routed)
New profiles: skip

To                         Action      From
--                         ------      ----
22/tcp                     ALLOW IN    Anywhere
21/tcp                     DENY IN     Anywhere
80/tcp                     ALLOW IN    Anywhere
22/tcp (v6)                ALLOW IN    Anywhere (v6)
21/tcp (v6)                DENY IN     Anywhere (v6)
80/tcp (v6)                ALLOW IN    Anywhere (v6)
```

10. Get a numbered list of added rules:

    ```
    $ sudo ufw status numbered
    ```

```
ubuntu@ubuntu:~$ sudo ufw status numbered
Status: active

     To                        Action      From
     --                        ------      ----
[ 1] 22/tcp                    ALLOW IN    Anywhere
[ 2] 21/tcp                    DENY IN     Anywhere
[ 3] 80/tcp                    ALLOW IN    Anywhere
[ 4] 22/tcp (v6)               ALLOW IN    Anywhere (v6)
[ 5] 21/tcp (v6)               DENY IN     Anywhere (v6)
[ 6] 80/tcp (v6)               ALLOW IN    Anywhere (v6)
```

11. You can also allow all ports in a range by specifying a port range:

    ```
    $ sudo ufw allow 1050:5000/tcp
    ```

12. If you want to open all ports for a particular IP address, use the following command:

```
$ sudo ufw allow from 10.0.2.100
```

13. Alternatively, you can allow an entire subnet, as follows:

```
$ sudo ufw allow from 10.0.2.0/24
```

14. You can also allow or deny a specific port for a given IP address:

```
$ sudo ufw allow from 10.0.2.100 to any port 2222
$ sudo ufw deny from 10.0.2.100 to any port 5223
```

15. To specify a protocol in the preceding rule, use the following command:

```
$ sudo ufw deny from 10.0.2.100 proto tcp to any port 5223
```

16. Deleting rules:

```
$ sudo ufw delete allow ftp
```

17. Delete rules by specifying their numbers:

```
$ sudo ufw status numbered
$ sudo ufw delete 2
```

18. Add a new rule at a specific number:

```
$ sudo ufw insert 1 allow 5222/tcp        # Inserts a rule at
number 1
```

19. If you want to reject outgoing FTP connections, you can use the following command:

```
$ sudo ufw reject out ftp
```

20. UFW also supports application profiles. To view all application profiles, use the following command:

```
$ sudo ufw app list
```

21. Get more information about the app profile using the following command:

```
$ sudo ufw app info OpenSSH
```

22. Allow the application profile as follows:

```
$ sudo ufw allow OpenSSH
```

23. Set ufw logging levels [off|low|medium|high|full] with the help of the following command:

```
$ sudo ufw logging medium
```

24. View firewall reports with the `show` parameter:

```
$ sudo ufw show added     # list of rules added
$ sudo ufw show raw    # show complete firewall
```

25. Reset `ufw` to its default state (all rules will be backed up by UFW):

```
$ sudo ufw reset
```

There's more...

UFW also provides various configuration files that can be used:

▶ `/etc/default/ufw`: This is the main configuration file.

▶ `/etc/ufw/sysctl.conf`: These are the kernel network variables. Variables in this file override variables in `/etc/sysctl.conf`.

▶ `/var/lib/ufw/user[6].rules or /lib/ufw/user[6].rules` are the rules added via the `ufw` command.

▶ `/etc/ufw/before.init` are the scripts to be run before the UFW initialization.

▶ `/etc/ufw/after.init` are the scripts to be run after the UFW initialization.

See also

▶ Check logging section of the UFW community page for an explanation of UFW logs at `https://help.ubuntu.com/community/UFW`

▶ Check out the UFW manual pages with the following command:

```
$ man ufw
```

Securing against brute force attacks

So you have installed minimal setup of Ubuntu, you have setup SSH with public key authentication and disabled password authentication, and you have also allowed only single non-root user to access the server. You also configured a firewall, spending an entire night understanding the rules, and blocked everything except a few required ports. Now does this mean that your server is secured and you are free to take a nice sound sleep? Nope.

Servers are exposed to the public network, and the SSH daemon itself, which is probably the only service open, and can be vulnerable to attacks. If you monitor the application logs and access logs, you can find repeated systematic login attempts that represent brute force attacks.

Fail2ban is a service that can help you monitor logs in real time and modify iptables rules to block suspected IP addresses. It is an intrusion-prevention framework written in Python. It can be set to monitor logs for SSH daemon and web servers. In this recipe, we will discuss how to install and configure fail2ban.

Getting ready

You will need access to a root account or an account with similar privileges.

How to do it...

Follow these steps to secure against brute force attacks:

1. Fail2ban is available in the Ubuntu package repository, so we can install it with a single command, as follows:

   ```
   $ sudo apt-get update
   $ sudo apt-get install fail2ban
   ```

2. Create a copy of the `fail2ban` configuration file for local modifications:

   ```
   $ sudo cp /etc/fail2ban/jail.conf /etc/fail2ban/jail.local
   ```

3. Open a new configuration file in your favorite editor:

   ```
   $ sudo nano /etc/fail2ban/jail.local
   ```

4. You may want to modify the settings listed under the `[DEFAULT]` section:

   ```
   # The DEFAULT allows a global definition of the options. They can be overridden
   # in each jail afterwards.

   [DEFAULT]
   ignoreip = 127.0.0.1/8
   bantime  = 600
   findtime = 600
   maxretry = 3
   ```

5. Add your IP address to the ignore IP list.

6. Next, set your e-mail address if you wish to receive e-mail notifications of the ban action:

   ```
   destemail = you@provider.com
   sendername = Fail2Ban
   mta = sendmail
   ```

7. Set the required value for the `action` parameter:

   `action = $(action_mwl)s`

8. Enable services you want to be monitored by setting `enable=true` for each service. SSH service is enabled by default:

   `[ssh]`

   `enable = true`

```
[ssh]

enabled   = true
port      = ssh
filter    = sshd
logpath   = /var/log/auth.log
maxretry = 6
```

9. Set other parameters if you want to override the default settings.

10. Fail2ban provides default configuration options for various applications. These configurations are disabled by default. You can enable them depending on your requirement.

11. Restart the `fail2ban` service:

    `$ sudo service fail2ban restart`

12. Check iptables for the rules created by fail2ban:

    `$ sudo iptables -S`

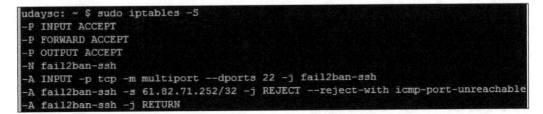

```
udaysc: ~ $ sudo iptables -S
-P INPUT ACCEPT
-P FORWARD ACCEPT
-P OUTPUT ACCEPT
-N fail2ban-ssh
-A INPUT -p tcp -m multiport --dports 22 -j fail2ban-ssh
-A fail2ban-ssh -s 61.82.71.252/32 -j REJECT --reject-with icmp-port-unreachable
-A fail2ban-ssh -j RETURN
```

13. Try some failed SSH login attempts, preferably from some other system.

14. Check iptables again. You should find new rules that reject the IP address with failed login attempts:

```
udaysc: ~ $ sudo iptables -S
-P INPUT ACCEPT
-P FORWARD ACCEPT
-P OUTPUT ACCEPT
-N fail2ban-ssh
-A INPUT -p tcp -m multiport --dports 22 -j fail2ban-ssh
-A fail2ban-ssh -s 12.166.225.156/32 -j REJECT --reject-with icmp-port-unreachab
le
-A fail2ban-ssh -j RETURN
```

How it works...

Fail2ban works by monitoring the specified log files as they are modified with new log entries. It uses regular expressions called filters to detect log entries that match specific criteria, such as failed login attempts. Default installation of fail2ban provides various filters that can be found in the /etc/fail2ban/filter.d directory. You can always create your own filters and use them to detect log entries that match your criteria.

Once it detects multiple logs matching with the configured filters within the specified timeout, fail2ban adjusts the firewall settings to reject the matching IP address for configured time period.

There's more...

Check out the article about defending against brute force attacks at http://www.la-samhna.de/library/brutessh.html.

The preceding articles shows multiple options to defend against SSH brute force attacks. As mentioned in the article, you can use iptables to slow down brute force attacks by blocking IP addresses:

```
$ iptables -A INPUT -p tcp --dport 22 -m state --state NEW -m
recent --set --name SSH -j ACCEPT

$ iptables -A INPUT -p tcp --dport 22 -m recent --update --seconds
60 --hitcount 4 --rttl --name SSH -j LOG --log-prefix "SSH_brute_force "

$ iptables -A INPUT -p tcp --dport 22 -m recent --update --seconds
60 --hitcount 4 --rttl --name SSH -j DROP
```

These commands will create an iptables rule to permit only three SSH login attempts per minute. After three attempts, whether they are successful or not, the attempting IP address will be blocked for another 60 seconds.

Discussing Ubuntu security best practices

In this recipe, we will look at some best practices to secure Ubuntu systems. Linux is considered to be a well secured operating system. It is quite easy to maintain the security and protect our systems from unauthorized access by following a few simple norms or rules.

Getting ready

You will need access to a root or account with `sudo` privileges. These steps are intended for a new server setup. You can apply them selectively for the servers already in productions.

How to do it...

Follow these steps to discuss Ubuntu security best practices:

1. Install updates from the Ubuntu repository. You can install all the available updates or just select security updates, depending on your choice and requirement:

   ```
   $ sudo apt-get update
   $ sudo apt-get upgrade
   ```

2. Change the root password; set a strong and complex root password and note it down somewhere. You are not going to use it every day:

   ```
   $ sudo passwd
   ```

3. Add a new user account and set a strong password for it. You can skip this step if the server has already set up a non-root account, like Ubuntu:

   ```
   $ sudo adduser john
   $ sudo passwd john
   ```

4. Add a new user to the `Sudoers` group:

   ```
   $ sudo adduser john sudo
   ```

5. Enable the public key authentication over SSH and import your public key to new user's `authorized_keys` file.

6. Restrict SSH logins:

   1. Change the default SSH port:

      ```
      port 2222
      ```

   2. Disable root login over SSH:

      ```
      PermitRootLogin no
      ```

3. Disable password authentication:

```
PasswordAuthentication no
```

4. Restrict users and allow IP address:

```
AllowUsers john@(your-ip) john@(other-ip)
```

7. Install fail2ban to protect against brute force attacks and set a new SSH port in the fail2ban configuration:

```
$ sudo apt-get install fail2ban
```

8. Optionally, install UFW and allow your desired ports:

```
$ sudo ufw allow from <your-IP> to any port 22 proto tcp
$ sudo ufw allow 80/tcp
$ sudo ufw enable
```

9. Maintain periodic snapshots (full-disk backups) of your server. Many cloud service providers offer basic snapshot tools.

10. Keep an eye on application and system logs. You may like to set up log-monitoring scripts that will e-mail any unidentified log entry.

How it works...

The preceding steps are basic and general security measures. They may change according to your server setup, package selection, and the services running on your server. I will try to cover some more details about specific scenarios. Also, I have not mentioned application-specific security practices for web servers and database servers. A separate recipe will be included in the respective chapters. Again, these configurations may change with your setup.

The steps listed earlier can be included in a single shell script and executed at first server boot up. Some cloud providers offer an option to add scripts to be executed on the first run of the server. You can also use centralized configuration tools such as Ansible, Chef/Puppet, and some others. Again, these tools come with their own security risks and increase total attack surface. This is a tradeoff between ease of setup and server security. Make sure that you select a well-known tool if you choose this route.

I have also mentioned creating single user account, except root. I am assuming that you are setting up your production server. With production servers, it is always a good idea to restrict access to one or two system administrators. For production servers, I don't believe in setting up multiple user accounts just for accountability or even setting LDAP-like centralized authentication methods to manage user accounts. This is a production environment and not your backyard. Moreover, if you follow the latest trends in immutable infrastructure concepts, then you should not allow even a single user to interfere with your live servers. Again, your mileage may vary.

Another thing that is commonly recommended is to set up automated and unattended security updates. This depends on how trusted your update source is. You live in a world powered by open source tools where things can break. You don't want things to go haywire without even touching the servers. I would recommend setting up unattended updates on your staging or test environment and then periodically installing updates on live servers, manually. Always have a snapshot of the working setup as your plan B.

You may want to skip host-based firewalls such as UFW when you have specialized firewalls protecting your network. As long as the servers are not directly exposed to the Internet, you can skip the local firewalls.

Minimize installed packages and service on single server. Remember the Unix philosophy, *do one thing and do it well,* and follow it. By minimizing the installed packages, you will effectively reduce the attack surface, and maybe save little on resources too. Think of it as a house with a single door verses a house with multiple doors. Also, running single service from one server provides layered security. This way, if a single server is compromised, the rest of your infrastructure remains in a safe state.

Remember that with all other tradeoffs in place, you cannot design a perfectly secured system, there is always a possibility that someone will break in. Direct your efforts to increase the time required for an attacker to break into your servers.

See also

- *First 5 Minutes Troubleshooting A Server* at `http://devo.ps/blog/troubleshooting-5minutes-on-a-yet-unknown-box/`

- Try to break in your own servers at `http://www.backtrack-linux.org/`

- What Can Be Done To Secure Ubuntu Server? at `http://askubuntu.com/questions/146775/what-can-be-done-to-secure-ubuntu-server`

3
Working with Web Servers

In this chapter, we will cover the following recipes:

- ▶ Installing and configuring the Apache web server
- ▶ Serving dynamic contents with PHP
- ▶ Hosting multiple websites with a virtual domain
- ▶ Securing web traffic with HTTPS
- ▶ Installing Nginx with PHP_FPM
- ▶ Setting Nginx as a reverse proxy
- ▶ Load balancing with Nginx
- ▶ Setting HTTPs on Nginx
- ▶ Benchmarking and performance tuning of Apache
- ▶ Securing the web server
- ▶ Troubleshooting the web server

Introduction

A web server is a tool that publishes documents on a network, generally the Internet. HTTP is called a language of the Internet and web servers, apart from browsers, are native speakers of HTTP. Web servers generally listen on one or multiple ports for requests from clients and accept requests in the form of URLs and HTTP headers. On receiving a request, web servers look for the availability of the requested resource and return the contents to the client. The term web server can refer to one or multiple physical servers or a software package, or both of them working together.

Some well known web servers include the Apache web server, Microsoft IIS, and Nginx. Apache web server is the most popular web server package available across platforms such as Windows and Linux. It is an open source project and freely available for commercial use. Nginx, which is again an open source web server project, started to overcome the problems in a high-load environment. Because of its lightweight resource utilization and ability to scale even on minimal hardware, Nginx quickly became a well known name. Nginx offers a free community edition as well as a paid commercial version with added support and extra features. Lastly, Microsoft IIS is a web server specifically designed for Windows servers. Apache still has the major share in the web server market, with Nginx rapidly taking over with some other notable alternatives such as lighttpd and H2O.

Apache is a modularized web server that can be extended by dynamically loading extra modules as and when required. This provides the flexibility to run a bare minimum web server or a fully featured box with modules to support compression, SSL, redirects, language modules, and more. Apache provides multiple connection processing **algorithms** called **multi-processing modules** (**MPM**). It provides an option to create a separate single threaded process for each new request (mpm_prefork), a multi-threaded process that can handle multiple concurrent requests (mpm_worker), or the latest development of mpm_event, which separates the active and idle connections.

Nginx can be considered the next generation of web servers. Its development started to solve the **C10k** problem, that is, handling ten thousand connections at a time. Apache, being a process-driven model, has some limitations when handling multiple concurrent connections. Nginx took advantage of the **event-driven** approach with asynchronous, non-blocking connection handling algorithms. A new connection request is handled by a worker process and placed in an event loop where they are continuously checked for events. The events are processed asynchronously. This approach enables Nginx to run with a much lower memory footprint and lower CPU use. It also eliminates the overload of starting a new process for a new connection. A single worker process started by Nginx can handle thousands of concurrent connections.

> It is possible that some terms used throughout this chapter are unknown to you. It is not possible to explain everything in a Cookbook format. A quick Google search for a term will give you more details on them.

Both Apache and Nginx can be configured to process dynamic contents. Apache provides respective language processors such as mod_php and mod_python to process dynamic contents within the worker process itself. Nginx depends on external processors and uses CGI protocols to communicate with external processors. Apache can also be configured to use an external language processor over CGI, but the choice depends on performance and security considerations.

While both Apache and Nginx provide various similar features, they are not entirely interchangeable. Each one has its own pros and cons. Where Nginx excels at serving static contents, Apache performs much better processing dynamic contents. Many web administrators prefer to use Apache and Nginx together.

 Nginx is commonly used as a frontend caching/reverse proxy handling client requests and serving static contents, while Apache is used as a backend server processing dynamic contents.

Nginx handles a large number of connections and passes limited requests of dynamic contents to backend Apache servers. This configuration also allows users to scale horizontally by adding multiple backend servers and setting Nginx as a load balancer.

In this chapter, we will be working with both Apache and Nginx servers. We will learn how to set up Apache with PHP as a language for dynamic contents. We will look at some important configurations of Apache. Later, we will set up Nginx with an optional PHP processor, PHP_FPM, and configure Nginx to work as a reverse proxy and load balancer. We will also look at performance and security configurations for both the servers.

Installing and configuring the Apache web server

In this recipe, we will simply install the Apache web server from the Ubuntu package repository. We will also look at the basic configuration options and set up our first web page.

Getting ready

You will need access to a root account or an account with `sudo` privileges.

I will be using Apache to refer to the Apache web server. The Apache web server is the most popular project by the Apache Foundation and is generally known as just Apache.

How to do it...

Follow these steps to install and configure the Apache web server:

1. Install Apache2 from the Ubuntu package repository:

   ```
   $ sudo apt-get update
   $ sudo apt-get install apache2
   ```

2. Check if Apache2 has installed successfully. The command `wget` should download the `index.html` file:

```
$ wget 127.0.0.1
```

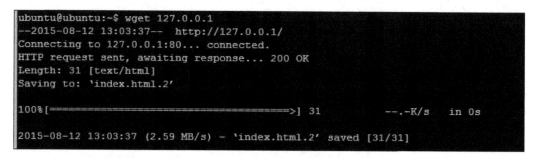

```
ubuntu@ubuntu:~$ wget 127.0.0.1
--2015-08-12 13:03:37--  http://127.0.0.1/
Connecting to 127.0.0.1:80... connected.
HTTP request sent, awaiting response... 200 OK
Length: 31 [text/html]
Saving to: 'index.html.2'

100%[===================================>] 31          --.-K/s   in 0s

2015-08-12 13:03:37 (2.59 MB/s) - 'index.html.2' saved [31/31]
```

3. You can also open a browser on a local machine and point it to the server IP address. You should see a default **It works!** page customized for Ubuntu:

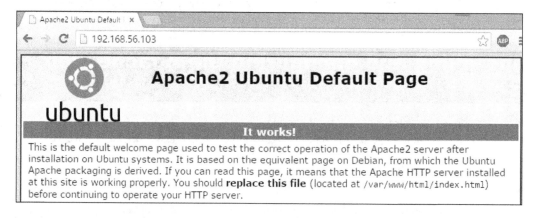

4. Now, let's proceed with creating our first virtual host. First create a directory structure. Change the directory to `/var/www/` and create a new directory for the contents of our site:

```
$ cd /var/www
```

```
$ sudo mkdir example.com
```

5. Change the ownership and group of the directory `example.com`:

```
$ sudo chown ubuntu:www-data example.com
```

6. Set the file permissions to secure web contents:

```
$ sudo chmod 750 example.com
```

7. Create the required directories under the `example.com` directory:

```
$ cd example.com
$ mkdir public_html
```

8. Create a `index.html` file under the `public_html` directory:

```
$ echo '<b>Hello World ...</b>' > public_html/index.html
```

9. Next, we need to set up a new virtual host under the Apache configuration.

10. Copy the default **Virtual Host** file under `/etc/apache2/sites-available` and use it as a starting point for our configuration:

```
$ cd /etc/apache2/sites-available
$ sudo cp 000-default.conf example.com.conf
```

11. Edit `example.com.conf` to match it with the following example. Change the parameters as per your requirements:

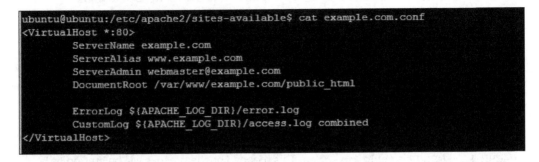

```
ubuntu@ubuntu:/etc/apache2/sites-available$ cat example.com.conf
<VirtualHost *:80>
        ServerName example.com
        ServerAlias www.example.com
        ServerAdmin webmaster@example.com
        DocumentRoot /var/www/example.com/public_html

        ErrorLog ${APACHE_LOG_DIR}/error.log
        CustomLog ${APACHE_LOG_DIR}/access.log combined
</VirtualHost>
```

12. Save the changes and exit `example.com.conf`.

13. If you are using the same port as the default `VirtualHost`, do not forget to disable the default one:

```
$ sudo a2dissite 000-default.conf
```

14. Finally, enable our new `VirtualHost` with `a2ensite` and reload Apache:

```
$ sudo a2ensite example.com.conf
$ sudo service apache2 reload
```

15. Start your browser and point it to the domain or IP address of your server:

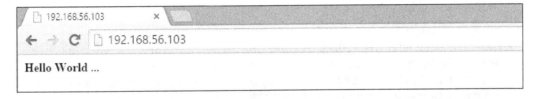

How it works...

The Apache package for Ubuntu is included in the default package repository. We need a single command to install the Apache web server. Installation creates a structure of configuration files under `/etc/apache2` and a sample web page under `/var/www/html`.

As mentioned in the default **It works!** page, Apache2 does not use a single configuration file such as `httpd.conf` in older versions, but rather separates its configuration across multiple configuration files. These files are named after their respective uses. `apache2.conf` is now a main configuration file and creates a central configuration by including all other files.

`conf-available`, `mods-available,` and `sites-available` contain configuration snippets and other files for global configurations, modules, and virtual hosts respectively. These configurations are selectively activated under their enabled counterparts with symbolic links for each configuration to be enabled.

`envvars` contains all environment variables and default values for Apache to work.

`ports.conf` defines the ports Apache should listen on.

The default web page is created under the `/var/www/html` directory.

In this recipe, we have created our virtual host for the domain name `example.com` and hosted it under the directory `/var/www/example.com`. Next, we have to change the owner and default group of this directory to the user, ubuntu and group, `www-data`. This grants full access to the user `ubuntu` and allows read and execute access to the group `www-data`. If you have observed the contents of the `envvars` file, you may have noticed that the variable `APACHE_RUN_GROUP` is set to `www-data`. This means Apache process will be started as the group `www-data`. By setting a default group, we have allowed Apache process to read the contents of the `example.com` directory. We have also enabled write access to the `logs` directory so that Apache processes can log to this directory.

After creating the virtual host configuration and setting the respective options, all we need to do is enable a new virtual host or site. Apache2 provides the respective commands to enable or disable configurations, modules, and sites. `a2ensite` will be used to enable the site from options available under `sites-available`. Basically, this will create a symbolic link under the `sites-enabled` directory to a specified site configuration. Similarly, `a2dissite` will disable the site by removing the symbolic link from the `sites-enabled` directory. Similar commands are available to work with configurations and modules.

There's more...

You may want to get rid of the warning that says `Could not reliably determine the server's fully qualified domain name`. This warning appears because the Apache process could not find the default FQDN for this server. You can set the default FQDN simply by creating a new configuration file and then enabling this new configuration:

1. Create a new file under the `conf-available` directory:

   ```
   $ sudo vi /etc/apache2/conf-available/fqdn.conf
   ```

2. Add a server name variable to this file:

   ```
   ServerName  localhost
   ```

3. Save the changes and enable this configuration:

   ```
   $ sudo a2enconf fqdn
   ```

4. Reload the Apache server:

   ```
   $ sudo service apache2 reload
   ```

HTTP version 2 support

If you are looking for HTTP2 support, Apache does provide a separate module for that. Apache version 2.4.17 ships with a module, `mod_http2`, that implements the latest HTTP version, HTTP2. It is still an experimental implementation and needs to be enabled manually. This version of Apache (2.4.17) is available with Ubuntu Xenial (16.04) in the default package repository. If you are using Ubuntu 14.04, you can use the external repository as follows:

```
$ sudo add-apt-repository -y ppa:ondrej/apache2
```

Once the required version of Apache is installed, you can enable `mod_http2` as follows:

```
$ sudo a2enmod http2
```

Next, edit the specific virtual host file to enable the HTTP2 protocol for a specific site. Note that you need to configure your site to use an SSL/TLS connection:

```
<VirtualHost *:443>

    Protocols h2 http/1.1

    ...

</VirtualHost>
```

Finally, restart your Apache server:

```
$ sudo service apache2 restart
```

H2O, the new name in web servers, is developed around the HTTP2 protocol. It does support both HTTP 1.1 and a stable implementation of the HTTP2 protocol. You may want to check this out as your local or development server.

See also

You can read more by following the links:

- There is a good Q and A about permissions for web directory at `http://serverfault.com/questions/357108/what-permissions-should-my-website-files-folders-have-on-a-linux-webserver`

- You can find more details about installing the Apache web server at `https://help.ubuntu.com/lts/serverguide/httpd.html`

- Apache official documentation - `http://httpd.apache.org/docs/2.4/`

Serving dynamic contents with PHP

In this recipe, we will learn how to install PHP and set it to work alongside the Apache web server. We will install PHP binaries and then the Apache module `mod_php` to support PHP-based dynamic contents.

Getting ready

You will need access to a root account or an account with `sudo` privileges.

The Apache web server should be installed and working properly.

How to do it...

Follow these steps to serve dynamic contents with PHP:

1. Install PHP7 and the Apache module for PHP support:

   ```
   $ sudo apt-get update
   $ sudo apt-get install -y php7.0 libapache2-mod-php7.0
   ```

2. Check if PHP is properly installed and which version has been installed:

   ```
   $ php -v
   ```

```
ubuntu@ubuntu:~$ php -v
PHP 7.0.4-7ubuntu2 (cli) ( NTS )
Copyright (c) 1997-2016 The PHP Group
Zend Engine v3.0.0, Copyright (c) 1998-2016 Zend Technologies
    with Zend OPcache v7.0.6-dev, Copyright (c) 1999-2016, by Zend Technologies
```

3. Create `index.php` under the `public_html` directory of our site:

   ```
   $ cd /var/www/example.com/public_html
   $ vi index.php
   ```

4. Add the following contents to `index.php`:

   ```
   <?php echo phpinfo(); ?>
   ```

5. Save and exit the `index.php` file.

6. Open `example.com.conf` from `sites-available`:

   ```
   $ sudo vi /etc/apache2/sites-available/example.com.conf
   ```

7. Add the following line under the `VirtualHost` directive:

   ```
   DirectoryIndex index.php index.html
   ```

```
ubuntu@ubuntu:~$ cat /etc/apache2/sites-available/example.com.conf
<VirtualHost *:80>
        ServerName example.com
        ServerAlias www.example.com
        ServerAdmin webmaster@example.com
        DirectoryIndex index.php index.html
        DocumentRoot /var/www/example.com/public_html
```

8. Save the changes and reload Apache:

   ```
   $ sudo service apache2 reload
   ```

9. Now, access your site with your browser, and you should see a page with information regarding the installed PHP:

PHP Version 7.0.4-7ubuntu2	
System	Linux ubuntu 4.4.0-21-generic #37-Ubuntu SMP Mon Apr 18 18:33:37 UTC
Server API	Apache 2.0 Handler
Virtual Directory Support	disabled
Configuration File (php.ini) Path	/etc/php/7.0/apache2
Loaded Configuration File	/etc/php/7.0/apache2/php.ini

How it works...

Here, we have installed PHP binaries on our server along with the Apache module `libapache2-mod-php7.0` to support dynamic content coded in PHP. A module, mod_php, runs inside Apache process and processes PHP scripts from within Apache itself. For mod_php to work, Apache needs to run with the `mpm_prefork` module. PHP setup completes all these settings and restarts the Apache server:

```
Creating config file /etc/php/7.0/apache2/php.ini with new version
Module mpm_event disabled.
Enabling module mpm_prefork.
apache2_switch_mpm Switch to prefork
apache2_invoke: Enable module php7.0
Setting up php7.0 (7.0.4-7ubuntu2) ...
ubuntu@ubuntu:~$
```

After we have installed PHP and mod_php, we simply need to create a PHP script. We have created `index.php` with little code to display `phpinfo`. At this stage, if you have both `index.html` and `index.php` under the same directory; by default, `index.html` will take over and be rendered first. You will need to explicitly specify `index.php` to access the page as `http://127.0.0.1/index.php`. We have set a directive, `DirectoryIndex`, under Apache Virtual Host to set `index.php` as a default index file.

PHP settings

All PHP settings are listed under its own configuration file, `php.ini`. PHP comes with two sets of configurations, as follows:

/usr/lib/php/7.0/php.ini-development

The `/usr/lib/php/7.0/php.ini-productionDevelopment` file is customized for a development environment and enables options like `display_errors`. For production systems, you can use the configuration file, `php.ini-production`.

The preceding files can be treated as a reference configuration that ships with the PHP installation. A copy of `php.ini-production` can be found under `/etc/php/7.0`. Apache and CLI configurations are separated in respective directories. You can directly edit settings under these files or simply use default files by creating a symbolic link to the development or production file as follows:

```
$ cd /etc/php/7.0/apache2
$ sudo mv php.ini php.ini.orig
$ sudo ln -s /usr/lib/php/7.0/php.ini-development php.ini
```

There's more...

Along with PHP, Apache supports various other scripting languages for dynamic content. You can install modules for Perl, Python, Ruby, and other scripting languages.

Add Python support:

```
$ sudo apt-get install libapache2-mod-python
```

Add Perl support:

```
$ sudo apt-get install libapache2-mod-perl2
```

Add Ruby support:

```
$ sudo apt-get install libapache2-mod-passenger
```

Installing the LAMP stack

If you are interested in installing the entire LAMP stack, then Ubuntu provides a single command to do so. Use the following command to install Apache, PHP, and MySQL collectively:

```
$ sudo apt-get install lamp-server^
```

Notice the caret symbol at the end of the command. If you miss this symbol, apt will return an error saying `package not found`.

> `lamp-server` is set in the Ubuntu repository as a task to install and configure Apache, PHP, and MySQL collectively. The caret symbol in `apt-get` command is used to specify the task rather than the package. Alternatively, you can use the `tasksel` command as `$ sudo tasksel install lamp-server`. **Tasksel** is a program used to ease the installation of packages that are commonly used together.

Upgrading PHP under Ubuntu 14

As of Ubuntu 14.10, Ubuntu does not provide a package for PHP7 in its repository, but you can use a Debian package repository to upgrade your PHP version. This repository is maintained by Ondřej Surý.

Use the following commands to upgrade to PHP 7:

```
$ sudo apt-get install software-properties-common
$ sudo add-apt-repository ppa:ondrej/php
$ sudo apt-get update
$ sudo apt-get install php7.0
```

Check the PHP version after installation completes:

```
$ php -v
```

Hosting multiple websites with a virtual domain

Setting multiple domains on a single server is a very commonly asked question. In fact, it is very easy to do this with virtual host. In this recipe, we will set up two domains on a single server and set up a sub-domain as well. We will also look at IP-based virtual hosts.

Getting ready

You will need access to a root account or an account with `sudo` privileges.

You will need the Apache server installed and working. This recipe describes configuration for Apache version 2.4

You may need a DNS set up if you want to access configured domains over the Internet.

We will set up two domains, namely `example1.dom` and `example2.com`, and a sub-domain, `dev.example1.com`.

How to do it...

Follow these steps to host multiple websites with a virtual domain:

1. Change the directory to `/var/www` and create a directory structure for the required domains and sub-domain. Also create a blank `index.html` for each domain:

   ```
   $ cd /var/www
   $ sudo mkdir -p example1.com/public_html
   $ sudo touch example1.com/public_html
   $ sudo cp -R example1.com example2.com
   $ sudo cp -R example1.com dev.example1.com
   ```

2. Change the directory ownership and file permissions on the newly created directories:

```
$ sudo chown -R ubuntu:www-data example*
$ sudo chown -R ubuntu:www-data dev.example1.com
$ chmod 750 -R example*
$ chmod 750 -R dev.example1.com
```

 Note the use of the wildcard syntax (chmod 750 -R example*). You can use a similar syntax with various other commands in Linux and save some repeated typing or copy and paste work.

3. Edit the index.html file for each domain with the respective text:

```
ubuntu@ubuntu:/var/www$ cat example1.com/public_html/index.html
<b>Hello from example1.com</b>
ubuntu@ubuntu:/var/www$ cat example2.com/public_html/index.html
<b>Hello from example2.com</b>
ubuntu@ubuntu:/var/www$ cat dev.example1.com/public_html/index.html
<b>Hello from developers at dev.example1.com</b>
```

4. Next, we need to create virtual host configuration for each domain. Change the directory to /etc/apache2/sites-available and copy the default virtual host file 000-default.conf:

```
$ cd /etc/apache2/sites-available
$ sudo cp 000-default.conf example1.com.conf
```

5. Edit the new virtual host file and set ServerName, DocumentRoot, and other variables to match your environment. The final file should look something like this:

```
<VirtualHost *:80>
    ServerName example1.com
    ServerAlias www.example1.com
    DocumentRoot /var/www/example1.com/public_html
    ...
</VirtualHost>
```

6. Now copy this virtual host file to create example2.com.conf and dev.example1.com.conf and modify the respective settings in each of them. You need to update the serverName, serverAlias, and DocumentRoot parameters.

7. Here, we are done with the setup and configuration part. Now enable the virtual hosts and reload the Apache server for the settings to take effect:

```
$ sudo a2ensite example*
$ sudo a2ensite dev.example1.com.conf
$ sudo service apache2 reload
```

8. You can check all enabled virtual hosts with the following command:

```
$ sudo a2query -s
```

9. Next, to test our setup, we need to configure the hosts' setup on the local system. Open and edit the `/etc/hosts` file and add host entries. If you have Windows as your local system, you can find the `hosts` file under `%systemroot%\System32\drivers\etc`:

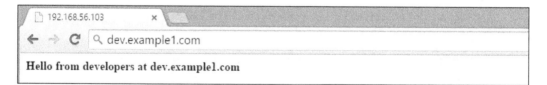

```
                                            hosts - Notepad
File   Edit   Format   View   Help
127.0.0.1           localhost
192.168.56.103     example1.com
192.168.56.103     example2.com
192.168.56.103     dev.example1.com
```

10. Finally, try to access domains by their names. You should see text entered in the respective `index.html` files for each domain:

```
 192.168.56.103          ×
 ←  →  C    dev.example1.com

Hello from developers at dev.example1.com
```

How it works...

Multiple domain hosting works with the concept of **NamedVirtualHost**. We have configured virtual hosts with **ServerName** and **ServerAlias**. When a client sends a request with a domain name, it sends a host name in the request headers. This host name is used by Apache to determine the actual virtual host to serve this request. If none of the available virtual hosts match the requested host header, then the default virtual host or the first virtual host will be used to serve the request.

In this example, we have used hosts file to map test domain names with local IP. With the actual domain name, you need to point DNS servers to the IP address of your web server. Generally, all popular hosting providers host their own DNS servers. You need to add these DNS servers to your domain setting with domain registrar. Then, on your hosting side, you need to set respective **A records** and **CNAME** records. An A record points to an IP address and the CNAME record is an alias for the A record used for pointing a subdomain to an A record. Your hosting provider should give you details on how to configure domains and subdomains.

In previous versions of Apache server, you might need to enable `NameVirtualHost` under the configuration file. Find a line similar to `#NameVirtualHost 172.20.30.40` and uncomment it by removing the # symbol at the start.

You can also set up IP-based virtual hosts. If you have multiple IP addresses available on your server, you can set the virtual host to listen on a particular IP address. Use the following steps to set up an IP-based virtual host:

1. Get a list of the available IP addresses:

```
$ ifconfig | grep "inet addr"
ubuntu@ubuntu:~$ ifconfig | grep "inet addr"
inet addr:10.0.2.15  Bcast:10.0.2.255  Mask:255.255.255.0
inet addr:192.168.56.102  Bcast:192.168.56.255
Mask:255.255.255.0
inet addr:127.0.0.1  Mask:255.0.0.0
```

2. Edit the virtual host configuration and set it to match the following:

```
Listen 80
<VirtualHost 192.168.56.102>
        DocumentRoot /var/www/example1.com/public_html
        ServerName example1.com
</VirtualHost>
```

See also

▶ Apache documentation at `https://httpd.apache.org/docs/2.2/vhosts/examples.html`

▶ Refer to the *Installing and configuring the Apache web server* recipe for the installation and configuration of the Apache web server.

Securing web traffic with HTTPS

HTTP is a non-secure protocol commonly used to communicate over the Web. The traffic is transferred in plain text form and can be captured and interpreted by a third-party attacker. **Transport Layer Security** and **Secure Socket Layer** protocols (**TLS/SSL**) can be used to secure the traffic between client and server. These protocols encapsulate normal traffic in an encrypted and secure wrapper. It also validates the identity of the client and server with SSL keys, certificates, and certification authorities.

When HTTP is combined with TLS or SSL, it is abbreviated as HTTPS or HTTP secure. Port 443 is used as a standard port for secured HTTP communication. Nearly all leading web servers provide inbuilt support for enabling HTTPS. Apache has a module called mod_ssl that enables the use of HTTPS.

To set up your servers with SSL/TLS encrypted traffic, you will need an SSL certificate and a key pair that can be used to encrypt traffic. Generally, the certificate and keys are obtained from a trusted signing authority. They charge you some fees to verify your ownership of the web property and allocate the required signed certificates. You can also generate self-signed certificates for internal use. Few certification authorities provide a free SSL certificate. Recently, Mozilla has started a free and automated certificate authority named *Let's Encrypt*. At the time of writing, the service is in public beta and has started allocating certificates. Let's Encrypt offers a client that can be used to obtain certificates and set up automated renewal. You can also find various unofficial clients for Apache and Nginx servers.

In this recipe, we will learn how to create our own self-signed certificate and set up the Apache server to serve contents over a secure channel.

Getting ready

You will need access to a root account or an account with sudo privileges. I assume that you have the Apache server preinstalled. You will also need OpenSSL installed.

Make sure your firewall, if any, allows traffic on port 443. Check *Chapter 2, Networking, Securing network with uncomplicated firewall* recipe for more details on Uncomplicated Firewall.

How to do it...

Follow these steps to secure web traffic with HTTPS:

1. First, we will start by creating a self-signed SSL certificate. Create a directory under /etc/apache2 to hold the certificate and key:

   ```
   $ sudo mkdir /etc/apache2/ssl
   ```

2. Change to the new directory and enter the following command to create a certificate and SSL key:

```
$ cd /etc/apache2/ssl
$ sudo openssl req -x509 -nodes -days 365 \
-newkey rsa:2048 -keyout ssl.key -out ssl.crt
```

3. This will prompt you to enter some information about your company and website. Enter the respective details and press *Enter* for each prompt:

```
Country Name (2 letter code) [AU]:IN
State or Province Name (full name) [Some-State]:MH
Locality Name (eg, city) []:MUM
Organization Name (eg, company) [Internet Widgits Pty Ltd]:example
Organizational Unit Name (eg, section) []:tech
Common Name (e.g. server FQDN or YOUR name) []:example.com
Email Address []:admin@example.com
```

4. After you are done with it, you can check the generated certificate and key:

```
$ ls -1
```

```
ubuntu@ubuntu:/etc/apache2/ssl$ ls -1
total 8
-rw-r--r-- 1 root root 1391 Aug 12 14:55 ssl.crt
-rw-r--r-- 1 root root 1704 Aug 12 14:55 ssl.key
```

5. Next, we need to configure Apache to use SSL. We will enable SSL for the previously created virtual host.

6. Open the Virtual Host configuration file, `example.com.conf`. After removing comments, it should look similar to the following:

```
ubuntu@ubuntu:~$ cat /etc/apache2/sites-available/example.com.conf
<VirtualHost *:80>
        ServerName example.com
        ServerAlias www.example.com
        ServerAdmin webmaster@example.com
        DirectoryIndex index.php index.html
        DocumentRoot /var/www/example.com/public_html

        ErrorLog ${APACHE_LOG_DIR}/error.log
        CustomLog ${APACHE_LOG_DIR}/access.log combined
</VirtualHost>
```

7. Now, copy the entire `<VirtualHost *:80> ... </VirtualHost>` tag and paste it at the end of the file.

8. Under the newly copied contents, change the port from `80` to `443`.

9. Add the following lines below the `DocumentRoot` line. This will enable SSL and specify the path to the certificate and key:

   SSLEngine on

   SSLCertificateFile /etc/apache2/ssl/ssl.crt

   SSLCertificateKeyFile /etc/apache2/ssl/ssl.key

10. The final file should look something like this:

```
ubuntu@ubuntu:~$ cat /etc/apache2/sites-available/example.com.conf
<VirtualHost *:80>
        ServerName example.com
        ServerAlias www.example.com
        ServerAdmin webmaster@example.com
        DirectoryIndex index.php index.html
        DocumentRoot /var/www/example.com/public_html

        ErrorLog ${APACHE_LOG_DIR}/error.log
        CustomLog ${APACHE_LOG_DIR}/access.log combined
</VirtualHost>

<VirtualHost *:443>
        ServerName example.com
        ServerAlias www.example.com
        ServerAdmin webmaster@example.com
        DirectoryIndex index.php index.html
        DocumentRoot /var/www/example.com/public_html

        SSLEngine on
        SSLCertificateFile /etc/apache2/ssl/ssl.crt
        SSLCertificateKeyFile /etc/apache2/ssl/ssl.key

        ErrorLog ${APACHE_LOG_DIR}/error.log
        CustomLog ${APACHE_LOG_DIR}/access.log combined
</VirtualHost>
```

11. Save the changes, exit `example.com.conf`, and enable the `mod_ssl` module on the Apache server:

    $ sudo a2enmod ssl

12. Next, enable the Virtual Host `example.com`. If it's already enabled, it will return a message saying `site example.com already enabled`:

    $ sudo a2ensite example.com.conf

13. Reload the Apache server for the changes to take effect:

    $ sudo service apache2 reload

14. Now, open your browser on the client system and point it to your domain name or IP address with HTTPS at the start:

    ```
    https://example.com
    ```

15. Your browser may return an error saying **Invalid Certification Authority**. This is fine as we are using a self-signed certificate. Click **Advanced** and then click **Proceed to example.com** to open a specified page:

16. Once the page is loaded completely, find the padlock icon in the upper right corner of the browser and click on it. The second section with the green lock icon will display the encryption status. Now your communication with the server is encrypted and secure:

How it works...

We have created a self-signed certificate to secure an HTTP communication. The key will be used to encrypt all communication with clients. Another thing to note is that we have defined a separate Virtual Host entry on port 443. This Virtual Host will be used for all requests that are received over port 443. At the same time, we have allowed non-secured HTTP communication for the same Virtual Host. To disable non-secure communication on port 80, you can simply comment out the original Virtual Host configuration. Alternatively, you can separate both configurations into two files and enable or disable with the a2ensite and a2dissite commands.

Some of the parameters used for generating a key and certificate are as follows:

 ▶ - nodes specifies that we do not want to use a passphrase for a key.

 ▶ - days this specifies the number of days the certificate is valid for. Our certificate is valid for 365 days, that is, a year.

 ▶ - newkey rsa:2048 this option is used to generate a certificate along with a private key. rsa:2048 specifies the 2048 bit long RSA private key.

I have modified the existing Virtual Host entry to demonstrate the minimal configuration required to enable secure HTTP communication. You can always use the default secure Virtual Host configuration available under sites-available/default-ssl.conf. This file provides some additional parameters with respective comments.

The certificate created in this recipe will not be trusted over the Internet but can be used for securing local or internal communication. For production use, it is advisable to get a certificate signed from an external, well known **certification authority**. This will avoid the initial errors in browsers.

There's more...

To get a signed certificate from an external certification authority, you will need a CSR document.

The following are the steps to generate a CSR:

1. Generate a key for the CSR:

    ```
    $ openssl genrsa -des3 -out server.key 2048
    ```

2. You will be asked to enter a passphrase for the key and then verify it. They will be generated with name server.key.

3. Now, remove the passphrase from the key. We don't want to enter a passphrase each time a key is used:

```
$ openssl rsa -in server.key -out server.key.insecure
$ mv server.key server.key.secure
$ mv server.key.insecure server.key
```

4. Next, create the CSR with the following command:

```
$ openssl req -new -key server.key -out server.csr
```

5. A CSR file is created with the name `server.csr`, and now you can submit this CSR for signing purposes.

See also

▸ Refer to the *Installing and configuring the Apache web server* recipe for the installation and configuration of the Apache web server.

▸ Check out the certificates and security in the Ubuntu server guide at `https://help.ubuntu.com/lts/serverguide/certificates-and-security.html`

▸ How to set up client verification at `http://askubuntu.com/questions/511149/how-to-setup-ssl-https-for-your-site-on-ubuntu-linux-two-way-ssl`

▸ Apache documentation on SSL configuration at `http://httpd.apache.org/docs/2.4/ssl/ssl_howto.html`

▸ Free SSL certificate with Mozilla Let's Encrypt at `https://letsencrypt.org/getting-started/`

▸ Easily generate SSL configuration for your web server at Mozilla SSL Configuration Generator at `https://mozilla.github.io/server-side-tls/ssl-config-generator/`

Installing Nginx with PHP_FPM

In this recipe, we will learn how to install and set up Nginx as a web server. We will also install PHP to be able to serve dynamic content. We need to install PHP_FPM (FastCGI Process Manager), as Nginx doesn't support the native execution of PHP scripts. We will install the latest stable version available from the Nginx package repository.

Getting ready

You will need access to a root account or an account with `sudo` privileges.

How to do it...

Follow these steps to install Nginx with PHP_FPM:

1. Update the `apt` package repository and install Nginx. As of writing this Ubuntu 16.04 repository contains latest stable release of Nginx with version 1.10.0:

   ```
   $ sudo apt-get update
   $ sudo apt-get install nginx
   ```

2. Check if Nginx is properly installed and running:

   ```
   $ sudo service nginx status
   ```

3. Check the installed version of Nginx:

   ```
   $ nginx -v
   ```

4. You may want to point your browser to the server IP or domain. You should see a default Nginx welcome page:

5. Next, proceed with installing PHP_FPM:

   ```
   $ sudo apt-get install php7.0-fpm
   ```

6. Configure Nginx to use the PHP processor. Nginx sites are listed at `/etc/nginx/sites-available`. We will modify the default site:

   ```
   $ sudo nano /etc/nginx/sites-available/default
   ```

7. Find a line stating the priority of the `index` file and add `index.php` as a first option:

   ```
   index index.php index.html index.htm;
   ```

8. Next, add the following two `location` directives:

```
location / {
    try_files $uri $uri/ /index.php;
}
location ~ \.php$ {
    include fastcgi_params;
    fastcgi_param SCRIPT_FILENAME
    $document_root$fastcgi_script_name;
    fastcgi_param QUERY_STRING    $query_string;
    fastcgi_pass unix:/var/run/php/php7.0-fpm.sock;
}
```

9. Save the changes and exit the file. It should look similar to this:

```
server {
        listen 80 default_server;
        listen [::]:80 default_server;
        root /var/www/html;
        index index.php index.html index.htm;
        server_name _;
        location / {
                try_files $uri $uri/ /index.php;
        }
        location ~ \.php$ {
                include fastcgi_params;
                fastcgi_param SCRIPT_FILENAME
                $document_root$fastcgi_script_name;
                fastcgi_param QUERY_STRING $query_string;
                fastcgi_pass unix:/var/run/php/php7.0-fpm.sock;
        }
}
```

10. Change the PHP settings to disable `PATH_TRANSLATED` support. Find an option, `cgi.fix_pathinfo`, and uncomment it with the value set to `0`:

```
$ sudo nano /etc/php/7.0/fpm/php.ini
cgi.fix_pathinfo=0
```

11. Now, restart PHP_FPM and Nginx for the changes to take effect:

```
$ sudo service php7.0-fpm restart
$ sudo service nginx restart
```

12. Create an `index.php` file with some PHP code in it at the path mentioned in the default site configuration:

    `$ sudo nano /var/www/html/index.php`

    `<?php phpinfo(); ?>`

13. Open your browser and point it to your server. You should see the result of your PHP script:

PHP Version 7.0.4-7ubuntu2.1

System	Linux server-01 4.4.0-22-generic #40-Ubuntu SMP Thu May 12 22:03:46 UT
Server API	FPM/FastCGI
Virtual Directory Support	disabled
Configuration File (php.ini) Path	/etc/php/7.0/fpm
Loaded Configuration File	/etc/php/7.0/fpm/php.ini
Scan this dir for additional .ini files	/etc/php/7.0/fpm/conf.d

How it works...

Here, we have installed the latest stable version of the Nginx server with PHP_FPM to support dynamic content scripted with PHP. The Ubuntu repository for version 16.04 contains the latest stable release of Nginx, So installing Nginx is as easy as a single command. If you are interested in more recent versions Nginx maintains their own package repository for mainline packages. You just need to add repository, the rest of the installation process is similar to a single `apt-get install nginx` command.

If you are running the Apache server on the same machine, you may want to change the default port Nginx runs on. You can find these settings under site configurations, located at `/etc/nginx/sites-available`. Nginx creates default site configuration with the filename set to `default`. Find the lines that start with `listen` and change the port from its default, `80`, to any port number of your choice.

After installing Nginx, we need to configure it to support dynamic content. Here, we have selected PHP as a dynamic content processor. PHP is a popular scripting language and very commonly used with web servers for dynamic content processing. You can also add support for other modules by installing their respective processors. After installing PHP_FPM, we have configured Nginx to use PHP_FPM and pass all PHP requests to the FPM module on a socket connection.

We have used two location blocks in configuration. The first block search is for static content, such as files and directories, and then if nothing matches, the request is forwarded to `index.php`, which is in turn forwarded to the FastCGI module for processing. This ensures that Nginx serves all static content without executing PHP, and only requests that are not static files and directories are passed to the FPM module.

The following is a brief description of the parameters used under FastCGI configuration:

- The parameter `try_files` configures Nginx to return `404` pages, that is, the *page not found* error, for any requests that do not match website content. This is limited to static files.

- With the parameter `fastcgi_param`, you can forward the script name and query string to the PHP FPM process.

- One more optional parameter is `cgi.fix_pathinfo=0`, under the PHP configuration file `php.ini`. By default, PHP is set to search for the exact script filename and then search for the closest match if the exact name is not found. This may become a security risk by allowing an attacker to execute random scripts with simple guesswork for script names. We have disabled this by setting its value to `0`.

Finally, after we restart PHP_FPM and Nginx, our server is ready to process static as well as dynamic content. All static content will be handled by Nginx itself, and requests for URLs that end with `.php` will be forwarded to PHP_FPM for processing. Nginx may cache the processed result for future use.

There's more...

If you are running Ubuntu 12.10, you may need to install the following dependencies before adding the Nginx repository to the installation sources:

1. Install `python-software-properties` and `software-properties-common`:

   ```
   $ sudo apt-get install python-software-properties
   $ sudo apt-get install software-properties-common
   ```

2. You may want to remove your Apache installation completely. Use the following commands to remove Apache:

   ```
   $ sudo service apache2 stop
   $ sudo apt-get remove --purge apache2 apache2-utils apache2.2-bin apache2-common
   ```

Nginx maintains their own package repositories for stable and mainline releases. These repositories can be used to get the latest updates of Nginx as and when available. Use the stable repository, - `$ sudo add-apt-repository ppa:nginx/stable`.

Use the mainline repository - `$ sudo add-apt-repository ppa:nginx/development`.

See also

▶ Common Nginx pitfalls at `http://wiki.nginx.org/Pitfalls`

▶ Nginx Quick start guide at `http://wiki.nginx.org/QuickStart`

Setting Nginx as a reverse proxy

Apache and Nginx are two popular open source web servers. Both are very powerful, but at the same time have their own disadvantages as well. Apache is not good at handling high load environments with multiple concurrent requests and Nginx does not have inbuilt support for dynamic content processing. Many administrators overcome these problems by using both Apache and Nginx together. Nginx handles all incoming requests and only passes requests for dynamic content to Apache. Additionally, Nginx can provide a catching option which enables the server to respond to a request with results from a similar previous request. This helps to reduce the overall response time and minimize the load sent to Apache.

In this recipe, we will learn how to set up a web server configured with a reverse proxy. We will use Nginx as a reverse proxy, which will serve all static content and pass the requests for dynamic content to Apache.

Getting ready

You will need access to a root account or an account with `sudo` privileges.

I assume that Apache is installed and running with a virtual host, `example.com`.

How to do it...

Follow these steps to set Nginx as a reverse proxy:

1. Install Nginx with the following command:

    ```
    $ sudo apt-get update
    $ sudo apt-get install nginx
    ```

2. Create a new site configuration under `/etc/nginx/sites-available` and add the following content to it:

    ```
    $ sudo nano /etc/nginx/sites-available/reverse_proxy
    server {
      listen 80;
    ```

```
    root /var/www/example.com;
    index index.php index.html index.htm;


    server_name example.com;


    location / {
        try_files $uri $uri/ /index.php;
    }


    location ~ \.php$ {
        proxy_set_header X-Real-IP    $remote_addr;
        proxy_set_header X-Forwarded-For $remote_addr;
        proxy_set_header Host $host;
        proxy_pass http://127.0.0.1:8080;
    }
    location ~* \.(js|css|jpg|jpeg|png|svg|html|htm)$ {
        expires      30d;
    }


    location ~ /\.ht {
        deny all;
    }
}
```

3. Enable this new configuration by creating a symbolic link under `sites-enabled`:

   ```
   $ sudo ln -s /etc/nginx/sites-available/reverse_proxy \
   /etc/nginx/sites-enabled/reverse_proxy
   ```

4. Optionally, disable the default site by removing the symbolic link from `sites-enabled`:

   ```
   $ sudo rm /etc/nginx/sites-enabled/default
   ```

5. Next, we need to change the Apache settings to listen on port `8080`. This will leave port `80` to be used by Nginx:

   ```
   $ sudo nano /etc/apache2/ports.conf
   listen 127.0.0.1:8080
   ```

6. Also change `NameVirtualHost`, if you are using it:

   NameVirtualHost 127.0.0.1:8080

7. Change the virtual hosts settings to listen on port `8080`:

   ```
   $ sudo nano /etc/apache2/sites-available/example.com
   <VirtualHost 127.0.0.1:8080>
     ServerName example.com
     ServerAdmin webmaster@example.com
     DocumentRoot /var/www/example.com/public_html
   </VirtualHost>
   ```

8. Save the changes and restart Apache for the changes to take effect:

   ```
   $ sudo service apache2 restart
   ```

9. Now, restart Nginx:

   ```
   $ sudo service nginx restart
   ```

10. Check for open ports with the following command:

    ```
    $ sudo netstat -pltn
    ```

```
ubuntu@ubuntu:~$ sudo netstat -pltn | egrep '(apache|nginx)'
tcp        0      0 127.0.0.1:8080          0.0.0.0:*               LISTEN      4753/apache2
tcp        0      0 0.0.0.0:80              0.0.0.0:*               LISTEN      3962/nginx
tcp6       0      0 :::80                   :::*                    LISTEN      3962/nginx
tcp6       0      0 :::443                  :::*                    LISTEN      4753/apache2
ubuntu@ubuntu:~$
```

11. Open your browser and point it to the IP address of your server. It should load the page configured under the Apache virtual host, `example.com`.

How it works...

With the `proxy_pass` parameter, we have simply asked Nginx to pass all requests for PHP scripts to Apache on `127.0.0.1` on port `8080`. Then, we set Apache to listen on the loopback IP and port `8080`, which will receive requests forwarded by Nginx and process them with an internal PHP processor. All non-PHP content will still be served by Nginx from the `/var/www` directory. The `try_files $uri $uri/ /index.php;` option sets Nginx to search for the file with a specified name and then look for the folder; lastly, if both file and folder are not found, send the request to `index.php`, which will then be processed by Apache.

Other options used with proxy pass ensures that Apache and PHP scripts receive the actual hostname and IP of the client and not of the Nginx server. You can use an additional module named `libapache2-mod-rpaf` on Apache. This module provides an option to set a proxy IP address and rename the parameters sent by the proxy server. You can install the module with the following command:

```
$ sudo apt-get install libapache2-mod-rpaf
```

The configuration file for this module is available at `/etc/apache2/mods-available/rpaf.conf`.

You can find various other proxy options and their respective explanations in the Nginx documentation at `http://nginx.org/en/docs/http/ngx_http_proxy_module.html`

Finally, with Nginx set as a frontend, Apache will not have to interact directly with HTTP clients. You may want to disable some of the Apache modules that will not be used in this setup:

```
$ sudo a2dismod deflate cgi negotiation autoindex
```

As always, do not forget to reload Apache after any changes.

There's more...

Nginx can be set to cache the response received from the backend server and thereby minimize repeated requests on backend servers, as well as the response time. Nginx can cache the content in local files and serve new requests from the cache. The cache can be invalidated or even disabled based on the request received. To enable caching, add the following settings to the Nginx site configuration:

```
  proxy_cache_path /data/nginx/cache levels=1:2 keys_zone=backend-
cache:8m max_size=50m;
 proxy_cache_key "$scheme$request_method$host$request_uri$args";
  server {
    ## add other settings heres
   location / {
     proxy_pass 127.0.0.1:8080;
     proxy_cache backend-cache;
     proxy_cache_bypass $http_cache_control;
     add_header X-Proxy-Cache $upstream_cache_status;
     proxy_cache_valid  200 302  10m;
     proxy_cache_valid  404      1m;
   }
 }
```

You may need to create the proxy path directory `/data/nginx/cache` and set the appropriate file permissions. Set the directory ownership to `www-data` and restrict permissions to `700`. You can use any location for cache data and not necessarily `/data/nginx/cache`.

This configuration sets the cache validity of 10 minutes, which is quite a lengthy period. This will work if you have static content that rarely changes. Instead, if you are serving dynamic content that is frequently updated, then you can take advantage of microcaching by setting the cache validity to a very small period of a few seconds. Add the following parameters to further improve your caching configuration for microcaching:

- `proxy_cache_lock on`: Queues additional requests while the cache is being updated
- `proxy_cache_use_stale updating`: Uses stale data while the cache is being updated

HAProxy and Varnish

HAProxy and Varnish are other popular options for the reverse proxy and the caching proxy, respectively. Both of them can offer improved performance when compared with Nginx. HAProxy can also be used as a Layer 4 and Layer 7 load balancer. We covered HAProxy in *Chapter 2, Networking*, in the *Load Balancing with HAProxy* recipe.

See also

- Nginx admin guide on reverse proxies at `https://www.nginx.com/resources/admin-guide/reverse-proxy/`
- Understanding Nginx proxying, load balancing, and caching at `https://www.digitalocean.com/community/tutorials/understanding-nginx-http-proxying-load-balancing-buffering-and-caching`
- Nginx proxy module documentation at `http://nginx.org/en/docs/http/ngx_http_proxy_module.html`

Load balancing with Nginx

When an application becomes popular and the number of requests increases beyond the capacity of a single server, we need to scale horizontally. We can always increase the capacity (vertical scaling) of a server by adding more memory and processing power, but a single server cannot scale beyond a certain limit. While adding separate servers or replicas of the application server, we need a mechanism which directs the traffic between these replicas. The hardware or software tool used for this purpose is known as a load balancer. Load balancers work as transparent mechanisms between the application server and client by distributing the requests between available instances. This is a commonly used technique for optimizing resource utilization and ensuring fault tolerant applications.

Nginx can be configured to work as an efficient Layer 7 as well as Layer 4 load balancer. Layer 7 is application layer of HTTP traffic. With Layer 4 support, Nginx can be used to load balance database servers or even XMPP traffic. With version 1.9.0, Nginx has enabled support for Layer 4 load balancing in their open source offerings.

In this recipe, we will learn how to set up Nginx as a load balancer.

Getting ready

You will need access to a root account or an account with `sudo` privileges.

You will need a minimum of three servers, as follows:

- An Nginx server, which will be set as a load balancer
- Two or more application servers with a similar code base set up on all

How to do it...

Follow these steps to set load balancing with Nginx:

1. I assume that you already have Nginx installed. If not, you can refer to the *Installing Nginx with PHP_FPM* recipe of this chapter.

2. Now, create a new configuration file under `/etc/nginx/sites-available`. Let's call it `load_balancer`:

   ```
   $ sudo nano /etc/nginx/sites-available/load_balancer
   ```

3. Add the following lines to this `load_balancer` file. This is the minimum configuration required to get started with load balancing:

   ```
   upstream backend {
     server srv1.example.com;
     server srv2.example.com;
     server 192.168.1.12:8080;
     # other servers if any
   }
   server {
     listen 80;
     location / {
       proxy_pass http://backend;
     }
   }
   ```

4. Enable this configuration by creating a symlink to `load_balancer` under `sites-enabled`:

   ```
   $ sudo ln -s /etc/nginx/sites-available/load_balancer
   /etc/nginx/sites-enabled/load_balancer
   ```

5. You may want to disable all other sites. Simply remove the respective links under `sites-enabled`.

6. Check the configuration for syntax errors:

   ```
   $ sudo nginx -t
   ```

```
ubuntu@ubuntu:~$ sudo nginx -t
nginx: the configuration file /etc/nginx/nginx.conf syntax is ok
nginx: configuration file /etc/nginx/nginx.conf test is successful
ubuntu@ubuntu:~$
```

7. Now, reload Nginx for the changes to take effect:

   ```
   $ sudo service nginx reload
   ```

8. Yes, you are ready to use a load balancer. Open your favorite browser and point it to the IP of your Nginx server. You should see the contents of `example.com` or whatever domain you have used.

How it works...

We have created a very basic configuration for a load balancer. With this configuration, Nginx takes the traffic on port `80` and distributes it between `srv1.example.com` and `srv2.example.com`. With an upstream directive, we have defined a pool of servers that will actually process the requests. The upstream directive must be defined in a HTTP context. Once the upstream directive is defined, it will be available for all site configurations.

 All configuration files defined under `sites-available` are combined in the main configuration file, `/etc/nginx/nginx.conf`, under the HTTP directive. This enables us to set other directives in `site-specific` configurations without specifying the HTTP block.

When defining servers under an `upstream` directive, you can also use the IP address and port of the application server. This is an ideal configuration, especially when both the load balancer and the application servers are on the same private network, and this will help minimize the communication overhead between Nginx and backend servers.

Next, under the `server` block, we have configured Nginx to `proxy_pass` all requests to our `backend` pool.

While setting backend servers, we have not explicitly specified any load balancing algorithm. Nginx provides various load balancing algorithms that define the server that will receive a particular request. By default, Nginx uses a round-robin algorithm and passes requests to each available server in sequential order. Other available options are as follows:

- `least_connection`: This passes the request to the host with the fewest active connections.

- `least_time`: Nginx chooses the host with the lowest latency. This option is available with Nginx plus.

- `ip_hash`: A hash of clients' IP addresses, and is used to determined the host to send the request to. This method guarantees that requests with the same IP address are served by the same host, unless the selected host is down.

Hash uses a user defined key to generate a hash value and then uses the hash to determine the processing host.

There's more...

Nginx provides various other load balancing features, such as weighted load balancing, active and passive health checks, backup servers, and session persistence. With the latest commits to the open source version, it now supports TCP load balancing as well. These settings can be updated at runtime with the help of HTTP APIs. The following are a few examples of different load balancing configurations:

- Set server weights:

```
upstream app-servers {
    server srv1.example.com weight 3;
    server srv2.example.com;
}
```

- Health checkups and backup servers:

```
upstream app-servers {
    server srv1.example.com max_fails 3 fail_timeout 10;
    server srv2.example.com fail_timeout 50;
    192.168.1.12:8080 backup;
}
```

▶ Session persistence with cookies:

```
upstream app-servers {
    server srv1.example.com;
    server srv2.example.com;
    sticky cookie srv_id expires=1h domain=.example.com
path=/;
}
```

Check the Nginx load balancing guide for various other load balancing options and their respective details.

See also

▶ Nginx admin guide for load balancers at https://www.nginx.com/resources/admin-guide/load-balancer

Setting HTTPs on Nginx

In this recipe, we will learn how to enable HTTPs communication on the Nginx server.

Getting ready

You will need access to a root account or an account with `sudo` privileges.

How to do it...

Follow these steps to set HTTPs on Nginx:

1. Obtain a certificate and the related keys from a certification authority or create a self-signed certificate. To create a self-signed certificate, refer to the *Securing web traffic with HTTPS* recipe in this chapter.

2. Create a directory to hold all certificate and keys:

   ```
   $ sudo mkdir -p /etc/nginx/ssl/example.com
   ```

3. Move the certificate and keys to the preceding directory. Choose any secure method, such as SCP, SFTP, or any other.

4. Create a virtual host entry or edit it if you already have one:

   ```
   $ sudo nano /etc/nginx/sites-available/example.com
   ```

5. Match your virtual host configuration with the following:

```
server {
  listen 80;
  server_name example.com www.example.com;
  return 301 https://$host$request_uri;
}
server {
  listen 443 ssl;
  server_name example.com www.example.com;

  root /var/www/example.com/public_html;
  index index.php index.html index.htm;

  ssl on;
  ssl_certificate
  /etc/nginx/ssl/example.com/server.crt;

  ssl_certificate_key
  /etc/nginx/ssl/example.com/server.key;

  # if you have received ca-certs.pem from Certification
  Authority
  #ssl_trusted_certificate /etc/nginx/ssl/example.com/ca-
  certs.pem;

  ssl_session_cache shared:SSL:10m;
  ssl_session_timeout 5m;
  keepalive_timeout    70;

  ssl_ciphers "HIGH:!aNULL:!MD5 or HIGH:!aNULL:!MD5:!3DES";
  ssl_prefer_server_ciphers on;
  ssl_protocols  TLSv1.2 TLSv1.1 TLSv1;
  add_header Strict-Transport-Security "max-age=31536000";

  location / {
    try_files $uri $uri/ /index.php;
  }
```

```
        location ~ \.php$ {
          include fastcgi_params;
          fastcgi_pass unix:/var/run/php/php7.0-fpm.sock;
        }
      }
```

6. Enable this configuration by creating a symbolic link to it under `sites-enabled`:

    $ sudo ln -s /etc/nginx/sites-available/example.com /etc/nginx/sites-enabled/example.com

7. Check the configuration for syntax errors:

    $ sudo nginx -t

8. Reload Nginx for the changes to take effect:

    $ sudo service nginx reload

9. Open your browser and access the site with domain or IP with HTTPS.

How it works...

When you know some basic configuration parameters, Nginx is quite simple to set up. Here, we have taken a few SSL settings from the default configuration file and added a simple redirection rule to redirect non-HTTPs traffic on port 80 to port 443. The first `server` block takes care of the redirection.

In addition to specifying the server certificate and keys, we have enabled session resumption by setting the cache to be shared across the Nginx process. We also have a timeout value of 5 minutes.

All other settings are common to the Nginx setup. We have allowed the virtual host to match with `example.com`, as well as `www.example.com`. We have set the index to search `index.php`, followed by `index.html` and others. With `location` directives, we have set Nginx to search for files and directories before forwarding the request to a PHP processor. Note that if you create a self-signed certificate, you will notice your browser complaining about invalid certification authority.

See also

▶ Nginx HTTPs guide at `http://nginx.org/en/docs/http/configuring_https_servers.html`

Benchmarking and performance tuning of Apache

In this recipe, we will learn some performance tuning configurations that may help to squeeze out the last bit of performance from the available hardware. Before diving into performance tuning, we need to evaluate our servers and set a benchmark which can be used to measure improvements after any changes. We will be using a well known HTTP benchmarking tool, **Apache Bench** (**ab**). Various other benchmarking tools are available and each one has its own feature set. You can choose the one that best suits your needs.

Getting ready

You will need two systems: one with the web server software installed and another to run Apache Bench. You will need root access or access to an account with similar privileges.

You will also need to modify a few network parameters to handle a large network load. You will also need to set a higher open files limit, in `limits.conf`, on both systems. Check the *Tuning TCP Stack* recipe in *Chapter 2, Networking*.

How to do it...

1. Install the Apache Bench tool. This is available with the package `apache2-utils`:

   ```
   $ sudo apt-get install apache2-utils
   ```

2. If you need to, you can check all the available options of the `ab` tool as follows:

   ```
   $ ab -h
   ```

3. Now we are ready to generate network load. Execute the following command to start `ab`:

   ```
   $ ab -n 10000 -c 200 -t 2 -k "http://192.168.56.103/index.php"
   ```

It will take some time to complete the command depending on the parameters. You should see similar results to the following (partial) output:

```
Total transferred:      16739619 bytes
HTML transferred:       16700040 bytes
Requests per second:    117.96 [#/sec] (mean)
Time per request:       1695.491 [ms] (mean)
Time per request:       8.477 [ms] (mean, across all concurrent requests)
Transfer rate:          8170.87 [Kbytes/sec] received

Connection Times (ms)
              min  mean[+/-sd] median   max
Connect:        0    44  33.6     64      81
Processing:    44   815 363.9    983    1617
Waiting:       44   784 360.2    944    1592
Total:        122   859 340.5   1046    1675
```

Additionally, you may want to benchmark your server for CPU, memory, and IO performance. Check the *Setting performance benchmarks* recipe in *Chapter 13, Performance Monitoring*.

Now that we have a benchmark for server performance with stock installation, we can proceed with performance optimization. The following are some settings that are generally recommended for performance tuning:

- Apache related settings:
  - Remove/disable any unused modules
  - Enable mod_gzip/mod_deflate
  - Turn HostnameLookups off
  - Use IP address in configuration files
  - Use persistence connection by enabling keepalive, then set keepalive timeout
  - Limit the uses of AllowOverride or completely disable it with AllowOverride none
  - Disable ExtendedStatus; this is useful while testing but not in production

- Nginx related settings:
  - Set worker_processes to the count of your CPU cores or simply set it to auto
  - Set the number of worker_connections to test multiple values to find the best match for your servers
  - Set the keepalive_requests and keepalive_timeout values; these reduce the overhead of creating new connections
  - Enable idle connections with upstream servers by setting the keepalive value

- Enable log buffering with buffer and flush parameters to `access_log`; this will reduce IO requests while logging
- Reduce the log-level - you can set it to warn the user or display an error while in production
- Set the `sendfile` directive to use an efficient `sendfile()` call from the operating system
- Enable caching and compression
- Make sure that you track the performance changes after each set of modifications; this way you will have exact knowledge regarding what worked and what not
- You should also tune the TCP stack. The details of the TCP stack settings are covered in *Chapter 2, Networking*.

There's more...

Various other tools are available for benchmarking different features of the web server. The following are some well known tools, as well as a few latest additions:

- **Httperf**: A web server benchmarking tool with some advanced options
- **Perfkit**: a cloud benchmark tool by Google
- **Wrk**: `https://github.com/wg/wrk`
- **H2load**: HTTP2 load testing tool at `https://nghttp2.org/documentation/h2load-howto.html`

See also

- Apache performance tuning guide at `https://httpd.apache.org/docs/2.4/misc/perf-tuning.html`
- Nginx performance tuning guide at `https://www.nginx.com/blog/tuning-nginx/`

Securing the web server

In this recipe, we will learn some steps for securing web server installation.

Getting ready

You will need access to a root account or an account with `sudo` privileges.

You may need to have a web server stack installed and running.

How to do it...

Follow these steps to secure the web server:

1. Disable any unwanted modules. You can check all enabled modules with the following command:

    ```
    $ a2query -m
    ```

2. Disable modules with the following command:

    ```
    $ sudo a2dismod status
    ```

3. Hide the web server's identity. For Apache, edit `/etc/apache2/conf-available/security.conf` and set the following values:

    ```
    ServerSignature Off
    ServerTokens Prod
    ```

4. You may want to check other options under `security.conf`.

5. Next, disable the Apache server status page:

    ```
    $ sudo a2dismod status
    ```

6. For Nginx, edit `/etc/nginx/nginx.conf` and uncomment the following line:

    ```
    # server_tokens off;
    ```

7. In production environments, minimize the detail shown on error pages. You can enable the PHP Suhosin module and strict mode.

8. Disable directory listing. On Apache, add the following line to the virtual host configuration:

    ```
    <Directory /var/www/example.com>
      Options -Indexes
    </Directory>
    ```

9. You can also disable directory listing globally by setting `Options -Indexes` in `/etc/apache2/apache2.conf`.

10. Restrict access to the following directories:

```
<Directory /var/www/ >
   Order deny,allow    # order of Deny and Allow
   Deny from all    # Deny web root for all
</Directory>
```

11. Disable directory level settings and the use of `.htaccess`. This also helps improve performance:

```
<Directory />
   AllowOverride None    # disable use of .htaccess
</Directory>
```

12. Disable the following symbolic links:

```
<Directory />
   Options -FollowSymLinks
</Directory>
```

13. You can also install `mod_security` and `mod_evasive` for added security. `mod_security` acts as a firewall by monitoring traffic in real time, whereas `mod_evasive` provides protection against Denial of Service attacks by monitoring request data and requester IP.

14. For Apache, you can install `mod_security` as a plugin module as follows:

```
$ sudo apt-get install libapache2-modsecurity
$ sudo a2enmod mod-security
```

15. On Nginx, you need to first compile `mod_security` and then compile Nginx with `mod_security` enabled.

16. Turn of server side includes and CGI scripts:

```
<Directory />
   Options -ExecCGI -Includes
</Directory>
```

17. Limit request body, headers, request fields, and max concurrent connections; this will help against DOS attacks.

18. Set the following variables on Apache:

    `TimeOut`

    `KeepAliveTimeout`

    `RequestReadTimeout`

    `LimitRequestBody`

    `LimitRequestFields`

    `LimitRequestFieldSize`

    `LimitRequestLine`

    `MaxRequestWorkers`

19. For Nginx, configure the following variables to control buffer overflow attacks:

    `client_body_buffer_size`

    `client_header_buffer_size`

    `client_max_body_size`

    `large_client_header_buffers`

20. Enable logging and periodically monitor logs for any new or unrecognized events:

    ```
    <VirtualHost *:80>
      ErrorLog /var/log/httpd/example.com/error_log
      CustomLog /var/log/httpd/example.com/access_log combined
    </VirtualHost>
    ```

21. Set up HTTPs and set it to use modern ciphers. You can also disable the use of SSL and enforce TLS.

How it works...

In this recipe, I have listed the various options available to make your web server more secure. It is not necessary to set all these settings. Disabling some of these settings, especially `FollowSymlinks` and `AllowOverride`, may not suit your requirements or your environment. You can always choose the settings that apply to your setup.

Various settings listed here are available in their respective configuration files, mostly under `/etc/apache2` for the Apache web server and `/etc/nginx` for the Nginx server.

Also, do not forget to reload or restart your server after setting these options.

You should also set your Ubuntu environment to be more secure. You can find more details on securing Ubuntu in *Chapter 2, Networking*.

See also

▸ Installing `mod_evasive` at `https://www.linode.com/docs/websites/apache-tips-and-tricks/modevasive-on-apache`

▸ Apache security tips at `http://httpd.apache.org/docs/2.4/misc/security_tips.html`

▸ Setting up `mod_security` at `https://www.digitalocean.com/community/tutorials/how-to-set-up-mod_security-with-apache-on-debian-ubuntu`

Troubleshooting the web server

In this recipe, we will cover some common issues with Apache and Nginx and list the basic steps for overcoming those issues. The steps mentioned here are general troubleshooting methods; you may need to change them based on your setup and environment.

Getting ready

You may need root level access to your web server system.

How to do it...

Web server problems can be grouped in a few broad categories, such as a server not working, a particular domain or virtual host is not accessible, problems with a specific module configuration, and access denied errors. The following section lists each of these problems and their possible solutions.

Web server not accessible

1. The first step is to check your local Internet connection. Try to access the server from another system from another network.

2. Check if the DNS settings point to your web server.

3. If your network is working properly, then try to ping to the server IP address.

4. On the web server, check the firewall or any other tool that may block communication.

5. Open a `telnet` connection to web server on port `80`, or whatever port you have used for web server. If you see output similar to following screenshot, then your web server is working:

```
ubuntu@ubuntu:~$ telnet 192.168.56.103 80
Trying 192.168.56.103...
Connected to 192.168.56.103.
Escape character is '^]'.
```

6. Make sure that the web server port is not being used by some other process:

```
$ sudo netstat -plutn
```

```
Active Internet connections (only servers)
Proto Recv-Q Send-Q Local Address           Foreign Address         State       PID/Program name
tcp        0      0 127.0.0.1:8080          0.0.0.0:*               LISTEN      1069/apache2
tcp        0      0 0.0.0.0:80              0.0.0.0:*               LISTEN      994/nginx
tcp        0      0 0.0.0.0:22              0.0.0.0:*               LISTEN      948/sshd
tcp6       0      0 :::22                   :::*                    LISTEN      948/sshd
```

7. If required, reload or restart the web server process:

```
$ sudo service apache2 reload/restart
```

8. Check the Apache/Nginx logs listed under the `/var/log/` directory and view the entire file in a scrollable format:

```
$ less /var/log/apache2/error.log
```

9. See the continuous stream of logs as they are added to the log file:

```
$ tail -f /var/log/nginx/error.log
```

10. You may want to run Apache with extended log levels. Find the variable `LogLevel` in `/etc/apache2/apache2.conf` and set its value to `debug`:

```
$ sudo nano /etc/apache2/apache2.conf
```

```
LogLevel debug
```

11. Run Apache in debug single process mode:

```
$ sudo apache2ctl -X  # debug mode single worker
```

Virtual host not accessible

1. Make sure you have enabled virtual host configuration:

```
ubuntu@ubuntu:~$ a2query -s
example.com (enabled by site administrator)
```

2. Check the virtual host configuration for any syntax errors:

```
ubuntu@ubuntu:~$ sudo apache2ctl -t
Syntax OK
```

3. On Nginx, use the following command:

```
ubuntu@ubuntu:~$ sudo nginx -t
nginx: the configuration file /etc/nginx/nginx.conf syntax
is ok
nginx: configuration file /etc/nginx/nginx.conf test is
successful
```

4. Check the virtual host's details and other Apache configurations:

```
$ sudo apache2ctl -S
```

```
ubuntu@ubuntu:~$ sudo apache2ctl -S
VirtualHost configuration:
127.0.0.1:8080            example.com (/etc/apache2/sites-enabled/example.com.conf:1)
ServerRoot: "/etc/apache2"
Main DocumentRoot: "/var/www"
Main ErrorLog: "/var/log/apache2/error.log"
Mutex default: dir="/var/lock/apache2" mechanism=fcntl
Mutex mpm-accept: using_defaults
Mutex watchdog-callback: using_defaults
Mutex ssl-stapling: using_defaults
Mutex ssl-cache: using_defaults
PidFile: "/var/run/apache2/apache2.pid"
Define: DUMP_VHOSTS
Define: DUMP_RUN_CFG
User: name="www-data" id=33
Group: name="www-data" id=33
```

5. Make sure your virtual host IP and port configuration matches the one defined with `NamedVirtualHost`.

6. Check `DocumentRoot` - does it point to proper files?

   ❑ On Apache:

   ```
   <VirtualHost *:80>
        DocumentRoot /var/www/html
   <VirtualHost>
   ```

   ❑ On Nginx:

   ```
   server {
        root /usr/share/nginx/html;
   }
   ```

7. Crosscheck your `ServerName` and `ServerAlias` variables - do they match your domain name?

   ❑ On Apache, these settings should look similar to this:

   ```
   <VirtualHost *:80>
       ServerName example.com
       ServerAlias www.example.com
   </virtualHost>
   ```

   ❑ On Nginx, the `ServerName` is defined as this:

   ```
   server {
       server_name example.com www.example.com;
   }
   ```

Access denied or forbidden errors

Check directory permissions for the virtual host root directory. Are they accessible to the web server? Check the web server user and group (commonly `www-data`) have ready permissions. If required, you can set permissions with `chown` and `chmod` commands.

```
ubuntu@ubuntu:~$ ls -l /var/www/
drwxr-x--- 3 ubuntu www-data 4096 Aug  4 23:00 example.com
drwxr-xr-x 2 ubuntu www-data 4096 Aug  2 23:04 public_html
```

Secondly, make sure that you have properly set directory permissions in the virtual host configuration. Are they restricting file access?

Use the following commands to set directory permissions in the virtual host configuration:

```
<Directory /var/www/>
    AllowOverride None
    Order Deny,Allow
    Deny from all
</Directory>
```

Apache downloads .php files

Make sure that the `mod_php` module is installed and enabled:

```
ubuntu@ubuntu:~$ ls -l /etc/apache2/mods-available | grep php
-rw-r--r-- 1 root root  897 Jul  2 21:26 php7.0.conf
-rw-r--r-- 1 root root   59 Jul  2 21:26 php7.0.load

ubuntu@ubuntu:~$ a2query -m | grep php
php7.0 (enabled by maintainer script)
```

4
Working with Mail Servers

In this chapter, we will cover the following recipes:

- ▸ Sending e-mails with Postfix
- ▸ Enabling IMAP and POP3 with Dovecot
- ▸ Adding e-mail accounts
- ▸ Mail filtering with spam-assassin
- ▸ Troubleshooting the mail server
- ▸ Installing the Zimbra mail server

Introduction

In this chapter, we will learn how to set up an e-mail server. We will be using Postfix MTA to send e-mails and Dovecot to enable receiving e-mails. We will also install the Zimbra e-mail server, which is all-in-one one package to set up sending and receiving e-mails and web access. By the end of this chapter, you will be able to send e-mails with your own e-mail server.

Sending e-mails with Postfix

In this recipe, we will set up Postfix **Mail Transfer Agent** (**MTA**). This will be a very basic setup which will enable us to send and receive e-mails from our server. Postfix is an open source MTA which routes e-mails to their destination. It is a default MTA for Ubuntu and is available in Ubuntu's main package repository.

Getting ready

You will need access to a root account or an account with `sudo` privileges.

A domain name (FQDN) is required while configuring Postfix. You can configure your local server for testing, but make sure that you set the proper host entries and hostname.

How to do it...

Follow these steps to send e-mails with Postfix:

1. Install Postfix and `mailutils` with the following commands:

   ```
   $ sudo apt-get update
   $ sudo apt-get install postfix mailutils -y
   ```

2. The installation process will prompt you to enter some basic configuration details. When asked for **General type of mail configuration:**, select **Internet Site** and then click on **<Ok>**:

3. On the next screen, enter your domain name, for example, `mail.example.com`, and answer the other questions. You can leave them with default values:

4. After installation completes, we need to modify the Postfix configuration under
    `/etc/postfix/main.cf`:

    ```
    $ sudo nano /etc/postfix/main.cf
    ```

5. Set `myhostname` to point to your domain name:

    `myhostname = mail.example.com`

6. Ensure `mynetworks` is set to the local network. This will secure your server
    from spammers:

    ```
    mynetworks = 127.0.0.0/8 [::ffff:127.0.0.0]/104 [::1]/128
    ```

7. Also check `mydestination`. It should contain your domain name:

    `mydestination = example.com, ubuntu, localhost.localdomain,`
    `localhost`

```
myhostname = mail.example.com
alias_maps = hash:/etc/aliases
alias_database = hash:/etc/aliases
myorigin = /etc/mailname
mydestination = mail.example.com, ubuntu, localhost.localdomain, localhost
relayhost =
mynetworks = 127.0.0.0/8 [::ffff:127.0.0.0]/104 [::1]/128
```

8. Change the mail storage format to `Maildir` from the default `mbox`. Search and
    uncomment the following line:

    `home_mailbox = Maildir/`

9. Optionally, you can change the TLS keys used by Postfix. Find the `TLS parameters`
    section and point the variables to your key path:

```
# TLS parameters
smtpd_tls_cert_file=/etc/ssl/certs/ssl-cert-snakeoil.pem
smtpd_tls_key_file=/etc/ssl/private/ssl-cert-snakeoil.key
smtpd_use_tls=yes
```

10. Save the configuration file and exit.

11. Now, reload Postfix for the changes to take effect:

    ```
    $ sudo service postfix reload
    ```

    Test if everything is working as expected. Open a telnet connection to the mail server:

    ```
    $ telnet localhost 25
    ```

You should see an output similar to the following screenshot:

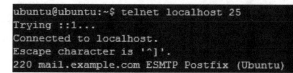

```
ubuntu@ubuntu:~$ telnet localhost 25
Trying ::1...
Connected to localhost.
Escape character is '^]'.
220 mail.example.com ESMTP Postfix (Ubuntu)
```

12. Now, send your first e-mail from this server. Type `sendmail user@domain` and press *Enter*. Then, type your message, and when done with that press *Ctrl + D* to send an e-mail.

13. To read your e-mails, log in with the user you send e-mails to. Start the mail program with the command `mail`. This should show you a list of e-mails received by this user account. The output should look similar to following screenshot:

```
root@ubuntu:~# mail
"/var/mail/root": 1 message 1 new
>N   1 ubuntu             Tue Sep  1 15:34  10/375
?
```

14. To read any e-mail, type in the mail number and press *Enter*. Type `q` followed by *Enter* to quit the mail reader.

How it works...

Postfix installation is quite a simple task; you need to be sure that you have configured the proper settings and then you are up and running in minutes. The Postfix installation process itself prompts for basic settings.

> If you miss providing configuration during installation, you can always recall the same dialogue box with the `reconfigure` command as follows:
>
> `$ sudo dpkg-reconfigure postfix`

Other parameters include `mynetworks` and `mydestination`. With `mynetwork`, we have restricted the uses of the mail server to the local network. Only users on the local network can use this server to send and receive e-mails. The parameter `mydestination` specifies the domain names that Postfix is going to serve. For all other domains that are not listed under `mydestination`, Postfix will simply act as a forwarder.

We have configured Postfix to use the `Maildir` format for storing e-mails. This is a new storage format and provides various improvements over the default format, `mbox`. Also, `Maildir` is used by various IMAP and POP servers. With `Maildir`, each new message is stored in a separate file. This avoids file locking when working with messages and provides protection against mailbox corruption.

Now if you send an e-mail to a local domain, it will be delivered to the inbox of the respective user, which can be read with `mail` command. If you send e-mails to an external mail server, such as Gmail, chances are your mail gets delivered to spam. You need to include a number of different parameters in your e-mail headers and then make sure that your server IP is not blacklisted. It would be a good idea to use an external mail server such as Mail Chimp or Gmail for sending e-mails.

See also

▸   An article by Jeff Atwood on sending e-mails through code. This may help you get your e-mails out of spam: `http://blog.codinghorror.com/so-youd-like-to-send-some-email-through-code/`

▸   Mailbox formats: `http://wiki.dovecot.org/MailboxFormat`

▸   The difference between port 465 and 587: `http://stackoverflow.com/questions/15796530/what-is-the-difference-between-ports-465-and-587`

Enabling IMAP and POP3 with Dovecot

In this recipe, we will learn how to install and set up Dovecot to enable accessing e-mails over IMAP and POP3 protocols. This will enable mail clients such as thunderbird to download e-mails on a user's local system.

Getting ready

You will need access to a root account or an account with `sudo` privileges

Make sure that you have set up Postfix and are able to send and receive e-mails on your server.

You may need an e-mail client to connect to and test the Dovecot setup.

How to do it...

Follow these steps to enable IMAP and POP3 with Dovecot:

1. First, install the Dovecot binaries from the Ubuntu main repository:

    ```
    $ sudo apt-get update
    ```

    ```
    $ sudo apt-get install dovecot-imapd dovecot-pop3d
    ```

2. You will be prompted for a hostname to be used for certificate generation. Type in a full hostname, for example `mail.example.com`. You can skip this step if you already have certificates.

3. Next, proceed with configuring Dovecot. Open the file `/etc/dovecot/dovecot.conf`:

    ```
    $ sudo nano /etc/dovecot/dovecot.conf
    ```

4. Find the `Enable installed protocols` section and add a new line to set the protocols that you want Dovecot to support:

    ```
    protocols = pop3 pop3s imap imaps
    ```

5. Open `/etc/dovecot/conf.d/10-mail.conf` and set the mailbox to be used. Dovecot supports `mbox` as well as `Maildir`. Make sure you set the correct path of your `mail` directory:

    ```
    mail_location = mbox:~/mail:INBOX=/var/spool/mail/%u
    ```

6. Open `/etc/dovecot/conf.d/10-ssl.conf` and uncomment or change the following lines to enable SSL authentication. Here, I have used certificates created by Postfix. You can use your own certificates or use the one generated by Dovecot:

    ```
    ssl = yes
    ssl_cert = < /etc/ssl/certs/ssl-cert-snakeoil.pem
    ssl_key =</etc/ssl/private/ssl-cert-snakeoil.key
    ```

7. Restart the Dovecot daemon:

    ```
    $ sudo service dovecot restart
    ```

8. Test Dovecot by creating a telnet connection. You should see an output similar to the following:

    ```
    $ telnet localhost pop3
    ```

```
ubuntu@ubuntu:~$ telnet localhost pop3
Trying ::1...
Connected to localhost.
Escape character is '^]'.
+OK Dovecot (Ubuntu) ready.
```

How it works...

Dovecot is one of the most popular **Mail Delivery Agents (MDA)** with support for IMAP and POP3 protocols. It works with both major mailbox formats, namely mbox and Maildir. The installation process is simple, and a minimal configuration can get you started with your own IMAP or POP3 service.

Dovecot developers have tried to simplify the configuration by separating it across various small files for each section. All these configuration files are located under /etc/dovecot/conf.d. If you prefer to use a single configuration file, you can replace the default file with the entire working configuration. To get all enabled configurations, use the doveconf -n command:

```
# mv /etc/dovecot/dovecot.conf /etc/dovecot/dovecot.conf.old
# doveconf -n > /etc/dovecot/dovecot.conf
```

In this recipe, we have configured Dovecot to support POP3, POP3 secure, IMAP, and IMAP secure. You can choose a single protocol or any combination of them. After setting protocol support, we have set the mailbox type to mbox. If you are using Maildir as your mailbox format, instead replace the mailbox setting with following line:

```
mail_location = maildir:~/Maildir
```

Now, when a user wants to check his e-mails, they need to authenticate with the Dovecot server. At this stage, only users with a user account on the server will be able to access their e-mails with Dovecot. To support users without creating a user account, we will need to set up Virtual Users, which is covered in the next recipes.

If you plan to skip SSL setup, you may need to enable plain text authentication under the configuration file, /etc/dovecot/conf.d/10-auth.conf. Find and uncomment the following line and set it to no:

```
disable_plaintext_auth = yes
```

The default setting is to allow plain text authentication over SSL connections only. That means the clients that do not support SSL will not be allowed to log in.

See also

▶ Dovecot wiki Quick-configuration at http://wiki2.dovecot.org/QuickConfiguration

Adding e-mail accounts

In this recipe, we will learn how to add e-mail accounts to Postfix. The easiest way to add a new e-mail account to Postfix is to add a new user account on your server. Postfix will check for user accounts and deliver e-mails to respective users. We will create a virtual user setup so that we do not need to create user accounts for each e-mail user.

Getting ready

You will need access to a root account or an account with `sudo` privileges.

I assume that you have completed your basic Postfix setup and that it is working properly.

How to do it...

Follow these steps to add e-mail account:

1. Create a new user account:

    ```
    $ useradd -s /usr/bin/nologin -m vmail
    ```

2. Get the UID and GID for this account:

    ```
    $ grep vmail /etc/passwd
    vmail:x:1001:1001::/home/vmail:/usr/bin/nologin
    ```

    ```
    ubuntu@ubuntu:~$ grep vmail /etc/passwd
    vmail:x:1001:1001::/home/vmail:/usr/bin/nologin
    ubuntu@ubuntu:~$
    ```

3. Create a base directory layout for domains and users:

    ```
    $ sudo mkdir -p /home/vmail/example.org/bob
    $ sudo mkdir -p /home/vmail/example.net/alice
    ```

4. Allow only the user vmail to access these files:

    ```
    $ sudo chown -R vmail:vmail /home/vmail
    $ chmod -R 700 /home/vmail
    ```

5. Next, configure Postfix. Edit `/etc/postfix/main.cf` and add the following lines:

    ```
    virtual_mailbox_base = /home/vmail
    virtual_mailbox_domains = /etc/postfix/virtual_domains
    virtual_mailbox_maps = hash:/etc/postfix/virtual_maps
    virtual_alias_maps = hash:/etc/postfix/virtual_alias
    virtual_uid_maps = static:1001   # user ID for user vmail
    virtual_gid_maps = static:1001   # group ID for user vmail
    ```

6. Create the file `virtual_domains` under /etc/postfix:

   ```
   $ sudo nano /etc/postfix/virtual_domains
   ```

   ```
   example.org
   example.net
   ```

7. Create the `virtual_maps` file:

   ```
   $ sudo nano /etc/postfix/virtual_maps
   bob@example.org   example.org/bob/
   alice@example.org   example.org/alice/
   @example.org   example.org/catchall/   # catch all address
   ```

8. Create the `virtual_alias` file and optionally set a `redirect`:

   ```
   $ sudo nano /etc/postfix/virtual_alias
   # redirect emails for tim to bob
   ```

   ```
   tim@example.org   bob@example.org
   ```

9. Now generate database of virtual maps and aliases by hashing respective files:

   ```
   $ sudo postmap /etc/postfix/virtual_maps
   $ sudo postmap /etc/postfix/virtual_alias
   ```

10. Reload Postfix and send an e-mail to the newly created address:

    ```
    $ sudo postfix reload
    $ sendmail bob@example.org
    ```

How it works...

Here, we have created a virtual mailbox setup to enable our Postfix server to serve multiple domains as well as add e-mail users without creating user accounts on the server. All e-mails received by virtual users will be stored under the home directory of the vmail user (virtual_ mailbox_base in Postfix configuration). When you need to add a new e-mail account, simply add the e-mail address with its respective domain to the virtual_maps file. In case you need to support a new domain, you can easily add it to the virtual_domains file.

The third file we used is virtual_alias. You can set e-mail forwarding in this file. It is handy when you need to create a new alias for an e-mail address or forward e-mails to one or multiple accounts. We have set a catchall entry in the virtual_alias file; this setting will redirect all e-mails received on nonexistent accounts to catchall@example.org, which can be checked by the domain administrator.

There's more...

Using files for virtual users and domains is good for getting started with setup. But once you need to add more and more user accounts and domains it is a good idea to move the users and domains to a database server. This can be easily done by changing the lookup table type. Postfix supports a variety of lookup table types, which include LDAP, MySQL, PGSQL, memcache, SQLite, and many others.

To use MySQL as a backend database, complete the following steps:

1. Create respective tables for `virtual_domain`, `virtual_maps`, and `virtual_alias`.

2. Change the Postfix configuration to use MySQL as a lookup table:

   ```
   virtual_mailbox_domains = mysql:/etc/postfix/mysql-virtual-domains
   virtual_mailbox_maps = mysql:/etc/postfix/mysql-virtual-maps
   virtual_alias_maps = mysql:/etc/postfix/mysql-virtual-alias
   ```

3. Add the respective details to each file using the following commands:

   ```
   $ sudo nano /etc/postfix/mysql-virtual-domains

   user = mysql_user
   password = mysql_password
   hosts = 127.0.0.1
   dbname = mysql_db_name
   query = SELECT 1 FROM virtual_domains WHERE name='%s'

   $ sudo nano /etc/postfix/mysql-virtual-maps

   . . .
   query = SELECT 1 FROM virtual_users WHERE email='%s'

   $ sudo nano /etc/postfix/mysql-virtual-alias

   . . .
   query = SELECT destination FROM virtual_aliases WHERE
   source='%s'
   ```

4. You can test your mapping with the following command. This should output 1 as a result:

   ```
   $ postmap -q bob@example.org mysql:/etc/postfix/mysql-virtual-maps
   ```

5. Finally, restart the Postfix daemon.

Web console for virtual mailbox administration

The **Vimbadmin** package provides a web console for virtual mailbox administration. It is a PHP-based open source package. You can get source code and installation instructions at `https://github.com/opensolutions/ViMbAdmin`.

See also

- ▶ Postfix guide at `http://www.postfix.org/VIRTUAL_README.html`
- ▶ Postfix lookup table types at `http://www.postfix.org/DATABASE_README.html#types`

Mail filtering with spam-assassin

In this recipe, we will learn how to install and set up a well-known e-mail filtering program, spam-assassin.

Getting ready

You will need access to a root account or an account with `sudo` privileges.

You need to have Postfix installed and working.

How to do it...

Follow these steps to filter mail with spam-assassin:

1. Install spam-assassin with the following command:

   ```
   $ sudo apt-get update
   $ sudo apt-get install spamassassin spamc
   ```

2. Create a user account and group for spam-assassin:

   ```
   $ sudo groupadd spamd
   $ sudo useradd -g spamd -s /usr/bin/nologin \
   -d /var/log/spamassassin -m spamd
   ```

3. Change the default settings for the spam daemon. Open `/etc/default/spamassassin` and update the following lines:

   ```
   ENABLED=1
   SAHOME="/var/log/spamassassin/"
   OPTIONS="--create-prefs --max-children 5 --username spamd -
   -helper-home-dir ${SAHOME} -s ${SAHOME}spamd.log"
   PIDFILE="${SAHOME}spamd.pid"
   CRON=1
   ```

4. Optionally, configure spam rules by changing values in `/etc/spamassassin/local.cf`:

```
trusted_networks 10.0.2.   # set your trusted network
required_score 3.0     # 3 + will be marked as spam
```

5. Next, we need to change the Postfix settings to pass e-mails through spam-assassin. Open `/etc/postfix/master.cf` and find the following line:

```
smtp         inet   n      -        -        -        -
smtpd
```

6. Add the content filtering option:

```
-o content_filter=spamassassin
```

```
# ==========================================================================
# service type  private unpriv  chroot  wakeup  maxproc command + args
#               (yes)   (yes)   (yes)   (never) (100)
# ==========================================================================
smtp        inet  n       -       -       -       -       smtpd
-o content_filter=spamassassin
```

7. Define the content filter block by adding the following lines to the end of the file:

```
spamassassin unix -     n       n       -       -
pipe
        user=spamd argv=/usr/bin/spamc -f -e
        /usr/sbin/sendmail -oi -f ${sender} ${recipient}
```

```
spamassassin unix -     n       n       -       -       pipe
        user=spamd argv=/usr/bin/spamc -f -e
        /usr/sbin/sendmail -oi -f ${sender} ${recipient}
```

8. Finally, restart spam-assassin and Postfix:

```
$ sudo service spamassassin start
```

```
$ sudo service postfix reload
```

9. You can check spam-assassin and mail logs to verify that spam-assassin is working properly:

```
$ less /var/log/spamassassin/spamd.log
```

```
$ less /var/log/mail.log
```

How it works...

Spam filtering works with the help of a piping mechanism provided by Postfix. We have created a new Unix pipe which will be used to filter e-mails. Postfix will pass all e-mails through this pipe, which will be then scanned through spam-assassin to determine the spam score. If given e-mail scores below the configured threshold, then it passes the filter without any modification; otherwise, spam-assassin adds a spam header to the e-mail.

Spam-assassin works with a Bayesian classifier to classify e-mails as spam or not spam. Basically, it checks the content of the e-mail and determines the score based on content.

There's more...

You can train spam-assassin's Bayesian classifier to get more accurate spam detections.

The following command will train spam-assassin with spam contents (--spam):

```
$ sudo sa-learn --spam -u spamd --dir ~/Maildir/.Junk/* -D
```

To train with non-spam content, use the following command (--ham):

```
$ sudo sa-learn --ham -u spamd --dir ~/Maildir/.INBOX/* -D
```

If you are using the mbox format, replace --dir ~/Maildir/.Junk/* with the option --mbox.

See also

▶ Sa-learn - train SpamAssassin's Bayesian classifier at https://spamassassin.apache.org/full/3.2.x/doc/sa-learn.html and https://wiki.apache.org/spamassassin/BayesInSpamAssassin

▶ Learn about Bayesian classification at https://en.wikipedia.org/wiki/Naive_Bayes_classifier

Troubleshooting the mail server

Sometimes you may face problems such as e-mails not being sent, delayed delivery or mail bouncing, issues while fetching e-mails, and login failures. In this recipe, we will learn how to identify the exact problem behind these issues. We will learn how to use debugging tools and read the logs of Postfix and Dovecot.

Getting ready

You will need access to a root account or an account with `sudo` privileges.

It is assumed that you have already installed Postfix and Dovecot servers.

How to do it...

Follow these steps to troubleshoot the mail server:

1. Start with checking the status of Postfix and Dovecot. If you get output that says `stop/waiting` or `not running` then the respective service is not running:

   ```
   $ sudo service postfix status
   $ sudo service dovecot status
   ```

   ```
   ubuntu@ubuntu:~$ sudo service postfix status
    * postfix is running
   ubuntu@ubuntu:~$ sudo service dovecot status
   dovecot start/running, process 5260
   ```

2. Try to restart the respective services. Restarting may give you error messages. Also check for startup logs under `/var/log/mail.log`:

   ```
   $ sudo service postfix restart
   $ less /var/log/mail.log
   ```

3. You can use a `tail` command to monitor the stream of logs while the service is running. You can easily filter the output of `tail` by piping it to a `grep` command:

   ```
   $ tail -f /var/log/mail.log
   ```

   Use `grep` to only view selected logs:

   ```
   $ tail -f /var/log/mail.log | grep "dovecot"
   ```

   ```
   ubuntu@ubuntu:~$ tail -f /var/log/mail.log | grep dovecot
   Sep  1 16:17:45 ubuntu dovecot: anvil: Warning: Killed with signal 15 (by pid=1 uid=
   0 code=kill)
   Sep  1 16:17:45 ubuntu dovecot: log: Warning: Killed with signal 15 (by pid=1 uid=0
   code=kill)
   Sep  1 16:17:45 ubuntu dovecot: master: Dovecot v2.2.9 starting up (core dumps disab
   led)
   Sep  1 16:18:14 ubuntu dovecot: pop3-login: Aborted login (no auth attempts in 9 sec
   s): user=<>, rip=::1, lip=::1, secured, session=<RUB/Sa0eIAAAAAAAAAAAAAAAAAAAAAAAB>
   ```

4. Use `grep -v` to filter/remove selected logs:

```
$ tail -f /var/log/mail.log | grep -v "dovecot"
```

```
ubuntu@ubuntu:~$ tail -f /var/log/mail.log | grep -v dovecot
Sep  1 16:50:15 ubuntu postfix/smtp[5426]: 5DA06380726: to=<root@example.com>, relay
=none, delay=4733, delays=4713/0.01/20/0, dsn=4.4.3, status=deferred (Host or domain
 name not found. Name service error for name=example.com type=MX: Host not found, tr
y again)
```

5. You can check other log files such as `/var/log/mail.err` and `/var/log/upstart/dovecot.log`.

   You may want to enable verbose logging to get detailed debugging information. To enable debug mode on Dovecot, edit `10-logging.conf` and enable `auth_verbose` and `mail_debug` variables:

   ```
   $ sudo nano /etc/dovecot/conf.d/10-logging.conf
   ```

   ```
   auth_verbose = yes
   mail_debug = yes
   ```

   Restart Dovecot:

   ```
   $ sudo service dovecot restart
   ```

6. To enable verbose logging on Postfix, edit `master.cf` file and add the `-v` argument:

   ```
   $ sudo nano /etc/postfix/master.cf
   ```

   ```
   smtp      inet  n     -       -       -       smtpd
   -v
   ```

   Restart Postfix.

7. Turn off chroot operations:

   ```
   $ sudo nano /etc/postfix/master.cf
   ```

   ```
   smtp      inet  n     -       n       -       -       smtpd
   ```

8. Check user account with Dovecot:

   ```
   $ doveadm username useremail@example.com
   ```

9. If you have set virtual users, check if they are working properly:

   ```
   $ postmap -q bob@example.org mysql:/etc/postfix/mysql-virtual-maps
   ```

10. Check respective ports used by Postfix and Dovecot. Postfix uses ports `25`, `465`, `587` and Dovecot uses port `993` and `995`:

    ```
    $ telnet localhost 993
    ```

11. Check `netstat` to make sure services are listening:

    ```
    $ sudo netstat -plutn
    ```

```
ubuntu@ubuntu:~$ sudo netstat -plutn
Active Internet connections (only servers)
Proto Recv-Q Send-Q Local Address           Foreign Address         State       PID/Program name
tcp        0      0 0.0.0.0:143             0.0.0.0:*               LISTEN      5260/dovecot
tcp        0      0 0.0.0.0:22              0.0.0.0:*               LISTEN      776/sshd
tcp        0      0 0.0.0.0:25              0.0.0.0:*               LISTEN      5687/master
tcp        0      0 0.0.0.0:993             0.0.0.0:*               LISTEN      5260/dovecot
tcp        0      0 0.0.0.0:995             0.0.0.0:*               LISTEN      5260/dovecot
tcp        0      0 0.0.0.0:110             0.0.0.0:*               LISTEN      5260/dovecot
tcp6       0      0 :::143                  :::*                    LISTEN      5260/dovecot
```

12. Check for DNS resolution and MX records:

    ```
    $ host -t mx example.com
    ```

13. Check if spam filters and antivirus scanners are working properly.

See also

▸ Postfix debugging - `http://www.postfix.org/DEBUG_README.html`

▸ Postfix book (troubleshooting) at `http://www.postfix-book.com/debugging.html`

▸ Dovecot troubleshooting at `http://wiki2.dovecot.org/WhyDoesItNotWork`

Installing the Zimbra mail server

Until now, we have installed Postfix, Dovecot, spam-assassin, and other tools separately. In this recipe, we will learn how to install the Zimbra collaboration server, which covers all tools in a single package. The Zimbra server contains Postfix, MySQL, OpenLDAP, ClamAV, and Spam-Assassin, Calendar, and various other features. Zimbra provides a paid option as well as an open source version. We will be installing an open source version of the Zimbra server in single server mode.

Getting ready

As always, you will need access to a root account or an account with `sudo` privileges.

For Zimbra to work properly, you will need the following minimum configuration for your server:

▸ At least 1.5 GHz of CPU 2 GHz recommended

▸ Minimum 8 GB of memory

▸ Minimum 10 GB of storage 20 GB recommended

You will need to set proper DNS and MX records for your domain.

You will also need various ports, as follows:

- Postfix/LMTP 25, 7025
- HTTP 80, 443
- POP3 110, 995
- IMAP 143, 993
- LDAP 389

How to do it...

Follow these steps to install Zimbra collaboration server:

1. Install the dependency packages before starting with the Zimbra installation:

   ```
   $ sudo apt-get update
   $ sudo apt-get install libperl5.18 libaio1 unzip pax sysstat
   sqlite3 libgmp10
   ```

2. Download and extract the Zimbra open source package using the following command:

   ```
   $ wget https://files.zimbra.com/downloads/8.6.0_GA/zcs-
   8.6.0_GA_1153.UBUNTU14_64.20141215151116.tgz
   $ tar -zxvf zcs-8.6.0_GA_1153.UBUNTU14_64.20141215151116.tgz
   $ cd zcs-8.6.0_GA_1153.UBUNTU14_64.20141215151116
   ```

3. Make sure you have set the proper hostname and hosts entries in respective files:

   ```
   $ cat /etc/hosts
   127.0.0.1 localhost
   119.9.107.28    mail.server.local       mail
   $ cat /etc/hostname
   mail.server.local
   ```

4. Start the Zimbra installation by executing the installer:

   ```
   $ sudo ./install.sh
   ```

5. The installation process will ask you to agree with License Agreement. Type y and press *Enter* to continue:

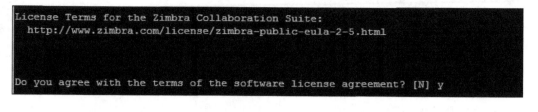

```
License Terms for the Zimbra Collaboration Suite:
  http://www.zimbra.com/license/zimbra-public-eula-2-5.html



Do you agree with the terms of the software license agreement? [N] y
```

6. On acceptance of agreement, Zimbra will check for dependencies and then ask for the component selection. I have chosen to skip a few components. Type y when asked for confirmation:

```
Select the packages to install

Install zimbra-ldap [Y] y

Install zimbra-logger [Y] y
```

7. Type y when asked for package selection confirmation.

8. The installation process will take some time. As installation completes, the Zimbra configuration menu will be displayed. Here, you need to set an admin account password:

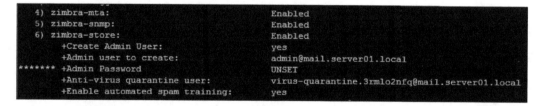

```
  4) zimbra-mta:                        Enabled
  5) zimbra-snmp:                       Enabled
  6) zimbra-store:                      Enabled
      +Create Admin User:               yes
      +Admin user to create:            admin@mail.server01.local
****** +Admin Password                 UNSET
      +Anti-virus quarantine user:      virus-quarantine.3rmlo2nfq@mail.server01.local
      +Enable automated spam training:  yes
```

9. On the main menu, select 6 to choose `zimbra-store` and then type 4 for the admin password. The new prompt will ask for the admin account password:

```
Select, or 'r' for previous menu [r] 4

Password for admin@mail.server01.local (min 6 characters): [Vfs7tvEVf] password
```

10. Then, type `r` to come back to the main menu and then type `a` to apply settings, and again press *Enter* to save settings:

```
*** CONFIGURATION COMPLETE - press 'a' to apply
Select from menu, or press 'a' to apply config (? - help) a
Save configuration data to a file? [Yes]
Save config in file: [/opt/zimbra/config.8466]
Saving config in /opt/zimbra/config.8466...done.
The system will be modified - continue? [No] y
```

11. Finally, apply all configurations when asked. Zimbra will ask you to send installation notification to Zimbra. Choose `Yes` by typing `y` to notify Zimbra:

```
Notify Zimbra of your installation? [Yes] y
Notifying Zimbra of installation via http://www.zimbra.com/cgi-bin/notify.cgi?VER=8.6.0_
GA_1153_UBUNTU14_64&MAIL=admin@mail.server01.local

Notification complete
```

12. Now you can access your Zimbra server with the domain name of your server or IP address. Your browser may prompt for a non-trusted server certificate, as shown in the following screenshot:

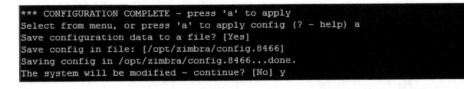

13. You can access the **Inbox** panel on port `7071`, `https://yourserver.tld:7071`.

How it works...

Zimbra combines various commonly used packages in a single package and provides a web interface to work with them. It reduces the efforts required in installing and configuring all tools separately. For any additional features, you can always switch to the Zimbra collaboration server, Network Edition.

There's more...

If you are planning to use Zimbra on your local network, you will need a DNS server set up. Alternatively, you can use the tool `dnsmasq`. It is a small package that sets up a quick DNS environment on your local network.

See also

▶ Zimbra open source features at `https://www.zimbra.com/open-source/features`

5
Handling Databases

In this chapter, we will cover the following recipes:

- ▶ Installing relational databases with MySQL
- ▶ Storing and retrieving data with MySQL
- ▶ Importing and exporting bulk data
- ▶ Adding users and assigning access rights
- ▶ Installing web access for MySQL
- ▶ Setting backups
- ▶ Optimizing MySQL performance – queries
- ▶ Optimizing MySQL performance – configuration
- ▶ Creating MySQL replicas for scaling and high availability
- ▶ Troubleshooting MySQL
- ▶ Installing MongoDB
- ▶ Storing and retrieving data with MongoDB

Introduction

In this chapter, we will learn how to set up database servers. A database is the backbone of any application, enabling an application to efficiently store and retrieve crucial data to and from persistent storage. We will learn how to install and set up relational databases with MySQL and NoSQL databases with MongoDB.

MySQL is a popular open source database server used by various large scale applications. It is a mature database system that can be scaled to support large volumes of data. MySQL is a relational database and stores data in the form of rows and columns organized in tables. It provides various storage engines, such as MyISAM, InnoDB, and in-memory storage. MariaDB is a fork of a MySQL project and can be used as a drop-in replacement for MySQL. It was started by the developers of MySQL after Oracle took over Sun Microsystems, the owner of the MySQL project. MariaDB is guaranteed to be open source and offers faster security releases and advanced features. It provides additional storage engines, including XtraDB by Percona and Cassandra for the NoSQL backend. PostgreSQL is another well-known name in relational database systems.

NoSQL, on the other hand, is a non-relational database system. It is designed for distributed large-scale data storage requirements. For some types of data, it is not efficient to store it in the tabular form offered by relational database systems, for example, data in the form of a document. NoSQL databases are used for these types of data. Some emerging NoSQL categories are document storage, key value store, BigTable, and the graph database.

In this chapter, we will start by installing MySQL, followed by storing and manipulating data in MySQL. We will also cover user management and access control. After an introduction to relational databases, we will cover some advanced topics on scaling and high availability. We will learn how to set up the web administration tool, PHPMyAdmin, but the focus will be on working with MySQL through command line access. In later recipes, we will also cover the document storage server, MongoDB.

Installing relational databases with MySQL

In this recipe, we will learn how to install and configure the MySQL database on an Ubuntu server.

Getting ready

You will need access to a root account or an account with `sudo` privileges.

Make sure that the MySQL default port 3306 is available and not blocked by any firewall.

How to do it...

Follow these steps to install the relational database MySQL:

1. To install the MySQL server, use the following command:

```
$ sudo apt-get update
$ sudo apt-get install mysql-server-5.7
```

The installation process will download the necessary packages and then prompt you to enter a password for the MySQL root account. Choose a strong password:

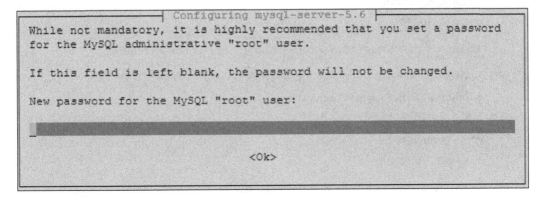

2. Once the installation process is complete, you can check the server status with the following command. It should return an output similar to the following:

```
$ sudo service mysql status
mysql.service - MySQL Community Server
   Loaded: loaded (/lib/systemd/system/mysql.service
   Active: active (running) since Tue 2016-05-10 05:
```

3. Next, create a copy of the original configuration file:

```
$ cd /etc/mysql/mysql.conf.d
$ sudo cp mysqld.cnf mysqld.cnf.bkp
```

4. Set MySQL to listen for a connection from network hosts. Open the configuration file /etc/mysql/mysql.conf.d/mysqld.cnf and change bind-address under the [mysqld] section to your server's IP address:

```
$ sudo nano /etc/mysql/mysql.conf.d/mysqld.cnf
bind-address = 10.0.2.6
```

```
# Instead of skip-networking the default is now to listen only on
# localhost which is more compatible and is not less secure.
bind-address             = 10.0.2.6
#
```

 For MySQL 5.5 and 5.6, the configuration file can be found at /etc/mysql/my.cnf

5. Optionally, you can change the default port used by the MySQL server. Find the [mysqld] section in the configuration file and change the value of the port variable as follows:

```
port = 30356
```

Make sure that the selected port is available and open under firewall.

6. Save the changes to the configuration file and restart the MySQL server:

```
$ sudo service mysql restart
```

7. Now open a connection to the server using the MySQL client. Enter the password when prompted:

```
$ mysql -u root -p
```

8. To get a list of available commands, type \h:

```
mysql> \h
```

```
List of all MySQL commands:
Note that all text commands must be first on line and end with ';'
?         (\?) Synonym for `help'.
clear     (\c) Clear the current input statement.
connect   (\r) Reconnect to the server. Optional arguments are db and host.
delimiter (\d) Set statement delimiter.
edit      (\e) Edit command with $EDITOR.
ego       (\G) Send command to mysql server, display result vertically.
```

How it works...

MySQL is a default database server available in Ubuntu. If you are installing the Ubuntu server, you can choose MySQL to be installed by default as part of the LAMP stack. In this recipe, we have installed the latest production release of MySQL (5.7) from the Ubuntu package repository. Ubuntu 16.04 contains MySQL 5.7, whereas Ubuntu 14.04 defaults to MySQL version 5.5.

If you prefer to use an older version on Ubuntu 16, then use following command:

```
$ sudo add-apt-repository 'deb http://archive.ubuntu.com/ubuntu
trusty universe'
$ sudo apt-get update
$ sudo apt-get install mysql-server-5.6
```

After installation, configure the MySQL server to listen for connections from external hosts. Make sure that you open your database installation to trusted networks such as your private network. Making it available on the Internet will open your database to attackers.

There's more...

Securing MySQL installation

MySQL provides a simple script to configure basic settings related to security. Execute this script before using your server in production:

```
$ mysql_secure_installation
```

This command will start a basic security check, starting with changing the `root` password. If you have not set a strong password for the root account, you can do it now. Other settings include disabling remote access to the root account and removing anonymous users and unused databases.

MySQL is popularly used with PHP. You can easily install PHP drivers for MySQL with the following command:

```
$ sudo apt-get install php7.0-mysql
```

See also

▶   The Ubuntu server guide mysql page at
    `https://help.ubuntu.com/14.04/serverguide/mysql.html`

Storing and retrieving data with MySQL

In this recipe, we will learn how to create databases and tables and store data in those tables. We will learn the basic **Structured Query Language** (**SQL**) required for working with MySQL. We will focus on using the command-line MySQL client for this tutorial, but you can use the same queries with any client software or code.

Getting ready

Ensure that the MySQL server is installed and running. You will need administrative access to the MySQL server. Alternatively, you can use the root account of MySQL.

How to do it...

Follow these steps to store and retrieve data with MySQL:

1. First, we will need to connect to the MySQL server. Replace `admin` with a user account on the MySQL server. You can use root as well but it's not recommended:

    ```
    $ mysql -u admin -h localhost -p
    ```

2. When prompted, enter the password for the `admin` account. If the password is correct, you will see the following MySQL prompt:

```
ubuntu@ubuntu:~$ mysql -u admin -h localhost -p
Enter password:
Welcome to the MySQL monitor.  Commands end with ; or \g.
Your MySQL connection id is 7
Server version: 5.7.12-0ubuntu1 (Ubuntu)
```

3. Create a database with the following query. Note the semi-colon at the end of query:

   mysql > create database myblog;

4. Check all databases with a `show` databases query. It should list `myblog`:

   mysql > show databases;

```
mysql> show databases;
+--------------------+
| Database           |
+--------------------+
| information_schema |
| myblog             |
| mysql              |
| performance_schema |
| replication_test   |
+--------------------+
5 rows in set (0.03 sec)
```

5. Select a database to work with, in this case `myblog`:

   mysql > use myblog;

   Database changed

6. Now, after the database has changed, we need to create a table to store our data. Use the following query to create a table:

```
CREATE TABLE `articles` (
  `id` int(11) NOT NULL AUTO_INCREMENT,
  `title` varchar(255) NOT NULL,
  `content` text NOT NULL,
  `created_at` timestamp NOT NULL DEFAULT
CURRENT_TIMESTAMP,
  PRIMARY KEY (`id`)
) ENGINE=InnoDB AUTO_INCREMENT=1;
```

7. Again, you can check tables with the `show tables` query:

```
mysql > show tables;
```

```
mysql> show tables;
+------------------+
| Tables_in_myblog |
+------------------+
| articles         |
+------------------+
1 row in set (0.00 sec)
```

8. Now, let's insert some data in our table. Use the following query to create a new record:

```
mysql > INSERT INTO `articles` (`id`, `title`, `content`,
`created_at`)
VALUES (NULL, 'My first blog post', 'contents of article',
CURRENT_TIMESTAMP);
```

```
mysql> INSERT INTO `articles` (`id`, `title`, `content`, `created_at`)
    -> VALUES (NULL, 'My first blog post', 'contents of article', CURRENT_TIMEST
AMP);
Query OK, 1 row affected (0.04 sec)
```

9. Retrieve data from the table. The following query will select all records from the articles table:

```
mysql > Select * from articles;
```

```
mysql> select * from articles;
+----+----------------------+---------------------+---------------------+
| id | title                | content             | created_at          |
+----+----------------------+---------------------+---------------------+
|  1 | New title            | contents of article | 2015-09-15 16:42:26 |
|  2 | My second  blog post | contents of blog 2  | 2015-09-15 16:44:15 |
+----+----------------------+---------------------+---------------------+
2 rows in set (0.00 sec)
```

10. Retrieve the selected records from the table:

```
mysql > Select * from articles where id = 1;
```

11. Update the selected record:

```
mysql > update articles set title="New title" where id=1;
```

```
mysql> update articles set title = "New title" where id = 1;
Query OK, 1 row affected (0.01 sec)
Rows matched: 1  Changed: 1  Warnings: 0
```

12. Delete the record from the `articles` table using the following command:

```
mysql > delete from articles where id = 2;
```

How it works...

We have created a relational database to store blog data with one table. Actual blog databases will need additional tables for comments, authors, and various entities. The queries used to create databases and tables are known as **Data Definition Language** (**DDL**), and queries that are used to select, insert, and update the actual data are known as **Data Manipulation Language** (**DML**).

MySQL offers various data types to be used for columns such as `tinyint`, `int`, `long`, `double`, `varchar`, `text`, `blob`, and so on. Each data type has its specific use and a proper selection may help to improve the performance of your database.

Importing and exporting bulk data

In this recipe, we will learn how to import and export bulk data with MySQL. Many times it happens that we receive data in CSV or XML format and we need to add this data to the database server for further processing. You can always use tools such as MySQL workbench and phpMyAdmin, but MySQL provides command-line tools for the bulk processing of data that are more efficient and flexible.

How to do it...

Follow these steps to import and export bulk data:

1. To export a database from the MySQL server, use the following command:

    ```
    $ mysqldump -u admin -p mytestdb > db_backup.sql
    ```

2. To export specific tables from a database, use the following command:

    ```
    $ mysqldump -u admin -p mytestdb table1 table2 >
    table_backup.sql
    ```

3. To compress exported data, use `gzip`:

    ```
    $ mysqldump -u admin -p mytestdb | gzip > db_backup.sql.gz
    ```

4. To export selective data to the CSV format, use the following query. Note that this will create `articles.csv` on the same server as MySQL and not your local server:

    ```
    SELECT id, title, contents FROM articles
    INTO OUTFILE '/tmp/articles.csv'
    FIELDS TERMINATED BY ',' ENCLOSED BY '"'
    LINES TERMINATED BY '\n';
    ```

5. To fetch data on your local system, you can use the MySQL client as follows:

   ❑ Write your query in a file:

   ```
   $ nano query.sql
   select * from articles;
   ```

   ❑ Now pass this query to the `mysql` client and collect the output in CSV:

   ```
   $ mysql -h 192.168.2.100 -u admin -p myblog < query.sql > output.csv
   ```

   The resulting file will contain tab separated values.

6. To import an SQL file to a MySQL database, we need to first create a database:

   ```
   $ mysqladmin -u admin -p create mytestdb2
   ```

7. Once the database is created, import data with the following command:

   ```
   $ mysql -u admin -p mytestdb2 < db_backup.sql
   ```

8. To import a CSV file in a MySQL table, you can use the `Load Data` query. The following is the sample CSV file:

```
ubuntu@ubuntu:~$ cat /tmp/articles.csv
"1","New title","contents of article"."2015-09-15 16:42:26"
"2","My second blog post","contents of blog 2"."2015-09-15 16:44:15"
ubuntu@ubuntu:~$
```

Now use the following query from the MySQL console to import data from CSV:

```
LOAD DATA INFILE 'c:/tmp/articles.csv'
INTO TABLE articles
FIELDS TERMINATED BY ','  ENCLOSED BY '"'
LINES TERMINATED BY \n IGNORE 1 ROWS;
```

See also

▸ MySQL select-into syntax at
https://dev.mysql.com/doc/refman/5.6/en/select-into.html

▸ MySQL load data infile syntax at
https://dev.mysql.com/doc/refman/5.6/en/load-data.html

▸ Importing from and exporting to XML files at
https://dev.mysql.com/doc/refman/5.6/en/load-xml.html

Adding users and assigning access rights

In this recipe, we will learn how to add new users to the MySQL database server. MySQL provides very flexible and granular user management options. We can create users with full access to an entire database or limit a user to simply read the data from a single database. Again, we will be using queries to create users and grant them access rights. You are free to use any tool of your choice.

Getting ready

You will need a MySQL user account with administrative privileges. You can use the MySQL root account.

How to do it...

Follow these steps to add users to MySQL database server and assign access rights:

1. Open the MySQL shell with the following command. Enter the password for the admin account when prompted:

   ```
   $ mysql -u root -p
   ```

2. From the MySQL shell, use the following command to add a new user to MySQL:

   ```
   mysql> create user 'dbuser'@'localhost' identified by
   'password';
   ```

3. You can check the user account with the following command:

   ```
   mysql> select user, host, password from mysql.user where
   user = 'dbuser';
   ```

   ```
   mysql> select user, host, password from mysql.user where user = 'blog_admin';
   +------------+-----------+--------------------------------------------+
   | user       | host      | password                                   |
   +------------+-----------+--------------------------------------------+
   | blog_admin | localhost | *59C70DA2F3E3A5BDF46B68F5C8B8F25762BCCEF0  |
   +------------+-----------+--------------------------------------------+
   1 row in set (0.00 sec)
   ```

4. Next, add some privileges to this user account:

   ```
   mysql> grant all privileges on *.* to 'dbuser'@'localhost'
   with grant option;
   ```

5. Verify the privileges for the account as follows:

   ```
   mysql> show grants for 'dbuser'@'localhost'
   ```

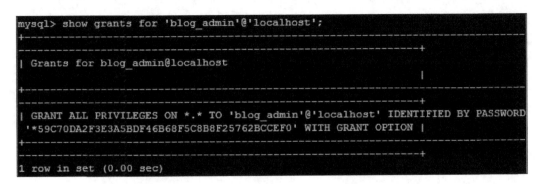

```
mysql> show grants for 'blog_admin'@'localhost';
+---------------------------------------------------------------------+
| Grants for blog_admin@localhost                                     |
+---------------------------------------------------------------------+
| GRANT ALL PRIVILEGES ON *.* TO 'blog_admin'@'localhost' IDENTIFIED BY PASSWORD
 '*59C70DA2F3E3A5BDF46B68F5C8B8F25762BCCEF0' WITH GRANT OPTION |
+---------------------------------------------------------------------+
1 row in set (0.00 sec)
```

6. Finally, exit the MySQL shell and try to log in with the new user account. You should log in successfully:

```
mysql> exit
$ mysql -u dbuser -p
```

How it works...

MySQL uses the same database structure to store user account information. It contains a hidden database named MySQL that contains all MySQL settings along with user accounts. The statements create user and grant work as a wrapper around common insert statements and make it easy to add new users to the system.

In the preceding example, we created a new user with the name dbuser. This user is allowed to log in only from localhost and requires a password to log in to the MySQL server. You can skip the identified by 'password' part to create a user without a password, but of course, it's not recommended.

To allow a user to log in from any system, you need to set the host part to a %, as follows:

```
mysql> create user 'dbuser'@'%' identified by 'password';
```

You can also limit access from a specific host by specifying its FQDN or IP address:

```
mysql> create user 'dbuser'@'host1.example.com' identified by 'password';
```

Or

```
mysql> create user 'dbuser'@'10.0.2.51' identified by 'password';
```

Note that if you have an anonymous user account on MySQL, then a user created with username'@'% will not be able to log in through localhost. You will need to add a separate entry with username'@'localhost.

Next, we give some privileges to this user account using a `grant` statement. The preceding example gives all privileges on all databases to the user account `dbuser`. To limit the database, change the database part to `dbname.*`:

```
mysql> grant all privileges on dbname.* to 'dbuser'@'localhost' with
grant option;
```

To limit privileges to certain tasks, mention specific privileges in a `grant` statement:

```
mysql> grant select, insert, update, delete, create
    -> on dbname.* to 'dbuser'@'localhost';
```

The preceding statement will `grant select`, `insert`, `update`, `delete`, and `create` privileges on any table under the `dbname` database.

There's more...

Similar to preceding add user example, other user management tasks can be performed with SQL queries as follows:

Removing user accounts

You can easily remove a user account with the `drop` statement, as follows:

```
mysql> drop user 'dbuser'@'localhost';
```

Setting resource limits

MySQL allows setting limits on individual accounts:

```
mysql> grant all on dbname.* to 'dbuser'@'localhost'
    ->        with max_queries_per_hour 20
    ->            max_updates_per_hour 10
    ->            max_connections_per_hour 5
    ->            max_user_connections 2;
```

See also

▶   MySQL user account management at `https://dev.mysql.com/doc/refman/5.6/en/user-account-management.html`

Installing web access for MySQL

In this recipe, we will set up a well-known web-based MySQL administrative tool—phpMyAdmin.

Getting ready

You will need access to a root account or an account with `sudo` privileges.

You will need a web server set up to serve PHP contents.

How to do it...

Follow these steps to install web access for MySQL:

1. Enable the `mcrypt` extension for PHP:

   ```
   $ sudo php5enmod mcrypt
   ```

2. Install `phpmyadmin` with the following commands:

   ```
   $ sudo apt-get update
   $ sudo apt-get install phpmyadmin
   ```

3. The installation process will download the necessary packages and then prompt you to configure `phpmyadmin`:

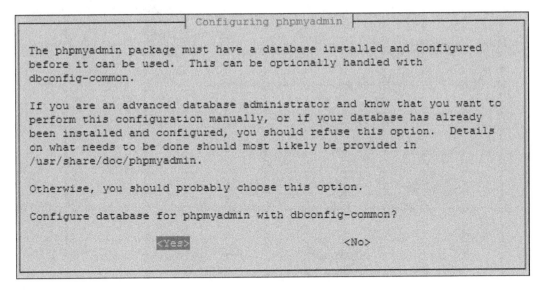

4. Choose `<yes>` to proceed with the configuration process.

5. Enter the MySQL admin account password on the next screen:

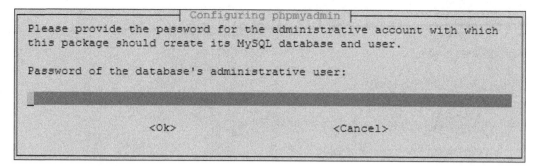

6. Another screen will pop up; this time, you will be asked for the new password for the `phpmyadmin` user. Enter the new password and then confirm it on the next screen:

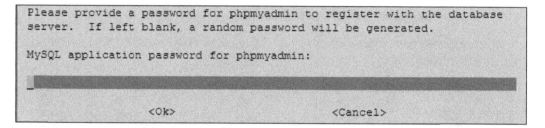

7. Next, `phpmyadmin` will ask for web server selection:

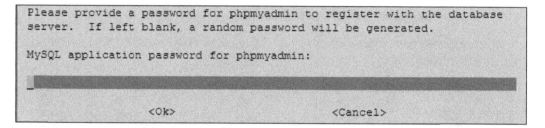

8. Once the installation completes, you can access phpMyAdmin at `http://server-ip/phpmyadmin`. Use your admin login credentials on the login screen. The `phpmyadmin` screen will look something like this:

How it works...

PHPMyAdmin is a web-based administrative console for MySQL. It is developed in PHP and works with a web server such as Apache to serve web access. With PHPMyAdmin, you can do database tasks such as create databases and tables; select, insert, update data; modify table definitions; and a lot more. It provides a query console which can be used to type in custom queries and execute them from same screen.

With the addition of the Ubuntu software repository, it has become easy to install PHPMyAdmin with a single command. Once it is installed, a new user is created on the MySQL server. It also supports connecting to multiple servers. You can find all configuration files located in the `/etc/phpmyadmin` directory.

There's more...

If you want to install the latest version of phpMyAdmin, you can download it from their official website, `https://www.phpmyadmin.net/downloads/`. You can extract downloaded contents to your web directory and set MySQL credentials in the `config.inc.php` file.

See also

- Read more about phpMyAdmin in the Ubuntu server guide at `https://help.ubuntu.com/lts/serverguide/phpmyadmin.html`
- Install and secure phpMyAdmin at `https://www.digitalocean.com/community/tutorials/how-to-install-and-secure-phpmyadmin-on-ubuntu-14-04`

Setting backups

In this recipe, we will learn how to back up the MySQL database.

Getting ready

You will need administrative access to the MySQL database.

How to do it...

Follow these steps to set up the backups:

1. Backing up the MySQL database is the same as exporting data from the server. Use the `mysqldump` tool to back up the MySQL database as follows:

   ```
   $ mysqldump -h localhost -u admin -p mydb > mydb_backup.sql
   ```

2. You will be prompted for the admin account password. After providing the password, the backup process will take time depending on the size of the database.

3. To back up all databases, add the `--all-databases` flag to the preceding command:

   ```
   $ mysqldump --all-databases -u admin -p alldb_backup.sql
   ```

4. Next, we can restore the backup created with the `mysqldump` tool with the following command:

   ```
   $ mysqladmin -u admin -p create mydb
   $ mysql -h localhost -u admin -p mydb < mydb_backup.sql
   ```

5. To restore all databases, skip the database creation part:

   ```
   $ mysql -h localhost -u admin -p < alldb_backup.sql
   ```

How it works...

MySQL provides a very general tool, `mysqldump`, to export all data from the database server. This tool can be used with any type of database engine, be it MyISAM or InnoDB or any other. To perform an online backup of InnoDB tables, `mysqldump` provides the `--single-transaction` option. With this option set, InnoDB tables will not be locked and will be available to other applications while backup is in progress.

Oracle provides the MySQL Enterprise backup tool for MySQL Enterprise edition users. This tool includes features such as incremental and compressed backups. Alternatively, Percona provides an open source utility known as **Xtrabackup**. It provides incremental and compressed backups and many more features.

Some other backup methods include copying MySQL table files and the `mysqlhotcopy` script for InnoDB tables. For these methods to work, you may need to pause or stop the MySQL server before backup.

You can also enable replication to mirror all data to the other server. It is a mechanism to maintain multiple copies of data by automatically copying data from one system to another. In this case, the primary server is called **Master** and the secondary server is called **Slave**. This type of configuration is known as Master-Slave replication. Generally, applications communicate with the Master server for all read and write requests. The Slave is used as a backup if the Master goes down. Many times, the Master-Slave configuration is used to load balance database queries by routing all read requests to the Slave server and write requests to the Master server. Replication can also be configured in Master-Master mode, where both servers receive read-write requests from clients.

See also

- MySQL backup methods at `http://dev.mysql.com/doc/refman/5.6/en/backup-methods.html`
- Percona XtraBackup at `https://www.percona.com/doc/percona-xtrabackup/2.2/index.html`
- MySQL binary log at `http://dev.mysql.com/doc/refman/5.6/en/binary-log.html`

Optimizing MySQL performance – queries

MySQL performance optimizations can be divided into two parts. One is query optimization and the other is MySQL server configuration. To get optimum results, you have to work on both of these parts. Without proper configuration, queries will not provide consistent performance; on the other hand, without proper queries and a database structure, queries may take much longer to produce results.

In this recipe, we will learn how to evaluate query performance, set indexes, and identify the optimum database structure for our data.

Getting ready

You will need access to an admin account on the MySQL server.

You will need a large dataset to test queries. Various tools are available to generate test data. I will be using test data available at `https://github.com/datacharmer/test_db`.

How to do it...

Follow these steps to optimize MySQL performance:

1. The first and most basic thing is to identify key columns and add indexes to them:

   ```
   mysql> alter table salaries add index (salary);
   ```

2. Enable the slow query log to identify long-running queries. Enter the following commands from the MySQL console:

   ```
   mysql> set global log_slow_queries = 1;

   mysql> set global slow_query_log_file =
   '/var/log/mysql/slow.log';
   ```

3. Once you identify the slow and repeated query, execute that query on the database and record query timings. The following is a sample query:

   ```
   mysql> select count(*) from salaries where salary between
   30000 and 65000 and from_date > '1986-01-01';
   ```

   ```
   mysql> select count(*) from salaries where salary between 30000 and 65000 and fr
   om_date > '1986-01-01';
   +----------+
   | count(*) |
   +----------+
   |  1646072 |
   +----------+
   1 row in set (3.67 sec)
   ```

4. Next, use `explain` to view the query execution plan:

   ```
   mysql> explain select count(*) from salaries where salary
   between 30000 and 65000 and from_date > '1986-01-01';
   ```

   ```
   mysql> explain select count(*) from salaries where salary between 30000 and 6500
   0 and from_date > '1986-01-01';
   +----+-------------+----------+------+---------------+------+---------+------+--------+-------------+
   | id | select_type | table    | type | possible_keys | key  | key_len | ref  | rows   | Extra       |
   +----+-------------+----------+------+---------------+------+---------+------+--------+-------------+
   |  1 | SIMPLE      | salaries | ALL  | NULL          | NULL | NULL    | NULL | 2756234 | Using where |
   +----+-------------+----------+------+---------------+------+---------+------+--------+-------------+
   1 row in set (0.04 sec)
   ```

5. Add required indexes, if any, and recheck the query execution plan. Your new index should be listed under `possible_keys` and key columns of `explain` output:

```
mysql> alter table `salaries` add index (  `from_date` ) ;
```

6. If you found that MySQL is not using a proper index or using another index than expected then you can explicitly specify the index to be used or ignored:

```
mysql> select * from salaries use index (salaries) where
salary between 30000 and 65000 and from_date > '1986-01-
01';
```

```
mysql> select * from salaries where salary between 30000
and 65000 and from_date > '1986-01-01' ignore index
(from_date);
```

Now execute the query again and check query timings for any improvements.

7. Analyze your data and modify the table structure. The following query will show the minimum and maximum length of data in each column. Add a small amount of buffer space to the reported maximum length and reduce additional space allocation if any:

```
mysql> select * from `employees` procedure analyse();
```

The following is the partial output for the `analyse()` procedure:

```
| employees.employees.emp_no      | 10001       | 499999      |            5 |
      6 |              0 |    0 | 253321.7634 |           | 300552.3312 | MEDIUM
INT(6) UNSIGNED NOT NULL |
| employees.employees.birth_date | 1952-02-01 | 1965-02-01 |           10 |
   10 |              0 |    0 | 10.0000     | NULL      |             | DATE N
OT NULL                  |
| employees.employees.first_name | Aamer       | Zvonko      |            3 |
   14 |              0 |    0 | 6.2157      | NULL      |             | VARCHA
R(14) NOT NULL           |
```

8. Check the database engines you are using. The two major engines available in MySQL are MyISAM and InnoDB:

```
mysql> show create table employees;
```

How it works...

MySQL uses SQL to accept commands for data processing. The query contains the operation, such as `select`, `insert`, and `update`; the target that is a table name; and conditions to match the data. The following is an example query:

```
select * from employee where id = 1001;
```

In the preceding query, `select  *` is the operation asking MySQL to select all data for a row. The target is the `employee` table, and `id = 1001` is a condition part.

Once a query is received, MySQL generates query execution plan for it. This step contains various steps such as parsing, preprocessing, and optimization. In parsing and pre-processing, the query is checked for any syntactical errors and the proper order of SQL grammar. The given query can be executed in multiple ways. Query optimizer selects the best possible path for query execution. Finally, the query is executed and the execution plan is stored in the query cache for later use.

The query execution plan can be retrieved from MySQL with the help of the `explain` query and explain extended. Explain executes the query until the generation of the query execution plan and then returns the execution plan as a result. The execution plan contains table names used in this query, key fields used to search data, the number of rows needed to be scanned, and temporary tables and file sorting used, if any. The query execution plan shows possible keys that can be used for query execution and then shows the actual key column used. **Key** is a column with an index on it, which can be a primary index, unique index, or non-unique index. You can check the MySQL documentation for more details on query execution plans and `explain` output.

If a specific column in a table is being used repeatedly, you should consider adding a proper index to that column. **Indexes** group similar data together, which reduces the look up time and total number of rows to be scanned. Also keep in mind that indexes use large amounts of memory, so be selective while adding indexes.

Secondly, if you have a proper index set on a required column and the query optimization plan does not recognize or use the index, you can force MySQL to use a specific index with the `USE INDEX index_name` statement. To ignore a specific index, use the statement `IGNORE INDEX index_name`.

You may get a small improvement with table maintenance commands. **Optimize table** is useful when a large part of the table is modified or deleted. It reorganizes table index data on physical storage and improves I/O performance. **Flush table** is used to reload the internal cache. **Check table** and **Analyze table** check for table errors and data distribution respectively. The improvements with these commands may not be significant for smaller tables. Reducing the extra space allocated to each column is also a good idea for reducing total physical storage used. Reduced storage will optimize I/O performance as well as cache utilization.

You should also check the storage engines used by specific tables. The two major storage engines used in MySQL are MyISAM and InnoDB. InnnoDB provides full transactional support and uses row-level locking, whereas MyISAM does not have transaction support and uses table-level locking. MyISAM is a good choice for faster reads where you have a large amount of data with limited writes on the table. MySQL does support the addition of external storage engines in the form of plugins. One popular open source storage engine is **XtraDB** by Percona systems.

There's more...

If your tables are really large, you should consider partitioning them. Partitioning tables distributes related data across multiple files on disk. Partitioning on frequently used keys can give you a quick boost. MySQL supports various different types of partitioning such as hash partitions, range partitions, list partitions, key partitions, and also sub-partitions.

You can specify hash partitioning with table creation as follows:

```
create table employees (
    id int not null,
    fname varchar(30),
    lname varchar(30),
    store_id int
) partition by hash(store_id) partitions 4;
```

Alternatively, you can also partition an existing table with the following query:

```
mysql> alter table employees partition by hash(store_id) partitions
4;
```

Sharding MySQL

You can also shard your database. Sharding is a form of horizontal partitioning where you store part of the table data across multiple instances of a table. The table instance can exist on the same server under separate databases or across different servers. Each table instance contains parts of the total data, thus improving queries that need to access limited data. Sharding enables you to scale a database horizontally across multiple servers.

The best implementation strategy for sharding is to try to avoid it for as long as possible. Sharding requires additional maintenance efforts on the operations side and the use of proxy software to hide sharding from an application, or to make your application itself sharding aware. Sharding also adds limitations on queries that require access to the entire table. You will need to create cross-server joins or process data in the application layer.

See also

- ▸ The MySQL optimization guide at https://dev.mysql.com/doc/refman/5.6/en/optimization.html
- ▸ MySQL query execution plan information at https://dev.mysql.com/doc/refman/5.6/en/execution-plan-information.html
- ▸ InnoDB storage engine at https://dev.mysql.com/doc/refman/5.6/en/innodb-storage-engine.html
- ▸ Other storage engines available in MySQL at https://dev.mysql.com/doc/refman/5.6/en/storage-engines.html

- ▸ Table maintenance statements at `http://dev.mysql.com/doc/refman/5.6/en/table-maintenance-sql.html`
- ▸ MySQL test database at `https://github.com/datacharmer/test_db`

Optimizing MySQL performance – configuration

MySQL has hundreds of settings that can be configured. Version 5.7 ships with many improvements in default configuration values and requires far fewer changes. In this recipe, we will look at some of the most important parameters for tuning MySQL performance.

Getting ready

You will need access to a root account or an account with `sudo` privileges.

You will need access to a root account on the MySQL server.

How to do it...

Follow these steps to improve MySQL configuration:

1. First, create a backup of the original configuration file:

```
$ cd /etc/mysql/mysql.conf.d
$ sudo cp mysqld.cnf mysqld.cnf.bkp
```

2. Now open `my.cnf` for changes:

```
$ sudo nano /etc/mysql/mysql.conf.d/mysqld.cnf
```

3. Adjust the following settings for your InnoDB tables:

```
innodb_buffer_pool_size = 512M  # around 70% of total ram
innodb_log_file_size  = 64M
innodb_file_per_table = 1
innodb_log_buffer_size = 4M
```

4. If you are using MyISAM tables, set the key buffer size:

```
key_buffer_size = 64M
```

5. Enable the slow query log:

```
slow_query_log = 1
slow_query_log_file = /var/lib/mysql/mysql-slow.log
long_query_time = 2
```

6. Disable the query cache:

```
query_cache_size = 0
```

7. Set the maximum connections as per your requirements:

   ```
   max_connections = 300
   ```

8. Increase the temporary table size:

   ```
   tmp_table_size = 32M
   ```

9. Increase `max_allowed_packet` to increase the maximum packet size:

   ```
   max_allowed_packet = 32M
   ```

10. Enable binary logging for easy recovery and replication:

    ```
    log_bin = /var/log/mysql/mysql-bin.log
    ```

11. Additionally, you can use `mysqltuner.pl`, which gives general recommendations about the MySQL best practices:

    ```
    $ wget http://mysqltuner.pl/ -O mysqltuner.pl
    $ perl mysqltuner.pl
    ```

How it works...

The preceding example shows some important settings for MySQL performance tuning. Ensure that you change one setting at a time and assess its results. There is no silver bullet that works for all, and similarly, some of these settings may or may not work for you. Secondly, most settings can be changed at runtime with a `SET` statement. You can test settings in runtime and easily reverse them if they do not work as expected. Once you are sure that settings work as expected, you can move them to the configuration file.

The following are details on the preceding settings:

- `innodb_buffer_pool_size`: the size of the cache where InnoDB data and indexes are cached. The larger the buffer pool, the more data can be cached in it. You can set this to around 70% of available physical memory as MySQL uses extra memory beyond this buffer. It is assumed that MySQL is the only service running on server.

- `log_file_size`: the size of the redo logs. These logs are helpful in faster writes and crash recovery.

- `innodb_file_per_table`: This determines whether to use shared table space or separate files for each table. MySQL 5.7 defaults this setting to ON.

- `key_buffer_size`: determines the key buffer for MyISAM tables.

- `slow_query_log` and `long_query_time` enable slow query logging and set slow query time respectively. Slow query logging can be useful for identifying repeated slow queries.

- `Query_cache_size` caches the result of a query. It is identified as a bottleneck for concurrent queries and MySQL 5.6 disables it by default.

- ▶ `max_connections` sets the number of maximum concurrent connections allowed. Set this value as per your application's requirements. Higher values may result in higher memory consumption and an unresponsive server. Use connection pooling in the application if possible.

- ▶ `max_allowed_packet` sets the size of the packet size that MySQL can send at a time. Increase this value if your server runs queries with large result sets. `mysqld` set it to `16M` and `mysqldump` set it to `24M`. You can also set this as a command-line parameter.

- ▶ `log_bin` enables binary logging, which can be used for replication and also for crash recovery. Make sure that you set proper rotation values to avoid large dump files.

There's more...

MySQL performance tuning primer script: This script takes information from show status and show variables statements. It gives recommendations for various settings such as slow query log, max connections, query cache, key buffers, and many others. This shell script is available at `http://day32.com/MySQL`.

You can download and use this script as follows:

```
$ wget http://day32.com/MySQL/tuning-primer.sh
$ sh tuning-primer.sh
```

Percona configuration wizard

Percona systems provide a developer-friendly, web-based configuration wizard to create a configuration file for your MySQL server. The wizard is available at `http://tools.percona.com`

MySQL table compression

Depending on the type of data, you can opt for compressed tables. Compression is useful for tables with long textual contents and read-intensive workloads. Data and indexes are stored in a compressed format, resulting in reduced I/O and a smaller database size, though it needs more CPU cycles to compress and uncompress data. To enable compression, you need an InnoDB storage engine with `innodb_file_per_table` enabled and the file format set to Barracuda. Check MySQL documents for more details on InnoDB compression at `https://dev.mysql.com/doc/innodb/1.1/en/innodb-compression.html`.

See also

- ▶ MySQL tuner script at `https://github.com/major/MySQLTuner-perl`
- ▶ MySQL docs at `https://dev.mysql.com/doc/refman/5.7/en/optimization.html`

▶ InnoDB table compression at `https://dev.mysql.com/doc/refman/5.7/en/innodb-table-compression.html`

Creating MySQL replicas for scaling and high availability

When your application is small, you can use a single MySQL server for all your database needs. As your application becomes popular and you get more and more requests, the database starts becoming a bottleneck for application performance. With thousands of queries per second, the database write queue gets longer and read latency increases. To solve this problem, you can use multiple replicas of the same database and separate read and write queries between them.

In this recipe, we will learn how to set up replication with the MySQL server.

Getting ready

You will need two MySQL servers and access to administrative accounts on both.

Make sure that port 3306 is open and available on both servers.

How to do it...

Follow these steps to create MySQL replicas:

1. Create the replication user on the Master server:

   ```
   $ mysql -u root -p
   mysql> grant replication slave on *.* TO
   'slave_user'@'10.0.2.62' identified by 'password';
   mysql> flush privileges;
   mysql> quit
   ```

2. Edit the MySQL configuration on the Master server:

   ```
   $ sudo nano /etc/mysql/my.cnf
   [mysqld]
   bind-address = 10.0.2.61     # your master server ip
   server-id = 1
   log-bin = mysql-bin
   binlog-ignore-db = "mysql"
   ```

3. Restart MySQL on the Master server:

```
$ sudo service mysql restart
```

4. Export MySQL databases on the Master server. Open the MySQL connection and lock the database to prevent any updates:

```
$ mysql -u root -p
mysql> flush tables with read lock;
```

5. Read the Master status on the Master server and take a note of it. This will be used shortly to configure the Slave server:

```
mysql> show master status;
```

```
mysql> show master status;
+--------------------+----------+--------------+------------------+-------------
| File               | Position | Binlog_Do_DB | Binlog_Ignore_DB | Executed_Gt
+--------------------+----------+--------------+------------------+-------------
| mysql-bin.000010 |     2214 |              | mysql            |
+--------------------+----------+--------------+------------------+-------------
1 row in set (0.00 sec)
```

6. Open a separate terminal window and export the required databases. Add the names of all the databases you want to export:

```
$ mysqldump -u root -p --databases testdb  >
master_dump.sql
```

7. Now, unlock the tables after the database dump has completed:

```
mysql> UNLOCK TABLES;

mysql> quit;
```

8. Transfer the backup to the Slave server with any secure method:

```
$ scp master_backup.sql
ubuntu@10.0.2.62:/home/ubuntu/master_backup.sql
```

9. Next, edit the configuration file on the Slave server:

```
$ sudo nano /etc/mysql/my.cnf
[mysqld]
bind-address = 10.0.2.62
server-id = 2
relay_log=relay-log
```

10. Import the dump from the Master server. You may need to manually create a database before importing dumps:

```
$ mysqladmin -u admin -p create testdb
$ mysql -u root -p < master_dump.sql
```

11. Restart the MySQL server:

```
$ sudo service mysql restart
```

12. Now set the Master configuration on the Slave. Use the values we received from `show master status` command in step 5:

```
$ mysql -u root -p

mysql > change master to

master_host='10.0.2.61', master_user='slave_user',

master_password='password', master_log_file='mysql-bin.000010',

master_log_pos=2214;
```

13. Start the Slave:

```
mysql> start slave;
```

14. Check the Slave's status. You should see the message `Waiting for master to send event` under `Slave_IO_state`:

```
mysql> show slave status\G
```

```
mysql> show slave status\G
*************************** 1. row ***************************
           Slave_IO_State: Waiting for master to send event
              Master_Host: 10.0.2.6
              Master_User: slave_user
              Master_Port: 3306
            Connect_Retry: 60
          Master_Log_File: mysql-bin.000010
      Read_Master_Log_Pos: 2214
```

Now you can test replication. Create a new database with a table and a few sample records on the Master server. You should see the database replicated on the Slave immediately.

How it works...

MySQL replication works with the help of binary logs generated on the Master server. MySQL logs any changes to the database to local binary logs with a lightweight buffered and sequential write process. These logs will then be read by the slave. When the slave connects to the Master, the Master creates a new thread for this replication connection and updates the slave with events in a binary log, notifying the slave about newly written events in binary logs.

On the slave side, two threads are started to handle replication. One is the IO thread, which connects to the Master and copies updates in binary logs to a local log file, `relay_log`. The other thread, which is known as the SQL thread, reads events stored on `relay_log` and applies them locally.

In the preceding recipe, we have configured Master-Slave replication. MySQL also supports Master-Master replication. In the case of Master-Slave configuration, the Master works as an active server, handling all writes to database. You can configure slaves to answer read queries, but most of the time, the slave server works as a passive backup server. If the Master fails, you manually need to promote the slave to take over as Master. This process may require downtime.

To overcome problems with Master - Slave replication, MySQL can be configured in **Master-Master** relation, where all servers act as a Master as well as a slave. Applications can read as well as write to all participating servers, and in case any Master goes down, other servers can still handle all application writes without any downtime. The problem with Master-Master configuration is that it's quite difficult to set up and deploy. Additionally, maintaining data consistency across all servers is a challenge. This type of configuration is lazy and asynchronous and violates ACID properties.

In the preceding example, we configured the `server-id` variable in the `my.cnf` file. This needs to be unique on both servers. MySQL version 5.6 adds another UUID for the server, which is located at `data_dir/auto.cnf`. If you happen to copy `data_dir` from Master to host or are using a copy of a Master virtual machine as your starting point for a slave, you may get an error on the slave that reads something like **master and slave have equal mysql server UUIDs**. In this case, simply remove `auto.cnf` from the slave and restart the MySQL server.

There's more...

You can set MySQL load balancing and configure your database for high availability with the help of a simple load balancer in front of MySQL. HAProxy is a well known load balancer that supports TCP load balancing and can be configured in a few steps, as follows:

1. Set your MySQL servers to Master - Master replication mode.

2. Log in to `mysql` and create one user for `haproxy` health checks and another for remote administration:

   ```
   mysql> create user 'haproxy_admin'@'haproxy_ip';

   mysql> grant all privileges on *.* to 'haproxy_admin'@'haproxy_ip'
   identified by 'password' with
   grant option;

   mysql> flush privileges;
   ```

3. Next, install the MySQL client on the HAProxy server and try to log into the `mysql` server with the `haproxy_admin` account.

4. Install HAProxy and configure it to connect to `mysql` on the TCP port:

```
listen mysql-cluster
    bind haproxy_ip:3306
    mode tcp
    option mysql-check user haproxy_check
    balance roundrobin
    server mysql-1 mysql_srv_1_ip:3306 check
    server mysql-2 mysql_srv_2_ip:3306 check
```

5. Finally, start the `haproxy` service and try to connect to the `mysql` server with the `haproxy_admin` account:

```
$ mysql -h haproxy_ip -u hapoxy_admin -p
```

See also

▸   MySQL replication configuration at http://dev.mysql.com/doc/refman/5.6/en/replication.html

▸   How MySQL replication works at https://www.percona.com/blog/2013/01/09/how-does-mysql-replication-really-work/

▸   MySQL replication formats at http://dev.mysql.com/doc/refman/5.5/en/replication-formats.html

Troubleshooting MySQL

In this recipe, we will look at some common problems with MySQL and learn how to solve them.

Getting ready

You will need access to a root account or an account with `sudo` privileges.

You will need administrative privileges on the MySQL server.

How to do it...

Follow these steps to troubleshoot MySQL:

1. First, check if the MySQL server is running and listening for connections on the configured port:

   ```
   $ sudo service mysql status
   $ sudo netstat -pltn
   ```

2. Check MySQL logs for any error messages at `/var/log/mysql.log` and `mysql.err`.

3. You can try to start the server in interactive mode with the `verbose` flag set:

   ```
   $ which mysqld
   /usr/sbin/mysqld
   $ sudo /usr/sbin/mysqld --user=mysql --verbose
   ```

4. If you are accessing MySQL from a remote system, make sure that the server is set to `listen` on a public port. Check for `bind-address` in `my.cnf`:

   ```
   bind-address   = 10.0.247.168
   ```

5. For any access denied errors, check if you have a user account in place and if it is allowed to log in from a specific IP address:

   ```
   mysql> select user, host, password from mysql.user where user = 'username';
   ```

6. Check the user has access to specified resources:

   ```
   mysql > grant all privileges on databasename.* to 'username'@'%';
   ```

7. Check your firewall is not blocking connections to MySQL.

8. If you get an error saying `mysql server has gone away`, then increase `wait_timeout` in the configuration file. Alternatively, you can re-initiate a connection on the client side after a specific timeout.

9. Use a `repair table` statement to recover the crashed MyISAM table:

   ```
   $ mysql -u root -p
   mysql> repair table databasename.tablename;
   ```

10. Alternatively, you can use the `mysqlcheck` command to repair tables:

    ```
    $ mysqlcheck -u root -p --auto-repair \
    --check --optimize databasename
    ```

▶ InnoDB troubleshooting at `https://dev.mysql.com/doc/refman/5.7/en/innodb-troubleshooting.html`

Installing MongoDB

Until now, we have worked with the relational database server, MySQL. In this recipe, we will learn how to install and configure MongoDB, which is a not only SQL (NoSQL) document storage server.

Getting ready

You will need access to a root account or an account with `sudo` privileges.

How to do it...

To get the latest version of MongoDB, we need to add the MongoDB source to Ubuntu installation sources:

1. First, import the MongoDB GPG public key:

    ```
    $ sudo apt-key adv \
    --keyserver hkp://keyserver.ubuntu.com:80 \
    --recv 7F0CEB10
    ```

2. Create a `list` file and add an install source to it:

    ```
    $ echo "deb http://repo.mongodb.org/apt/ubuntu
    "$(lsb_release
    -sc)"/mongodb-org/3.0 multiverse" | sudo tee
    /etc/apt/sources.list.d/mongodb-org-3.0.list
    ```

3. Update the `apt` repository sources and install the MongoDB server:

    ```
    $ sudo apt-get update
    $ sudo apt-get install -y mongodb-org
    ```

4. After installation completes, check the status of the MongoDB server:

    ```
    $ sudo service mongod status
    ```

5. Now you can start using the MongoDB server. To access the Mongo shell, use the following command:

    ```
    $ mongo
    ```

How it works...

We have installed the MongoDB server from the MongoDB official repository. The Ubuntu package repository includes the MongoDB package in it, but it is not up to date with the latest release of MongoDB. With GPG keys, Ubuntu ensures the authenticity of the packages being installed. After importing the GPG key, we have created a `list` file that contains the installation source of the MongoDB server.

After installation, the MongoDB service should start automatically. You can check logs at `/var/log/mongodb/mongod.log`.

See also

> ▸ MongoDB installation guide at `http://docs.mongodb.org/manual/tutorial/install-mongodb-on-ubuntu/`

Storing and retrieving data with MongoDB

In this recipe, we will look at basic CRUD operations with MongoDB. We will learn how to create databases, store, retrieve, and update stored data. This is a recipe to get started with MongoDB.

Getting ready

Make sure that you have installed and configured MongoDB. You can also use the MongoDB installation on a remote server.

How to do it...

Follow these steps to store and retrieve data with MongoDB:

1. Open a shell to interact with the Mongo server:

   ```
   $ mongo
   ```

2. To open a shell on a remote server, use the command given. Replace `server_ip` and `port` with the respective values:

   ```
   $ mongo server_ip:port/db
   ```

3. To create and start using a new database, type `use dbname`. Since schemas in MongoDB are dynamic, you do not need to create a database before using it:

   ```
   > use testdb
   ```

4. You can type `help` in Mongo shell to get a list of available commands and help regarding a specific command:

   > `help`: Let's insert our first document:

   > `db.users.insert({'name':'ubuntu','uid':1001})`

```
> db.users.insert({'name':'ubuntu','uid':1001})
WriteResult({ "nInserted" : 1 })
>
```

5. To view the created database and collection, use the following commands:

   > **show dbs**

```
> show dbs
local    0.078GB
test     0.078GB
testdb   0.078GB
>
```

   > **show collections**

```
> show collections
system.indexes
users
>
```

6. You can also insert multiple values for a key, for example, which groups a user belongs to:

   > `db.users.insert({'name':'root','uid':1010, 'gid':[1010, 1000, 1111]})`

7. Check whether a document is successfully inserted:

   > `db.users.find()`

```
> db.users.find()
{ "_id" : ObjectId("55f7d9b28b756ea94f93a10d"), "name" : "root", "uid" : 1010, "
gid" : [ 1010, 1000, 1111 ] }
{ "_id" : ObjectId("560ce2a7cf3368a229826104"), "name" : "root", "uid" : 1010, "
gid" : [ 1010, 1000, 1111 ] }
>
```

8. To get a single record, use `findOne()`:

   > `db.users.findOne({uid:1010})`

9. To update an existing record, use the `update` command as follows:

   > **db.users.update({name:'ubuntu'}, {$set:{uid:2222}})**

10. To remove a record, use the `remove` command. This will remove all records with a name equal to `ubuntu`:

    > **db.users.remove({'name':'ubuntu'})**

11. To drop an entire collection, use the `drop()` command:

    > **db.users.drop()**

12. To drop a database, use the `dropDatabase()` command:

    > **db.users.dropDatabase()**

How it works...

The preceding examples show very basic CRUD operations with the MongoDB shell interface. MongoDB shell is also a JavaScript shell. You can execute all JS commands in a MongoDB shell. You can also modify the shell with the configuration file, `~/.mongorc.js`. Similar to shell, MongoDB provides language-specific drivers, for example, MongoDB PHP drivers to access MongoDB from PHP.

MongoDB works on the concept of collections and documents. A collection is similar to a table in MySQL and a document is a set of key value stores where a key is similar to a column in a MySQL table. MongoDB does not require any schema definitions and accepts any pair of keys and values in a document. Schemas are dynamically created. In addition, you do not need to explicitly create the collection. Simply type a collection name in a command and it will be created if it does not already exist. In the preceding example, `users` is a collection we used to store all data. To explicitly create a collection, use the following command:

```
> use testdb
> db.createCollection('users')
```

You may be missing the `where` clause in MySQL queries. We have already used that with the `findOne()` command:

```
> db.users.findOne({uid:1010})
```

You can use `$lt` for less than, `$lte` for less than or equal to, `$gt` for greater than, `$gte` for greater than or equal to, and `$ne` for not equal:

```
> db.users.findOne({uid:{$gt:1000}})
```

In the preceding example, we have used the `where` clause with the equality condition `uid=1010`. You can add one more condition as follows:

```
> db.users.findOne({uid:1010, name:'root'})
```

To use the or condition, you need to modify the command as follows:

```
> db.users.find ({$or:[{name:'ubuntu'}, {name:'root'}]})
```

You can also extract a single key (column) from the entire document. The find command accepts a second optional parameter where you can specify a select criteria. You can use values 1 or 0. Use 1 to extract a specific key and 0 otherwise:

```
> db.users.findOne({uid:1010}, {name:1})
```

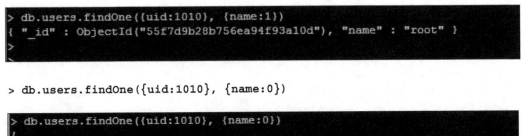

```
> db.users.findOne({uid:1010}, {name:1})
{ "_id" : ObjectId("55f7d9b28b756ea94f93a10d"), "name" : "root" }
>
```

```
> db.users.findOne({uid:1010}, {name:0})
```

```
> db.users.findOne({uid:1010}, {name:0})
{
        "_id" : ObjectId("55f7d9b28b756ea94f93a10d"),
        "uid" : 1010,
        "gid" : [
                1010,
                1000,
                1111
        ]
}
>
```

There's more...

You can install a web interface to manage the MongoDB installation. There are various open source web interfaces listed on Mongo documentation at http://docs.mongodb.org/ecosystem/tools/administration-interfaces/.

When you start a mongo shell for the first time, you may see a warning message regarding transperent_hugepage and defrag. To remove those warnings, add the following lines to /etc/init/mongod.conf, below the $DAEMONUSER /var/run/mongodb.pid line:

```
if test -f /sys/kernel/mm/transparent_hugepage/enabled; then
  echo never > /sys/kernel/mm/transparent_hugepage/enabled
fi
if test -f /sys/kernel/mm/transparent_hugepage/defrag; then
  echo never > /sys/kernel/mm/transparent_hugepage/defrag
fi
```

Find more details on this Stack Overflow post at `http://stackoverflow.com/questions/28911634/how-to-avoid-transparent-hugepage-defrag-warning-from-mongodb`

See also

- Mongo CRUD tutorial at `https://docs.mongodb.org/manual/applications/crud/`
- MongoDB query documents at `https://docs.mongodb.org/manual/tutorial/query-documents/`

6
Network Storage

In this chapter, we will cover the following recipes:

- ▶ Installing the Samba server
- ▶ Adding users to the Samba server
- ▶ Installing the secure FTP server
- ▶ Synchronizing files with Rsync
- ▶ Performance tuning the Samba server
- ▶ Troubleshooting the Samba server
- ▶ Installing the Network File System

Introduction

Often we need to store a lot of data and local systems don't have enough space. Sometimes, we need to quickly share this data across multiple systems and users. Also, when you have a big network, chances are you have Linux systems as well as Windows or Mac. Centralized networked storage can help to solve these storage and sharing problems. Linux provides various options, such as Samba and NFS, to host a centralized storage server and share data across multiple computers.

In this chapter, we will learn how to set up a centralized storage system. We will set up the Samba server and NFS server. We will learn how to enable synchronization with Rsync and set Windows clients to access storage servers.

Installing the Samba server

In this recipe, we will learn how to install Samba as our network storage server. Samba is a collection of open source applications that implement **Server Message Block** (**SMB**) and **Common Internet File System** (**CIFS**) protocols on Unix systems. This allows Samba to be accessible across different types of network system. Samba provides various other functionalities, such as a domain controller for the networks of Windows systems. In this recipe, we will focus on using Samba as a storage server.

Getting ready

You will need access to a root account or an account with `sudo` privileges

If your server is using any firewall system, make sure to open the necessary network ports. Samba runs on TCP 139 and 445 and UDP ports 137 and 138. Check *Chapter 2, Networking*, for more details on firewall configuration.

How to do it...

Follow these steps to install the Samba server:

1. Install the Samba server with the following command:

    ```
    $ sudo apt-get update
    $ sudo apt-get install samba -y
    ```

2. After installation is complete, you can check the Samba version with the following command:

    ```
    $ smbd --version
    ```

3. Next, we need to configure Samba to enable sharing on the network. First, create a backup of the original configuration file:

    ```
    $ sudo cp /etc/samba/smb.conf /etc/samba/smb.conf.orignl
    ```

4. Next, open `smb.conf` and replace its contents with the following:

    ```
    [global]
    workgroup = WORKGROUP
    server string = Samba Server
    netbios name = ubuntu
    security = user
    map to guest = bad user
    ```

```
dns proxy = no
[Public]
path = /var/samba/shares/public
browsable =yes
writable = yes
guest ok = yes
read only = no
create mask = 644
```

5. Next, we need to create a shared directory:

   ```
   $ sudo mkdir -p /var/samba/shares/public
   ```

6. Change the directory permissions to make it world writable:

   ```
   $ sudo chmod 777 /var/samba/shares/public
   ```

7. Restart the Samba service for the changes to take effect:

   ```
   $ sudo service smbd restart
   ```

Now you can access this Samba share on the Windows client. Open Windows Explorer and in the address bar, type in \\ubuntu or \\your-server-ip. You should see the shared directory, Public, as follows:

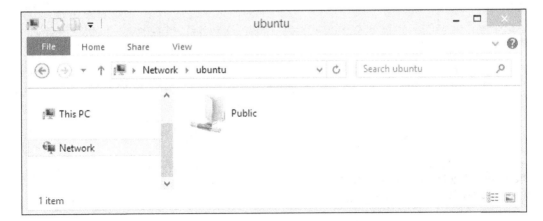

How it works...

Samba is quite an old technology, especially in the age of Cloud storage such as Dropbox and Amazon S3. However, when it comes to private networking, Samba offers a hassle-free setup and is always available for free. All you need is a small server with some free storage space. The release of Samba 4 has added **Active Directory** (**AD**) support. Now it's possible to set up Windows AD on Linux servers. Support for AD comes with a wide range of other features, including DNS for name resolution, centralized storage, and authentication with LDAP and Kerberos.

As you can see in the preceding example, setting up Samba is quick and easy, and you can easily get started with network storage within minutes. We can install the Samba server with a single command, as Samba packages are available in the Ubuntu default package repository. After installation, we have created a new quick and dirty configuration file which defines a few parameters, such as the server name (`netbios name`) and a share definition. We have created a publicly-shared directory where everyone can read and write the contents.

Once you are done with installation and initial testing, make sure that you remove public sharing and enable authenticated access to your Samba shares. You don't want the server to fill up with data from unknown people. In the next recipes, we will take a closer look at user management and access control for Samba shares.

There's more...

To secure your Samba installation and limit access to your local network or subnet, you can use the following configuration parameters:

```
[globals]
hosts deny = ALL
hosts allow = xxx.xxx.xxx.xxx/yy 127.
interfaces = eth0 lo
bind interfaces only = Yes
```

This configuration limits Samba to listen only on listed interfaces. In this case, its `eth0`, the Ethernet network, and `lo`, localhost. Connection requests from all other hosts are denied.

Tools for personal file sharing

If you need a simple file sharing tool for your personal use and do not want to set up and configure Samba, then you can try using a tool named OwnCloud. It is very similar to Dropbox and is open source. It gives you web access to all your files and documents. Plus, you get desktop and mobile client apps to sync all files to a remote server.

Another good tool is BitTorrent Sync. Again, this is a file synchronization tool, but this time it is peer-to-peer file synchronization. If you really care about the privacy and security of data, then this tool is made for you. All files are synchronized between two or more systems (say, your desktop and laptop) without the use of any centralized server.

See also

▶ Ubuntu server guide for Samba at `https://help.ubuntu.com/lts/serverguide/samba-fileserver.html`

Adding users to the Samba server

In the previous recipe, we installed the Samba server and created a public share accessible to everyone. In this recipe, we will learn how to add authentication to the Samba server and password protect shared directories.

Getting ready

You will need access to a root account or an account with `sudo` privileges.

Make sure that the Samba server is installed and running.

How to do it...

Follow these steps to add users to the Samba server:

1. Create a new user account. You can use any existing account or add a new Samba only account with the following command. Change `smbuser` to your desired username:

   ```
   $ sudo useradd -d /home/smbuser -s /sbin/nologin smbuser
   ```

2. Now, we need to allocate a Samba password to this new user. First, enter your `sudo` password, followed by the new password for your Samba account, and then verify the password:

   ```
   $ sudo smbpasswd -a smbuser
   ```

```
ubuntu@ubuntu:/var/samba/shares/public$ sudo smbpasswd -a smbuser
[sudo] password for ubuntu:
New SMB password:
Retype new SMB password:
ubuntu@ubuntu:/var/samba/shares/public$
```

3. Create a shared directory for this user and change its ownership:

    ```
    $ sudo chown smbuser:smbuser /var/samba/share/smbuser
    ```

4. Next, edit the Samba configuration to add the preceding share:

    ```
    [Private]
    path = /var/samba/shares/smbuser
    browsable = yes
    writable = yes
    valid users = smbuser
    ```

5. Save the changes to the configuration file and reload the Samba server:

    ```
    $ sudo service smbd reload
    ```

6. Now, check in Windows Explorer. You should see the new shared directory. On trying to open that directory, you will be asked for a Samba username and password:

How it works...

Samba allows various different types of configuration for shared resources. In the previous recipe, we learned how to set up a public share, and in this recipe we have created a private share for a single user. We have created a new user with the `nologin` permission. This will allow `smbuser` to access only the Samba shared directory and nothing else. You can also use existing user accounts on the Ubuntu server.

After adding a user, we set a password to be used with the Samba server. Samba maintains a database of passwords separately from Ubuntu passwords. You can enable or disable Samba users with the following commands:

- Enable a Samba user:

  ```
  $ sudo smbpasswd -e username
  ```

- Disable a Samba user:

  ```
  $ sudo smbpasswd -d username
  ```

- Remove a Samba user:

  ```
  $ sudo smbpasswd -x username
  ```

To enable multiple users to access a shared resource, you can specify the list of users under the valid users line, as follows:

```
valid users = userone, usertwo, userthree
```

Similarly, you can limit write permissions to a set of users, as follows:

```
write list = userone, usertwo
```

Samba also supports the sharing of users, home directories. This will enable users to create shares for all existing Ubuntu users with a single block of configuration. Add the following lines to the Samba configuration to enable the sharing of home directories:

```
[homes]
browseable = No
valid users = %S
```

After this configuration, user's home directories will be available at //server-name/user-name. You will be required to provide a username and password to access these shares. Home directories are by default shared as read only. To enable write permissions, add the following line to the preceding block:

```
writable = yes
```

Note that on Windows, you will not be able to access multiple home directories from a single Windows system. Windows does not allow multiple user authentications to a single host.

Alternatively, to share a directory with a group of users, you can use group sharing. Use the following line to share a directory with a group of users:

```
path=/var/samba/shares/group-share
valid users = @groupname
```

Then, set group ownership on the directory, `group-share`:

```
$ sudo chgrp groupname /var/samba/shares/group-share
```

There are some other directives such as `create mask`, `directory mask`, `force user`, and `force group`. These directives can be used to determine the permissions and ownership of the newly created files under Samba share.

After any changes to the Samba configuration file, use `testparm` to check the configuration for any syntax errors:

```
$ testparm
```

It should show the Loaded services file `OK` message, as listed in following screenshot:

```
ubuntu@ubuntu:~$ testparm
Load smb config files from /etc/samba/smb.conf
rlimit_max: increasing rlimit_max (1024) to minimum Windows limit (16384)
Processing section "[Private]"
Loaded services file OK.
Server role: ROLE_STANDALONE
Press enter to see a dump of your service definitions

[global]
        server string = Samba Server %v
```

There's more...

With the release of version 4, Samba can be set as a domain controller. Check the official documentation for more details at the following link:

```
https://wiki.samba.org/index.php/Setup_a_Samba_Active_Directory_
Domain_Controller
```

You can also configure the Samba server to authenticate against the LDAP server. LDAP installation and configuration is covered in *Chapter 14, Centralized Auth Service*. For more details on Samba and LDAP integration, check out the Ubuntu server guide at `https://help.ubuntu.com/lts/serverguide/samba-ldap.html`.

See also

▶ Linux home server Samba guide at `http://www.brennan.id.au/18-Samba.html#useraccounts`

Installing the secure FTP server

In this recipe, we will learn how to install the **File Transfer Protocol** (**FTP**) server and configure it to use SSL encryption.

Getting ready

You will need access to a root account or an account with `sudo` privileges.

How to do it...

Follow these steps to install the secure FTP server:

1. Install `vsftpd` with the following command:

   ```
   $ sudo apt-get update
   $ sudo apt-get install vsftpd
   ```

2. After installation, we can configure `vsftpd` by editing `/etc/vsftpd.conf`.

3. First create the SSL certificate for the FTP server:

   ```
   sudo openssl req -x509 -nodes -days 365 -newkey rsa:2048 -keyout /etc/ssl/private/vsftpd.pem -out /etc/ssl/private/vsftpd.pem
   ```

4. Next, configure Vsftpd. Add or edit the following lines in `vsftpd.conf`:

   ```
   anonymous_enable=no
   local_enable=yes
   write_enable=yes
   chroot_local_user=yes
   Add the SSL certificate created in the previous step:
   rsa_cert_file=/etc/ssl/private/vsftpd.pem
   rsa_private_key_file=/etc/ssl/private/vsftpd.pem
   ssl_enable=yes
   ssl_ciphers=high
   force_local_data_ssl=yes
   force_local_logins_ssl=yes
   ```

5. Save and exit the configuration file.

6. Restart the Vsftpd server:

   ```
   $ sudo service vsftpd restart
   ```

7. Now you can use any FTP client that supports the SFTP protocol to connect to your FTP server. The following is the configuration screen for SFTP client FileZilla:

How it works...

FTP is an insecure protocol and you should avoid using it, especially in a production environment. Limit use of FTP to downloads only and use more secure methods, such as SCP, to upload and transfer files on servers. If you have to use FTP, make sure that you have disabled anonymous access and enable SFTP to secure your data and login credentials.

In this recipe, we have installed Vsftpd, which is a default FTP package in the Ubuntu repository. Vsftpd stands for very secure FTP daemon, and it is designed to protect against possible FTP vulnerabilities. It supports both FTP and SFTP protocols.

As Vsftpd is available in the Ubuntu package repository, installation is very simple, using only a single command. After Vsftpd installed, we created an SSL certificate to be used with an FTP server. With this configuration, we will be using the SFTP protocol, which is more secure than FTP. You can find more details about SSL certificates in *Chapter 3, Working with Web Servers*.

Under the Vsftpd configuration, we have modified some settings to disable anonymous logins, allowed local users to use FTP, enabled write access, and used chroot for local users. Next, we have set a path for previously generated SSL certificates and enabled the use of SSL. Additionally, you can force the use of TLS over SSL by adding the following lines to the configuration file:

```
ssl_tlsv1=yes
ssl_sslv2=no
ssl_sslv3=no
```

There's more...

This recipe covers FTP as a simple and easy-to-use tool for network storage. FTP is inherently insecure and you must avoid its use in a production environment. Server deployments can easily be automated with simple Git hooks or the sophisticated integration of continuous deployment tools such Chef, Puppet, or Ansible.

See also

▸ Ubuntu server FTP guide at `https://help.ubuntu.com/lts/serverguide/ftp-server.html`

Synchronizing files with Rsync

In this recipe, we will learn how to use the Rsync utility to synchronize files between two directories or between two servers.

How to do it...

Follow these steps to synchronize files with Rsync:

1. Set up key-based authentication between source and destination servers. We can use password authentication as well, which is described later in this recipe.

2. Create a sample directory structure on the source server. You can use existing files as well:

   ```
   ubuntu@src$ mkdir sampledir

   ubuntu@src$ touch sampledir/file{1..10}
   ```

3. Now, use the following command to synchronize the entire directory from the source server to your local system. Note the / after `sampledir`. This will copy contents of `sampledir` in the `backup`. Without /, the entire `sampledir` will be copied to the `backup`:

```
ubuntu@dest$ rsync -azP -e ssh
ubuntu@10.0.2.8:/home/ubuntu/sampledir/ backup
```

As this is the first time, all files from `sampledir` on the remote server will be downloaded in a `backup` directory on your local system. The output of the command should look like the following screenshot:

```
ubuntu@dest:~$ rsync -azP -e ssh ubuntu@10.0.2.8:/home/ubuntu/sampledir/ backup
receiving incremental file list
./
file1
             0 100%    0.00kB/s    0:00:00 (xfr#1, to-chk=22/24)
file10
             0 100%    0.00kB/s    0:00:00 (xfr#2, to-chk=21/24)
file11
```

4. You can check the downloaded files with the `ls` command:

```
$ ls -l backup
```

5. Add one new file on the remote server under `sampledir`:

```
ubuntu@src$ touch sampledir/file22
```

6. Now re-execute the `rsync` command on the destination server. This time, `rsync` will only download a new file and any other update files. The output should look similar to the following screenshot:

```
ubuntu@dest$ rsync -azP -e ssh
ubuntu@10.0.2.8:/home/ubuntu/sampledir backup
```

```
ubuntu@dest:~$ rsync -azP -e ssh ubuntu@10.0.2.8:/home/ubuntu/sampledir/ backup
receiving incremental file list
./
file22
             0 100%    0.00kB/s    0:00:00 (xfr#1, to-chk=7/25)
ubuntu@dest:~$
```

7. To synchronize two local directories, you can simply specify the source and destination path with `rsync`, as follows:

```
$ rsync /var/log/mysql ~/mysql_log_backup
```

How it works...

Rsync is a well known command line file synchronization utility. With Rsync, you can synchronize files between two local directories, as well as files between two servers. This tool is commonly used as a simple backup utility to copy or move files around systems. The advantage of using Rsync is that file synchronization happens incrementally, that is, only new and modified files will be downloaded. This saves bandwidth as well as time. You can quickly schedule a daily backup with a cron and Rsync. Open a cron jobs file with `ctontab-e` and add the following line to enable daily backups:

```
$ crontab -e     # open crontab file
@daily rsync -aze ssh ubuntu@10.0.2.50:/home/ubuntu/sampledir
/var/backup
```

In the preceding example, we have used a pull operation, where we are downloading files from the remote server. Rsync can be used to upload files as well. Use the following command to push files to the remote server:

```
$ rsync -azP -e ssh backup
ubuntu@10.0.2.50:/home/ubuntu/sampledir
```

Rsync provides tons of command line options. Some options that are used in the preceding example are -a, a combination of various other flags and stands for achieve. This option enables recursive synchronization and preserves modification time, symbolic links, users, and group permissions. Option -z is used to enable compression while transferring files, while option -P enables progress reports and the resumption of interrupted downloads by saving partial files.

We have used one more option, -e, which specifies which remote shell to be used while downloading files. In the preceding command, we are using SSH with public key authentication. If you have not set public key authentication between two servers, you will be asked to enter a password for your account on the remote server. You can skip the -e flag and rsync will use a non-encrypted connection to transfer data and login credentials.

Note that the SSH connection is established on the default SSH port, port 22. If your remote SSH server runs on a port other than 22, then you can use a slightly modified version of the preceding command as follows:

```
rsync -azP -e "ssh -p port_number" source destination
```

Anther common option is --exclude, which specifies the pattern for file names to be excluded. If you need to specify multiple exclusion patterns, then you can specify all such patterns in a text file and include that file in command with the options --exclude-from=filename. Similarly, if you need to include some specific files only, you can specify the inclusion pattern with options --include=pattern or --include-from=filename.

Exclude a single file or files matching with a single pattern:

```
$ rsync -azP --exclude 'dir*' source/ destination/
```

Exclude a list of patterns or file names:

```
$ rsync -azP --exclude-from 'exclude-list.txt' source/
destination/
```

By default, Rsync does not delete destination files, even if they are deleted from the source location. You can override this behavior with a `--delete` flag. You can create a backup of these files before deleting them. Use the `--backup` and `--backup-dir` options to enable backups. To delete files from the source directory, you can use the `--remove-source-files` flag. Another handy option is `--dry-run`, which simulates a transfer with the given flags and displays the output, but does not modify any files. You should use `--dry-run` before using any deletion flags.

Use this to remove source files with `--dry-run`:

```
$ rsync --dry-run --remove-source-files -azP source/
destination/
```

There's more...

Rsync is a great tool to quickly synchronize the files between source and destination, but it does not provide bidirectional synchronization. It means the changes are synchronized from source to destination and not vice versa. If you need bi-directional synchronization, you can use another utility, Unison. You can install Unison on Debian systems with the following command:

```
$ sudo apt-get -y install unison
```

Once installed, Unison is very similar to Rsync and can be executed as follows:

```
$ unison /home/ubuntu/documents
ssh://10.0.2.56//home/ubuntu/documents
```

You can get more information about Unison in the manual pages with the following command:

```
$ man unison
```

If you wish to have your own Dropbox-like mirroring tool which continuously monitors for local file changes and quickly replicates them to network storage, then you can use Lsyncd. Lsyncd is a live synchronization or mirroring tool, which monitors the local directory tree for any events (with inotify and `fsevents`), and then after few seconds spawns a synchronization process to mirror all changes to a remote location. By default, Lsyncd uses Rsync for synchronization.

As always, Lsyncd is available in the Ubuntu package repository and can be installed with a single command, as follows:

```
$ sudo apt-get install lsyncd
```

To get more information about Lsyncd, check the manual pages with the following command:

```
$ man lsyncd
```

See also

▶ Ubuntu Rsync community page at `https://help.ubuntu.com/community/rsync`

Performance tuning the Samba server

In this recipe, we will look at Samba configuration parameters in order to get optimum performance out of your Samba installation.

Getting ready

You will need root access or an account with `sudo` privileges.

It is assumed that you have installed the Samba server and it is properly working.

How to do it...

1. Open the Samba configuration file located at `/etc/samba/smb.conf`:

   ```
   $ sudo vi /etc/samba/smb.conf
   ```

2. Add or edit the following options under the `global` section of the configuration file:

   ```
   [global]
   log level = 1
   socket options = TCP_NODELAY IPTOS_LOWDELAY SO_RCVBUF=131072 SO_SNDBUF=131072 SO_KEEPALIVE
   read raw = Yes
   write raw = Yes
   strict locking = No
   oplocks = yes
   max xmit = 65535
   dead time = 15
   ```

```
getwd cache = yes
aio read size = 16384
aio write size = 16384
use sendfile = true
```

3. Save the configuration file and restart the Samba service:

    ```
    $ sudo service smbd restart
    ```

How it works...

The Samba server provides various configuration parameters. It uses TCP sockets to connect with clients and for data transfer. You should compare Samba's performance with similar TCP services such as FTP.

The preceding example lists some commonly used configuration options for Samba. Some of these options may work for you and some of them may not. The latest Samba version ships with default values for these options that work fairly well for common network conditions. As always, test these options one at a time or in a group, and benchmark each modification to get optimum performance.

The explanation for the preceding is as follows:

- ▶ `log level`: The default log level is set to `0`. Samba produces a lot of debugging information and writing all this to disk is a slow operation. Increasing the log level results in increased logs and poor performance. Unless you are debugging the server, it is good to have the log level set to the lowest value.

- ▶ `socket options`: These are the TCP/IP stack level options.

- ▶ `read raw` and `write raw`: These options enable Samba to use large read and writes to a network up to 64 KB in a single request. Some older clients may have issues with raw reads and writes. Check your setup before using these options.

- ▶ `dead time` and `so_keepalive`: These options set periodic checks for dead connections and close such connections and free unused memory.

- ▶ `oplocks`: This allows clients to cache files locally and results in overall performance improvement. The default setting disables `oplocks`.

- ▶ `aio read size` and `aio write size`: This **Asynchronous IO (AIO)** allows Samba to read and write asynchronously when a file's size is bigger than the specified size values.

You can find various other options and respective explanations in the Samba manual pages. Use the following command to open the manual pages on your server:

```
$ man smbd
```

Troubleshooting the Samba server

In this recipe, we will look at the various tools available for troubleshooting Samba shares.

How to do it...

Samba troubleshooting can be separated in to three parts: network connectivity, Samba process issues, and Samba configuration issues. We will go through each of them step by step. As a first step for troubleshooting, let's start with network testing.

Checking network connectivity

Follow these steps to check network connectivity:

1. Send ping requests to the Samba server to check network connectivity:

    ```
    $ ping samba-server-ip
    ```

2. Check name resolution. Ping the Samba server by its name. Windows uses netbios for name resolution:

    ```
    $ ping samba-server-name
    ```

3. Check the Samba configuration for network restrictions. Temporarily open Samba to all hosts.

4. Use tcpdump to check Samba network communication. Start tcpdump as follows and let it run for some time while accessing the Samba server from clients. All packets will be logged in a file named tcpdump in the current directory:

    ```
    $ sudo tcpdump -p -s 0 -w tcpdumps port 445 or port 139
    ```

    ```
    ubuntu@ubuntu:~$ sudo tcpdump -p -s 0 -w tcpdumps port 445 or port 139
    [sudo] password for ubuntu:
    tcpdump: listening on eth0, link-type EN10MB (Ethernet), capture size 65535 byte
    s
    ```

5. If you know the client IP address, you can filter tcpdumps with the following command:

    ```
    $ sudo tcpdump -s 0 -w tcpdumps host client_IP
    ```

6. Connect to the Samba process with `telnet`:

   `$ echo "hello" | telnet localhost 139`

```
ubuntu@ubuntu:~$ echo "hello" | telnet localhost 139
Trying ::1...
Connected to localhost.
Escape character is '^]'.
Connection closed by foreign host.
```

7. Check whether your Samba server uses a firewall. If so, check the allowed ports on your firewall. If the firewall is on, make sure you have allowed the Samba ports as follows:

```
ubuntu@ubuntu:~$ sudo ufw show added
Added user rules (see 'ufw status' for running firewall):
ufw allow 139
ufw allow 445
ubuntu@ubuntu:~$
```

8. Try connecting to FTP or a similar TCP service on the Samba server. This may identify the problems with the TCP stack.

9. Use `nmblookup` to test `netbios name` resolution for Windows systems.

Checking the Samba service

Follow these steps to check Samba service:

1. Check whether the Samba service has started properly:

   `$ sudo service samba status`

2. Use `netstat` to check the Samba daemon is listening on the network:

   `$ sudo netstat -plutn`

```
ubuntu@ubuntu:~$ sudo netstat -plutn | grep smbd
tcp        0      0 0.0.0.0:445            0.0.0.0:*               LISTEN
704/smbd
tcp        0      0 0.0.0.0:139            0.0.0.0:*               LISTEN
704/smbd
tcp6       0      0 :::445                 :::*                    LISTEN
704/smbd
tcp6       0      0 :::139                 :::*                    LISTEN
704/smbd
```

3. Use `ps` to check the Samba processes. Look for the process name, `smbd`, in the output of the following command:

```
$ ps aux
```

4. Use `strace` to view the Samba process logs. This will list all filesystem activities by `smbd` process:

```
$ strace smbd
```

Checking Samba logs

Follow these steps to check Samba logs:

1. Check Samba log files for any warning or errors.

2. Increase the log level to get more debugging information:

```
[global]
log level = 3
```

3. Enable logging for a specific client with client-specific configuration. First, set the following options under `smb.conf` to enable client-specific configuration:

```
[global]
    log level = 0
    log file = /var/log/samba/log.%m
    include = /etc/samba/smb.conf.%m
```

4. Now create a new configuration file for a specific client:

```
$ sudo vi /etc/samba/smb.conf.client1
[global]
log level = 3
```

5. Similarly, you can create separate logs for each Samba user:

```
[global]
    log level = 0
    log file = /var/log/samba/log.%u
    include = /etc/samba/smb.conf.%u
```

Checking Samba configuration

Follow these steps to check Samba configuration:

1. Check the registered users and accounts in the Samba server user database with the `pdbedit` command:

   ```
   $ sudo pdbedit -L
   ```

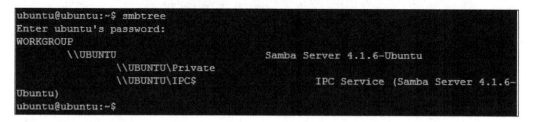

```
ubuntu@ubuntu:~$ sudo pdbedit -L
smbuser:1001:
ubuntu:1000:ubuntu
ubuntu@ubuntu:~$
```

2. Check the shares with the `smbtree` command:

```
ubuntu@ubuntu:~$ smbtree
Enter ubuntu's password:
WORKGROUP
        \\UBUNTU                            Samba Server 4.1.6-Ubuntu
                \\UBUNTU\Private
                \\UBUNTU\IPC$                       IPC Service (Samba Server 4.1.6-
Ubuntu)
ubuntu@ubuntu:~$
```

3. Use the `testparm` command to find any errors in the Samba configuration:

   ```
   $ testparm
   ```

4. Check for allowed users and group names. Make sure that group names start with the @ symbol.

5. Back up your configuration files and then use minimal configuration to test Samba:

   ```
   [global]
        workgroup = WORKGROUP
        security = user
        browsable = yes
   [temp]
        path = /tmp
        public = yes
   ```

> Publicly writable directories are not good for server security.
> Remove the preceding configuration as soon as testing is finished.

6. Test your configuration with `smbcclient`. It should list all Samba shares:

```
$ smbclient -L localhost -U%
```

```
ubuntu@ubuntu:~$ smbclient -L localhost -U%
Domain=[WORKGROUP] OS=[Unix] Server=[Samba 4.1.6-Ubuntu]

        Sharename       Type        Comment
        ---------       ----        -------
        IPC$            IPC         IPC Service (Samba Server 4.1.6-Ubuntu)
        Private         Disk
Domain=[WORKGROUP] OS=[Unix] Server=[Samba 4.1.6-Ubuntu]
```

See also

▶ Samba docs troubleshooting at `https://www.samba.org/samba/docs/using_samba/ch12.html`

Installing the Network File System

Network File System (**NFS**) is a distributed filesystem protocol that allows clients to access remote files and directories as if they are available on the local system. This allows client systems to leverage large centrally shared storage. Users can access the same data from any system across the network. A typical setup for NFS includes a server that runs the NFS daemon, nfsd, and lists (export) files and directories to be shared. A client system can mount these exported directories as their local file system.

In this recipe, we will learn how to install the NFS server and client systems.

Getting ready

You will need two Ubuntu systems: one as a central NFS server and another as a client. For this recipe, we will refer to the NFS server with the name Host and the NFS client with the name Client. The following is an example IP address configuration for the Host and Client systems:

```
Host - 10.0.2.60
Client - 10.0.2.61
```

You will need access to a root account on both servers, or at least an account with sudo privileges.

How to do it...

Follow these steps to install NFS:

1. First, we need to install the NFS server:

    ```
    $ sudo apt-get update
    $ sudo apt-get install nfs-kernel-server
    ```

2. Create the directories to be shared:

    ```
    $ sudo mkdir /var/nfs
    ```

3. Add this directory to NFS exports under /etc/exports:

    ```
    $ sudo nano /etc/exports
    ```

4. Add the following line to /etc/exports:

    ```
    /var/nfs      *(rw,sync,no_subtree_check)
    ```

5. Save and close the exports file.

6. Now, restart the NFS service:

    ```
    $ sudo service nfs-kernel-server restart
    ```

7. Next, we need to configure the client system to access NFS shares.

8. Create a mount point for NFS shares.

9. Install the nfs-common package on the client side:

    ```
    $ sudo apt-get install nfs-common
    $ sudo mkdir -p /var/nfsshare
    ```

10. Mount the NFS shared directory on the newly-created mount point:

    ```
    $ sudo mount 10.0.2.60:/var/nfs /var/nfsshare
    ```

11. Confirm the mounted share with the following command:

    ```
    $ mount -t nfs
    ```

12. Now, change the directory to /var/nfsshare, and you are ready to use NFS.

How it works...

In the preceding example, we have installed the NFS server and then created a directory that will share with clients over the network. The configuration file `/etc/exports` contains all NFS shared directories. The syntax to add new exports is as follows:

```
directory_to_share    client_IP_or_name(option1, option2,
option..n)
```

The options used in exports are as follows:

- ▶ `rw`: This enables read/write access. You can enable read-only access with the `ro` option.

- ▶ `sync`: This forces the NFS server to write changes to disk before replying to requests. sync is the default option; you can enable async operations by explicitly stating async. Async operations may get a little performance boost but at the cost of data integrity.

- ▶ `no_subtree_check`: This disables subtree checking, which provides more stable and reliable NFS shares.

You can check the `exports` documentation for more export options. Use the `man` command to open the `exports` manual pages, as follows:

```
$ man exports
```

In the preceding example, we have used the `mount` command to mount the NFS share. Once the client system has restarted, this mount will be removed. To remount the NFS share on each reboot, you can add the following line to `/etc/fstab` file:

```
10.0.2.60:/var/nfs   /var/nfsshare    nfs4    _netdev,auto  0  0
```

To mount all shares exported by the NFS server, you can use the following command:

```
$ sudo mount 10.0.2.60:/ /var/nfsshare
```

There's more...

NFS 4.1 adds support for pNFS, which enables clients to access the storage device directly and in parallel. This architecture eliminates scalability and performance issues with NFS deployments.

See also

► NFS exports options at `http://manpages.ubuntu.com/manpages/trusty/man5/exports.5.html`

► Parallel NFS at `http://www.pnfs.com/`

► NFS documentation in manual pages, by using the following command:

```
$ man nfs
```

7
Cloud Computing

In this chapter, we will cover the following recipes:

- ▶ Creating virtual machine with KVM
- ▶ Managing virtual machines with virsh
- ▶ Setting up your own cloud with OpenStack
- ▶ Adding a cloud image to OpenStack
- ▶ Launching a virtual instance with OpenStack
- ▶ Installing Juju a service orchestration framework
- ▶ Managing services with Juju

Introduction

Cloud computing has become the most important terminology in the computing sphere. It has reduced the effort and cost required to set up and operate the overall computing infrastructure. It has helped various businesses quickly start their business operations without wasting time planning their IT infrastructure, and has enabled really small teams to scale their businesses with on-demand computing power.

The term **cloud** is commonly used to refer to a large network of servers connected to the Internet. These servers offer a wide range of services and are available for the general public on a pay-per-use basis. Most cloud resources are available in the form of **Software as a Service (SaaS)**, **Platform as a Service (PaaS)**, or **Infrastructure as a Service (IaaS)**. A SaaS is a software system hosted in the cloud. These systems are generally maintained by large organizations; a well-known example that we commonly use is Gmail and the Google Docs service. The end user can access these application through their browsers. He or she can just sign up for the service, pay the required fees, if any, and start using it without any local setup. All data is stored in the cloud and is accessible from any location.

PaaS provide a base platform to develop and run applications in the cloud. The service provider does the hard work of building and maintaining the infrastructure and provides easy-to-use APIs that enable developers to quickly develop and deploy an application. Heroku and the Google App Engine are well-known examples of PaaS services.

Similarly, IaaS provides access to computing infrastructure. This is the base layer of cloud computing and provides physical or virtual access to computing, storage, and network services. The service builds and maintains actual infrastructure, including hardware assembly, virtualization, backups, and scaling. Examples include Amazon AWS and the Google Compute Engine. Heroku is a platform service built on top of the AWS infrastructure.

These cloud services are built on top of virtualization. Virtualization is a software system that enables us to break a large physical server into multiple small virtual servers that can be used independently. One can run multiple isolated operating systems and applications on a single large hardware server. Cloud computing is a set of tools that allows the general public to utilize these virtual resources at a small cost.

Ubuntu offers a wide range of virtualization and cloud computing tools. It supports hypervisors, such as KVM, XEN, and QEMU; a free and open source cloud computing platform, OpenStack; the service orchestration tool Juju and machine provisioning tool MAAS. In this chapter, we will take a brief look at virtualization with KVM. We will install and set up our own cloud with OpenStack and deploy our applications with Juju.

Creating virtual machine with KVM

Ubuntu server gives you various options for your virtualization needs. You can choose from KVM, XEN, QEMU, VirtualBox, and various other proprietary and open source tools. KVM, or Kernel virtual machine, is the default hypervisor on Ubuntu. In this recipe, we will set up a virtual machine with the help of KVM. Ubuntu, being a popular cloud distribution provides prebuilt cloud images that can be used to start virtual machines in the cloud. We will use one of these prebuilt images to build our own local virtual machine.

Getting ready

As always, you will need access to the root account or an account with sudo privileges.

How to do it...

Follows these steps to install KVM and launch a virtual machine using cloud image:

1. To get started, install the required packages:

   ```
   $ sudo apt-get install kvm cloud-utils \
   genisoimage bridge-utils
   ```

Before using KVM, you need to check whether your CPU
supports hardware virtualization, which is required by KVM.
Check CPU support with the following command:

```
$ kvm-ok
```

You should see output like this:

```
INFO: /dev/kvm exists
```

KVM acceleration can be used.

2. Next, download the cloud images from the Ubuntu servers. I have selected the Ubuntu 14.04 Trusty image:

```
$ wget http://cloud-
images.ubuntu.com/releases/trusty/release/ubuntu-14.04-server-
cloudimg-amd64-disk1.img -O trusty.img.dist
```

This image is in a compressed format and needs to be converted into an uncompressed format. This is not strictly necessary but should save on-demand decompression when an image is used. Use the following command to convert the image:

```
$ qemu-img convert -O qcow2 trusty.img.dist trusty.img.orig
```

3. Create a copy-on-write image to protect your original image from modifications:

```
$ qemu-img create -f qcow2 -b trusty.img.orig trusty.img
```

4. Now that our image is ready, we need a cloud-config disk to initialize this image and set the necessary user details. Create a new file called user-data and add the following data to it:

```
$ sudo vi user-data
#cloud-config
password: password
chpasswd: { expire: False }
ssh_pwauth: True
```

This file will set a password for the default user, ubuntu, and enable password authentication in the SSH configuration.

5. Create a disk with this configuration written on it:

```
$ cloud-localds my-seed.img user-data
```

6. Next, create a network bridge to be used by virtual machines. Edit `/etc/network/interfaces` as follows:

```
auto eth0
iface eth0 inet manual


auto br0
iface br0 inet dhcp
    bridge_ports eth0
```

 On Ubuntu 16.04, you will need to edit files under the `/etc/network/interfaces.d` directory. Edit the file for `eth0` or your default network interface, and create a new file for `br0`. All files are merged under `/etc/network/interfaces`.

7. Restart the networking service for the changes to take effect. If you are on an SSH connection, your session will get disconnected:

```
$ sudo service networking restart
```

8. Now that we have all the required data, let's start our image with KVM, as follows:

```
$ sudo kvm -netdev bridge,id=net0,br=br0 \
-net user -m 256 -nographic \
-hda trusty.img -hdb my-seed.img
```

This should start a virtual machine and route all input and output to your console. The first boot with `cloud-init` should take a while. Once the boot process completes, you will get a login prompt. Log in with the username `ubuntu` and the password specified in user-data.

9. Once you get access to the shell, set a new password for the user `ubuntu`:

```
$ sudo passwd ubuntu
```

After that, uninstall the cloud-init tool to stop it running on the next boot:

```
$ sudo apt-get remove cloud-init
```

Your virtual machine is now ready to use. The next time you start the machine, you can skip the second disk with the cloud-init details and route the system console to VNC, as follows:

```
$ sudo kvm -netdev bridge,id=net0,br=br0 \
-hda trusty.img \
-m 256 -vnc 0.0.0.0:1 -daemonize
```

How it works...

Ubuntu provides various options to create and manage virtual machines. The previous recipe covers basic virtualization with KVM and prebuilt Ubuntu Cloud images. KVM is very similar to desktop virtualization tools such as VirtualBox and VMware. It comes as a part of the Qemu emulator and uses hardware acceleration features from the host CPU to boost the performance of virtual machines. Without hardware support, the machines need to run inside the Qemu emulator.

After installing KVM, we have used Ubuntu cloud image as our pre-installed boot disk. Cloud images are prebuilt operating system images that do not contain any user data or system configuration. These images need to be initialized before being used. Recent Ubuntu releases contain a program called cloud-init, which is used to initialize the image at first boot. The cloud-init program looks for the metadata service on the network and queries user-data once the service is found. In our case, we have used a secondary disk to pass user data and initialize the cloud image.

We downloaded the prebuilt image from the Ubuntu image server and converted it to uncompressed format. Then, we created a new snapshot with the backing image set to the original prebuilt image. This should protect our original image from any modifications so that it can be used to create more copies. Whenever you need to restore a machine to its original state, just delete the newly created snapshot images and recreate it. Note that you will need to use the cloud-init process again during such restores.

This recipe uses prebuilt images, but you can also install the entire operating system on virtual machines. You will need to download the required installation medium and attach a blank hard disk to the VM. For installation, make sure you set the VNC connection to follow the installation steps.

There's more...

Ubuntu also provides the `virt-manager` graphical interface to create and manage KVM virtual machines from a GUI. You can install it as follows:

```
$ sudo apt-get install virt-manager
```

Alternatively, you can also install Oracle VirtualBox on Ubuntu. Download the `.deb` file for your Ubuntu version and install it with `dpkg -i`, or install it from the package manager as follows:

1. Add the Oracle repository to your installation sources. Make sure to substitute `xenial` with the correct Ubuntu version:

   ```
   $ sudo vi /etc/apt/sources.list
   deb http://download.virtualbox.org/virtualbox/debian xenial
   contrib
   ```

2. Add the Oracle public keys:

```
wget -q
https://www.virtualbox.org/download/oracle_vbox_2016.asc -O- |
sudo apt-key add -
```

3. Install VirtualBox:

```
$ sudo apt-get update && sudo apt-get install virtualbox-5.0
```

See also

▶ VirtualBox downloads: `https://www.virtualbox.org/wiki/Linux_Downloads`

▶ Ubuntu Cloud images on a local hypervisor: `https://help.ubuntu.com/community/UEC/Images#line-105`

▶ The Ubuntu community page for KVM: `https://help.ubuntu.com/community/KVM`

Managing virtual machines with virsh

In the previous recipe, we saw how to start and manage virtual machines with KVM. This recipe covers the use of Virsh and virt-install to create and manage virtual machines. The `libvirt` Linux library exposes various APIs to manage hypervisors and virtual machines. Virsh is a command-line tool that provides an interface to libvirt APIs.

To create a new machine, Virsh needs the machine definition in XML format. virt-install is a Python script to easily create a new virtual machine without manipulating bits of XML. It provides an easy-to-use interface to define a machine, create an XML definition for it and then load it in Virsh to start it.

In this recipe, we will create a new virtual machine with virt-install and see how it can be managed with various Virsh commands.

Getting ready

You will need access to the root account or an account with `sudo` privileges.

▶ Install the required packages, as follows:

```
$ sudo apt-get update
$ sudo apt-get install -y qemu-kvm libvirt-bin virtinst
```

▶ Install packages to create the cloud init disk:

```
$ sudo apt-get install genisoimage
```

- Add your user to the `libvirtd` group and update group membership for the current session:

```
$ sudo adduser ubuntu libvirtd
$ newgrp libvirtd
```

How to do it...

We need to create a new virtual machine. This can be done either with an XML definition of the machine or with a tool called virt-install. We will again use the prebuilt Ubuntu Cloud images and initialize them with a secondary disk:

1. First, download the Ubuntu Cloud image and prepare it for use:

```
$ mkdir ubuntuvm && cd ubuntuvm
$ wget -O trusty.img.dist \
http://cloud-images.ubuntu.com/releases/trusty/release/ubuntu-
14.04-server-cloudimg-amd64-disk1.img
$ qemu-img convert -O qcow2 trusty.img.dist trusty.img.orig
$ qemu-img create -f qcow2 -b trusty.img.orig trusty.img
```

2. Create the initialization disk to initialize your cloud image:

```
$ sudo vi user-data
#cloud-config
password: password
chpasswd: { expire: False }
ssh_pwauth: True
$ sudo vi meta-data
instance-id: ubuntu01;
local-hostname: ubuntu
$ genisoimage -output cidata.iso -volid cidata -joliet \
-rock user-data meta-data
```

3. Now that we have all the necessary data, let's create a new machine, as follows:

```
$ virt-install --import --name ubuntu01 \
--ram 256 --vcpus 1 --disk trusty.img \
--disk cidata.iso,device=cdrom \
--network bridge=virbr0 \
--graphics vnc,listen=0.0.0.0 --noautoconsole -v
```

This should create a virtual machine and start it. A display should be opened on the local VNC port 5900. You can access the VNC through other systems available on the local network with a GUI.

> You can set up local port forwarding and access VNC from your local system as follows:
>
> ```
> $ ssh kvm_hostname_or_ip -L 5900:127.0.0.1:5900
> $ vncviewer localhost:5900
> ```

4. Once the cloud-init process completes, you can log in with the default user, ubuntu, and the password set in user-data.

5. Now that the machine is created and running, we can use the virsh command to manage this machine. You may need to connect virsh and qemu before using them:

```
$ virsh connect qemu:///system
```

6. Get a list of running machines with virsh list. The --all parameter will show all available machines, whether they are running or stopped:

```
$ virsh list --all # or virsh --connect qemu:///system list
```

7. You can open a console to a running machine with virsh as follows. This should give you a login prompt inside the virtual machine:

```
$ virsh console ubuntu01
```

To close the console, use the *Ctrl +]* key combination.

8. Once you are done with the machine, you can shut it down with virsh shutdown. This will call a shutdown process inside the virtual machine:

```
$ virsh shutdown ubuntu01
```

You can also stop the machine without a proper shutdown, as follows:

```
$ virsh destroy ubuntu01
```

9. To completely remove the machine, use virsh undefine. With this command, the machine will be deleted and cannot be used again:

```
$ virsh destroy ubuntu01
```

How it works...

Both the `virt-install` and `virsh` commands collectively give you an easy-to-use virtualization environment. Additionally, the system does not need to support hardware virtualization. When it's available, the virtual machines will use KVM and hardware acceleration, and when KVM is not supported, Qemu will be used to emulate virtual hardware.

With `virt-install`, we have easily created a KVM virtual machine. This command abstracts the XML definition required by libvirt. With a list of various parameters, we can easily define all the components with their respective configurations. You can get a full list of `virt-install` parameters with the `--help` flag.

> The `virtinst` package, which installs `virt-install`, also contains some more commands, such as `virt-clone`, `virt-admin`, and `virt-xml`. Use tab completion in your bash shell to get a list of all `virt-*` commands.

Once the machine is defined and running, it can be managed with `virsh` subcommands. Virsh provides tons of subcommands to manage virtual machines, or domains as they are called by libvirt. You can start or stop machines, pause and resume them, or stop them entirely. You can even modify the machine configuration to add or remove devices as needed, or create a clone of an existing machine. To get a list of all machine (domain) management commands, use `virsh help domain`.

Once you have your first virtual machine, it becomes easier to create new machines using the XML definition from it. You can dump the XML definition with `virsh dumpxml machine`, edit it as required, and then create a new machine using XML configuration with `virsh create configuration.xml`.

There are a lot more options available for the `virsh` and `virt-install` commands; check their respective manual pages for more details.

There's more...

In the previous example, we used cloud images to quickly start a virtual machine. You do not need to use cloud machines, and you can install the operating system on your own using the respective installation media.

Download the installation media and then use following command to start the installation. Make sure you change the -c parameter to the downloaded ISO file, along with the location:

```
$ sudo virt-install -n ubuntu -r 1024 \
--disk path=/var/lib/libvirt/images/ubuntu01.img,bus=virtio,size=4 \
-c ubuntu-16.04-server-i386.iso \
--network network=default,model=virtio
--graphics vnc,listen=0.0.0.0 --noautoconsole -v
```

The command will wait for the installation to complete. You can access the GUI installation using the VNC client.

Forward your local port to access VNC on a KVM host. Make sure you replace 5900 with the respective port from virsh vncdisplay node0:

```
$ ssh kvm_hostname_or_ip -L 5900:127.0.0.1:5900
```

Now you can connect to VNC at `localhost:5900`.

Easy cloud images with uvtool

Ubuntu provides another super easy tool named uvtool. This tool focuses on the creation of virtual machines out of Ubuntu Cloud images. It synchronizes cloud images from Ubuntu servers to your local machine. Later, these images can be used to launch virtual machines in minutes. You can install and use uvtool with the following commands:

```
$ sudo apt-get install uvtool
```

Download the Xenial image from the cloud images:

```
$ uvt-simplestreams-libvirt sync release=xenial arch=amd64
```

Start a virtual machine:

```
$ uvt-kvm create virtsys01
```

Finally, get the IP of a running system:

```
$ uvt-kvm ip virtsys01
```

Check out the manual page with the `man uvtool` command and visit the official uvtool page at `https://help.ubuntu.com/lts/serverguide/cloud-images-and-uvtool.html` for more details.

See also

- ▸ Check out the manual pages for virt-install using `$ man virt-install`
- ▸ Check out the manual pages for virsh using `$ man virsh`
- ▸ The official Libvirt site: `http://libvirt.org/`
- ▸ The Libvirt documentation on Ubuntu Server guide: `https://help.ubuntu.com/lts/serverguide/libvirt.html`

Setting up your own cloud with OpenStack

We have already seen how to create virtual machines with KVM and Qemu, and how to manage them with tools such as virsh and virt-manager. This approach works when you need to work with a handful of machines and manage few hosts. To operate on a larger scale, you need a tool to manage host machines, VM configurations, images, network, and storage, and monitor the entire environment. OpenStack is an open source initiative to create and manage a large pool of virtual machines (or containers). It is a collection of various tools to deploy IaaS clouds. The official site defines OpenStack as an operating system to control a large pool of compute, network, and storage resources, all managed through a dashboard.

OpenStack was primarily developed and open-sourced by Rackspace, a leading cloud service provider. With its thirteenth release, Mitaka, OpenStack provides tons of tools to manage various components of your infrastructure. A few important components of OpenStack are as follows:

- ▸ **Nova**: Compute controller
- ▸ **Neutron**: OpenStack networking
- ▸ **Keystone**: Identity service
- ▸ **Glance**: OpenStack image service
- ▸ **Horizon**: OpenStack dashboard
- ▸ **Cinder**: Block storage service
- ▸ **Swift**: Object store
- ▸ **Heat**: Orchestration program

OpenStack in itself is quite a big deployment. You need to decide the required components, plan their deployment, and install and configure them to work in sync. The installation itself can be a good topic for a separate book. However, the OpenStack community has developed a set of scripts known as DevStack to support development with faster deployments. In this recipe, we will use the DevStack script to quickly install OpenStack and get an overview of its workings. The official OpenStack documentation provides detailed documents for the Ubuntu based installation and configuration of various components. If you are planning a serious production environment, you should read it thoroughly.

Getting ready

You will need a non-root account with `sudo` privileges. The default account named `ubuntu` should work.

The system should have at least two CPU cores with at least 4 GB of RAM and 60 GB of disk space. A static IP address is preferred. If possible, use the minimal installation of Ubuntu.

 If you are performing a fresh installation of Ubuntu Server, press *F4* on the first screen to get installation options, and choose **Install Minimal System**. If you are installing inside a virtual machine, choose **Install Minimal Virtual Machine**. You may need to go to the installation menu with the *Esc* key before using *F4*.

DevStack scripts are available on GitHub. Clone the repository or download and extract it to your installation server. Use the following command to clone:

```
$ git clone https://git.openstack.org/openstack-dev/devstack \
-b stable/mitaka --depth 1
$ cd devstack
```

You can choose to get the latest release by selecting the master branch. Just skip the `-b stable/mitaka` option from the previous command.

How to do it...

Once you obtain the DevStack source, it's as easy as executing an installation script. Before that, we will create a minimal configuration file for passwords and basic network configuration:

1. Copy the sample configuration to the root of the `devstack` directory:

    ```
    $ cp samples/local.conf
    ```

2. Edit `local.conf` and update passwords:

    ```
    ADMIN_PASSWORD=password
    DATABASE_PASSWORD=password
    RABBIT_PASSWORD=password
    SERVICE_PASSWORD=$ADMIN_PASSWORD
    ```

3. Add basic network configuration as follows. Update IP address range as per your local network configuration and set `FLAT_INTERFACE` to your primary Ethernet interface:

    ```
    FLOATING_RANGE=192.168.1.224/27
    ```

```
FIXED_RANGE=10.11.12.0/24
FIXED_NETWORK_SIZE=256
FLAT_INTERFACE=eth0
```

Save the changes to the configuration file.

4. Now, start the installation with the following command. As the Mitaka stable branch has not been tested with Ubuntu Xenial (16.04), we need to use the FORCE variable. If you are using the master branch of DevStack or an older version of Ubuntu, you can start the installation with the ./stack.sh command:

```
$ FORCE=yes ./stack.sh
```

The installation should take some time to complete, mostly depending on your network speed. Once the installation completes, the script should output the dashboard URL, keystone API endpoint, and the admin password:

```
This is your host IP address: 192.168.1.10
This is your host IPv6 address: ::1
Horizon is now available at http://192.168.1.10/dashboard
Keystone is serving at http://192.168.1.10:5000/
The default users are: admin and demo
The password: password
ubuntu@ubuntu:~/devstack$
```

5. Now, access the OpenStack dashboard and log in with the given username and password. The admin account will give you an admin interface. The login screen looks like this:

6. Once you log in, your admin interface should look something like this:

Now, from this screen, you can deploy new virtual instances, set up different cloud images, and configure instance flavors.

How it works...

We used DevStack, an unattended installation script, to install and configure basic OpenStack deployment. This will install OpenStack with the bare minimum components for deploying virtual machines with OpenStack. By default, DevStack installs the identity service, Nova network, compute service, and image service. The installation process creates two user accounts, namely `admin` and `dummy`. The `admin` account gives you administrative access to the OpenStack installation and the `dummy` account gives you the end user interface. The DevStack installation also adds a Cirros image to the image store. This is a basic lightweight Linux distribution and a good candidate to test OpenStack installation.

The default installation creates a basic flat network. You can also configure DevStack to enable Neutron support, by setting the required options in the configuration. Check out the DevStack documentation for more details.

There's more...

Ubuntu provides its own easy-to-use OpenStack installer. It provides options to install OpenStack, along with LXD support and OpenStack Autopilot, an enterprise offering by Canonical. You can choose to install on your local machine (all-in-one installation) or choose a **Metal as a Service** (**MAAS**) setup for a multinode deployment. The single-machine setup will install OpenStack on multiple LXC containers, deployed and managed through Juju. You will need at least 12 GB of main memory and an 8-CPU server. Use the following commands to get started with the Ubuntu OpenStack installer:

```
$ sudo apt-get update
$ sudo apt-get install conjure-up
$ conjure-up openstack
```

While DevStack installs a development-focused minimal installation of OpenStack, various other scripts support the automation of the OpenStack installation process. A notable project is OpenStack Ansible. This is an official OpenStack project and provides production-grade deployments. A quick GitHub search should give you a lot more options.

See also

- ▸ A step-by-step detailed guide to installing various OpenStack components on Ubuntu server: `http://docs.openstack.org/mitaka/install-guide-ubuntu/`
- ▸ DevStack Neutron configuration: `http://docs.openstack.org/developer/devstack/guides/neutron.html`
- ▸ OpenStack Ansible: `https://github.com/openstack/openstack-ansible`
- ▸ A list of OpenStack resources: `https://github.com/ramitsurana/awesome-openstack`
- ▸ Ubuntu MaaS: `http://www.ubuntu.com/cloud/maas`
- ▸ Ubuntu Juju: `http://www.ubuntu.com/cloud/juju`
- ▸ Read more about LXD and LXC in *Chapter 8, Working with Containers*

Adding a cloud image to OpenStack

In the previous recipe, we installed and configured OpenStack. Now, to start using the service, we need to upload virtual machine images. The OpenStack installation uploads a test image named Cirros. This is a small Linux distribution designed to be used as a test image in the cloud. We will upload prebuilt cloud images available from Ubuntu.

Getting ready

Make sure you have installed the OpenStack environment and you can access the OpenStack dashboard with valid credentials. It is not necessary to have an admin account to create and upload images.

Select the cloud image of your choice and get its download URL. Here, we will use the Trusty Ubuntu Server image. The selected image format is QCOW2, though OpenStack support various other image formats. The following is the URL for the selected image:

```
https://cloud-images.ubuntu.com/trusty/current/trusty-server-
cloudimg-amd64-disk1.img
```

How to do it...

The OpenStack dashboard provides a separate section for image management. You can see the images that are already available and add or remove your own images. Follow these steps to create your own image:

1. Log in to your OpenStack dashboard. On successful login, you should get an **Overview** page for your account.

2. Now, from the left-hand side **Project** menu, under the **Compute** submenu, click on **Images**:

This should show you a list of all publicly available images—something like this:

	Image Name	Type	Status	Public	Protected	Format	Size	Actions
☐	Ubuntu Xenial	Image	Active	Yes	No	QCOW2	289.8 MB	Launch ▾
☐	cirros-0.3.4-x86_64-uec-ramdisk	Image	Active	Yes	No	ARI	3.6 MB	

(Tabs: ⚓ Project (0) ↪ Shared with Me (0) 👥 Public (4) ＋ Create Image 🗑 Delete Images)

3. Click on the **Create Image** button to add a new image. This should open a popup box with various details. Here, you can choose to add an image URL or enter an image path if you have downloaded the image to your local machine.

4. Fill in the name and other required details. Under **Image Source**, select the image location, and in the next box, **Image Location**, enter the URL for the Ubuntu Cloud image.

5. Under **Format**, select the image format of your selected image. In this case, it's **QCOW2**.

6. Enter amd64 under **Architecture**. Make sure you match this with your selected image.

7. Enter the minimum disk and RAM size. As we have selected an Ubuntu image, the minimum disk size should be 5 GB and minimum RAM 256 MB. These values will affect the selection of instance flavors while creating a new instance.

8. Finally, click on the **Create Image** button to save the details and add the image to OpenStack. This will download the image from the source URL and save it in the image repository. The resulting image will be listed under the **Project** tab, as follows:

	Image Name	Type	Status	Public	Protected	Format	Size	Actions
☐	Ubuntu Trusty	Image	Active	No	No	QCOW2	247.7 MB	Launch ▾

(Tabs: ⚓ Project (1) ↪ Shared with Me (0) 👥 Public (4) ＋ Create Image 🗑 Delete Images)

Displaying 1 item

Now, the image is ready can be used to launch new cloud instances.

How it works...

OpenStack is a cloud virtualization platform and needs operating system images to launch virtual machines in the cloud. The Glance OpenStack imaging service provides the image-management service. It supports various types of image, including Qemu format, raw disk files, ISO images, and images from other virtualization platforms, as well as Docker images. Like every other thing in OpenStack, image management works with the help of APIs provided by Glance.

OpenStack, being a cloud platform, is expected to have ready-to-use images that can be used to quickly start a virtual instance. It is possible to upload the operating system installation disk and install the OS to a virtual instance, but that would be a waste of resources. Instead, it is preferable to have prebuilt cloud images. Various popular operating systems provide their respective cloud images, which can be imported to cloud systems. In the previous example, we used the Ubuntu Cloud image for the Ubuntu Trusty release.

We imported the image by specifying its source URI. Local image files can also be uploaded by selecting the image file as an image source. You can also build your own images and upload them to the image store to be used in the cloud. Along with the image source, we need to provide a few more parameters, which include the type of the image being uploaded and the minimum resource requirements of that image. Once the image has been uploaded, it can be used to launch a new instance in the cloud. Also, the image can be marked as public so that it is accessible to all OpenStack users. You will need specific rights for your OpenStack account to create public images.

There's more...

OpenStack images can also be managed from the command line with the client called `glance`. To access the respective APIs from the command line, you need to authenticate with the Glance server. Use the following steps to use `glance` from the command line:

1. First, add authentication parameters to the environment:

```
export OS_USERNAME=demo
export OS_PASSWORD=password
export OS_AUTH_URL=http://10.196.69.158/identity
export OS_TENANT_ID=8fe52bb13ca44981aa15d9b62e9133f4
```

> DevStack makes things even easier by providing a script,
> openrc. It's located under the root directory of DevStack and
> can be used as follows:
>
> **$ source openrc demo   # source openrc username**
>
> You are then ready, without multiple export commands.

2. Now, use the following command to obtain the image list for the specified user:

   $ glance image-list

```
ubuntu@ubuntu:~$ glance image-list
+--------------------------------------+----------------------------------+
| ID                                   | Name                             |
+--------------------------------------+----------------------------------+
| 6948c538-7f52-4439-8e81-e26cdefc8b08 | cirros-0.3.4-x86_64-uec          |
| ad7a5ef1-f500-4e5d-a44e-22710c066938 | cirros-0.3.4-x86_64-uec-kernel   |
| c1b1b13e-1d4c-49c4-8dd6-0e25c3c12ba1 | cirros-0.3.4-x86_64-uec-ramdisk  |
| abf59bb4-68e6-4b89-8b77-8fdaeff7163e | Ubuntu Trusty                    |
| ffddf013-5f6c-4c47-b4fe-e087957680fd | Ubuntu Xenial                    |
+--------------------------------------+----------------------------------+
```

You can get a list of available command-line options with glance help.

See also

▸ Read more about OpenStack image management: http://docs.openstack.org/image-guide/

▸ Command-line image management: http://docs.openstack.org/user-guide/common/cli_manage_images.html

▸ Dashboard image management: http://docs.openstack.org/user-guide/dashboard_manage_images.html

▸ Glance documentation: http://docs.openstack.org/developer/glance/

Launching a virtual instance with OpenStack

Now that we have OpenStack installed and have set our desired operating system image, we are ready to launch our first instance in a self-hosted cloud.

Getting ready

You will need credentials to access the OpenStack dashboard.

Uploading your own image is not necessary; you can use the default Cirros image to launch the test instance.

Log in to the OpenStack dashboard and set the SSH key pair in the **Access & Security** tab available under the **Projects** menu. Here, you can generate a new key pair or import your existing public key.

> If you generate a new key pair, a file with the .pem extension will be downloaded to your local system. To use this key with PuTTy, you need to use PuTTYgen and extract the public and private keys.

How to do it...

OpenStack instances are the same virtual machines that we launch from the command line or desktop tools. OpenStack give you a web interface to launch your virtual machines from. Follow these steps to create and start a new instance:

1. Select the **Instance** option under the **Projects** menu and then click on the **Launch Instance** button on the right-hand side. This should open a modal box with various options, which will look something like this:

Details *	Please provide the initial hostname for the instance, the availability zone where instance count. Increase the Count to create multiple instances with the same se
Source *	Instance Name *
Flavor *	
Network Ports	Availability Zone
Key Pair	nova ▾
	Count *

2. Now, start filling in the necessary details. All fields that are marked with * are required fields. Let's start by naming our instance. Enter the name in the **Instance Name** field.

3. Set the value of **Count** to the number of instances you want to launch. We will leave it at the default value of **1**.

4. Next, click on the **Source** tab. Here, we need to configure the source image for our instance. Set **Select Boot Source** to **Image** and select **No** for **Create New Volume**. Then, from the **Available Images** section, search the desired image and click on the button with the **+** sign to select the image. The list should contain our recently uploaded image. The final screen should look something like this:

Select Boot Source				Create New Volume		
Image			▾	Yes	No	
Allocated						
Name	Updated		Size	Type	Visibility	
> Ubuntu Trusty	6/4/16 11:26 AM		247.69 MB	qcow2	Private	−

5. Next, on the **Flavor** tab, we need to select the desired resources for our instance. Select the desired flavor by clicking on the **+** button. Make sure that the selected row does not contain any warning signs.

6. Now, from the **Key Pair** tab, select the SSH key pair that we just created. This is required to log in to your instance.

7. Finally, click on the **Launch Instance** button from the bottom of the modal box. A new instance should be created and listed under the instances list. It will take some time to start; wait for the **Status** column to show **Active**:

	Instance Name = ▾				Filter	⚙ Launch Instance	🗑 Delete Insta

	Instance Name	Image Name	IP Address	Size	Key Pair	Status	Availability Zone	Task	Power State	Time since created
☐	First Instance	Ubuntu Trusty	10.11.12.6	m1.small	demo	Active	nova	None	Running	1 minute

Displaying 1 item

8. You are now ready to access your virtual instance. Log in to your host console and try to ping the IP address of your instance. Then, open an SSH session with the following command:

```
$ ssh -i your_key ubuntu@instance_ip
```

This should give you a shell inside your new cloud instance. Try to ping an external server, such as an OpenDNS server, from within an instance to ensure connectivity.

To make this instance available on your local network, you will need to assign a floating IP address to it. Click on the drop-down arrow from the **Actions** column and select **Associate Floating IP**. This should add one more IP address to your instance and make it available on your local network.

How it works...

OpenStack instances are the same as the virtual machines that we build and operate with common virtualization tools such as VirtualBox and Qemu. OpenStack provides a central console for deploying and managing thousands of such machines on multiple hosts. Under the hood, OpenStack uses the same virtualization tools as the others. The preferred hypervisor is KVM, and if hardware acceleration is not available, Qemu emulation is used. OpenStack supports various other hypervisors, including VMware, XEN, Hyper-V, and Docker. In addition, a lightervisor, LXD, is on its way to a stable release. Other than virtualization, OpenStack adds various other improvements, such as image management, block storage, object storage, and various network configurations.

In the previous example, we set various parameters before launching a new instance; these include the instance name, resource constraints, operating system image, and login credentials. All these parameters will be passed to the underlying hypervisor to create and start the new virtual machine. A few other options that we have not used are volumes and networks. As we have installed a very basic OpenStack instance, new developments in network configurations are not available for use. You can update your DevStack configuration and install the OpenStack networking component Neutron.

Volumes, on the other hand, are available and can be used to obtain disk images of the desired size and format. You can also attach multiple volumes to a single machine, providing extended storage capacity. Volumes can be created separately and do not depend on the instance. You can reuse an existing volume with a new instance, and all data stored on it will be available to the new instance.

Here, we have used a cloud image to start a new instance. You can also choose a previously stored instance snapshot, create a new volume, or use a volume snapshot. The volume can be a permanent volume, which has its life cycle separate from the instance, or an ephemeral volume, which gets deleted along with the instance. Volumes can also be attached at instance runtime or even removed from an instance, provided they are not a boot source.

Other options include configuration and metadata. The configuration tab provides an option to add initialization scripts that are executed at first boot. This is very similar to cloud-init data. The following is a short example of a cloud-init script:

```
#cloud-config
package_update: true
package_upgrade: true
password: password
chpasswd: { expire: False }
ssh_pwauth: True
ssh_authorized_keys:
  - your-ssh-public-key-contents
```

This script will set a password for the default user (ubuntu in the case of Ubuntu images), enable password logins, add an SSH key to authorize keys, and update and upgrade packages.

The metadata section adds arbitrary data to instances in the form of key-value pairs. This data can be used to identify an instance from a group and automate certain tasks.

Once an instance has been started, you have various management options from the **Actions** menu available on the instance list. From this menu, you can create instance snapshots; start, stop, or pause instances; edit security groups; get the VNC console; and so on.

There's more...

Similar to the `glance` command-line client, a compute client is available as well and is named after the compute component. The `nova` command can be used to create and manage cloud instances from the command line. You can get detailed parameters and options with the `nova help` command or, to get help with a specific subcommand, `nova help <subcommand>`.

See also

- The cloud-init official documentation: `https://cloudinit.readthedocs.io/en/latest/`
- More on cloud-init: `https://help.ubuntu.com/community/CloudInit`
- OpenStack instance guide: `http://docs.openstack.org/user-guide/dashboard_launch_instances.html`
- Command-line cheat sheet: `http://docs.openstack.org/user-guide/cli_cheat_sheet.html#compute-nova`

Installing Juju a service orchestration framework

Up to now in this chapter, we have learned about virtualization and OpenStack for deploying and managing virtual servers. Now, it's time to look at a service-modeling tool, Juju. Juju is a service-modeling tool for Ubuntu. Connect it to any cloud service, model your application, and press deploy—done. Juju takes care of lower-level configuration, deployments, and scaling, and even monitors your services.

Juju is an open source tool that offers a GUI and command-line interface for modeling your service. Applications are generally deployed as collections of multiple services. For example, to deploy WordPress, you need a web server, a database system, and perhaps a load balancer. Service modeling refers to the relations between these services. Services are defined with the help of **charms**, which are collections of configurations and deployment instructions, such as dependencies and resource requirements. The Juju store provides more than 300 predefined and ready-to-use charms.

Once you model your application with the required charms and their relationships, these models can be stored as a bundle. A bundle represents a set of charms, their configurations, and their relationships with each other. The entire bundle can be deployed to a cloud or local system with a single command. Also, similar to charms, bundles can be shared and are available on the Juju store.

This recipe covers the installation of Juju on Ubuntu Server. With the release of Xenial, the latest Ubuntu release, Canonical has also updated the Juju platform to version 2.0.

Getting ready

You need access to the root account or an account with `sudo` privileges.

Make sure you have the SSH keys generated with your user account. You can generate a new key pair with the following command:

```
$ ssh-keygen -t rsa -b 2048
```

How to do it...

Juju 2.0 is available in the Ubuntu Xenial repository, so installation is quite easy. Follow these steps to install Juju, along with LXD for local deployments:

1. Install Juju, along with the LXD and ZFSUtils packages. On Ubuntu 16, LXD should already be installed:

   ```
   $ sudo apt-get update
   $ sudo apt-get install juju-2.0 lxd zfsutils-linux
   ```

2. The LXD installation creates a new group, lxd, and adds the current user to it. Update your group membership with newgrp so that you don't need to log out and log back in:

```
$ newgrp lxd
```

3. Now, we need to initialize LXD before using it with Juju. We will create a new ZFS pool for LXD and configure a local lxd bridge for container networking with NAT enabled:

```
$ sudo lxd init
Name of the storage backend to use (dir or zfs): zfs
Create a new ZFS pool (yes/no)? yes
Name of the new ZFS pool: lxdpool
Would you like to use an existing block device (yes/no)? no
Size in GB of the new loop device (1GB minimum): 20
Would you like LXD to be available over the network (yes/no)? no
Do you want to configure the LXD bridge (yes/no)? yes
```

LXD has been successfully configured.

4. Now that LXD has been configured, we can bootstrap Juju and create a controller node. The following command will bootstrap Juju with LXD for local deployments:

```
$ juju bootstrap juju-controller lxd
```

This command should take some time to finish as it needs to fetch the container image and the install Juju tools inside the container.

5. Once the bootstrap process completes, you can check the list of controllers, as follows:

```
$ juju list-controllers
CONTROLLER              MODEL     USER          SERVER
local.juju-controller*  default   admin@local
10.155.16.114:17070
```

6. You can also check the LXD container created by Juju using the lxc list command:

```
$ lxc list
```

7. From Juju 2.0 onwards, every controller will install the Juju GUI by default. This is a web application to manage the controller and its models. The following command will give you the URL of the Juju GUI:

```
$ juju gui
...
https://10.201.217.65:17070/gui/2331544b-1e16-49ba-8ac7-
2f13ea147497/
...
```

8. You may need to use port forwarding to access the web console. Use the following command to quickly set up iptables forwarding:

    ```
    $ sudo iptables -t nat -A PREROUTING -p tcp --dport 17070 -j
    DNAT \
    --to-destination 10.201.217.65:17070
    ```

9. You will also need a username and password to log in to the GUI. To get these details, use the following command:

    ```
    $ juju show-controller --show-passwords juju-controller
    ...
    accounts:
        admin@local:
            user: admin@local
            password: 8fcb8aca6e22728c6ac59b7cba322f39
    ```

When you log in to the web console, it should look something like this:

Now, you are ready to use Juju and deploy your applications either with a command line or from the web console.

How it works...

Here, we installed and configured the Juju framework with LXD as a local deployment backend. Juju is a service-modeling framework that makes it easy to compose and deploy an entire application with just a few commands. Now, we have installed and bootstrapped Juju. The bootstrap process creates a controller node on a selected cloud; in our case, it is LXD. The command provides various optional arguments to configure controller machines, as well as pass the credentials to the bootstrap process. Check out the bootstrap help menu with the `juju bootstrap --help` command.

We have used LXD as a local provider, which does not need any special credentials to connect and create new nodes. When using pubic cloud providers or your own cloud, you will need to provide your username and password or access keys. This can be done with the help of the `add-credentials <cloud>` command. All added credentials are stored in a plaintext file: `~/.local/share/juju/credentials.yaml`. You can view a list of available cloud credentials with the `juju list-credentials` command.

The controller node is a special machine created by Juju to host and manage data and models related to an environment. The container node hosts two models, namely admin and default, and the admin model runs the Juju API server and database system. Juju can use multiple cloud systems simultaneously, and each cloud can have its own controller node.

From version 2.0 onwards, every controller node installs the Juju GUI application by default. The Juju GUI is a web application that provides an easy-to-use visual interface to create and manage various Juju entities. With its simple interface, you can easily create new models, import charms, and set up relations between them. The GUI is still available as a separate charm and can be deployed separately to any machine in a Juju environment. The command-line tools are more than enough to operate Juju, and it is possible to skip the installation of the GUI component using the `--no-gui` option with the `bootstrap` command.

There's more...

In the previous example, we used LXD as a local deployment backend for Juju. With LXD, Juju can quickly create new containers to deploy applications. Along with LXD, Juju supports various other cloud providers. You can get a full list of supported cloud providers with the `list-clouds` option:

```
$ juju list-clouds
```

Juju also provides the option to fetch updates to a supported cloud list. With the `update-clouds` subcommand, you can update your local cloud with the latest developments from Juju.

Along with public clouds, Juju also supports OpenStack deployments and MaaS-based infrastructures. You can also create your own cloud configuration and add it to Juju with the `juju add-cloud` command. Like with LXD, you can use virtual machines or even physical machines for Juju-based deployments. As far as you can access the machine with SSH, you can use it with Juju. Check out the cloud-configuration manual for more details: `https://jujucharms.com/docs/devel/clouds-manual`

See also

 ▸ Read more about Juju concepts at `https://jujucharms.com/docs/devel/juju-concepts`
 ▸ Get to know Juju-supported clouds or how to add your own at `https://jujucharms.com/docs/devel/clouds`
 ▸ The Juju GUI: `https://jujucharms.com/docs/devel/controllers-gui`
 ▸ Juju controllers: `https://jujucharms.com/docs/devel/controllers`
 ▸ Refer to *Chapter 8, Working with Containers* for more details about LXD containers
 ▸ Learn how to connect Juju to a remote LXD server: `https://insights.ubuntu.com/2015/11/16/juju-and-remote-lxd-host/`

Managing services with Juju

In the previous recipe, we learned how to install the Juju service orchestration framework. Now, we will look at how to use Juju to deploy and manage a service.

Getting ready

Make sure you have installed and bootstrapped Juju.

How to do it...

We will deploy a sample WordPress installation with a load balancer. The MySQL service will be used as the database for WordPress. Both services are available in the Juju Charm store.

Follow these steps to manage services with Juju:

1. Let's start by deploying the WordPress service with `juju deploy`. This should give you the following output:

   ```
   $ juju deploy wordpress
   Added charm "cs:trusty/wordpress-4" to the model.
   Deploying charm "cs:trusty/wordpress-4" with the charm series
   "trusty".
   ```

2. Now, deploy a MySQL service to store WordPress contents:

   ```
   $ juju deploy mysql
   Added charm "cs:trusty/mysql-38" to the model.
   Deploying charm "cs:trusty/mysql-38" with the charm series
   "trusty".
   ```

3. Now, you can use `juju status` to confirm your deployed services. It should show you the deployed services, their relations, and respective machine statuses, as follows:

   ```
   $ juju status
   ```

```
ubuntu@ubuntu:~$ juju status
[Services]
NAME         STATUS       EXPOSED CHARM
mysql        maintenance  false   cs:trusty/mysql-38
wordpress    unknown      false   cs:trusty/wordpress-4

[Relations]
SERVICE1     SERVICE2   RELATION     TYPE
mysql        mysql      cluster      peer
wordpress    wordpress  loadbalancer peer
```

4. Now that both services have been deployed, we need to connect them together so that `wordpress` can use the database service. Juju calls this a relation, and it can be created as follows:

   ```
   $ juju add-relation mysql wordpress
   ```

5. Finally, we need to expose our `wordpress` service so that it can be accessed outside our local network. By default, all charms start as unexposed and are accessible only on a local network:

   ```
   $ juju expose wordpress
   ```

You can get the IP address or DNS name of the `wordpress` instance with the `juju status` command from the `Machines` section. Note that in a local LXD environment, you may need a forwarded port to access WordPress.

How it works...

In this example, we deployed two separate services using Juju. Juju will create two separate machines for each of them and deploy the service as per the instructions in the respective charms. These two services need to be connected with each other so that `wordpress` knows the existence of the MySQL database. Juju calls these connections relations. Each charm contains a set of hooks that are triggered on given events. When we create a relation between WordPress and MySQL, both services are informed about it with the `database-relation-changed` hook. At this point, both services can exchange the necessary details, such as MySQL ports and login credentials. The WordPress charm will set up a MySQL connection and initialize a database.

Once both services are ready, we can expose them to be accessed on a public network. Here, we do not need MySQL to be accessible by WordPress users, so we have only exposed the `wordpress` service. WordPress can access MySQL internally, with the help of a relation.

You can use the Juju GUI to visualize your model and add or remove charms and their relations. At this point, if you open a GUI, you should see your charms plotted on the graph and connected with each other through a small line, indicating a relation. The GUI also provides an option to set constraints on a charm and configure charm settings, if any.

Note that both charms internally contain scaling options. WordPress is installed behind an Nginx reverse proxy and can be scaled with extra units as and when required. You can add new units to the service with a single command, as follows:

```
$ juju add-unit mysql -n 1
```

There's more...

When you no longer need these services, the entire model can be destroyed with the `juju destroy-model <modelname>` command. You can also selectively destroy particular services with the `remove-service` command and remove relations with `remove-relations`. Check out the Juju manual page for tons of commands that are not listed in the Juju help menu.

See also

▶ How to create your own charm: `https://jujucharms.com/docs/stable/authors-charm-writing`

▶ More about hooks: `https://jujucharms.com/docs/stable/authors-hook-environment`

8
Working with Containers

In this chapter, we will cover the following recipes:

- ▸ Installing LXD, the Linux container daemon
- ▸ Deploying your first container with LXD
- ▸ Managing LXD containers
- ▸ Managing LXD containers – advanced options
- ▸ Setting resource limits on LXD containers
- ▸ Networking with LXD
- ▸ Installing Docker
- ▸ Starting and managing Docker containers
- ▸ Creating images with a Dockerfile
- ▸ Understanding Docker volumes
- ▸ Deploying WordPress using a Docker network
- ▸ Monitoring Docker containers
- ▸ Securing Docker containers

Introduction

Containers are quite an old technology and existed in the form of chroot and FreeBSD Jails. Most of us have already used containers in some form or other. The rise of Docker gave containers the required adoption and popularity. Ubuntu has also released a new tool named LXD with Ubuntu 15.04.

A container is a lightweight virtual environment that contains a process or set of processes. You might already have used containers with chroot. Just as with containers, we create an isolated virtual environment to group and isolate a set of processes. The processes running inside the container are isolated from the base operating system environment, as well as other containers running on the same host. Such processes cannot access or modify anything outside the container. A recent development in the Linux kernel to support namespaces and cgroups has enabled containers to provide better isolation and resource-management capabilities.

One of the reasons for the widespread adoption of containers is the difference between containers and hypervisor-based virtualization, and the inefficiencies associated with virtual machines. A VM requires its own kernel, whereas containers share the kernel with the host, resulting in a fast and lightweight isolated environment. Sharing the kernel removes much of the overhead of VMs and improves resource utilization, as processes communicate with a single shared kernel. You can think of containers as OS-level virtualization.

With containers, the entire application can be started within milliseconds, compared to virtual minutes. Additionally, the image size becomes much smaller, resulting in easier and faster cloud deployments. The shared operating system results in smaller footprints, and saved resources can be used to run additional containers on the same host. It is normal to run hundreds of containers on your laptop.

However, containerization also has its own shortcomings. First, you cannot run cross-platform containers. That is, containers must use the same kernel as the host. You cannot run Windows containers on a Linux host, and vice versa. Second, the isolation and security is not as strong as hypervisor-based virtualization. Containers are largely divided into two categories: OS containers and application containers. As the name suggests, application containers are designed to host a single service or application. Docker is an application container. You can still run multiple processes in Docker, but it is designed to host a single process.

OS containers, on the other hand, can be compared to virtual machines. They provide user space isolation. You can install and run multiple applications and run multiple processes inside OS containers. LXC on Linux and Jails on BSD are examples of OS containers.

In this chapter, we will take a look at LXC, an OS container, and Docker, an application container. In the first part of the chapter, we will learn how to install LXC and deploy a containerized virtual machine. In subsequent recipes, we will work with Docker and related technologies. We will learn to create and deploy a container with Docker.

Installing LXD, the Linux container daemon

LXC is a system built on the modern Linux kernel and enables the creation and management of virtual Linux systems or containers. As discussed earlier, LXC is not a full virtualization system and shares the kernel with the host operating system, providing lightweight containerization. LXC uses Linux namespaces to separate and isolate the processes running inside containers. This provides much better security than simple chroot-based filesystem isolation. These containers are portable and can easily be moved to another system with a similar processor architecture.

Ubuntu 15.04 unveiled a new tool named LXD, which is a wrapper around LXC. The official page calls it a container hypervisor and a new user experience for LXC. Ubuntu 16.04 comes preinstalled with its latest stable release, LXD 2.0. With LXD, you no longer need to work directly with lower-level LXC tools.

LXD adds some important features to LXC containers. First, it runs unprivileged containers by default, resulting in improved security and better isolation for containers. Second, LXD can manage multiple LXC hosts and can be used as an orchestration tool. It also supports the live migration of containers across hosts.

LXD provides a central daemon named LXD and a command-line client named `lxc`. Containers can be managed with the command-line client or the REST APIs provided by the LXD daemon. It also provides an OpenStack plugin, nova-compute-lxd, to deploy containers on the OpenStack cloud.

In this recipe, we will learn to install and configure the LXD daemon. This will set up a base for the next few recipes in this chapter.

Getting ready

You will need access to the root account or an account with `sudo` privileges.

Make sure that you have enough free space available on disk.

How to do it...

Ubuntu 16.04 ships with the latest release of LXD preinstalled. We just need to initialize the LXD daemon to set the basic settings.

1. First, update the `apt` cache and try to install LXD. This should install updates to the LXD package, if any:

    ```
    $ sudo apt-get update
    $ sudo apt-get install lxd
    ```

If you are using Ubuntu 14.04, you can install LXD using the following command:

```
$ sudo apt-get -t trusty-backports install lxd
```

2. Along with LXD, we will need one more package named ZFS—the most important addition to Ubuntu 16.04. We will be using ZFS as a storage backend for LXD:

```
$ sudo apt-get install zfsutils-linux
```

3. Once LXD has been installed, we need to configure the daemon before we start using it. Use `lxd init` to start the initialization process. This will ask some questions about the LXD configuration:

```
$ sudo lxd init
Name of the storage backend to use (dir or zfs): zfs
Create a new ZFS pool (yes/no)? yes
Name of the new ZFS pool: lxdpool
Would you like to use an existing block device (yes/no)? no
Size in GB of the new loop device (1GB minimum): 10
Would you like LXD to be available over the network (yes/no)?
no
Do you want to configure the LXD bridge (yes/no)? yes
Warning: Stopping lxd.service, but it can still be activated
by: lxd.socket
LXD has been successfully configured.
```

Now, we have our LXD setup configured and ready to use. In the next recipe, we will start our first container with LXD.

How it works...

Ubuntu 16.04 comes preinstalled with LXD and makes it even easier to start with system containers or operating system virtualization. In addition to LXD, Ubuntu now ships with inbuilt support for ZFS (OpenZFS), a filesystem with support for various features that improve the containerization experience. With ZFS, you get faster clones and snapshots with copy-on-write, data compression, disk quotas, and automated filesystem repairs.

LXD is a wrapper around lower-level LXC or Linux containers. It provides the REST API for communicating and managing LXC components. LXD runs as a central daemon and adds some important features, such as dynamic resource restrictions and live migrations between multiple hosts. Containers started with LXD are unprivileged containers by default, resulting in improved security and isolation.

This recipe covers the installation and initial configuration of the LXD daemon. As mentioned previously, LXD comes preinstalled with Ubuntu 16. The installation commands should fetch updates to LXD, if any. We have also installed `zfsutils-linux`, a user space package to interact with ZFS. After the installation, we initialized the LXD daemon to set basic configuration parameters, such as the default storage backend and network bridge for our containers.

We selected ZFS as the default storage backend and created a new ZFS pool called `lxdpool`, backed by a simple loopback device. In a production environment, you should opt for a physical device or separate partition. If you have already created a ZFS pool, you can directly name it by choosing `no` for `Create new ZFS pool`. To use a separate storage device or partition, choose `yes` when asked for block storage.

> Use the following commands to get ZFS on Ubuntu 14.04:
> ```
> $ sudo apt-add-repository ppa:zfs-native/stable
> $ sudo apt-get update && sudo apt-get install ubuntu-zfs
> ```

ZFS is the recommended storage backend, but LXD also works with various other options, such as **Logical Volume Manager** (**LVM**) and **btrfs** (pronounced "butter F S"), that offer nearly the same features as ZFS or a simple directory-based storage system.

Next, you can choose to make LXD available on the network. This is necessary if you are planning a multi-host setup and support for migration. The initialization also offers to configure the `lxdbr0` bridge interface, which will be used by all containers. By default, this bridge is configured with IPv6 only. Containers created with the default configuration will have their `veth0` virtual Ethernet adapter attached to `lxdbr0` through a NAT network. This is the gateway for containers to communicate with the outside world. LXD also installs a local DHCP server and the `dnsmasq` package. DHCP is used to assign IP addresses to containers, and `dnsmasq` acts as a local name-resolution service.

If you misplace the network bridge configuration or need to update it, you can use the following command to get to the network configuration screen:

```
$ sudo dpkg-reconfigure -p medium lxd
```

There's more...

The LXD 2.0 version, which ships with Ubuntu 16, is an LTS version. If you want to get your hands on the latest release, then you can install stable versions from the following repository:

```
$ sudo add-apt-repository ppa:ubuntu-lxc/lxd-stable
```

For development releases, change the PPA to `ppa:ubuntu-lxc/lxd-git-master`.

For more information, visit the LXC download page at `https://linuxcontainers.org/lxc/downloads/`.

If you still want to install LXC, you can. Use the following command:

```
$ sudo apt-get install lxc
```

This will install the required user space package and all the commands necessary to work directly with LXC. Note that all LXC commands are prefixed with `lxc-`, for example, `lxc-create` and `lxc-info`. To get a list of all commands, type `lxc-` in your terminal and press *Tab* twice.

See also

- ▸ For more information, check the LXD page of the Ubuntu Server guide: `https://help.ubuntu.com/lts/serverguide/lxd.html`
- ▸ The LXC blog post series is at `https://www.stgraber.org/2013/12/20/lxc-1-0-blog-post-series/`
- ▸ The LXD 2.0 blog post series is at `https://www.stgraber.org/2016/03/11/lxd-2-0-blog-post-series-012/`
- ▸ Ubuntu 16.04 switched to Systemd, which provides its own container framework, systemd-nspawn; read more about systemd containers on its Ubuntu man page at `http://manpages.ubuntu.com/manpages/xenial/man1/systemd-nspawn.1.html`
- ▸ See how to get started with systemd containers at `https://community.flockport.com/topic/32/systemd-nspawn-containers`

Deploying your first container with LXD

In this recipe, we will create our first container with LXD.

Getting ready

You will need access to the root account or an account with `sudo` privileges.

How to do it...

LXD works on the concept of remote servers and images served by those remote servers. Starting a new container with LXD is as simple as downloading a container image and starting a container out of it, all with a single command. Follow these steps:

1. To start your first container, use the `lxc launch` command, as follows:

   ```
   $ lxc launch ubuntu:14.04/amd64 c1
   ```

   LXC will download the required image (`14.04/amd64`) and start the container. You should see the progress like this:

   ```
   ubuntu@ubuntu:~$ lxc launch ubuntu:14.04/amd64 c1
   Creating c1
   Retrieving image: 100%
   Starting c1
   ubuntu@ubuntu:~$
   ```

2. As you can see in the screenshot, `lxc launch` downloads the required image, creates a new container, and then starts it as well. You can see your new container in a list of containers with the `lxc list` command, as follows:

   ```
   $ lxc list
   ```

```
ubuntu@ubuntu:~$ lxc list
+------+---------+----------------------+------+------------+-----------+
| NAME | STATE   |         IPV4         | IPV6 |    TYPE    | SNAPSHOTS |
+------+---------+----------------------+------+------------+-----------+
| c1   | RUNNING | 10.201.233.13 (eth0) |      | PERSISTENT | 0         |
+------+---------+----------------------+------+------------+-----------+
ubuntu@ubuntu:~$
```

3. Optionally, you can get more details about the containers with the `lxc info` command:

   ```
   $ lxc info c1
   ```

4. Now that your container is running, you can start working with it. With the `lxc exec` command, you can execute commands inside a container. Use the following command to obtain the details of Ubuntu running inside a container:

```
$ lxc exec c1 -- lsb_release -a
```

```
ubuntu@ubuntu:~$ lxc exec c1 -- lsb_release -a
No LSB modules are available.
Distributor ID: Ubuntu
Description:    Ubuntu 14.04.4 LTS
Release:        14.04
Codename:       trusty
```

5. You can also open a bash shell inside a container, as follows:

```
$ lxc exec c1 -- bash
```

How it works...

Creating images is a time-consuming task. With LXD, the team has solved this problem by downloading the prebuilt images from trusted remote servers. Unlike LXC, where images are built locally, LXD downloads them from the remote servers and keep a local cache of these images for later use. The default installation contains three remote servers:

- **Ubuntu**: This contains all Ubuntu releases
- **Ubuntu-daily**: This contains all Ubuntu daily builds
- **images**: This contains all other Linux distributions

You can get a list of available remote servers with this command:

```
$ lxc remote list
```

Similarly, to get a list of available images on a specific remote server, use the following command:

```
$ lxc image list ubuntu:
```

In the previous example, we used 64-bit Ubuntu 14.04 from one of the preconfigured remote servers (`ubuntu:`). When we start a specific container, LXD checks the local cache for the availability of the respective image; if it's not available locally, the required images gets fetched from the remote server and cached locally for later use. These images are kept in sync with remote updates. They also expire if not used for a specific time period, and expired images are automatically removed by LXD. By default, the expiration period is set to 10 days.

You can find a list of various configuration parameters for LXC and LXD documented on GitHub at `https://github.com/lxc/lxd/blob/master/doc/configuration.md`.

The `lxc launch` command creates a new container and then starts it as well. If you want to just create a container without starting it, you can do that with the `lxc init` command, as follows:

```
$ lxc init ubuntu:xenial c2
```

All containers (or their `rootfs`) are stored under the `/var/lib/lxd/containers` directory, and images are stored under the `/var/lib/lxd/images` directory.

 All LXD containers are non-privileged containers by default. You do not need any special privileges to create and manage containers. On the other hand, LXD does support privileged containers as well.

While starting a container, you can specify the set of configuration parameters using the `--config` flag. LXD also supports configuration profiles. Profiles are a set of configuration parameters that can be applied to a group of containers. Additionally, a container can have multiple profiles. LXD ships with two preconfigured profiles: `default` and `docker`.

To get a list of profiles, use the `lxc profile list` command, and to get the contents of a profile, use the `lxc profile show <profile_name>` command.

Sometimes, you may need to start a container to experiment with something—execute a few random commands and then undo all the changes. LXD allows us to create such throwaway or ephemeral containers with the `-e` flag. By default, all LXD containers are permanent containers. You can start an ephemeral container using the `--ephemeral` or `-e` flag. When stopped, an ephemeral container will be deleted automatically.

With LXD, you can start and manage containers on remote servers as well. For this, the LXD daemon needs to be exposed to the network. This can be done at the time of initializing LXD or with the following commands:

```
$ lxc config set core.https_address "[::]"
$ lxc config set core.trust_password some-password
```

Next, make sure that you can access the remote server and add it as a remote for LXD with the `lxc remote add` command:

```
$ lxc remote add remote01 192.168.0.11  #  lxc remote add name server_ip
```

Now, you can launch containers on the remote server, as follows:

```
$ lxc launch ubuntu:xenial remote01:c1
```

There's more...

Unlike LXC, LXD container images do not support password-based SSH logins. The container still has the SSH daemon running, but login is restricted to a public key. You need to add a key to the container before you can log in with SSH. LXD supports file management with the `lxc file` command; use it as follows to set your public key inside an Ubuntu container:

```
$ lxc file push ~/.ssh/id_rsa.pub \
c1/home/ubuntu/.ssh/authorized_keys \
--mode=0600 --uid=1000
```

Once the public key is set, you can use SSH to connect to the container, as follows:

```
$ ssh ubuntu@container_IP
```

Alternatively, you can directly open a root session inside a container and get a bash shell with `lxc exec`, as follows:

```
$ lxc exec c1 -- bash
```

See also

- ▸ The LXD getting started guide: `https://linuxcontainers.org/lxd/getting-started-cli/`
- ▸ The Ubuntu Server guide for LXC: `https://help.ubuntu.com/lts/serverguide/lxd.html`
- ▸ Container images are created using tools such as debootstrap, which you can read more about at `https://wiki.debian.org/Debootstrap`
- ▸ Creating LXC templates from scratch: `http://wiki.pcprobleemloos.nl/using_lxc_linux_containers_on_debian_squeeze/creating_a_lxc_virtual_machine_template`

Managing LXD containers

We have installed LXD and deployed our first container with it. In this recipe, we will learn various LXD commands that manage the container lifecycle.

Getting ready...

Make sure that you have followed the previous recipes and created your first container.

How to do it...

Follow these steps to manage LXD containers:

1. Before we start with container management, we will need a running container. If you have been following the previous recipes, you should already have a brand new container running on your system. If your container is not already running, you can start it with the `lxc start` command:

   ```
   $ lxc start c1
   ```

2. To check the current state of a container, use `lxc list`, as follows:

   ```
   $ lxc list c1
   ```

   This command should list only containers that have c1 in their name.

3. You can also set the container to start automatically. Set the `boot.autostart` configuration option to `true` and your container will start automatically on system boot. Additionally, you can specify a delay before autostart and a priority in the autostart list:

   ```
   $ lxc config set c1 boot.autostart true
   ```

4. Once your container is running, you can open a bash session inside a container using the `lxc exec` command:

   ```
   $ lxc exec c1 -- bash
   root@c1:~# hostname
   c1
   ```

   This should give you a root shell inside a container. Note that to use bash, your container image should have a bash shell installed in it. With alpine containers, you need to use `sh` as the shell as alpine does not contain the bash shell.

5. LXD provides the option to pause a container when it's not being actively used. A paused container will still hold memory and other resources assigned to it, but not receive any CPU cycles:

```
$ lxc pause c1
```

```
ubuntu@ubuntu:~$ lxc list c1
+--------+--------+----------------------+--------+------------+-----------+
| NAME   | STATE  |         IPV4         | IPV6   |    TYPE    | SNAPSHOTS |
+--------+--------+----------------------+--------+------------+-----------+
| c1     | FROZEN | 10.201.233.13 (eth0) |        | PERSISTENT | 0         |
+--------+--------+----------------------+--------+------------+-----------+
```

6. Containers that are paused can be started again with `lxc start`.

7. You can also restart a container with the `lxc restart` command, with the option to perform a stateful or stateless restart:

```
$ lxc restart --stateless c1
```

8. Once you are done working with the container, you can stop it with the `lxc stop` command. This will release all resources attached to that container:

```
$ lxc stop c1
```

At this point, if your container is an ephemeral container, it will be deleted automatically.

9. If the container is no longer required, you can explicitly delete it with the `lxc delete` command:

```
$ lxc delete c1
```

There's more...

For those who do not like to work with command line tools, you can use a web-based management console known as LXD GUI. This package is still in beta but can be used on your local LXD deployments. It is available on GitHub at `https://github.com/dobin/lxd-webgui`.

See also

▸ Get more details about LXD at `https://www.stgraber.org/2016/03/19/lxd-2-0-your-first-lxd-container-312/`

▸ LXC web panel: `https://lxc-webpanel.github.io/install.html`

Managing LXD containers – advanced options

In this recipe, we will learn about some advanced options provided by LXD.

How to do it...

Follow these steps to deal with LXD containers:

1. Sometimes, you may need to clone a container and have it running as a separate system. LXD provides a `copy` command to create such clones:

   ```
   $ lxc copy c1 c2    # lxc copy source destination
   ```

   You can also create a temporary copy with the `--ephemeral` flag and it will be deleted after one use.

2. Similarly, you can create a container, configure it as per you requirements, have it stored as an image, and use it to create more containers. The `lxc publish` command allows you to export existing containers as a new image. The resulting image will contain all modifications from the original container:

   ```
   $ lxc publish c1 --alias nginx    # after installing nginx
   ```

   The container to be published should be in the stopped state. Alternatively, you can use the `--force` flag to publish a running container, which will internally stop the container before exporting.

3. You can also move the entire container from one system to another. The `move` command helps you with moving containers across hosts. If you move a container on the same host, the original container will be renamed. Note that the container to be renamed must not be running:

   ```
   $ lxc move c1 c2 # container c1 will be renamed to c2
   ```

4. Finally, we have the snapshot and restore functionality. You can create snapshots of the container or, in simple terms, take a backup of its current state. The snapshot can be a stateful snapshot that stores the container's memory state. Use the following command to create a snapshot of your container:

   ```
   $ lxc snapshot c1 snap1   # lxc snapshot container cnapshot
   ```

5. The `lxc list` command will show you the number of snapshots for a given container. To get the details of every snapshot, check the container information with the `lxc info` command:

   ```
   $ lxc info c1
   ...
   ```

```
Snapshots:
    c1/shap1 (taken at 2016/05/22 10:34 UTC) (stateless)
```

 You can skip the snapshot name and LXD will name it for you. But, as of writing this, there's no option to add a description with snapshots. You can use the filename to describe the purpose of each snapshot.

6. Once you have the snapshots created, you can restore it to go back to a point or create new containers out of your snapshots and have both states maintained. To restore your snapshot, use `lxc restore`, as follows:

    ```
    $ lxc restore c1 snap1    # lxc restore container snapshot
    ```

7. To create a new container out of your snapshot, use `lxc copy`, as follows:

    ```
    $ lxc copy c1/snap1 c4  # lxc copy container/snapshot
    new_container
    ```

8. When you no longer need a snapshot, delete it with `lxc delete`, as follows:

    ```
    $ lxc delete c1/snap1      # lxc delete container/snapshot
    ```

How it works...

Most of these commands work with the `rootfs` or `root` filesystem of `containers`. The `rootfs` is stored under the `/var/lib/lxd/containers` directory. Copying creates a copy of the `rootfs` while deleting removes the `rootfs` for a given container. These commands benefit with the use of the ZFS file system. Features such as copy-on-write speed up the copy and snapshot operations while reducing the total disk space use.

Setting resource limits on LXD containers

In this recipe, we will learn to set resource limits on containers. LXD uses the cgroups feature in the Linux kernel to manage resource allocation and limits. Limits can be applied to a single container through configuration or set in a profile, applying limits to a group of containers at once. Limits can be dynamically updated even when the container is running.

How to do it...

We will create a new profile and configure various resource limits in it. Once the profile is ready, we can use it with any number of containers. Follow these steps:

1. Create a new profile with the following command:

   ```
   $ lxc profile create cookbook
   Profile cookbook created
   ```

2. Next, edit the profile with `lxc profile edit`. This will open a text editor with a default profile structure in YML format:

   ```
   $ lxc profile edit cookbook
   ```

   Add the following details to the profile. Feel free to select any parameters and change their values as required:

   ```
   name: cookbook
   config:
     boot.autostart: "true"
     limits.cpu: "1"
     limits.cpu.priority: "10"
     limits.disk.priority: "10"
     limits.memory: 128MB
     limits.processes: "100"
   description: A profile for Ubuntu Cookbook Containers
   devices:
     eth0:
       nictype: bridged
       parent: lxdbr0
       type: nic
   ```

   Save your changes to the profile and exit the text editor.

3. Optionally, you can check the created profile, as follows:

   ```
   $ lxc profile show cookbook
   ```

   ```
   ubuntu@ubuntu:~$ lxc profile show cookbook
   name: cookbook
   config:
     boot.autostart: "true"
     limits.cpu: "1"
     limits.cpu.priority: "10"
     limits.disk.priority: "10"
   ```

4. Now, our profile is ready and can be used with a container to set limits. Create a new container using our profile:

```
$ lxc launch ubuntu:xenial c4 -p cookbook
```

5. This should create and start a new container with the cookbook profile applied to it. You can check the profile in use with the lxc info command:

```
$ lxc info c4
```

```
ubuntu@ubuntu:~$ lxc info c4
Name: c4
Architecture: x86_64
Created: 2016/05/22 17:44 UTC
Status: Running
Type: persistent
Profiles: cookbook
Pid: 13300
```

6. Check the memory limits applied to container c4:

```
$ lxc exec c4 -- free -m
```

7. Profiles can be updated even when they are in use. All containers using that profile will be updated with the respective changes, or return a failure message. Update your profile as follows:

```
$ lxc profile set cookbook limits.memory 256MB
```

How it works...

LXD provides multiple options to set resource limits on containers. You can apply limits using profiles or configure containers separately with the lxc config command. The advantage of creating profiles is that you can have various parameters defined in one central place, and all those parameters can be applied to multiple containers at once. A container can have multiple profiles applied and also have configuration parameters explicitly set. The overlapping parameters will take a value from the last applied profile. Also the parameters that are set explicitly using lxc config will override any values set by profiles.

The LXD installation ships with two preconfigured profiles. One is **default**, which is applied to all containers that do not receive any other profile. This contains a network device for a container. The other profile, named **docker**, configures the required kernel modules to run Docker inside the container. You can view the parameters of any profile with the lxc profile show profile_name command.

In the previous example, we used the `edit` option to edit the profile and set multiple parameters at once. You can also set each parameter separately or update the profile with the `set` option:

```
$ lxc profile set cookbook limits.memory 256MB
```

Similarly, use the `get` option to read any single parameter from a profile:

```
$ lxc profile get cookbook limits.memory
```

Profiles can also be applied to a running container with `lxc profile apply`. The following command will apply two profiles, `default` and `cookbook`, to an existing container, c6:

```
$ lxc profile apply c6 default,cookbook
```

 We could have skipped the network configuration in the `cookbook` profile and had our containers use the default profile along with `cookbook` to combine both configurations.

Updating the profiles will update the configuration for all container using that profile. To modify a single container, you can use `lxc config set` or pass the parameters directly to a new container using the `-c` flag:

```
$ lxc launch ubuntu:xenial c7 -c limits.memory=64MB
```

Similar to `lxc profile`, you can use the edit option with `lxc config` to modify multiple parameters at once. The same command can also be used to configure or read server parameters. When used without any container name, the command applies to the LXD daemon.

There's more...

The `lxc profile` and `lxc config` commands can also be used to attach local devices to containers. Both commands provide the option to work with various devices, which include network, disk IO, and so on. The simplest example will be to pass a local directory to a container, as follows:

```
$ lxc config device add c1 share disk \
source=/home/ubuntu path=home/ubuntu/shared
```

- Read more about setting resource limits at `https://www.stgraber.org/2016/03/26/lxd-2-0-resource-control-412`
- For more details about LXC configuration, check the help menu for the `lxc profile` and `lxc config` commands, as follows:

```
$ lxc config --help
```

Networking with LXD

In this recipe, we will look at LXD network setup. By default, LXD creates an internal bridge network. Containers are set to access the Internet through **Network Address Translation** (**NAT**) but are not accessible from the Internet. We will learn to open a service on a container to the Internet, share a physical network with a host, and set a static IP address to a container.

Getting ready

As always, you will need access to the root account or an account with `sudo` privileges.

Make sure that you have created at least one container.

How to do it...

By default, LXD sets up a NAT network for containers. This is a private network attached to the `lxdbr0` port on the host system. With this setup, containers get access to the Internet, but the containers themselves or the services running in the containers are not accessible from an outside network. To open a container to an external network, you can either set up port forwarding or use a bridge to attach the container directly to the host's network:

1. To set up port forwarding, use the `iptables` command, as follows:

   ```
   $ sudo iptables -t nat -A PREROUTING -p tcp -i eth0 \
   --dport 80 -j DNAT --to 10.106.147.244:80
   ```

   This will forward any traffic on the host TCP port `80` to the containers' TCP port `80` with the IP `10.106.147.244`. Make sure that you change the port and IP address as required.

2. You can also set a bridge that connects all containers directly to your local network. The bridge will use an Ethernet port to connect to the local network. To set a bridge network with the host, we first need to create a bridge on the host and then configure the container to use that bridge adapter.

   To set up a bridge on the host, open the `/etc/network/interfaces` file and add the following lines:

   ```
   auto br0

   iface br0 inet dhcp

       bridge_ports eth0
   ```

   Make sure that you replace `eth0` with the name of the interface connected to the external network.

3. Enable IP forwarding under `sysctl`. Find the following line in `/etc/sysctl.conf` and uncomment it:

   ```
   net.ipv4.ip_forward=1
   ```

4. Start a new bridge interface with the `ifup` command:

   ```
   $ sudo ifup br0
   ```

 Note that if you are connected to a server over SSH, your connection will break. Make sure to have a snapshot of the working state before changing your network configuration.

5. If required, you can restart the networking service, as follows:

   ```
   $ sudo service networking restart
   ```

6. Next, we need to update the LXD configuration to use our new bridge interface. Execute a reconfiguration of the LXD daemon and choose `<No>` when asked to create a new bridge:

   ```
   $ sudo dpkg-reconfigure -p medium lxd
   ```

```
Would you like to setup a network bridge for LXD containers now?

                 <Yes>                          <No>
```

7. Then on the next page, choose `<Yes>` to use an existing bridge:

```
Do you want to use an existing bridge?

              <Yes>                              <No>
```

8. Enter the name of the newly created bridge interface:

```
A valid network interface name (e.g. lxdbr0).

Bridge interface name:

br0_

                        <Ok>
```

This should configure LXD to use our own bridge network and skip the internal bridge. You can check the new configuration under the default profile:

```
$ lxc profile show default
```

```
description: Default LXD profile
devices:
  eth0:
    name: eth0
    nictype: bridged
    parent: br0
    type: nic
```

9. Now, start a new container. It should receive the IP address from the router on your local network. Make sure that your local network has DHCP configured:

```
ubuntu@ubuntu:~$ lxc list
+------+---------+----------------------+------+------------+-----------+
| NAME | STATE   |         IPV4         | IPV6 |    TYPE    | SNAPSHOTS |
+------+---------+----------------------+------+------------+-----------+
| c5   | RUNNING | 192.168.0.104 (eth0) |      | PERSISTENT | 0         |
+------+---------+----------------------+------+------------+-----------+
```

How it works...

By default, LXD sets up a private network for all containers. A separate bridge, lxdbr0, is set up and configured in the default profile. This network is shared (NAT) with the host system, and containers can access the Internet through this network. In the previous example, we used IPtables port forwarding to make the container port 80 available on the external network. This way, containers will still use the same private network, and a single application will be exposed to the external network through the host system. All incoming traffic on host port 80 will be directed to the container's port 80.

You can also set up your own bridge connected to the physical network. With this bridge, all your containers can connect to and be directly accessible over your local network. Your local DHCP will be used to assign IP addresses to containers. Once you create a bridge, you need to configure it with LXD containers either through profiles or separately with container configuration. In the previous example, we reconfigured the LXD network to set a new bridge.

> If you are using virtual machines for hosting containers and want to set up a bridge, then make sure that you have enabled promiscuous mode on the network adapter of the virtual machine. This can be enabled from the network settings of your hypervisor. Also, a bridge setup may not work if your physical machine is using a wireless network.

LXD supports more advanced network configuration by attaching the host eth interface directly to a container. The following settings in the container configuration will set the network type to a physical network and use the host's eth0 directly inside a container. The eth0 interface will be unavailable for the host system till the container is live:

```
$ lxc config device add c1 eth0 nic nictype=physical parent=eth0
```

There's more...

LXD creates a default bridge with the name lxdbr0. The configuration file for this bridge is located at /etc/default/lxd-bridge. This file contains various configuration parameters, such as the address range for the bridge, default domain, and bridge name. An interesting parameter is the additional configuration path for dnsmasq configurations.

The LXD bridge internally uses dnsmasq for DHCP allocation. The additional configuration file can be used to set up various dnsmasq settings, such as address reservation and name resolution for containers.

Edit `/etc/default/lxd-bridge` to point to the dnsmasq configuration file:

```
# Path to an extra dnsmasq configuration file
LXD_CONFILE="/etc/default/dnsmasq.conf"
```

Then, create a new configuration file called `/etc/default/dnsmasq.conf` with the following contents:

```
dhcp-host=c5,10.71.225.100
server=/lxd/10.71.225.1
#interface=lxdbr0
```

This will reserve the IP `10.71.225.100` for the container called `c5`, and you can also ping containers with that name, as follows:

```
$ ping lxd.c5
```

See also

- Read more about bridge configuration at `https://wiki.debian.org/LXC/SimpleBridge`
- Find out more about LXD bridge at the following links:
  - `https://insights.ubuntu.com/2016/04/07/lxd-networking-lxdbr0-explained/`
  - `http://askubuntu.com/questions/754323/lxd-2-0-local-networking`
  - `https://insights.ubuntu.com/2015/11/10/converting-eth0-to-br0-and-getting-all-your-lxc-or-lxd-onto-your-lan/`
- Read more about dnsmasq at `https://wiki.debian.org/HowTo/dnsmasq`
- Sample dnsmasq configuration file: `http://oss.segetech.com/intra/srv/dnsmasq.conf`
- Check the dnsmasq manual pages with the `man dnsmasq` command

Installing Docker

In last few recipes, we learned about LXD, an operating system container service. Now, we will look at a hot new technology called Docker. Docker is an application container designed to package and run a single service. It enables developers to enclose an app with all dependencies in an isolated container environment. Docker helps developers create a reproducible environment with a simple configuration file called a Dockerfile. It also provides portability by sharing the Dockerfile, and developers can be sure that their setup will work the same on any system with the Docker runtime.

Docker is very similar to LXC. Its development started as a wrapper around the LXC API to help DevOps take advantage of containerization. It added some restrictions to allow only a single process to be running in a container, unlike a whole operating system in LXC. In subsequent versions, Docker changed its focus from LXC and started working on a new standard library for application containers, known as **libcontainer**.

It still uses the same base technologies, such as Linux namespaces and control groups, and shares the same kernel with the host operating system. Similarly, Docker makes use of operating system images to run containers. Docker images are a collection of multiple layers, with each layer adding something new to the base layer. This something new can include a service, such as a web server, application code, or even a new set of configurations. Each layer is independent of the layers above it and can be reused to create a new image.

Being an application container, Docker encourages the use of a microservice-based distributed architecture. Think of deploying a simple **WordPress** blog. With Docker, you will need to create at least two different containers, one for the MySQL server and the other for the WordPress code with PHP and the web server. You can separate PHP and web servers in their own containers. While this looks like extra effort, it makes your application much more flexible. It enables you to scale each component separately and improves application availability by separating failure points.

While both LXC and Docker use containerization technologies, their use cases are different. LXC enables you to run an entire lightweight virtual machine in a container, eliminating the inefficiencies of virtualization. Docker enables you to quickly create and share a self-dependent package with your application, which can be deployed on any system running Docker.

In this recipe, we will cover the installation of Docker on Ubuntu Server. The recipes after that will focus on various features provided by Docker.

Getting ready

You will need access to the root account or an account with sudo privileges.

How to do it...

Recently, Docker released version 1.11 of the Docker engine. We will follow the installation steps provided on the Docker site to install the latest available version:

1. First, add a new gpg key:

```
$ sudo apt-key adv --keyserver hkp://p80.pool.sks-
keyservers.net:80 --recv-keys
58118E89F3A912897C070ADBF76221572C52609D
```

2. Next, add a new repository to the local installation sources. This repository is maintained by Docker and contains Docker packages for 1.7.1 and higher versions:

```
$ echo "deb https://apt.dockerproject.org/repo ubuntu-xenial
main" | \
sudo tee /etc/apt/sources.list.d/docker.list
```

> If you are using an Ubuntu version other than 16.04 (Xenial), then make sure that you replace the repository path with the respective codename. For example, on Ubuntu 14.04 (Trusty), use the following repository:
>
> deb https://apt.dockerproject.org/repo ubuntu-trusty main

3. Next, update the apt package list and install Docker with the following commands:

```
$ sudo apt-get update
$ sudo apt-get install docker-engine
```

4. Once the installation completes, you can check the status of the Docker service, as follows:

```
$ sudo service docket status
```

5. Check the installed Docker version with docker version:

```
$ sudo docker version
Client:
 Version:      1.11.1
 API version:  1.23
 ...
Server:
 Version:      1.11.1
 API version:  1.23
 ...
```

6. Download a test container to test the installation. This container will simply print a welcome message and then exit:

```
$ sudo docker run hello-world
```

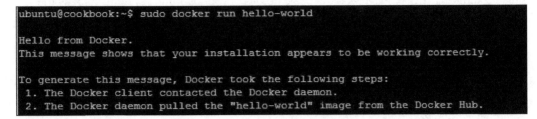

```
ubuntu@cookbook:~$ sudo docker run hello-world

Hello from Docker.
This message shows that your installation appears to be working correctly.

To generate this message, Docker took the following steps:
 1. The Docker client contacted the Docker daemon.
 2. The Docker daemon pulled the "hello-world" image from the Docker Hub.
```

7. At this point, you need to use `sudo` with every Docker command. To enable a non-sudo user to use Docker, or to simply avoid the repeated use of `sudo`, add the respective usernames to the `docker` group:

```
$ sudo gpasswd -a ubuntu docker
```

 The `docker` group has privileges equivalent to the root account. Check the official Docker installation documentation for more details.

Now, update group membership, and you can use Docker without the `sudo` command:

```
$ newgrp docker
```

How it works...

This recipe installs Docker from the official Docker repository. This way, we can be sure to get the latest version. The Ubuntu 16.04 repository also contains the package for Docker with version 1.10. If you prefer to install from the Ubuntu repository, it's an even easier task with a single command, as follows:

```
$ sudo apt-get install docker.io
```

As of writing this, Docker 1.11 is the latest stable release and the first release to have been built on Open Container Initiative standards. This version is built on **runc** and **containerd**.

There's more...

Docker provides a quick installation script, which can be used to install Docker with a single command. This scripts reads the basic details of your operating system, such as the distribution and version, and then executes all the required steps to install Docker. You can use the bootstrap script as follows:

```
$ sudo curl -sSL https://get.docker.com | sudo sh
```

Note that with this command, the script will be executed with `sudo` privileges. Make sure you cross-check the script's contents before executing it. You can download the script without executing it, as follows:

```
$ curl -sSL https://get.docker.com -o docker_install.sh
```

See also

- The Docker installation guide: `http://docs.docker.com/installation/ubuntulinux/`
- Operating system containers versus application containers: `https://blog.risingstack.com/operating-system-containers-vs-application-containers/`
- What Docker adds to lxc-tools: `http://stackoverflow.com/questions/17989306/what-does-docker-add-to-lxc-tools-the-userspace-lxc-tools`
- A curated list of Docker resources: `https://github.com/veggiemonk/awesome-docker`

Starting and managing Docker containers

So, we have installed the latest Docker binary. In this recipe, we will start a new container with Docker. We will see some basic Docker commands to start and manage Docker containers.

Getting ready

Make sure that you have installed Docker and set your user as a member of the Docker group.

You may need `sudo` privileges for some commands.

How to do it...

Let's create a new Docker container and start it. With Docker, you can quickly start a container with the `docker run` command:

1. Start a new Docker container with the following command:

   ```
   $ docker run -it --name dc1 ubuntu /bin/bash
   Unable to find image 'ubuntu:trusty' locally
   trusty: Pulling from library/ubuntu
   6599cadaf950: Pull complete
   23eda618d451: Pull complete
   ...
   Status: Downloaded newer image for ubuntu:trusty
   root@bd8c99397e52:/#
   ```

   Once a container has been started, it will drop you in a new shell running inside it. From here, you can execute limited Ubuntu or general Linux commands, which will be executed inside the container.

2. When you are done with the container, you can exit from the shell by typing `exit` or pressing *Ctrl + D*. This will terminate your shell and stop the container as well.

3. Use the `docker ps` command to list all the containers and check the status of your last container:

   ```
   $ docker ps -a
   ```

   ```
   ubuntu@cookbook:~$ docker ps -a
   CONTAINER ID          IMAGE                        COMMAND              CREATED
               STATUS                  PORTS               NAMES
   708fea034cbe          ubuntu                       "/bin/bash"           59 second
   s ago        Exited (0) 28 seconds ago                 dc1
   7c289a54b60b          hello-world                  "/hello"              7 minutes
    ago        Exited (0) 7 minutes ago                  condescending_bo
   ```

   By default, `docker ps` lists all running containers. As our container is no longer running, we need to use the `-a` flag to list all available containers.

4. To start the container again, you can use the `docker start` command. You can use the container name or ID to specify the container to be started:

   ```
   $ docker start -ia dc1
   ```

   ```
   ubuntu@cookbook:~$ docker start -ia dc1
   root@708fea034cbe:/#
   root@708fea034cbe:/# exit
   exit
   ubuntu@cookbook:~$
   ```

   The `-i` flag will start the container in interactive mode and the `-a` flag will attach to a terminal inside the container. To start a container in detached mode, use the `start` command without any flags. This will start the container in the background and return to the host shell:

   ```
   $ docker start dc1
   ```

5. You can open a terminal inside a detached container with `docker attach`:

   ```
   $ docker attach dc1
   ```

6. Now, to detach a terminal and keep the container running, you need the key combinations *Ctrl + P* and *Ctrl + Q*. Alternatively, you can type `exit` or press *Ctrl + C* to exit the terminal and stop the container.

7. To get all the details of a container, use the `docker inspect` command with the name or ID of the container:

   ```
   $ docker inspect dc1 | less
   ```

   This command will list all the details of the container, including container status, network status and address, and container configuration files.

    Use `grep` to filter container information. For example, to get the IP address from the `docker inspect` output, use this:

   ```
   $ docker inspect dc1 | grep-iipaddr
   ```

8. To execute a command inside a container, use `docker exec`. For example, the following command gets the environment variables from the `dc1` container:

   ```
   $ docker exec dc1 env
   ```

This one gets the IP address of a container:

```
$ docker exec dc1 ifconfig
```

```
ubuntu@cookbook:~$ docker exec dc1 ifconfig
eth0      Link encap:Ethernet  HWaddr 02:42:ac:11:00:02
          inet addr:172.17.0.2  Bcast:0.0.0.0  Mask:255.255.0.0
          inet6 addr: fe80::42:acff:fe11:2/64 Scope:Link
          UP BROADCAST RUNNING MULTICAST  MTU:1500  Metric:1
          RX packets:8 errors:0 dropped:0 overruns:0 frame:0
```

9. To get the processes running inside a container, use the docker top command:

```
$ docker top dc1
```

```
ubuntu@cookbook:~$ docker top dc1
UID                 PID                 PPID                C
STIME               TTY                 TIME                CMD
root                6495                866                 0
05:23               pts/12              00:00:00            /bin/bash
```

10. Finally, to stop the container, use docker stop, which will gracefully stop the container after stopping processes running inside it:

```
$ docker stop dc1
```

11. When you no longer need the container, you can use docker rm to remove/delete it:

```
$ docker rm dc1
```

 Want to remove all stopped containers with a single command? Use this:

```
$ docker rm $(dockerps -aq)
```

How it works...

We started our first Docker container with the docker run command. With this command, we instructed the Docker daemon to start a new container with an image called Ubuntu, start an interactive session (-i), and allocate a terminal (-t). We also elected to name our container with the --name flag and execute the /bin/bash command inside a container once it started.

The Docker daemon will search for Ubuntu images in the local cache or download the image from Docker Hub if the specified image is not available in the local cache. Docker Hub is a central Docker image repository. It will take some time to download and extract all the layers of the images. Docker maintains container images in the form of multiple layers. These layers can be shared across multiple container images. For example, if you have Ubuntu running on a server and you need to download the Apache container based on Ubuntu, Docker will only download the additional layer for Apache as it already has Ubuntu in the local cache, which can be reused.

Docker provides various other commands to manage containers and images. We have already used a few of them in the previous example. You can get the full list of all available commands from the command prompt itself, by typing `docker` followed by the *Enter* key. All commands are listed with their basic descriptions. To get more details on any specific subcommand, use its `help` menu, as follows:

```
$ docker rmi --help
```

There's more...

Docker images can be used to quickly create `runc` containers, as follows:

```
$ sudo apt-get install runc
$ mkdir -p runc/rootfs && cd runc
$ docker run --name alpine alpine sh
$ docker export alpine > alpine.tar
$ tar -xf alpine.tar -C rootfs
$ runc spec
$ sudo runc start alpine
```

See also

- Docker run documentation: `http://docs.docker.com/engine/reference/commandline/run/`
- Check manual entries for any Docker command: `$ man docker create`

Creating images with a Dockerfile

This recipe explores image creation with Dockerfiles. Docker images can be created in multiple ways, which includes using Dockerfiles, using `docker commit` to save the container state as a new image, or using `docker import`, which imports chroot directory structure as a Docker image.

In this recipe, we will focus on **Dockerfiles** and related details. Dockerfiles help in automating identical and repeatable image creation. They contain multiple commands in the form of instructions to build a new image. These instructions are then passed to the Docker daemon through the `docker build` command. The Docker daemon independently executes these commands one by one. The resulting images are committed as and when necessary, and it is possible that multiple intermediate images are created. The build process will reuse existing images from the image cache to speed up build process.

Getting ready

Make sure that your Docker daemon is installed and working properly.

How to do it...

1. First, create a new empty directory and enter it. This directory will hold our Dockerfile:

   ```
   $ mkdir myimage
   ```

   ```
   $ cd myimage
   ```

2. Create a new file called `Dockerfile`:

   ```
   $ touch Dockerfile
   ```

3. Now, add the following lines to the newly created file. These lines are the instructions to create an image with the Apache web server. We will look at more details later in this recipe:

   ```
   FROM ubuntu:trusty

   MAINTAINER ubuntu server cookbook


   # Install base packages

   RUN apt-get update && apt-get -yq install apache2 && \

   apt-get clean && \

   rm -rf /var/lib/apt/lists/*


   RUN echo "ServerName localhost" >>
   /etc/apache2/apache2.conf


   ENV APACHE_RUN_USER www-data

   ENV APACHE_RUN_GROUP www-data

   ENV APACHE_LOG_DIR /var/log/apache2
   ```

```
ENV APACHE_PID_FILE /var/run/apache2.pid

ENV APACHE_LOCK_DIR /var/www/html


VOLUME ["/var/www/html"]

EXPOSE 80

CMD ["/usr/sbin/apache2", "-D", "FOREGROUND"]
```

4. Save the changes and start the `docker build` process with the following command:

   `$ docker build.`

This will build a new image with Apache server installed on it. The build process will take a little longer to complete and output the final image ID:

```
Step 12 : CMD /usr/sbin/apache2 -D FOREGROUND
 ---> Running in d75bff891353
 ---> e9cfe1181171
Removing intermediate container d75bff891353
Successfully built e9cfe1181171
```

5. Once the image is ready, you can start a new container with it:

   `$ docker run -p 80:80 -d image_id`

   Replace `image_id` with the image ID from the result of the build process.

6. Now, you can list the running containers with the `docker ps` command. Notice the `ports` column of the output:

    `$ docker ps`

```
ubuntu@cookbook:~$ docker run -p 80:80 -d e9cfe1181171
255c06f2478db50e33a501535c19880d825153fd6134f507514d6dfd525d1d75
ubuntu@cookbook:~$ docker ps
CONTAINER ID       IMAGE            COMMAND                CREATED
     STATUS                PORTS                NAMES
255c06f2478d       e9cfe1181171       "/usr/sbin/apache2 -D"   6 seconds ago
     Up 4 seconds          0.0.0.0:80->80/tcp    sad_keller
ubuntu@cookbook:~$
```

Apache server's default page should be accessible at your host domain name or IP address.

How it works...

A Dockerfile is a document that contains several commands to create a new image. Each command in a Dockerfile creates a new container, executes that command on the new container, and then commits the changes to create a new image. This image is then used as a base for executing the next command. Once the final command is executed, Docker returns the ID of the final image as an output of the `docker build` command.

This recipe demonstrates the use of a Dockerfile to create images with the Apache web server. The Dockerfile uses a few available instructions. As a convention, the instructions file is generally called **Dockerfile**. Alternatively, you can use the `-f` flag to pass the instruction file to the Docker daemon. A Dockerfile uses the following format for instructions:

`# comment`

`INSTRUCTION argument`

All instructions are executed one by one in a given order. A Dockerfile must start with the FROM instruction, which specifies the base image to be used. We have started our Dockerfile with **Ubuntu:trusty** as the base image. The next line specifies the maintainer or the author of the Dockerfile, with the MAINTAINER instruction.

Followed by the author definition, we have used the RUN instruction to install Apache on our base image. The RUN instruction will execute a given command on the top read-write layer and then commit the results. The committed image will be used as a starting point for the next instruction. If you've noticed the RUN instruction and the arguments passed to it, you can see that we have passed multiple commands in a chained format. This will execute all commands on a single image and avoid any cache-related problems. The apt-get clean and rm commands are used to remove any unused files and minimize the resulting image size.

After the RUN command, we have set some environment variables with the ENV instruction. When we start a new container from this image, all environment variables are exported to the container environment and will be accessible to processes running inside the container. In this case, the process that will use such a variable is the Apache server.

Next, we have used the VOLUME instruction with the path set to /var/www/html. This instruction creates a directory on the host system, generally under Docker root, and mounts it inside the container on the specified path. Docker uses volumes to decouple containers from the data they create. So even if the container using this volume is removed, the data will persist on the host system. You can specify volumes in a Dockerfile or in the command line while running the container, as follows:

```
$ docker run -v /var/www/html image_id
```

You can use docker inspect to get the host path of the volumes attached to container.

Finally, we have used the EXPOSE instruction, which will expose the specified container port to the host. In this case, it's port 80, where the Apache server will be listening for web requests. To use an exposed port on the host system, we need to use either the -p flag to explicitly specify the port mapping or the -P flag, which will dynamically map the container port to the available host port. We have used the -p flag with the argument 80:80, which will map the container port 80 to the host port 80 and make Apache accessible through the host.

The last instruction, CMD, sets the command to be executed when running the image. We are using the executable format of the CMD instruction, which specifies the executable to be run with its command-line arguments. In this case, our executable is the Apache binary with -D FOREGROUND as an argument. By default, the Apache parent process will start, create a child process, and then exit. If the Apache process exits, our container will be turned off as it no longer has a running process. With the -D FOREGROUND argument, we instruct Apache to run in the foreground and keep the parent process active. We can have only one CMD instruction in a Dockerfile.

The instruction set includes some more instructions, such as ADD, COPY, and ENTRYPOINT. I cannot cover them all because it would run into far too many pages. You can always refer to the official Docker site to get more details. Check out the reference URLs in the *See also* section.

There's more...

Once the image has been created, you can share it on Docker Hub, a central repository of public and private Docker images. You need an account on Docker Hub, which can be created for free. Once you get your Docker Hub credentials, you can use `docker login` to connect your Docker daemon with Docker Hub and then use `docker push` to push local images to the Docker Hub repository. You can use the respective `help` commands or manual pages to get more details about `docker login` and `docker push`.

Alternatively, you can also set up your own local image repository. Check out the Docker documents for deploying your own registry at `https://docs.docker.com/registry/deploying/`.

 GitLab, an open source Git hosting server, now supports container repositories. This feature has been added in GitLab version 8.8. Refer to *Chapter 11, Git Hosting*, for more details and installation instructions for GitLab.

We need a base image or any other image as a starting point for the Dockerfile. But how do we create our own base image?

Base images can be created with tools such as **debootstrap** and **supermin**. We need to create a distribution-specific directory structure and put all the necessary files inside it. Later, we can create a tarball of this directory structure and import the tarball as a Docker image using the `docker import` command.

See also

- ▶ Dockerfile reference: `https://docs.docker.com/reference/builder/`
- ▶ Dockerfile best practices: `https://docs.docker.com/articles/dockerfile_best-practices`
- ▶ More Dockerfile best practices: `http://crosbymichael.com/dockerfile-best-practices.html`
- ▶ Create a base image: `http://docs.docker.com/engine/articles/baseimages/`

Understanding Docker volumes

One of the most common questions seen on Docker forums is how to separate data from containers. This is because any data created inside containers is lost when the container gets deleted. Using `docker commit` to store data inside Docker images is not a good idea. To solve this problem, Docker provides an option called data volumes. Data volumes are special shared directories that can be used by one or more Docker containers. These volumes persist even when the container is deleted. These directories are created on the host file system, usually under the `/var/lib/docker/` directory.

In this recipe, we will learn to use Docker volumes, share host directories with Docker containers, and learn basic backup and restore tricks that can be used with containers.

Getting ready

Make sure that you have the Docker daemon installed and running. We will need two or more containers.

You may need `sudo` privileges to access the `/var/lib/docker` directory.

How to do it...

Follow these steps to understand Docker volumes:

1. To add a data volume to a container, use the `-v` flag with the `docker run` command, like so:

   ```
   $ docker run -dP -v /var/lib/mysql --name mysql\
   -e MYSQL_ROOT_PASSWORD= passwdmysql:latest
   ```

   This will create a new MySQL container with a volume created at `/var/lib/mysql` inside the container. If the directory already exists on the volume path, the volume will overlay the directory contents.

2. Once the container has been started, you can get the host-specific path of the volume with the `docker inspect` command. Look for the `Mounts` section in the output of `docker inspect`:

   ```
   $ docker inspect mysql
   ```

```
    "Mounts": [
        {
            "Name": "99999cdfbab177220de964b63c6f6a3a283b68067765d9199fb7bd09350
1d548",
            "Source": "/var/lib/docker/volumes/99999cdfbab177220de964b63c6f6a3a2
83b68067765d9199fb7bd093501d548/_data",
            "Destination": "/var/lib/mysql",
            "Driver": "local",
            "Mode": "",
            "RW": true
        }
```

3. To mount a specific directory from the host system as a data volume, use the following syntax:

    ```
    $ mkdir ~/mkdir
    $ docker run -dP -v ~/mysql:/var/lib/mysql \
    --name mysql mysql:latest
    ```

    This will create a new directory named `mysql` at the home path and mount it as a volume inside a container at `/var/lib/mysql`.

4. To share a volume between multiple containers, you can use named volume containers.

    First, create a container with a volume attached to it. The following command will create a container with its name set to `mysql`:

    ```
    $ docker run -dP -v /var/lib/mysql --name mysql\
    -e MYSQL_ROOT_PASSWORD= passwd mysql:latest
    ```

5. Now, create a new container using the volume exposed by the `mysql` container and list all the files available in the container:

    ```
    $ docker run --rm --volumes-from mysql ubuntu ls -l
    /var/lib/mysql
    ```

```
ubuntu@cookbook:~$ docker run --rm --volumes-from mysql ubuntu ls -l /var/lib/my
sql
total 188444
-rw-r----- 1 999 999       56 Nov 10 06:10 auto.cnf
-rw-r----- 1 999 999     1319 Nov 10 06:10 ib_buffer_pool
-rw-r----- 1 999 999 50331648 Nov 10 06:10 ib_logfile0
-rw-r----- 1 999 999 50331648 Nov 10 06:10 ib_logfile1
-rw-r----- 1 999 999 79691776 Nov 10 06:10 ibdata1
```

6. To back up data from the `mysql` container, use the following command:

```
$ docker run --rm--volumes-from mysql -v ~/backup:/backup \
$ tar cvf /backup/mysql.tar /var/lib/mysql
```

7. Docker volumes are not deleted when containers are removed. To delete volumes along with a container, you need to use the `-v` flag with the `docker rm` command:

```
$ dockerrm -v mysql
```

How it works...

Docker volumes are designed to provide persistent storage, separate from the containers' life cycles. Even if the container gets deleted, the volume still persists unless it's explicitly specified to delete the volume with the container. Volumes can be attached while creating a container using the `docker create` or `docker run` commands. Both commands support the `-v` flag, which accepts volume arguments. You can add multiple volumes by repeatedly using the volume flag. Volumes can also be created in a Dockerfile using the `VOLUME` instruction.

When the `-v` flag is followed by a simple directory path, Docker creates a new directory inside a container as a data volume. This data volume will be mapped to a directory on the host filesystem under the `/var/lib/docker` directory. Docker volumes are read-write enabled by default, but you can mark a volume to be read-only using the following syntax:

```
$ docker run -dP -v /var/lib/mysql:ro --name mysql mysql:latest
```

Once a container has been created, you can get the details of all the volumes used by it, as well as its host-specific path, with the `docker inspect` command. The `Mounts` section from the output of `docker inspect` lists all volumes with their respective names and paths on the host system and path inside a container.

Rather than using a random location as a data volume, you can also specify a particular directory on the host to be used as a data volume. Add a host directory along with the volume argument, and Docker will map the volume to that directory:

```
$ docker run -dP -v ~/mysql:/var/lib/mysql \
--name mysql mysql:latest
```

In this case, `/var/lib/mysql` from the container will be mapped to the `mysql` directory located at the user's home address.

Need to share a single file from a host system with a container? Sure, Docker supports that too. Use `docker run -v` and specify the file source on the host and destination inside the container. Check out following example command:

```
$ docker run --rmd -v ~/.bash_history:/.bash_history ubuntu
```

The other option is to create a named data volume container or data-only container. You can create a named container with attached volumes and then use those volumes inside other containers using the `docker run --volumes-from` command. The data volumes container need not be running to access volumes attached to it. These volumes can be shared by multiple containers, plus you can create temporary, throwaway application containers by separating persistent data storage. Even if you delete a temporary container using a named volume, your data is still safe with a volume container.

From Docker version 1.9 onwards, a separate command, `docker volume`, is available to manage volumes. With this update, you can create and manage volumes separately from containers. Docker volumes support various backend drivers, including AUFS, OverlayFS, BtrFS, and ZFS. A simple command to create a new volume will be as follows:

```
$ docker volume create --name=myvolume
$ docker run -v myvolume:/opt alpine sh
```

See also

 ▶ The Docker volumes guide: `http://docs.docker.com/engine/userguide/dockervolumes/`

 ▶ Clean up orphaned volumes with this script: `https://github.com/chadoe/docker-cleanup-volumes`

Deploying WordPress using a Docker network

In this recipe, we will learn to use a Docker network to set up a WordPress server. We will create two containers, one for MySQL and the other for WordPress. Additionally, we will set up a private network for both MySQL and WordPress.

How to do it...

Let's start by creating a separate network for WordPress and the MySQL containers:

1. A new network can be created with the following command:

    ```
    $ docker network create wpnet
    ```

2. Check whether the network has been created successfully with `docker network ls`:

    ```
    $ docker network ls
    ```

```
ubuntu@cookbook:~$ docker network create wpnet
d2405dfb37f4d450e09b0f62ca097fd85da9017016184a8ee038c5e27e5b30cd
ubuntu@cookbook:~$ docker network ls
NETWORK ID          NAME          DRIVER
d3c35f350f8e        bridge        bridge
fd9b429d3539        none          null
b9e3d814828e        host          host
d2405dfb37f4        wpnet         bridge
```

3. You can get details of the new network with the `docker network inspect` command:

    ```
    $ docker network inspect wpnet
    ```

```
ubuntu@cookbook:~$ docker network inspect wpnet
[
    {
        "Name": "wpnet",
        "Id": "d2405dfb37f4d450e09b0f62ca097fd85da9017016184a8ee038c5e27e5b30cd"

        "Scope": "local",
        "Driver": "bridge",
        "IPAM": {
            "Driver": "default",
            "Config": [
                {}
            ]
        },
        "Containers": {},
        "Options": {}
```

4. Next, start a new MySQL container and set it to use wpnet:

    ```
    $ docker run --name mysql -d \
    -e MYSQL_ROOT_PASSWORD=password \
    --net wpnet mysql
    ```

5. Now, create a container for WordPress. Make sure the `WORDPRESS_DB_HOST` argument matches the name given to the MySQL container:

```
$ docker run --name wordpress -d -p 80:80 \
--net wpnet\
-e WORDPRESS_DB_HOST=mysql\
-e WORDPRESS_DB_PASSWORD=password wordpress
```

6. Inspect `wpnet` again. This time, it should list two containers:

```
"Containers": {
    "278abce759709f28a45dac29fc79ca13104a7be5bdb45c3bfff326a3ae6a6262":
{
        "EndpointID": "84ce992c28743857d3ca478bcaead36262f58f5d81433a9dd
46e06ef63913910",
        "MacAddress": "02:42:ac:12:00:02",
        "IPv4Address": "172.18.0.2/16",
        "IPv6Address": ""
    },
    "d0318648190de753188f9d8aa42c5f58e0333f2b503ddb6c9e260ac98e37be2e":
{
        "EndpointID": "dc3aa8f8b0c01ef9c7080fc875dd7a2e4d1a5e3d459249d64
ed5fd117b8faa1a",
        "MacAddress": "02:42:ac:12:00:03",
        "IPv4Address": "172.18.0.3/16",
        "IPv6Address": ""
    }
},
```

Now, you can access the WordPress installation at your host domain name or IP address.

How it works...

Docker introduced the **container networking model** (**CNM**) with Docker version 1.9. CNM enables users to create small, private networks for a group of containers. Now, you can set up a new software-assisted network with a simple `docker network create` command. The Docker network supports bridge and overlay drivers for networks out of the box. You can use plugins to add other network drivers. The bridge network is a default driver used by a Docker network. It provides a network similar to the default Docker network, whereas an overlay network enables multihost networking for Docker clusters.

This recipe covers the use of a bridge network for wordpress containers. We have created a simple, isolated bridge network using the `docker network` command. Once the network has been created, you can set containers to use this network with the `--net` flag to `docker run` command. If your containers are already running, you can add a new network interface to them with the `docker network connect` command, as follows:

```
$ # docker network connect network_name container_name
$ docker network connect wpnet mysql
```

Similarly, you can use `docker network disconnect` to disconnect or remove a container from a specific network. Additionally, this network provides an inbuilt discovery feature. With discovery enabled, we can communicate with other containers using their names. We used this feature while connecting the MySQL container to the wordpress container. For the `WORDPRESS_DB_HOST` parameter, we used the container name rather than the IP address or FQDN.

If you've noticed, we have not mentioned any port mapping for the `mysql` container. With this new wpnet network, we need not create any port mapping on the MySQL container. The default MySQL port is exposed by the `mysql` container and the service is accessible only to containers running on the wpnet network. The only port available to the outside world is port `80` from the wordpress container. We can easily hide the WordPress service behind a load balancer and use multiple wordpress containers with just the load balancer exposed to the outside world.

There's more...

Docker also supports links to create secure communication links between two or more containers. You can set up a WordPress site using linked containers as follows:

1. First, create a `mysql` container:

    ```
    $ docker run --name mysql -d \
    -e MYSQL_ROOT_PASSWORD=password mysql
    ```

2. Now, create a `wordpress` container and link it with the `mysql` container:

    ```
    $ docker run --name wordpress -d -p 80:80 --link mysql:mysql
    ```

    And you are done. All arguments for `wordpress`, such as DB_HOST and ROOT_PASSWORD, will be taken from the linked `mysql` container.

The other option to set up WordPress is to set up both WordPress and MySQL in a single container. This needs process management tools such as **supervisord** to run two or more processes in a single container. Docker allows only one process per container by default.

See also

You can find the respective Dockerfiles for MySQL and WordPress containers at the following addresses:

- ▶ Docker Hub WordPress: `https://hub.docker.com/_/wordpress/`
- ▶ Docker Hub MySQL: `https://hub.docker.com/_/mysql/`
- ▶ Docker networking: `https://blog.docker.com/2015/11/docker-multi-host-networking-ga/`
- ▶ Networking for containers using libnetwork: `https://github.com/docker/libnetwork`

Monitoring Docker containers

In this recipe, we will learn to monitor Docker containers.

How to do it...

Docker provides inbuilt monitoring with the `docker stats` command, which can be used to get a live stream of the resource utilization of Docker containers.

1. To monitor multiple containers at once using their respective IDs or names, use this command:

```
$ docker stats mysql f9617f4b716c
```

```
CONTAINER              CPU %                   MEM USAGE / LIMIT    MEM %
  NET I/O                 BLOCK I/O
mysql                  0.03%                    438.5 MB / 4.145 GB  10.58%
  2.656 kB / 1.301 kB    32.49 MB / 290.1 MB
wordpress              0.00%                    84.7 MB / 4.145 GB   2.04%
  1.301 kB / 1.36 kB     54.92 MB / 49.15 kB
```

> If you need to monitor all running containers, use the following command:
> ```
> $ docker stats $(dockerps -q)
> ```

2. With `docker logs`, you can fetch logs of your application running inside a container. This can be used similarly to the `tail -f` command:

```
$ docker logs -f ubuntu
```

3. Docker also records state change events from containers. These events include start, stop, create, kill, and so on. You can get real-time events with `docker events`:

```
$ docker events
```

To get past events, use the `--since` flag with `docker events`:

```
$ docker events --since '2015-11-01'
```

4. You can also check the changes in the container filesystem with the `docker diff` command. This will list newly added (A), changed (C), or deleted (D) files.

```
$ docker diff ubuntu
```

5. Another useful command is `docker top`, which helps look inside a container. This commands displays the processes running inside a container:

```
$ docker top ubuntu
```

How it works...

Docker provides various inbuilt commands to monitor containers and the processes running inside them. It uses native system constructs such as namespaces and cgroups. Most of these statistics are collected from the native system. Logs are directly collected from running processes.

Need something more, possibly a tool with graphical output? There are various such tools available. One well-known tool is **cAdvisor** by Google. You can run the tool itself as a Docker container, as follows:

```
docker run -d -p 8080:8080 --name cadvisor \
  --volume=/:/rootfs:ro \
  --volume=/var/run:/var/run:rw \
  --volume=/sys:/sys:ro \
  --volume=/var/lib/docker/:/var/lib/docker:ro \
google/cadvisor:latest
```

Once the container has been started, you can access the UI at your server domain or IP on port `8080` or any other port that you use. cAdvisor is able to monitor both LXC and Docker containers. In addition, it can report host system resources.

There's more...

Various external tools are available that provide monitoring and troubleshooting services. **Sysdig** is a similar command-line tool that can be used to monitor Linux systems and containers. Read some examples of using sysdig at `https://github.com/draios/sysdig/wiki/Sysdig%20Examples`.

Also, check out Sysdig Falco, an open source behavioral monitor with container support.

See also

- ▶ Docker runtime metrics at `http://docs.docker.com/v1.8/articles/runmetrics/`
- ▶ cAdvisor at GitHub: `https://github.com/google/cadvisor`

Securing Docker containers

In this recipe, we will learn Docker configurations that may result in slightly improved security for your containers. Docker uses some advanced features in the latest Linux kernel, which include kernel namespaces to provide process isolation, control groups to control resource allocation, and kernel capabilities and user namespaces to run unprivileged containers. As stated on the Docker documentation page, Docker containers are, by default, quite secure.

This recipe covers some basic steps to improve Docker security and reduce the attack surface on the Ubuntu host as well as the Docker daemon.

How to do it...

The first and most common thing is to use the latest versions of your software. Make sure that you are using the latest Ubuntu version with all security updates applied and that your Docker version is the latest stable version:

1. Upgrade your Ubuntu host with the following commands:

   ```
   $ sudo apt-get update
   $ sudo apt-get upgrade
   ```

2. If you used a Docker-maintained repository when installing Docker, you need not care about Docker updates, as the previous commands will update your Docker installation as well.

3. Set a proper firewall on your host system. Ubuntu comes preinstalled with UFW; you simply need to add the necessary rules and enable the firewall. Refer to *Chapter 2, Networking* for more details on UFW configuration.

   On Ubuntu systems, Docker ships with the **AppArmor** profile. This profile is installed and enforced with a Docker installation. Make sure you have AppArmor installed and working properly. AppArmor will provide better security against unknown vulnerabilities:

   ```
   $ sudo apparmor_status
   ```

4. Next, we will move on to configure the Docker daemon. You can get a list of all available options with the `docker daemon --help` command:

   ```
   $ docker daemon --help
   ```

5. You can configure these settings in the Docker configuration file at `/etc/default/docker`, or start the Docker daemon with all required settings from the command line.

6. Edit the Docker configuration and add the following settings to the `DOCKER_OPTS` section:

   ```
   $ sudo nano /etc/default/docker
   ```

7. Turn off inter-container communication:

   ```
   --icc=false
   ```

8. Set default ulimit restrictions:

   ```
   --default-ulimitnproc=512:1024 --default-ulimitnofile=50:100
   ```

9. Set the default storage driver to overlayfs:

   ```
   ---storage-driver=overlay
   ```

10. Once you have configured all these settings, restart the Docker daemon:

    ```
    $ sudo service docker restart
    ```

11. Now, you can use the security bench script provided by Docker. This script checks for common security best practices and gives you a list of all the things that need to be improved.

12. Clone the script from the Docker GitHub repository:

    ```
    $ git clone https://github.com/docker/docker-bench-security.git
    ```

13. Execute the script:

```
$ cd docker-bench-security
$ sh docker-bench-security.sh
```

```
[INFO] 1 - Host Configuration
[WARN] 1.1   - Create a separate partition for containers
[PASS] 1.2   - Use an updated Linux Kernel
[PASS] 1.5   - Remove all non-essential services from the host - Network
[PASS] 1.6   - Keep Docker up to date
[INFO] 1.7   - Only allow trusted users to control Docker daemon
```

Try to fix the issues reported by this script.

14. Now, we will look at Docker container configurations.

The most important part of a Docker container is its image. Make sure that you download or pull the images from a trusted repository. You can get most of the images from the official Docker repository, Docker Hub.

15. Alternatively, you can build the images on your own server. Dockerfiles for the most popular images are quite easily available and you can easily build images after verifying their contents and making any changes if required.

When building your own images, make sure you don't add the root user:

```
RUN group add -r user && user add -r -g user user
USER user
```

16. When creating a new container, make sure that you configure CPU and memory limits as per the containers requirements. You can also pass container-specific ulimit settings when creating containers:

```
$ docker run --cpu-shares1024 --memory 512 --cpuset-cpus 1
```

17. Whenever possible, set your containers to read-only:

```
$ docker run --read-only
```

18. Use read-only volumes:

```
$ docker run -v /shared/path:/container/path:ro ubuntu
```

19. Try not to publish application ports. Use a private Docker network or Docker links when possible. For example, when setting up WordPress in the previous recipe, we used a Docker network and connected WordPress and MySQL without exposing MySQL ports.

20. You can also publish ports to a specific container with its IP address. This may create problems when using multiple containers, but is good for a base setup:

```
$ docker run -p 127.0.0.1:3306:3306 mysql
```

See also

▸ Most of these recommendations are taken from the Docker security cheat sheet at https://github.com/konstruktoid/Docker/blob/master/Security/

▸ The Docker bench security script: https://github.com/docker/docker-bench-security

▸ The Docker security documentation: http://docs.docker.com/engine/articles/security/

9
Streaming with Ampache

In this chapter, we will cover the following recipes:

- ▶ Installing the Ampache server
- ▶ Uploading contents and creating catalogs
- ▶ Setting on-the-fly transcoding
- ▶ Enabling API access for remote streaming
- ▶ Streaming music with Ampache

Introduction

This chapter covers the installation and configuration of the open source audio and video streaming service, Ampache. It is a web-based streaming application that allows you to upload your own audio/video contents and access them across multiple Internet-enabled devices. You can easily set up your home media server using Ampache and your old personal computer running Ubuntu. We will focus on installing Ampache on the Ubuntu server, but you can install Ampache on any Linux distribution of your choice.

Installing the Ampache server

This recipe covers the installation of the Ampache server. It is a simple PHP-based web application. Once installed and set up, you can use a web interface to play your audio/video files or use any of the various popular streaming clients to stream content over the intranet or even the Internet.

Getting ready

We will be using Ubuntu Server 16.04, but you can choose to have any version of Ubuntu.

Additionally, we will need the Samba server. It will be used as shared network storage.

As always, access to a root account or an account with `sudo` privileges will be required.

How to do it...

Ampache is a web application developed in PHP. We will start the installation with the LAMP stack. This recipe covers installation with the Apache web server, but you can choose any other web server:

1. Install the LAMP stack if it's not already installed:

    ```
    $ sudo apt-get update
    $ sudo apt-get install apache2 mysql-server-5.5 php7 \
    php7-mysql php7-curl libapache2-mod-php7
    ```

     For more details on Apache and PHP installation, check
    Chapter 3, Working with Web Server.

2. Next, download the latest Ampache server source code. Ampache is a PHP application:

    ```
    $ wget https://github.com/ampache/ampache/archive/3.8.0.tar.gz
    Extract achieve contents under a web root directory
    $ tar -xf 3.8.0.tar.gz -C /var/www
    $ mv /var/www/ampache-3.8.0 /var/www/ampache
    ```

3. We also need to create some configuration files. You can use the default configuration that ships with the Ampache setup and rename the existing files:

    ```
    $ cd /var/www/ampache
    $ mv rest/.htaccess.dist rest/.htaccess
    $ mv play/.htaccess.dist play/.htaccess
    $ mv channel/.htaccess.dist channel/.htaccess
    ```

4. The Ampache web setup will save the configuration under the `config` directory. It will need write access to that directory:

   ```
   $ chmod 777 -R config
   ```

5. Next, we need to configure the Apache web server, enable `mod_rewrite`, and set a virtual host pointing to the Ampache directory.

6. Enable `mod_rewrite` with the following command:

   ```
   $ sudo a2enmod rewrite
   ```

7. Create a new virtual host configuration:

   ```
   $ cd /etc/apache2/sites-available/
   $ sudo vi ampache.conf
   ```

8. Add the following lines to `ampache.conf`:

   ```
   <VirtualHost *:80>
       DocumentRoot /var/www/ampache
         <Directory /var/www/ampache/>
       DirectoryIndex index.php
       AllowOverride All
       Order allow,deny
       Allow from all
     </Directory>
     ErrorLog ${APACHE_LOG_DIR}/error.log
     LogLevel warn
     CustomLog ${APACHE_LOG_DIR}/access.log combined
   </VirtualHost>
   ```

9. Now, disable any default configuration that is using port `80`, or alternatively you can use a port other than `80` for Ampache installation.

10. Reload the Apache server for the changes to take effect:

    ```
    $ sudo service apache2 reload
    ```

Here, we have installed and configured the base setup. Now, we can move on to configuration through a web-based installer. You can access the web installer at the domain name or IP address of your server. The installer should greet you with a big Ampache logo and a language selection box; something similar to the following:

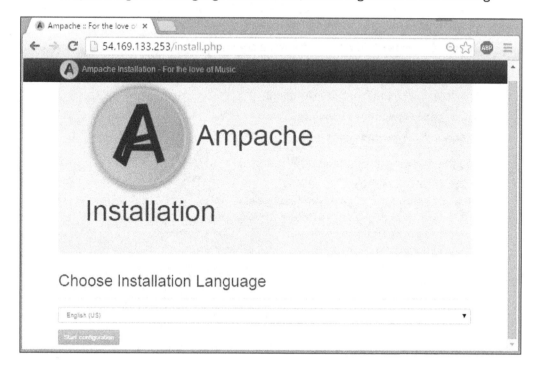

11. Select the language of your choice and click the **Start configuration** button.

12. On the next page, Ampache will check all the requirements and show you a list of settings that need to be fixed. These are mostly the configuration changes and file permissions.

13. Most of these requirements should already be marked with a green **OK** button. You need to fix things that are marked in red. The requirements screen will look as follows:

14. Click the **Continue** button when you are done reviewing all the requirements.

15. On the next page, you need to configure the MySQL settings. Fill in the necessary details and select **Create Database User** to create a new Ampache user under the MySQL server:

16. Click **Insert Database** to configure database settings.

17. The next screen will confirm the database settings and write the configuration changes to a file under the `config` directory. You can choose to change the installation type and enable transcoding configuration from this screen. Once done, click the **Continue** button to write the configuration file. If you see any errors, scroll to the bottom of the page and click the **write** button to write config changes.

18. Finally, the web setup will ask for admin account credentials for the Ampache server. The **Create Admin Account** form will be shown with **Username** and **Password** fields, as follows. Set the admin account username and password and click the **Create Account** button:

Create Admin Account

Username	admin
Password	Password
Confirm Password	Confirm Password

Create Account

19. Once the account is created, the Ampache installation script will redirect you to the web player screen. If it shows a login screen, use the admin account credentials created in the last step to log in. The landing page of the web player will be rendered as follows:

You have completed the Ampache setup process. Now you need to upload content and enjoy your own streaming server. We will learn to create a catalog and upload content in the next recipe.

How it works...

Ampache is a web application written in PHP. We have downloaded the latest Ampache code and set it to work with our web server using Virtual Host configuration. Ampache provides sample `htaccess` files that set required redirection rules. We have enabled respective rules by renaming the sample files. If you are using a web server other than Apache, make sure you check the Ampache documentation for your web server. It supports Nginx and lighttpd as web servers.

Ampache has made it easy to cross-check all requirements and configure your database connection using the web installer. The installer checks for the required PHP settings and extensions and returns a simple page with things that need to fixed. Next, we can configure database settings and push schema directly from the web installer.

Once everything is configured, the web installer returns the login page, from where you can access the Ampache server.

There's more...

The Ampache community have created a Docker image for the Ampache server. If you have a Docker system set up, you can quickly get started with Ampache with its Docker image.

You can get the Dockerfile at `https://github.com/ampache/ampache-docker`.

Ampache is also available in the Ubuntu package repository and can be installed with the following single command:

```
$ sudo apt-get install ampache mysql-server-5.5
```

The currently available version of Ampache is 3.6. If you don't care about the latest and greatest updates, you can use the Ubuntu repository for quick and easy installation.

See also

- ▶ Ampache installation guide: `https://github.com/ampache/ampache/wiki/Installation`

Uploading contents and creating catalogs

So, we have installed the Ampache streaming server. Now, we will learn how to upload our audio/video content and create our first catalog.

Getting ready

You will need audio and video files to be uploaded on your server and enough space to save all this content. I will be using podcasts from Ubuntu podcasts in the MP3 format.

Upload all content to your Ampache server and note the directory path. I will be using the `podcasts` directory under `home` for my user.

Open the Ampache server homepage and log in with admin credentials.

How to do it...

Ampache provides the admin page, where you can perform all administrative tasks, such as catalogue management, user management, and other configurations. We will create a new catalogue from the admin panel and then point it to already uploaded content:

1. From your Ampache homepage, click on the admin icon in the upper-left corner of the screen. This should list all administrative tools:

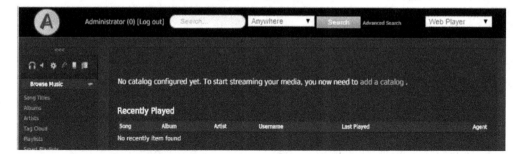

2. Now, click on the **Add a Catalog** link. This should load the **Add a Catalog** page:

3. Enter the catalog name. Use a name that describes your content. I will use Ubuntu podcasts.

4. Set the **Catalog Type** to local, as we will be loading content from your local filesystem.

5. Enter the path for your MP3 (or video) files, /home/ubuntu/podcasts in my case.

6. Click on the **Add Catalog** button. This will create a new catalog and import all content to it. The process will check for meta tags and try to collect more information about the content. It will take some time to process all the files and add details to the Ampache database:

7. Finally, click **Continue** to complete catalog creation and go to the catalog list:

8. Once catalog creation is complete, you can go to the homepage by clicking the home icon (first) in the upper-left of the screen and then clicking on the song title link. This should list all the files available under your catalog directory:

Song Title	Artist	Album	Tags	Time	Rating	Fav.	Action
Episode 36 - The One in Massapequa	Ubuntu UK Podcast	Season 07	Podcast	33:26	⊘★★★★★1	♥	
Episode 37 - The One on the Last Night	Ubuntu UK Podcast	Season 07	Podcast	28:25	⊘★★★★★1	♥	
Episode 38 - The Last One	Ubuntu UK Podcast	Season 07	Podcast	57:30	⊘★★★★★1	♥	

9. From this song list, you can play songs/podcasts, add or remove ratings, add them to playlists, and more:

How it works...

Catalog creation simply reads the content from the upload directory and adds the respective details to the MySQL database. The process tries to gather more details about content using information collected from meta tags and track titles or file names. This information is then used to group the content by artist and album. Note that Ampache is not tagging software where you upload random content and receive a well-organized media library. For Ampache to work well, you need to have properly tagged and well-organized content.

Setting on-the-fly transcoding

Transcoding means converting media from one format to another. Suppose your music files are in a format different to MP3 and your media player only understands MP3 format. In that case, you need to convert your music files to MP3. This conversion task is done by transcoder programs. There are various transcoding programs available, such as `ffmpeg` and `avconv`. These programs need codec before they can convert media from source format to destination format. We need to separately install and configure these components.

Ampache supports on-the-fly transcoding of media files. That is, your music that is not in an MP3 format can be converted into the MP3 format just before it is delivered to your music player, and your high definition video content can be optimized for mobile consumption to reduce bandwidth use.

In this recipe, we will learn how to install and configure transcoding programs with Ampache.

Getting ready

Make sure you have working a setup of the Ampache server.

You will need access to a root account or an account with root privileges.

How to do it...

Ampache depends on external libraries for transcoding to work. We will first install the dependencies and then configure Ampache to work with them:

1. First, add the `ffmpeg` PPA to the Ubuntu installation sources:

   ```
   $ sudo apt-add-repository ppa:mc3man/trusty-media
   $ sudo apt-get update
   ```

2. Now, install `ffmpeg` and other required codecs:

   ```
   $ sudo apt-get install flac mp3splt lame faad ffmpeg vorbis-tools
   ```

3. Next, we need to configure Ampache and enable transcoding. Open the configuration file located at `/var/www/ampache/config/ampache.cfg.php`, find the following lines in the file, and uncomment them:

   ```
   max_bit_rate = 576
   min_bit_rate = 48
   transcode_flac = required
   transcode_mp3 = allowed
   encode_target = mp3
   transcode_cmd = "ffmpeg"
   ```

   Here, we have set `ffmpeg` for the encoding/decoding of media files. You can choose any encoder of your choice. Change the value of `transcode_cmd` respectively.

4. Next, enable debug mode to get details of the transcoding. Find the debug section in the configuration file and set it as follows:

   ```
   debug = true
   Enable log file path which is, by default, set to null
   log_path = "/var/log/ampache"
   ```

5. Save the changes to the configuration file and reload the Apache web server:

```
$ sudo service apache2 reload
```

Now your transcoding setup should be working. You should be able to upload media in a different format and play it as MP3 or other respective formats.

It often happens that we have content in a format that is not supported by the device we are using for playback. Maybe the device does not have the required codec or the hardware is not capable of playing a high bit rate. We may even need to convert content to a lower bit rate and reduce the bandwidth used to stream. The transcoding feature of Ampache helps us to cover these scenarios.

With transcoding, you can convert the content to the desired device-supported format before actually starting the streaming. This is called on-the-fly transcoding. The contents are encoded in a new format as and when needed. Once the conversion is completed, the new format can be cached for repeat use. In the above example, we set Ampache to convert FLAC files to MP3 using the ffmpeg tool. Now whenever we request a file that is originally available in the FLAC format, Ampache will convert it to MP3 before streaming it to our device.

Ampache uses external, well-established media conversion tools for transcoding. Any tool that works with the Ubuntu command line can be configured to work with Ampache. Refer to the Ampache configuration file to get more details and configuration examples.

Enabling API access for remote streaming

A streaming client needs to get the details of the media available on the streaming server. The client needs to authenticate with server access the catalog and list of songs and even request offline access to store media locally. With Ampache, we can use its REST and XML APIs. Through these APIs, clients can communicate with Ampache. You can even write your own client tool using any of the supported APIs.

This recipe covers the setup process for streaming content to remote devices. As of writing this, Ampache allows all users to use all available APIs. We will learn how to modify this setting and configure it to limit access based on user accounts.

Getting ready

Open Ampache in your browser and log in with admin credentials.

How to do it...

We will create a separate user account for remote streaming. From the Ampache homepage, click on the admin icon in the top-left corner and then click on the **Add User** link from the **User Tools** section. An add user menu will be shown that looks like this:

![Adding a New User screen showing Username, Full Name, E-mail, Website, Password, Confirm Password, User Access Level, and Avatar fields with an Add User button]

1. Fill in the **Username, E-mail,** and **Password** fields for the new user account and set **User Access** to User.

2. Click the **Add User** button to create this user and then click **Continue**.

3. We will use this new user account to log in from the remote client.

4. Next, we need to configure access rights and allow this user to use APIs to stream music.

5. Click on the admin icon and then click on the **Add ACL** link under the **Access Control** section.

![Add Access Control List screen showing Name, Level, User, ACL Type fields and IPv4 or IPv6 Addresses with Start and End fields and a Create ACL button]

6. Set the name for this access control list.

7. Set level to **Read/Write**.

8. Set the user to the user account created in the previous step.

9. Set **ACL type** to `Stream Access`.

10. Set the start and end IP addresses to `0.0.0.0` and `255.255.255.255` respectively.

11. Click **Create ACL** to save the settings.

12. Click on the **Add ACL** link again and repeat the preceding settings, except, for **ACL Type** that choose `API/RPC`.

13. Now you can use Ampache streaming from your mobile client. When asked for your username and password, use our new user account, and for the streaming server URL, use your Ampache FQDN followed by `/ampache`, for example:

    `http://myampachehost.com/ampache`

14. If your client needs an API key, you can generate one from the **User Tools** section.

15. Click on the **Browse Users** link and then select the user account in question. Click the edit icon to update user details and then click on the generate API key icon.

16. Finally, click the **Update User** button to save your changes.

How it works...

By default, the Ampache server creates an Access Control List that allows all access to all users. It is a good idea to create a separate user and grant only the required permissions. Here, we have created a new user account with access to the REST API and to stream content. This will allow better control over users and content, as well as allow us to set various user-specific default settings, such as default bitrate and encoding formats.

Streaming music with Ampache

We have set up the Ampache server and configured it for streaming. In this recipe, we will learn how to set up an Android client to play content from our Ampache server.

Getting ready

You will need an Android or iOS phone or tablet. We will focus on the configuration of an Android client, but the same configuration should work with an iOS device, and even desktop clients such as VLC.

How to do it...

Follow these steps to stream music with Ampache:

1. First, install Just Player on your Android device. It is an Ampache client and uses XML APIs to stream content from Ampache. It is available from the Play Store.

2. Once installed, open the settings of Just Player and search for Ampache under cloud player.

3. We need to add our Ampache server details here. Enter the server URL as the domain name or IP address of your Ampache server and append /ampache at the end, for example:

   ```
   http://myampacheserver.com/ampache
   ```

4. Next, enter the username and password in their respective fields. You can use the user account created in the last recipe.

5. Click **Check** to confirm the settings and then save.

Now you should be able to access your Ampache songs on your Android device or phone.

10

Communication Server with XMPP

In this chapter, we will cover the following recipes:

- ▶ Installing Ejabberd
- ▶ Creating users and connecting with the XMPP client
- ▶ Configuring the Ejabberd installation
- ▶ Creating web client with Strophe.js
- ▶ Enabling group chat
- ▶ Chat server with Node.js

Introduction

Extensible Messaging and Presence Protocol (**XMPP**) is a communication protocol that provides near-real-time message passing between two or more entities. XMPP is based on XML and transfers data in predefined formats that are known to server as well as client systems. Being an XML-based protocol, you can easily extend XMPP to suit your requirements. It also provides various standard extensions to extend the base functionality of the XMPP server.

In this chapter, we will learn how to set up our own XMPP server. The main focus will be on implementing a simple chat application. In later recipes, we will also look at a Node.js and socket-based alternative to implementing the messaging server.

We will be working with a popular XMPP server **Ejabberd**. It is a well-known XMPP implementation supported by ProcessOne. Ejabberd is based on Erlang, a functional programming language specifically designed for soft real-time communication.

Installing Ejabberd

In this recipe, we will learn how to install the Ejabberd XMPP server. We will be using an integrated installation package that is available from the Ejabberd download site. You can also install Ejabberd from the Ubuntu package repository, but that will give you an older, and probably outdated, version.

Getting ready

You will need an Ubuntu server with root access or an account with `sudo` privileges.

How to do it...

The following are the steps to install Ejabberd:

1. Download the Ejabberd installer with the following command. We will be downloading the 64-bit package for Debian-based systems.

2. Make sure you get the updated link to download the latest available version:

   ```
   $ wget https://www.process-one.net/downloads/downloads-
   action.php?file=/ejabberd/15.11/ejabberd_15.11-0_amd64.deb -O
   ejabberd.deb
   ```

3. Once the download completes, you will have an installer package with the `.deb` extension. Use the `dpkg` command to install Ejabberd from this package:

   ```
   $ sudo dpkg -i ejabberd.deb
   ```

4. When installation completes, check the location of the Ejabberd executable:

   ```
   $ whereis ejabberd
   ```

```
ubuntu@ubuntu:~$ whereis ejabberd
ejabberd: /opt/ejabberd-15.11/bin/ejabberd.init /opt/ejabberd-15.11/bin/ejabberd
.service
ubuntu@ubuntu:~$
```

5. Now you can start the Ejabberd server, as follows:

   ```
   $ sudo /opt/ejabberd-15.11/bin/ejabberdctl start
   ```

6. The `start` command does not create any output. You can check the server status with the `ejabberdctl status` command:

`$ sudo /opt/ejabberd-15.11/bin/ejabberdctl status`

```
ubuntu@ubuntu:/opt/ejabberd-15.11$ sudo bin/ejabberdctl start
ubuntu@ubuntu:/opt/ejabberd-15.11$ sudo bin/ejabberdctl status
The node ejabberd@localhost is started with status: started
ejabberd 15.11 is running in that node
ubuntu@ubuntu:/opt/ejabberd-15.11$
```

7. Now your XMPP server is ready to use. Ejabberd includes a web-based admin panel. Once the server has started, you can access it at `http://server_ip:5280/admin`. It should ask you to log in, as shown in the following screenshot:

```
← → C   🗅 127.0.0.1:5280/admin                          ☆  ≡

                    Authentication Required          ✕

                    The server http://127.0.0.1:5280 requires a username and
                    password. The server says: ejabberd.


                    User Name:  |

                    Password:


                                              Log In      Cancel
```

8. The admin panel is protected with a username and password. Ejabberd installation creates a default administrative user account with the username and password both set to `admin`.

In older versions of Ejabberd, you needed to create an admin account before logging in. The Ejabberd configuration file grants all admin rights to the username admin. The following command will help you to create a new admin account:

`$ sudo ejabberdctl register_user admin ubuntu password`

9. To log in, you need a JID (XMPP ID) as a username, which is a username and hostname combination. The hostname of my server is `ubuntu` and the admin JID is `admin@ubuntu`. Once you have entered the correct username and password, an admin console will be rendered as follows:

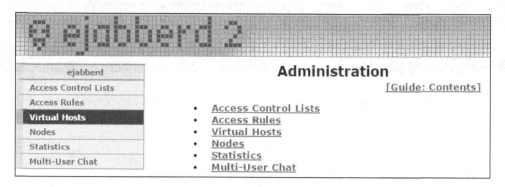

How it works...

Ejabberd binaries are available as a Debian package. It includes a minimum Erlang runtime and all other dependencies. You can download the latest package from the Ejabberd download page.

The installer unpacks all the contents at the `/opt/ejabberd-version` directory. You can get an exact location of the installation with the `whereis` command. All executable files are generally located under the `bin` directory. We will mostly be working with `ejabberdctl`, which is a command line administrative tool. It provides various options to manage and monitor Ejabberd installation. You can see the full list of supported options by entering `ejabberdctl` without any options.

The following screenshot shows the partial output of executing `ejabberdctl` without any options:

If the server is not running, you will only see options to start the server or launch a debug console.

If you have noticed, I am using `sudo` with each `ejabberdctl` command. You can avoid the use of the `sudo` command by switching to the `ejabberd` user, which is created at the time of Ejabberd installation. The installer creates a system user account, `ejabberd`, and sets its `home` directory to the Ejabberd installation directory, `/opt/ejabberd-version`. You will still need to use `sudo` to switch user accounts as the `ejabberd` user has no password set. Use the following command to log in as the `ejabberd` user:

$ sudo su ejabberd

In addition to creating the system user to run the Ejabberd process, the installer also creates an `ejabberd` admin account. The username and password for the administrator account is set to `admin/admin`. Make sure that you change this password before using your server in production. The installation process also creates a default XMPP host. The hostname is set to match your server hostname. It can be modified from the configuration file.

Once the server has started, you can access the handy web administrative console to manage most of the Ejabberd settings. You can add new users, create access control lists and set access rules, check the participating servers (`node`), and all hosted XMPP domains (`host`). Additionally, you can enable or disable Ejabberd modules separately for each domain. That means if you are using the same server to host `xmpp1.example1.com` and `xmpp2.example2.com`, you can enable a multi-user chat for `xmpp1.example1.com` and disable the same module for `xmpp2.example2.com`.

See also

▶ Ejabberd download page at `https://www.process-one.net/en/ejabberd/downloads/`

Creating users and connecting with the XMPP client

We have installed the XMPP server, Ejabberd. In this recipe, we will learn how to add new user accounts to the Ejabberd server. We will also learn how to configure the XMPP client and connect to our server.

Getting ready

Make sure that you have installed the Ejabberd server and it is running properly.

Additionally, you will need XMPP client software. You can choose from multiple free and open source clients such as pidgin, PSI, Adium, Gajim, and many more. I will be using PSI as it provides various low-level administrative features.

How to do it...

Ejabberd supports multiple methods for registering a new user account. These include adding a new user from the command line, creating a new user from the admin panel, and allowing clients to register with the server using in-band registration. Here, we will create a new user from a command line admin tool. Later in this recipe, I will briefly explain another two methods.

Follow these steps to create a user account and connect it with a XMPP client:

1. Use the following command to register a new user using the `ejabberdctl` command:

   ```
   $ # ejabberdctl register username host password
   $ sudo ejabberdctl register user1 ubuntu password
   ```

   ```
   ejabberd-15.11$ sudo bin/ejabberdctl register user1 ubuntu password
   [sudo] password for ubuntu:
   User user1@ubuntu successfully registered
   ejabberd-15.11$
   ```

2. You can get a list of registered users with the `registered_users` option to `ejabberdctl`:

   ```
   $ # ejabberdctl  registered_users host
   $ sudo ejabberdctl registered_users ubuntu
   ```

   ```
   ejabberd-15.11$ sudo bin/ejabberdctl registered_users ubuntu
   admin
   user1
   ejabberd-15.11$
   ```

3. Now you can create a connection to the server with the XMPP client and your new account. Download and install the XMPP client tool, PSI.

4. Open PSI, click the **General** tab, and then select **Account Setup**. This will open the **XMPP Accounts** window, which looks something like this:

5. Click the **Add** button in the **XMPP Accounts** window. This will open another window named **Add Accounts**:

6. Now, in the **Add Account** window, enter the name for this connection, or you can choose to keep the name as **Default**. Click the **Add** button to open one more window.

7. In the newly opened window, enter the account details that we created with the ejabberdctl command:

	Psi: Account Properties	?	×

Name: Default

| Account | Details | Privacy | Connection | Misc. |

Account

XMPP Address: user 1@ubuntu

Example: juliet@capulet.com

Password: ••••••• Change...

Settings

☐ Automatically connect on startup

☐ Automatically connect after sleep

☐ Automatically reconnect if disconnected

☑ Log message history

Save   Cancel

8. On the **Account** tab, enter the full XMPP address (JID) and password for your account.

If your server IP address is mapped with a domain name and your JID refers to the same domain, you can click **Save** and the account setup is completed for you. If not, you need to provide a server IP or FQDN in the **Connection** tab.

9. Click on the **Connection** tab, then click to check the **Manually Specify Server Host/ Port:** checkbox, and then enter the server IP or FQDN and change the port to match your configuration:

| Account | Details | Privacy | Connection | Misc. |

Connection proxy: None ▼ Edit...

☐ Compress traffic (if possible)

☑ Send "keep-alive" packets (to prevent timeouts)

☑ Manually Specify Server Host/Port:

Host: 127.0.0.1| Port: 5222

Encrypt connection: When available ▼

Allow plaintext authentication: Over encrypted connection ▼

10. Next, click the **Save** button to complete the account setup and then click **Close** to close the account setup window. Your account will be listed in the main window of **Psi**, as follows:

```
Psi  –  □  ✕

General  Status  View

Default 🔒 (0/0)
⭐ user1



🕊▼  ⭐ Offline  ▼
```

11. Now you are ready to connect to your XMPP server. Select the listed account and change the drop-down box at the bottom to **Online**. This will start the connection process and set the user status as Online.

12. The PSI client will show a prompt regarding self-signed certificates if you are using the default certificate provided by Ejabberd. Click **Trust this certificate** to proceed.

It will take a few seconds to complete the connection process. Once connected, your PSI status will change to **Online**:

13. Now click **General** menu to add XMPP contacts or to join a group chat or to send a message to existing contact. To change your Instant Messaging account status, click on the **Status** menu and select your desired option.

How it works...

The preceding example demonstrates the account creation and client setup process for connecting with the XMPP server. We have used an administrative command to create an XMPP account and then configured client software to use the existing account.

You can also create a new account from the Ejabberd web console. The web console lists all the configured hostnames under the Virtual Hosts section, and each host lists options for user and access management, and other administration tools. Both these options need the server administrator to create an account.

Additionally, XMPP supports an extension that enables a user to self-register with the server. This is called in-band registration (xep-0077), where a user can send his registration request with his desired username, password, and other details, such as email, and the server creates a new user account. This is useful with public XMPP servers where administrators cannot handle all registration requests. The Ejabberd server supports in-band registration with the mod_register plugin, which is enabled by default. From the client side, you can use any XMPP client that supports in-band registration. If you have noticed, PSI also supports in-band registration and provides an option to register a new account in the **Add Account** process:

Psi: Add Account

Please choose a friendly **Name** that Psi can use to refer to this account.

Click the **Register New Account** checkbox if you want Psi to try and create an account for you on a remote

Name: Default_1

☐ Register new account

There's more...

When it is an XMPP administration task, PSI is a handy tool. It provides a debug console where you can monitor all XML data transfers between the client and server, as well as send arbitrary XML stanzas to the server. You can access the XML console from right-clicking the menu of your PSI account. Once opened, check **Enable** checkbox to enable traffic monitoring. The **XML Console** looks similar to the following screenshot:

XML Console

```
</iq>

<!-- TS:2015-12-07T10:21:08--><iq from="user1@ubuntu/Lenovo-PC" type="result" xml:lang="en"
to="user1@ubuntu/Lenovo-PC" id="aacba">
<query xmlns="jabber:iq:version">
<name>Psi</name>
<version>0.15</version>
<os>Windows NT</os>
</query>
</iq>
```

Filter

☑ Message   ☑ Presence   ☑ IQ   JID: [   ]

☑ Enable   Dump Ringbuf   Clear   XML Input...   Close

XML Console also allows the filtering of traffic based on packet type. Button **Dump Ringbuf** can be used to dump any traffic before opening the **XML Console**.

Another option is service discovery from the right-click menu. You need to log in as an administrator to see all the options under service discovery. From here, you can monitor user accounts and various services that are available on the server. The **Service Discovery** window looks something like this:

See also

▶   A list of XMPP client tools at `https://xmpp.org/xmpp-software/clients/`

Configuring the Ejabberd installation

Ejabberd comes with various default settings that make it easy to get started. We can install Ejabberd and start using it as soon as installation completes. This works when we are testing our setup, but when we need a production server, we need to make a number of changes to the default installation. Ejabberd provides a central configuration file through which we can easily configure our XMPP installation.

This recipe covers the basic configuration of the Ejabberd server.

Getting ready

Make sure that you have installed the Ejabberd server.

You will need access to a root account or an account with `sudo` privileges.

How to do it...

Ejabberd configuration files are located under the `conf` directory in the Ejabberd installation. On the Ubuntu server, it should be `/opt/ejabberd-version/conf`.

Follow these steps to configure the Ejabberd installation:

1. Open the `ejabberd.yml` file. It contains configuration settings in the YML format.

2. Let us start by setting the domain for our XMPP service. This is located under the `SERVED HOSTNAMES` section in the configuration file. The default setting uses the server hostname as a host for the XMPP service.

3. Add a fully qualified domain name under the `hosts` section. You can choose to keep the default host entry or remove it:

```
###.    ===================
###'    SERVED HOSTNAMES

hosts:
  - "ubuntu"
  - "xmpp.example.com"
```

4. Next, you may want to change the default ports for XMPP connections. Search for the `LISTENING PORTS` section in `ejabberd.yml` and change the respective ports. I will use the default port configuration. The following is the configuration snippet listing `port 5222`:

```
###.    ===============
###'    LISTENING PORTS
listen:
  -
    port: 5222
    module: ejabberd_c2s
    certfile: "/opt/ejabberd-15.11/conf/server.pem"
    starttls: true
```

5. The `LISTENING PORTS` section contains different port configurations, each serving a separate service. Three of them are enabled by default and serve a client to server connection (`5222`), server to server connection (`5269`), and HTTP module for admin console and `http_bind` service (`5280`).

6. The same section contains the parameter named `certfile`, which specifies the SSL certificate file to be used while creating client connections. The default settings point to a certificate created by the Ejabberd installation process. You can change it to your own signed certificate.

7. Also note the shaper and access settings. These settings specify the connection throttling and access control settings used for the client to server connections respectively.

8. At the end of the `LISTENING PORTS` section, there is a configuration for `BOSH` (port `5280`) connections, as well as the web admin panel. This section also enables web socket connections with the `ejabberd_http_ws` module.

9. Under the `AUTHENTICATION` section, you can configure the authentication mechanism to be used. By default, Ejabberd uses `internal` authentication but it can be set to use `external` scripts, system-level authentication, external databases, or even a centralized LDAP service. The following is the list of all supported options:

```
###.  ===============
###'  AUTHENTICATION

auth_method: internal
## auth_method: external
## auth_method: odbc
## auth_method: pam
## auth_method: ldap
```

10. Default `internal` authentication works well enough and we will proceed with it. If you are planning to use a different authentication mechanism, make sure that you comment out `internal` authentication.

11. You can also enable anonymous login support, where clients can open an XMPP connection without a username and password. Simply uncomment the respective settings from Anonymous login support:

12. Next, under the DATABASE SETUP section, you can set Ejabberd to use an external database system. Ejabberd supports all leading relational database systems, including SQLite. The following is the list of all supported database systems:

13. The default database settings use an inbuilt database server known as **Mnesia**. It provides in-memory and disk-based storage and can be easily replicated across Ejaberd nodes. Mnesia works well even for very busy XMPP operations.

14. To define an admin user, search for the ACCESS CONTROL LISTS section and add your desired username and hostname under the admin users list:

```
###.    =====================
###'    ACCESS CONTROL LISTS
acl:
  admin:
    user:
      - "admin": "ubuntu"
```

This same section includes a list of blocked users.

You can also define your own access control lists, which can be used to restrict permissions to specific hostnames or users. The Access Rules section define the rules applicable to listed ACLs.

15. Finally, under the `modules` section, you can configure the modules to be used by Ejabberd. Modules are plugins to extend the functionality of the Ejabberd server. Comment out the modules that you are not planning to use. You can also enable or disable any module in runtime from the web admin panel. The following is the partial list of modules:

```
## Modules enabled in all ejabberd virtual hosts.
modules:
  mod_adhoc: {}
  mod_admin_extra: {}
  mod_announce: # recommends mod_adhoc
    access: announce
  mod_blocking: {} # requires mod_privacy
  mod_caps: {}
  mod_carboncopy: {}
```

Each module is named after respective XEPs (XMPP extensions). You can get details of the functionality of any module by looking for the related XEP. Also check the Ejabberd documentation to find out the dependencies between modules.

16. Once you are done with all the configuration, you can restart the Ejabberd server with `ejabberdctl restart` or reload configuration changes with the `ejabberdctl reload_config` command:

```
$ sudo bin/ejabberdctl reload_config
```

How it works...

Most of the core settings of Ejabberd are controlled through the configuration file, `ejabberd.yml`. Alternatively, you can change settings with the `ejabberdctl` command, but those settings will not persist after restart. If you need the settings to be permanent, change them in the configuration file. You can always reload the configuration file changes without restarting the server.

While editing the configuration file, make sure that you follow the indentation and spacing as shown in examples. Ejabberd configuration follows the YML format and any change in spacing will leave that setting undefined. The good news is that the latest version of Ejabberd will prompt you about any mistakes in configuration.

There's another file named `ejabberdctl.cfg` that contains Erlang runtime settings. You may need to update those parameters while performance tuning the Ejabberd server.

There's more...

The Ejabberd server is highly extensible and customizable thanks to its modular architecture. Most Ejabberd features are implemented as external modules. Modules are pluggable components that can be used to extend core functionality. These modules can be enabled or disabled as per requirements and do not affect the core functionality. Ejabberd modules are written in either Erlang or Elixir.

Ejabberd modules work with the hook mechanism implemented in the Ejabberd core. Hooks are nothing but simple events such as message received, user logged in, and connection time out. You can get a full list of supported hooks in the Ejabberd documentation, although it may not be a complete list. Each hook gets its own handler chain, with each handler assigned with a priority number. When you enable a module, it registers a given handler with a respective hook and a position or priority in the handler chain. When a hook is triggered by an event, it executes each handler in a chain, one after another. Additionally, a handler function may request to stop processing hooks and not to execute any further handlers.

The Ejabberd administrative command `ejabberdctl` provides an option to search for and install external modules. Ejabberd takes care of downloading the module, compiling, and installing it. You can even write your own module and add it to the local repository for installation. Check Ejabberd's developer documents for more details on module development.

See also

- List of XMPP extensions at `http://xmpp.org/xmpp-protocols/xmpp-extensions/`
- Ejabberd document at link - `https://www.process-one.net/docs/ejabberd/guide_en.html`
- Ejabberd developer documentation at `http://docs.ejabberd.im/developer/modules/`
- Ejabberd hooks at `http://docs.ejabberd.im/developer/hooks/`

Creating web client with Strophe.js

In this recipe, we will learn how to use web technologies to create a web-based XMPP client. I will demonstrate the use of the popular JavaScript library **StropheJS** to create a basic web client and connect to the XMPP server.

Strophe is a collection of libraries that can be used to communicate with the XMPP server. It contains **libstrophe**, which is a C-based implementation of XMPP client functionalities, and Strophe.js, which is a JavaScript implementation. Strophe provides core XMPP client functionality and can be extended with custom modules. The community has contributed various extensions to support additional XMPP functions.

With a limit on page count, I will focus on a simple demo of Strophe.js where we download the code and modify an example to connect with our XMPP server.

Getting ready

You will need the XMPP server installed and running. You can also use public XMPP servers, but make sure that you register with them and obtain your username (JID) and password.

You will need at least two user accounts to communicate with each other.

As we are using a web-based connection, it needs a **Bidirectional-streams Over Synchronous HTTP (BOSH)** extension enabled on the XMPP server. Ejabberd supports this functionality with `mod_http_bind` and it should be enabled by default.

Download and extract the latest source achieve from the Strophe.js site: `http://strophe.im/strophejs/`.

Optionally, you will need a web server set up to access a web client.

How to do it...

I assume the source code is located in the StropheJS directory. We will use one of the examples shipped with the StropheJS source:

1. Change the directory to `examples` under the extracted StropheJS code. This directory contains multiple examples, demonstrating different features of StropheJS. We will use `echobot.js` and `echobot.html` as our starting point.

2. Open `echobot.js` and change the `BOSH_SERVICE` URL on the first line, as follows:

   ```
   var BOSH_SERVICE = 'http://hostname:5280/http-bind';
   ```

3. Replace the hostname with your XMPP domain or XMPP server IP address. For example, if your XMPP server is available at `xmpp.mysrv.com`, then the `BOSH_SERVICE` URL will be as follows:

   ```
   var BOSH_SERVICE = 'http://xmpp.mysrv.com:5280/http-bind';
   ```

4. Optionally, you can enable debug logging to watch actual data exchanged between client and server. Find the `$(document).ready()` section and uncomment the following lines:

```
// uncomment the following lines to spy on the wire
traffic.
connection.rawInput = function (data) { log('RECV: ' +
data); };
connection.rawOutput = function (data) { log('SEND: ' +
data); };
```

5. Save the changes to `echobot.js` and open `echobot.html` in your browser. You should see a page with two text fields, one for **JID** and another for **Password**:

6. Enter your JID (XMPP username) and respective password and click **connect**.

7. Now, Strophe.js will try to open an XMPP connection and log in with the given details. If the connection is successful, you should see the following screen:

8. The last line includes your JID, with a unique identifier for the current session appended at the end. This form of JID is also called **full JID**.

9. Open a separate client connection with, say, PSI, log in with some other user, and send a message on your given JID. This should print your message on the web page and the same message will be echoed back to the sender. Your web page should look similar to the following screenshot:

← → C ☐ file:///C:/Users/user/Desktop/strophejs/examples/echobot.html ☆ ≡

JID: admin@ubuntu   Password: •••••   connect

Strophe is connecting.
Strophe is connected.
ECHOBOT: Send a message to admin@ubuntu/8551152211449319057231360 to talk to me.
ECHOBOT: I got a message from user1@ubuntu/Lenovo-PC: Hii
ECHOBOT: I sent user1@ubuntu/Lenovo-PC: Hii

> When you are done playing around, click **disconnect** to properly close the XMPP connection.

How it works...

Strophe.js is a JavaScript-based XMPP client library that makes it easy to write your own web-based XMPP clients. Strophe handles all actual communication parts, such as the encoding and decoding of XML stanzas, the connection procedure, and so on. You can use simple APIs provided by Strophe to create your client. Strophe.js uses jQuery to work with the HTML DOM, so if you are familiar with jQuery you will feel at home when working with Strophe.

If you browse through the code in echobot.js, you will see two main event handlers: onConnect and onMessage. These event handlers are attached to specific events and are executed when that event occurs. The onConnect handler is attached to a connection object to capture any change in connection state, and onMessage is attached as a handler for message events. It will be triggered when our client receives any message from the server.

If you are interested in the syntax for the addHandler function, it is as follows:

```
addHandler: function (handler,ns,name,type,id,from,options)
```

The `handler` parameter is the actual function to manipulate an incoming message object; `ns` is the XMPP namespace and can be used to receive packets only from a certain namespace. It defaults to jabber:client, the name parameter, which is the name of an element to act upon—in our case, it is `message`. You can use `iq` or `presence` to receive respective data types. Other parameters add more filtering options, where you can specify a specific ID for the message, type of the message packet (chat or normal or group, defaults to chat) and other options.

The handler function `onMessage` gets triggered whenever a `connection` object receives a new message from the server. Then, it parses the received data and extracts all required information. As it is an echo bot, it simply reads the message and echoes it back to the sender. The new message packet is generated with the following lines:

```
var reply = $msg({to: from, from: to, type: 'chat'})
    .cnode(Strophe.copyElement(body));
```

The message is passed to a `connection` object with the following lines, which in turn sends it to the server:

```
connection.send(reply.tree());
```

The last section initiates the Strophe client on page load (`ready`). When we click on the **connect** button, a `click` handler in this section gets triggered and opens a new connection with the XMPP server. The same button is changed to disconnect so that we can send a proper disconnect request to the server.

There's more...

Strophe.js supports WebSocket-based XMPP connections, and the latest version of Ejabberd has also added support for WebSockets. WebSockets provides noticeable performance improvements and reduces connection time over BOSH connections. In the preceding example, we have used the BOSH protocol, which can be replaced with WebSocket simply by changing the `BOSH_SERVICE` URL as follows:

```
var BOSH_SERVICE = 'ws:// hostname:5280/websocket';
```

If you need a secure WebSocket connection, use the `wss` protocol instead of:

```
wsvar BOSH_SERVICE = 'wss:// hostname:5280/websocket';
```

You should check other examples, mainly `prebind` and `restore`. Both demonstrate connection features that can help in reducing connection delay.

See also

- ▸ StropheJS official page at `http://strophe.im/strophejs/`
- ▸ StropheJS GitHub repo at `https://github.com/strophe/strophejs`
- ▸ StropheJS API documentation at `http://strophe.im/strophejs/doc/1.1.3/files/strophe-js.html`
- ▸ StropheJS plugins at `https://github.com/metajack/strophejs-plugins`

Enabling group chat

In this recipe, we will learn how to set up and use the group chat feature of XMPP. Group chat is also called **Multi User Chat** (**MUC**). Ejabberd supports MUC with the help of an extension and is enabled by default.

Getting ready

You will need the Ejabberd server set up and running. Make sure you have enabled MUC with the `mod_muc` and `mod_muc_admin` modules.

You will need two users for the group chat. One of them needs to have admin rights to set up MUC and create rooms.

Check your XMPP client for the support of MUC or conference protocol. I will be using PSI as a client for this recipe.

How to do it...

For multi-user chat, we need two or more users logged in on the server at the same time, plus a chat room. Let's first set up our chat client with user accounts and create a chat room.

Follow these steps to enable group chat:

1. Open PSI and set up two different accounts. Log in to the XMPP server and set the **Status** to **Online**. Your PSI window should look something like this:

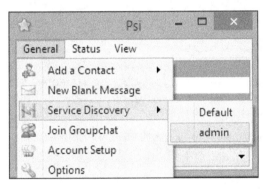

2. You can access the MUC statistics on the Ejabberd web panel to check available rooms.

3. Now we will create our first chat room. In PSI, click the **General** menu, select **Service Discovery**, and then select your **admin** account:

4. This will open a **Service Discovery** window with a list of all administrative services on your Ejabberd XMPP server:

5. Look for the **Chatrooms** node under the **Name** column and double-click it to browse its options. A new window will pop up, which should look something like this:

6. Now type the name of the chat room you want to create under the **Room information** section. Set your nickname as it should be displayed to other participants and click the **Join** button.

7. This will open a new window for your chat room. You will notice the chat room name on the title bar of the window. As the user admin created this room, he is assigned as a moderator:

8. For now, the admin is the only participant in this room. Repeat the same steps with other user accounts to get them to join this room. Make sure that you use the same room name again. Once a new user joins the room, the admin user will get notified. Both users can see each other in the participants section:

xmppmuc@conference.ubuntu		admin

Topic:

*** 2015-12-07
[11:39:28] *** New room created
[11:40:56] *** user1 (user1@ubuntu/Lenovo-PC) has joined the room as a participant

Moderators (1)
🌟 admin
Participants (1)
🌟 user1
Visitors

> [You can always share your room name with other users to let them in.]

How it works...

A group chat works in a similar way to a one on one chat. In a one-on-one chat, we send a message to the JID of a specific user, while in a multi-user chat we send a message to the JID of a chat room. As the message is received on room ID, XMPP takes care of forwarding it to all participants in that room.

There's more...

By default, XMPP chat rooms are not persistent and will be deleted when all participants leave that room. PSI uses the default configuration to quickly create a new chat room. Once the chat room is created, you can configure it in the same chat room window. Click on the options button, the downward triangle in the upper-right corner of the chat room window, and then select **Configure room**:

Room Configuration

Affiliations | General

Room title:

Room description:

Make room persistent: ☐

Make room public searchable: ✔

Make participants list public: ✔

On the first tab, you can set members, administrators, and ban user accounts. On the **General** tab, you can set other room configurations. You can mark a room as persistent and make it private password-protected. This tab contains a number of other options; check them at your leisure.

You may have noticed we have used an admin account to create a chat room. You can allow non-admin users to act as an MUC admin. Open the Ejabberd configuration and search for `muc_admin` configuration. Add your desired username below the admin entry and set it to **allow**.

See also

> ▸ Candy - JavaScript-based multi-user chat client at `https://candy-chat.github.io/candy/`
> ▸ Strophe.js MUC plugin at `https://github.com/metajack/strophejs-plugins/tree/master/muc`

Chat server with Node.js

Up to now, this chapter has covered XMPP and its usages. It is a good, mature protocol with multiple servers developed around it. Sometimes, however, you may need to set up a quick application that uses a simple message transfer, or develop a small chat application for your team. For such projects, XMPP servers may turn out to be overkill. You may not use all the features of XMPP and waste resources, even for a basic setup. Plus, developing an XMPP application is a time consuming process.

In this case, you can quickly start using Node.js-based socket communication. Node.js has gained popularity in the developer community. It is a framework developed in a commonly known language, JavaScript. In this recipe, we will learn how to develop a message passing application using Node.js sockets. We will use Socket.io, a popular Node.js library, to work with sockets and a demo app provided by Socket.io.

Getting ready

You will need access to a root account or an account with `sudo` privileges.

How to do it...

We are going to set up a Node.js-based application, so we need to install Node.js on our Ubuntu server.

Follow these steps to install Node.js:

1. Install Node.js with the following command:

   ```
   $ sudo apt-get update
   $ sudo apt-get install nodejs
   ```

2. Optionally, check your Node.js version:

   ```
   $ node -v
   ```

3. Next, download the sample application from the Socket.io GitHub repo:

   ```
   $ wget https://github.com/rauchg/chat-
   example/archive/master.zip
   ```

4. Unzip the downloaded contents. This will create a new directory named
   `chat-sample-master`:

   ```
   $ unzip master.zip
   ```

5. Change the path to the newly created directory:

   ```
   $ cd chat-sample-master
   ```

6. Next, we will need to install the dependencies for this sample application. Use the
   following Node.js command to install all dependencies.

   ```
   $ npm install
   ```

7. This will fetch all dependencies and install them in the `node_modules` directory
   under `chat-sample-master`. Once the `install` command completes, you can
   start your application with the following command:

   ```
   $ node index.js
   ubuntu: ~/chat-example-master $ node index.js listening on
   *:3000
   ```

8. This will start an inbuilt HTTP server and set it to listen on default port `3000`. Now you
   can access the app at `http://server-ip:3000`. The screen will look similar to the
   following image:

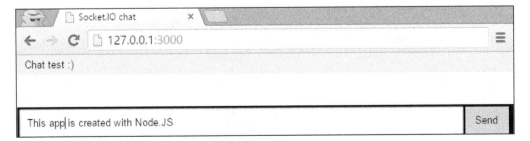

9. Open another instance in a separate browser window and start sending your messages.

How it works...

We have set up a very simple application that listens on a given Node.js socket. To send a message, we have used the `socket.emit()` function, which writes the data from text box to socket:

```
$('form').submit(function(){
        socket.emit('chat message', $('#m').val());
        ...
});
```

When this message is received on the server side, the server writes it to all connected sockets, resulting in a group chat scenario:

```
io.on('connection', function(socket){
  socket.on('chat message', function(msg){
    io.emit('chat message', msg);
  });
});
```

Similarly, to receive a message, we keep listening on the socket, and when an event chat message happens, we write the received data to an HTML page as a message:

```
socket.on('chat message', function(msg){
        $('#messages').append($('<li>').text(msg));
});
```

This is very basic application and can be extended easily to implement one-on-one chat. All we need is a unique ID for all clients and a little modification to the interface to separate messages. Right now, the message is sent as it is; you can collect the message and create a JSON object to contain sender and receiver IDs, plus any additional information.

The advantage of using NodeJS is quick and easy development. JavaScript is a commonly used language and you can easily get support from the large community. You can always develop the application as per your requirements. The disadvantage is regarding scaling; you will need to code the clustering mechanism on your own, whereas for XMPP, clustering is implemented by nearly all leading servers.

There's more...

The Node.js setup available with the Ubuntu repository is not the latest one. You can download the latest version from the node official download page.

Download NodeJS binaries for Linux. Choose your desired version by visiting the NodeJS download page. As of writing this, the latest stable version is 5.1:

```
$ wget https://nodejs.org/download/release/v5.1.0/node-v5.1.0-linux-x64.tar.xz
```

Extract binaries and move it to `/use/local` so that it is accessible globally:

```
$ tar Jxv --strip=1 -C /usr/local/
```

Check the node version with the following command:

```
$ node -v
```

See also

- ▶ Node.js download page: `https://nodejs.org/en/download`
- ▶ Node: how to install: `https://github.com/nodejs/help/issues/41`
- ▶ Sample chat application on GitHub: `https://github.com/rauchg/chat-example`

11
Git Hosting

In this chapter, we will cover the following recipes:

- ▶ Installing Git
- ▶ Creating a local repository with Git CLI
- ▶ Storing file revisions with Git commit
- ▶ Synchronizing the repository with a remote server
- ▶ Receiving updates with Git pull
- ▶ Creating repository clones
- ▶ Installing GitLab, your own Git hosting
- ▶ Adding users to the GitLab server
- ▶ Creating a repository with GitLab
- ▶ Automating common tasks with Git hooks

Introduction

In this chapter, we will learn how to set up a popular version control system: Git. A version control system, also known as revision control system, can be thought of as a repository of files that record every single change in a file. Every update to a file or set of files is recorded as a new version, with some metadata about that specific modification. Metadata contains details of who made the change, a small comment explaining why the change was made, details on exactly what changed in each file, and a timestamp. You can easily switch back to an older version when needed.

Version control systems are generally used to track software source code, but they can be used with virtually any type of file. It is necessary for collaborative work where two or more people are working on the same file. Everyone maintains their own local copy of each file and works on them. When a person satisfactorily completes his work, he sends the updated file to the central repo. Others can synchronize their local copies with this central repo and receive any updates. If two people happen to modify the same file at the same time, they can choose what to keep and what to remove before sending updates to the central repository. If any issue happens with the latest updates, source code can be replaced with previous known-to-work versions. This allows you to track the changes over time and find the cause of the problem.

Over time, multiple version control systems have been developed; some are **centralized version control systems** (**CVCS**) and others are distributed version control systems. Centralized systems consist of a single central server that hosts all the versions and updates. Everyone sends new changes to the central server and gets updates from it. This makes it easy to administer the repository and enable fine-grained control, but it also becomes a candidate for a single point of failure. If a central server goes down, no one can push changes or get updates. CVS and Subversion are well known centralized version control systems.

Distributed version control systems, on the other hand, overcome this problem by distributing a full copy of the repository on each participating system. If a central server goes down, a copy from any client can be sent to the server to restore it. One can even choose to promote a client as a new server. Git, Mercurial, and Bazaar are examples of distributed version control systems. Bazaar is sponsored and developed by Canonical, the developer of Ubuntu. It is primarily focused on community-supported open source software development.

In this chapter, we will focus on Git, a popular version control system. It was primarily developed by Linus Torvalds to support the development of the Linux kernel. Git is influenced by the lessons learned from other version control systems. It was developed with the aim to support large projects, such as the Linux kernel, and the need for a fully distributed system and high speed. Later, GitHub, a social network for code and developers, ensured the widespread adoption of Git.

In this chapter, we will learn how to work with Git. Starting with the basics, such as installing Git and using it locally, we will also cover some advanced features of Git. We will also set up our own Git hosting with GitLab, an open source tool.

Installing Git

This recipe covers the installation of Git binaries on the Ubuntu server. As always, we will install the latest available Git package.

Getting ready

You will need access to a root account or an account with `sudo` privileges.

How to do it...

Git maintains a separate repository of the latest binaries on Launchpad. We will use PPA for this repository,to install the latest Git version:

1. Add PPA to the Ubuntu installation source:

   ```
   $ sudo add-apt-repository ppa:git-core/ppa
   ```

2. Update the `apt` repository cache:

   ```
   $ sudo apt-get update
   ```

3. Now, install Git with a simple `apt-get install git` command:

   ```
   $ sudo apt-get install git -y
   ```

4. Once installation completes, you can check the Git version with the following command. You can cross check the version with the official Git download page:

   ```
   $ git version
   ```

5. Now introduce yourself to Git by providing your name and email address. Git will add this information to every commit message made by you:

   ```
   $ git config --global user.name "Your Name"
   $ git config --global user.email "email@domain.com"
   ```

6. You can cross-check the configuration by using the `--list` parameter to `git config`:

   ```
   $ git config --list
   ```

7. Use `git help` to get a list of the basic daily use commands:

   ```
   $ git help
   ```

How it works...

Here, we have the installed the latest Git version from the repository maintained by Git developers. The Ubuntu default package repository contains the Git package, but often it is not updated. Ubuntu 14.04 still provides Git version 1.9.1.

Once the Git packages are installed, you need to identify yourself to Git. This information is used to tag the commits created by you. We have globally set the username and email with the `git config` command. Now, whenever you create a new commit in any repository on this system, the commit will get tagged with your username and email. This helps in tracking who did what, especially when you are working in a large group. You can get a list of configuration settings with the command `git config --list`, and the output should look something like the following:

```
$ git config --list
user.name=yourname
user.email=youremail@example.com
```

If you execute the same command from within a repository directory, the list will show some extra settings specific to that repository:

```
~/sample-repo$ git config --list
user.name=yourname
user.email=youremail@example.com
core.repositoryformatversion=0
core.filemode=true
core.bare=false
core.logallrefupdates=true
```

Now, if you are not already familiar with Git, you can make use of the `git help` command to get documentation and manual pages. The default help menu lists commonly used commands with a short description. You can get a list of all available commands with the same `git help` command and a flag, `-a`.

```
$ git help -a
```

Additionally, the installation contains some guides or manual pages to help you get started with Git. To get a list of the available guides, use:

```
$ git help -g
```

The common Git guides are as follows:

- ▸ `attributes`: Defines attributes per path
- ▸ `glossary`: A Git glossary
- ▸ `ignore`: Specifies intentionally untracked files to ignore

To open a particular guide, use the `git help guidename` or the `man git [guidename]` command:

```
$ git help everyday # or man giteveryday
```

There's more...

Git has become a mainstream version control system, especially after the rise of the social coding site **GitHub**. There are other well-known version control systems available, such as Subversion and Mercurial. Facebook uses a modified version of Mercurial for their internal code hosting. Bazaar is another distributed version control system sponsored and developed by Canonical, the force behind Ubuntu. Bazaar provides tight integration with Launchpad, a collaborative development platform by Canonical.

You can get more details about Bazaar on their official page at `http://bazaar.canonical.com/en/`.

See also

You can read more by following these links:

- **Git basics**: `https://git-scm.com/book/en/v2/Getting-Started-Git-Basics`
- **Git book**: `https://git-scm.com/book/en/v2`
- Check out the Git interactive tutorial at: `https://try.github.io` and `http://git.rocks/`
- **Launchpad**: `https://launchpad.net/`

Creating a local repository with Git CLI

Now that we have the Git binaries installed, let's take a step forward and create our first local Git repository.

Getting ready

Make sure that you have installed Git.

How to do it...

We will take a common path by starting a new pet project, where we will simply create a new local directory, add some files to it, and then realize, *Ohh I am gonna need a version control system*:

1. So, yes, quickly create your new project:

   ```
   $ mkdir mynewproject
   $ touch mynewproject /index.html
   $ touch mynewproject /main.js
   $ touch mynewproject/main.css
   ```

2. Add some sample content to these files by editing them:

   Now you need to create a Git repository for this project. Sure, Git covered you with the `git init` command.

3. Make sure you are in the project directory and then initialize a new repository, as follows:

   ```
   $ cd mynewproject
   $ git init
   ```

This will initialize a new empty repository under the project directory. A new hidden directory gets created with the name `.git`. This directory will contain all the metadata of your Git repository and all revisions of every single file tracked by Git.

How it works...

Here, we have used the `git init` command to initialize a new repository on our local system. The files created before initializing a repo are optional; you can always skip that step and directly use `git init` to create a new local repository. Later, when you need to push (synchronize) this repo with a remote hosted repository, you can simply use the `git remote add` command. We will see examples of `git remote add` in the next recipes.

With the `git init` command, you can also create a bare repository by using the `--bare` flag. The difference between a normal repository and a bare repository is that a **bare repository** does not have a working copy. You cannot use a bare repository directly to edit and commit files. Unlike a normal repository, where revision history, tags, and head information is stored in a separate .git directory, a bare repo stores all this data in the same directory. It is meant to be a central shared repository where multiple people can commit their changes. You need to clone these types of repositories to access and edit files. The changes can be pushed using the `git push` command from the cloned copy.

There's more...

You can also use `git clone` to clone existing repositories. The repository can be local or remote. The `clone` command will replicate the contents of a parent repository, including revision history and other details. We will see more details of `git clone` in the next recipes.

See also

You can read more by following these links:

▸   **Git init**: `https://git-scm.com/docs/git-init`

▸   **Git clone**: `https://git-scm.com/docs/git-clone`

Storing file revisions with Git commit

We have initialized a new repository for our project. Now we will learn how to store file modifications using `git add` and `git commit`.

Getting ready

Make sure you have initialized a new git repository and created sample files under your project directory. Follow the previous recipes to get more details.

How to do it...

Now that we have a new repo initialized for our project, let's go ahead and check in our files.

1. Before we add any files, simply check the current status of the repo with the `git status` command. This should list all the files under the `Untracked files` list, as follows:

    ```
    $ git status
    ```

    ```
    ubuntu@ubuntu:~/mynewproject$ git status
    On branch master

    Initial commit

    Untracked files:
      (use "git add <file>..." to include in what will be committed)

            index.html
            main.css
            main.js

    nothing added to commit but untracked files present (use "git add" to track)
    ```

As shown by `git status`, none of our files are being tracked by `Git`. We need to add those files before Git tracks any changes to them.

2. Let's add all the files to the tracking list with `git add`:

   `$ git add .`

   This command does not create any output, but stages all untracked files to be added to the repo. The symbol (`.`) specifies the current directory and processes all files under the current directory. You can also specify file name(s) to add specific files.

3. Now check the git status again. This time, it will show newly added files marked by green text and a message saying `Changes to be committed`:

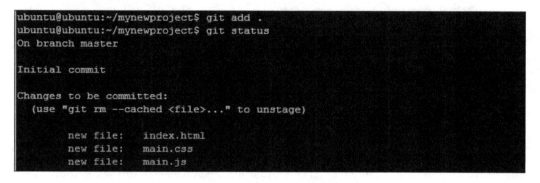

```
ubuntu@ubuntu:~/mynewproject$ git add .
ubuntu@ubuntu:~/mynewproject$ git status
On branch master

Initial commit

Changes to be committed:
  (use "git rm --cached <file>..." to unstage)

        new file:   index.html
        new file:   main.css
        new file:   main.js
```

4. Next, commit the current state of the files with the `git commit` command. Commit means asking Git to save the current state of staged files:

   `$ git commit -m "First commit"`

```
ubuntu@ubuntu:~/mynewproject$ git commit -m "First commit"
[master (root-commit) 4459fcc] First commit
 3 files changed, 0 insertions(+), 0 deletions(-)
 create mode 100644 index.html
 create mode 100644 main.css
 create mode 100644 main.js
ubuntu@ubuntu:~/mynewproject$
```

The `git commit` command will display details of updates to the repository, along with the commit ID (`4459fcc`). In this case, we have added three new files without any new insertion or deletion of contents.

5. Now if you check the `git status` again, it should show the `nothing to commit` message:

```
$ git status

On branch master

nothing to commit, working directory clean
```

6. Next, make some changes in any file and check the repo status again. This time, it should show the modified files as follows:

```
ubuntu@ubuntu:~/mynewproject$ git status
On branch master
Changes not staged for commit:
  (use "git add <file>..." to update what will be committed)
  (use "git checkout -- <file>..." to discard changes in working directory)

        modified:   index.html

no changes added to commit (use "git add" and/or "git commit -a")
```

7. You can check the exact differences to the previous version and current modifications with the `git diff` command. Use `git diff` without any file name to get all modifications in all files, or use it with a file name to check specific files:

```
$ git diff
```

```
ubuntu@ubuntu:~/mynewproject$ git diff index.html
diff --git a/index.html b/index.html
index e69de29..398a696 100644
--- a/index.html
+++ b/index.html
@@ -0,0 +1,9 @@
+<!DOCTYPE html>
+<html>
+<head>
+        <title>Git demo</title>
+</head>
+<body>
+        <h2>My new project :)</h2>
+</body>
+</html>
```

8. Now you can repeat the add and commit process to store these changes. We have modified an existing file without creating new files. We can use the -a flag with git commit to stage changes and commit them in a single command, as follows:

```
$ git commit -a -m "index.html updated"
```

The -a flag will stage all modified files and commit will proceed with newly staged contents. Note that this only works with modified files. If you have created any new file, you need to use git add to stage them.

How it works...

This recipe uses two primary commands: git add and git commit. The first one stages the content for the next commit, and the second actually stores the current state of the content. The git add command is used to add new files, stage updates to existing files, and remove any entries of deleted files. All these modifications to the current working tree are staged for the next commit. The command can be used multiple times to stage multiple modifications. Additionally, you can stage all files under the current directory at once by adding a single file, naming it explicitly, or even choosing a single line from a bunch of updates in the single file.

Once the modifications are staged, you can use git commit to store the updates. When the changes are committed, Git stores the updates in the revision history and changes Git Head to point to the latest revision. All updated files are stored in the form of a **binary large object** (**blob**) as a new snapshot. The commit process also triggers some hooks or events that can be used to execute external scripts to carry out some additional functions. Later in this chapter, we will discuss Git hooks in more detail.

Other than git add and git commit, we have used git status and git diff commands. As the name suggests, git status shows the current status of the repository in question. It lists all files that have been modified after the last commit, newly created or deleted files, and any updates that have already been staged. The git diff command can be used to list all modifications to a given file. It compares the current state of a file against its last committed or indexed state. Note that you can use git diff before indexing any file with git add.

There's more...

Another useful command is git checkout. It can be used to discard any modifications and restore a file to its previous state, or restore the deleted file to its known revision.

Synchronizing the repository with a remote server

Up to now, we have learned how to create a local Git repository and add or update files to it. In this recipe, we will learn how to set up a remote repo and synchronize local code with it. We will be using GitHub to host our remote repository; feel free to choose any other code hosting service.

Getting ready

You will need a GitHub account. Sign up for a free account if you do not already have one.

How to do it...

To create a new repository on GitHub, log in to your GitHub account and create a new public repository:

1. Click the **Create repository** button. Make sure that the checkbox **Initialize this repository with a README** is unchecked. The new repository form should look something like this:

2. On the next page, you will be given an option to initialize this repository. We already have a local repository, so we will use the ... **or push an existing repository from the command line** option:

...or create a new repository on the command line

```
echo # mynewproject >> README.md
git init
git add README.md
git commit -m "first commit"
git remote add origin https://github.com/sawantuday/mynewproject.git
git push -u origin master
```

...or push an existing repository from the command line

```
git remote add origin https://github.com/sawantuday/mynewproject.git
git push -u origin master
```

---

3. Copy both commands and execute them on a local Git repository:

```
$ git remote add origin https://github.com/sawantuday/
mynewproject.git
```

```
$ git push -u origin master
```

The first command, `git remote`, adds a reference to the remote repository on GitHub and sets it as its origin. The next command, `git push`, synchronizes all local content with the remote repository. The `git push` command will show the details, as follows:

```
ubuntu@ubuntu:~/mynewproject$ git remote add origin https://github.com/sawantuda
y/mynewproject.git
ubuntu@ubuntu:~/mynewproject$ git push -u origin master
Username for 'https://github.com': sawantuday
Password for 'https://sawantuday@github.com':
Counting objects: 3, done.
Compressing objects: 100% (2/2), done.
Writing objects: 100% (3/3), 225 bytes | 0 bytes/s, done.
Total 3 (delta 0), reused 0 (delta 0)
To https://github.com/sawantuday/mynewproject.git
 * [new branch]      master -> master
Branch master set up to track remote branch master from origin.
```

4. You will be prompted to authenticate with your GitHub account from the command line. Enter your GitHub username and password. This ensures that you are allowed to push the changes to the repository. Alternatively, you can add your local SSH public key to your GitHub account to avoid manual authentication.

Now you can use your GitHub repository to share code with others or clone it to some other system. On the GitHub page, check the code tab to take a look at files in the repository.

How it works...

Local repositories are good for personal work. A single person can work with them easily. A centrally hosted repository is required when you need to share the code base with a group of people. Everyone can make a local copy of the central code base and send their changes back to the central copy. GitHub solves this problem by hosting repositories that are accessible over the Internet. You can simply create a free public repository and share its URL with colleagues. Through access control, you can select who can check in their code. You can also set up your own centrally hosted repository. All you need is a system accessible over your network or Internet.

Here, we have created a central shared repository on GitHub. GitHub provides various options to initialize a repository and add code to it. As we already have our local repository ready, we just need to add a reference to the remote repo and synchronize our changes with `git push`. The `git remote` command is used to add a reference to the remote repository. We have set the remote repository as **origin,** that is, the default remote repository. When using `git push` or `git pull` commands, if we do not specify any remote name it is assumed to be origin. Also, by default, Git marks the first remote as origin.

Next, we used Git push to push or synchronize our local contents to a remote copy. We have explicitly mentioned the remote name as origin and the remote branch as master. By default, Git always pushes to a remote named origin and branch master.

There's more...

You can create your own remote copy on a local shared server. All you need is a normal user account on that server.

Log in to the shared server and create a bare repository with the following command:

```
$ git init --bare shared_repo
```

This will create an empty bare repository under the shared_repo directory. If you check its contents, you will find all Git-specific files and directories.

Now you can clone this repo from your workstation or use the `git remote add` command to add a remote to your already initialized repository. Use the following command to clone the repo. Replace the username with the user account on a shared server:

```
$ git clone ssh://user@ server_ip_or_name/full/path/to/repo
```

This command will ask for the password of the user account you have used in the username. Additionally, you can remove the password prompt by setting key-based **SSH** authentication with a shared server.

GitHub pages

You can host your own simple static website with GitHub for free. All you need is a Git repository hosted on GitHub. Follow these steps to get your own GitHub page:

1. Create a new repository with the name `username.github.io`, where `username` should be your GitHub username.

2. Clone this repository to your local system. If you already have a project created on your local system, you can add this repository as a remote. Check this recipe for how to add a remote.

3. Create `index.html` if you do not have one. Add some content to `index.html`.

4. Stage all content, commit to the local repository, and then push to GitHub.

5. Next, point your browser to username.github.io. You should see the content of index.html.

GitHub pages works with websites generated using static website generators such as Jeykyll, Hugo, and Octopress. By default, you get a `github.io` sub-domain, but you can use your own domain name as well.

See also

Check the manual pages for git remote and git push with `man git-remote` and `man git-push` respectively:

▸ Read more about generating SSH keys: `https://help.github.com/articles/generating-ssh-keys/`

▸ Get free hosting for your static website at GitHub pages: `https://pages.github.com/`

Receiving updates with Git pull

In the last recipe, we learned how to set up a remote repository and send local changes to a remote using the `git push` command. The story is not complete yet. When the repository is shared by multiple people, everyone will push their own changes. The central repository will keep on updating. When you want to synchronize or push your changes to the central repo, you need to download any updates made by other users and then push your modifications on top of that. A git pull command will be used to pull down any updates to the remote central repository to your local repository.

This recipe covers the git pull command. We will use this command to resolve a rejected push, but it is generally used simply to update your local copy.

Getting ready

You will need one central remote repository; it may be hosted on GitHub or anywhere else.

Secondly, you will need two local copies of the central repo. Use the `git clone` command to create a local replica of the remote repository. These two copies are used for demonstration purposes; in the real world, you will already have multiple copies with different users of your repository:

```
$ git clone https://github.com/sawantuday/mynewproject.git local_copy_1
$ git clone https://github.com/sawantuday/mynewproject.git local_copy_2
```

Now enter `local_copy_1`, create a new file with random content and then commit and push the changes back to the remote repository:

```
$ cd local_copy_1
$ echo "// Modifications by user 1" >> index.php
$ git add .
$ git commit -m "Index.php created with comments"
$ git push origin master
```

Your push command should complete without any errors or warnings.

Next, enter `local_copy_2` and create a new file with random contents:

```
$ cd local_copy_2
$ echo "\\ Modifications by user 2" >> main.php
```

How to do it...

Suppose you are user two working on a copy, `local_copy_2`. You cloned the repository and started working with the code base. In the meantime, user one completed his work and pushed his changes back to the central repo. Now, after you have completed your work, you are ready to send updates to the remote repo:

1. Commit your modifications to the local repository:

   ```
   $ git add .
   ```

   ```
   $ git commit -m "main.php created with comments"
   ```

```
ubuntu@ubuntu:~/local_copy_2$ git add .
ubuntu@ubuntu:~/local_copy_2$ git commit -m "main.php created with comments"
[master e84e941] main.php created with comments
 1 file changed, 1 insertion(+)
 create mode 100644 main.php
ubuntu@ubuntu:~/local_copy_2$
```

2. Try to push your commit to the central repo:

   ```
   $ git push origin master
   ```

   This time, your push should fail, saying someone else had already updated the remote repository. Git will give you details of a rejected push, as follows:

```
ubuntu@ubuntu:~/local_copy_2$ git push origin master
Username for 'https://github.com': sawantuday
Password for 'https://sawantuday@github.com':
To https://github.com/sawantuday/mynewproject.git
 ! [rejected]        master -> master (fetch first)
error: failed to push some refs to 'https://github.com/sawantuday/mynewproject.git'
hint: Updates were rejected because the remote contains work that you do
hint: not have locally. This is usually caused by another repository pushing
hint: to the same ref. You may want to first integrate the remote changes
hint: (e.g., 'git pull ...') before pushing again.
hint: See the 'Note about fast-forwards' in 'git push --help' for details.
```

3. Now you need to pull remote changes; first, with git pull, merge any potential conflicts, and then try to push again:

```
$ git pull origin master
```

```
ubuntu@ubuntu:~/local_copy_2$ git pull origin master
remote: Counting objects: 3, done.
remote: Compressing objects: 100% (2/2), done.
remote: Total 3 (delta 0), reused 3 (delta 0), pack-reused 0
Unpacking objects: 100% (3/3), done.
From https://github.com/sawantuday/mynewproject
 * branch            master      -> FETCH_HEAD
   4459fcc..585f879  master      -> origin/master
Merge made by the 'recursive' strategy.
 index.php | 1 +
 1 file changed, 1 insertion(+)
 create mode 100644 index.php
```

4. You will be asked to enter a merge message in **nano** or a similar editor. Simply accept the pre-filled message and save the file by pressing *Ctrl + O*, then press *Enter* to save, and then *Ctrl + X* to exit.

5. Now try to push again. This time it should complete successfully:

```
$ git push origin master
```

How it works...

As we saw in the previous example, git pull is used to pull the remote modifications to the local repository. It is a good idea to use git pull before starting your work on the local copy. This way you can be sure that you have all remote updates in your local repository, thus reducing the chances of a rejected push.

The git pull command can be used any time, even to simply update your local codebase with the remote copy. I have used it in a commit and push flow just to demonstrate the rejected push and merge scenario.

The example demonstrates the simple automated merge. It may happen that both user one and user two are working on the same file and incidentally modify the same part of the code. Git will report a Merge conflict, as follows:

```
Unpacking objects: 100% (3/3), done.
From https://github.com/sawantuday/mynewproject
 * branch            master      -> FETCH_HEAD
   e762fed..6e3e1f4  master      -> origin/master
Auto-merging index.php
CONFLICT (content): Merge conflict in index.php
Automatic merge failed; fix conflicts and then commit the result.
ubuntu@ubuntu:~/local_copy_2$
```

Now, in this case, Git may not be able to automatically merge both updates. It will combine both updates in single file and mark them in a special format, as follows:

```
<<<<<< HEAD
// Modifications by user 2 index.php
// generating conflicts
=======
// Modifications by user 1 inde.php
>>>>>> 6e3e1f4f6360d0b2a5f1eab6f8c1f1aedc2135d4
```

In this case, you need to decide what to keep and what to remove. Once you are done with solving conflicts, remove the special tags added by Git and commit the conflicting file. After that, you can push your updates along with the new commit for merging.

See also

You can read more by following these links:

- **Git pull**: https://git-scm.com/docs/git-pull
- **Git merge**: https://git-scm.com/docs/git-merge
- **Git fetch**: https://git-scm.com/docs/git-fetch

Creating repository clones

Git clone allows you to create a copy of your repository in a new directory or location. It can be used to replicate a remote repository on your local system or create a local clone to be shared over an intranet. This recipe covers the `git clone` command. We will learn to create a clone of a remote repository and then take a look at various transport protocols supported by Git for cloning.

Getting ready

You will need Git binaries installed on your local system, plus a remote repository. Note down the full path (clone URL) of the remote repository.

How to do it...

Create a clone of the repository with the `git clone` command, as follows:

```
$ git clone ssh://ubuntu@192.168.0.100:22/home/ubuntu/cookbook.git \
ubuntu_cookbook
```

You will be asked to enter a password for the user account `ubuntu`.

This command will create a new directory named `ubuntu_cookbook` and clone the repository cookbook.git into this directory.

How it works...

As seen in the previous example, the `git clone` command will create a new copy of an existing repository. The repository can be a local repository or one located on a remote server. Git supports various protocols to transfer the content between two systems. This includes well-known protocols such as SSH, HTTP/S, and rsync. In addition, Git provides a native transport protocol named Git. Note that the Git protocol does not require any authentication and should be used carefully. In the previous example, we have used the SSH protocol. When working with local repositories, you can use `file///path/to/repo.git` or even an absolute path `/path/to/repo.git` format.

Cloning requires a single argument, which is the path of the repository to be cloned. You can skip the destination directory and Git will create a clone in a new directory named after the repository name.

You can also create a new **bare clone** with the `--bare` option of the `git clone` command. This is useful for creating a shared central clone that is used by a group of people.

Another important option is the **depth** clone. When cloning a large repository that contains years of work, and you do not really need the entire history of the repository, the option `--depth` can be used to copy only a specified number of revisions. This will help you in quickly downloading just the tip of an entire repository, and will save you some bandwidth by avoiding unnecessary downloads. The syntax for the `--depth` option is as follows:

```
git clone --depth 1 https://github.com/torvalds/linux.git mylinux
```

See also

You can read more by following these links:

▶ **Git clone**: `https://git-scm.com/docs/git-clone`

Installing GitLab, your own Git hosting

Up to now in this chapter, we have worked with the Git **command line interface** (**CLI**). It is a very flexible and powerful interface. This recipe covers the installation of a web interface for Git repositories. We will install GitLab, an open source self-hosted Git server. Through GitLab, you can do most administrative tasks, such as creating new repositories, managing access rights, and monitoring history. You can easily browse your files or code and quickly make small edits. GitLab is also adding support for collaboration tools.

Getting ready

You will need access to a root account or an account with `sudo` privileges

Make sure you check out the minimum requirements for installation. You can use a single core 1 GB server for an installation with less than 100 users. An server with 2 cores and 2 GB RAM is recommended.

Also check the available disk space. The installer itself takes around 400 MB of disk space.

How to do it...

We will use the recommended Omnibus Package Installer. It provides a .deb package for Debian/Ubuntu systems. Additionally, the omnibus installation takes care of housekeeping tasks such as restarting the worker process to maintain memory use. If you choose to follow the manual installation process, you can get the detailed installation guide from the GitLab documentation:

1. First, we will need to download the installer package. Download the latest installer package from the GitLab download page at `https://packages.gitlab.com/gitlab/gitlab-ce`:

   ```
   $ wget https://packages.gitlab.com/gitlab/gitlab-ce/packages/
   ubuntu/xenial/gitlab-ce_8.7.1-ce.1_amd64.deb/download
   ```

2. Once download completes, install GitLab using the `dpkg` command, as follows:

   ```
   $ sudo dpkg -i gitlab-ce_8.7.1-ce.1_amd64.deb
   ```

3. After installation, use the following command to configure GitLab:

   ```
   $ sudo gitlab-ctl reconfigure
   ```

4. Optionally, check the system status with the `gitlab-ctl status` command. It should return a list of processes and their respective PIDs, as follows:

```
ubuntu@ubuntu:~$ sudo gitlab-ctl status
[sudo] password for ubuntu:
run: gitlab-workhorse: (pid 806) 57803s; run: log: (pid 805)
57803s
run: logrotate: (pid 31438) 202s; run: log: (pid 810) 57803s
run: nginx: (pid 813) 57803s; run: log: (pid 812) 57803s
run: postgresql: (pid 817) 57803s; run: log: (pid 811) 57803s
```

5. Then, open your browser and point it to your server IP or hostname. You will be asked to set a new password for the administrator account. Once you set a new password, use `root` as the username and your password to login.

How it works...

GitLab is a Ruby-based web application that provides centralized hosting for your Git repositories. We have installed an open source community edition of GitLab using their Omnibus installer. It is an integrated installer package that combines all dependencies and default settings. The installer combines Nginx, Redis, Sidekiq, Unicorn, and PostgreSQL. Unfortunately, the community edition with the Omnibus installer does not support switching to the MySQL database server. To use MySQL, you need to follow the manual installation process and compile GitLab from source, along with other various dependencies.

The configuration file is located at `/etc/gitlab/gitlab.rb`. It is quite a lengthy file and contains numerous parameters, separated by each component. Some important settings to look at include `external_url`, where you can set your domain name, **database** settings, if you are planning to use external PostgreSQL setup, and **email** server settings, to set up your outgoing email server. If you choose to modify any settings, you will need to reconfigure the installation using the `gitlab-ctl reconfigure` command. You can get a list of enabled configurations using the `gitlab-ctl show-config` command.

The GitLab Omnibus package ships with some extra components: **GitLab CI,** a continuous integration service, and **GitLab mattermost**, an integrated installation of mattermost that provides an internal communication functionality with a chat server and file sharing. GitLab CI is enabled by default and can be accessed at `http://ci.your-gitlab-domain.com`. You can enable mattermost from the configuration file and then access it at `http://mattermost.your-gitlab-domain.com`.

There's more...

Git provides an inbuilt web interface to browse your repositories. All you need is a repository, web server, and the following command:

```
$ git instaweb --httpd apache2  # defaults to lighttpd
You can access the page at http://server-ip:1234
```

Check the GitWeb documentation for more details at `https://git-scm.com/docs/gitweb`.

See also

Check out the requirements for GitLab installation: `https://github.com/gitlabhq/gitlabhq/blob/master/doc/install/requirements.md`.

Adding users to the GitLab server

We have set up our own Git hosting server with GitLab, but it still contains a single admin user account. You can start using the setup and create a new repository with an admin account, but it is a good idea to set up a separate non-root account. In this recipe, we will cover the user management and access control features of the GitLab server.

Getting ready

Make sure you have followed the previous recipe and installed the GitLab server.

Login to GitLab with your root or admin account.

You will need to configure the email server before creating a user account. You can use an external email service, such as sendgrid or mailgun. Update your GitLab email server configuration and reconfigure the server for the changes to take effect.

How to do it...

The default landing page for GitLab is a projects page. The same page is listed even when you log in as root. To create a new user, we need to access the admin area:

1. To open the admin console, click on the admin area icon located at the top-right corner of the screen. Alternatively, you can add `/admin` to the base URL and access the admin area.

   The admin dashboard will greet you with details about your installation and the features and components list. The left-hand menu will list all available options.

2. Click on the **Users** menu to get user account-related options.

3. Next, click on the big green **New User** button to open a new user form.

   Now fill in the required details such as name, username, and email. The form should looks something like this:

New user

Account

Name	
	* required
Username	
	* required
Email	
	* required

4. You cannot set a password for a new user account on the create user form. The reset password link will be mailed to the user at a given email ID. A new user can set his password through that link:

Password

Password	Reset link will be generated and sent to the user. User will be forced to set the password on first sign in.

5. Under the **Access** section, you can mark this user as admin and set a limit on projects created by him:

Access

Projects limit	10
Can create group	☑
Admin	☐

6. Next, under the profile section, you can add some more details for this user account.

7. Now, click on the **Create User** button at the bottom-left of the form. This will save the given details and trigger a password reset email. A screen will change to the **User Details** page where you can see the account details, groups, and projects of a given user, as well as other details. From the same page, you can block or remove the user account.

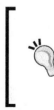
A little workaround if you do not have email server set up is to click on the edit button on the user details page. This will open the same form as add new user, with the password fields enabled. Type in the new password, then confirm them, and click on the **Save changes** button. You have set the password for your new user without a reset email or the email server.

The new user account is ready to be used. Open the login page in a new window or private browser and use the email or username and newly set password to log in.

Creating a repository with GitLab

Now that we have set up our own Git hosting and created a new user account, we can start using our Git hosting by creating a new Git repository.

Getting ready

This recipe uses the GitLab setup. Make sure that you have followed the previous recipe and installed your GitLab server.

Log in with your user account on the GitLab server. You can choose the admin account, but a normal user account is recommended.

If you need to use SSH to clone and push to your repositories, you will need to set up your SSH key. From the dashboard, click on **Profile Settings** and then select **SSH Keys** to add a new SSH key. Check *Chapter 2, Networking*, for more details on how to create an SSH key.

How to do it...

In the previous recipe, we learned how to create a local repository and then push it to the remote. Here, we will first create a remote or hosted repository and then clone it to our local system:

1. Log in to your GitLab account. You will be greeted with the Welcome screen detailing your projects.

2. Click on the **NEW PROJECT** button to create a new repository:

Welcome to GitLab!

Self hosted Git management application.

You don't have access to any projects right now.

You can create up to **10 projects.**

+ NEW PROJECT

3. On a new screen, enter the project or repository name in the project path field. Add an optional descriptive message and select the proper checkbox to make your repository public or private:

Project path	ubuntu-cookbook-gitlab			
Import project from	○ GITHUB	☙ BITBUCKET	♥ GITLAB.COM	🗐 GITORIOUS.ORG
	git ANY REPO BY URL			
Description (optional)	Awesome project			

4. Next, click on the **Create Project** button to create a new repository. This will redirect you to the repository page.

A URL for your repository is listed, with some details on how to use your new repository. You can use HTTP URL if you have not set up SSH keys. Additionally, you may need to replace the hostname with the server IP from the repository URL:

ubuntu-cookbook-gitlab

sample repo

★ 0   SSH   HTTP   git@ubuntu:user1/ubuntu-cookbook-g   ❂   ➕

5. Alternatively, you can create a readme file from the GitLab interface itself. Click on the **README** link to open a file editor in your browser.

When you clone the private repository using its HTTP URL, a local Git daemon will ask you for the username and password details for authentication.

Automating common tasks with Git hooks

One of the more interesting features of Git is hooks. With hooks, you can tie an arbitrary script to various Git events. Whenever a particular event, such as a `git commit` or `git push`, occurs, the script attached to that event gets executed.

Typically, an event consists of several steps, and a script can be attached to each of these steps. The most common steps are pre-event and post-event, with pre hooks executed before the event and post hooks after the event. A pre hook, such as pre-commit, is generally used to cross-check the updates and can approve or reject an actual event. A post hook is used to execute additional activities after an event, such as start a built process when a new push is received or a notification sent.

Every Git repository consists of a `.git/hooks` directory with sample scripts. You can start using those hooks by removing the `.sample` extension from the script name. Additionally, the hook scripts belong to a single repository instance and do not get copied with the repository clone. So, if you add some hooks to your local repository and then push changes to the remote, the hooks will not get replicated on the remote. You will need to manually copy those scripts on the remote system. Built-in sample hooks generally use the shell scripts, but you can use any scripting language, such as Python or even PHP.

In this recipe, we will learn how to use Git hooks. We will create our own post-commit hook that deploys to a local web server.

Getting ready

We will need a local web server installed. I have used an Apache installation; feel free to use your favorite server:

1. Set up a new virtual host under Apache and enable it:

```
$ cd /var/www/
$ sudo mkdir git-hooks-demo
$ sudo chown ubuntu:ubuntu git-hooks-demo
$ cd git-hooks-demo
```

2. Create index.html and add the following contents to it:

```
$ vi index.html
```

```
<!DOCTYPE html>
<html>
<head><title>Git hooks demo</title></head>
  <body>
    <h2>Deployed Manually </h2>
  </body>
</html>
```

3. Create the virtual host configuration:

```
$ cd /etc/apache2/sites-available
$ sudo cp 000-default.conf git-hooks-demo.conf
```

4. Open the virtual host configuration, git-hooks-demo.conf, and replace its contents with following:

```
<VirtualHost *:80>
  DocumentRoot /var/www/git-hooks-demo/html
</VirtualHost>
```

5. Check the initial version by visiting your IP address in your browser.

6. Next, initialize a Git repository under the home directory:

```
$ cd ~/
$ mkdir git-hooks-repo
$ cd git-hooks-repo
$ git init
```

7. Copy index.html from the web root to the repository:

```
$ cp /var/www/git-hooks-demo/index.html .
```

Now we are equipped with the basic requirements to create our Git hook.

How to do it...

Git hooks are located under the `.git/hooks` directory. We will create a new post commit hook that deploys the latest commit to our local web server. We will be using a shell script to write our hook:

1. Create a new file under the `.git/hooks` directory of your repository:

   ```
   $ touch .git/hooks/post-commit
   ```

2. Add the following contents to our `post-commit` hook:

   ```bash
   #!/bin/bash
   echo "Post commit hook started"
   WEBROOT=/var/www/git-hooks-demo
   TARBALL=/tmp/myapp.tar
   echo "Exporting repository contents"
   git archive master --format=tar --output $TARBALL
   mkdir $WEBROOT/html_new
   tar -xf $TARBALL -C $WEBROOT/html_new --strip-components 1
   echo "Backup existing setup"
   mv $WEBROOT/html $WEBROOT/backups/html-'date +%Y-%m-%d-%T'
   echo "Deploying latest code"
   mv $WEBROOT/html_new $WEBROOT/html
   exit 0
   ```

3. We need to set executable permissions to a `post-commit` file so that Git can execute it:

   ```
   $ chmod +x .git/hooks/post-commit
   ```

4. Now, update the `index.html` content. Change the line `<h2>Deployed Manually </h2>` to `<h2>Deployed using Git Hooks </h2>`.

5. Commit the changes as usual. We have edited the existing file, so staging and committing can be done in a single command, as follows:

   ```
   $ git commit -a -m "deployed using hooks"
   ```

This time, the `git commit` result should output all echo statements from our `git hook`. It should look as follows:

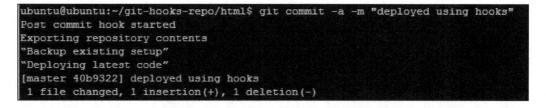

```
ubuntu@ubuntu:~/git-hooks-repo/html$ git commit -a -m "deployed using hooks"
Post commit hook started
Exporting repository contents
"Backup existing setup"
"Deploying latest code"
[master 40b9322] deployed using hooks
 1 file changed, 1 insertion(+), 1 deletion(-)
```

You can check the latest deployed `index.html` by visiting the IP address of your system:

How it works...

We have created a simple post commit hook that exports all files from the Git repository, backs up the existing live site, and replaces it with new contents. This is a very simple shell script, set to execute after each commit event on the local repository. A script that starts with a hash bang signature defines that the script is expecting bash runtime. Later, we defined the `WEBROOT` and `TARBALL` variables, which contain the full path for the **web-root** directory and backup location respectively. Next, we created an archive of all the files with the `git archive` command. This command creates an archive of a named tree; a tree can be a specific commit ID or a branch. We have used a master branch for our export. The contents are exported in a tarball format with the export location set using the `--output` parameter. Once we have the tarball in place, we need to replace the live site with contents from the tarball. We have also taken a backup of the running site, just in case anything goes wrong.

This is a very primitive script and deploys only to the local server. To deploy on a remote server, you will need to use some synchronization tools such as **rsync** to update the content on a remote server. Make sure you are using an SSH connection for your deployments to live servers. Many blogs advise you to have a Git instance running on a live web server and setting it to deploy the live site using a `post-receive` hook. This can be an option for staging or a demo server, but on a live server I would try to avoid installing any tool other than a web server. Any additional packages will increase the effective attack surface and may compromise the security of your servers. Who knows whether Git contains some unknown shocks (remember shell shock?)

Note that we are creating a backup on each new commit. You may end up with an out of disk space error if your deployment is big or if you are doing frequent commits. That is not a big problem, though. The script can be easily modified to delete any directories created X days before. You can even choose to keep the last, say, 10 backups and delete others.

As we are deploying to a local web server, we have set the script to be a `post-commit` hook. If you choose to deploy it on a remote server, then make sure you set the script as a post receive or update script. We commit on a local repository and push updates to the remote server.

As we have seen, this is a plain shell script, and you can easily use any bash command in this script. Additionally, you can execute the script manually using the `sh script.sh` command or the short hand notation, `./script.sh`. This will help in debugging the script and monitoring the output without the need to create any Git commits. Also make sure that the script file is set as executable and that all directories you are working with are writable by your user account.

If you are using remote repositories hosted with GitHub or GitLab, they provide a webhook feature which works similar to Git hooks. You will need to set a script accessible over the Web through a URL. When a particular event happens, GitLab will make a `POST` request to a given URL with the relevant event data.

See also

- ▶ Read more about Git hooks at `https://git-scm.com/docs/githooks`
- ▶ Customizing Git hooks at `https://git-scm.com/book/en/v2/Customizing-Git-Git-Hooks`

12
Collaboration Tools

In this chapter, we will cover the following recipes:

- ▶ Installing the VNC Server
- ▶ Installing Hackpad, a collaborative document editor
- ▶ Installing Mattermost – a self-hosted slack alternative
- ▶ Installing OwnCloud, self-hosted cloud storage

Introduction

This chapter covers various collaboration tools. Collaboration enables people to share thoughts and solve problems collectively. With the help of the Internet, we can communicate quickly and more effectively. Tools such as WhatsApp and Slack have changed the way we communicate personally, as well as in corporate life. Services such as Google Docs hosts our documents in the cloud, which can then be shared with multiple people and simultaneously modified by them. Need a comment on your latest edit? Click that chat button and send your request. Need to discuss face to face? Click another button to start video call. Need to send a long detailed message? Yes, we've got e-mail services.

Most of these services are hosted by Internet giants and available as **SAAS** (**Software as a Service**) products. Simply choose subscription plans and start using them. Many of these services even offer free basic plans. The only problem with these services is you've got to trust a service provider with your data. All your messages, emails, photos, and important documents are hosted with some third party.

In this chapter, we will learn to how set up various open source tools on our own servers. We have already installed an email and instant messaging service, central Git hosting, and a file server. This chapter will focus on more advanced collaboration tools. We will cover the VNC server to share your desktop, the OwnCloud server for document and file sharing, and Mattermost, an open source Slack alternative.

Installing the VNC server

VNC (Virtual Network Computing) enables us to access the GUI of a remote system over a secured network. The VNC client installed on a local system captures the input events of a mouse and keyboard and transfers them to the remote VNC server. Those events are executed on a remote system and the output is sent back to the client. VNC is a desktop sharing tool and is generally used to access the desktop system for remote administration and technical support.

With Ubuntu server, we rarely need a desktop environment. However, if you are a newbie administrator or quite unfamiliar with the command line environment, then GUI becomes a handy tool for you. Plus, you may want to deploy a shared remote desktop environment where people can collaborate with each other. This recipe covers the installation of the VNC server on Ubuntu Server 14.04. We will install a GUI component that is required by VNC and then install and configure the VNC server.

Getting ready

You will need access to a root account or an account with sudo privileges.

How to do it...

The Ubuntu server and cloud editions generally ship with a minimal installation footprint and do not contain GUI components. We will use Gnome-core as our desktop component. Gnome-core is a part of an open source desktop environment.

1. Access the server shell and use the following command to install `gnome-core`:

    ```
    $ sudo apt-get update
    $ sudo apt-get install gnome-core -y
    ```

    This will take some time as the command needs to download a bunch of components and install them.

2. Once Gnome is installed, we can proceed with VNC server installation using the following command:

    ```
    $ sudo apt-get install vnc4server -y
    ```

3. When installation completes, start a new VNC session by using the following command:

    ```
    $ vncserver
    ```

As this is the first time we have started VNC, you will be prompted to set up a password. This session will also create a few configuration files required for VNC. Your screen should look similar to the screenshot below:

```
ubuntu@ubuntu:~$ vncserver

You will require a password to access your desktops.

Password:
Verify:

New 'ubuntu:1 (ubuntu)' desktop is ubuntu:1

Creating default startup script /home/ubuntu/.vnc/xstartup
Starting applications specified in /home/ubuntu/.vnc/xstartup
Log file is /home/ubuntu/.vnc/ubuntu:1.log
```

1. Next, we will edit the default configuration files created by our first session, kill the VNC process, and then edit the configuration file:

   $ vncserver -kill :1

   Killing Xvnc4 process ID 2118

2. Edit the default configuration file and set it to use the Gnome session. Open ~/.vnc/xstartup and uncomment or add the following line to it:

   $ nano ~/.vnc/xstartup

   #!/bin/sh

   # Uncomment the following two lines for normal desktop:

   unset SESSION_MANAGER

   # exec /etc/X11/xinit/xinitrc

   #[-x /etc/vnc/xstartup] && exec /etc/vnc/xstartup

   #[-r $HOME/.Xresources] && xrdb $HOME/.Xresources

   #xsetroot -solid grey

   #vncconfig -iconic &

   #x-terminal-emulator -geometry 80x24+10+10 -ls -title "$VNCDESKTOP Desktop" &

   #x-window-manager &

   metacity &

   gnome-settings-daemon &

   gnome-panel &

3. Optionally, disable the Gnome startup script. This will stop Gnome from starting with a system boot and you will see a CLI login instead of the new Gnome-based graphical login screen. Open `/etc/init/gdm.conf` and comment out the following lines:

```
$ sudo nano /etc/init/gdm.conf

#start on ((filesystem

#              and runlevel [!06]

#              and started dbus

#              and plymouth-ready)

#          or runlevel PREVLEVEL=S)
```

4. Save all modifications in configuration files and start a new VNC session. This time, we will add screen resolution and color depth options:

```
$ vncserver -geometry 1366x768 -depth 24
```

```
ubuntu@ubuntu:~$
ubuntu@ubuntu:~$ vncserver -geometry 1366x768 -depth 24

New 'ubuntu:1 (ubuntu)' desktop is ubuntu:1

Starting applications specified in /home/ubuntu/.vnc/xstartup
Log file is /home/ubuntu/.vnc/ubuntu:1.log
```

5. Next, from your local system, install the VNC client software and open it. I have used the TightVNC client. Enter your server IP address and a VNC desktop number to be connected. Here, we have created a single session to a sample IP address, which will be `192.168.0.1:1`:

6. Click **Connect**; you will be prompted for a password to authenticate your session:

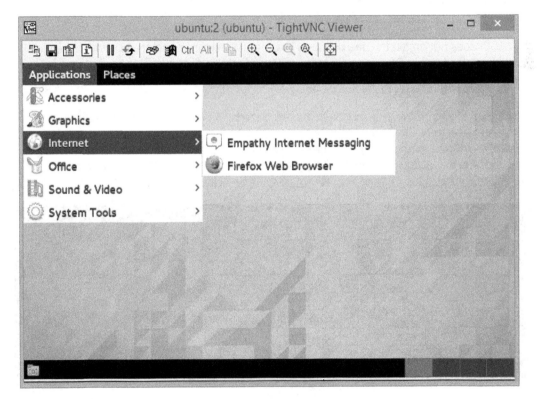

7. Enter the password that we created while starting the first session. You should see a desktop screen with a basic Gnome theme. The following is the scaled screenshot of the VNC viewer:

How it works...

VNC works with a client-server model. We have installed the VNC server daemon on our Ubuntu Server and a client on the local system. The server daemon communicates with the GUI buffer or frame buffer on the server side and transfers that buffer data to the client. The client renders that buffer in specially designed software called the VNC viewer. In addition to rendering the remote buffer, the VNC client or viewer captures mouse and keyboard (input) events happening over the client window. Those events are then sent to the VNC server, which applies them to the current graphics frame and any updates are sent back to client.

The pevious example uses simple Gnome-core components. This is a basic graphics suite which contains graphics drives, plus some other tools such as the Firefox browser and an instant messaging client. You can even choose to have a limited setup and install selective, required selected required Gnome packages as follows:

```
$ sudo apt-get install gnome-panel gnome-settings-daemon \
metacity nautilus gnome-terminal
```

This GUI does not match the one provided by Ubuntu Desktop. If you prefer to have the same experience as Ubuntu Desktop, you can separately install a package, `ubuntu-desktop`:

```
$ sudo apt-get install ubuntu-desktop
```

VNC does support multiple sessions to a single server. You may have noticed in the connection address used previously that we used **:1** to represent the first session or display. This is shorthand for the full port number, which is `5901` for the first session, `5092` for the second, and so on. You can use the full port or just the last digit to refer to a session. Notice the change in desktop number when we start multiple VNC sessions:

```
ubuntu@ubuntu:~$ vncserver -geometry 640x480 -depth 24

New 'ubuntu:1 (ubuntu)' desktop is ubuntu:1

Starting applications specified in /home/ubuntu/.vnc/xstartup
Log file is /home/ubuntu/.vnc/ubuntu:1.log

ubuntu@ubuntu:~$ vncserver -geometry 640x480 -depth 24

New 'ubuntu:2 (ubuntu)' desktop is ubuntu:2

Starting applications specified in /home/ubuntu/.vnc/xstartup
Log file is /home/ubuntu/.vnc/ubuntu:2.log
```

Additionally, you can start a new VNC session for different users with its own password. Simply log in or switch (su user1) to the user account, start `vncserver`, set the password, and you are done.

See also

▶ How VNC works on Stack Overflow - `http://stackoverflow.com/questions/4833152/how-realvnc-works`

Installing Hackpad, a collaborative document editor

In this recipe, we will install a collaborative document editor, Hackpad. It is a document editor based on an open source editor, EtherPad. Hackpad was acquired by Dropbox, and in early 2015 they open sourced its code.

Getting ready

You will need a system with at least 2 GB of memory.

As always, you will need an account with super user privileges.

How to do it...

Hackpad is a web application based on Java. We will need to install the JDK; **Scala**, which is another programming language; and MySQL as a data store. We will start by installing dependencies and then cloning the Hackpad repository from GitHub.

1. Install JDK and Scala. The installation document mentions Sun JDK as a requirement but it works with Open JDK.

   ```
   $ sudo apt-get update
   $ sudo apt-get install openjdk-7-jdk scala -y
   ```

2. Install the MySQL server. You can get more details on MySQL installation in the chapter handling the database:

   ```
   $ sudo apt-get install mysql-server-5.6
   ```

3. Next, clone the Hackpad repository. You can choose not to install Git and download the ZIP archive of Hackpad from GitHub:

   ```
   $ git clone https://github.com/dropbox/hackpad.git
   ```

4. This will create a new directory, `hackpad`. Before we run the build script, we need to set some configuration parameters to match our environment. Change the directory to `hackpad` and edit the `bin/exports.sh` file as follows:

   ```
   export SCALA_HOME="/usr/share/java"
   export SCALA_LIBRARY_JAR="$SCALA_HOME/scala-library.jar"
   export JAVA_HOME="/usr/share/java"
   ```

5. Next, create a configuration file as a copy of the default configuration, as follows:

```
$ cp etherpad/etc/etherpad.localdev-default.properties \
etherpad/etc/etherpad.local.properties
```

6. Edit the newly created configuration, get the admin email address, and search for the following line in `etherpad/etc/etherpad.local.properties`:

```
etherpad.superUserEmailAddresses =
__email_addresses_with_admin_access__
```

Replace it with:

```
etherpad.superUserEmailAddresses = admin@yourdomain.tld
```

Optionally, you can set the project to production mode by setting `isProduction` to `true`:

```
devMode = false
verbose = true
etherpad.fakeProduction = false
etherpad.isProduction = true
```

7. If you are using a domain name other than localhost, then configure the same with the following option:

```
topdomains =yourdomain.tld,localhost
```

8. Set your email host settings. You will need an email address to receive your registration confirmation email. However, this is not a hard requirement for initial setup:

```
smtpServer = Your SMTP server
smtpUser = SMTP user
smtpPass = SMTP password
```

9. Next, run a build script from the bin directory:

```
$ ./bin/build.sh
```

10. Once the build completes, set up the MySQL database. The script will create a new database named `hackpad` and a MySQL user account. You will be asked to enter your MySQL root account password:

```
$ ./contrib/scripts/setup-mysql-db.sh
```

```
ubuntu@ubuntu:~/hackpad$ ./contrib/scripts/setup-mysql-db.sh
Creating database hackpad...
Enter password:
Granting priviliges...
Enter password:
Success
ubuntu@ubuntu:~/hackpad$
```

11. Finally, you can start the server by executing `run.sh` from the bin directory:

    $ ./bin/run.sh

    This will take a few seconds to start the application. Once you see the HTTP server is listening to the line, you can access Hackpad at `http://yourdomain.tld:9000`:

```
ubuntu@ubuntu:~/hackpad$
ubuntu@ubuntu:~/hackpad$ ./bin/run.sh
./bin/run.sh: line 30: /home/ubuntu/hackpad/etherpad/data/etherpad.pid: No such
file or directory
Maximum ram: 1701M
Maximum thread count: 283
Using config file: ./etc/etherpad.local.properties
OpenJDK 64-Bit Server VM warning: Cannot open file ./data/logs/backend/jvm-gc.lo
g due to No such file or directory

Using mysql database type.
Establishing mysql connection (this may take a minute)...
mysql connection established.
Building cache for live migrations...
HTTP server listening on http://localhost:9000/
```

12. Access Hackpad and register with an email address that is used for an admin account. If you have set up an email server, you should receive a confirmation email containing a link to activate your account.

    If you have not set up email server access to the MySQL database to get your authentication token, open the MySQL client and use the following queries to get your token. The MySQL password for the Hackpad account is taken from the configuration file:

    ```
    $ mysql -h localhost -u hackpad -ppassword
    mysql> use hackpad;
    mysql> select * from email_signup;
    ```

13. Select your token from the row matching your email address and replace it in the following URL. In this case, the auth toke is `PgEJoGAiL3E2ZD12FqMc`:

    ```
    http://yourdomain.com:9000/ep/account/validate-
    email?email=user@youremail.com&token=your_auth_token_from_db
    ```

    The full auth URL for my admin account will look like this:

    ```
    http://localhost.local:9000/ep/account/validate-email?email=admin@
    localhost.local&token= PgEJoGAiL3E2ZD12FqMc
    ```

14. Open this URL in the browser and your account registration will be confirmed. You will be logged in to your Hackpad account.

    Once you log in to your new account, Hackpad will start with a welcome screen listing all the default pads that looks something like the following:

    You can click any of them and start editing or create a new document. When opened, you will get a full page to add contents, with basic text editing options in the top bar:

The document can be shared using the invite box or simply by sharing the URL.

How it works...

As mentioned before, Hackpad is a collaborative editor based on an open source project, EtherPad. It allows you to create online documents directly in your browser. In the same way as Google Docs, you can use Hackpad to create and store your documents in the cloud. Plus, you can access Hackpad from any device. All your documents will be rendered in a proper format suitable for your device.

When you log in for the first time, the home screen will greet you with stock pads. You can edit existing pads or start a new one from the top bar. An editor will give you a basic text editing setting, plus options to create lists and add comments. You can even add data in a tabular format. Click on the gear icon from the top bar and it will give you options to view document history, get an embedded link, or delete the document.

Every change in the document will be marked with your username, and if two or more people are working with the document at the same time, then the specific line being edited by each user is marked with the user's tag:

On the right-hand side of the document, you can see the options to invite your peers to collaborate on this document. You can invite people using their email address. Make sure that you have configured your email server before using this feature. Alternatively, the invites are also shown in a chat window with clickable links, as shown in the following screenshot:

At the bottom of the document, you can find all activity logs about the new initiation and the editing of this document. There is an option to chat with participating people directly from the same window. It is located at the bottom corner of the right-hand side; it's the small bar with a chat icon named after your domain. This provides one-to-one chat, as well as a group chat:

localhost	□ LOCALHOST CHAT (2 ONLINE)	⚙
🗍 admin		*January 8, 2016*
🗍 uday	admin: Hey UD	12:15
	admin: Check out the document shared with you	12:16

> Note that this setup does not work with IP addresses. You will need a domain name that maps to an IP address. You can set localhost files to set up local domain mappings, or use a local DNS server for your internal network.

There's more

Hackpad is a collaborative document editor. You can add snippets of code in a given document but not entire code files. To edit your code, you can use an open source Cloud IDE named Cloud 9 IDE. Check out the GitHub repo at `https://github.com/c9/core/`. Alternatively, you can get Docker images set up quickly and play around with the IDE.

Using Hackpad with Docker

The Hackpad setup contains a Docker file as well. If you have Docker installed, you can build a Docker image for Hackpad. Simply change your directory to `Hackpad git repo` and build a Docker image with the following command:

```
$ docker build -t hackpad
```

See also

Read more about Hackpad at the following links:

- ▸ Hackpad with Docker at `https://github.com/dropbox/hackpad/blob/master/DOCKER.md`
- ▸ Hackpad repo at `https://github.com/dropbox/hackpad`
- ▸ Etherpad at `http://etherpad.org/`
- ▸ Cloud 9 IDE at `https://c9.io/`

Installing Mattermost – a self-hosted slack alternative

This recipe covers another open source collaboration tool, Mattermost. **Mattermost** is a modern communication tool that includes one-to-one chat, group chat IRC-like channels, file sharing, and a super-fast search functionality. It can be thought of as a modern IRC tool. Mattermost is well known as an open source Slack alternative, but the Mattermost website says it is not limited to being a Slack alternative. You can find a list of features at `http://www.mattermost.org/features`.

The GitHub repository contains a step-by-step guide for installing Mattermost on production servers. We will use the same guide as our base.

Getting ready

You will need a 64-bit Ubuntu server and access to an account with sudo privileges. Mattermost prebuilt binaries are available only on a 64-bit platform. If you are running 32-bit Ubuntu, you will need to compile Mattermost from source. We will use MySQL as a database for Mattermost. I will use the same server for the database and Mattermost. You may want to separate these services on two different servers for better performance.

Create a separate MySQL user account and database for Mattermost. I will use the lowercase `mattermost` as a database name as well as a username.

Additionally, you will need a proxy if you are planning to load balance multiple Mattermost instances or have a secure setup with SSL enabled.

You will need a separate storage directory for shared multimedia contents. You should use a separate large volume specifically assigned for this purpose. Make sure that the directory is owned by the current user. To keep things simple, I will use a data directory under the current user's home, that is, `/home/ubuntu/mattermost-data`.

How to do it...

Mattermost is based on Golang as a backend and React, a JavaScript framework, for the frontend. Golang is capable of creating self-sufficient independent binaries. We will download the prebuilt package available on GitHub. As of writing this, the latest stable version is 1.3.0:

1. Download the Mattermost archive with the following command:

   ```
   $ wget
   https://github.com/mattermost/platform/releases/download/v1.3.
   0/mattermost.tar.gz
   ```

2. Extract content from the archive. This will create a new directory named `mattermost`:

   ```
   $ tar -xf mattermost.tar.gz
   ```

3. Next, edit the Mattermost configuration file located under the `config` directory:

   ```
   $ cd mattermost
   ```

   ```
   $ vi config/config.json
   ```

4. It is already configured to use MySQL as a data source. We need to set our username and password details for the database. Search for the SqlSettings section and replace the content of the `DataSource` parameter with the following line:

   ```
   "DataSource": "mattermost:
   password@tcp(localhost:3306)/mattermost?charset=utf8mb4,utf
   8"
   ```

5. Next, search for the FileSettings section and set the `Directory` parameter to the directory we created for multimedia content:

   ```
   "Directory":"/home/ubuntu/mattermost-data/"
   ```

6. Now, run the Mattermost server with the following command, and wait for the server to start listening:

   ```
   $./bin/platform
   ```

7. Now you can access the Mattermost service at the hostname of your server at `http://server_ip_or_host:8065`. However, the service is still running from the console and will be terminated when we close the terminal.

8. Terminate this process by pressing *Ctrl + C* and set a startup daemon so that we can start Mattermost in the backend and automatically start the service on system reboot.

9. Create a new upstart configuration under the `/etc/init` directory:

```
$ sudo nano /etc/init/mattermost.conf
```

10. Add the following content to the newly created file:

```
start on runlevel [2345]
stop on runlevel [016]
respawn
chdir /home/ubuntu/mattermost
setuid ubuntu
exec bin/platform
```

11. Now you can start Mattermost with any of the following commands:

```
$ sudo start mattermost
```

Or

```
$ sudo service mattermost start
```

Optionally, if you want to load balance the Mattermost service using Nginx or HAProxy in front of it, please refer to *Chapter 3, Working with Web Servers,* for detail on how to do so. The use of a load balancer will also give you an option to enable SSL security for all communication.

12. Once you start the Mattermost service and access the homepage, you will be asked to sign up. Create an account with an email address and you can start using your own Mattermost instance. You can access the server at `http://yourserver:8065`.

How it works...

Mattermost is all about team communication and collaboration. When you access the Mattermost server for the first time and sign up with your email address, you will get an option to create a new team or join existing teams.:

Mattermost

All team communication in one place, searchable and accessible anywhere

> Email Address

Create Team

Find my teams

To join an existing team, you need to submit your email address and Mattermost will reply with links to the team page where you are a member. If you have not yet created a team, simply proceed with signup. On signup, after you have entered your email address, you will be asked to select a team name and URI or a web address for your team page. Enter a good name for your team and click **Next**:

Team Name

ubuntu cookbook

Name your team in any language. Your team name shows in menus and headings.

Next >

On the next page, you will be asked to choose a URL for your team page. The box should be pre-filled with a suggested URL. Feel free to change it if you have a better idea:

Team URL

http://54.169.15.171:...   ubuntu-cookbook

Choose the web address of your new team:

- Short and memorable is best
- Use lowercase letters, numbers and dashes
- Must start with a letter and can't end in a dash

Next >

Once you are done with signup, you will be greeted with a welcome message and a simple walkthrough of the Mattermost service. Once you are done with the introduction, you will land on the Town Square channel. This is a prebuilt public channel accessible to all users. There's one more prebuilt channel named Off-Topic listed on the left side menu. You can create your own public channel, create a Private Group, or have a one-to-one chat through Direct Messages.

Beginning of Town Square

Welcome to Town Square!

This is the first channel teammates see when they sign up - use it for posting updates everyone needs to know.

&+ Invite others to this team   / Set a header

Write a message...

Before you start using the service, invite some more users to your team. Click on the **Invite others to this team** link or click on your username at the top left and then select the Invite New Member link. Here, you can enter the email and name of a single member to invite them. Optionally, you can get a team invite link, which can be shared with a group:

Team Invite Link   ✕

Send teammates the link below for them to sign-up to this team site.

http://54.169.15.171:8065/signup_user_complete/?
id=cwh9amzt6inq5f7q4pxu1bucfo

Copy Link   Close

The username menu on the left gives you some more options. You can update team settings, manage team members, and even create a new team altogether. You will need to be a team admin to access these options. If you are part of multiple teams, then you can see an option to switch to a different team.

The team members will receive all communication in public channels. A user can decide to be a part of a channel or leave it and not receive any communication from a specific channel. Other options are Private group and Direct messages. In private groups, you can communicate and share with selected people and not the entire team, whereas in a direct message, as the name suggests, it is a one-to-one chat.

Every single message shared using Mattermost is archived and stored on the Mattermost server. Users can access their respective communication history and even search for a specific message, or documents from a specific user. Shared documents also become part of the archive and are available for later use. The search menu is available at the top-right corner of the screen.

The first user to sign up on Mattermost will get additional admin rights and can access the System Console (from the username menu) to configure system settings and set global defaults. Here, you can configure the database, set your email server and configure email notifications, configure default team settings, check system logs, and much more. When using Mattermost in production mode, make sure that you have configured the SMTP service under email settings and enabled email notifications. You can also enable email verification where account activation will need a user to verify their email address.

There's more ...

The Mattermost service provides an option to integrate with various other popular services. One such service we have worked with is the GitLab server. While working with Git, we have seen the installation process of the GitLab omnibus package. The omnibus package contains Mattermost as a configurable component. If you have GitLab installed through the Omnibus package, check its configuration to enable the Mattermost service. Alternatively, you can configure GitLab integration from the Mattermost settings as well.

From version 1.1, Mattermost added support for web hooks to integrate with external services. Mattermost supports both incoming and outgoing hooks. Incoming hooks can pull events from external services and vice versa. These hooks are compatible with Slack APIs and the tools developed to work with Slack should work with self-hosted Mattermost as well.

See also

Read more about Mattermost by following these resources:

- Mattermost features: `http://www.mattermost.org/features`
- Installation on Ubuntu: `http://docs.mattermost.com/install/prod-ubuntu.html`
- Mattermost Dockerfile: `https://hub.docker.com/r/mattermost/platform/`
- Mattermost web-hooks: `http://www.mattermost.org/webhooks/`
- Mattermost Source Code on GitHub: `https://github.com/mattermost/platform`

Installing OwnCloud, self-hosted cloud storage

OwnCloud is a self-hosted file storage and synchronization service. It provides client tools to upload and sync all your files to a central storage server. You can access all your data through a well-designed web interface, which can be accessed on any device of your choice. In addition to a simple contact service, OwnCloud supports contacts, email, and calendar synchronization. Plus, all your data is stored on your own server, making it a more secure option.

In this recipe, we will learn how to install the OwnCloud service on the Ubuntu server. We will be working with a basic OwnCloud setup that includes file sharing and storage. Later, you can add separate plugins to extend the capability of your OwnCloud installation.

Getting ready

You will need access to an account with sudo privileges.

How to do it...

OwnCloud is a PHP-based web application. Its dependencies include a web server, PHP runtime, and a database server. We will use the installation package provided by OwnCloud. The package takes care of all dependencies, plus it will help in updating our installation whenever a new version is available. We will install the latest stable version of OwnCloud. As of writing this, OwnCloud does not provide any packages for Ubuntu 16.04. I have used the package for Ubuntu 15.10:

1. Add the OwnCloud repository public key to your Ubuntu server:

   ```
   $ wget
   https://download.owncloud.org/download/repositories/stable/Ubu
   ntu_15.10/Release.key -O owncloud.key

   $ sudo apt-key add - < owncloud.key
   ```

2. Next, add the OwnCloud repository to installation sources. Create a new source list:

   ```
   $ sudo touch /etc/apt/sources.list.d/owncloud.list
   ```

3. Add an installation path to the newly created source list:

   ```
   $ sudo nano /etc/apt/sources.list.d/owncloud.list

   deb
   http://download.owncloud.org/download/repositories/stable/Ubun
   tu_15.10/ /
   ```

4. Update installation sources with the `apt-get update` command:

```
$ sudo apt-get update
```

5. Install the OwnCloud package. This will download and install all dependencies, download the OwnCloud package, and set up the Apache web server virtual host configuration. By default, OwnCloud use SQLite as a default database. This can be changed at the signup page:

```
$ sudo apt-get install owncloud
```

6. Once installed, you can access your OwnCloud installation at `http://your_server/owncloud`. This will open the registration page for an admin account. Enter the admin username and password for a new account. The first user to register will be marked as the admin of the OwnCloud instance.

> Your server may return a **Not Found** error for the preceding URL. In that case, you need to configure Apache and point it to the OwnCloud setup. Open the default virtual host file `/etc/apache2/sites-available/000-default.conf` and change `DocumentRoot` to match the following:
>
> `DocumentRoot /var/www/owncloud`
>
> Reload the Apache server for the changes to take effect. Now you should be able to access OwnCloud at `http://your_server`.

The same page contains a warning saying the default database is SQLite. Click the configure database link; this will show you the option to enter database connection details. Enter all the required details and click submit.

Once registration completes, you will be redirected to the OwnCloud homepage. If you need any help, this page contains the OwnCloud user manual. You can start uploading content or create new text files right from the homepage.

Optionally, install OwnCloud desktop and mobile applications to sync files across all your devices.

How it works...

OwnCloud is a web application that enables you to synchronize and share files across the web. Store a backup of all your files on a central OwnCloud server, or use it as a central place to send and receive files. OwnCloud also provides native applications for all platforms so that you can easily replicate the necessary data across all your devices. Once you have logged in to your account, OwnCloud will list the default directory structure with a PDF file for the user manual. The screen should look similar to the following:

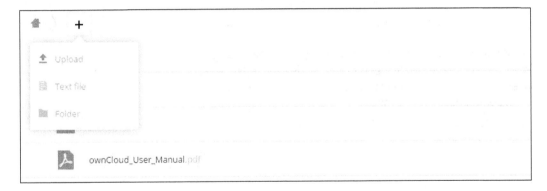

With the recent updates, OwnCloud has removed various default packages and reduced the overall binary size. For now, the default installation contains a file browser, an activity monitor, and a gallery. The file browser supports the uploading, viewing, and sharing of files. You can create new text files and open PDF files right from the browser:

Default features can be extended from the **Apps** submenu accessible from the **Files** link at the top, left of the screen. It gives you a list of installed and enabled or disabled apps. Plus, you can search for apps across categories such as Multimedia, Productivity, Games, and Tools. Choose your desired category, scroll to the desired app and click enable to install a new component:

OwnCloud also allows flexible user management. When logged in as an admin user, you can access the Users menu from the top-right login section of the screen. Under users, you can create a new user, assign them to a group, create a new group, and even set the disk quota allowed:

Next is the admin section, which is again accessible to users from the admin group at the top-right of the screen. This section lists all the administrative settings relating to the core OwnCloud setup, as well as for installed apps. Each section contains a link to detailed documentation. The important part of the settings is the email server setup. By default, OwnCloud uses default PHP-based emails. It is recommended you set up an SMTP service. You can use external SMTP service providers, such as MailChimp, or set up your own SMTP server. At the bottom of the admin settings page, you can see some links to improve your OwnCloud experience. This includes performance tuning the OwnCloud setup, security guidelines, theme support, and so on.

See also

- OwnCloud repositories: `https://download.owncloud.org/download/repositories/stable/owncloud/`

- OwnCloud admin manual: `https://doc.owncloud.org/server/8.2/admin_manual/`

13
Performance Monitoring

In this chapter, we will cover the following recipes:

- ▶ Monitoring the CPU
- ▶ Monitoring memory and swap
- ▶ Monitoring the network
- ▶ Monitoring storage
- ▶ Setting performance benchmarks

Introduction

When starting a new server, we tend to use stock images of the Ubuntu server and default installation process. The focus is on developing and improving the application code. The base operating system is not given much attention until we hit some performance issues. Once you reach the tip of application level optimizations and have collected all low-hanging fruit, the next obvious target is system monitoring and resource optimization. In this chapter, we will focus on various performance monitoring tools. We will learn to use various tools to track down the bottlenecks and then briefly look at possible solutions.

The chapter is separated in various recipes, and each covers the monitoring of a single system resource, such as the CPU and memory. At the end of the chapter, we will learn how to set up a performance baseline and use it to compare different configurations of system parameters.

Monitoring the CPU

Modern CPUs generally do not become bottlenecks for performance. The processing power is still far ahead of the data transfer speeds of I/O devices and networks. Generally, the CPU spends a big part of processing time waiting for synchronous IO to fetch data from the disk or from a network device. Tracking exact CPU usage is quite a confusing task. Most of the time, you will find higher CPU use, but in reality, the CPU is waiting for data to become available.

In this recipe, we will focus on tracking CPU performance. We will look at some common tools used to get CPU usage details.

Getting ready

You may need `sudo` privileges to execute some commands.

How to do it...

Let's start with the most commonly used monitoring command that is `top` command. The `top` command shows a summarized view of various resource utilization metrics. This includes CPU usage, memory and swap utilization, running processes, and their respective resource consumption, and so on. All metrics are updated at a predefined interval of three seconds.

Follow these steps to monitor the CPU:

1. To start top, simply type in `top` in your command prompt and press *Enter*:

   ```
   $ top
   ```

```
top - 20:22:53 up 10:53,  2 users,  load average: 0.25, 0.52, 0.53
Tasks: 107 total,   3 running, 102 sleeping,   2 stopped,   0 zombie
%Cpu(s):  9.1 us, 13.1 sy,  0.0 ni, 54.8 id,  0.0 wa,  0.0 hi, 22.9 si,  0.0 st
KiB Mem:   4047976 total,   657272 used,  3390704 free,    40836 buffers
KiB Swap:  1044476 total,        0 used,  1044476 free.   465296 cached Mem

  PID USER      PR  NI    VIRT    RES    SHR S  %CPU %MEM     TIME+ COMMAND
 8292 ubuntu    20   0   40016  12268   6448 R  80.8  0.3   1:44.48 python
    8 root      20   0       0      0      0 S  17.2  0.0   0:25.68 rcuos/0
    3 root      20   0       0      0      0 S   2.3  0.0   0:04.27 ksoftirqd/0
    7 root      20   0       0      0      0 S   1.3  0.0   0:18.50 rcu_sched
```

2. As you can see in the preceding screenshot, a single Python process is using 80% of CPU time. The CPU is still underutilized, with 58% time in idle processes:

Optionally, you can use the `htop` command. This is the same process monitor as top, but a little easier to use, and it provides text graphs for CPU and memory utilization. You will need to install htop separately:

```
$ sudo apt-get install htop      # one time command
$ htop
```

```
  1  [||||||||||||||||           43.1%]    Tasks: 40, 29 thr; 1 running
  2  [|||||||||||||              31.4%]    Load average: 0.14 0.25 0.15
Mem[|||||||||||              577/3953MB]    Uptime: 00:06:31
Swp[                           0/1019MB]

  PID USER       PRI  NI  VIRT   RES   SHR S CPU% MEM%   TIME+  Command
 2171 ubuntu      20   0 40016 12240  6420 S 51.1  0.3  0:04.12 python -m SimpleH
 2172 ubuntu      20   0 25744  3568  3032 R  2.3  0.1  0:00.17 htop
  918 root        20   0  251M 15012 12492 S  0.8  0.4  0:01.26 /usr/bin/docker -
 1225 mysql       20   0 1108M  461M 13744 S  0.0 11.7  0:03.57 /usr/sbin/mysqld
```

3. While top is used to get an overview of all running processes, the command `pidstat` can be used to monitor CPU utilization by an individual process or program. Use the following command to monitor CPU consumed by MySQL (or any other task name):

```
$ pidstat -C mysql
```

```
ubuntu@ubuntu:~$ pidstat -C mysql
Linux 3.16.0-30-generic (ubuntu)         01/16/2016      _x86_64_        (2 CPU)

08:39:30 PM    UID      PID   %usr %system  %guest    %CPU  CPU  Command
08:39:30 PM    105     8458   0.00    0.00    0.00    0.00    1  mysqld
ubuntu@ubuntu:~$
```

4. With `pidstat`, you can also query statistics for a specific process by its process ID or PID, as follows:

```
$ pidstat -p 1134
```

5. The other useful command is `vmstat`. This is primarily used to get details on virtual memory usages but also includes some CPU metrics similar to the `top` command:

```
ubuntu@ubuntu:~$ vmstat 1
procs -----------memory---------- ---swap-- -----io---- -system-- ------cpu-----
 r  b   swpd   free    buff  cache   si   so    bi    bo   in   cs us sy id wa st
 1  0      0 2933084  41284 466000    0    0     6     5   27   33  1  0 98  0
0
 0  0      0 2933068  41284 466000    0    0     0     0   40   77  0  1 99  0
0
 0  0      0 2933068  41284 466000    0    0     0     0   25   57  0  0 100  0
 0
```

6. Another command for getting processor statistics is `mpstat`. This returns the same statistics as `top` or `vmstat` but is limited to CPU statistics. Mpstat is not a part of the default Ubuntu installation; you need to install the `sysstat` package to use the `mpstat` command:

   $ sudo apt-get install sysstat -y

7. By default, `mpstat` returns combined averaged stats for all CPUs. Flag `-P` can be used to get details of specific CPUs. The following command will display statistics for processor one (0) and processor two (1), and update at an interval of 3 seconds:

   $ mpstat -P 0,1 3

```
ubuntu@ubuntu:~$ mpstat -P 0,1
Linux 3.16.0-30-generic (ubuntu)        01/16/2016     _x86_64_        (2 CPU)

08:50:32 PM  CPU    %usr   %nice    %sys %iowait    %irq   %soft  %steal  %guest
  %gnice   %idle
08:50:32 PM    0    0.36    0.00    0.36    0.15    0.00    0.55    0.00    0.00
    0.00   98.58
08:50:32 PM    1    2.24    0.00    0.22    0.09    0.00    0.00    0.00    0.00
    0.00   97.45
```

8. One more command, `sar` (**System Activity Reporter**), gives details of system performance.

   The following command will extract the CPU metrics recorded by `sar`. Flag `-u` will limit details to CPU only and `-P` will display data for all available CPUs separately. By default, the `sar` command will limit the output to CPU details only:

   $ sar -u -p ALL

```
ubuntu@ubuntu:~$ sar -u -P ALL
Linux 3.16.0-30-generic (ubuntu)        01/23/2016       _x86_64_        (2 CPU)

08:34:56 AM        LINUX RESTART

08:35:01 AM     CPU     %user    %nice   %system   %iowait    %steal    %idle
08:45:01 AM     all     2.38     0.00      6.99      1.20      0.00    89.42
08:45:01 AM       0     1.32     0.00     10.16      1.35      0.00    87.17
08:45:01 AM       1     3.38     0.00      4.00      1.07      0.00    91.55

Average:        CPU     %user    %nice   %system   %iowait    %steal    %idle
Average:        all     2.38     0.00      6.99      1.20      0.00    89.42
Average:          0     1.32     0.00     10.16      1.35      0.00    87.17
Average:          1     3.38     0.00      4.00      1.07      0.00    91.55
```

9. To get current CPU utilization using `sar`, specify the interval, and optionally, counter values. The following command will output 5 records at an interval of 2 seconds:

   ```
   $ sar -u 2 5
   ```

```
ubuntu@ubuntu:~$ sar -u 2 5
Linux 3.16.0-30-generic (ubuntu)        01/23/2016       _x86_64_        (2 CPU)

08:49:30 AM     CPU     %user    %nice   %system   %iowait    %steal    %idle
08:49:32 AM     all     0.25     0.00      0.00      0.00      0.00    99.75
08:49:34 AM     all     0.00     0.00      0.25      0.00      0.00    99.75
08:49:36 AM     all     0.00     0.00      0.25      0.00      0.00    99.75
08:49:38 AM     all     0.00     0.00      0.00      0.00      0.00   100.00
08:49:40 AM     all     0.25     0.00      0.25      0.00      0.00    99.50
Average:        all     0.10     0.00      0.15      0.00      0.00    99.75
```

10. All this data can be stored in a file specified by the (-o) flag. The following command will create a file named `sarReport` in your current directory, with details of CPU utilization:

    ```
    $ sar -u -o sarReport 3 5
    ```

Other options include flag –u, to limit the counter to CPU, and flag A, to get system-wide counters that include network, disk, interrupts, and many more. Check `sar` manual (man `sar`) to get specific flags for your desired counters.

How it works...

This recipe covers some well known CPU monitoring tools, starting with the very commonly used command, `top`, to the background metric logging tool SAR.

In the preceding example, we used top to get a quick summarized view of the current state of the system. By default, top shows the average CPU usage. It is listed in the third row of top output. If you have more than one CPU, their usage is combined and displayed in one single column. You can press *1* when top is running to get details of all available CPUs. This should expand the CPU row to list all CPUs. The following screenshot shows two CPUs available on my virtual machine:

```
top - 20:31:17 up 11:01,  2 users,  load average: 0.27, 0.19, 0.36
Tasks: 106 total,   3 running, 101 sleeping,   2 stopped,   0 zombie
%Cpu0  : 24.4 us, 24.1 sy,  0.0 ni,  1.3 id,  0.0 wa,  0.0 hi, 50.2 si,  0.0 st
%Cpu1  :  0.0 us,  1.4 sy,  0.0 ni, 98.6 id,  0.0 wa,  0.0 hi,  0.0 si,  0.0 st
KiB Mem:   4047976 total,    658196 used,   3389780 free,     40960 buffers
KiB Swap:  1044476 total,         0 used,   1044476 free.    465456 cached Mem

  PID USER      PR  NI    VIRT    RES    SHR S  %CPU %MEM     TIME+ COMMAND
 8292 ubuntu    20   0   40016  12268   6448 R  88.4  0.3   2:41.84 python
    8 root      20   0       0      0      0 S  10.6  0.0   0:36.30 rcuos/0
```

The CPU row shows various different categories of CPU utilization, and the following is a list of their brief descriptions:

- `us`: Time spent in running user space processes. This reflects the CPU consumption by your application.

- `sy`: Time taken by system processes. A higher number here can indicate too many processes, and the CPU is spending more time process scheduling.

- `ni`: Time spent with user space processes that are assigned with execution priority (nice value).

- `id`: Indicates the time spent in idle mode, where the CPU is doing nothing.

- `wa`: Waiting for IO. A higher value here means your CPU is spending too much time handling IO operations. Try improving IO performance or reducing IO at application level.

- `hi/si`: Time spent in hardware interrupts or software interrupts.

- `st`: Stolen CPU cycles. The hypervisor assigned these CPU cycles to another virtual machine. If you see a higher number in this field, try reducing the number of virtual machines from the host. If you are using a cloud service, try to get a new server, or change your service provider.

The second metric shown is the process level CPU utilization. This is listed in a tabular format under the column head, %CPU. This is the percentage of CPU utilization by each process. By default, the top output is automatically sorted in descending order of CPU utilization. Processes that are using higher CPU get listed at top. Another column, named TIME+, displays total CPU time used by each process. Check the processes section on the screen, which should be similar to the following screenshot:

PID	USER	PR	NI	VIRT	RES	SHR	S	%CPU	%MEM	TIME+	COMMAND
8292	ubuntu	20	0	40016	12268	6448	R	87.6	0.3	3:30.06	python
8	root	20	0	0	0	0	S	10.9	0.0	0:45.80	rcuos/0
3	root	20	0	0	0	0	S	1.3	0.0	0:06.15	ksoftirqd/0
7	root	20	0	0	0	0	S	0.3	0.0	0:25.41	rcu_sched
9	root	20	0	0	0	0	R	0.3	0.0	0:12.98	rcuos/1
1725	ubuntu	20	0	105744	4900	3824	S	0.3	0.1	0:04.17	sshd
8383	ubuntu	20	0	24828	2976	2540	R	0.3	0.1	0:00.35	top

If you have noticed the processes listed by top you should see that top itself is listed in the process list. Top is considered as a separate running process and also consumes CPU cycles.

> To get help on the **top** screen, press *H*; this will show you various key combinations to modify top output. For additional details, check out the manual pages with the command, man top. When you are done with top, press *Q*, to exit or use the exit combination, *Ctrl + C*.

With top, you can get a list of processes or tasks that are consuming most of the CPU time. To get more details of these tasks, you can use the command, pidstat. By default, pidstat shows CPU statistics. It can be used with a process name or **process ID** (**pid**). With pidstat, you can also query memory usages, IO statistics, child processes, and various other process related details. Check the manual page for pidstat using the command man pidstat.

Both commands, top as well as pidstat, give a summarized view of CPU utilization. Top output is refreshed at a specific interval and you cannot extract utilization details over a specific time period. Here comes the other handy command that is vmstat. When run without any parameters, vmstat outputs a single line with memory and CPU utilization, but you can ask vmstat to run infinitely and update the latest metrics at specific intervals using the delay parameter. All the output lines are preserved and can be used to compare the system stats for a given period. The following command will render updated metrics every 5 seconds:

```
$ vmstat 5
```

Optionally, specify the count after delay parameter to close `vmstat` after specific repetitions. The following command will update the stats 5 times at 1 second intervals and then exit:

```
$ vmstat 1 5
```

The details provided by `vmstat` are quite useful for real-time monitoring. The tool `sar` helps you to store all this data in log files and then extract specific details whenever needed. **Sar** collects data from various internal counters maintained by the Linux kernel. It collects data over a period of time which can be extracted when required. Using `sar` without any parameters will show you the data extracted from the previously saved file. The data is collected in a binary format and is located at the `/var/log/sysstat` directory. You may need to enable data collection in the `/etc/default/sysstat` file. When the stats collection is enabled, `sar` automatically collects data every 10 minutes. Sar is again available from the package `sysstat`. Along with the `sar` package, `sysstat` combines two utilities: command `sa1` to record daily system activity data in a binary format, and command `sa2` to extract that data to a human readable format. All data collected by `sar` can be extracted in a human readable format using the `sa2` command. Check the manual pages for both commands to get more details.

There's more...

Similar to sar, one more well-known tool is **collectd**. It gathers and stores system statistics, which can later be used to plot graphs.

See also

- Get information on your system CPU with the following command:

  ```
  $ less /proc/cpuinfo
  ```

- Details on /proc file system: `http://tldp.org/LDP/Linux-Filesystem-Hierarchy/html/proc.html`

Monitoring memory and swap

Memory is another important component of system performance. All files and data that are currently being used are kept in the system main memory for faster access. The CPU performance also depends on the availability of enough memory. Swap, on the other hand, is an extension to main memory. Swap is part of persistent storage, such as hard drives or solid state drives. It is utilized only when the system is low on main memory.

In this chapter, we will learn how to monitor system memory and swap utilization.

Getting ready

You may need `sudo` privileges for some commands.

How to do it...

In the last recipe, we used commands `top` and `vmstat` to monitor CPU utilization. These commands also provided details of memory usage. Let's start with the `top` command again:

1. Run the `top` command and check for the `Mem` and `Swap` rows:

```
top - 09:03:20 up 29 min,  2 users,  load average: 0.00, 0.01, 0.05
Tasks: 114 total,   1 running, 113 sleeping,   0 stopped,   0 zombie
%Cpu(s):  0.3 us,  0.2 sy,  0.0 ni, 99.5 id,  0.0 wa,  0.0 hi,  0.0 si,  0.0 st
KiB Mem:   4047976 total,   914372 used,  3133604 free,    26112 buffers
KiB Swap:  1044476 total,        0 used,  1044476 free.   297272 cached Mem
```

2. The **memory** line displays the size of total available memory, size of used memory, free memory, and the memory used for buffers and the file system cache. Similarly, **swap** row should display the allocated size of the swap if you have enabled the swapping. Along with these two lines, `top` shows per process memory utilization as well. The columns VIRT, RES, SHR, and %MEM all show different memory allocation for each process:

```
  PID USER      PR  NI    VIRT    RES    SHR S  %CPU %MEM     TIME+ COMMAND
 1225 mysql     20   0 1134984 473080  13744 S   0.7 11.7   0:08.93 mysqld
 2171 ubuntu    20   0   40016  12240   6420 S   0.3  0.3   1:06.74 python
 2374 ubuntu    20   0   24828   2972   2528 R   0.3  0.1   0:00.55 top
    1 root      20   0   33744   4316   2684 S   0.0  0.1   0:05.08 init
    2 root      20   0       0      0      0 S   0.0  0.0   0:00.01 kthreadd
    3 root      20   0       0      0      0 S   0.0  0.0   0:03.36 ksoftirqd/0
```

3. Similar to the `top` command, you can query memory statistics for a specific PID or program by using the `pidstat` command. By default, `pidstat` displays only CPU statistics for a given process. Use flag `-r` to query memory utilization and page faults:

```
$ pidstat -C mysql -r
```

4. Next, we will go through the `vmstat` command. This is an abbreviation of virtual memory statistics. Enter the command `vmstat` in your console and you should see output similar to the following screenshot:

```
ubuntu@ubuntu:~$ vmstat
procs -----------memory---------- ---swap-- -----io----- -system-- ------cpu-----
 r  b   swpd   free   buff  cache   si   so    bi    bo   in   cs us sy id wa st
 1  0      0 3133432 26204 297436    0    0    78    19  121  156  1  2 95  1
0
```

Using `vmstat` without any option returns a single line report of `memory`, `swap`, `io`, and CPU utilization. Under the `memory` column, it shows the amount of swap, free memory, and the memory used for cache and buffers. It also display a separate `swap` column with **Swap In** (`si`) and **Swap Out** (`so`) details.

5. To get detailed statistics of memory and event counters, use flag `-s`. This should display a table, as follows:

```
$ vmstat -s
```

```
ubuntu@ubuntu:~$ vmstat -s
      4047976 K total memory
       915040 K used memory
       586468 K active memory
       251360 K inactive memory
      3132936 K free memory
        26288 K buffer memory
       297540 K swap cache
      1044476 K total swap
            0 K used swap
      1044476 K free swap
```

6. Another handy command is `free`, which displays the amount of used and available memory in the system. Use it as follows, with the `-h` flag to get human-friendly units:

```
$ free -h
```

```
ubuntu@ubuntu:~$ free -h
              total        used        free      shared  buff/cache   available
Mem:           992M         37M        708M        3.2M        245M        921M
Swap:          1.0G          0B        1.0G
ubuntu@ubuntu:~$
```

7. Finally, command `sar` can give you periodic reports of memory utilization. Simply enable `sar` to collect all reports and then extract memory reports from it or set a specific command to log only memory and swap details.

8. Finally, use `sar` to monitor current memory and swap utilizations. The following command will query the current memory (`-r`) and swap (`-S`) utilization:

   `$ sar -rS 1 5`

```
ubuntu@ubuntu:~$ sar -rS 1 5
Linux 3.16.0-30-generic (ubuntu)         01/23/2016       _x86_64_        (2 CPU)

09:19:16 AM kbmemfree kbmemused  %memused kbbuffers  kbcached  kbcommit   %commi
t   kbactive    kbinact    kbdirty
09:19:17 AM   3132956    915020     22.60     26416    297676    910312     17.8
8    586880     251420         40

09:19:16 AM kbswpfree kbswpused  %swpused kbswpcad   %swpcad
09:19:17 AM   1044476         0      0.00        0      0.00
```

9. For more details on using `sar`, check *Monitoring the CPU* recipe or read the manual pages using the `man sar` command. The command `sar` is available in the package `sysstat`; you will need to install it separately if not already installed.

10. All these tools show process-level memory statistics. If you are interested in memory allocation inside a particular process, then the command `pmap` can help you. It reports the memory mapping of a process, including details of any shared libraries in use and any program extensions with their respective memory consumptions. Use `pmap` along with the PID you want to monitor as follows:

    `$ sudo pmap -x 1322`

> All information displayed by `pmap` is read from a file named `maps` located in the `/proc/ file` system. You can directly read the file as follows:
>
> `$ sudo cat /proc/1322/maps`

How it works...

System memory is the primary storage for processes in execution. It is the fastest available storage medium, but is volatile and limited in storage space. The limited storage is generally extended with the help of slower, disk-based Swap files. Processes that are not being actively executed are swapped to disk so that active processes get more space in the faster main memory. Similar to other operating systems, Ubuntu provides various tools to monitor system-wide memory utilization as well as memory uses by process. Commonly used tools include top, vmstat, and free.

We have used the `top` command to monitor CPU uses and know that top provides a summarized view of system resource utilization. Along with a CPU summary, top also provides the memory statistics. This includes overall memory utilization plus per process usage. The summary section in the `top` output displays the total available and used memory. It also contains a separate row for swap. By default, all Ubuntu systems enable the swap partition with nearly the same size as main memory. Some cloud service providers disable the cache for performance reasons.

The details section of top shows per process memory usage separated into multiple columns:

- Column `VIRT` shows the virtual memory assigned to a task or process; this includes memory assigned for program code, data, and shared libraries, plus memory that is assigned but not used.

- Column `RES` shows the non-swapped physical memory used by processes. Whereas column `SHR` shows the amount of shared memory, this is the memory that can be shared with other processes through shared libraries.

- The column `%MEM` shows the percentage of main memory assigned to a specific process. This is a percentage of `RES` memory available to task out of total available memory.

- By default, all memory values are shown in the lowest units, KB. This can be changed using the key combination, *Shift + E* for summary rows and *E* for process columns.

Similar to `top`, the command `ps` lists running processes but without refreshing the list. Without any options, `ps` shows the list of processes owned by the current user. Use it as follows to get a list of all running processes:

```
$ ps aux
```

Sometimes it is useful to monitor a specific process over a period of time. Top shows you a list of all running processes and `ps` gives you a one-time list. The following command will help you monitor a single program within `top`:

```
$ top -p $(pgrep process-name | head -20 | tr "\\n"
"," | sed 's/,$//')
```

The command `vmstat` gives you overall detail regarding memory and swap utilization. The memory column shows the amount of available memory. Next to the memory column, the swap column indicates the amount of memory read from disk (`si`) or written to disk (`so`) per second. Any activity in the `si` and `so` columns indicates active swap utilization. In that case, you should either increase the physical memory of the system or reduce the number of processes running. Large numbers under the swap column may also indicate higher CPU utilization, where the CPU waits for IO operations (`wa`) to complete. As seen before, you can specify the delay and interval options to repeatedly query `vmstat` reports.

One more command, named `free`, shows the current state of system memory. This shows overall memory utilization in the first row and swap utilization in the second row. You may get confused by looking at the lower values in the `free` column and assume higher memory uses. Part of free memory is being used by Linux to improve file system performance by caching frequently used files. The memory used for file caching is reflected in the `buff/cache` column and is available to other programs when required. Check the last column, named `available`, for the actual free memory.

 If you are on Ubuntu 14.04 or lower, the output of the `free` command will contain three rows, with overall memory utilization in the first row, actual memory utilization with cache and buffer adjustments in the second, and swap listed in the third row.

The second row of `free` output displays the swap utilization. You may see swap being used under the `used` column. This is the amount of swap allocated but not effectively used. To check if your system is effectively swapping, use the command `vmstat 1` and monitor `si/so` columns for any swap activity.

System swapping behavior also depends on the value of the kernel parameter named `vm.swappiness`. Its value can range between 0 to 100, where 0 configures the kernel to avoid swapping as much as possible and 100 sets it to swap aggressively. You can read the current `swappiness` value using the following command:

```
$ sudo sysctl vm.swappiness
vm.swappiness = 60
```

To modify the `swappiness` value for the current session, use the `sysctl` command with a new value, as follows. It is a good idea to use lower values and avoid swapping as much as possible:

```
$ sudo sysctl vm.swappiness=10
vm.swappiness = 10
```

To permanently set `swappiness`, you need to edit the `/etc/sysctl.conf` file and add or uncomment `vm.swappiness=10` to it. Once the file is updated, use the following command to read and set a new value from the configuration file:

```
$ sudo sysctl -p
```

Check the `swapon` and `swapoff` commands if you need to enable swapping or disable it.

There's more...

Most of these statistics are read from the `/proc` partition. The two main files listing details of memory and swap are `/proc/meminfo` and `/proc/swaps`.

The command `lshw` (list hardware) can give you the details of actual hardware. This includes the physical memory configuration, the firmware version, CPU details, such as clock speed, the cache, and various other hardware information. Use `lshw` as follows:

```
$ sudo lshw
```

See also

▶ Check the `swapon` and `swapoff` commands to enable or disable swap files:

```
$ man swapon
$ man swapoff
```

Monitoring the network

When we are talking about a server, its network is the most important resource. Especially in the cloud network, when it is the only communication channel to access the server and connect with other servers in the network. The network comes under an Input/Output device category. Networks are generally slow in performance and are an unreliable communication channel. You may lose some data while in transit, data may be exposed to external entities, or a malicious guy can update original data before it reaches you.

The Ubuntu server, as well as Linux in general, provides tons of utilities to ease network monitoring and administration. This recipe covers some inbuilt tools to monitor network traffic and its performance. We will also look at a few additional tools that are worth a space on your system.

Getting ready

Some commands may need `sudo` access.

You may need to install a few tools.

How to do it...

1. We will start with a commonly used command, that is, `ifconfig`. We mostly use this command to read the network configuration details such as the IP address. When called without any parameters, `ifconfig` displays details of all active network interfaces as follows:

```
ubuntu@ubuntu:~$ ifconfig
docker0    Link encap:Ethernet  HWaddr 56:84:7a:fe:97:99
           inet addr:172.17.42.1  Bcast:0.0.0.0  Mask:255.255.0.0
           UP BROADCAST MULTICAST  MTU:1500  Metric:1
           RX packets:0 errors:0 dropped:0 overruns:0 frame:0
           TX packets:0 errors:0 dropped:0 overruns:0 carrier:0
           collisions:0 txqueuelen:0
           RX bytes:0 (0.0 B)  TX bytes:0 (0.0 B)

eth0       Link encap:Ethernet  HWaddr 08:00:27:ea:fe:96
           inet addr:10.0.2.8  Bcast:10.0.2.255  Mask:255.255.255.0
```

2. These details contain the IP address assigned to each network interface, its hardware address, the **maximum packet size** (MTU) and basic statistics of **received** (RX) and **transmitted** (TX) packets, and the count of errors or dropped packets, and so on.

3. If you are only interested in quick network statistics, use `ifconfig` with flag `-s`, as follows:

```
ubuntu@ubuntu:~$ ifconfig -s
Iface   MTU Met   RX-OK RX-ERR RX-DRP RX-OVR    TX-OK TX-ERR TX-DRP TX-OVR Flg
docker0    1500 0       0      0     0 0            0      0      0      0 B
MU
eth0       1500 0  150716      0     0 0       151045      0      0      0 B
MRU
lo        65536 0      56      0     0 0           56      0      0      0 L
RU
```

4. If you do not see a specific network interface listed in the active list, then query for all available interfaces with the `-a` option to `ifconfig`.

5. Another commonly used command is `ping`. It sends ICMP requests to a specified host and waits for the reply. If you query for a host name, `ping` will get its IP address from DNS. This also gives you confirmation that the DNS is working properly. Ping also gives you the latency of your network interface. Check for the `time` values in the output of the `ping` command:

```
ubuntu@ubuntu:~$ ping www.google.com -c 4
PING www.google.com (74.125.200.99) 56(84) bytes of data.
64 bytes from sa-in-f99.1e100.net (74.125.200.99): icmp_seq=1 ttl=44 time=1011 m
s
64 bytes from sa-in-f99.1e100.net (74.125.200.99): icmp_seq=2 ttl=44 time=273 ms
64 bytes from sa-in-f99.1e100.net (74.125.200.99): icmp_seq=3 ttl=44 time=268 ms
64 bytes from sa-in-f99.1e100.net (74.125.200.99): icmp_seq=4 ttl=44 time=326 ms

--- www.google.com ping statistics ---
4 packets transmitted, 4 received, 0% packet loss, time 3012ms
rtt min/avg/max/mdev = 268.283/470.026/1011.957/313.726 ms, pipe 2
```

6. Next, comes `netstat`. It is mainly used to check network connections and routing tables on the system. The commonly used syntax is as follows:

   `$ sudo netstat -plutn`

```
ubuntu@ubuntu:~$ sudo netstat -plutn
Active Internet connections (only servers)
Proto Recv-Q Send-Q Local Address          Foreign Address         State
PID/Program name
tcp        0      0 0.0.0.0:111             0.0.0.0:*               LISTEN
711/rpcbind
tcp        0      0 0.0.0.0:80              0.0.0.0:*               LISTEN
1487/nginx
tcp        0      0 0.0.0.0:38512           0.0.0.0:*               LISTEN
_
```

7. The preceding command should list all TCP (`-t`) / UDP (`-u`) connections, plus any ports that are actively listening (`-l`) for connection. The flag, `-p`, queries the program name responsible for a specified connection. Note that flag `-p` requires sudo privileges. Also check flag `-a` to get all listening as well as non-listening sockets, or query the routing table information with flag `-r` as follows:

   `$ netstat -r`

```
ubuntu@ubuntu:~$ netstat -r
Kernel IP routing table
Destination     Gateway         Genmask         Flags  MSS Window  irtt Iface
default         10.0.2.1        0.0.0.0         UG       0 0         0 eth0
10.0.2.0        *               255.255.255.0   U        0 0         0 eth0
172.17.0.0      *               255.255.0.0     U        0 0         0 docker0
ubuntu@ubuntu:~$
```

8. You can also get protocol level network statistics using the `netstat` command as follows:

   ```
   $ netstat -s
   ```

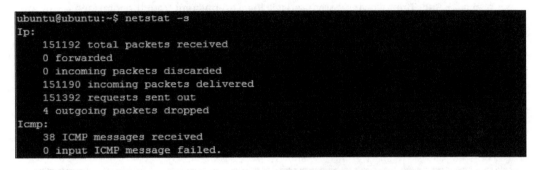

```
ubuntu@ubuntu:~$ netstat -s
Ip:
    151192 total packets received
    0 forwarded
    0 incoming packets discarded
    151190 incoming packets delivered
    151392 requests sent out
    4 outgoing packets dropped
Icmp:
    38 ICMP messages received
    0 input ICMP message failed.
```

9. One more utility very similar to `netstat` is `ss`. It displays detailed TCP socket information. Use `ss` without any parameters to get a list of all the sockets with a state established.

10. Another command, `lsof`, gives you a list of all open files. It includes the files used for network connections or sockets. Use with flag `-i` to list all network files, as follows:

    ```
    $ sudo lsof -i
    ```

```
ubuntu@ubuntu:~$ sudo lsof -i
COMMAND    PID    USER    FD   TYPE DEVICE SIZE/OFF NODE NAME
rpcbind    711    root    6u   IPv4 10803     0t0   UDP *:sunrpc
rpcbind    711    root    7u   IPv4 10806     0t0   UDP *:858
rpcbind    711    root    8u   IPv4 10807     0t0   TCP *:sunrpc (LISTEN)
rpcbind    711    root    9u   IPv6 10808     0t0   UDP *:sunrpc
rpcbind    711    root    10u  IPv6 10809     0t0   UDP *:858
```

11. To filter output, use flag -s with protocol and state as filter options:

    ```
    $ sudo lsof -iTCP -sTCP:LISTEN
    ```

12. Next, we will look at a well-known tool, tcpdump. It collects network traffic and displays it to a standard output or dump in a file system. You can dump the content of the packets for any network interface. When no interface is specified, tcpdump defaults to the first configured interface, which is generally eth0. Use it as follows to get a description of packets exchanged over eth0:

    ```
    $ sudo tcpdump -i eth0
    ```

13. To log raw packets to a file, use flag -w. These logged packets can later be read with the -r flag. The following command will log 100 packets from the interface eth0 to the file tcpdump.log:

    ```
    $ sudo tcpdump -i eth0 -w tcpdump.log -c 100
    $ tcpdump -r tcpdump.log
    ```

14. Next, to get statistics of network traffic, use the command sar. We have already used sar to get CPU and memory statistics. To simply extract all network statistics, use sar as follows:

    ```
    $ sar -n ALL 1 5
    ```

```
ubuntu@ubuntu:~$ sar -n ALL 1 5
Linux 3.16.0-30-generic (ubuntu)        01/23/2016      _x86_64_        (2 CPU)

09:41:54 AM     IFACE   rxpck/s   txpck/s   rxkB/s   txkB/s   rxcmp/s   txcmp/
s    rxmcst/s   %ifutil
09:41:55 AM      eth0     0.00      0.00     0.00     0.00     0.00      0.0
0      0.00      0.00
09:41:55 AM   docker0     0.00      0.00     0.00     0.00     0.00      0.0
0      0.00      0.00
09:41:55 AM        lo     0.00      0.00     0.00     0.00     0.00      0.0
0      0.00      0.00
```

15. This will log all network statistics at an interval of 1 second. You can also enable periodic logging in the file /etc/default/sysstat. For network specific usage of sar, check flag -n in the man pages.

16. There is one more utility named collectl which is similar to sar. In the same way as sar, you will need to separately install this command as well:

    ```
    $ sudo apt-get install collectl
    ```

17. Once installed, use `collectl` with the -s flag and value sn to get statistics about the network. Using it without any parameters gives you statistics for the CPU, disk, and network:

```
ubuntu@ubuntu:~$ collectl -s sn
defined(@array) is deprecated at /usr/share/collectl/formatit.ph line 3149.
        (Maybe you should just omit the defined()?)
waiting for 1 second sample...
#<----------Network---------><------Sockets----->
#  KBIn  PktIn  KBOut  PktOut  Tcp  Udp  Raw Frag
      0      6      0       0   71    0    0    0
      1     10      1       8   71    0    0    0
      0      8      0       3   71    0    0    0
```

How it works...

This recipe covers various network monitoring commands including the commonly used `ifconfig` and `ping`, `netstat`, `tcpdump`, and `collectl`.

If you have been working with Linux systems for a while, you should have already used the basic network commands, `ifconfig` and `ping`. **Ifconfig** is commonly used to read network configuration and get details of network interfaces. Apart from its basic use, `ifconfig` can also be used to configure the network interface. See *Chapter 2, Networking*, to get more details on network configuration. With `netstat`, you can get a list of all network sockets and their respective processes using those socket connections. With various parameters, you can easily separate active or listening connections and even separate connections with the protocol being used by the socket. Additionally, `netstat` provides details of routing table information and network statistics as well. The command `ss` provides similar details to netstat and adds some more information. You can use `ss` to get memory usages of socket (-m) and the process using that particular socket (-p). It also provides various filtering options to get the desired output. Check the manual pages of `ss` with the command, `man ss`.

There's more...

Following are some more commands that can be useful when monitoring network data. With a limit on page count, it is not possible to cover them all, so I am simply listing the relevant commands:

Many of these commands need to be installed separately. Simply type in the command if it's not available, and Ubuntu will help you with a command to install the respective package.

- ► `nethogs`: Monitors per process bandwidth utilization
- ► `ntop` / `iftop`: Top for network monitoring
- ► `iptraf`: Monitors network interface activity
- ► `vnstat`: Network traffic monitoring with logging
- ► `ethtool`: Queries and configures network interfaces
- ► `nicstat` / `ifstat` / `nstat`: Network interface statistics
- ► `tracepath`: Traces a network route to destination host

Monitoring storage

Storage is one of the slowest components in a server's system, but is still the most important component. Storage is mainly used as a persistence mechanism to store a large amount of processed/unprocessed data. A slow storage device generally results in heavy utilization of read write buffers and higher memory consumption. You will see higher CPU usage, but most of the CPU time is spent waiting for I/O requests.

The recent developments of the flash storage medium have vastly improved storage performance. Still, it's one of the slowest performing components and needs proper planning— I/O planning in the application code, plus enough main memory for read write buffers.

In this recipe, we will learn to monitor storage performance. The main focus will be on local storage devices rather than network storage.

Getting ready

As always, you will need `sudo` access for some commands.

Some of the commands many not be available by default. Using them will prompt you if the command is not available, along with the process necessary to install the required package.

Install the `sysstat` package as follows. We have already used it in previous recipes:

```
$ sudo apt get install sysstat
```

How to do it...

1. The first command we will look at is `vmstat`. Using `vmstat` without any option displays an `io` column with two sub entries: bytes in (`bi`) and bytes out (`bo`). Bytes in represents the number of bytes read in per second from the disk and bytes out represents the bytes written to the disk:

```
ubuntu@ubuntu:~$ vmstat
procs -----------memory---------- ---swap-- -----io---- -system-- ------cpu-----
 r  b   swpd   free   buff  cache   si   so    bi    bo   in   cs us sy id wa st
 1  0      0 3123824  27100 300008    0    0    35     9   66   94  1  1 98  1
0
ubuntu@ubuntu:~$
```

2. Vmstat also provides two flags, `-d` and `-D`, to get disk statistics. Flag `-d` displays disk statistics and flag `-D` displays a summary view of disk activity:

```
ubuntu@ubuntu:~$ vmstat -D
        27 disks
         3 partitions
     18203 total reads
      4881 merged reads
   1232378 read sectors
   2471384 milli reading
      7315 writes
      3128 merged writes
```

3. There's one more option, `-p`, that displays partition-specific disk statistics. Use the command `lsblk` to get a list of available partitions and then use the `vmstat -p` partition:

```
ubuntu@ubuntu:~$ lsblk
NAME                      MAJ:MIN RM   SIZE RO TYPE MOUNTPOINT
sda                         8:0    0    20G  0 disk
├─sda1                      8:1    0   243M  0 part /boot
├─sda2                      8:2    0     1K  0 part
└─sda5                      8:5    0  19.8G  0 part
  ├─ubuntu--vg-root (dm-0) 252:0   0  18.8G  0 lvm  /
  └─ubuntu--vg-swap_1 (dm-1) 252:1 0  1020M  0 lvm  [SWAP]
ubuntu@ubuntu:~$ vmstat -p sda5
sda5          reads    read sectors   writes    requested writes
              7098        625450        2026        168776
```

4. Another command, `dstat`, is a nice replacement for `vmstat`, especially for disk statistics reporting. Use it with flag `-d` to get disk read writes per seconds. If you have multiple disks, you can use `dstat` to list their stats separately:

   ```
   $ dstat -d -D total,sda
   ```

5. Next, we will look at the command `iostat`. When used without any options, this command displays basic CPU utilization, along with read write statistics for each storage device:

   ```
   ubuntu@ubuntu:~$ iostat
   Linux 3.16.0-30-generic (ubuntu)          01/23/2016          _x86_64_          (2 CPU)

   avg-cpu:   %user    %nice %system %iowait   %steal   %idle
              0.62     0.04    1.07    0.53     0.00    97.74

   Device:              tps   kB_read/s   kB_wrtn/s    kB_read    kB_wrtn
   sda                 1.88       58.81       15.84     314884      84806
   dm-0                3.14       58.23       15.84     311785      84800
   dm-1                0.04        0.17        0.00        896          0
   ```

6. The column `tps` specifies the I/O requests sent to a device per second, and `kb_read/s` and `kb_wrtn/s` specifies per second blocks read and blocks written respectively. `kb_read` and `kb_wrtn` shows the total number of blocks read and written.

7. Some common options for `iostat` include `-d`, that displays disk only statistics, `-g` that displays statistics for a group of devices, flag `-p` to display partition specific stats, and `-x` to get extended statistics. Do not forget to check the manual entries for `iostat` to get more details.

8. You can also use the command `iotop`, which is very similar to the `top` command but it displays disk utilization and relevant processes.

9. The command `lsof` can display the list of all open files and respective processes using that file. Use `lsof` with the process name to get files opened by that process:

   ```
   $ lsof -c sshd
   ```

   ```
   ubuntu@ubuntu:~$ sudo lsof -c sshd
   COMMAND   PID    USER    FD    TYPE         DEVICE SIZE/OFF    NODE NAME
   sshd     1254    root    cwd    DIR         252,0    4096       2 /
   sshd     1254    root    rtd    DIR         252,0    4096       2 /
   sshd     1254    root    txt    REG         252,0  766784   11349 /usr/sbin/ssh
   d
   sshd     1254    root    mem    REG         252,0   47712  655587 /lib/x86_64-1
   inux-gnu/libnss_files-2.19.so
   ```

10. To get a list of files opened by a specific PID, use the following command: `$ lsof -p 1134`. Or, to get a list of files opened by a specific user, use the `$ lsof -u ubuntu` command.

All these commands provide details on the read write performance of a storage device. Another important detail to know is the availability of free space. To get details of space utilization, you can use command `df -h`. This will list a partition-level summary of disk space utilization:

```
ubuntu@ubuntu:~$ df -h
Filesystem                     Size  Used Avail Use% Mounted on
/dev/mapper/ubuntu--vg-root    19G   2.8G   15G  16% /
none                          4.0K      0  4.0K   0% /sys/fs/cgroup
udev                          2.0G   4.0K  2.0G   1% /dev
tmpfs                         396M   604K  395M   1% /run
none                          5.0M      0  5.0M   0% /run/lock
none                          2.0G      0  2.0G   0% /run/shm
none                          100M      0  100M   0% /run/user
/dev/sda1                     236M    38M  186M  17% /boot
```

11. Finally, you can use the `sar` command to track disk performance over a period of time. To get real-time disk activity, use `sar` with the `-d` option, as follows:

    `$ sar -d 1`

```
ubuntu@ubuntu:~$ sar -d 1
Linux 3.16.0-30-generic (ubuntu)        01/23/2016      _x86_64_        (2 CPU)

10:10:33 AM          DEV       tps  rd_sec/s  wr_sec/s  avgrq-sz  avgqu-sz     awai
t     svctm     %util
10:10:34 AM       dev8-0      0.00      0.00      0.00      0.00      0.00      0.0
0     0.00      0.00
10:10:34 AM     dev252-0      0.00      0.00      0.00      0.00      0.00      0.0
0     0.00      0.00
10:10:34 AM     dev252-1      0.00      0.00      0.00      0.00      0.00      0.0
0     0.00      0.00
```

12. Use flag `-F` to get details on file system utilization and flag `-S` to display swap utilization. You can also enable sar logging and then extract details from those logs. Check the previous recipes in this chapter for how to enable sar logging. Also check manual entries for sar to get details of various options.

Setting performance benchmarks

Until now, in this chapter we have learned about various performance monitoring tools and commands. This recipe covers a well-known performance benchmarking tool: **Sysbench**. The purpose of performance benchmarking is to get a sense of system configuration and the resulting performance. Sysbench is generally used to evaluate the performance of heavy load systems. If you read the Sysbench introduction, it says that Sysbench is a benchmarking tool to evaluate a system running database under intensive load. It is also being used as a tool to evaluate the performance of multiple cloud service providers.

The current version of Sysbench supports various benchmark tests including CPU, memory, IO system, and OLTP systems. We will primarily focus on CPU, memory, and IO benchmarks.

Getting ready

Before using Sysbench, we will need to install it. Sysbench is available in the Ubuntu package repository with a little older (0.4.12) version. We will use the latest version (0.5) from Percona Systems, available in their repo.

To install Sysbench from the Percona repo, we need to add the repo to our installation sources. Following are the entries for Ubuntu 14.04 (trusty). Create a new file under `/etc/apt/source.list.d` and add the following lines to it:

```
$ sudo vi /etc/apt/sources.list.d/percona.list
deb http://repo.percona.com/apt trusty main
deb-src http://repo.percona.com/apt trusty main
```

Next, add the PGP key for the preceding repo:

```
$ sudo apt-key adv --keyserver keys.gnupg.net --recv-keys
1C4CBDCDCD2EFD2A
```

Now we are ready to install the latest version of Sysbench from the Percona repo. Remember to update the `apt` cache before installation:

```
$ sudo apt-get update
$ sudo apt-get install sysbench
```

Once installed, you can check the installed version with the `--version` flag to `sysbench`:

```
$ sysbench --version
sysbench 0.5
```

How to do it...

Now that we have Sysbench installed, let's start with performance testing our system:

1. Sysbench provides a prime number generation test for CPU. You can set the number of primes to be generated with the option `--cpu-max-prime`. Also set the limit on threads with the `--num-threads` option. Set the number of threads equal to the amount of CPU cores available:

```
$ sysbench --test=cpu --num-threads=4 \
--cpu-max-prime=20000 run
```

2. The test should show output similar to the following screenshot:

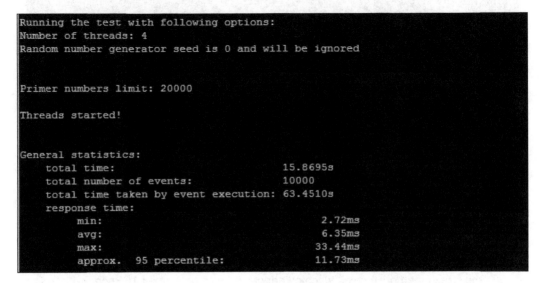

```
Running the test with following options:
Number of threads: 4
Random number generator seed is 0 and will be ignored


Primer numbers limit: 20000

Threads started!


General statistics:
    total time:                          15.8695s
    total number of events:              10000
    total time taken by event execution: 63.4510s
    response time:
        min:                                 2.72ms
        avg:                                 6.35ms
        max:                                33.44ms
        approx.   95 percentile:            11.73ms
```

3. Following are the extracted parts of the result from multiple tests with a different thread count on a system with a dual core CPU. It is clear that using two threads give better results:

Threads	1	2	3	4
Total time	33.0697s	15.4335s	15.6258s	15.7778s

4. Next, we will run a test for main memory. The memory tests provides multiple options, such as block-size, total data transfer, type of memory operations, and access modes. Use the following command to run memory tests:

```
$ sysbench --test=memory --memory-block-size=1M \
--num-threads=2 \
--memory-total-size=100G --memory-oper=read run
```

5. Following is part of the output from the memory test:

```
Threads started!

Operations performed: 102400 (1663868.39 ops/sec)

102400.00 MB transferred (1663868.39 MB/sec)


General statistics:
    total time:                          0.0615s
    total number of events:              102400
    total time taken by event execution: 0.0569s
```

6. If you have enabled huge page support, set the memory test support allocation from the huge page pool with the parameter, `--memory-hugetlb`. By default, it's set to off.

7. Next comes the storage performance test. This test also provides you with a number of options to test disk read write speeds. Depending on your requirements, you can set parameters like block-size, random or sequential read writes, synchronous or asynchronous IO operations, and many more.

8. For the `fileio` test we need a few sample files to test with. Use the `sysbench` `prepare` command to create test files. Make sure to set a total file size greater than the size of memory to avoid caching effects. I am using a small 1GBnode with 20G disk space, so I am using 15 files of 1G each:

```
$ sysbench --test=fileio --file-total-size=15G \
--file-num=15 prepare
```

```
ubuntu@ubuntu:~$ sysbench --test=fileio --file-total-size=15G --file-num=15 prep
are
sysbench 0.5:  multi-threaded system evaluation benchmark

15 files, 1048576Kb each, 15360Mb total
Creating files for the test...
Extra file open flags: 0
Creating file test_file.0
Creating file test_file.1
```

9. Once the test preparation is complete, you can run the `fileio` test with different options, depending on what you want to test. The following command will perform random write operations for `60` seconds:

```
$ sysbench --test=fileio --file-total-size=15G \
--file-test-mode=rndwr --max-time=60 \
--file-block-size=4K --file-num=15 --num-threads=1 run
```

```
Operations performed:  0 reads, 10000 writes, 1500 Other = 11500 Total
Read 0b  Written 39.062Mb  Total transferred 39.062Mb  (1.2449Mb/sec)
  318.69 Requests/sec executed

General statistics:
    total time:                          31.3789s
    total number of events:              10000
    total time taken by event execution: 0.1245s
```

10. To perform random read operations, change `--file-test-mode` to `rndrd`, or to perform sequential read operations, use `seqrd`. You can also combine read write operations with `rndrw` or `seqrewr`. Check the help menu for more options.

> To get a full list of available options, enter the `sysbench` command without any parameter. You can also query details of a specific test with `sysbench --test=<name> help`. For example, to get help with I/O tests, use:
>
> `$ sysbench --test=fileio help`

11. When you are done with the `fileio` test, execute the `cleanup` command to delete all sample files:

```
$ sysbench --test=fileio cleanup
```

12. Once you have gathered various performance details, you can try updating various performance tuning parameters to boost performance. Make sure you repeat related tests after each change in parameter. Comparing results from multiple tests will help you to choose the required combination for best performance and a stable system.

There's more...

Sysbench also supports testing MySQL performance with various tests. In the same way as the `fileio` test, Sysbench takes care of setting a test environment by creating tables with data. When using Sysbench from the Percona repo, all OLTP test scripts are located at `/usr/share/doc/sysbench/tests/db/`. You will need to specify the full path when using these scripts. For example:

```
$ sysbench --test=oltp
```

The preceding command will change to the following:

```
$ sysbench --test=/usr/share/doc/sysbench/tests/db/oltp.lua
```

Graphing tools

Sysbench output can be hard to analyze and compare, especially with multiple runs. This is where graphs come in handy. You can try to set up your own graphing mechanism, or simply use prebuilt scripts to create graphs for you. A quick Google search gave me two good, looking options:

- A Python script to extract data from Sysbench logs: `https://github.com/tsuna/sysbench-tools`
- A shell script to extract Sysbench data to a CSV file, which can be converted to graphs: `http://openlife.cc/blogs/2011/august/one-liner-condensing-sysbench-output-csv-file`

More options

There are various other performance testing frameworks available. Phoronix Test Suite, Unixbench, and Perfkit by Google are some popular names. Phoronix Test Suite focuses on hardware performance and provides a wide range of performance analysis options, whereas Unixbench provides an option to test various Linux systems. Google open-sourced their performance toolkit with a benchmarker and explorer to evaluate various cloud systems.

See also

- Get more details on benchmarking with Sysbench at `https://wiki.mikejung.biz/Benchmarking`

- Sysbench documentation at `http://imysql.com/wp-content/uploads/2014/10/sysbench-manual.pdf`

- A sample script to run batch run multiple Sysbench tests at `https://gist.github.com/chetan/712484`

- Sysbench GitHub repo at `https://github.com/akopytov/sysbench`

- Linux performance analysis in 60 seconds. A good read for what to check when you are debugging a performance issue at `http://techblog.netflix.com/2015/11/linux-performance-analysis-in-60s.html`

14
Centralized Authentication Service

In this chapter, we will cover the following recipes:

- ▶ Installing OpenLDAP
- ▶ Installing phpLDAPadmin
- ▶ Ubuntu server logins with LDAP
- ▶ Authenticating Ejabberd users with LDAP

Introduction

When you have a large user base using multiple services across the organization, a centralized authentication service becomes a need rather than a luxury. It becomes necessary to quickly add new user accounts across multiple services when a new user comes in, and deactivate the respective access tokens when a user leaves the organization. A centralized authentication service enables you to quickly respond by updating the user database on a single central server.

Various different services are available to set up centralized authentication. In this chapter, we will learn how to set up a centralized authentication service using a **Lightweight Directory access Protocol** (**LDAP**). A directory is a special database designed specifically for high volume lookups. LDAP directories are tree-based data structures, also known as **Directory Information Trees** (**DIT**). Each node in a tree contains a unique entry with its own set of attributes.

LDAP is specifically designed for high volume read systems with limited write activities. These directories are commonly used for storing details of users with their respective access control lists. Some examples include shared address books, shared calendar services, centralized authentication for systems such as Samba, and storage DNS systems. LDAP provides lightweight access to the directory services over the TCP/IP stack. It is similar to the X.500 OSI directory service, but with limited features and limited resource requirements. For more details on LDAP, check out the OpenLDAP admin guide at `http://www.openldap.org/doc/admin24/intro.html`.

Installing OpenLDAP

This recipe covers the installation and initial configuration of LDAP. The Ubuntu package repository makes the installation easy by providing the required packages for the LDAP service.

Getting ready

You will need access to a root account or an account with `sudo` privileges.

How to do it...

Let's start with installing the LDAP package and helper utilities:

1. Update your repository using the `apt-get update` command and then install the OpenLDAP package, `slapd`:

    ```
    $ sudo apt-get update
    $ sudo apt-get install slapd ldap-utils
    ```

2. You will be asked to enter the admin password and to confirm it.

3. The installation process simply installs the package without any configuration. We need to start the actual configuration process with the reconfiguration of the `slapd` package. Use the following command to start the re-configuration process:

    ```
    $ sudo dpkg-reconfigure slapd
    ```

4. This command will ask you a series of questions including the domain name, admin account, password, database type, and others. Match your answers as follows:

    - Omit LDAP server configuration – NO.

❏ DNS Domain name – Enter your domain name. You can use any domain name. For this setup, I will be using example.com. This domain name will determine the top structure of your directory:

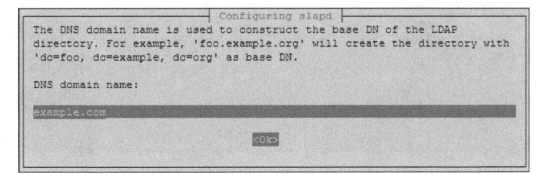

❏ Organization name – Enter your organization name. I am using example as my organization.

❏ Admin password – Enter a password for the admin account. It can be the same as the one entered during installation, or a totally different one. Make sure you note this password as it will be used to access the admin account.

❏ Database backend – HDB

```
────────────────┤ Configuring slapd ├────────────────
The HDB backend is recommended. HDB and BDB use similar storage formats,
but HDB adds support for subtree renames. Both support the same
configuration options.

In either case, you should review the resulting database configuration
for your needs. See /usr/share/doc/slapd/README.DB_CONFIG.gz for more
details.

Database backend to use:

                          BDB
                          HDB
```

❏ Remove the database when slapd is purged - this is about removing the database in case you uninstall the slapd package. Choose NO as you don't want the database to be deleted:

❏ Move old database - YES

> ❏ Allow the LDAPv2 protocol - unless you are planning to use some old tools, choose NO:

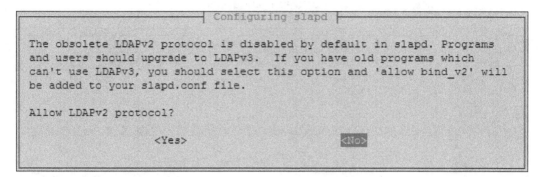

```
                         Configuring slapd
  ┌─────────────────────────────────────────────────────────────────────┐
  │ The obsolete LDAPv2 protocol is disabled by default in slapd. Programs │
  │ and users should upgrade to LDAPv3.  If you have old programs which    │
  │ can't use LDAPv3, you should select this option and 'allow bind_v2' will │
  │ be added to your slapd.conf file.                                     │
  │                                                                       │
  │ Allow LDAPv2 protocol?                                                │
  │                                                                       │
  │             <Yes>                              <No>                   │
  └─────────────────────────────────────────────────────────────────────┘
```

5. Once you have answered all the questions, the process will reconfigure the LDAP service. Now your LDAP service is installed and ready to use:

```
ubuntu@ubuntu:~$ sudo dpkg-reconfigure slapd
 * Stopping OpenLDAP slapd                                        [ OK ]
   Moving old database directory to /var/backups:
   - directory unknown... done.
   Creating initial configuration... done.
   Creating LDAP directory... done.
 * Starting OpenLDAP slapd                                        [ OK ]
Processing triggers for libc-bin (2.19-0ubuntu6.6) ...
ubuntu@ubuntu:~$
```

6. Now you can use utility commands to query existing data. To test whether the LDAP service is installed and running properly, use the `ldapsearch -x` command. You should see output similar to following screenshot:

```
ubuntu@ubuntu:~$ ldapsearch -x
# extended LDIF
#
# LDAPv3
# base <> (default) with scope subtree
# filter: (objectclass=*)
# requesting: ALL
#
```

7. Use `ldapsearch` as follows to query our newly added domain, `example.com`:

```
$ ldapsearch -x -LLL -H ldap:/// -b dc=example,dc=com dn
```

```
ubuntu@ubuntu:~$ ldapsearch -x -LLL -H ldap:/// -b dc=example,dc=com dn
dn: dc=example,dc=com

dn: cn=admin,dc=example,dc=com

ubuntu@ubuntu:~$
```

8. The following command will query the default content for `example.com`:

```
$ ldapsearch -x -LLL -b dc=example,dc=com
```

```
ubuntu@ubuntu:~$ ldapsearch -x -LLL -b dc=example,dc=com
dn: dc=example,dc=com
objectClass: top
objectClass: dcObject
objectClass: organization
o: example
dc: example

dn: cn=admin,dc=example,dc=com
objectClass: simpleSecurityObject
objectClass: organizationalRole
cn: admin
description: LDAP administrator
```

The `ldap-utils` package also provides more commands to configure the LDAP service, but it is quite a lengthy and complex task. In the next recipe, we will learn how to set up a web-based admin interface that make things a little easier.

How it works...

With the respective packages available in the Ubuntu package repository, installing **OpenLDAP** is quite an easy task. All we have to do is install the required binaries and then configure the LDAP system to serve our desired domain. We have installed two packages: one is `slapd`, the LDAP daemon, and the other is `ldap-utils`, which provides various commands to work with the LDAP daemon. After installation is complete, we have re-configured LDAP to match our required directory setup. We have chosen to go with LDAPv3 API and disabled LDAPv2. If you have any older systems working with LDAPv2, then you will need to enable support for old APIs.

▸ Open LDAP admin guide at `http://www.openldap.org/doc/admin24/intro.html`

▸ Ubuntu OpenLDAP guide at `https://help.ubuntu.com/lts/serverguide/openldap-server.html`

▸ LDAP protocol RFC at `http://www.rfc-editor.org/rfc/rfc2251.txt`

▸ LDAP protocol technical details at `http://www.rfc-editor.org/rfc/rfc3377.txt`

▸ Get more help with LDAP configuration using the `man ldap.conf` command.

Installing phpLDAPadmin

In the previous recipe, we installed the LDAP service, but working with LDAP using the command line interface is quite a complex and lengthy task. This recipe covers the installation of a user interface, phpLDAPadmin. The `phpldapadmin` package provides an easy-to-use web-based user interface for the LDAP service.

Getting ready

Make sure that you have the LDAP service installed and running.

How to do it...

Follow these steps to install phpLDAPadmin:

1. The Ubuntu package repository makes things easy again by providing the package for phpLDAPadmin. The web interface can be quickly installed in a single command as follows:

    ```
    $ sudo apt-get install phpldapadmin
    ```

2. The installation process takes care of installing all dependencies including PHP and the Apache web server. It also creates necessary configurations and sets up Apache with the required settings for phpLDAPadmin. Once installation is complete, you can access the admin interface at `http://youServerIP/phpldapadmin`.

3. Before we access the admin page, let's make some small changes in the configuration file. The file is located at `/etc/phpldapadmin/config.php`. By default, phpLDAPadmin shows warning messages for unused template files. These warning messages get shown in the main interface before the actual content. To hide them, search for `hide_template_warning` in the configuration file and set it to `true`. You will also need to uncomment the same line:

```
$config->custom->appearance['hide_template_warning'] =
true;
```

4. The other settings should have already been set by the installation process. You can cross-check the following settings:

```
$servers->setValue('server','host','127.0.0.1');

$servers->setValue(
    'login','bind_id',
    'cn=admin,dc=example,
    dc=com'
);

$servers->setValue(
    'server','base',array('dc=example,dc=com')
);
```

5. Once you are done with the configuration file changes, save and close it and then access the admin interface through your browser:

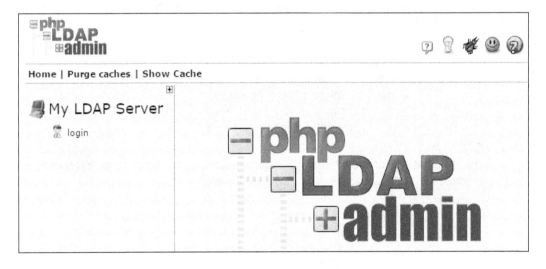

6. Click on the **login** link on the left of the page to get the login dialogue box. The username (**Login DN**) field is already filled with details for the admin account. Make sure the details match the domain you have set up. Enter the password for the admin account and click the **Authenticate** button:

Warning: This web connection is unencrypted.

Login DN:

cn=admin,dc=example,dc=com

Password:

Anonymous

Authenticate

 You can also log in as an anonymous user. In the login box, do not enter a password, click to check the **Anonymous** checkbox, and then click the **Authenticate** button. This gives you a read-only view, which is quite useful when you just need to verify some details.

7. You should have noticed the warning on the login box saying the `connection is unencrypted`. This is just a reminder that you are using the admin console over a non-HTTPs connection. You can set up Apache with SSL certificates to get an encrypted, secure connection with your LDAP server. Check *Chapter 3, Working with Web Servers*, for more details on how to set up SSL certificates on the Apache web server.

8. Once you log in to phpLDAPadmin, you can see the domain listed in the left-hand side menu. Click on the domain link to view its details.

9. Next, click on the small plus link (**+**) to expand the domain link and see its children. With the default settings, it should show only the admin account:

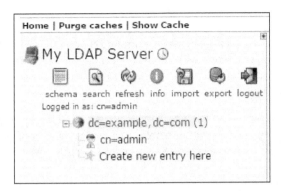

10. Along with the link for the admin account, you will see an option to create a new entry. Clicking on this link will show you a list of templates for the new entry:

Select a template for the creation process

Templates:
- Courier Mail: Account
- Courier Mail: Alias
- Generic: Address Book Entry
- Generic: DNS Entry
- Generic: LDAP Alias
- Generic: Organisational Role
- Generic: Organisational Unit
- Samba: Domain
- Samba: Group Mapping
- Samba: Machine
- Sendmail: Alias
- Sendmail: Cluster
- Sendmail: Domain
- Sendmail: Relays

While clicking on some of these templates, for example *Generic: User Account*, you may notice a PHP error saying `Error trying to get non-existent value`. The form rendering fails and you cannot see the complete form the with submit button. This is a small bug and can be fixed with a small edit.

Open `/usr/share/phpldapadmin/lib/TemplateRender.php`.

Search for the following line:

```
$default = $this->getServer()
->getValue('appearance','password_hash');
```

Now update the preceding command as follows:

```
$default = $this->getServer()
->getValue('appearance','password_hash_custom');
```

Now you are ready to create groups and respective user accounts on your LDAP server.

How it works...

In this recipe, we have installed a web-based administration console for the LDAP server. The `ldap-utils` package provides various commands to work with the LDAP server, but it is quite a complex and lengthy task. A graphical user interface gives you a better listing of all options and existing configurations, making things a little easier.

The phpLDAPadmin package is a PHP/Apache-based web application that provides a graphical interface for the LDAP server. It displays all options and configurations in an easy-to-use graphical format and passes all user actions to LDAP APIs.

There's more...

Apache directory studio is another user interface for LDAP administration. It is a desktop application based on Java. You can get more details at `https://directory.apache.org/studio/`.

See also

  ▶   A StackOverflow answer for the phpLDAPadmin error message at `http://stackoverflow.com/a/21195761/1012809`

Ubuntu server logins with LDAP

So, we have installed and configured our own centralized auth server with LDAP. Now is the time to use LDAP to authenticate client logins. In this recipe, we will set up a separate Ubuntu server to use our LDAP server for authenticating users.

Getting ready

You will need a new Ubuntu server to be set as an LDAP client. Also, `sudo` privileges are needed for the initial setup.

Make sure you have followed the previous recipes and have set up your LDAP server.

How to do it...

1. We will need to install the LDAP client-side package on the client system. This package will install all the required tools to authenticate with the remote LDAP server:

   ```
   $ sudo apt-get update
   $ sudo apt-get install ldap-auth-client nscd
   ```

2. The installation process will ask you some questions regarding your LDAP server and its authentication details. Answer those questions as follows:

   - LDAP server URI: `ldap://you-LDAP-server-IP`: Make sure you change the protocol line from `ldapi:///` to `ldap://`

   - `Distinguished name of search base`: Match this to the domain set on the LDAP server in the format `dc=example,dc=com`

   - `LDAP version to use`: 3

   - `Make local root database admin`: Yes

   - `Does LDAP database require login`: No

   - `LDAP account for root`: `cn=admin,dc=example,dc=com`

   - `LDAP root account password`: The password for the LDAP admin account

3. Next, we need to change the authentication configuration to check with the LDAP server. First, run the following command to set the **name service switch** file `/etc/nsswitch.conf`:

   ```
   $ sudo auth-client-config -t nss -p lac_ldap
   ```

4. This will change `/etc/nsswitch.conf` as follows:

```
# /etc/nsswitch.conf
#
# Example configuration of GNU Name Service Switch functionality.
# If you have the `glibc-doc-reference' and `info' packages installed, try:
# `info libc "Name Service Switch"' for information about this file.

# pre_auth-client-config # passwd:        compat
passwd: files ldap
# pre_auth-client-config # group:         compat
group: files ldap
# pre_auth-client-config # shadow:        compat
shadow: files ldap
```

5. Next, add the following line to `/etc/pam.d/common-session`. This will create a local home directory for LDAP users. Edit the `common-session` file and add the following line at the end of the file:

   session required   pam_mkhomedir.so umask=0022 skel=/etc/skel

6. Now restart the `nscd` service with the following command:

   $ sudo /etc/init.d/nscd restart

   Now you should be able to log in with the user account created on your LDAP server. I have set up an **Organizational Unit** (**OU**) named **users** and created an admin user under it:

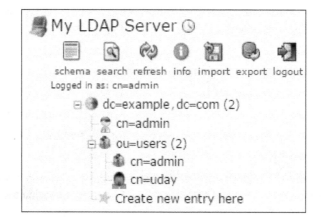

7. Next, change the login to the newly created LDAP user account with the `su username` command. You will need to enter a password that is configured on LDAP server. As this is a first-time login for this new user, our PAM settings have created a new home directory for him:

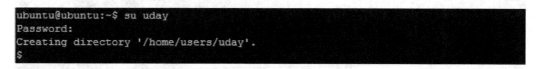

This new user is a member of the admin group on the LDAP server, so he will get `sudo` privileges on the local server as well.

You can always use a default login prompt to log in with LDAP users, as well as local user accounts that already exist on the server.

How it works...

Here we have configured the Ubuntu server to authenticate with our centralized LDAP system. This is not limited to the Ubuntu server and you can configure the Ubuntu desktop in a similar way as well. Using a centralized authentication makes it easy to administer hundreds of user accounts from a single place. A user can still log in as a local user if he has any local credentials.

Using centralized authentication enables you to log in from any system. You will get the same access rights and permissions from any terminal. Additionally, if the LDAP configuration supports roaming profiles then all your data will be replicated to any new system you log in from. You may have noticed the home directory for the LDAP user account is located in the /home/users directory and not in /home. This separates your account from any local users.

Finally, the groups and roles configured on the LDAP server also apply on the system you are logging in from. So, if the user is assigned admin rights on the LDAP server, he will get admin rights, including sudo privileges, on the system he is logged in from. This is because Ubuntu contains a default group named admin with sudo privileges. When a user logs in with his LDAP account, the groups and roles assigned to his LDAP account are matched with local groups and roles. You can either disable such groups from any remote systems, or set the proper access rights on the LDAP server itself.

See also

▶   The Ubuntu community page for LDAP client authentication at
    https://help.ubuntu.com/community/LDAPClientAuthentication

Authenticating Ejabberd users with LDAP

In this recipe, we will learn to set up the Ejabberd server to authenticate the user with our LDAP server. Until now, we have set up the LDAP server and used it to log in to the Ubuntu server with a user account created on the LDAP server. This recipe covers the configuration of an external service to work with our LDAP installation.

The Ejabberd server provides built-in support for LDAP-based authentication. You can use LDAP for user authentication as well as vCard storage. As stated in the Ejabberd admin guide, Ejabberd use LDAP as a read-only data source. We cannot create new user accounts in the LDAP directory, but we can change passwords if the mod_register module is enabled.

Getting ready

You will need the Ejabberd service installed and running. Go through *Chapter 10, Communication Server with XMPP*, for details on the installation and configuration of the Ejabberd server.

Create a user account on the LDAP server to be used with Ejabberd.

How to do it...

As Ejabberd provides inbuilt support for LDAP-based authentication, we simply need to edit configurations and set the `auth` method to LDAP. If you have used a Debian package for the Ejabberd installation, your Ejabberd should be installed in `/opt/ejabberd-version` directory and the configuration can be found at `/etc/ejabberd-version/conf`. If you have installed Ejabberd from source, all configuration files are located in the `/etc/ejabberd` directory:

1. Open `ejabberd.yml` from your Ejabberd configuration directory and search for Authentication. With the default settings, it should contain the following line indicating internal authentication:

   ```
   auth_method: internal
   ```

2. Comment out that line by changing it as follows:

   ```
   ## auth_method: internal
   ```

3. Next, find Authentication using LDAP. This section contains a few parameters and configures communication with the LDAP server. Search and update the following parameters:

   ```
   ldap_servers:
     - "domain/IP of LDAP server"
   ldap_port: 389
   ldap_rootdn: "cn=admin,dc=example,dc=com"
   ldap_password: "password"
   ldap_base: "ou=ejabberd,dc=example,dc=com"
   ```

   I have used a default admin account to authenticate with the LDAP server itself. In a production environment, you should change it to a different account. With a default LDAP setup, you can skip the `ldap_rootdn` and `ldap_password` settings to enable anonymous connection.

4. Next, under the `ldap_base` parameter, I have restricted users to the Organizational Unit named `Ejabberd`. Only the user accounts that are configured under the `Ejabberd` unit can log in with the Ejabberd server.

5. Now, save the configuration file changes and close the file, and then restart the Ejabberd server with the following command:

```
$ sudo /opt/ejabberd-version/bin/ejabberdctl restart
```

6. If the server fails to restart, check the log files for any configuration errors. Alternatively, you can use the `reload_config` option to `ejabberdctl` to update the in-memory configuration without restarting:

```
$ sudo /opt/ejabberd-version/bin/ejabberdctl reload_config
```

7. Once the server has started, you can log in with your LDAP accounts. You will need a JID to log in with Ejabberd, which is a combination of a UID from the LDAP server and any host configured on Ejabberd, for instance, uday@cookbook.com, where uday is the **UID** on LDAP and cookbook.com is the **host** served by Ejabberd server. The domain entries on the LDAP server and Ejabberd need not match.

The following is the default host entry for my Ejabberd installation:

```
## hosts: Domains served by ejabberd.
## You can define one or several, for example:
## hosts:
##   - "example.net"
##   - "example.com"
##   - "example.org"
##
hosts:
  - "ubuntu"
```

8. Now you can log in to Ejabberd with your LDAP username. Here is the account set up in my chat client with the JID uday@ubuntu, where uday is my LDAP user and ubuntu is the Ejabberd host:

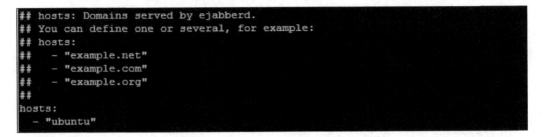

Once all things are set up, you should be able to connect to the Ejabberd server using your LDAP user account.

How it works...

Here, we have set up Ejabberd as an example of LDAP-based authentication. Similar to Ejabberd, various other systems support centralized authentication through LDAP with either built-in support or with a plug-in module. Make sure that you create a proper directory structure with organizational units, roles, and separate users in proper groups. Also use a separate user account for authenticating with the LDAP server itself. You need to set the respective LDAP credentials in the Ejabberd configuration file. If somehow your Ejabberd server gets compromised, then the LDAP server credentials are readily available to an attacker. To limit the risk, using separate and limited accounts is a good idea. Ejabberd also supports anonymous authentication with the LDAP server and mostly uses it as a read-only database. So, even if you skip the authentication details (depending on the LDAP configuration), Ejabberd should work well and authenticate your users.

Ejabberd also provides good enough debug logging, where you can see the actual communication with the LDAP server. You will need to set logging to debug mode in the Ejabberd configuration. The log files are located in the `/opt/ejabberd-version/logs` directory or the `/var/log/ejabberd` directory, depending on the source of the Ejabberd installation.

See also

- ► Ejabberd docs LDAP section at `https://www.process-one.net/docs/ejabberd/guide_en.html#ldap`

Module 2

CentOS 7 Linux Server Cookbook, Second Edition

Over 80 recipes to get up and running with CentOS 7 Linux server

1
Installing CentOS

In this chapter, we will cover:

- ▶ Downloading CentOS and confirming the checksum on Windows or OS X
- ▶ Creating USB installation media on Windows or OS X
- ▶ Performing an installation of CentOS using the graphical installer
- ▶ Running a netinstall over HTTP
- ▶ Installing CentOS using a kickstart file
- ▶ Re-installing the boot loader
- ▶ Troubleshooting the system in rescue mode
- ▶ Getting started and customizing the boot loader
- ▶ Updating the installation and enhancing the minimal install with additional administration and development tools

Introduction

This chapter is a collection of recipes that covers the basic practice of installing the CentOS 7 operating system. The purpose of this chapter is to show you how quickly you can get CentOS up and running whilst enabling you to customize your installation with a few 'tricks of the trade' thrown in for good measure.

Downloading CentOS and confirming the checksum on Windows or OS X

In this recipe, we will learn how to download and confirm the checksum of one or more CentOS 7 disk images using a typical Windows or OS X desktop computer. CentOS is made available in various formats by HTTP, FTP, or the rsync protocol from a series of mirror sites located across the world or via the BitTorrent network. For downloading very important files from the Internet, such as operating system images, it is considered best practices to validate those files' checksum, in order to ensure that any resulting media would function and perform as expected when installing. This also makes certain that the files are genuine and come from the original source.

Getting ready

To complete this recipe, it is assumed that you are using a typical Windows-based (Windows 7, Windows Vista, or similar) or OS X computer with full administration rights. You will need an Internet connection to download the required installation files and also need access to a standard DVD/CD disk burner with the appropriate software, in order to create the relevant installation disks from the image files. For the purpose of this recipe, it is assumed that all the downloads will be stored on Windows in your personal `C:\Users\<username>\Downloads` folder, or if using an OS X system, in the `/Users/<username>/Downloads` folder.

How to do it...

Regardless of the type of installation files you download, the following techniques can be applied to all the image files supplied by the CentOS project:

1. Let's begin by visiting `http://www.centos.org` in a web browser and navigate to the button link **Get CentOS Now**. Then click the link **list of the current mirrors** in the text.

2. The mirror sites are categorized, so from the resulting list of links, choose a mirror that is geographically near your current location. For example, if you are in London (UK), you can choose a mirror from **EU** and **United Kingdom**. Now choose a mirror site by selecting either the HTTP or the FTP link.

3. Having made your selection, you will now see a list of directories of all the available CentOS versions. To proceed, simply click the appropriate folder that reads 7. Next, you will see an additional list of directories, such as `atomic`, `centosplus`, `cloud`, and so on. We proceed by choosing the `isos` directory.

4. CentOS 7 currently only supports the 64-bit architecture, so browse to the only directory available labeled `x86_64`, which is a container for the 64-bit version.

5. You will now be presented with a series of files available for download. Begin by downloading a copy of the valid checksum result identified as `md5sum.txt`.

6. If you are new to CentOS or are intending to follow the recipes found throughout this book, then the minimal installation is ideal. This contains the least amount of packages to have a functional system, so choose the following (XXXX is the month stamp of this release):

    ```
    CentOS-7-x86_64-Minimal-XXXX.iso
    ```

7. On a Windows-based system only (on Mac, this tool is already available in the system), visit `http://mirror.centos.org/centos/dostools/` in your browser and download the program `md5sum.exe`.

8. Now on Windows, open the command prompt (typically found at **Start | All Programs | Accessories | Command Prompt**) and type the following commands into the window that will open (press the *Enter* key at the end of all the lines):

    ```
    cd downloads
    dir
    ```

9. On OS X, open the program **Finder | Applications | Utilities | Terminal**, then type the following commands (press the *Enter* key at the end of all the lines):

    ```
    cd ~/Downloads
    ls
    ```

10. You should now see all the files in your download folder (including all the downloaded CentOS installation image files, the md5sum.txt file and on Windows, the md5sum. exe program).

11. Based on the file names shown, modify the following command in order to check the checksum of your downloaded ISO image file. On Windows, type the following command (change the XXXX month stamp accordingly):

    ```
    md5sum.exe CentOS-7-x86_64-Minimal-XXXX.iso
    ```

12. On OS X, use instead:

    ```
    md5 CentOS-7-x86_64-Minimal-XXXX.iso
    ```

13. Press the *Return* key to proceed and then wait for the command prompt to respond. The response is known as the MD5 sum and the result could look like the following:

    ```
    d07ab3e615c66a8b2e9a50f4852e6a77  CentOS-7-x86_64-Minimal-
    1503-01.iso
    ```

14. Now look at the the sum and compare against the relevant listing for your particular image file in `md5sum.txt` (open in a text editor). If both the numbers match, then you can be confident that you have indeed downloaded a valid CentOS image file. If not, your downloaded file is probably corrupted, so please restart this procedure by downloading the image file again.

15. When you have finished, simply burn your image file(s) to a blank CD-ROM or DVD-ROM using your preferred desktop software, or create a USB installation media from it, as we will show you in the next recipe in this chapter.

How it works...

So what have we learned from this experience?

The act of downloading a CentOS installation image is just the first step towards building the perfect server. Although this process is very simple, many do forget the need to confirm the checksum. In this book, we will work with the minimal installation image, but you should be aware that there are other installation options available to you, such as NetInstall, DVD, Everything, and various LiveCDs.

Creating USB installation media on Windows or OS X

In this recipe, we will learn how to create a USB installation media on Windows or OS X. Nowadays, more and more server systems, desktop PCs, and laptops get shipped without any optical drive. Installing a new operating system, such as CentOS Linux using USB devices gets essential for them as no other installation option is available, as there is no other way to boot the installation media. Also, installing CentOS using USB media can be considerably faster than using the CD/DVD approach.

Getting ready

Before we begin, it is assumed that you have followed the previous recipe in which you were shown how to download a minimal CentOS image and confirm the checksum of the relevant image files. It is also assumed that all the downloads (including the downloaded ISO file) are stored on Windows in your `C:\Users\<username>\Downloads` folder or if using a OS X system, in the `/Users/<username>/Downloads` folder. Next, you will need a free USB device which can be discovered by your operating system, with enough total space, and which is empty or with data on it that can be discarded. The total space of the USB device needed for preparing as an installation media for CentOS 7 for the minimal version must be roughly 700 megabyte. If you are working on a Windows computer, you will need a working Internet connection to download additional software. On OS X, you need an administrator user account.

How to do it...

To begin this recipe, start up your Windows or OS X operating system, then connect a free USB device with enough capacity, and wait until it gets discovered by **File Manager** under Windows or **Finder** under OS X.

1. On a Windows based system, we need to download an additional software called `dd`. Visit `http://www.chrysocome.net/dd` in your favorite browser. Now download the latest `dd-XX.zip` file you can find there, with `XX` being the latest stable version number. For example, `dd-0.5.zip`.

2. On Windows, navigate to your `Downloads` folder using **File Manager**. Here you will find the `dd-05.zip` file. Right-click on it and click on **Extract All**, and extract the `dd.exe` file without creating any subdirectory.

3. On Windows, open the command prompt (typically found at **Start | All Programs | Accessories | Command Prompt**) and type the following commands:

```
cd downloads
dd.exe --list
```

4. On OS X, open the program **Finder | Applications | Utilities | Terminal**, and then type the following commands:

```
cd ~/Downloads
diskutil list
```

5. On Windows, to spot the name of the right USB device you want to use as installation media, look into the output of the command under the `removable media` section. Below that, you should find a line starting with `Mounting on` and then a drive letter, for example, `\.\e:`. This cryptic written drive letter is the most important part we need in the next step, so please write it down.

6. On OS X, the device path can be found in the output of the former command and has the format of `/dev/disk<number>`, where `number` is a unique identifier of the disk. The disks are numbered, starting with zero (`0`). Disk `0` is likely to be the OS X recovery disk, and disk `1` is likely to be your main OS X installation. To identify your USB device, try to compare the `NAME`, `TYPE`, and `SIZE` columns to the specifications of your USB stick. If you have identified the device name, write it down, for example, `/dev/disk3`.

7. On Windows, type the following command, assuming your USB device selected as a installation media has the Windows device name `\\.\e:` (change this as required and be careful what you type – this can create tremendous data loss). Also, substitute `XXXX` with the correct `iso` file version number in the next command:

```
dd.exe if=CentOS-7-x86_64-Minimal-XXXX.iso of=\\.\e: bs=1M
```

8. On OS X, you need two commands which will ask for the administrator password (replace `XXXX` and `disk3` with the correct version number and the correct USB device path):

```
sudo diskutil unmountDisk /dev/disk3
sudo dd if=./CentOS-7-x86_64-Minimal-XXXX.iso of=/dev/disk3 bs=1m
```

9. After the dd program finishes, there will be some output statistics on how long it took and how much data has been transferred during the copy process. On OS X, ignore any warning messages about the disk not being readable.

10. Congratulations! You now have created your first CentOS 7 USB installation media. You now can safely remove the USB drive in Windows or OS X, and physically unplug the device and use it as a boot device for installing CentOS 7 on your target machine.

How it works...

So what have we learned from this experience?

The purpose of this recipe was to introduce you to the concept of creating an exact copy of a CentOS installation ISO file on a USB device, using the dd command-line program. The dd program is a Unix based tool which can be used to copy bits from a source to a destination file. This means that the source gets read bit by bit and written to a destination without considering the content or file allocation; it just involves reading and writing pure raw data. It expects two file name based arguments: input file (if) and output file (of). We will use the CentOS image file as our input filename to clone it exactly 1:1 to the USB device, which is accessible through its device file as our output file parameter. The bs parameter defines the block size, which is the amount of data to be copied at once. Be careful, it is an absolute expert tool and overwrites any existing data on your target while copying data on it without further confirmation or any safety checks. So at least double-check the device drive letters of your target USB device and never confuse them! For example, if you have a second hard disk installed at D: and your USB device at E: (on OS X, at /dev/disk2 and /dev/disk3 respectively) and you confuse the drive letter E: with D: (or /dev/disk3 with /dev/disk2), your second hard disk would be erased with little to no chances of recovering any lost data. So handle with care! If you're in doubt of the correct output file device, never start the dd program!

In conclusion, it is fair to say that there are other far more convenient solutions available for creating a USB installation media for CentOS 7 than the dd command, such as the Fedora Live USB Creator. But the purpose of this recipe was not only to create a ready-to-use CentOS USB installer but also to get you used to the dd command. It's a common Linux command that every CentOS system administrator should know how to use. It can be used for a broad variety of daily tasks. For example, for securely erasing hard disks, benchmarking network speed, or creating random binary files.

Performing an installation of CentOS using the graphical installer

In this recipe, we will learn how to perform a typical installation of CentOS using a new graphical installer interface introduced in CentOS 7. In many respects, this is considered to be the recommended approach to installing your system, as it not only provides you with the ability to create the desired hard disk partitions but also to customize your installation in lots of ways (for example, keyboard layout, package selection, installation type, and so on). Your installation will then form the basis of a server on which you can build, develop, and run any type of service you may want to provide in the future.

Getting ready

Before we begin, it is assumed that you have followed the previous recipe in which you were shown how to download a CentOS image, confirm the checksum of the relevant image files, and create the relevant installation optical disks or USB media. Your system must be a 64 bit (x64_86) architecture, must have at least 406 MB RAM to load the graphical installer 1 GB or more is recommended if installing a graphical window manager such as Gnome), and have at least 10 GB free hard disk space.

How to do it...

To begin this recipe, insert your installation media (CD/DVD or USB device), restart the computer, and press the correct key for selecting the boot device during startup. Then choose the inserted device from the list (for many computers, this can be reached using *F11* or *F12* but can be different on your system. Please refer to your motherboard's manual).

1. On the welcome splash screen, the option **Test this media & install CentOS 7** is preselected and we will use this option. When you are ready, press the *Return* key to proceed.

2. After loading some initial files, the installer then starts to test the installation media. A single test should take between 30 seconds to five minutes and will report if there are any errors on your installation media. When this process is complete, the system will finally load the graphical installer.

3. The CentOS installer will now present the graphical installation welcome screen. From this point onwards, you can use your keyboard and mouse (the latter is highly recommended), but remember to enable the number lock on your keyboard if you intend to use the keypad.

4. On the left side you see the main language category and on the right side, the sub-languages for the installer. You can also search for a language using the textbox on the left bottom. All changes to your language settings will take effect immediately, so when you are ready, choose the **Continue** button to proceed.

5. Now we reach the main installation menu, which is called **Installation summary**.

6. Most options shown here already have some predefined values and can be used without changing, others which do not have any default value and which need your attention are labeled with a red exclamation mark like the **Installation Destination** under **System** category. So let's click on it using the mouse.

7. After clicking the **Installation Destination** button, you will see a graphical list of all the hard disk devices currently connected to your computer, which you can use for installing the operating system on. You can select your target hard disk by clicking on the correct hard disk symbol. It will then put a check mark on it. If you are unsure about the right hard disk, try to identify it by comparing its brand and total size shown in the menu. Before the installation can proceed, you must select a hard disk. Be careful and choose your target hard disk wisely as it will erase any existing data on it during the installation. When you are ready, click the **Done** button.

8. If your selected hard disk already contained data, then when clicking on **Done,** you may see what could be described as a warning/error message. The message may read: **You don't have enough space available to install CentOS**. Don't worry! This is to be expected and the message is simply asking you to re-initialize your hard disk because CentOS can only be installed on an empty disk. In most cases, especially if you have more than one partition on the hard disk, simply click on **Reclaim space** which will show a new window with a detailed list of all the partitions on this drive. Here just click on **Delete All** and then again on **Reclaim space** to discard any data on this disk, which will complete the task of disk initialization and enable you to proceed to the next step. When finished, click the **Done** button.

9. Back at the **Installation Summary** screen, the exclamation mark on the **Installation Destination** item should be gone now.

10. Optionally, we can click on **Network & Hostname** under **System category**. On the following page, on the left side, you can choose the primary network adapter you would like to connect to the Internet and select it by clicking on it. For the selected device, click on the switch on the right side to enable and connect it automatically using the **On** position of the switch. Finally, before closing this submenu, change the hostname in its text field to something appropriate. Click **Done**.

11. Now back at the **Installation Summary** screen, all the important settings have been made or have got predefined values, and all the exclamation marks are gone. If you are happy with these settings, click on the **Start installation** button or change the settings appropriately.

12. On the next screen, you will be required to create and confirm a root password for the root user while the new system gets installed in the background. Choose a secure password with not less than six characters.

13. Here on this screen you can also create a standard user account which is highly recommended. If you create a new user do not check **Make this user administrator**. When you are ready, click **Done** (if you entered a weak password, you have to confirm this by clicking twice)

14. CentOS will now partitionate and format your hard disk in the background and resolve any dependencies, and the installer will begin writing to the hard disk. This may take some time, but a progress bar will indicate the status of your installation. When finished, the installer will inform you that the entire process is complete and that the installation was successful. So when you are ready, click on the **Reboot** button. Now release your installation media from the drive.

15. Congratulations! You have now installed CentOS 7 on your computer.

How it works...

In this recipe, you have discovered how to install the CentOS 7 operating system. Having covered the typical approach to the graphical installation process, you are now in a position to develop the server with additional configuration changes and packages that will suit the role you intend the server to fulfill. This graphical installer has been built with the aim to be very intuitive and flexible, and makes installation very easy as it will guide the user through some mandatory tasks that he has to fulfill before the installation of the main system can be started.

Running a netinstall over HTTP

In this recipe, we will learn how to initiate the process of running a netinstall over HTTP (using the URL method) in order to install CentOS 7. It is a process in which a small image file is used to boot the computer and let the user select and install only the software packages and services he wants and nothing more over a network connection thus providing great flexibility.

Getting ready

Before we begin, it is assumed that you already know how to download and checksum a CentOS 7 installation image and how to create the relevant installation media from it. For this recipe here, we will need to download and create installation media for the netinstall image (download the latest CentOS-7-x86_64-NetInstall-XXXX.iso file) instead of the minimal ISO shown in another recipe in this chapter. Also, it is assumed that you have at least gone through the graphical installation procedure once to exactly know how to boot from your installation media and work with the installer program.

How to do it...

To begin this recipe, insert your prepared netinstall media, boot your computer from it, and wait for the welcome screen to appear:

1. On the welcome splash screen, the option **Test this media & install CentOS 7** is preselected and we will use this option. When you are ready, press the *Return* key to proceed.

2. After the tests finish, the graphical installer will load and present the typical graphical installation summary screen.

 Here the installer should be configured exactly as in the normal graphical installation recipe, besides the following mandatory changes to the **Network & Host name** and **Installation source** menu items (which is shown by the red exclamation marks).

3. Before we can install CentOS over the network, we have to make sure that we have a working network connection. Therefore, you should first click on the **Network & Host name** menu entry and activate one of your network adapters to the connected state. Refer to the normal installation recipe for more details.

4. Next, click on **Installation source** to enter the settings. As we will be installing over HTTP (also referred to as the URL method), you should leave the default **On the network** selected in the **Which installation source would you like to use?** section.

5. Now type in the following URL in the standard `http://` textfield, which we will use to download all the required installation packages at `http://mirror.centos.org/centos/7/os/x86_64/`.

6. Alternatively, you can also use a personal repository which you would have to create in advance (see *Chapter 4, Managing Packages with YUM*)

7. When you are ready, click on **Done** to start the initialization process.

8. On success, the installer will begin to retrieve the appropriate `install.img` file. This may take several minutes to complete, but once resolved, a progress bar will indicate all the download activity. When this process finishes successfully, the exclamation mark at the **installation source** will go away but another one will pop up which will tell the user that it is missing the **software selection**. Click on it and choose whatever fits your need. As for the purpose of this recipe, just select **Minimal install** under **Base environment** and then click on **Done**.

9. If the **Which installation source** would you like to use stays greyed out and cannot be changed, then there are connection problems with your network adapter. If this is the case, go back to configure **Network & Hostname** and change the network settings until the connected state can be reached.

10. CentOS 7 will now install the operating system the usual way and will congratulate you when this process finishes. It may be slower than installing from a physical installation media since all the packages have to be retrieved from the Internet.

How it works...

The purpose of this recipe was to introduce you to the concept of the CentOS network installation process, in order to show you just how simple this approach can be. By completing this recipe you have not only saved time by limiting your initial download to those files that are required by the installation process, but you have also been able to take advantage of the full graphical installation method without the need for a complete DVD suite.

Installing CentOS 7 using a kickstart file

While installing CentOS 7 manually using the graphical installer utility is fine on a single server, doing so on a multiple number of systems can be tedious. Kickstart files can automate the installation process of a server system and here we will show how this can be done. They are simple text based configuration files which provide detailed and exact instructions on how the target system should be set up and installed (for example, which keyboard layout or additional software packages to install).

Getting ready

To successfully complete this recipe, you will need access to an already installed CentOS 7 system to retrieve the kickstart configuration file we want to work with and use for automated installation. On this pre-installed CentOS server, you also need a working Internet connection to download additional software.

Next, we will need to download and create installation media for the DVD or the Everything image (download the latest `CentOS-7-x86_64-DVD-XXXX.iso` or `CentOS-7-x86_64-Everything-XXXX.iso` file), instead of the minimal iso file shown in another recipe in this chapter. Then you need another USB device which must be read and writable on Linux systems (formatted as FAT16, FAT32, EXT2, EXT3, EXT4, or XFS filesystem).

How to do it...

For this recipe to work, we first need physical access to an existing kickstart file from another finished CentOS 7 installation, which we will use as a template for a new CentOS 7 installation.

1. Log in as root on the existing CentOS 7 system and make sure the kickstart configuration file exists by typing the following command and pressing the *Return* key to execute (this will show you the details of the file):

   ```
   ls -l /root/anaconda-ks.cfg
   ```

2. Next, physically plug in a USB device and then type the following command, which will give you a list of all the hard disk devices currently connected to the computer:

   ```
   fdisk -l
   ```

3. Try to identify the device name by comparing its size, partitions, and identified filesystems with the specifications of your USB device. The device name will be of kind /dev/sdX, where X is an alphabetical character, such as b, c, d, e, ... and so on. If you cannot find the right device name for your USB media using the fdisk command, try the following trick: run fdisk -l twice - first with plugged-out and then with plugged-in USB device and compare how the second output changed - it has one device name more than the first output: your device name of interest !

4. If you have found the right device name in the list, create a directory to mount it to the current filesystem:

   ```
   mkdir /mnt/kickstart-usb
   ```

5. Next, actually mount the stick to this folder, assuming that your USB partition of choice is at /dev/sdc1 (change this as required):

   ```
   mount /dev/sdc1 /mnt/kickstart-usb
   ```

6. Now we will create our working copy of the kickstart file on the USB device for customizing:

   ```
   cp /root/anaconda-ks.cfg /mnt/kickstart-usb
   ```

7. Next, open the copied kickstart file on the USB device with your favorite text editor (here we will use the editor nano, if you have not installed it yet type yum install nano):

   ```
   nano /mnt/kickstart-usb/anaconda-ks.cfg
   ```

8. We will now modify the file for installing CentOS on a new target system. In nano, use the up and down arrow keys to go to the line which starts with (<your_hostname> will be the name of the hostname you gave during installation e.g. minimal.home):

   ```
   network --hostname=<your_hostname>
   ```

9. Now edit the `<your_hostname>` string to give it a new unique hostname. For example, add a `-2` to the end of any existing name, as shown next:

   network   --hostname=minimal-2.home

10. Next, move the cursor down using the up and down arrow keys until it stops at the line which says `%packages`. Append the following lines right below it (you can further customize this and provide additional packages that you want to install automatically):

    mariadb-server

    httpd

    rsync

    net-tools

11. Now save and close the file, to do this in the nano editor use the key combination *Ctrl+o* (which means, hold down the *Ctrl* key on the keyboard and then the *o* key without releasing the *Ctrl* key) to write the changes. Then press *Return* to confirm the filename and *Ctrl+x* to exit the editor.

12. Next, install the following CentOS package:

    yum install system-config-kickstart

13. Now we validate the syntax of our kickstart file using the `ksvalidator` program, which is included in the package we just installed:

    ksvalidator /mnt/kickstart-usb/anaconda-ks.cfg

14. If the `config` file is error-free, unmount the USB stick now by using the following commands:

    cd

    umount /mnt/kickstart-usb

15. When you get a new command prompt again, unplug the USB device with the kickstart file for using on the target machine physically from the system.

16. Now you need physical access to the target machine you want to install CentOS on, using the kickstart file just created. Disconnect any other external file storage(s) that you do not need during the installation.

17. Power on the computer and put in your prepared CentOS installation media (must be a CentOS DVD or Everything installation disk image prepared on a CD/DVD disc or a USB device installer). Also connect to the computer the USB stick containing the kickstart file you just created in the earlier steps (if you using a USB drive for installing CentOS then you will need two free USB ports in total to complete this recipe).

18. Next, start the server and press the correct key during the initial bootup screen, associated with booting the CentOS installation media you just connected.

19. After the CentOS installer starts loading, the common standard CentOS 7 installation welcome screen will show up and the option **Test this media & install CentOS 7** will be pre-selected by the cursor.

20. Next, press the *Esc* key on your keyboard once to switch to the `boot: prompt`.

21. Now we are ready to start the kickstart installation. To do this, you need to know the exact partition name on the USB device where the kickstart file is located. Type the following command, assuming that your partition is at `/dev/sdc1` (change this as required), and press the *Return* key to start the kickstart installation process:

    ```
    linux ks=hd:sdc1:/anaconda-ks.cfg
    ```

 If you cannot find out the right device and partition name of the USB stick, you have to start the target system in rescue mode (refer to the *Troubleshooting the system in rescue mode* recipe) to identify the right device name and partition number by comparing its size, partitions, and identified filesystems with the specifications of your stick.

22. The new system now gets installed automatically using the instructions from the provided kickstart file. You can watch the installation output messages as it is showing the user detailed installation progress.

23. If the system has finished installing, reboot the system and log in to your new machine to verify that the new system has been setup the way we described using the kickstart file.

How it works...

In this recipe, you have seen that every server running a CentOS 7 installation keeps the kickstart file in its root directory, which contains detailed information on how the system had been set up during the installation. The kickstart files can be used to automate the installations of multiple systems with the same configuration. This can save a lot of time doing repetitive work as no user interaction during installation is needed. Also, we can use this method if the target machines don't meet the minimum requirement in RAM for graphical based installations but when needed other features the text mode installer does not provide such as custom partitioning of the system. Kickstart configuration files are simple plain text files which can be created manually from scratch. Because there are quite a number of different commands available to construct your system using the kickstart syntax, we used an existing file as a template and customized it to fit our needs, instead of starting out completely new. We did not use the minimal installation image to drive our kickstart installation because we installed some extra packages not included on the minimal ISO file, such as the Apache webserver.

Getting started and customising the boot loader

When you turn on your computer, the boot loader is the first program that starts up and is responsible for loading and transferring control to an underlying operating system. Nowadays, almost any modern Linux distribution uses the **GRand Unified Bootloader version 2** (**GRUB2**) for starting the system. It has a lot of flexibility in configuration and supports a lot of different operating systems. In this recipe, we will show how to customize the GRUB2 boot loader by disabling the waiting time of the menu display and therefore improving the time it takes for booting the system.

Getting ready

To complete this recipe, you will require access to an already installed CentOS 7 operating system (minimal or any other CentOS 7 installation type will work) with root privileges. Also, you need to have some basic experiences with a text based editor, such as nano, for changing the configuration files.

How to do it...

We begin this recipe by opening the main GRUB2 configuration file with our text editor of choice and modifying it.

1. First log in as root into your system and create a copy of the GRUB2 configuration file for backup and rollback, if needed. Press the *Return* key to finish:

    ```
    cp /etc/default/grub /etc/default/grub.BAK
    ```

2. Open the main GRUB2 configuration file that we want to edit with the following command and press the *Return* key (here we will use the editor nano, if you have not installed it yet type `yum install nano`):

    ```
    nano /etc/default/grub
    ```

3. Press the *Return* key in the first line where the cursor is at to insert a new line at the top, and then insert the following line:

    ```
    GRUB_HIDDEN_TIMEOUT=0
    ```

4. Add a # sign to the beginning of the following line, as shown:

    ```
    GRUB_TIMEOUT=0
    ```

5. Now save the file in the nano using *Ctrl+o* (and *Return* to confirm the filename to save). Use *Ctrl+x* to exit the editor and then run the following command:

    ```
    dmesg | grep -Fq "EFI v"
    ```

6. If the preceding command does not produce any output, run the following command:

   `grub2-mkconfig -o /boot/grub2/grub.cfg`

7. Otherwise, if there is an output, run:

   `grub2-mkconfig -o /boot/efi/EFI/centos/grub.cfg`

8. If `grub2-mkconfig` is successful, it will print `Done`. Now reboot your system using the following command:

   `reboot`

9. During the rebooting process, you will notice that the GRUB2 boot menu will not appear any more and the system will boot up faster.

How it works...

Having completed this recipe, we now know how to customize the GRUB2 boot loader. In this very easy recipe, we only showed you very basic modifications to the boot loader but it can do much more! It supports a broad variety of filesystems and can boot almost any compatible operating system. This is also particularly useful if you plan to run multiple operating systems on the same machine. To learn more about GRUB2's configuration file syntax type the `info grub2 | less` command and go to the section `6.1 Simple configuration handling` (read the recipe *Navigating text files with less* in *Chapter 2, Configuring the System* to learn how to browse this document).

Troubleshooting the system in rescue mode

We all make mistakes and this is especially true for novice Linux system administrators. Linux can have a steep learning curve and sooner or later there will be a point in your career where your CentOS installation does not start up due to broad number of reasons, including hardware problems or human mistakes such as configuration errors. If this has happened to you then you can use the CentOS rescue mode in order to boot an otherwise unbootable system and try to undo your mistakes or find out the root of the problems. In this recipe, we will show you three common use cases when to use this option:

▶ Accessing the filesystem for recovering important data or undoing changes to configuration files if CentOS is not booting up

▶ Changing the root password if you forgot it

▶ Re-installing the boot loader which can be damaged when installing another operating system on the same harddisk where CentOS is installed

Getting ready

To complete this recipe, you will require a standard installation media (CD/DVD or USB device) of the CentOS 7 operating system. For recovering the data from the system, you will need to connect some sort of external storage device to the system, such as an external hard disk or a working network connection to another computer to copy all your precious data to a different location.

How to do it...

To begin this recipe, you should boot your server from the CentOS installation CD/DVD or the USB device and wait until the first welcome splash screen appears with the cursor waiting at the **Test this media & install CentOS 7** menu option.

Reaching rescue mode

1. From the main menu, use the down arrow key to select **Troubleshooting** and then press the *Return* key to proceed.

2. On the **Troubleshooting** screen, use the down arrow key to highlight **Rescue a CentOS system**. When you are ready, press the *Return* key to proceed.

3. After some loading time, we enter the rescue screen, which includes various confirmation sub-screens. To begin this section, use the left and right arrow keys to choose **Continue** and press the *Return* key to proceed.

4. On the first sub-screen, choose **OK** and press the *Return* key to proceed.

5. Again, in the following sub-screen, choose **OK** and press the *Return* key to proceed.

6. On the next screen, choose the **Start** shell and by using the *Tab* key, highlight **OK** and press the *Return* key to proceed.

7. By completing the preceding steps, you will launch a shell session. You will notice this at the bottom of your display. The current status of the shell session will read as follows:

    ```
    bash-4.2#
    ```

8. At the prompt, type the following instruction to change the root filesystem, before pressing the *Return* key to complete your request:

    ```
    chroot /mnt/sysimage
    ```

9. Congratulations! You just reached the rescue mode. To exit it at any time, simply type the following command and then press the *Return* key to complete your request (don't do this right now as this will restart the system):

    ```
    reboot
    ```

10. After the basic rescue mode is reached, we have the following options, depending on the type of problem.

Accessing the filesystem

If you are now in the rescue mode and need to backup important files from the filesystem, you need a destination location for the data transfer. For transferring the data we want to recover from the server to another computer please physically connect an external USB device to it. You can also use network storages for the recovery. For example, you could import an NFS server share and copy data to it. Refer to the *Working with NFS* recipe in *Chapter 7, Building a Network*.

1. On the rescue mode command line, type in the following command, which will show you all the current partitions connected to the system, and then press the *Return* key to complete your request:

   ```
   fdisk -l
   ```

2. You now need to find out the right device name with the partition number of your connected device; comparing the total size or the filesystem output of the various devices with the specifications from your stick can help you in this process. You can also try the following trick: run the `fdisk -l` command twice, first with the plugged-in USB device and then again with the USB device unplugged, and compare the output of both the commands. It should be different by one device name which you are searching for!

3. If you have found the right device name in the list, create a directory to mount the stick to the filesystem:

   ```
   mkdir /mnt/hdd-recovery
   ```

4. Next, mount the disk partition to this folder. Here we assume that the USB device of interest has the device name sdd1 (please change if different on your system):

   ```
   mount /dev/sdd1 /mnt/hdd-recovery
   ```

5. The original system's hard disk's root partition has been mounted under a specific folder by the rescue system automatically (under /mnt/sysimage), if you need to access it for example to change configuration files which caused startup problems or make a full or partial backup. For example, if you need to backup your Apache webserver configuration files, use:

   ```
   cp -r /mnt/sysimage/etc/http /mnt/hdd-recovery
   ```

6. If you need to access the data that lives on partitions other than the currently mounted root partition, use `fdisk -l` to identify the partition of interest. Then create a directory and mount the partition to it and change to that directory to access your data similar you did when mounting the USB device.

7. To finish backing up the files, type:

   ```
   reboot
   ```

Accessing the filesystem

1. If you are in the rescue mode for changing the root password, just use the following command and provide a new password:

   ```
   passwd
   ```

2. To complete changing the password, type:

   ```
   reboot
   ```

Re-install the CentOS boot loader

1. We will now use the `fdisk` command to find the name of all the current partitions. To do this, type the following instruction and then press the *Return* key to complete your request:

   ```
   fdisk -l
   ```

2. Now run the following command:

   ```
   dmesg | grep -Fq "EFI v"
   ```

3. If the preceding command does not produce any output look for the * symbol in the `fdisk` listing in the boot column to find the correct start partition, and assuming that your boot disk is on `/dev/sda1` (change this as required), type the following:

   ```
   grub2-install /dev/sda
   ```

4. Otherwise, if there is an output, run instead:

   ```
   yum reinstall grub2-efi shim
   ```

5. If no error is reported, the console should respond as follows:

   ```
   # this device map was generated by anaconda
   (hd0) /dev/sda
   ```

6. The console output from the last step has confirmed that GRUB has now been successfully restored.

7. To reboot the computer, type:

   ```
   reboot
   ```

How it works...

There are a broad variety of problems which can be resolved by the tools provided through the rescue mode environment. Often these problems refer to booting problems but can also be from different types, such as forgetting the root password. Rescue mode can be a life-saver and an understanding of it is a very important skill to learn. It was felt that such a recipe should thus remain close at hand.

> Remember to always be careful when working with bootloader commands as improper use can make your operating system unbootable.

Updating the installation and enhancing the minimal install with additional administration and development tools

In this recipe, we will learn how to enhance the minimal install with additional tools that will give you a variety of administrative and development options, which in turn will prove vital during the lifetime of your server and which are essential for some recipes in this book. The minimal install is probably the most efficient way you can install a server, but having said that, a minimal install does require some additional features in order to make it a more compelling model.

Getting ready

To complete this recipe, you will require a minimal installation of the CentOS 7 operating system with root privileges and a connection to the Internet in order to facilitate the download of additional packages.

How to do it...

We will begin this recipe by updating the system.

1. To update the system, log in as root and type:

   ```
   yum -y update
   ```

2. CentOS will now search for the relevant updates and, if available, they will be installed. On completion and depending on what was updated (that is, kernel and new security features to name but a few), you can decide to reboot your computer. To do this, type:

   ```
   reboot
   ```

3. Your server will now reboot and return to the login screen. We will now complete this recipe and enhance our current installation with a series of package groups that will prove to be very useful in the future. To do this, log in as root and type:

   ```
   yum -y groupinstall "Base" "Development Libraries" "Development Tools"
   ```

   ```
   yum -y install policycoreutils-python
   ```

How it works...

The purpose of this recipe is to enhance the minimal installation of the CentOS 7 operating system and by doing this you have not only introduced yourself to the **Yellowdog Updater Modified (YUM)** package manager (something to which we will return to later on in this book), but you now have a system that is capable of running a vast amount of applications right out-of-the-box.

So what have we learned from this experience?

We started the recipe by updating the system in order to ensure that it is up to date. At this stage, it is often a good idea to reboot the system. It is not expected that we will do this very often but it is expected when updating for the first time after the installation of the operating system, as it is most likely that there are major changes available. The reason behind this is typically based on the desire to take advantage of a new kernel or revised security updates. In the next phase, the recipe showed you how to add a series of package groups that may prove to be more than useful in the future. To save time, we wrapped the instruction to install the three main package groups: Base, Development Libraries, and Development Tools. The preceding action alone installs over 200 individual packages, thereby giving your server the ability to compile the code and run a vast array of applications out-of -the-box, that you may need over the life time of your server. To see a list of all the packages within a group, for example, from Base, run the yum groupinfo Base command. Another package we installed was policycoreutils-python which provides tools and programs to manage the security enhanced access control to Linux, which we will use quite often throughout the chapters of this book.

2

Configuring the System

In this chapter, we will cover the following topics:

- ▶ Navigating text files with less
- ▶ Introduction to Vim
- ▶ Speaking the right language
- ▶ Synchronizing the system clock with NTP and the chrony suite
- ▶ Setting your hostname and resolving the network
- ▶ Becoming a superuser
- ▶ Building a static network connection
- ▶ Customizing your system banners and messages
- ▶ Priming the kernel

Introduction

This chapter is a collection of recipes that covers the basic practice of establishing the basic needs of a server. For many, building a server can often seem to be a daunting task, and so the purpose of this chapter is to provide you with an instant method to achieve the desired goals.

Navigating text files with less

Throughout this book, you will often use programs and tools that use the program less or a less-like navigation to view and read file content or display output. At first, the control can seem a bit unintuitive .Here, in this recipe, we will show you the basics of how to navigate through a file using less controls.

Getting ready

To complete this recipe, you will require a working installation of the CentOS 7 operating system with root privileges.

How to do it...

1. To begin, log in as root and type the following command to open a program that uses less for navigation:

    ```
    man man
    ```

2. To navigate, press the *up* and *down* key to scroll up and down one line at a time, the *spacebar* to scroll down a page, and the *b* key to scroll up a page. You can search within the text using the forward slash key, */*,followed by the search term, then press *Return* to search. Press *n* to jump to the next search result. Press the *q* key to exit.

How it works...

Here, in this short recipe, we have shown you the very basics of less navigation, which is essential for reading man pages and is used by a lot of other programs throughout this book to display text. We only showed you the basic commands and there is much more to learn. Please read the less manual to find out more on `man less` command.

Introduction to Vim

In this recipe, we will give you a very brief introduction to the text editor, Vim, which is used as the standard text editor throughout this book. You can also use any other text editor you prefer, such as nano or emacs, instead.

Getting ready

To complete this recipe, you will require a working installation of the CentOS 7 operating system with root privileges.

How to do it...

We will start this recipe by installing the `vim-enhanced` package, as it contains a tutorial you can use to learn working with Vim:

1. To begin, log in as root and install the following package:

   `yum install vim-enhanced`

2. Afterwards, type the following command to start the Vim tutorial:

   `vimtutor`

3. This will open the Vim tutorial in the Vim editor. To navigate, press the *up* and *down* key to scroll up and down single-line wise. To exit the tutorial, press the *Esc* key, then type `:q!`, followed by the *Return* key to exit.

4. You should now read through the file and go through the lessons to get a basic understanding of Vim, to learn how to edit your text documents.

How it works...

The tutorial shown in this recipe should be seen as a starting point from which to learn the basics for working with one of the most powerful and effective text editors available for Linux. Vim has a very steep learning curve, but after dedicating about half an hour to the vimtutor guide you should be able to do all the common text editing tasks without any problem, such as opening, editing, and saving text files.

Speaking the right language

In this recipe, we will show you how to change the language settings of your CentOS 7 installation for the whole system and for single users. The need to change this is rare but can be important, for example if we accidentally chose the wrong language during installation.

Getting ready

To complete this recipe, you will require a working installation of the CentOS 7 operating system with root privileges, and a console-based text editor of your choice. You should have read the *Navigating text files with less* recipe, because some commands in this recipe will use less for printing output.

How to do it...

There are two categories of settings that you have to adjust if you want to change the system-wide language settings of your CentOS 7 system. We begin by changing the system locale information and then the keyboard settings:

1. To begin, log in as root and type the following command to show the current locale settings for the console, graphical window managers (X11 layout), and also the current keyboard layout:

   ```
   localectl status
   ```

2. Next, to change these settings, we first need to know all the available locale and keyboard settings on this system (both commands use `less` navigation):

   ```
   localectl list-locales
   localectl list-keymaps
   ```

3. If you have picked the right locale from the output above in our example, `de_DE.utf8` and `keymap de-mac` (change to your own appropriate needs), you can change your locale and keyboard settings using:

   ```
   localectl set-locale LANG=de_DE.utf8
   localectl set-keymap de-mac
   ```

4. Now, verify the persistence of your changes using the same command again:

   ```
   localectl status
   ```

How it works...

As we have seen, the `localectl` command is a very convenient tool that can take care of managing all important language settings in a CentOS 7 system.

So what have we learned from this experience?

We started by logging in to our command line with the root user. Then, we ran the `localectl` command with the parameter `status`, which gave us an overview of the current language settings in the system. The output of this command showed us that language properties in a CentOS 7 system can be separated into locale (system locale) and keymap (VC keymap and all X11 layout properties) settings.

Locales on Linux are used to set the system's language as well as other language-specific properties. This can include texts from error messages, log output, user interfaces, and, if you are using a window manager such as Gnome, even **Graphical User Interfaces** (**GUI**). Locale settings can also define region-specific formatting such as paper sizes, numbers and their natural sorting, currency information, and so on. They also define character encoding, which can be important if you chose a language that has characters that cannot be found in the standard ASCII encoding.

Keymap settings on the other hand define the exact layout of each key on your keyboard.

Next, to change these settings, we first issued the `localectl` command with the `list-locales` parameter to retrieve a full list of all locales on the system, and `list-keymaps` to show a list of all keyboard settings available in the system. Locales as outputted from the `list-locales` parameter use a very compact annotation for defining a language:

Language[_Region] [.Encoding] [@Modificator]

Only the `Language` part is mandatory, all the rest is optional. Examples for language and region are: `en_US` for English and region United States or American English, `es_CU` would be language Spanish and Region Cuba or Cuban Spanish.

Encodings are important for special characters such as German umlaut or accents in the French language. The memory representation of these special characters can be interpreted differently depending on the used encoding type. In general UTF-8 should be used as it is capable of encoding almost any character in every language.

Modificators are used to change settings defined by the locale. For example, `sr_RS.utf8@latin` is used if you want to have Latin settings for serbian Serbia, which normally uses Cyrillic definitions. This will change to western settings such as sorting, currency information, and so on.

To change the actual locale, we used the `set-locale LANG=de_DE.utf8` parameter. Here, the encoding was selected to display proper German umlauts. Please note that we used the `LANG` option to set the same locale value (for example, `de_DE.utf8`) for all available locale options. If you don't want to have the same locale value for all available options, you can use a more fine-grained control over single locale options. Please refer to the locale description using the man page, `man 7 locale` (on minimal installation; you need to install all Linux documentation man pages before using the `yum install man-pages` command). You can set these additional options using a similar syntax, for example, to set the time locale use:

localectl set-locale LC_TIME="de_DE.utf8"

Next, we showed all available keymap codes using the `list-keymaps` parameter. As we have seen from running `localectl status`, the keymaps can be separated in non-graphical (VC keymap) and graphical (X11 layout) settings, which allows the flexible configuration of different keyboard layouts when using a window manager such as Gnome and for the console. Running `localectl` with the parameter, `set-keymap de-mac`, sets the current keymap to a German Apple Macintosh keyboard model. This command applies the given keyboard type to both the normal VC and the X11 keyboard mappings. If you want different mappings for X11 than for the console, use `localectl --no-convert set-x11-keymap cz-querty`, where we use `cz-querty` for the keymap code to a Czech querty keyboard model (change this accordingly).

There's more...

Sometimes, single system users need different language settings than the system's locale (which can only be set by the root user), according to their regional keyboard differences and for interacting with the system in their preferred human language. System-wide locales get inherited by every user as long as they are not overwritten by local environment variables.

 Changing system-wide locales does not necessarily have an effect on your user's locales if they have already defined something else for themselves.

To print all the current locale environment variables for any system user, we can use the command, `locale`. To set single environment variables with the appropriate variable name; for example, to set the time locale to US time we would use the following line:

```
export LC_TIME="en_US.UTF-8"
```

But, most likely we would want to change all the locales to the same value; this can be done by setting `LANG`. For example, to set all the locales to American English, use the following line:

```
export LANG="en_US.UTF-8"
```

To test the effect of locale changes, we can now produce an error message that will be shown in the language set by the `locale` command. Here is the different language output for changing locale from English to German:

```
export LANG="en_US.UTF-8"
ls !
```

The following output will be printed:

```
ls: cannot access !: No such file or directory
```

Now, change to German locale settings:

```
export LANG="de_DE.UTF-8"
ls !
```

The following output will be printed:

```
ls: Zugriff auf ! nicht möglich: Datei oder Verzeichnis nicht gefunden
```

Setting a locale in an active console using the `export` command will not survive closing the window or opening a new terminal session. If you want to make those changes permanent, you can set any locale environment variables, such as the `LANG` variable, in a file called `.bashrc` in your home directory, which will be read everytime a shell is opened. To change the locale settings permanently to `de_DE.UTF-8` in our example (change this to your own needs) use the following line:

```
echo "export LANG='de_DE.UTF-8'" >> ~/.bashrc
```

Synchronizing the system clock with NTP and the chrony suite

In this recipe, we will learn how to synchronize the system clock with an external time server using the **Network Time Protocol** (**NTP**) and the chrony suite. From the need to time-stamp documents, e-mails, and log files, to securing, running, and debugging a network, or to simply interact with shared devices and services, everything on your server is dependent on maintaining an accurate system clock, and it is the purpose of this recipe to show you how this can be achieved.

Getting ready

To complete this recipe, you will require a working installation of the CentOS 7 operating system with root privileges, a console-based text editor of your choice, and a connection to the Internet to facilitate downloading additional packages.

How to do it...

In this recipe, we will use the `chrony` service to manage our time synchronization. As chrony is not installed by default on CentOS minimal, we will start this recipe by installing it:

1. To begin, log in as root and install the `chrony` service, then start it and verify that it is running:

```
yum install -y chrony
systemctl start chronyd
systemctl status chronyd
```

2. Also, if we want to use chrony permanently, we will have to enable it on server startup:

```
systemctl enable chronyd
```

3. Next, we need to check whether the system already uses NTP to synchronize our system clock over the network:

```
timedatectl | grep "NTP synchronized"
```

4. If the output from the last step showed No for NTP synchronized, we need to enable it using:

```
timedatectl set-ntp yes
```

5. If you run the command (from step 3) again, you should see that it is now synchronizing NTP.

6. The default installation of chrony will use a public server that has access to the atomic clock, but in order to optimize the service we will need to make a few simple changes to streamline and optimize at what time servers are used. To do this, open the main chrony configuration file with your favorite text editor, as shown here:

```
vi /etc/chrony.conf
```

7. In the file, scroll down and look for the lines containing the following:

```
server 0.centos.pool.ntp.org iburst
server 1.centos.pool.ntp.org iburst
server 2.centos.pool.ntp.org iburst
server 3.centos.pool.ntp.org iburst
```

8. Replace the values shown with a list of preferred local time servers:

```
server 0.uk.pool.ntp.org iburst
server 1.uk.pool.ntp.org iburst
server 2.uk.pool.ntp.org iburst
server 3.uk.pool.ntp.org iburst
```

> Visit http://www.pool.ntp.org/ to obtain a list of local servers geographically near your current location. Remember, the use of three or more servers will have a tendency to increase the accuracy of the NTP service.

9. When complete, save and close the file before synchronizing your server using the sytstemctl command:

```
systemctl restart chronyd
```

10. To check whether the modifications in the `config` file were successful, you can use the following command:

    systemctl status chronyd

11. To check whether chrony is taking care of your system time synchronization, use the following:

    chronyc tracking

12. To check the network sources chrony uses for synchronization, use the following:

    chronyc sources

How it works...

Our CentOS 7 operating system's time is set on every boot based on the hardware clock, which is a small-battery driven clock located on the motherboard of your computer. Often, this clock is too inaccurate or has not been set right, therefore it's better to get your system time from a reliable source over the Internet (that uses real atomic time). The chrony daemon, `chronyd`, sets and maintains system time through a process of synchronization with a remote server using the NTP protocol for communication.

So, what have we learned from this experience?

As a first step, we installed the `chrony` service, since it is not available by default on a CentOS 7 minimal installation. Afterwards, we enabled the synchronization of our system time with NTP using the `timedatectl set-ntp yes` command.

After that, we opened the main chrony configuration file, `/etc/chrony.conf`, and showed how to change the external time servers used. This is particularly useful if your server is behind a corporate firewall and have your own NTP server infrastructure.

Having restarted the service, we then learned how to check and monitor our new configuration using the `chronyc` command. This is a useful command line tool (c stands for client) for interacting and controlling a chrony daemon (locally or remotely). We used the `tracking` parameter with `chronyc`, which showed us detailed information of the current NTP synchronization process with a specific server. Please refer to the man pages of the `chronyc` command if you need further help about the properties shown in the output (`man chronyc`).

We also used the `sources` parameter with the `chronyc` program, which showed us an overview of the used NTP time servers.

You can also use the older `date` command to validate correct time synchronization. It is important to realize that the process of synchronizing your server may not be instantaneous, and it can take a while for the process to complete. However, you can now relax in the full knowledge that you now know how to install, manage and synchronize your time using the NTP protocol.

There's more...

In this recipe, we set our system's time using the `chrony` service and the NTP protocol. Usually, system time is set as **Coordinated Universal Time** (**UTC**) or world time, which means it is one standard time used across the whole world. From it, we need to calculate our local time using time zones. To find the right time zone, use the following command (read the *Navigating textfiles with less* recipe to work with the output):

```
timedatectl list-timezones
```

If you have found the right time zone, write it down and use it in the next command; for example, if you are located in Germany and are near the city of Berlin, use the following command:

```
timedatectl set-timezone Europe/Berlin
```

Use `timedatectl` again to check if your local time is correct now:

```
timedatectl | grep "Local time"
```

Finally, if it is correct, you can synchronize your hardware clock with your system time to make it more precise:

```
hwclock --systohc
```

Setting your hostname and resolving the network

The process of setting the hostname is typically associated with the installation process. If you ever need to change it or your server's **Domain Name System** (**DNS**) resolver, this recipe will show you how.

Getting ready

To complete this recipe, you will require a working installation of the CentOS 7 operating system with root privileges, and a console-based text editor of your choice.

How to do it...

To begin this recipe, we shall start by accessing the system as root and opening the following file in order to name or rename your current server's hostname:

1. Log in as root and type in the following command to see the current hostname:
   ```
   hostnamectl status
   ```

2. Now, change the hostname value to your preferred name. For example, if you want to call your server `jimi`, you would type (change appropriately):

    ```
    hostnamectl set-hostname jimi
    ```

> Static hostnames are case-sensitive and restricted to using an Internet-friendly alphanumeric string of text. The overall length should be no longer than 63 characters, but try to keep it much shorter.

3. Next, we need the IP address of the server. Type in the following command to find it (you need to identify the correct network interface in the output):

    ```
    ip addr list
    ```

4. Afterwards, we will set the **Fully Qualified Domain Name** (**FQDN**), in order to do this, we will need to open and edit the hosts file:

    ```
    vi /etc/hosts
    ```

5. Here, you should add a new line appropriate to your needs. For example, if your server's hostname was called jimi, (with an IP address of `192.168.1.100`, and a domain name of `henry.com`) your final line to append will look like this:

    ```
    192.168.1.100        jimi.henry.com jimi
    ```

> For a server found on a local network only, it is advisable to use a non-Internet based top-level address. For example, you could use `.local` or `.lan`, or even `.home`, and by using these references you will avoid any confusion with the typical `.com`, `.co.uk`, or `.net` domain names.

6. Next, we will open the `resolv.conf` file, which is responsible for configuring static DNS server addresses that the system will use:

    ```
    vi /etc/resolv.conf
    ```

7. Replace the content of the file with the following:

    ```
    # use google for dns
    nameserver 8.8.8.8
    nameserver 8.8.4.4
    ```

8. When complete, save and close your file before rebooting your server to allow the changes to take immediate effect. To do this, return to your console and type:

    ```
    reboot
    ```

9. On a successful reboot, you can now check your new hostname and FQDN by typing the following commands and waiting for the response:

```
hostname --fqdn
```

10. To test if we can resolve domain names to IP addresses using our static DNS server addresses, use the following command:

```
ping -c 10 google.com
```

How it works...

A hostname is a unique label created to identify a machine on a network. It is restricted to alphanumeric-based characters, and making a change to your server's hostname can be achieved by using the `hostnamectl` command. A DNS server is used to translate domain names to IP addresses. There are several public DNS servers available; in a later recipe, we will build our own DNS service.

So, what have we learned from this experience?

In the first stage of the recipe, we changed the current hostname used by our server with the `hostnamectl` command. This command can set three different types of hostnames. Using the command with the `set-hostname` parameter will set the same name for all three hostnames: the high-level `pretty` hostname, which might include all kinds of special characters (for example, `Lennart's Laptop`), the static hostname which is used to initialize the kernel hostname at boot (for example `lennarts-laptop`), and the transient hostname, which is a default received from network configurations.

Following this, we set the FQDN of our server. A FQDN is the hostname along with a domain name after it. A domain name gets important when you are running a private DNS, or allowing external access to your server. Besides using a DNS server setting the FQDN can be achieved by updating the hosts file found at `/etc/hosts`.

This file is used by CentOS to map hostnames to an IP address, and it is often found to be incorrect on a new, un-configured, or recently installed server. For this reason, we first had to find out the IP address of the server using `ip addr list`.

An FQDN should consist of a short hostname and the domain name. Based on the example shown in this recipe, we set the FQDN for a server named `henry`, whose IP address is `192.168.1.100` and domain name is `henry.com`.

Saving this file would arguably complete this process. However, because the kernel makes a record of the hostname during the boot process, there is no choice but to reboot your server before you can use the changed settings.

Next, we opened the system's `resolv.conf` file, which keeps the IP addresses of the system's DNS servers. If your server does not use or have any DNS records, your system is not able to use domain names for network destinations in any program at all. In our example, we entered the public Google DNS server IP addresses, but you are allowed to use any DNS server you want or have to use (often in a cooperate environment, behind a firewall, you have to use internal DNS server infrastructures). On a successful reboot, we confirmed your new settings by using the `hostname` command, which can print out the hostname or the FQDN based on the parameters given.

So, in conclusion, you can say that this recipe has not only served to show you how to rename your server and resolve the network, but has also showed you the difference between a hostname and domain name:

As we have learned, a server is not only known by the use of a shorter, easier-to-remember, and quicker-to-type single-word-based host name, it also consists of three values separated with a period (for example jimi.henry.com). The relationship between these values may have seemed strange at first, especially where many people would have seen them as a single value, but by completing this recipe you have discovered that the domain name remains distinct from the hostname by virtue of being determined by the resolver subsystem, and it is only by putting them together that your server will yield the FQDN of the system as a whole.

There's more...

The hosts file consists of a list of IP addresses and corresponding hostnames, and if your network contains computers whose IP addresses are not listed in an existing DNS record, then in order to speed up your network it is often recommended that you add them to this file.

This can be achieved on any operating system, but to do this on CentOS, simply open the hosts file in your favorite text editor, as shown next:

vi /etc/hosts

Now, scroll down to the bottom of the file and add the following values by substituting the domain names and IP addresses shown here with something more appropriate to your own needs:

```
192.168.1.100     www.example1.lan
192.168.1.101     www.example2.lan
```

You can even use external address such as:

```
83.166.169.228   www.packtpub.com
```

This method provides you with the chance to create mappings between domain names and IP addresses without the need to use a DNS, and it can be applied to any workstation or server. The list is not restricted by size, and you can even employ this method to block access to certain websites by simply re-pointing all requests to visit a known website to a different IP address. For example, if the real address of `www.website.com` is `192.168.1.200` and you want to restrict access to it, then simply make the following changes to the hosts file on the computer that you want to block from access:

```
127.0.0.1     www.website.com
```

It isn't failsafe, but in this instance anyone trying to access `www.website.com` on this system will automatically be sent to `127.0.0.1`, which is your local network address, so this will just block access.

When you have finished, remember to save and close your file in the usual way before proceeding to enjoy the benefits of faster and safer domain name resolution across any available network.

Building a static network connection

In this recipe, we will learn how to configure a static IP address for a new or existing CentOS server.

While a dynamically assigned IP address or DHCP reservation may be fine for most desktop and laptop users, if you are setting up a server, it is often the case that you will require a static IP address. From web pages to e-mail, databases to file sharing, a static IP address will become a permanent location from which your server will deliver a range of applications and services, and it is the intention of this recipe to show you how easily it can be achieved.

Getting ready

To complete this recipe, you will require a working installation of the CentOS 7 operating system with root privileges and a console-based text editor of your choice.

How to do it...

For the purpose of this recipe, you will be able to find all the relevant files in the directory, `/etc/sysconfig/network-scripts/`. First, you need to find out the correct name of the network interface that you want to set as static. If you need to set more than one network interface as static, repeat this recipe for every device.

1. To do this, log in as root and type the following command to get a list of all of your system's network interfaces:

   ip addr list

2. If you have only one network card installed, it should be very easy to find out its name; just select the one not named `lo` (which is the loopback device). If you got more than one, having a look at the IP addresses of the different devices can help you choose the right one. In our example, the device is called `enp0s3`.

3. Next, make a backup of the network interface configuration file (change the `enp0s3` part accordingly, if your network interface is named differently):

    ```
    cp /etc/sysconfig/network-scripts/ifcfg-enp0s3/etc/sysconfig/
    network-scripts/ifcfg-enp0s3.BAK
    ```

4. When you are ready to proceed, open the following file in your favorite text editor by typing what is shown next:

    ```
    vi /etc/sysconfig/network-scripts/ifcfg-enp0s3
    ```

5. Now, work down the file and apply the following changes:

    ```
    NM_CONTROLLED="no"

    BOOTPROTO=none

    DEFROUTE=yes

    PEERDNS=no

    PEERROUTES=yes

    IPV4_FAILURE_FATAL=yes
    ```

6. Now, add your IP information by customizing the values of `XXX.XXX.XXX.XXX` as required:

    ```
    IPADDR=XXX.XXX.XXX.XXX

    NETMASK= XXX.XXX.XXX.XXX

    BROADCAST= XXX.XXX.XXX.XXX
    ```

7. We must now add a default gateway. Typically, this should be the address of your router. To do this, simply add a new line at the bottom of the file, as shown next, and customize the value as required:

    ```
    GATEWAY=XXX.XXX.XXX.XXX
    ```

8. When ready, save and close the file before repeating this step for any remaining Ethernet devices that you want to make static. When doing this, remember to assign a different IP address to each device.

9. When finished, save and close this file before restarting your network service:

    ```
    systemctl restart network
    ```

How it works...

In this recipe, you have seen the process associated with changing the state of your server's IP address from a dynamic value obtained from an external DHCP provider, to that of a static value assigned by you. This IP address will now form a unique network location from which you will be able to deliver a whole host of services and applications. It is a permanent modification, and yes, you could say that the process itself was relatively straightforward.

So, what have we learned from this experience?

Having started the recipe by identifying your network interface name of choice and creating a backup of the original Ethernet configuration files, we then opened the configuration file located at `/etc/sysconfig/network-scripts/ifcfg-XXX` (with `XXX` being the name of your interface, for example, `enp0s3`). As being static no longer requires the services of the network manager, we disabled `NM_CONTROLLED` by setting the value to `no`. Next, as we are in the process of moving to a static IP address, `BOOTPROTO` has been set to `none`, as we are no longer using DHCP. To complete our configuration changes, we then moved on to add our specific network values and set the IP address, the netmask, broadcast, and the default gateway address.

In order to assist the creation of a static IP address, the default gateway is a very important setting in as much as it allows the server to contact the wider world through a router.

When finished, we were asked to save and close the file before repeating this step for any remaining Ethernet devices. Having done this, we were then asked to restart the network service in order to complete this recipe and to enable our changes to take immediate effect.

Becoming a superuser

In this recipe, we will learn how to provide nominated users or groups with the ability to execute a variety of commands with elevated privileges.

On CentOS Linux, many files, folders, or commands can only be accessed or executed by a user called `root`, which is the name of the user who can control everything on a Linux system. Having one root user per system may suit your needs, but for those who want a greater degree of flexibility, a solid audit trail, and the ability to provide a limited array of administrative capabilities to a select number of trusted users, you have come to the right place. It is the purpose of this recipe to show you how to activate and configure the **sudo** (**superuser do**) command.

Getting ready

To complete this recipe, you will require a minimal installation of the CentOS 7 operating system with root privileges. It is assumed that your server maintains one or more users (other than root) who qualify for this escalation in powers. If you did not create a system user account during installation, please do so by first applying the recipe, *Managing users and their groups*, in *Chapter 3, Managing the System*.

How to do it...

To start this recipe, we will first test the sudo command with a non-privileged user.

1. To begin, log in to your system using a non-root user account, then type the following to verify that sudo is not enabled (use your user account's password when asked):

   sudo ls /var/log/audit

2. This will print the following error output with <username>, which is the user you are currently logged in with:

   <username> is not in the sudoers file.   This incident will be reported.

3. Now, log out the system user using the command:

   logout

4. Next, log in as root and use the following command to give the non-root user sudo power (change <username> appropriately):

   usermod -G wheel <username>

5. Now, you can test if sudo is working by logging out root again and re-logging in the user from step 1, and then trying again:

   sudo ls /var/log/audit

6. Congratulations, you've now set a normal user to have sudo powers and can view and execute files and directories restricted to the root user.

How it works...

Unlike some Linux distributions, CentOS does not provide sudo by default. Instead, you are typically allowed to access restricted parts of the system with the root user only. This offers a certain degree of security, but for a multi-user server there is little to no flexibility unless you simply provide these individuals with full administrative root access permissions. This is not advisable, and for this reason it was the purpose of this recipe to show you how to provide one or more users with the right to execute commands with elevated privileges.

So, what did we learn from this experience?

We started by logging in to the system with a normal user account having no root privileges or sudo powers. With this user, we then tried to list a directory that normally only the root user is allowed to see, so we applied the `sudo` command on it. It failed, giving us the error that we are not in the sudoers list.

The `sudo` command provides nominated users or groups with the ability to execute a command as if they were the root user. All actions are recorded (in a file called `/var/log/secure`), so there will be a trace of all the commands and arguments used.

We then logged in as the true root user and added a group called wheel to the system user that we wanted sudo rights for. This group is used as a special administration group and every member of it is granted sudo rights automatically.

From now on, the nominated user can implement sudo in order to execute any command with elevated privileges. To do this, the user would be required to type the word `sudo` before any command, for example, they could run the following command:

sudo yum update

They will be asked to confirm their user password (not the root password!), and after successful authentication the program will be executed as the user root.

Finally, we can say that there are three ways to become root on a CentOS Linux system:

First, to log in as the true user root to the system. Second, you can use the command, `su - root`, while any normal system user is logged in, giving the root user's password to switch to a root shell prompt permanently. Third, you can give a normal user sudo rights so that they can execute single commands using their own passwords as if they were the root user, while staying logged in as themselves.

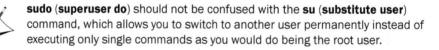

sudo (superuser do) should not be confused with the **su (substitute user)** command, which allows you to switch to another user permanently instead of executing only single commands as you would do being the root user.

The `sudo` command allows great flexibility for servers that have a lot of users, where one administrator is not enough to manage the whole system.

Customizing your system banners and messages

In this recipe, we will learn how to display a welcome message if a user successfully logs in to our CentOS 7 system using SSH or console, or opens a new terminal window in a graphical window manager. This is often used to show the user informative messages, or for legal reasons.

Getting ready

To complete this recipe, you will require a minimal installation of the CentOS 7 operating system with root privileges and a console-based text editor of your choice.

How to do it...

1. To begin, log in to your system using your root user account and create the following new file with your favorite text editor:

   ```
   vi /etc/motd
   ```

2. Next, we will put in the following content in this new file:

   ```
   ##############################################
   # This computer system is for authorized users only.
   # All activity is logged and regularly checked.
   # Individuals using this system without authority or
   # in excess of their authority are subject to
   # having all their services revoked...
   ##############################################
   ```

3. Save and close this file.

4. Congratulations, you have now set a banner message for whenever a user successfully logs in to the system using ssh or a console.

How it works...

For legal reasons, it is strongly recommended that computers display a banner before allowing users to log in; lawyers suggest that the offense of unauthorized access can only be committed if the offender knows at the time that the access he intends to obtain is unauthorized. Login banners are the best way to achieve this. Apart from this reason, you can provide the user with useful system information.

So, what did we learn from this experience?

We started this recipe by opening the file, `/etc/motd`, which stands for message of the day; this content will be displayed after a user logged in a console or ssh. Next, we put in that file a standard legal disclaimer and saved the file.

There's more...

As we have seen, the `/etc/motd` file displays static text after a user successfully logs in to the system. If you want to also display a message when an ssh connection is first established, you can use ssh banners. The banner behavior is disabled in the ssh daemon configuration file by default, which means that no message will be displayed if a user establishes an ssh connection. To enable this feature, log in as root on your server and open the `/etc/ssh/sshd_config` file using your favorite text editor, and put in the following content at the end of the file:

Banner /etc/ssh-banner

Then, create and open a new file called `/etc/ssh-banner`, and put in a new custom ssh greeting message.

Finally, restart your ssh daemon using the following line:

systemctl restart sshd.service

The next time someone establishes an ssh connection to your server, this new message will be printed out.

The `motd` file can only print static messages and some system information details, but it is impossible to generate real dynamic messages or use bash commands in it if a user successfully logs in.

Also, `motd` does not work in non-login shells, such as when you open a new terminal within a graphical window manager. In order to achieve this, we can create a custom script in the `/etc/profile.d` directory. All scripts in this directory get executed automatically if a user logs in to the system. First, we delete any content in the `/etc/motd` file, as we don't want to display two welcome banners. Then, we open the new file, `/etc/profile.d/motd.sh`, with our text editor and create a custom message, such as the following, where we can use bash commands and write little scripts (use the back ticks to run bash shell commands in this file):

```
#!/bin/bash
echo -e "
###############################
#
# Welcome to `hostname`, you are logged in as `whoami`
# This system is running `cat /etc/redhat-release`
```

```
# kernel is `uname -r`
# Uptime is `uptime | sed 's/.*up ([^,]*), .*/1/'`
# Mem total `cat /proc/meminfo | grep MemTotal | awk {'print $2'}` kB
###################################"
```

Priming the kernel

The Linux kernel is a program that constitutes the central core of the operating system. It can directly access the underlying hardware and make it available to the user to work with it using the shell.

In this recipe, we will learn how to prime the kernel by working with dynamically loaded kernel modules. Kernel modules are device driver files (or filesystem driver files) that add support for specific pieces of hardware so that we can access them.

You will not work very often with kernel modules as a system administrator, but having a basic understanding of them can be beneficial if you have a device driver problem or an unsupported piece of hardware.

Getting ready

To complete this recipe, you will require a minimal installation of the CentOS 7 operating system with root privileges.

How to do it...

1. To begin, log in to your system using your root user account, and type the following command in order to show the status of all Linux kernel modules currently loaded:

   `lsmod`

2. In the output, you will see all loaded device drivers (module); let's see if a cdrom and floppy module have been loaded:

   `lsmod | grep "cdrom\|floppy"`

3. On most servers, there will be the following output:

   ```
   cdrom                    42556  1 sr_mod
   floppy                   69417  0
   ```

4. Now, we want to show detailed information about the sr_mod cdrom module:

   `modinfo sr_mod`

5. Next, unload these two modules from the kernel (you can only do this if the module and hardware have been found and loaded on your system; otherwise skip this step):

    ```
    modprobe -r -v sr_mod floppy
    ```

6. Check if the modules have been unloaded (output should be empty now):

    ```
    lsmod | grep "cdrom\|floppy"
    ```

7. Now, to show a list of all kernel modules available on your system, use the following directory where you can look around:

    ```
    ls /lib/modules/$(uname -r)/kernel
    ```

8. Let's pick a module from the subfolder `/lib/modules/$(uname -r)/kernel/drivers/` called `bluetooth` and verify that it is not loaded yet (output should be empty):

    ```
    lsmod | grep btusb
    ```

9. Get more information about the module:

    ```
    modinfo btusb
    ```

10. Finally, load this bluetooth USB module:

    ```
    modprobe btusb
    ```

11. Verify again that it is loaded now:

    ```
    lsmod | grep "btusb"
    ```

How it works...

Kernel modules are the drivers that your system's hardware needs to communicate with the kernel and operating system (also, they are needed to load and enable filesystems). They are loaded dynamically, which means that only the drivers or modules are loaded at runtime, which reflects your own custom specific hardware.

So, what did we learn from this experience?

We started using the `lsmod` command to view all the currently loaded kernel modules in our system. The output shows three columns: the module name, the amount of RAM the module occupies while loaded, and the number of processes this module is used by and a list of dependencies of other modules using it. Next, we checked if the `cdrom` and `floppy` modules have been loaded by the kernel yet. In the output, we saw that the `cdrom` module is dependent on the `sr_mod` module. So, next we used the `modinfo` command to get detailed information about it. Here, we learned that `sr_mod` is the SCSI `cdrom` driver.

Since we only need the floppy and cdrom drivers while we first installed the base system we can now disable those kernel modules and save us some memory. We unloaded the modules and their dependencies with the `modprobe -r` command and rechecked whether this was successful by using `lsmod` again.

Next, we browsed the standard kernel module directory (for example, `/lib/modules/$(uname -r)/kernel/drivers`). The `uname` substring command prints out the current kernel version so that it makes sure that we are always listing the current kernel modules after having installed more than one version of the kernel on our system.

This kernel module directory keeps all the available modules on your system structured and categorized using subdirectories. We navigated to `drivers/bluetooth` and picked the `btusb` module. Doing `modinfo` on the `btusb` module, we found out that it is the generic bluetooth USB driver. Finally, we decided that we needed this module, so we loaded it using the `modprobe` command again.

There's more...

It's important to say that loading and unloading kernel modules using the `modprobe` command is not persistent; this means that if you restart the system, all your changes to kernel modules will be gone. To load a kernel module at boot time create a new executable script file, `/etc/sysconfig/modules/<filename>.modules`, where `<filename>` is a name of your choice. There you put in `modprobe` execution commands just as you would on the normal command line. Here is an example of additionally loading the bluetooth driver on startup, for example `/etc/sysconfig/modules/btusb.modules`:

```
#!/bin/sh
if [ ! -c /dev/input/uinput ] ; then
exec /sbin/modprobe btusb >/dev/null 2>&1
fi
```

Finally, you need to make your new module file executable via the following line:

```
chmod +x /etc/sysconfig/modules/btusb.modules
```

Recheck your new module settings with `lsmod` after reboot.

To remove a kernel module at boot time for example `sr_mod`, we need to blacklist the module's name using the `rdblacklist` kernel boot option. We can set this option by appending it to the end of the `GRUB_CMDLINE_LINUX` directive in the GRUB2 configuration file `/etc/default/grub` so it will look like:

```
GRUB_CMDLINE_LINUX="rd.lvm.lv=centos/root rd.lvm.lv=centos/swap
crashkernel=auto rhgb quiet rdblacklist=sr_mod"
```

If you need to blacklist multiple modules, the `rdblacklist` option can be specified multiple times like `rdblacklist=sr_mod rdblacklist=nouveau`.

Next recreate the GRUB2 configuration using the `grub2-mkconfig` command (to learn more read the *Getting started and customizing the boot loader* recipe in *Chapter 1, Installing CentOS*).

```
grub2-mkconfig -o /boot/grub2/grub.cfg
```

Finally we also need to `blacklist` the module name using the blacklist directive in a new `.conf` file of your choice in the `/etc/modprobe.d/` directory for example:

```
echo "blacklist sr_mod" >> /etc/modprobe.d/blacklist.conf
```

3
Managing the System

In this chapter, we will cover the following topics:

- ▸ Knowing and managing background services
- ▸ Troubleshooting background services
- ▸ Tracking system resources with journald
- ▸ Configuring journald to make it persistent
- ▸ Managing users and their groups
- ▸ Scheduling tasks with cron
- ▸ Synchronizing files and doing more with rsync
- ▸ Maintaining backups and taking snapshots
- ▸ Monitoring important server infrastructure
- ▸ Taking control with Git and Subversion

Introduction

This chapter is a collection of recipes that provides for the need to maintain a performance-based server solution. From monitoring your free disk space, to working with system services and managing the synchronization of remote files, the purpose of this chapter is to show you how quickly and easily you can get to grips with the task of server maintenance.

Knowing and managing your background services

Linux system services are one of the most fundamental concepts of every Linux server. They are programs which run continuously in your system, waiting for external events to process something or do it all the time. Normally, when working with your server, a system user will not notice the existence of such a running service because it is running as a background process and is therefore not visible. There are many services running all the time on any Linux server. These can be a web server, database, FTP, SSH or printing, DHCP, or LDAP server to name a few. In this recipe, we will show you how to manage and work with them.

Getting ready

To complete this recipe, you will require a working installation of the CentOS 7 operating system with root privileges, a console-based text editor of your choice, and a connection to the Internet to facilitate the download of additional packages. Some commands shown here use *less* navigation in their output. Read the *Navigating text files with less* recipe from *Chapter 2, Configuring the System* to learn how to browse them.

How to do it...

systemctl is a program that we will use to manage all our background service tasks in a CentOS 7 system. Here, we will show you how to use it, taking the Apache web server service as an example in order to get familiar with it. For a full explanation of Apache, read *Chapter 12, Providing Web Services*:

1. First, we log in as root and install the Apache web server package:

   ```
   yum install httpd
   ```

2. Next we will check Apache's service status:

   ```
   systemctl status httpd.service
   ```

3. Start the webserver service in the background and print out it's status again:

   ```
   systemctl start httpd.service
   systemctl status httpd.service
   ```

4. Next, let's print out a list of all services currently running in the background of your system; in this list, you should identify the httpd service you just started:

   ```
   systemctl -t service -a --state running
   ```

5. Now, let's make a backup of the Apache configuration file:

   ```
   cp /etc/httpd/conf/httpd.conf /etc/httpd/conf/httpd.conf.BAK
   ```

6. Now, we will make some changes to the main Apache configuration file using sed:

```
sed -i 's/Options Indexes FollowSymLinks/Options -Indexes
+FollowSymLinks/g' /etc/httpd/conf/httpd.conf
```

7. Now, type the following command to stop and start the service and apply our changes:

```
systemctl stop httpd.service
systemctl start httpd.service
systemctl status httpd.service
```

8. Next, let's enable the `httpd` service to start automatically at boot time:

```
systemctl enable httpd.service
```

9. The last command will show how to restart a service:

```
systemctl restart httpd.service
```

How it works...

As we have seen, the `systemctl` utility can be used to take full control of your system's services. The `systemctl` is the control program for `systemd`, which is the system and service manager in CentOS 7 Linux. The `systemctl` command can be used for a variety of other tasks as well, but here we concentrate on managing services.

So, what have we learned from this experience?

We started this recipe by logging in as root and installed the Apache web server package as we want to use it for showing how to manage services in general using the `systemctl` program. Apache or the `httpd.service`, as it is called by `systemd`, is just an example we will use; other important services that might be running in a basic server environment could be `sshd.service`, `mariadb.service`, `crond.service`, and so on. Afterwards, we checked httpd's current status with the `systemctl status` command parameter. The output showed us two fields: **Loaded** and **Active**. The **Loaded** field tells us if it is currently loaded and if it will automatically be started at boot time; the **Active** field denotes whether the service is currently running or not. Next, we showed how to start a service using `systemctl`. The command's exact starting syntax for services is the `systemctl start <name of the service>.service`.

> By starting a service, the program gets detached from the terminal by forking off a new process that gets moved into the background where it runs as a non-interactive background process. This is sometimes called **daemon**.

Next, after we started the Apache webserver daemon, we then used systemctl's `status` parameter again to show how the status changes if we run it. The output shows us that it is currently loaded but disabled on reboot. We also see that it is running, along with the latest logging output from this service and other detailed information about the process. To get an overview of all status information for all services on the system, use `systemctl --type service --all`. A `systemctl` service must not be running all the time. Its state can also be stopped, degraded, maintained, and so on. Next, we used the following command to get a list of all currently running services on your system:

```
systemctl -t service -a --state running
```

As you can see here, we used the `-t` flag in order to filter only for type service units. As you may guess, `systemctl` can not only deal with service units, but also with a lot of other unit types. `systemd` units are resources `systemd` can manage using configuration files, and which encapsulate information about services, listening sockets, saved system state snapshots, mounting devices, and other objects that are relevant to the system. To get a list of all possible unit types, type `systemctl -t help`. These configuration unit files reside in special folders in the system, and the type they belong to can be read from the extension; all the service unit files have the file extension, `.service` (for example, device unit files have the extension, `.device`). There are two places where the system stores them. All the `systemd` unit files installed by the basic system during installation are in `/usr/lib/systemd/system`, all other services that come from installing packages such as Apache or for your own configurations should go to `/etc/systemd/system`. We can find our Apache service configuration file exactly at `/usr/lib/systemd/system/httpd.service`. Next, we showed the user how to stop a service, which is the opposite of starting it, using the syntax, `systemctl stop <name of the service>`. Finally, as a last step, we used systemctl's `restart` parameter, which just handles the stopping and starting of a service in one step with less typing. This is often useful if a service hangs and is unresponsive, and you quickly need to reset it to get it working. Before showing how to stop and restart a service, we did another important thing. While the Apache service was running, we changed its main service configuration file with the `sed` command, adding an `-Indexes` option that disables the directory web site file listings, and which is a common measure to increase the security of your web server. Since the Apache web server was already running and loading its configuration into memory during service startup, any changes to this file will never be recognized by the running service.

Normally, to apply any configuration file change, running services need a full service restart, because configuration files will normally only be loaded during startup initialization.

Now, imagine that your web server is reachable from the Internet and at the moment there are a lot of people accessing your web pages or applications in parallel. If you restart the Apache normally, the web server will be inaccessible for a while (as long as it takes to restart the server) as the process will actually end and afterwards start all over again. All the current users would get HTML 404 error pages if they were to request something at that moment. Also, all the current session information would have gone; imagine you have an online web shop where people use shopping carts or logging in. All this information would also be gone. To avoid the disruption of important services such as the Apache web server, some of these services have a `reload` option (but not every service has this feature!) that we can apply instead of the `restart` parameter. This option just reloads and applies the service's configuration file, while the service itself stays online and does not get interrupted during execution. For Apache, you can use the following command-line: `systemctl reload httpd.service`. To get a list of all the services that have the reload functionality, use the following lines:

```
grep -l "ExecReload" /usr/lib/systemd/system/*.service /etc/systemd/system/*.service
```

So, having completed this recipe, we can say that we now know how to work with the basic `systemctl` parameters to manage services. It can be a very powerful program and can be used for much more than only starting and stopping services. Also, in this recipe, we have used different names that all mean the same: system service, background process, or daemon.

There's more...

There is another important unit type called `target`. Targets are also unit files and there are quite a number of them already available in your system. To show them, use the following:

```
ls -a /usr/lib/systemd/system/*.target /etc/systemd/system/*.target
```

Simply said, targets are collections of unit files such as services or other targets. They can be used to create runlevel-like environments, which you may know from earlier CentOS versions. Runlevels define which services should be loaded at which system state. For example, there is a graphical state, or a rescue mode state, and so on. To see how the common runlevels correspond to our targets, run the following command, which shows us all the symbolic links between them:

```
ls -al /lib/systemd/system | grep runlevel
```

Targets can be dependent on other targets; to get a nice overview of target dependencies, we can run the following command to show all dependencies from the multi-user target to all the other targets (green means active and red means inactive):

```
systemctl list-dependencies multi-user.target
```

You can show the current target that we are in at the moment with:

```
systemctl get-default
```

You can also switch to another target:

```
systemctl set-default multi-user.target
```

Troubleshooting background services

Often, a big part of every system administrator's work is troubleshooting the server when something goes wrong. This is especially true for your system's services, as they are constantly running and processing information all the time. Services can be dependent on other services and on the server's system, and there will be situations in your administrator's life where the system services will fail or refuse to start. Here, in this recipe, we will show you how to troubleshoot them if something goes wrong.

Getting ready

To complete this recipe, you will require a working installation of the CentOS 7 operating system with root privileges and a console-based text editor of your choice; you should also have completed the *Knowing and managing your background services* recipe from this chapter, where we installed the Apache web server.

How to do it...

In order to show you how to troubleshoot services, we will introduce a random error in the Apache service's configuration file and then show you how to troubleshoot and fix it:

1. Log in as root and type the following command to append content to the `httpd.conf`:

   ```
   echo "THIS_IS_AN_ERRORLINE" >> /etc/httpd/conf/httpd.conf
   ```

2. Next, reload the `httpd` service and show its output:

   ```
   systemctl reload httpd.service
   systemctl status httpd.service -l
   ```

3. Let's revert this error line:

   ```
   sed -i 's/THIS_IS_AN_ERRORLINE//g' /etc/httpd/conf/httpd.conf
   ```

4. Now, restart the service again:

   ```
   systemctl reload httpd.service
   systemctl status httpd.service
   ```

How it works...

In this fairly short recipe, we showed you how an example service will behave if it contains errors, and what you can do to fix it to get you started. There are a lot of different scenarios where something can go wrong when services malfunction, and it can be a big part of a system administrator's job to solve those kinds of problem.

So, what have we learned from this experience?

We started this recipe by introducing a line of text in the main Apache configuration file, which does not contain any valid configuration syntax, and therefore the `httpd` service cannot interpret it. Then, we used the `systemctl reload` parameter to reload our server's configuration file. As said before, not all services have the reload option, so if your service of interest does not support this, use the `restart` parameter instead. Since Apache will try to reload the configuration file with our current changes, it will refuse to accept the new configuration because of the wrong syntax that we introduced. Since we are just reloading the configuration, the running Apache process will not be affected by this problem and will stay online using its original configuration. The `systemctl` parameter will print out the following error message, giving us a hint of what to do next:

Job for httpd.service failed. Take a look at systemctl status httpd. service and journalctl -xe for details.

As suggested by the error output, the `systemctl` status parameter is a very powerful tool to see what's going on behind the scenes with this service, and to try and find out the reason for any failure (here you can also see that Apache is still running). If you start the `systemctl status` with the `-l` flag, it prints out an even longer version of the output, which can help you even more.

The output of this command shows us the exact reason for failing the configuration reload, so we can easily trace down the cause of the problem (the output has been truncated):

AH00526: Syntax error on line 354 of /etc/httpd/conf/httpd.conf:

Invalid command ERRORLINE, perhaps misspelled or defined by a module, is not included in the server configuration.

This output is part of the complete `journald` log information. If you want to read more about it, please refer to the *Tracking system resources with journald* recipe in this chapter. So, with this very useful information from the output, we can easily spot the problem and redo the introduction of `ERRORLINE` using the `sed` command and reload the service again; this time everything will work fine.

So, in summary, we can say that the `systemctl status` command is a very comfortable command that can be tremendously helpful in finding out problems with your service. Most services are very sensitive to syntax errors, and sometimes it can be just a misplaced space character that caused the service to refuse to work. Therefore, system administrators must work precisely all the time.

Tracking system resources with journald

Log files contain system messages and output from services, the kernel, and all kinds of running applications. They can be very useful in many situations, for instance, to troubleshoot system problems and monitor services or other system resources, or doing security forensics after a breach of security. In this recipe, you will learn the basics of how to work with logging services using journald.

Getting ready

To complete this recipe, you will need a working installation of the CentOS 7 operating system with root privileges and a console-based text editor of your choice. Also, setting the time and date correctly is very crucial for the whole logging concept, so please apply the *Synchronizing the system clock with NTP and the chrony suite* recipe from *Chapter 2, Configuring the System* before using this recipe. Also, a basic knowledge of systemd and units can be advantageous. This is covered in the *Knowing and managing background services* recipe in this chapter. Journalctl uses *less* navigation to show output; please read the *Navigating text files with less* recipe from *Chapter 2, Configuring the System* if you don't know how to work with it.

How to do it...

On CentOS 7, we have a choice between two logging mechanisms called `rsyslog` and the `journald` log system, which is a component of the new `systemd` system manager, for viewing and managing logging information. Here, we will show you how to work with the `journalctl` command, which is the controlling client for the `journald` daemon:

1. To begin, log in as root and type the following command to view the whole journal log:

    `journalctl`

2. Next, we want to show only the messages within a specific time frame (change the date accordingly):

    `journalctl --since "2015-07-20 6:00:00" --until "2015-07-20 7:30:00"`

3. Afterwards, we want to filter the log system by all messages from the sshd service:

    `journalctl -u sshd.service --since "yesterday"`

4. Now, we want to show only messages with type error:

    `journalctl -p err -b`

5. To get the most verbose version of `journalctl`, use the `verbose` option:

    `journalctl -p err -b -o verbose`

6. To get a *current* view on the log output, use the following command (this is not *less* navigation—use the key combination *Ctrl+C* to exit this view):

```
journalctl -f
```

How it works...

In CentOS 7, we can use the new `journald` logging system, which is a part of the `systemd` system management. It is a centralized tool that will log just about everything on your system including all output from the early boot over kernel to services and all program messages. The main advantage over other logging mechanisms is that you don't have to configure logging for each of your services or other resources, because everything is already set up for all applications that are controlled and running through the centralized `systemd` system.

So, what have we learned from this experience?

We began our journey by running the `journalctl` command, which when applied without any parameters show us the complete journal log, which includes everything from starting your system and capturing the first boot log entries to the latest system messages in the order they appeared, appending new messages to the bottom (chronological order). If your system has been running for a while, it can contain hundreds of thousands of lines of logging data, and is very impractical to work with in this raw form.

This output is constantly captured by the `journald` daemon, but is not written to text files as other logging systems such as `rsyslog` do it. Instead, it uses a structured and indexed binary file, which stores a lot of additional meta information such as user Id, timestamp, and so on, and which makes it easy to transform into all kinds of different output formats. This can be very convenient if you want to further process journal information by another tool. As you cannot read binary files, you will need the client `journalctl` for it, which is used to query the `journald` database. Since it is almost impossible to parse through this sheer amount of data manually, we then take advantage of journalctl's rich filtering options. First, we used the `--since` and `--until` parameters to extract all log messages within a specific time frame. The syntax for specifying the time and date here is very flexible and understands phrases such as `yesterday` or `now`, but we stick with the simple date syntax, `YYYY-MM-DD HH:MM:SS`. Next, we used journalctl's `-u` parameter to filter log messages for a specific unit type. We used it to filter messages coming from the sshd daemon service. We added another filter using the `--since` parameter, which tightens the result of the `-u` unit filter even more, outputting only sshd service results that occurred yesterday. The next filter we applied was using the parameter string, `-p err -b`, which filters the log database by priority or log level. Every log message can have an associated priority that determines the importance of the message. To find out more about different log levels, refer to the manual using the command line `man 3 syslog` (if this manual is not available, install it by typing `yum install man-pages`). Our command will print out all log messages labeled as `error` or above, which includes: `error`, `critical`, `alert`, or `emergency`.

Next, we used the same command parameters but added `-o verbose`, which gives the most verbose output of logging information. Lastly we presented the `-f` parameter (for follow), which will give us a *live* view of the latest log messages and leaves this connection open, appending any new messages to the end of the output when they occur. This is often useful to see how the system reacts if you are currently testing out settings or starting/stopping services.

Summing up, one can say that, on CentOS 7, two logging systems do coexist: the older `rsyslog` and the newer `journald`, with the latter being your primary tool of choice for troubleshooting your system. But remember that on CentOS 7, `journald` is not a full replacement for `rsyslog` though. There are some `rsyslog` features that are missing in `journald`, and also there are lots of tools and scripts, such as log digesting tools or monitoring suites such as Nagios, that work exclusively with `rsyslog`.

System administrators often face a big challenge troubleshooting system errors or unexpected server behaviors. Often, it's not easy to find the single point of failure by searching through massive amounts of different log file texts while applying regular expression searches or Linux command line kung fu. Journald provides a very convenient alternative by providing a powerful and well-defined centralized querying system to get the log file analysis done quickly and efficiently!

Configuring journald to make it persistent

Journald's advantages over other logging systems such as `rsyslog` is that it is very efficient and logs just about everything on your system automatically without the need to configure anything, because it is a part of the `systemd` suite. The main disadvantage is that all `journald` log information will get lost after a system's restart. Journald logging can produce huge amounts of data and by default all logging information is only kept in memory, which is not very practicable if you need to access older log information or analyze causes of system crash reboots. Here, in this recipe, we show you how to configure `journald` to make it persistent.

Getting ready

To complete this recipe, you will require a minimal installation of the CentOS 7 operating system with root privileges and a console-based text editor of your choice.

How to do it...

To begin this recipe, we need to create a location that will hold our persistent journal database:

1. Log in as the root user and create the following directory:

    ```
    mkdir /var/log/journal
    ```

2. Next, add the new directory to `journald` to use it as a storage location and fix permissions:

```
systemd-tmpfiles --create --prefix /var/log/journal
```

3. Now, restart `journald`:

```
systemctl restart systemd-journald
```

4. Finally, to check whether the log survived the reboot, restart the computer and type the following:

```
journalctl --boot=-1
```

How it works...

We started this recipe by creating the new directory, `/var/log/journal`. By default, `journald` writes its log database to `/run/log/journal`, which is a directory only for runtime information, and its content does not survive system reboots. Afterwards, we used the `systemd-tmpfiles` command to set up our new directory for `journald`. Finally, we restarted the `journald` server daemon to apply our changes to the system. To test if persistence is working, restart your server and afterwards use `journalctl -boot=-1`. This will show us all journal information from the last boot. If persistence is not working, it will print out the following error; otherwise it will correctly show all journal messages before the last boot:

```
Failed to look up boot -1: Cannot assign requested address
```

In this fairly simple recipe, we have shown how to make `journald` persistent over system reboots. This is really useful if you need to review older log files from the past, which can sometimes help you find out problems, for example, the roots of past hardware failures.

Managing users and their groups

In this recipe, we will learn how to manage your system's users and groups on CentOS 7. Essential user and group managing skills are one of the most important CentOS system administrator fundamentals.

Getting ready

To complete this recipe, you will need a working installation of the CentOS 7 operating system with root privileges and a console-based text editor of your choice.

How to do it...

This recipe shows you how to manage users and groups by learning how to add, delete, and modify them:

1. To begin this recipe, we log in as root and type the following command to get a list of all the users known to the system: `cat /etc/passwd`.

2. Now, show the root user ID (**UID**) and group ID (**GID**):

   `id root`

3. Next, we will run the following command to add a new user to the system (exchange `your_new_username` with a username of your choice):

   `useradd your_new_username`

4. However, in order to complete this process, you will be expected to provide a suitable password. To do this, type the following command (change `your_new_username` with a username of choice) than enter a secure password when prompted:

   `passwd your_new_username`

   Passwords should not be less than six characters, but should not be longer than sixteen characters. They should consist of alphanumeric values, and for obvious reasons you must avoid the use of whitespaces. Do not use a dictionary-based word and refrain from using a known or obvious phrase.

5. Next, create a new group and give it a special name:

   `groupadd your_new_group`

6. Then, we add our new user to this new group:

   `usermod -G your_new_group your_new_username`

7. Finally, let's print the user ID and group IDs of our new user to see what has changed:

   `id your_new_username`

How it works...

The purpose of this recipe was to create a new user and group and show how to connect them together.

So, what did we learn from this experience?

First, we printed out the content of file /etc/passwd to show all the current users in the system. This list not only contains normal user-accounts that belong to real persons, but also accounts that are used to control and own a specific application or service. Then, we used the id command to display the unique user UID and GID for our existing user root. In Linux, every user can be identified by their UID and GID, and every file in the filesystem has specific permission settings that manage its access for the file owner, group owner, and the rest of the users. For each of those three groups, you can enable or disable read, write, and execute permissions using the command, chmod (use man chmod to learn more, and also check out man chown). The owner and group permissions correspond to a UID and GID that we can display for every file using ls -l.

Next, we issued the useradd command that required us to supply a suitable name for the new user, which in turn will enable the server to establish the new identity with a default set of values and criteria that includes a user ID, home directory, primary group (GID), and also set the default shell to bash. Completing this process is simply a matter of confirming a suitable password. To remove a user, there is the opposite command, userdel, which works similarly but can be given the option -f to remove the home directory instead of leave it on the system. Next, we used the groupadd command, which, as the name implies, will create a new group and associate a new unique GID to it. Afterwards, we made our user in question a member of the new group that we created before using the usermod -G command. As said before, each user has exactly one unique UID and GID. The first group is the primary group and is mandatory; however a user can belong to a number of different groups, which are then called secondary groups. The primary group is needed when creating a new file because it will set the GID and UID of the user creating it. To delete a group, we can use the groupdel command. Finally, we used the id command again on our new user to show its UID, primary GID, and the new secondary GID groups we added to it.

You are now able to fully control your user and groups with just a few commands: useradd, usermod, userdel, groupadd, groupmod, and groupdel.

Scheduling tasks with cron

In this recipe, we will investigate the role of server automation and the convenience of running specific tasks at predefined periods by introducing you to the time-based job scheduler known as cron. Cron allows for the automation of tasks by enabling the administrator to determine a predefined schedule based on any hour, any day, or any month. It is a standard component of the CentOS operating system, and it is the purpose of this recipe to introduce you to the concept of managing recurring tasks in order to take advantage of this invaluable tool and to make CentOS work for you.

Getting ready

To complete this recipe, you will require a minimal installation of the CentOS 7 operating system with root privileges, and a console-based text editor of your choice. The `crontab` program uses Vim for file editing. If you do not know how to work with Vim, go through the tutorial shown in the recipe *Introduction to Vim* in *Chapter 2, Configuring the System.*

How to do it...

The purpose of this recipe is to create a script that will write the time and date with a few words of your choice to a text file every five minutes. This may seem to be a relatively simple exercise, but the intention is to show you that, from such simplicity, cron can be used to do so much more that will make working with CentOS an absolute pleasure.

1. To begin this recipe, log in as root and create your first cron job by typing:

   ```
   crontab -e
   ```

2. We will now create a simple cron job that will write the date and time with the words `hello world` to a file located at `/root/cron-helloworld.txt` every five minutes. To do this, add the following line:

   ```
   */5 * * * * echo `date` "Hello world" >>$HOME/cron-
   helloworld.txt
   ```

3. When complete, simply save the file and exit the editor. The system will now respond with the following message:

   ```
   crontab: installing new crontab
   ```

4. The preceding message informs you that the server is now creating the new cron job and will automatically activate it. You can view the output of the script by reviewing the file found at `/root/cron-helloworld.txt` (you have to wait 5 minutes), or by monitoring the logfile found at `/var/log/cron` (use `tail -f /var/log/cron` and `Ctrl+C` to exit).

How it works...

Cron is the name of a program that enables CentOS users to execute commands or scripts automatically at a specified time and date. Cron's settings are kept in a user-specific file called `crontab`, and as we have seen in this recipe this file can be edited to create automated tasks as often as they are required.

So what did we learn from this experience?

The example used was very simple, but in many ways this was the purpose of this recipe. Crontab uses a daemon, `crond`, which runs constantly in the background and checks once a minute to see if any of the scheduled jobs need to be executed. If a task is found, then cron will execute it. To edit an existing `crontab` file or to create a new `crontab`, we use the `crontab -e` command. To view a list of current cron jobs, you can type `crontab -l`. Alternatively, to view a list of the current jobs for another user, you can type `crontab -u username -l`. Tasks or jobs are generally referred to as cron jobs, and by avoiding complication in our first script, it was the intention to show you that the nature of command construction was very simple. The formation of a cron job looks like this:

```
<minute> <hour> <day of the month> <month of the year> <day of the week>
<command>
```

Entries are separated by a single or tabbed space, and the allowed values are primarily numeric (that is, `0-59` for a minute, `0-23` for an hour, `1-31` for a day of the month, `1-12` for month of the year, and `0-7` for day of the week). However, in saying this, it is also true to say that there are more specific operators (/ , -) and cron-specific shortcuts (that is, `@yearly`, `@daily`, `@hourly`, and `@weekly`) that do allow for additional controls. For example, where the / operator is used to step through specified units, it can be read as *every*, so in our recipe the use of `*/5` will run the task every five minutes while the use of `*/1` runs the task every minute. As an addition to this, you should be aware that the use of this syntax will align all commands on the hour. So, with this in mind, the most suitable template or starting point for anyone wanting to write their first `cron` job is to start with a series of five asterisks followed by the command, like this:

```
* * * * * /absolute/path/to/script.sh
```

Then, proceed to configure the minute, hour, day, month, and day-of-the-week values as desired. For example, if you want a particular PHP script to run at 8 P.M. (20:00 hrs) on every weekday (Monday-Friday), it may look like this:

```
0 20 * * 1-5 /full/path/to/your/php/script.php
```

So, with this in mind, and by completing this recipe, you can see how cron can be used to manage a database backup, run a scheduled system backup, provide support to websites by activating scripts at predefined intervals, or run various bash scripts and a whole lot more.

There's more...

To delete or disable a cron job, it is simply a matter of either removing the instruction from an individual user's cron file or by placing a hash (#) at the beginning of the line. Individual cron files can be found at `/var/spool/cron/<username>`, and the use of the hash will either disable the cron job or allow you to write comments. To completely remove a `crontab` file, you can also use `crontab -r`. For example, if you want to remove the cron job created in the main recipe, you can log in as root and begin by typing the command, `crontab -e`. At this point, you may either remove the entire line or comment it out, as shown here:

```
# */15 * * * * echo `date` "Hello world" >>$HOME/cron-helloworld.txt
```

Next, save the file. There are also some special cron directories in the filesystem for system-wide cron jobs that will, if you drop a script file in it, run it automatically at a certain time point. The folders are called `cron.daily`, `cron.hourly`, `cron.weekly`, and `cron.monthly` in the `/etc` directory, and their names refer to the time point that they are run. Just remove the script from the folder if you don't want to execute it anymore. Take a look at the *Monitoring important server infrastructure* recipe for an example.

Synchronizing files and doing more with rsync

`rsync` is a program that can be used to synchronize files and directories across a variety of local and remote locations. It can interact with multiple operating systems, work over SSH, provide incremental backups, execute commands on a remote machine, and replace the need for the `cp` and `scp` commands. The `rsync` program is an invaluable asset for any system administrator who intends to run a server or manage a network of computers, as it not only simplifies the process of making backups in general, but it can be used to action a complete backup solution. For this reason, it is the purpose of this recipe to offer a suitable starting point for a small utility that will quickly become your trusted friend.

Getting ready

To complete this recipe, you will require a working installation of the CentOS 7 operating system with root privileges, a console-based text editor of your choice, and a connection to the Internet in order to facilitate the download of additional packages.

How to do it...

During the course of this recipe, it will be assumed that you know the location of the source files and directories that you wish to synchronize, and that a suitable destination is available:

1. To begin this recipe, log in as root and install `rsync` by typing:

   yum install rsync

2. Now, create a target directory for our synchronization (change the folder name appropriately):

   mkdir ~/sync-target

3. To begin the synchronization process, simply repeat the following command by modifying the value used for `/path/to/source/files/` with something more applicable to your needs:

   rsync -avz --delete /path/to/source/files/   ~/sync-target

4. Having used the *Return* key to confirm the preceding instruction, your system will now respond with a live report of what is being copied. When this process has finished, you can then compare both directories to see that the contents are exactly the same. To do this, use the `diff` command (if both are the same, no output will be written):

   diff -r /path/to/source/files/ ~/sync-target

How it works...

In this recipe, we considered the use of `rsync` through the command line. Of course, this is only one of the many ways that this tool can be used, but by using this approach we were able to explore a handful of the features provided by this very valuable utility.

So, what did we learn from this experience?

Rsync is not intended to be complicated. It is a fast and efficient file synchronization tool that is designed to be versatile by giving you complete access to an array of features on the command line. It can be used to maintain an exact copy (or mirror) of the `source` directory on the same machine or on a completely different system, and it does this by copying all the files once and then only updating the files that have changed the next time you run it. This can save tremendous bandwidth and should be your primary tool when copying data over the network. The use of the phrase, `--delete`, is important, as it instructs `rsync` to delete files on the target that do not exist in the source, while the chosen flags imply that `rsync` should use `-a` archive mode in order to recursively copy files and directories while keeping all permissions and time-based information; `-v)`verbosity mode so you can see what is happening; and `-z` to compress the data during the file transfer in order to save bandwidth and reduce the amount of time required to complete the entire process.

As you can see, `rsync` is very flexible and has many options that go beyond the purpose of this recipe, but if you want to exclude certain files you could always extend the original instruction by invoking the `--exclude` flag. By doing this, you tell `rsync` to back up an entire directory but ensure that it does not include a predefined pattern of files and folders. For example, if you are copying files from your server to a USB device and you do not want to include large files (such as an `.iso` image) or ZIP files, then your command may look similar to this:

```
rsync --delete -avz --exclude="*.zip" --exclude="*.iso"  /path/to/source/
/path/to/external/disk/
```

On a final note, there is the subject of verbosity. Verbosity is very useful, but a tendency to use bytes as its primary unit of measurement can be a source of confusion. So, in order to change this, you can invoke `rsync` with the –h (or human readable) option, as shown next:

```
rsync -avzh --exclude="home/path/to/file.txt" /home/ /path/to/external/
disk/
```

Maintaining backups and taking snapshots

In this recipe, we will show you how to do data backups, on a regular basis, that will take snapshots of some of your system's directory using the `crond` daemon. This will run the `rsync` program at regular intervals to implement a fully automated backup solution.

Getting ready

To complete this recipe, you will require a working installation of the CentOS 7 operating system with root privileges and a console-based text editor of your choice. It is also advantageous if you have read the *Synchronizing files and doing more with rsync* and *Scheduling tasks with cron* recipes in this chapter to get a deeper understanding of used commands.

How to do it...

It's important to install the `rsync` program on your server before proceeding with this recipe.

1. First, log in as root and create a directory where our backups will land:

   ```
   mkdir /backups
   ```

2. Now, we will create the following shell script file and open it for editing:

   ```
   mkdir ~/bin;vi ~/bin/mybackup.sh
   ```

3. Put in the following content, replacing /backups in the environment variable DEST and SOURCE with the one you would like to backup as well as the recipient's EMAIL:

```
#!/bin/bash
SBJT="cron backup report for `hostname -s` from $(date
+%Y%m%d:%T)"
FROM=root@domain
EMAIL=johndoe@internet.com
SOURCE=/root
DEST=/backups
LFPATH=/tmp
LF=$LFPATH/$(date +%Y%m%d_%T)_logfile.log
rsync --delete --log-file=$LF -avzq $SOURCE $DEST
(echo "$SBJT"; echo; cat $LF ) | sendmail -f $FROM -t $EMAIL
```

4. Make the script executable:

```
chmod a+x /root/bin/mybackup.sh
```

5. Now, open crontab using:

```
crontab -e
```

6. Next, create the following entry by adding the following line to the end of the document, then save and close it:

```
30 20 * * * /root/bin/mybackup.sh
```

How it works...

In this recipe, we have created a full automatic backup solution for a single system directory, which will create a snapshot of the files at a certain time point. At the time the backup process is complete you will receive an e-mail informing you that a backup has been made with a brief review of the actions taken.

So what did we learn from this experience?

We started this recipe by creating a directory where our backup will be placed. Next we created the actual script and filled it with some commands. Line 1 defines the file as a bash script, lines 2-6 are variables you can modify and customize to fit your own needs. lines 7-8 create a path and name for the log file based on the date, and line 9 calls rsync which will synchronize all our source files to the target directory /backups. It uses a special --log-file parameter which writes all output to the given file. The final line (10) sends the content of this log file to an email address.

Remember, you should customize the values as required (that is, change the e-mail address used, select a source directory, and choose a destination directory, and so on.). Before it can be used and executed by `cron`, we made it executable. Finally, we added this script as a cron job to run on a daily schedule at 20:30 hours. However, as this may be some hours away, if you would like to test your script right now, you can execute it on the command line using the following:

`/root/bin/mybackup.sh`

In conclusion, it will go without saying that a backup should be located on an external drive or on a separate partition, but having completed this introduction I think you will agree that `rsync` is ideally positioned in such a way that it will enable any server administrator to develop their own policy with regard to maintaining an effective backup of important data.

Monitoring important server infrastructure

In this recipe, we will use a small script that will monitor the available filesystem's disk space periodically using cron, and if it exceeds a certain percentage threshold the script will send out a mail with a warning message.

Getting ready

To complete this recipe, you will require a working installation of the CentOS 7 operating system with root privileges and a console-based text editor of your choice. You should have read the *Scheduling tasks with cron* recipe to have a basic understanding of the principles behind the cron system.

How to do it...

1. To begin this recipe, log in as root and create the following file that will contain our monitoring script:

    `vi /etc/cron.daily/monitor_disk_space.sh`

2. Now, put in the following content:

    ```
    #!/bin/bash
    EMAIL="root@localhost"
    THRESHOLD=70
    df -H | grep -vE '^Filesystem|tmpfs|cdrom' | awk '{ print $5 " "
    $6 }' | while read output;
    do
      usep=$(echo $output | awk '{ print $1}' | cut -d'%' -f1  )
      partition=$(echo $output | awk '{ print $2 }' )
    ```

```
    if [ $usep -ge $THRESHOLD ]; then

    (echo "Subject: Alert: Free space low on `hostname -s`, $usep %
used on $partition"; echo) |

    sendmail -t $EMAIL

    fi

done
```

3. Now, save the file and make it executable:

    ```
    chmod +x /etc/cron.daily/monitor_disk_space.sh
    ```

How it works...

We made this script executable and put it in the /etc/cron.daily directory, which is all we need to do to run this script automatically every day via the crond service.

This simple script showed us how easy it is to build monitoring scripts, and this can be a real alternative to installing and configuring big monitoring suites such as Nagios. You can use the shown script as a starting point to expand on, adding further resources that are important to monitor, such as CPU load, available RAM, and so on.

We used a script that executes the Linux command df, which is a tool to report file system disk space usage. From this command's output, the script then parsed the USE% column (with the Unix tools awk and cut), which gives us the total disk percentage used. This number will then be compared to a threshold the user can set by editing the script and changing the environment variable, THRESHOLD. If the extracted percentage number is higher than our threshold, there will be an email sent to the email address defined with the environment variable, EMAIL (change appropriately if needed).

Taking control with GIT and Subversion

Document revision control systems or version control systems, as they are sometimes called, are used for the management of changes to documents. These systems get more and more important these days as modern work often connects people from around the globe to collaborate and work together on all kinds of documents (for example, software source code) making it important to manage the file changes by different people using revisions. In this recipe, we will show you how to use modern version control systems such as GIT and Subversion to manage the versioning of config files.

Getting ready

To complete this recipe, you will require a working installation of the CentOS 7 operating system with root privileges, and a connection to the Internet in order to facilitate the download of additional packages.

How to do it...

Here in this recipe, we will put the complete main Linux configuration directory, /etc/, under version control of a Git repository to keep track of all our changes to configuration files:

1. To begin, log in as root, install Git, and configure it by providing an email address and username (please substitute your_username and your_email_address with real names):

```
yum install git
git config --global user.email  "your_email_address"
git config --global user.name "your_username"
```

2. Now, let's create a new repository in the /etc directory:

```
cd /etc/
git init
```

3. Now, after we have our new repository, let's add all the files in the /etc/ directory under version control:

```
git add *
```

4. To commit the files to the repository creating your first revision, type the following:

```
git commit -a -m "inital commit of the full /etc/ directory"
```

5. Now, let's change a file:

```
echo "FILE HAS CHANGED" >> yum.conf
```

6. Next, show the changes to your repository:

```
git status
```

7. Next, we will commit these changes and create a new revision of it:

```
git commit -a -m "changing yum.conf files"
```

8. Next, show all the commits so far:

```
git log --pretty=oneline --abbrev-commit
```

9. This will output the following commits on my system (the number hashes will be different on yours):

```
8069c4a changing yum.conf
5f0d50a inital commit of the full /etc directory
```

10. Based on the output from the earlier step, we will now show all the differences between the two revision numbers (change the number hashes on your system based on the output from the earlier step):

```
git diff 8069c4a 5f0d50a
```

11. To complete this recipe, we will revert our changes to the original file revision (the initial commit):

```
git checkout 5f0d50a
```

How it works

Here, in this recipe, we showed you how to use Git to manage changes to system config files in the /etc directory. This can be important, for example, if you are testing things out, so a lot of changes will be made to some configuration files and you will want to keep track of your changes, which is nice because you don't need to memorize every single step you have taken if you later have to revert the changes or go back to a specific revision, or compare different file versions.

So, what did we learn from this experience?

We started by installing Git and added a username and an e-mail address to its configuration, which is essential for using it later in the process. Then, we changed to the /etc directory and initialized (using the init parameter) a new empty Git project there, which is called repository and keeps track of all the files associated to it. This command will add a hidden .git directory to it, which will contain the complete file changes and revision information. Next, we added all the files (using the wildcard * operator) from this directory, including all sub-directories to the next revision. A revision is like a state the files are in at a given time point, and is identified by a unique hash ID such as 8069c4a. Then, we actually created a new revision using the commit parameter and supplied a meaningful message using the -m parameter. After we set up the Git repository and added all the files to it, every change to the files gets watched in the /etc directory. Next, we changed the main YUM configuration file in our repository by adding a random string to the end of it using the echo >> command. If we now use git's status parameter again, we see in the output that the Git system has notified that this file has been changed. We can now create a new revision with the changed file by using git's commit parameter again, using another meaningful message here stating that yum.conf has been changed. We then used the git log command. This will show us all the committed revisions with their unique md5 hash string IDs. With this ID, we can fuel the git diff command to see all the file changes between two revisions. To learn more about the output format, use man git-diff-files and read its section COMBINED DIFF FORMAT. In our last step, we used the checkout command to go to a specific file revision; here we reverted all our changes and went back to the original file state.

Git is a very powerful version management tool, and in this recipe we just scratched the surface of what can be done with it. To learn more about Git's wonderful techniques, such as branching, merging, pull requests, and so on, start with the Git tutorial pages by typing in man gittutorial.

There's more...

You can also use the program Subversion to bring your /etc directory under version control. Subversion is another common document revision control system whose main difference from Git is that it uses a centralized server to keep track of the file changes. Git is distributed, meaning that everybody working on a Git project will have the complete repository locally on their computer. Here, we will show you the exact steps necessary to use Subversion instead of Git for this purpose:

1. First, install Subversion and configure a new server directory for our /etc repository:

   ```
   yum install subversion
   mkdir -p /var/local/svn/etc-repos
   svnadmin create --fs-type fsfs /var/local/svn/etc-repos
   ```

2. Now, make an in-place import of the /etc filesystem to our new repository:

   ```
   svn mkdir file:///var/local/svn/etc-repos/etc
   -m "Make a directory in the repository to correspond to /etc"
   ```

3. Now, switch to the /etc directory and add all the files to a new revision:

   ```
   cd /etc
   svn checkout  file:///var/local/svn/etc-repos/etc ./
   svn add *
   ```

4. Now, create your first commit:

   ```
   svn commit -m "inital commit of the full /etc/ directory"
   ```

5. Next, change the yum.conf file:

   ```
   echo "FILE HAS CHANGED" >> yum.conf
   ```

6. Commit your changes to a new file revision:

   ```
   svn commit -m "changing yum.conf files"
   ```

7. Now, show the change log:

   ```
   svn log -r 1:HEAD
   ```

8. Show the file differences between our two commits (the first commit was the /etc import):

   svn diff -r 2:3

9. Finally, revert to the first revision of our yum.conf file:

   svn update -r 2 yum.conf

4
Managing Packages with YUM

In this chapter, we will cover the following topics:

- ▶ Using YUM to update the system
- ▶ Using YUM to search for packages
- ▶ Using YUM to install packages
- ▶ Using YUM to remove packages
- ▶ Keeping YUM clean and tidy
- ▶ Knowing your priorities
- ▶ Using a third-party repository
- ▶ Creating a YUM repository
- ▶ Working with the RPM package manager

Introduction

This chapter is a collection of recipes that provides a review of the tools required to grow your server. Package management is at the heart of any Linux-based system and the purpose of this chapter highlights the critical tools needed to manage software packages on a CentOS based server.

Using YUM to update the system

In this recipe, we will investigate the role of the **Yellowdog Updater, Modified** (**YUM**) package manager with regard to running a system update. Every once in a while, you may become aware of an update or may simply wish to discover if one exists. Applying patches and updates is a regular task for every server administrator, and an up-to-date system can help increase or ensure the security of your server as software bugs and vulnerabilities are found all the time and must be fixed promptly. In this recipe, you will learn how to achieve this with the help of YUM.

Getting ready

To complete this recipe, you will require a working installation of the CentOS 7 operating system with root privileges, a console-based text editor of your choice, and a connection to the Internet in order to facilitate the download of additional packages.

How to do it...

You can run this recipe, as often as required but it should be done frequently, based on a schedule of your own choosing in the full knowledge that on occasion, some updates may require a full system reboot:

1. Log in as root and check whether there are any updates for your installed packages. To do this, log in and type the following:

   ```
   yum check-update
   ```

2. If no updates are available, then the update process will end and no further work will need to be done. However, if updates are available, YUM will now return a list of all package updates from the repositories known to your system. To complete the update process, type the following command:

   ```
   yum -y update
   ```

3. By using the -y flag, the preceding command will now bypass the need to confirm the transaction summary, and your system will now undergo an immediate update process. When complete, you will be provided with a final report that identifies what dependencies have been installed and what packages have been updated.

4. Generally speaking, no further work is required and you may resume typical operations. However, if a new kernel has been installed, or an important security update has taken place, it may be necessary to reboot the system for the new changes to take effect. To do this, type the following:

   ```
   reboot
   ```

 While there is much debate as to whether an update will require a full system restart in practice, this is only to be considered after a kernel update, which is an update to glibc and particular security-based features that are activated during the boot process.

How it works...

YUM is the default package management system for CentOS and part of its role is to automatically calculate what packages may require updating, what dependencies are required, and to manage the entire process of updating your system in a very simple way.

So, what have we learned from this experience?

We started the recipe by checking to see if any updates were available to our system using the `yum` command with the `check-update` option. In this way, YUM will now check a central repository to confirm if an update is applicable to our system. A repository is a remote directory or website that contains prepared software packages and utilities. YUM will use this facility to automatically locate and obtain the correct **Red Hat Package Manager** (**RPM**) and dependencies, and if an update is available, then YUM will respond accordingly with a full summary of what packages and dependencies are available. For this reason, YUM is a very useful tool, and without doubt its mechanism does serve to simplify the processes associated with package management, because it can talk to repositories and this saves us from having to find and install new applications or updates manually. If there are updates available, the output will show us exactly which packages are affected, then we can proceed to update the system by using YUM's `update` parameter. In this instance, the preceding command includes the `-y` flag. This is done in order to circumvent the need to agree with the transaction summary given, and to confirm that we have already agreed to make these updates after running the previous check. Otherwise, you would simply confirm the requests by using the *Y* key.

There's more...

You can also use the update parameter to update single packages instead of the whole system by providing the package name like so: `yum update package_name`. YUM will serve to ensure that all of the requirements for an application are met during installation, and it will automatically install the packages for any dependencies that are not already present on your system. However, and I am sure you will be pleased to hear this, if a new application has requirements that conflict with existing software, YUM will abort the process without making any changes to your system. If you want to automate the updating of your system using a specific time interval, you can install the `yum-cron` package, which can be highly customized but is outside the scope of this book. To start after installation, use `man yum-cron`.

Using YUM to search for packages

In this recipe, we will investigate the role of using YUM to find a package. YUM was developed to improve the installation of RPM software packages, and it is used to access a growing list of packages that provide a full range of services offered by your server. YUM is simple to use, but if you are not sure what a package is called, then your duties as the server administrator can become that much harder. To overcome this, YUM maintains an extensive range of discovery tools and it is the purpose of this recipe to show you how to use this functionality in order to search through the various repositories and find the package you need.

Getting ready

To complete this recipe, you will require a working installation of the CentOS 7 operating system with root privileges, a console-based text editor of your choice, and a connection to the Internet.

How to do it...

This recipe will show you how to find one or more packages by invoking YUM's searching options. To do this, you will need to log in as the root user and complete the following process:

1. To search for a single package, replace the `keyword` value with the appropriate phrase, string, or parameter, and type the following:

   yum search keyword

2. Wait for a summary of the search results, and when a list is generated, you can query any package shown by simply replacing `package_name` with the appropriate value:

   yum info package_name

3. If the preceding results prove satisfactory, and you want to view a list of dependencies associated with the package in question, type the following:

   yum deplist package_name

How it works...

Searching for packages with YUM can be achieved in the same way as you would search for anything on the **World Wide Web** (**WWW**). The types of words you can search for can be as specific or as general as you like. They can even consist of full or partial words; having found a package that you may be interested in, you will have noticed that this recipe has also served to show you how to discover additional information about the package in question.

So, what have we learned from this experience?

YUM maintains extensive search features and it allows you to query packages by keyword, package name, and pathname. For example, if you want to locate the correct package for compiling C, Objective-C, and C++ code, you can use the `yum search compiler` query. When using these search terms on the command line, there are a number of related results, and each package carries a brief description that enables us to use a simple process of elimination in order to select the most obvious or the most relevant value. With this in mind, you can then query YUM using the `info` parameter to find out more about certain packages. This option reveals the full package details together with a detailed description of what functionality the package is intended to provide. Generally speaking, you may not need to know any further details.

However, there may be circumstances in which you want to know how this package interacts with the server as a whole (especially if you are working with source installations or troubleshooting broken packages), so we can use YUM's `deplist` parameter that can give quite a detailed report; if you do happen to have any broken packages, you could simply use this output to detail what dependencies you may or may not need to install in order to fix an underlying issue. This command is particularly useful when debugging dependencies or when working with source-based installations.

There's more...

Sometimes, you may not want to search for a specific package, and instead you may prefer to display the contents of your repositories in a catalog-style format. Again, this is easy to do and YUM provides for this functionality with the following commands. If you would like to simply list all the packages available to you from the current repositories used by your system, type `yum list all`. However, because this list may be quite exhaustive, you may prefer to page through the results by using `yum list all | less`. In a similar fashion, if you would simply like to list all the software currently installed on your system, type `yum list installed | less`. If you would like to determine which packages provide for a specific file or feature, simply run the following command at any time by substituting `your_filename_here` with something more relevant to your own needs: `yum provides your_filename_here`.

Using YUM to install packages

In this recipe, we will investigate the role of YUM in installing new packages on your server. An important task for every server administrator is the installation of applications and services. There are several different ways to achieve this, but the most effective method involves the YUM package manager. YUM is able to search through any number of repositories, automatically resolve package dependencies, and specify the installation of one or more packages. YUM is a modern and definitive way to install your packages on your server, and it is the purpose of this recipe to show you how it is done.

Getting ready

To complete this recipe, you will require a working installation of the CentOS 7 operating system with root privileges, a console-based text editor of your choice, and a connection to the Internet in order to facilitate the download of additional packages. It's also good if you have already found some interesting packages to install, which can be learned by using the instructions from the *Using YUM to search for packages* recipe.

How to do it...

This recipe will show you how to install one or more packages by invoking the YUM installation option. To do this, you will need to log in as the root user and complete the following process:

1. To install a single package, replace the `package_name` value with the appropriate value and type the following:

    ```
    yum install package_name
    ```

2. Your system will now provide a transaction report that will require your approval. So, when prompted, simply respond by using the *Y* or *N* key and press the *Return* key to either accept or decline the transaction, as shown as follows:

    ```
    Is this ok [y/d/N]: y
    ```

3. If you have declined the transaction, then no further work is required and you will exit the package management routine. However, if you have confirmed the transaction, then watch the progress of your installation, and in the end it will show you a `Complete!` message.

4. Congratulations! You now have successfully installed your package of choice.

How it works...

All packages are stored in the RPM package file format, and it is the role of YUM to provide access to those files that are stored in various repositories on the Internet. YUM is the power behind the package management for CentOS and it really does make the installation process very easy, but what have we learned from this experience?

Having invoked the `install` command, YUM will conduct a search of the various repositories in order to find the relevant headers and metadata associated with the package in question. For example, if you wanted to install a package called `wget`, you would begin by issuing the `install` command like so: `yum install wget`. YUM will then locate the package and generate a transaction summary that will not only indicate the required disk size and expected installation size, but will also indicate any necessary dependencies required by the requested package. YUM will then check several different repositories (`base`, `extras`, and `updates`) and, having resolved the need for any necessary dependencies, YUM will be asking us to confirm the request before continuing with the installation process. So, as you can see, by using the *Y* key, we will be providing YUM with the permission to fulfill the request, which in turn will result in the download, verification, and installation of the package(s) concerned.

There's more...

There are times when you may wish to install more than one package at a time. To do this, simply invoke the same `install` command, but instead of naming a single package, simply identify the full list of packages you may require in such a way that it forms a long shopping list:

```
yum install package_name1 package_name2 package_name3
```

The number of packages you can install in this way is unlimited, but always leave a single space between each package name and keep the command on a single line. For very long installation instructions, line-wrapping may occur.

You do not need to list the packages in any particular order and the request will be processed in exactly the same way as it was in the original recipe, and again after listing the transaction summary, it will remain pending until it is confirmed or declined. Again, use the Y key to confirm your request so that the process completes.

Using YUM to remove packages

In this recipe, we will investigate the role of using YUM with the intention of removing packages from your server. During the lifetime of your server, it is possible that certain applications and services may no longer be required. In such situations, it is typical that you will want to remove such packages in order to optimize your working environment, and it is the purpose of this recipe to show you how this is done.

Getting ready

To complete this recipe, you will require a working installation of the CentOS 7 operating system with root privileges, a console-based text editor of your choice, and a connection to the Internet.

How to do it...

This recipe will show you how to remove one or more packages by invoking the `yum remove` option. To do this, you will need to log in as the root user and complete the following process:

1. To remove a single package, replace the `package_name` value with the appropriate value and type the following:

   ```
   yum remove package_name
   ```

2. Wait for the transaction summary and confirmation prompt to be displayed, and then press either the *Y* key to confirm, or the *N* key to decline the transaction, as shown next:

    ```
    Is this ok [y/d/N]: y
    ```

3. If you have declined the transaction, then no further work is required and you will exit YUM. However, if you have confirmed the transaction, then simply watch the progress of package removal until it is confirmed and prints out a `Complete!` message.

How it works...

Applications that are no longer required can be removed with YUM. The process is very intuitive and similar to installing a new package, and it only requires you to confirm the name of the packages you want to remove.

So, what have we learned from this experience?

Having invoked the `remove` command, YUM will search your system to discover the relevant package; and by reading the package headers and metadata, it will also determine what dependencies this will affect. For example, if we wanted to remove a package called `wget`, we would begin by issuing the `remove` command like so: `yum remove wget`. YUM, in turn, would then locate the package details from your system and obtain a transaction summary that may include any necessary dependencies that are no longer required. The transaction printed out will remain pending until you instruct YUM to remove the package(s) concerned. When confirmed, YUM will complete the transaction, which in return will result in the removal of the package or packages. You should take extra care if the summary makes reference to any dependencies as these may be required by other RPMs. If you are concerned that certain dependencies should remain on the system, it is often a good idea to end the current transaction and simply de-activate or disable the software concerned. As with the `install` command, you can also remove multiple packages at a time, leaving a single space between the package names:

```
yum remove package_name1 package_name2 package_name3
```

Keeping YUM clean and tidy

In this recipe, we will investigate the role of YUM with regard to ensuring that the working cache remains current. As a part of its typical mode of operation, YUM will create a cache that consists of metadata and packages. These files are very useful, but over time, they will accumulate in size to such an extent that you may find that YUM is acting erratically or not as intended. The frequency of this happening can vary from system to system, but it generally implies that the YUM cache system requires your immediate attention. Such a situation can be quite frustrating, but it is the purpose of this recipe to provide a quick solution that will serve to assist you in cleaning the cache and restoring YUM to its original working state.

Getting ready

To complete this recipe, you will require a working installation of the CentOS 7 operating system with root privileges, a console-based text editor of your choice, and a connection to the Internet in order to facilitate the download of additional packages.

How to do it...

Before we begin, it is important to realize that, while we are troubleshooting a current problem, this same recipe can be run as often as required in order to keep YUM in an optimal working state:

1. We will begin this recipe by asking YUM to clean any cached package information. To do this, log in as root and type the following:

    ```
    yum clean packages
    ```

2. Allow time for your system to respond and when finished, type the following command to remove any cached XML-based metadata:

    ```
    yum clean metadata
    ```

3. Again, wait for YUM to respond and when ready, type the following command to remove any cached database files:

    ```
    yum clean dbcache
    ```

4. Following this, you will want to clean all the files to confirm the preceding instructions and to ensure that unnecessary disk space is not used. To do this, type the following line:

    ```
    yum clean all
    ```

5. Finally, you will want to rebuild the YUM cache by typing what is shown next:

    ```
    yum makecache
    ```

How it works...

YUM is a very powerful tool that is known for its ability to resolve package dependencies and automate the process of package management, but as with all things, there are times when even the best utilities can get confused and may report errors or behave erratically. Fixing this issue is relatively simple and the approach outlined in this recipe will also serve to keep your package manager in a healthy running state for the life of your operating system.

So, what have we learned from this experience?

During its typical operation, YUM will create a cache of metadata and packages that can be found at `/var/cache/yum`. These files are essential, but as they grow in size, this cache will ultimately serve to slow down the overall use of this utility and may even cause some issues. To address this situation, we started by using the following command to clean the current package-based cache using YUM's `clean packages` parameter options. We then followed this by cleaning the metadata cache using the command `clean metadata`, which will remove any excess XML-based files. YUM uses a SQLite database as a part of its normal operation, so the next step was to remove any remaining database files using the `clean dbcache` parameters. The next step was to clean all files associated with enabled repositories in order to reclaim any unused disk space: `yum clean all`. Finally, we restored YUM to its normal working state by rebuilding the cache using the `makecache` option.

There's more...

On a typical server, YUM is a great tool that will solve the most complex problems related to package dependencies and package management. However, in instances where you have knowingly mixed incompatible repositories or have used incomplete sources, there is a risk that YUM will not be able to help.

> Remember, in this situation, you should consider the following advice to be a temporary remedy only. A tendency to ignore any warnings provided by YUM will only lead to bigger problems later on.

If such instances occur, and if the error is RPM-based, as a temporary fix, you can skip broken packages by using the following command:

```
yum -y update --skip-broken
```

This command will allow YUM to continue working by bypassing any packages with errors, but as stated earlier this should be regarded as a temporary fix only. You should always be aware that a system with broken dependencies is not considered to be a healthy system. This situation is to be avoided at all costs, and under these circumstances fixing such errors should become your first priority.

Knowing your priorities

In this recipe, we will investigate the task of preparing YUM to manage additional repositories by installing a plugin known as **YUM priorities**. YUM has the ability to search, remove, install, retrieve, and update packages from various remote locations. Such features make YUM a powerful tool, but if you ever decide to add an additional third-party repository, there is a chance that conflicts will render the system unstable. Stability is one of the many advantages of using the CentOS operating system, and it is the purpose of this recipe to show you how this confidence can be maintained while simultaneously allowing for the addition of new repositories.

Getting ready

To complete this recipe, you will require a working installation of the CentOS 7 operating system with root privileges, a console-based text editor of your choice, and a connection to the Internet in order to facilitate the download of additional packages.

How to do it...

This recipe will show you how to prepare YUM in order to manage the process of using one or more third-party repositories by installing and configuring YUM priorities:

1. To begin this recipe, log in as root and type the following:

    ```
    yum install yum-plugin-priorities
    ```

2. Confirm the installation, and when complete type what is shown here:

    ```
    vi /etc/yum/pluginconf.d/priorities.conf
    ```

3. You should ensure that this file indicates that the plugin is enabled. It should show the instruction enabled = 1. It is not expected that you will need to change anything in this file, but if you have made any changes, simply save and close the file before proceeding.

4. We now need to establish a priority value for each repository. This is a numeric value in ascending order, where the highest priority is given the lowest number. To do this, open the following file as shown next:

    ```
    vi /etc/yum.repos.d/CentOS-Base.repo
    ```

5. Add the following line at the end of the [base] section:

    ```
    priority=1
    ```

6. Now, add the following line at the end of the [updates] section:

    ```
    priority=1
    ```

7. And finally, add the following line at the end of the [extras] section:

    ```
    priority=1
    ```

8. When complete, save and close the file before running a package update:

    ```
    yum update
    ```

How it works...

YUM priorities is a simple plugin that enables YUM to decide what repositories will assume the highest priority when installing and updating new packages. Using this plugin will reduce the chance of package confusion by ensuring that any particular package will always be installed or updated from the same repository. In this way, you can add an unlimited number of repositories and enable YUM to stay in control of package management.

So, what did we learn from this experience?

Enhancing YUM with this plugin was simply a matter of installing the `yum-plugin-priorities` package and ensuring that it was enabled in its configuration file. We then discovered that the priority is set in ascending order, where the lowest values are given precedence over all others. This, of course, serves to simplify the overall process, and for this reason, we ensured that the default repositories were given a value of 1 (`priority=1`). This will ensure that the default repositories maintain the highest priority, so when you do decide to add additional repositories you could assign them a priority value of 2, 3, 4... and 10, or more. On the other hand, it should be noted that we only set this value across three main sections: `[base]`, `[updates]`, and `[extras]`. In simple terms, this was only because the other sections are shown to be disabled. For example, you may have noticed that the `[centosplus]` section in `/etc/yum.repos.d/CentOS-Base.repo` include the following line: `enabled=0`, whereas the `[updates]` and `[extras]` sections show this value as `enabled=1`. Of course, if you intend to activate this repository, you will need to set a priority value for it, but for the purpose of this recipe such an action was not required. Finally, we ran a simple YUM package update in order to activate our revised settings.

So, as we can see, YUM priorities is an extremely flexible package that enables you to determine what repositories take priority when you want to expand your installation options. However, you should always be aware that YUM priorities may not be appropriate for your system, as you are giving it the power to decide what packages are to be ignored, what packages are installed, what packages are updated, and in what order and from which repository you will get them. For most users who tend not to stay away from the typical server functions, this may not be an immediate concern; you may even safely ignore this warning. But if stability and security are an overriding concern, and you do intend to use additional packages from external repositories, then you should give careful consideration to the use of this plugin or at least consider and research the integrity of the third-party repositories used.

Using a third-party repository

In this recipe, we will investigate the desire to take full advantage of the packages that are available to CentOS by installing both the EPEL and Remi repositories. CentOS is an enterprise-based operating system that prides itself on stability, and during the lifetime of your server, it is possible that not every piece of software you need can be found in the default repositories. It is also possible that you may require updated packages of current software, and for these reasons many server administrators choose to install both the EPEL and Remi repositories. These are not the only repositories available, but because they represent one of the most popular combinations, it is the purpose of this recipe to show you how both the EPEL and Remi repositories can be added to your system.

Getting ready

To complete this recipe, you will require a working installation of the CentOS 7 operating system with root privileges, a console-based text editor of your choice, and a connection to the Internet in order to facilitate the download of additional packages.

How to do it...

Before we start, it is assumed that you have followed the previous recipe that showed you how to install and activate YUM priorities.

1. To begin, log in as root and install the EPEL release repository using YUM:

    ```
    yum install epel-release
    ```

2. Next, from your home directory, type the following commands to download the remi release rpm package:

    ```
    curl -O http://rpms.famillecollet.com/enterprise/remi-release-7.
    rpm
    ```

     Please note that, while you are reading this, this URL may have changed; if so, please do some Internet research to find out if there is a new URL available.

3. The preceding file should now be located in your home folder. To proceed, type the following command:

    ```
    rpm -Uvh remi-release-7.rpm
    ```

4. After the installation is done, open the Remi repository file with your favorite text editor:

    ```
    vi /etc/yum.repos.d/remi.repo
    ```

5.   Change `enabled=0` to `enabled=1` and add the line `priority=10` to the end of the
     `[remi]` section.

6.   Now, open the EPEL repository file with your favorite text editor:

     vi /etc/yum.repos.d/epel.repo

7.   Again, change `enabled=0` to `enabled=1` if not set automatically and add the line
     `priority=10` in the `[epel]` section.

8.   To finish, update YUM as shown here:

     yum update

9.   If updates are available, choose *Y* to proceed. Having completed the update process,
     you will now be able to download and install packages from both the Remi and EPEL
     repositories as an addition to those that are used by default.

How it works...

In order to use and enjoy the benefits of a third-party repository, you are required to install and
enable it first using the YUM and RPM package manager.

So, what did we learn from this experience?

Having started the recipe, the task of installing both the Remi and EPEL repositories is
a remarkably smooth process. While the installation of the EPEL repository using YUM is
very safe to changes, the preceding URL for Remi is maintained at the discretion of the
repository owners, so you should always ensure that they are the most current. However,
having obtained the necessary repository setup file, it was then a matter of applying an RPM-
based command in order to install all necessary repository files on your system. Having done
this, we were then required to open the relevant configuration files of each of the installed
repositories and enable them (by changing `enabled=0` to `enabled=1`) and setting a priority
value (`priority=10`). While the former value will merely switch the repository on, the latter
one will be used by YUM to correctly identify which repositories were the most appropriate
when we called the `update` command. As it was discussed in the previous recipe regarding
YUM priorities, the simple rule of thumb is based on remembering the phrase "the lower the
number, the higher the priority." This, in itself (depending on your reasons), may not be a bad
thing to do, but for the purpose of this recipe, it is shown that the default CentOS repositories
should take priority over all others. Of course, you may disagree with this, and yes, there is
nothing stopping you from applying the same priority rule to a third-party supplier, but I do
caution you before diving in, and this is particularly the case if this is for a mission-critical
production server. Remember, if all the priority values are the same, then YUM will attempt
to download the latest version by default.

The reason for setting both Remi and EPEL to a higher value than the existing CentOS-based repositories is based on the need to consider security updates. Unless you have determined otherwise, it is always advised that the base files should come from CentOS first. This includes, but it is not limited to, Kernel updates, SELinux, and related packages. Third-party repositories should be used for additional packages that cannot be obtained from the original sources, or for access to particular updates that may not be available to the base release of CentOS. This may include packages such as Apache, MariaDB, or PHP. As a final footnote, you will have noticed that both Remi and EPEL repositories shared the same priority value. This is by design as these repositories are often viewed as partners. However, if you decide to begin mixing repositories, or use this recipe as a gateway to installing other repositories not mentioned here, then you should always do your research and evaluate every third-party on a case-by-case basis. The Remi and EPEL repositories are very popular, so if you do intend to add more third-party resources, read around the subject, choose your repositories carefully, and stay loyal.

There's more...

There are many other interesting repositories available for CentOS 7, such as ELRepo, which focuses on hardware-related packages such as filesystem drivers, graphics drivers, network drivers, sound drivers, and webcam or video drivers. Go to `http://elrepo.org` to learn how to install and access it.

Creating a YUM repository

If you maintain multiple CentOS servers in your local network and want to save Internet bandwidth or speed up the downloading of the same remote repository packages over and over again, or are within a very restrictive network environment where access to any remote CentOS repository is blocked for your clients, you might want to consider running your own YUM repository. Having your own repository is also an excellent solution if you want to rollout a few custom or unofficial RPM packages (for example in-house configuration files or programs) to your local crowd or if you just want to create an official CentOS 7 repository mirror site. Here in this recipe we will show you how to set up your own first YUM CentOS 7 repository and how to serve it to your local network.

Getting ready

To complete this recipe, you will require a working installation of the CentOS 7 operating system with root privileges, a console-based text editor of your choice, and a connection to the Internet to facilitate the download of additional packages. For this recipe to work, you will also need to place the CentOS 7 Everything DVD iso file image in your server's root home directory, if you haven't downloaded it yet, refer to a detailed description in the first recipe in *Chapter 1, Installing CentOS* (but download the latest `CentOS-7-x86_64-Everything-XXXX.iso` file instead of the minimal iso file). Also, we need a running Apache web server to share our YUM repository to our local network; please read the first recipe in *Chapter 12, Providing Web Services* in order to learn how to set it up.

How to do it...

To create our own YUM repository, we need the `createrepo` program, which is not installed on CentOS 7 by default. Let's begin our journey by installing it. In this example, we will use the IP address, `192.168.1.7`, for our YUM repository server:

1. Log in as root on your server and install the following package:

   ```
   yum install createrepo
   ```

2. Next, for every repository you want to share, create a subfolder beneath the Apache web root folder under `/var/www/html/repository/`, which will be publicly available when Apache is running; for example, to share the complete CentOS 7 `Everything` repository packages, you could use:

   ```
   mkdir -p /var/www/html/repository/centos/7.1
   ```

3. Now, put all your RPM package files of choice into the repository folders created here. In our example, we will put all RPM packages from the `Everything` iso image file into our new local repository location after we have mounted the content of the iso file to the filesystem:

   ```
   mount ~/CentOS-7-x86_64-Everything-1503-01.iso /mnt/
   ```

   ```
   cp -r /mnt/Packages/* /var/www/html/repository/centos/7.1/
   ```

4. Afterwards, we need to update the SELinux security contexts for all the new files copied into the Apache web root directory:

   ```
   restorecon -v -R /var/www/html
   ```

5. Now, for every repository we want to set up, run the following command:

   ```
   createrepo --database /var/www/html/repository/centos/7.1
   ```

6. Congratulations, you now have successfully created your first YUM repository, which can be accessed from any computer in the same network through the running Apache web server. In order to test it, log in as root to any other CentOS 7-based system that can ping our repository server and add our new repository to its YUM repository configuration directory:

    ```
    vi /etc/yum.repos.d/myCentosMirror.repo
    ```

7. Add the following content to this empty file (change the `baseurl` appropriately to fit your own needs):

    ```
    [myCentosMirror]
    name=my CentOS 7.1 mirror
    baseurl=http://192.168.1.7/repository/centos/7.1
    gpgcheck=1
    gpgkey=http://mirror.centos.org/centos/RPM-GPG-KEY-CentOS-7
    ```

8. Save and close the file, then test if your new repository is available (it should appear on the list) on your client:

    ```
    yum repolist | grep myCentosMirror
    ```

9. Now, to test our new YUM repository, we can try the following command:

    ```
    yum --disablerepo="*" --enablerepo="myCentosMirror" list available
    ```

How it works...

In this recipe, we have shown you how easy it is to install and set up a local YUM repository. However, we have only shown you how to create a mirror site of all the CentOS 7 Everything iso RPM packages, but you can repeat this process for creating YUM repositories of every kind of package that you want to share with your network.

So, what did we learn from this experience?

Setting up your own YUM repository was simply a matter of installing the `createrepo` package and copying all the RPM packages that you want to share into a subfolder of your choice beneath your Apache's document root directory (In our example, we had to mount the CentOS 7 Everything iso file to the filesystem, in order to access its included RPM package files that we want to share). As the Apache's document root directory is under the control of SELinux, afterwards we needed to set the security context for all the new RPM files in this directory to the `httpd_sys_content_t` type label; otherwise, no access through the web server would be possible. Finally, we needed to run the `createrepo` command on our new repository folder, which will create our new repository's metadata that is needed for any YUM client that wants to connect to the repository later to make queries to it.

Afterwards, to test our new repository, we created a new repository definition file on another CentOS 7 system that wants to use this new service and that must be in the same network as our YUM repository server. In this custom `.repo` configuration file, we put the correct URL path to the repository, enabled `gpg` checks, and took the standard CentOS 7 `gpgkey` so that our YUM client can proof the validity of the RPM packages official repository packages. Finally, we used the `yum` command with the `--disablerepo="*"` and `--enablerepo="myCentosMirror"` parameters, which will make sure to only use our new custom repository as a source. You can use these two parameters in combination with any other `yum` command such as `install`, `search`, `info`, `list`, and so on. This was just for testing; if you want to combine your new repository with the existing ones, please use YUM priorities for it (as shown in another recipe in this chapter).

There's more...

Now, before we announce our new centralized YUM repository to our network, we should first make an update of all the RPM packages that have changed since the release of the CentOS Everything iso. In order to do this, visit `http://www.centos.org` and choose a `rsync://` mirror link that is geographically near your current location. For example, if you are located in Germany one option could be `rsync://ftp.hosteurope.de/centos/` (for more detailed instructions on navigating the CentOS website, read the first recipe in *Chapter 1, Installing CentOS*). Also, before we can use the `rsync` protocol, we need to install the `rsync` package (`yum install rsync`), if not done already. Now, open the following empty script file `vi ~/update-myCentosMirror-repo.sh` file and put in the following content (replacing the `rsync://` location accordingly, if needed):

```
rsync -avz rsync://ftp.hosteurope.de/centos/7/os/x86_64/Packages/ /var/
www/html/repository/centos/7.1
```

```
restorecon -v -R /var/www/html
```

Now, make the file executable using `chmod +x ~/update-myCentosMirror-repo.sh`, and run it with `~/update-myCentosMirror-repo.sh`. This should update your repository to the latest version. Finally, to automate this process, let's create a cron job that will update our repository packages with the other mirror site every night at 2:30 am (open `crontab -e`):

```
30 2 * * * /root/update-myCentosMirror-repo.sh
```

Working with the RPM package manager

All software on a CentOS 7 system is distributed through RPM packages. Most of the time the YUM package manager is the first choice of any system administrator, performing software installation and maintenance, and is highly recommended whenever possible as it provides system integrity checks and has excellent package dependency resolution. In this recipe, we will show you an alternative way to manage your packages. We will be exploring the RPM package manager, which is a powerful tool used to build, install, query, verify, update, and erase individual RPM software packages. Though it is not as *intelligent* as YUM, as it cannot resolve package dependencies or work with repositories, it can be still relevant today since it provides very useful querying options that are not available in YUM, and it can be used to install single software packages manually.

Getting ready

To complete this recipe, you will require a working installation of the CentOS 7 operating system with root privileges, a console-based text editor of your choice, and a connection to the Internet in order to facilitate the download of additional RPM packages.

How to do it...

We start this recipe by downloading a `rpm` package from the Internet, which we will use to show you an example of how the `rpm` command works:

1. We will begin by logging in as root into the root's home directory and downloading the pipe view program from the EPEL repository, which cannot be found in the official CentOS repository:

   ```
   cd ~;curl -O http://dl.fedoraproject.org/pub/
   epel/7/x86_64/p/pv-1.4.6-1.el7.x86_64.rpm
   ```
   Please note that while you are reading this, the package URL may have changed.

2. After the download has been completed, we will install this package using the following `rpm` command:
   ```
   rpm -Uvh ~/pv-1.4.6-1.el7.x86_64.rpm
   ```

3. If the installation has finished, let's check if the installation of the package was successful by querying the RPM database:
   ```
   rpm -qa | grep "pv-"
   ```

4. You can also test the `pv` program directly (press *Ctrl+C* keys to quit):

```
dd if=/dev/urandom | pv | dd of=/dev/null
```

5. We can now use the `rpm` command's rich querying options to show useful information of the installed package:

```
rpm -qi pv
rpm -ql pv
rpm -qd pv
```

6. Finally, let's remove the package if you don't like or need it anymore:

```
rpm -e pv
```

How it works...

Here, in this recipe, we introduced you to the RPM package manager, which is the original program to manage RPM packages. The RPM package is a packaging standard for the distribution of software, and contains useful metadata in the file to verify the authorship (for example, using signature verification with PGP) and integrity of the software included. The installation of packages containing binary programs instead of manually compiling and building them from scratch is much easier and more consistent, but RPM packages can also contain any type of file, such as source code or just documentation files. As said in the introduction, the `rpm` command has six different modes of operation: building, installing, uninstalling, updating, querying, and verifying rpm packages. Here, in this recipe, we showed you how to use the most important five operations (we don't show building RPM's).

So, what have we learned from this experience?

We started by logging in as root and downloading the `pv` (pipe viewer) rpm package example from the non-official EPEL CentOS repository (EPEL contains high-quality add-on packages, thoroughly checked and officially conformed; see the *Using a third-party repository* recipe to learn more about the EPEL repository) manually using `curl`, because it is not available in the official repository but can be a very useful tool.

Although there are many RPM repositories and download sources on the Internet, for security and compatibility reasons, on productive systems you should consider installing only official CentOS 7 RPM packages from valid and reputable repositories and sources. In general, the packages contained are best tested and reviewed by many experts and users.

The downloaded package file's name can be read the following way, which follows the following non-mandatory naming convention for RHEL/CentOS packages:

`pv-1.4.6-1.x86_64.rpm` = **package name (pv)-version number (1.4.6)-release(1)-CPU architecture (x86_64)**

Next, we installed the downloaded `pv` package using the RPM package manager, which can be executed using the `rpm` command on the command line. We used it with the `-Uvh` command parameters together with the full name of the downloaded package rpm file.

> If using the rpm command for installing or upgrading rpm software packages, you should always use `-Uvh` with one exception; which are kernel packages. `-U` will remove old packages while updating, and this is not what you want if you install a new kernel. Use `-i` (for installing) here instead, as this will keep the old kernel files so that you can go back to an earlier version if you run into some problems.

`-U` is the parameter for installing or upgrading a package. If the package is not installed on the system, it will get installed; otherwise `rpm` tries to upgrade it if it the RPM package version is newer than the one installed. The `-v` parameter prints a more verbose output, while `-h` displays a nice progress bar. Installing the `pv` package when you have not enabled the EPEL repository on your system will get the following warning message:

`pv-1.6.0-1.x86_64.rpm: Header V3 DSA/SHA1 Signature, key ID 3fc56f51: NOKEY`

RPM will automatically check the validity of the package's signature before installing to make sure that the package's content has not been modified since it has been signed. Also, it checks that an RPM package is trustworthy, as it should be signed by an official third-party authority vendor using an encrypted key. You can ignore this message, as packages from the EPEL repository are from a secure source. To permanently trust EPEL sources, you can install its `gpg` public key on your system using the following command and getting rid of all future signature warning messages:

`rpm --import https://dl.fedoraproject.org/pub/epel/RPM-GPG-KEY-EPEL-7`

Having successfully installed the package, we now have a nice command line tool called `pv` to show the progress of data going through a Unix pipe, which can be useful if you are transferring huge amounts of data through pipelines where you normally never know the current state of progress. Afterwards, we queried the RPM database that stores information about all installed packages on a CentOS 7 system, using the `rpm` command with the `-q` flag. Working on the RPM database, we must use the true package name (`pv`) instead of the filename (`pv-1.4.6-1.x86_64.rpm`) that we used when we installed the packages in the first place. The same is true when removing an installed package; please specify the package name and not the version number or full filename.

To get detailed information about the installed package, `pv`, we used `-qi` (i for information), with the `-ql` parameter; we showed the full filename and path of all files in the package. `-qd` showed all the files in the package containing documentation. To read about more querying options, type `man rpm` and look under the PACKAGE QUERY OPTIONS section.

In summary, we can say that there are situations in a system administrator's life where one needs to install a piece of software that is not distributed through an official repository (for example, non-open-source, cutting-edge program or beta versions, software that have a license disallowing the ability to put it into a repository such as Java, or software from independent developers), and where one will have to download individual RPM packages and install them manually. Under the hood, YUM also depends and uses the RPM package manager in the background, so you are also able to use the YUM program to install rpm files (`yum install <filename.rpm>`). However, when it comes to querying your downloaded rpm files or installed packages on your system, there are situations where it's better to use the older `rpm` command without having to install additional YUM-based software such as `yum-utils`.

The biggest weakness of RPM is that it does not support repositories and is missing a dependency management system. If you work with RPM alone to install all your software on a CentOS system, you will easily run into package dependency problems where you cannot install a specific package because it relies on some other packages. Often, when you try to install the dependent packages, you need other packages that they depend on and so on. This can be very tedious work and should always be avoided by using YUM instead.

There's more...

The `rpm` command can not only be used to query the rpm database for information about installed packages, you can also use it to query rpm files that you downloaded. For example, use the `-qlp` parameter to show all files in a local `rpm` package file:

```
rpm -qlp ~/pv-1.4.6-1.el7.x86_64.rpm
```

To get detailed information about the package from the `rpm` file, use the `-qip` parameter, as shown here:

```
rpm -qip ~/pv-1.4.6-1.el7.x86_64.rpm
```

If you want to install an RPM package that you have downloaded locally and that has dependencies, you can use the `yum localinstall` command. This will install the local package once supplied with its filename, and will try to resolve all the dependencies from remote sources, for example:

```
wget http://location/to/a/rpm/package_name.rpm
yum localinstall package_name.rpm
```

5
Administering the Filesystem

In this chapter, we will cover the following topics:

- ▸ Creating a virtual block device
- ▸ Formatting and mounting a filesystem
- ▸ Using disk quotas
- ▸ Maintaining a filesystem
- ▸ Extending the capacity of the filesystem

Introduction

This chapter is a collection of recipes that provides for the need to drive a CentOS-based server solution. From formatting and mounting disks to extending a logical volume and maintaining your filesystem and disk quotas, the purpose of this chapter is to show you how quickly and easily you can get to grips with the task of managing the needs of its users in today's most demanding environments.

Creating a virtual block device

In this recipe, we will create a virtual block device that we will use to simulate real devices and partitions so that we can test-drive concepts and commands used in all later recipes in this chapter. Working with real disks and partitions often involves the risk of losing important data or even having to re-install your complete system. A virtual block device is ideal to learn the techniques and try things out before switching to "production mode". Later, if you have gained enough experience and feel safe, you can easily replace it with "real" hardware devices, partitions, and logical volumes (which is a part of LVM; see the later recipe). All you need to do is substitute your virtual device with "real" block device names.

Getting ready

To complete this recipe, you will require a minimal installation of the CentOS 7 operating system with root access. To create a virtual block device, you should have at least one gigabyte of free hard disk space that we will use temporarily to create and make. You can delete this reserved space later (or it will be automatically deleted on reboot). It's just for testing.

How to do it...

1. To begin, log in as `root` and create an empty file with the exact size of 1 gigabyte:

    ```
    dd if=/dev/zero of=/tmp/test-image.dd bs=1M count=1000
    ```

2. Now, let's create a loop device from the file we just created:

    ```
    losetup -fP  /tmp/test-image.dd
    ```

3. Next, print the generated loop device name:

    ```
    losetup -a
    ```

4. As this will be the first loop device created in the current system, the output will be as follows (`loop0` can be a different number if you have created a loop device before):

    ```
    /dev/loop0: [0035]:3714186 (/tmp/test-image.dd)
    ```

5. To get a list of all the block devices currently attached to the system, as well as important details, type the following:

    ```
    lsblk -io NAME,TYPE,SIZE,MOUNTPOINT,FSTYPE,MODEL
    ```

6. Now, let's create a new partition table of the type `gpt` on our new loop device (confirm the deletion of any data):

    ```
    parted /dev/loop0 mklabel gpt
    ```

7. Finally, create device maps from your loop device to make it more similar to real hard disk partitions:

```
kpartx -a /dev/loop0
```

How it works...

In this recipe, we have learned how to create a virtual block device that acts as a starting point for testing out how to create partitions, logical volumes, and filesystems in later recipes in this chapter.

So, what did we learn from this experience?

We started this recipe by creating a new empty file, which was one gigabyte in size, in the /tmp directory using the dd utility. dd is used to make exact copies of files (which is sometimes called cloning) and expects two parameters: an input file (the if parameter) and an output file (the of parameter). We used the zero device (/dev/zero) as our input file that returns an endless stream of bytes containing zero. We then limited the stream by defining a blocksize (bs) and count parameter. The bs defines the amount of data in bytes read at a time, while the count parameter counts how many repetitions of bs will be allowed. So, these arguments can be read as *stop the copying process when we reach a blocksize times count data received*. In our example, we used a blocksize of *1 Megabyte times 1000 = 1 Gigabyte*. This zero byte data was written to our output file (of) called /tmp/test-image.dd.

After we created this empty file, we created a temporary **loop** device with it. A loop device is just a pseudo-device that makes it possible to use a file as a **block device**. Often, such a file is a CD ISO image, and using it as a loop device will make it accessible as if it were a normal hardware drive. Any device that allows reading or writing data in blocks can be called a block device; in order to get a list of all available block devices in your system, we used the lsblk command, and as you can see, this includes our loop device as well. Standard loop device names start with the number zero, as in /dev/loop0.

Afterwards, we created a new **partition table** on our loop device using the parted command. A partition table is a table maintained on a disk by the operating system describing the partitions on it, and it must be created before we can create them. We used the partition table type gpt, but you can also use the old msdos type here instead.

Normally, when creating a partition table on a virtual block device, we cannot access individual partitions or make filesystems for different partitions on it, because the partitions cannot be addressed individually. Here we used the kpartx command to create device mappings from partition tables, which allows us later to access single partitions for creating filesystems using the notation, /dev/loop0p1, for partition 1 on loop device 0 and /dev/loop0p2 for partition 2 on loop device 0.

Congratulations, you have now created a brand new virtual block device with a standard partition table, which can be used and accessed as if it were a normal disk device.

There's more...

If we want to remove a virtual block device, we first have to unmount it from the filesystem if it is currently mounted (for example, `umount /dev/loo0p1`). Next, we need to detach the virtual block device file from the loop device using the `-d` parameter like so: `losetup -d /dev/loop0`. Afterwards, we can delete the block file if we want to: `rm /tmp/test-image.dd`.

Formatting and mounting a filesystem

In this recipe, you will be introduced to the standard CentOS filesystems **XFS**, **Ext4**, and **Btrfs**. Filesystems form one of the most fundamental parts of any operating system and nearly everything depends on them. Here, you will learn how to create different types of standard filesystems available in CentOS 7, and how to link them to your system so that we can access them afterwards for reading and writing. These two techniques are called **formatting** and **mounting** filesystems; while you do not do this very often, it remains one of the most fundamental Linux system administrator tasks.

Getting ready

To complete this recipe, you will require a minimal installation of the CentOS 7 operating system with root access. We will also use virtual block devices instead of real disk devices because it's better to demonstrate the usage of creating filesystems and formatting disks using "dummy" devices, instead of erasing your real hard disk contents. Therefore, you should have applied the *Creating a virtual block device* recipe and created a 1 Gigabyte virtual block device, which will be named `/dev/loop0` in this example.

If you want to apply this recipe for real disk devices, all you have to do is replace `/dev/loop0` with your correct partition—for logical volumes (lv) for example, `/dev/mapper/myServer/data`, for a SATA device `/dev/sdX`, or for an IDE-based hard disk name `/dev/hdX` (where X is a character `a-z`).

How to do it...

In our example, this block device is labeled at `/dev/loop0`. Please note that, if you have created more than one block device, your number could be different, so please change the name accordingly:

1. First, let's log in as `root` and show information about all currently available block devices:

   ```
   lsblk -io NAME,TYPE,SIZE,MOUNTPOINT,FSTYPE,MODEL
   ```

2. Now, recheck that we have a valid partition table installed on the device:

   ```
   parted /dev/loop0 print
   ```

3. The preceding line should print out the following content: `Partition Table: gpt`. If this is not the case, let's create a new partition table (confirm the deletion of any data):

    ```
    parted /dev/loop0 mklabel gpt
    ```

4. Now, we will create a new partition spanning the complete disk space with an `ext4` filesystem label (no filesystem will be installed yet; it's just a label):

    ```
    parted -a optimal /dev/loop0 mkpart primary ext4 2048KiB 100%
    ```

5. Print the partition table again to show the new partition we just created:

    ```
    parted /dev/loop0 print
    ```

6. Now, let's remove the partition:

    ```
    parted /dev/loop0 rm 1
    ```

7. We can also create a btrfs-labeled partition:

    ```
    parted -a optimal /dev/loop0 unit MB mkpart primary btrfs 2048KiB 100%
    ```

8. Afterwards, let's create an XFS-labeled partition spanning the whole disk:

    ```
    parted /dev/loop0 rm 1
    parted -a optimal /dev/loop0 mkpart primary xfs 2048KiB 100%
    ```

9. Now, show the block table again to see what we have changed:

    ```
    lsblk -io NAME,TYPE,SIZE,MOUNTPOINT,FSTYPE,MODEL
    ```

10. As we have only defined the partition type *label*, we still don't have a valid filesystem on our partition; so, in the next step, we format our disk using the correct type. We use XFS in our example. Please change `mkfs -t <type>` if you use `ext4` or `btrfs` instead:

    ```
    mkfs -t xfs /dev/loop0p1
    ```

11. Next, let's mount our virtual block device partition on the system, into the directory `/media/vbd-1`, and please change `-t <type>` if you use `ext4` or `btrfs` instead:

    ```
    mkdir /media/vbd-1
    mount -t xfs /dev/loop0p1  /media/vbd-1
    ```

12. Finally, test if we can read and write to the new filesystem:

    ```
    echo "this is a test" > /media/vbd-1/testfile.txt
    cat /media/vbd-1/testfile.txt
    ```

How it works...

Here, in this recipe, we showed the user how to create CentOS 7 standard partitions spanning the whole disk, and then we created some filesystems on them, which is called formatting, using different filesystem types. The standard filesystem available in CentOS 7 is XFS, but as we have learned in this recipe, there are lots of other ones available as well, including the popular ext4 and btrfs. XFS is a very robust and high-performing file system for large storage configurations; it is considered very mature and stable. Before CentOS 7, the standard file system was ext4, but it had some limitations and not the best performance when working with millions of files and is considered barely suitable for today's very large filesystems. btrfs is a relatively new filesystem and is included in CentOS 7, but at the time of writing it is still under development and should not be used for production systems. It is considered to be fully supported in later CentOS 7 minor releases and is likely to replace XFS as the standard CentOS filesystem type in the future, as it has a list of very promising features and enhancements, such as copy-on-write, which copies files each time you write to them, and which makes it possible to go back to former file versions.

So, what have we learned from this experience?

We started this recipe by using the `lsblk` command to print a list of all available block devices currently attached to the system. We used this command to check if our target block device that we want to use for installing partitions and filesystems on is available. In our example we will use the `/dev/loop0` device, please change this name if it's different on your system (as said before, you could also use a "real" disk block device, such as `/dev/sda`, but always be careful!). After confirming that we have our device ready, we used the `parted` command to check the partition table of the disk. A partition table is mandatory for any hard disk to keep track of the partition information on it. As you have seen, our primary tool for creating partition tables and partitions is *parted*, as it is the officially recommended CentOS 7 tool for these tasks, but there are other programs that do the same as well, such as `fdisk` or `gdisk`. If there is no partition table available, we must create one of type `gpt` using parted's `mklabel gpt` parameter.

Next, after we created the partition table, we put some partitions on it. Therefore, we issued parted's `mkpart` command with the `-a optimal primary ext4 2048KiB 100%` options.

 Be careful with the `parted` command all the time and recheck everything before executing, as most of its commands will completely destroy all the data currently stored on the disk.

This will create a new partition starting at 2,048 kilobytes (kb) until the end of the disk. We did not start at the very beginning of the disk (0%) as 2,048 kb is the start of the first sector on the disk to leave some space left to store some additional data. `-a optimal` aligns the partition to a multiple of the physical block size that will guarantee optimal performance. Next, we removed the partition again using the `rm` option and number 1, which refers to the first partition we just created. We recreated new partitions of type `btrfs` and finally `xfs`. After the disk is partitioned, we need an actual filesystem on it, as parted only labels the partition to a specific type, but does not do the actual formatting. To make the filesystem, we use the `mkfs` utility. You can either run it with the `-t` flag, as we did, or use a dot notation, such as `mkfs.xfs`, to specify the type you want to format it to. The `mkfs` command gives us a detailed output of what it has done, such as how many blocks have been written and so on.

Finally, after we have created the filesystem on our disk partition, we can use the `mount` command to make it available and work with it in our current system. `mount` either attaches or detaches a device's filesystem to our system's root filesystem. Therefore, we need to first create a directory to define where we want to attach it to. We use the directory, `/media/vbd-1`, as a parameter for the actual `mount` command with the syntax, `mount -t <file system type> <device> <dir>`. For almost all standard filesystems, you can skip the `-t` parameter as it will automatically detect the right type. To detach a filesystem from your system, you can use the `umount` command with the argument of the device you want to remove (you can also use the folder it's mounted to; both do work!). In our example, to unmount our loop device's first partition, type `umount /dev/loop0p1`.

After mounting our formatted partition device, we can access it like any other component beneath the root folder.

There's more...

In this recipe, we always use one partition spanning the complete available disk space. Often, you have more than one partition on a disk, so let's create this kind of layout instead. In this example, we create three 100 MB partitions on `/dev/loop0`:

1. First, let's delete our partition once again using the `rm` parameter so that we can add new ones:

   ```
   parted /dev/loop0 rm 1
   ```

2. Now, let's create three equal partitions:

   ```
   parted -a optimal /dev/loop0 unit MiB mkpart primary ext4 2048KiB 100
   parted -a optimal /dev/loop0 unit MiB mkpart primary ext4 100 200
   parted -a optimal /dev/loop0 unit MiB mkpart primary ext4 300 400
   ```

3. Let's review our layout:

    parted /dev/loop0 print

 Using the `gpt` partition table, we can create up to 128 primary partitions on any disk; when using the older `msdos` partition type, there is a maximum of four primary partitions. If you need more, you have to create extended partitions out of primary ones.

Using disk quotas

When administering a Linux multiuser system with many system users, it is wise to set some kind of restrictions or limits to the resources shared by the system. On a filesystem level, you can either restrict the available hard disk space or the total file number to a fixed size at a user, group, or directory level. The introduction of such rules can prevent people from "spamming" the system, filling up its free space, and generally your users will get more aware of the differentiation between important and unimportant data and will be more likely to keep their home directories tidy and clean. Here in this recipe, we will show you how to set up a **disk quota** limiting system for XFS filesystems, which puts restrictions on the amount of data your system's user accounts are allowed to store.

Getting ready

To complete this recipe, you will require a minimal installation of the CentOS 7 operating system with root access and a console-based text editor of your choice. For this recipe to work, and in order to set quotas, you will need at least one system user account next to your root account; if you don't have one yet, please refer to the recipe *Managing users and their groups* in *Chapter 3, Managing the System* to learn how to create one. Also, in the main recipe, it is expected that your CentOS 7 uses the XFS filesystem, which is standard on installation. Finally, your CentOS 7 installation needs to have been installed on a disk with at least 64 GB space, otherwise the installer will not create a *separate* logical /home volume, which is required in this recipe to make quotas work.

How to do it...

Here, we will learn how to set up a quota system for the XFS filesystem in two different ways: first, setting limits on the user and groups, and then on the directory (project) level. Disk quota systems have to be set on filesystem mount.

Enabling user and group quotas

1. To begin, log in as `root` and open the `fstab` file, which contains static mount information:

   ```
   vi /etc/fstab
   ```

2. Now, navigate the cursor to the line containing /home (with the *up* and *down* arrow keys) and move it to the word `defaults`, and then add the following text after `defaults`, separated by commas:

   ```
   ,uquota,gquota
   ```

3. The complete line will look like the following (your device name will be different, depending on your individual LVM name; here, it is `myserver`):

   ```
   /dev/mapper/myserver-home /home  XFS    defaults,uquota,gquota 0 0
   ```

4. Save and close the file, then remount the /home partition to activate the `quota` directive:

   ```
   umount /home;mount -a
   ```

5. Next, create a user quota on the total file size for a specific user named `john` (change appropriately to match a user available on your system):

   ```
   xfs_quota -x -c 'limit bsoft=768m bhard=1g john' /home/
   ```

6. Next, create a user quota for the total *amount* of files another user, `joe`, can have:

   ```
   xfs_quota -x -c 'limit isoft=1000 ihard=5000 joe' /home/
   ```

7. Let's create a file amount and size limit for everyone in the user group `devgrp` (the filesystem group `devgrp` must exist):

   ```
   xfs_quota -x -c 'limit -g bsoft=5g bhard=6g isoft=10000
   ihard=50000 devgrp' /home
   ```

8. Finally, show the whole quota report for the `home` volume:

   ```
   xfs_quota -x -c 'report -bi -h' /home
   ```

Enabling project (directory) quotas

In order to enable disk quotas for a single directory instead of user or group quotas, we have to add the project quota directive called `pquota` to the volume containing the directory. As we will use a directory called /srv/data for our project quota, we need to take the full underlying / root partition under quota control. For the root partition, we have to set quota flags as kernel boot options:

1. To begin with, open the following file as root after first making a backup of it:

   ```
   cp /etc/default/grub /etc/default/grub.BAK
   vi /etc/default/grub
   ```

2. Add the `rootflags=pquota` directive to the end of the line (add one whitespace character before it) starting with GRUB_CMDLINE_LINUX= before the closing double quote as shown here:

```
GRUB_CMDLINE_LINUX="rd.lvm.lv=centos/root rd.lvm.lv=centos/swap
crashkernel=auto rhgb quiet rootflags=pquota"
```

3. Save and close the file, and then rebuild the `grub` configuration with our new `boot` option:

```
grub2-mkconfig -o /boot/grub2/grub.cfg
```

4. Now, add the `pquota` flag to your root volume in `/etc/fstab` as well:

```
vi /etc/fstab
```

5. Navigate the cursor to the line containing the root mount point / and move it to the word `defaults`, and then add the following text, separated by a comma:

```
,prjquota
```

6. The complete line will look similar to the following:

```
/dev/mapper/myserver-root /          XFS     defaults,prjquota 0 0
```

7. Next, reboot your computer to apply your changes to the `root` volume:

```
reboot
```

8. After rebooting, make sure that the `root` volume has project quota enabled, which is defined as the `prjquota` flag in the volume's options (otherwise, if it is wrong and doesn't work, it will show as `noquota`):

```
cat /etc/mtab  | grep root
```

9. Next, let's create our target folder that we want to set quotas for:

```
mkdir /srv/data
```

10. We need to add a project name and an associated new, unique ID:

```
echo "myProject:1400" >> /etc/projid
```

11. Now, define that `/srv/data` will use quota rules from our project ID:

```
echo "1400:/srv/data" >> /etc/projects
```

12. Next, initialize the `project` quota for the `root` volume:

```
xfs_quota -xc 'project -s myProject' /
```

13. Finally, apply the following rule to create specific directory limits:

```
xfs_quota -x -c 'limit -p bsoft=1000m bhard=1200m myProject' /
```

14. Print out our quota rules for this device:

```
xfs_quota -x -c 'report -bi -h' /
```

How it works...

In this recipe, you learned how easy it is to set up a quota system on a user, group, or directory (project) level. Also, you have learned that there are two basic ways of defining quotas: either put a restriction on the *total file size* (called blocks), or a limit on the *number* of files (called inodes).

So, what have we learned from this experience?

We began this recipe by setting user and group quotas. As you have seen, a quota system can easily be enabled by adding associated directives to the partition of choice in the /etc/fstab file. Therefore, we began this recipe by opening this file and adding the special quota keywords for the XFS user, and group quotas to our /home partition. In order to apply these changes, we had to remount the filesystem using the mount command. As the quota system had been successfully started, we used the xfs_quota -x -c command line to set some quota limits on our enabled filesystem /home. -x enables expert mode while -c lets us run commands as arguments on the command line. When running xfs_quota without the -c option, you will get to an interactive prompt instead. First, we set some user limits for the users, john and joe. We did this by defining the following parameters with numbers: bsoft, bhard, isoft, ihard. As you can see, there are both soft and hard limits for file size (**blocks**) and file amount (**inodes**). Block quotas can be given in the typical metrics such as kilobyte (k), megabyte (m), and gigabyte (g), whereas an inode is a number. A soft limit is a threshold that, when crossed, prints out a warning message to the command line, whereas a hard limit will stop the user from adding any more data or files to the filesystem under quota protection. Afterwards, we set a group-based quota. If you use the -g flag, the limit will be defined for a group instead of the user. Using group rules can be very helpful to separate your users into different groups depending on the amount of files or total file size they should be allowed to have. Finally, we generated a report for all our current quota limits. The command we used there was 'report -bi -h', which generates reports for used filespace (-b for blocks) and the total amount of files (-i for inodes). -h specified that we want the output to be human-readable in megabytes or gigabytes.

To test that quotas work, let's create the following block and inode quotas for the user jack:

```
xfs_quota -x -c 'limit bhard=20m jack' /home/
xfs_quota -x -c 'limit ihard=1000 jack' /home/
```

Log in as the user jack (su - jack) and run the following command:

```
dd if=/dev/urandom of=~/test.dd bs=1M count=21
```

With this command, the user `john` will try to create a 21 megabyte size file, but when starting to write the twentieth megabyte, the following error message will appear:

```
dd: error writing '/home/jack/test.dd': Disk quota exceeded
```

Now, delete the `~/test.dd` file so that we can start another test. The same happens if you exceed your file amount limit. Test the following quota limit by trying to create 2,000 multiple files while the quota is limited to 1,000; do this by adding a lot of new files: `for i in {1..2000}; do touch ~/test$i.txt; done`. This results in the following error message:

```
touch: cannot touch '/home/jack/test1001.txt': Disk quota exceeded
```

To temporarily turn off user and group quota checking for a specific filesystem, you can run `xfs_quota -x -c 'off -u -g' /home/` (`-u` for user, `-g` for group) as `root` user. This is only temporary; to re-enable it, you need to remount the filesystem of interest, which is `umount /home; mount -a`. To remove a specific quota rule, just set its limit to zero, for example:

```
xfs_quota -x -c 'limit bhard=0 john' /home
```

Next, we set up quota on a *directory*, instead of the user/group level. This is a feature only XFS file systems are capable of; all other filesystems can only set quotas on a disk or partition level. Being able to control the disk usage of a directory hierarchy is useful if you do not otherwise want to set quota limits for a privileged user or groups. To activate directory quota, we first had to enable this as a kernel boot option because, by default, the root volume is flagged as `noquota`. Also, we added the `prjquota` directive in `/etc/fstab` to the root partition to make it work. If you want to learn more about kernel boot options, read the boot loader recipe in *Chapter 1, Installing CentOS*. To set file system flags for the root partition, we needed to reboot the system. After doing this, we made sure that the boot option has been set successfully by looking into the `mtab` file, which is a file that lists all currently mounted filesystems. Next, we set up a project name with an associated unique project ID (we randomly choose `1400`) in the `/etc/projid` file. In the next step, we applied this new project ID (`1400`) to a directory in the `/etc/projects` file called `/srv/data`. This system allows the application of specific project quota rules to many different directories. Afterwards, we initialized project quota for the root partition using the `project` option with the `xfs_quota` command, and then created a `limit` quota rule for this project name. All directories that are defined in the `/etc/projects` file under the corresponding project id are affected by this rule. This type of system can be used for fine-grain multiple folder quota rules. For every directory, you can set up a new project name or reuse a specific one, making this system very flexible.

In this recipe, we have created a block size hard limit of 1,200 megabytes for our project name, which is `myProject`. To test this quota, type the following:

```
dd if=/dev/zero of=/srv/data/dd.img bs=1M count=1201
```

This should stop `dd`, exactly after writing 1200 megabytes, with the following command line error message:

```
dd: error writing '/srv/data/dd.img': No space left on device
```

There's more...

As the name implies, the xfs_quota program shown in this recipe only works for XFS filesystems. If you want to use disk quotas on a user or group level for other file systems such as ext4 or btrfs, you have to install the quota package (yum install quota). Setting quotas works in a similar way to the steps shown in this recipe; please read the manual man quota to get you started.

Maintaining a filesystem

In this recipe, we will learn how to check the consistency and optionally repair CentOS 7 filesystems. Filesystem inconsistencies are rare events and filesystem checks normally are running automatically at boot time. But system administrators should also know how to run such tests manually, if they believe there is a problem with the filesystem.

Getting ready

To complete this recipe, you will require a working installation of the CentOS 7 operating system with root privileges. We will use virtual block devices instead of real disk devices because we *cannot* apply any file system check on a *mounted* disk. Therefore, you should have applied the *Formatting and mounting a filesystem* recipe and created a 1 gigabyte virtual block device with two partitions of half the total size: first, a partition with an XFS, and then another one with an ext4 filesystem. We will use the virtual block device named /dev/loop0 in this example.

As said before, these can be easily exchanged with real disk names.

How to do it...

1. To begin with, log in as root and show information about the current block devices attached to the system:

    ```
    lsblk -io NAME,TYPE,SIZE,MOUNTPOINT,FSTYPE,MODEL
    ```

2. Here, you should see two partitions on the loop0 device: /dev/loop0p1 and /dev/loop0p2. If you see that they are currently mounted to the system, unmount them now:

    ```
    umount /dev/loop0p1
    umount /dev/loop0p2
    ```

3. Now, let's check the XFS filesystem which in our example is loop0p1 (change appropriately):

    ```
    xfs_repair -n /dev/loop0p1
    ```

4. For the second partition on the disk that is ext4, we will use the following line:

```
fsck -f /dev/loop0p2
```

How it works...

In this recipe, we have learned how easy it is to run a filesystem check on a XFS or ext4 filesystem. The most important lesson you should have learned here is that you always have to *unmount* your disk partitions before running any filesystem checks!

So, what did we learn from this experience?

Since we cannot run any filesystem checks on any mounted device, if you want to check your system's disks and partitions, often you have to run such checks in the *rescue* mode where your filesystems are not mounted (for example, you cannot unmount the root partition to check because it's needed by the system all the time, whereas, for a separate home partition, it would be possible).

For the XFS file system, we use the `xfs_repair` tool, and for all others we will use the `fsck` program with the `-f` parameter (force) to check our filesystem.

It is important to note that we always need to run `fsck` instead of the specific `fsck.<file system type>` (such as `fsck.ext4`, `fsck.btrfs`), because it auto-detects the right tool for you. This is necessary because if you run the wrong specific `fsck.<file system type>` tool on the wrong filesystem (let's say running `fsck.ext4` on a btrfs filesystem), it can completely destroy it!

There's more...

So far, we have only showed you how to *check* a filesystem using `xfs_repair` and `fsck`. If some errors occur during the "checking" run on an XFS filesystem, run `xfs_repair` without the `-n` option—for example, use `xfs_repair /dev/loop0p1`. On a non-XFS partition, such as ext4, you would run `fsck` with the `-a` option (a for auto repair)—for example, `fsck -a /dev/loop0p2`. For `fsck`, if you got a lot of errors, it's best to use `-y` as well so that you do not have to confirm every error fix.

Now, let's simulate what would happen if we got a corrupted XFS filesystem using our virtual block device (*never* do this on any real disk partition!):

1. First, mount the `/dev/loop0p1` partition to your root filesystem:

```
mkdir /media/vbd-1
mount -t xfs /dev/loop0p1  /media/vbd-1
```

2. Next, create a large number of files on this mounted filesystem—for example, `2000` files:

```
for i in {1..2000}; do dd if=/dev/urandom bs=16 count=1 of=/media/vbd-1/file$i; done
```

3. Now, unmount the device and corrupt the filesystem using `dd`:

```
umount /dev/loop0p1
```

```
dd bs=512 count=10 seek=100 if=/dev/urandom of=/dev/loop0p1
```

4. Now, run a filesystem check:

```
xfs_repair -n /dev/loop0p1
```

5. This will most likely show you a list of corrupted files; in order to fix it, use the following line:

```
xfs_repair /dev/loop0p1
```

You can also simulate such a filesystem corruption on your ext4 virtual block device, and then repair it using `fsck -ay /dev/loop0p2`.

Extending the capacity of the filesystem

CentOS 7 uses the **Logical Volume Manager** (**LVM**) to organize the structure and available capacity of your partitions. It is a very dynamic and flexible system that can be extended or rearranged over time, and which is essential in today's most demanding and ever-changing environments. At the moment, buzzwords such as big data or cloud computing can be heard everywhere. Since massive amounts of data get produced all the time, storage requirements and disk space have to grow at the same steady pace. In this recipe, you will learn how to work with the LVM system and how to extend your physical drives, and also how to shrink and extend the capacity of your filesystems.

Getting ready

To complete this recipe, you will require a working installation of the CentOS 7 operating system with root privileges. We will use virtual block devices instead of real disk devices to show you from scratch how to set up a LVM first, and afterwards how to work with it. Please read the *Creating a virtual block device* recipe and create three 1 gigabyte virtual block devices with the GPT partition table, which will be labeled as `/dev/loop0`, `/dev/loop1`, and `/dev/loop2` in this example.

Again, feel free to use real disk devices if you feel ready for it.

How to do it...

First, we will start by creating an LVM test environment similar to the standard CentOS 7 LVM structure, which is set up during the installation of every server system:

1. First, let's log in as `root` and show information about our virtual block devices:

   ```
   lsblk -io NAME,SIZE
   ```

2. Next, create new partitions spanning the whole disk on each of the three virtual block devices (without a filesystem label):

   ```
   parted -a optimal /dev/loop0 mkpart primary  2048KiB 100%
   parted -a optimal /dev/loop1 mkpart primary  2048KiB 100%
   parted -a optimal /dev/loop2 mkpart primary  2048KiB 100%
   ```

3. Now, let's create LVM *physical volumes* on each of the loop devices (type `yes` to remove the `gpt` label):

   ```
   pvcreate /dev/loop0p1
   pvcreate /dev/loop1p1
   pvcreate /dev/loop2p1
   ```

4. Next, show information about our physical volumes:

   ```
   pvdisplay
   ```

5. Next, we will create a new LVM volume group on our first physical volume:

   ```
   vgcreate myVG1 /dev/loop0p1
   ```

6. Now, show information about the created group:

   ```
   vgdisplay myVG1
   ```

7. Afterwards, let's create some logical volumes on our first volume group, which will be treated as virtual partitions in our Linux system:

   ```
   lvcreate -L 10m  -n swap myVG1
   lvcreate -L 100m -n home myVG1
   lvcreate -L 400m -n root myVG1
   ```

8. Next, show information about the logical volumes:

   ```
   lvdisplay myVG1
   ```

9. Now, display how much free space our underlying volume group has left, which becomes important if you want to expand some logical volumes (see the section `Free  PE / Size` in the output):

   ```
   vgdisplay myVG1
   ```

10. Afterwards, let's create the filesystems on those new logical volumes:

```
mkswap /dev/myVG1/swap
mkfs.xfs /dev/myVG1/home
mkfs.xfs /dev/myVG1/root
```

11. Now, after we have created our test LVM system (which is very similar to the real CentOS LVM standard layout, but with smaller sizes), let's start working with it.

12. First, let's shrink the root partition, which is currently 400 megabytes (M) in size, by 200 megabytes, and afterwards, let's increase the home partition by 500 megabytes (confirm the possible data loss):

```
lvresize -L -200m /dev/myVG1/root
lvresize -L +500m /dev/myVG1/home
```

13. Use vgdisplay myVG1 again to see how the volume group's free space changes by running the previous commands (see Free   PE / Size).

14. Now, let's expand the XFS filesystem on the grown logical volume:

```
mkdir /media/home-test;mount /dev/myVG1/home /media/home-test
xfs_growfs /dev/myVG1/home
```

 It is very important not to use resize2fs for growing XFS filesystems, because it's incompatible and can corrupt them.

15. Now, let's say that after some time your data has grown again, and you need the home partition to be 1.5 gigabytes (G), but you only have 184.00 MiB left on the underlying volume group. First, we need to add our two prepared physical volumes from the beginning of this recipe to our volume group:

```
vgextend myVG1 /dev/loop1p1 /dev/loop2p1
vgdisplay myVG1
```

16. Afterwards, we have enough free space in our volume group (see Free   PE / Size) to expand our home logical volume (the volume must stay mounted):

```
lvresize -L +1500m /dev/myVG1/home
xfs_growfs /dev/myVG1/home
```

How it works...

Here, in this recipe, we have shown you how to work with the LVM for XFS partitions. It has been developed with the purpose of managing disk space on several hard disks dynamically. You can easily merge many physical hard disks together to make them appear as a single virtual hard disk to the system. This makes it a flexible and very scalable system in comparison to working with plain old static partitions. Traditional partitions are bound to, and cannot grow over, the total disk capacity they reside on, and their static partition layout cannot be changed easily. Also, we have introduced some important LVM technical terms that provide different abstraction layers to a hard disk, and which will be explained in this section so as to understand the concepts behind it: **physical volume (pv)**, **volume group (vg)**, and **logical volume (lv)**.

So, what did we learn from this experience?

We started this recipe by creating three virtual block devices of 1 gigabyte (G) each and then one partition spanning the whole device on each of them. Afterwards, we defined these single-partition devices as physical volumes (pv) using the `pvcreate` command. A pv is an LVM term that defines a storage unit in the LVM world. It must be defined on a partition, full drive, or loop device. A pv is just an abstraction of all the space available in the surrounding partition so that we can work with it on an LVM basis. Next, we created a volume group (vg) with the `vgcreate` command, where we also had to define a volume group name of our choice and put the first pv in it as a basic storage volume. As you can see, a vg is a container for at least one pv (we add more pv's later). Adding or removing pv's to or from a vg is the heart of the whole scalability concept of the LVM system. The pv's don't have to be all the same size, and it is possible to grow your vg over time by adding dozens of new physical drives all defined as pv. You can have more than one vg on your system, and you can identify them by the unique names you are giving to them. So, in summary, to extend the space of your vg, you have to create pv's out of physical drives, which you can then add to.

Finally, we created logical volumes (lv) on our vg, which can be seen and used like real physical partitions within a vg. Here, we created three lv's using the `lvcreate` command, by which we need to define the name of the vg (remember, there can be more than one vg on your system) that we want to put our target lv on, along with the size of the volume, as well as a name for it as the last parameter. You can add multiple lvs into a vg and you don't need to use the whole allocated space from the underlying free space of the vg. You can be very flexible with it. The best part is that your decision about your volumes' size and layout doesn't have to be fixed for all time; you can change them anytime later. It is a very dynamic system that can be extended and shrunk, deleted and created, without having to unmount the volume beforehand. But you have to remember that all lvs are bound to a vg, and it is not possible to create them without it or outside its spacial boundaries. If you need to extend an lv's space over the borders of the underlying vg, you have to extend the vg, as show in this recipe.

As you may have seen, for every LVM term, there is a "display" and "create" command, so it's easy to remember: `pvdisplay`, `vgdisplay`, `lvdisplay`, `pvcreate`, `vgcreate`, `lvcreate`.

After you have successfully created your lv's, you can work with them as you would with every other block device partition on your system. The only difference is that they reside in special device folders: `/dev/<vg name>/<lv name>` or `/dev/mapper/<vg name>/<lv name>`. For example, the home volume created in this example has the name `/dev/myVG1/home`. Finally, in order to use them as normal mount points, we created some test filesystems on them.

In the second part of this recipe, we showed you how to extend our vg and how to shrink and expand our lv's test system.

We started by using the `vgdisplay myVG1` command to show the currently available space on the vg. In the command output, we saw that our current volume group has a total of `996M` (VG Size), the allocated size from our lv's (swap, home, root) is `512M` (Alloc PE / Size), and the free size is `484M` (Free PE /Size). Next, we used the `lvresize` command to shrink and expand the logical volume's root and home. The `-L` parameter sets the new size of the volume, and with the + or - sign, the value is added to or subtracted from the actual size of the logical volume. Without it, the value is taken as an absolute one. Remember that we could only increase the home partition because the current volume layout does not occupy the complete vg's total space. After resizing, if we use the `vgdisplay` command again, we see that we now occupy more space in the vg; its free size has been decreased to `184M`. Since we expanded the `home` volume from `100M` to `500M` in total, we need to remember to expand its XFS filesystem too, since expanding a volume does not automatically expand its filesystem. Therefore, `400M` of the current volume are unallocated without any filesystem information. We used the command, `xfs_growfs`, which will, without defining a limit parameter, use the complete unallocated area for the XFS filesystem. If you want to resize any other filesystem type, such as ext4, you would use the `resize2fs` command instead.

Finally, we wanted to grow the home volume by `1.5G`, but we only have `184M` left on our vg to expand. This is where LVM really *shines*, because we can just add some more physical volumes to it (in the real world, you would just install new hard disks in your server and use them as pvs). We showed you how to *extend* the capacity of your vg by adding two 1G-sized pvs to it using the `vgextend` command. Afterwards, we used `vgdisplay` to see that our vg has now grown to 3G in total size, so finally we could extend our home lv as it would now fit into it. As a last step, we expanded the XFS file system once again to fill up the whole 2G home volume size.

Please remember, all the time, that if you use vg's with several physical hard disks, your data will be distributed among these. An LVM is not a RAID system and has no redundancy, so if one hard disk fails, your complete vg will fail too and your data will be lost! In order to deal with this problem, a proposed solution could be to use a physical RAID system for your hard disks and create an LVM on top of that.

6
Providing Security

In this chapter, we will cover the following topics:

- ▶ Locking down remote access and hardening SSH
- ▶ Installing and configuring fail2ban
- ▶ Working with a firewall
- ▶ Forging the firewall rules by example
- ▶ Generating self-signed certificates
- ▶ Using secure alternatives to FTP

Introduction

This chapter is a collection of recipes that provides a solid framework on which a server can be made secure in almost any environment. Security is the cornerstone of a good administrator, and this chapter illustrates how quickly and easily you can design and implement a series of checkpoints that will deliver the protection you need.

Locking down remote access and hardening SSH

In this recipe, we will learn how to provide additional security measures in order to harden the secure shell environment. The **Secure Shell (SSH)** is the basic toolkit that provides remote access to your server. The actual distance to the remote machine is negligible, but the shell environment enables you to perform maintenance, upgrades, the installation of packages and file transfers; you can also facilitate whatever action you need to carry out as the administrator in a secure environment. It is an important tool; as the gateway to your system, it is the purpose of this recipe to show you how to perform a few rudimentary configuration changes that will serve to protect your server from unwanted guests.

Getting ready

To complete this recipe, you will require a minimal installation of the CentOS 7 operating system with root privileges, a console-based text editor of your choice, and a connection to the Internet in order to download additional packages. It is assumed that your server already maintains at least one non-root-based administration account that can use the new features provided by this recipe.

How to do it...

The role of SSH will be vital if you are forced to administer your server from a remote location, and for this reason it is essential that a few basic steps are provided to keep it safe:

1. To begin, log in as `root` and create a backup of the original configuration file by typing the following command:

    `cp /etc/ssh/sshd_config /etc/ssh/sshd_config.bak`

2. Now, open the main `sshd` configuration file by typing the following:

    `vi /etc/ssh/sshd_config`

3. We shall begin by adjusting the time allowed to complete the login process, so scroll down and find the line that reads:

    `#LoginGraceTime 2m`

4. Uncomment this line and change its value to something more appropriate such as:

    `LoginGraceTime 30`

5. Now, scroll down a couple of more lines and find the line that reads as follows:

   `#PermitRootLogin yes`

6. Change this to the following:

   `PermitRootLogin no`

7. Find the following line:

   `X11Forwarding yes`

8. And change it to the following:

   `X11Forwarding no`

9. Save and close the file before restarting the SSH service, as shown here:

   `systemctl restart sshd`

10. At this stage, you may want to consider creating a new SSH session using the new settings before exiting the current session. This is to ensure that everything is working correctly and to avoid locking yourself out of the server accidentally. If you have difficulty starting a new SSH session, then simply return to the original session window and make the necessary adjustments (followed by a restart of the SSH service). However, if no difficulties have been encountered and you are on a successful secondary login, you may close the original shell environment by typing `exit`.

 Remember, having followed this recipe you should now find that root access to the shell is denied and you must log in using a standard user account. Any further work requiring root privilege will require the `su` or `sudo` command, depending on your preferences.

How it works...

SSH is a vital service that enables you to access your server remotely. A server administrator cannot work without it. In this recipe, you were shown how to make that service a little more secure.

So, what did we learn from this experience?

We began the recipe by creating a backup copy of our original main `sshd` configuration file. The next step was to open and edit it. The configuration file for SSH maintains a long list of settings that is ideal for most internal needs, but for a server in a production environment it is often advised that the default SSH configuration file will need changing to suit your particular needs. In this respect, the first step was to make a recommended change to the login grace time, `LoginGraceTime 30`. Instead of the default two minutes, the preceding value will allow only up to 30 seconds. This is the period of time where a user may be connected but will have not begun the authentication process; the lower the number, the fewer unauthenticated connections are kept open. Following this, we then removed the ability of a remote user to log in as the root user by using the `PermitRootLogin no` directive. In most cases, this is a must and a remote server should not allow a direct root login unless the server is in a controlled environment. The main reason behind this is to reduce the risk of getting hacked. The first thing every SSH hacker tries to crack is the password for the user root. If you disallow root login, an attacker needs to guess the user name as well, which is far more complex. The next setting simply disabled `X11Forwarding`. In situations like these, it is often a good idea to apply the phrase "if you do not use it, disable it". To complete the recipe, you were required to restart the SSH server in order to allow the changes to take immediate effect and start a new SSH session with the intention of making sure that the modifications did indeed work as expected. No system is ever safe, but having done this you can now relax, safe in the knowledge of having made the SSH server a little bit safer.

There's more...

There are a few more topics to cover to make your SSH server even more secure: we should change the SSH port number and show you how to limit SSH access to specific system users.

Changing the SSH port number of your server

Port 22 is the default port used by all SSH servers, and changing the port number used can go a small way to increase the overall security of your server. Again, open the main SSH daemon configuration file, `sshd_config`. Now, scroll down and locate the following line that reads:

```
#Port 22
```

Remove the leading # character (uncomment) and change the port number to another value by replacing XXXX with an appropriate port number:

```
Port XXXX
```

You must ensure that the new port number is not already in use, and when complete, save the file and close it. It is important to remember that any changes made here are reflected in your firewall configuration. So, we need to open the new port in firewalld as well. Set the new port via the environment variable NEWPORT (replace XXXX with your new SSH port), then execute the following sed command to change the SSH firewalld service file and reload the firewalld daemon afterwards (for details, read the firewall recipe in this chapter):

```
NEWPORT=XXXX
```

```
sed "s/port=\"22\"/port=\"$NEWPORT\"/g" /usr/lib/firewalld/services/
ssh.xml > /etc/firewalld/services/ssh.xml firewall-cmd --reload
```

Also, we have to tell SELinux (see *Chapter 14, Working with SELinux* to learn more about it) about the port change because it is restricted to port 22 by default. Make sure that the SELinux tools have been installed, then create a security label for our custom port, replacing XXXX with your changed port number:

```
yum install -y policycoreutils-python semanage port -a -t ssh_port_t -p
tcp XXXX
```

Finally restart the sshd service to apply our port change.

Limiting SSH access by user or group

By default, all valid users on the system are allowed to log in and enjoy the benefit of SSH. However, a more secure policy is to only allow a predetermined list of users or groups to log in. When henry, james, and helen represent valid SSH users on the system, in the sshd_config add this line to read as follows:

```
AllowUsers henry james helen
```

Alternatively, you can use the following method to enable any user that is a member of a valid administration group to log in. When admin represents a valid SSH group on the system, add this line to read as follows:

```
AllowGroups admin
```

When you have finished, save and close the file before restarting the SSH service.

Installing and configuring fail2ban

In this recipe, we will learn how to implement additional security measures for protecting the SSH server with a package called fail2ban. This is a tool that serves to protect a variety of services including SSH, FTP, SMTP, Apache, and many more against unwanted visitors. It works by reading log files for patterns based on failed login attempts and deals with the offending IP addresses accordingly. Of course, you may have already hardened your SSH server or another service on a direct application level, but it is the purpose of this recipe to show that, when faced with the possibility of Brute Force Attacks, an added layer of protection is always useful.

Getting ready

To complete this recipe, you will require a working installation of the CentOS 7 operating system with root privileges, a console-based text editor of your choice, and a connection to the Internet in order to download additional packages. In addition to this, it will be assumed that YUM is already configured to download packages from the EPEL repository (see *Chapter 4, Managing Packages with YUM*).

How to do it...

Fail2ban is not installed by default, and for this reason we will need to invoke the YUM package manager and download the necessary packages:

1. To begin this recipe, log in as `root` and type the following command:

   ```
   yum install fail2ban-firewalld fail2ban-systemd
   ```

2. Create a new configuration file in your favorite text editor, like so:

   ```
   vi  /etc/fail2ban/jail.local
   ```

3. Put in the following content:

   ```
   [DEFAULT]
   findtime = 900
   [sshd]
   enabled = true
   ```

4. Now, append the following line that defines the ban period. It is calculated in seconds, so adjust the time period to reflect a more suitable value. In this case, we have chosen this to be one hour:

   ```
   bantime  = 3600
   ```

5. Then, append the maximum number of login attempts:

   ```
   maxretry = 5
   ```

6. If you are running SSH over a custom port other than 22, you need to tell this to `fail2ban` as well (replace XXXX with your port number of choice) otherwise skip this step:

   ```
   port=XXXX
   ```

7. Now, save and close the file in the usual way before proceeding to enable the `fail2ban` service at boot. To do this, type the following command:

   ```
   systemctl enable fail2ban
   ```

8. To complete this recipe, you should now start the service by typing:

   ```
   systemctl start fail2ban
   ```

How it works...

`fail2ban` is designed to monitor users who repeatedly fail to log in correctly on your server, and its main purpose is to mitigate attacks designed to crack passwords and steal user credentials. It works by continuously reading your system's log files, and if this contains a pattern indicating a number of failed attempts, then it will proceed to act against the offending IP address. We all know that servers do not exist in isolation, and by using this tool, within a few minutes, the server will be running with an additional blanket of protection.

So, what did we learn from this experience?

`fail2ban` is not available from the standard CentOS repositories, and for this reason your server will need to have access to the EPEL repository. The installation of the `fail2ban` packages was very simple; besides the main `fail2ban` package, we installed two other packages to integrate it into CentOS 7's new `systemd` and firewalld server technologies. Next, for our local customization, we created a new `jail.local` file. We started specifying the `findtime` parameter for all targets (specified within the `[DEFAULT]` section), which is the amount of time a user has when attempting to log in. This value is measured in seconds and implies that, if a user fails to log in within the maximum number of attempts during the designated period, then they are banned. Next, we enabled `fail2ban` for the `sshd` daemon by adding a `[sshd]` section. In this section, we introduced the `bantime` value, which represents the total number of seconds that a host will be blocked from accessing the server if they are found to be in violation of the rules. Based on this, you were then asked to determine the maximum number of login attempts before blocking. Also, if you have changed your service's standard listening port, you have to define the custom port using the `port` directive. To test your settings, try to authenticate a user using SSH and provide a wrong password five times. On the sixth occasion, you should not be able to get back to the login prompt for one hour!

Protecting the `sshd` service from Brute Force Attacks is just the first step to get you started, and there is much more to learn with `failban`. To troubleshoot the service, please look at its log file at `/var/log/fail2ban.log`. To get some ideas about what can be done with it, open the following example `failban` config file: `less /etc/fail2ban/jail.conf`.

Working with a firewall

A firewall is a program that monitors and controls your system's network interfaces' incoming and outgoing network traffic, and can restrict the transmission to only useful and non-harmful data into and out of a computer system or network. By default, CentOS is made available with an extremely powerful firewall, built right into the kernel, called **netfilter**. While, in older versions of CentOS, we used the famous iptables application to control it, in version 7, the new standard netfilter management program has changed to a service called `firewalld`, which is already installed and enabled on every CentOS 7 server by default.

It is a very powerful service to take full control over your server's firewall security, and is much easier to work with than iptables. Its main advantages are that it features a better structured and more logical approach to managing and configuring every aspect of a modern firewall solution. Therefore, it will be the foundation of your server's security, and for this reason it is the purpose of this recipe to get you started on the fundamentals of firewalld quickly.

Getting ready

To complete this recipe, you will require a minimal installation of the CentOS 7 operating system with root privileges and a console-based text editor of your choice.

How to do it...

As the `firewalld` service is running on every CentOS 7 server by default, we can start directly working with the service by logging in to your server using the `root` user.

1. Type the following commands to query zone-related information:

```
firewall-cmd --get-zones | tr " " "\n"
firewall-cmd --list-all-zones
firewall-cmd --get-default-zone
firewall-cmd --list-all
```

2. We can switch to a different firewall `default` zone by using the following line:

```
firewall-cmd --set-default-zone=internal
```

3. Add a network interface to a `zone` temporarily:

```
firewall-cmd --zone=work --add-interface=enp0s8
```

4. Now, add a service to a `zone` temporarily:

```
firewall-cmd --zone=work --add-service=ftp
```

5. Test if adding the interface and service has been successful:

```
firewall-cmd --zone=work --list-all
```

6. Now, add the service permanently:

```
firewall-cmd --permanent --zone=work --add-service=ftp
firewall-cmd --reload
firewall-cmd --zone=work --list-all
```

7. Finally, let's create a new firewall zone by opening the following file:

```
vi /etc/firewalld/zones/seccon.xml
```

8. Now put in the following content:

```xml
<?xml version="1.0" encoding="utf-8"?>
<zone>
  <short>security-congress</short>
  <description>For use at the security congress. </description>
  <service name="ssh"/>
</zone>
```

9. Save and close, then reload the `firewall` config so that we can see the new zone:

   `firewall-cmd --reload`

10. Finally, check that the new zone is available:

    `firewall-cmd --get-zones`

How it works...

In comparison to iptables, the new firewalld system hides away the creation of sophisticated networking rules and has a very easy syntax that is less error-prone. It can dynamically reload netfilter settings at runtime without having to restart the complete service and we can have more than one firewall configuration set per system, which makes it great for working in changing network environments, such as for mobile devices like laptops. In this recipe, we have given you an introduction to the two fundamental building blocks of firewalld: the **zone** and the **service**.

So, what did we learn from this experience?

We started this recipe using `firewall-cmd` to get information about available firewall zones on the system. Firewalld introduces the new concept of network or firewall zones, which assigns different levels of trust to your server's network interfaces and their associated connections. In CentOS 7, there already exist a number of predefined firewalld zones, and all of these (for example, `private`, `home`, `public`, and so on, with the exception of the `trusted` zone) will block any form of incoming network connection to the server unless they are explicitly allowed using special rules attached to the zone (these rules are called firewalld services, which we will see later). We queried zone information using `firewall-cmd` with `--get-zones` or (more detailed) with the `--list-all-zones` parameter. Each of these zones acts as a complete and full firewall that you can use, depending on your system's environment and location. For example, as the name implies, the `home` zone is for use if your computer is located in home areas. If this is selected, you mostly trust all other computers and services on the networks to not harm your computer, whereas the public zone is more for use in public areas such as public access points and so on. Here, you do not trust the other computers and services on the network to not harm you. On CentOS 7, the standard `default` zone configuration set after installation is the `public` zone, which we displayed using the command's `--get-default-zone` parameter, and in more detail using `--list-all`.

Simply put, firewalld zones are all about controlling incoming connections to the server. Limiting outgoing connections with firewalld is also possible but is outside the scope of this book.

Also, to get more technical information about all currently available zones, we used the firewall client's `--list-all-zones` parameter. In the command's output, you will notice that a zone can have some associated networking interfaces and a list of services belonging to it, which are special firewall rules applied to incoming network connections. You may also notice that, while listing details of all zones and their associated services by default, all firewalld zones are very restrictive and barely allow anything to connect to the server at all. Also, another very important concept can be seen in the command's output from the above. Our `public` zone is marked as `default` and `active`. While the `active` zone is the one that is directly associated with a network interface, the `default` zone can really get important if you have multiple network adapters available. Here, it acts as a standard minimum firewall protection and fallback strategy, in case you missed to assign some active zone for every interface. For systems with only one network interface setting, the `default` zone will set the `active` zone automatically as well. To set a `default` zone, we used the `--set-default-zone` parameter and, to mark a zone as active for an interface, we used `--add-interface`. Please note that, if you don't specify the `--zone` parameter, most `firewall-cmd` commands will use the `default` zone to apply settings. Firewalld is listening on every network interface in your system, and waiting for new network packets to arrive. In summary we can say that if there is a new packet coming into a specific interface, the next thing firewalld has to do is find out which zone is the correct one associated with our network interface (using its active or if not available its default configuration); after finding it, it will apply all the service rules against the network packets belonging to it.

Next, we showed you how to work with firewalld services. Simply put, firewalld services are rules that open and allow a certain connection within our firewall to our server. Using such service file definitions allows the reusability of the containing rules because they can be added or removed to any zone. Also, using the predefined firewalld services already available in your system, as opposed to manually finding out and opening protocols, ports, or port ranges using a complicated iptables syntax for your system services of interest, can make your administrative life much easier. We added the `ftp` service to the `work` zone by invoking `--add-service`. Afterwards, we printed out details of the work zone using `--list-all`. Firewalld is designed to have a separated runtime and permanent configuration. While any change to the runtime configuration has immediate effect but will be gone, the permanent configuration will survive reload or restart of the firewalld service. Some commands such as switching the default zone are writing the changes into both configurations which mean they are immediately applied at runtime and are persistent over service restart. Other configuration settings such as adding a service to a zone are only writing to the runtime configuration. If you restart firewalld, reload its configuration, or reboot your computer, these temporary changes will be lost. To make those temporary changes permanent, we can use the `--permanent` flag with the `firewall-cmd` program call to write it to the permanent configuration file as well.

Other than with the runtime options, here the changes are not effective immediately, but only after a service restart/reload or system reboot. Therefore, the most common approach to apply permanent settings for such runtime-only commands is to first apply the setting with the `--permanent` parameter, and afterwards reload the firewall's configuration file to actually activate them.

Finally, we showed you how to create your own zone, which is just a XML file you have to create in the `/etc/firewalld/zones/` directory, and where we specified a name, description, and all the services that you want to activate. If you change something in any firewall configuration file, don't forget to reload the firewall config afterwards.

To finish this recipe, we will revert our permanent changes made to the `work` zone and reload firewalld to reset all the non-permanent changes we applied in this recipe:

```
firewall-cmd --permanent --zone=work --remove-service=ftp
firewall-cmd --reload
```

There's more...

To troubleshoot blocking services, instead of turning off the firewall completely, you should just switch `zone` to `trusted`, which will open all the incoming ports to the firewall:

```
firewall-cmd --set-default-zone=trusted
```

Once you have finished your tests, just switch back to the zone that you were in before, for example:

```
firewall-cmd --set-default-zone=public
```

Forging the firewall rules by example

In this recipe, we want to show you how to create your own firewalld service definitions or how to change existing ones, which any CentOS 7 system administrator should know if the predefined service files don't fit your system's need.

Getting ready

To complete this recipe, you will require a minimal installation of the CentOS 7 operating system with `root` privileges and a console-based text editor of your choice. We will be changing the SSH service's port number in firewalld, so make sure that you have configured the new port as shown in the recipe *Locking down remote access and hardening SSH*. Here, in our example, we have changed the port to `2223`. Also, we will create a new firewalld service for a small Python-based web server that we will use to demonstrate the integration of new system service's into firewalld. It's advantageous to grasp the basics of firewalld by working through the *Working with a firewall* recipe before starting here.

How to do it...

Here in this recipe, we will show you how to change and how to create new firewalld service definitions. In this recipe, it is considered that we are in the default public zone.

To change an existing firewalld service (ssh)

1. First, log in as `root` and copy the `ssh` service to the right place to edit it:

   ```
   cp /usr/lib/firewalld/services/ssh.xml /etc/firewalld/services
   ```

2. Next, open the `ssh` service definition file:

   ```
   vi /etc/firewalld/services/ssh.xml
   ```

3. Change the port from `22` to `2223`, then save the file and close it:

   ```
   <port protocol="tcp" port="2223"/>
   ```

4. Finally, reload the firewall:

   ```
   firewall-cmd --reload
   ```

To create your own new service

Perform the following steps to create your own new service:

1. Open a new file:

   ```
   vi /etc/firewalld/services/python-webserver.xml
   ```

2. Put in the following service definition:

   ```
   <?xml version="1.0" encoding="utf-8"?>
   <service>
     <short>Python Webserver</short>
     <description>For pythons webservers</description>
     <port port="8000" protocol="tcp"/>
   </service>
   ```

3. Save and close the file, and then finally reload the firewall:

   ```
   firewall-cmd --reload
   ```

4. Now, add this new service to our `default` zone:

   ```
   firewall-cmd --add-service=python-webserver
   ```

5. Afterwards, run the following command to start a simple Python web server in the foreground on port `8000` (press the key combination *Ctrl + C* to stop it):

   ```
   python -m SimpleHTTPServer 8000
   ```

6. Congratulations! Your new web server sitting at port `8000` can now be reached from other computers in your network:

```
http://<ip address of your computer>:8000/
```

How it works...

Here in this recipe, we have shown how easy it is to customize or define new firewalld services if the predefined needs to be changed, or for new system services that are not defined at all. Service definition files are simple XML files where you define rules for a given system service or program. There are two distinct directories where our firewalld service files live: `/usr/lib/firewalld/services` for all predefined services available from the system installation, and `/etc/firewalld/services` for all custom and user-created services.

So, what did we learn from this experience?

We started this recipe by making a working copy of the SSH firewalld service file in the right place at `/etc/firewalld/services`. We could just copy the original file because all files in this directory will overload the default configuration files from `/usr/lib/firewalld/services`. In the next step, we then modified it by opening it and changing the default port from `22` to `2223`. We have to do this every time we change a system's service standard listening port to make the firewall aware that it should allow network traffic to flow through the changed port. As you can see when opening this file, service files are simple XML text files with some mandatory and some optional tags and attributes. They contain a list of one or more ports and protocols that defines exactly what firewalld should enable if the service is connected to a zone. There can be another important setting in the XML file: helper modules. For example, if you open the SAMBA service file at `/usr/lib/firewalld/services/samba.xml`, you will see the tag, `<module name="nf_conntrack_netbios_ns"/>`. These are special kernel netfilter helper modules that can be dynamically loaded into the underlying kernel-based firewall, and which are needed for some system services, such as Samba or FTP, which create dynamic connections on temporary TCP or UDP ports instead of using static ports. After reloading the firewall configuration, we should now be able to test the connection from another computer in our network using the altered port.

In the second part of this recipe, we created a brand-new service file for a new system service, which is a simple Python web server listening on port 8000 displaying a simple directory content listing. Therefore, we created a simple XML service file for the Python web server including the right port 8000, restarted the firewall, and afterwards added this new service to our default public zone so that we can actually open connections through this service. You should now be able to browse to our web server's start page using another computer in the same network. However, as we did not use the `--permanent` flag, if you restart the firewalld daemon, the `python-webserver` service will be gone from the `public` zone (or you can also use the parameter, `--remove-service=python-webserver`).

In summary, we can say that the recommended firewall choice in CentOS 7 is firewalld, as all important system services have already been set up to use it via predefined service rules. You should remember that Linux firewalls are a very complex topic that can easily fill up a whole book, and you can do a lot more with the `firewall-cmd` that cannot be covered here in this book.

There's more...

Often, you just want to quickly open a specific port to test out things before writing your own custom-made service definition. In order to do this, you can use the following command line, which will open port `2888` using the tcp protocol temporarily on the `default` zone:

```
firewall-cmd --add-port=2888/tcp
```

Once you have finished your tests, just reload the firewall configuration to remove and close the specific port again.

Generating self-signed certificates

In this recipe, we will learn how to create self-signed **Secure Sockets Layer** (**SSL**) certificates using the OpenSSL toolkit. SSL is a technology used to encrypt messages between two ends of a communication (for example, a server and client) so that a third-party cannot read the messages sent between them. Certificates are not used for encrypting the data, but they are very important in this communication process to ensure that the party you are communicating with is exactly the one you suppose it to be. Without them, impersonation attacks would be much more common.

Getting ready

To complete this recipe, you will require a working installation of the CentOS 7 operating system with root privileges and a console-based text editor of your choice.

Generally speaking, if you are intending to use an SSL Certificate on a production server, you will probably want to purchase a SSL Certificate from a trusted Certificate Authority. There are many options open to you regarding what certificate best suits your requirements and your budget, but for the purpose of this recipe we will confine our discussion to a self-signed certificate that is more than adequate for any development server or internal network.

How to do it...

1. To begin, log in as `root` and go to the following directory so that we can use the Makefile to generate our intended certificates and keyfiles:

    `cd /etc/pki/tls/certs`

2. Now, to create a self-signed certificate with an embedded public key (both in the file, `server.crt`) along with its private key for the server (with the filename as `server.key`), type the following:

    `make server.crt`

3. You will then be asked for a password and will receive a series of questions, to which you should respond with the appropriate values. Complete all the required details by paying special attention to the common name value, which should reflect the domain name of the server or IP address that you are going to use this certificate for. For example, you may type:

    `mylocaldomainname.home`

4. To create a `pem` file that includes a self-signed certificate and a public and a private key in one file, and is valid for five years, type the following:

    `make server.pem DAYS=1825`

5. Now, let's create a key pair (a private key and self-signed certificate that includes the public key) for an Apache web server that we will need for enabling `https`, and which will be generated in `/etc/pki/tls/private/localhost.key` and `/etc/pki/tls/certs/localhost.crt` (use a secure password and repeat it in the second command):

    `make testcert`

6. To create a **Certificate Signing Request** (**CSR**) file instead of a self-signed certificate, use this:

    `make server.csr`

How it works...

Here in this recipe, we introduced you to the SSL technology that uses **public key cryptography (PKI)** (where two forms of keys exist: public and private). On the server, we store the private key and our clients get a public key. Every message sent from one end to the other is encrypted by the key belonging to one side and can only be decrypted by the corresponding key from the other. For example, a message encrypted with the server's private key can only be decrypted and read by the client's public key and vice versa. The public key is sent to the client through a certificate file, where it is part of the file. As said before, the public key is encrypting and decrypting the data and the certificate is not responsible for this, but rather for identifying a server against a client and making sure that you are actually connected to the same server you are trying to connect. If you want to set up secure services using SSL encryption in protocols such as FTPS, HTTPS, POP3S, IMAPS, LDAPS, SMTPS, and so on, you need a signed server certificate to work with. If you want to use these services for your business, and you want them to be trusted by the people who are using and working with them, for example, on the public Internet, your certificate should be signed from a official **certification authority (CA)**. Certificate prices are paid by subscription and can be very expensive. If you don't plan to offer your certificate or SSL-enabled services to a public audience, or you want to offer them only within a company's intranet or just want to test out things before buying, here you can also sign the certificate by yourselves (self-signed) with the OpenSSL toolkit.

> The only difference between a self-signed certificate and one coming from an official CA is that most programs using the certificate for communication will give you a warning that it does not know about the CA and that you should not trust it. After confirming the security risk, you can work with the service normally.

So, what did we learn from this experience?

We started this recipe by going to the standard location where all the system's certificates can be found in CentOS 7: `/etc/pki/tls/certs`. Here, we can find a Makefile, which is a helper script for conveniently generating public/private key pairs, SSL CSRs, and self-signed SSL test certificates. It works by hiding away from you complicated command line parameters for the OpenSSL program. It is very easy to use and will automatically recognize your target through the file extension of your file name parameter. So, it was a simple process to generate an SSL key pair by providing an output filename with the `.crt` extension. As said before, you will be asked for a password and a list of questions regarding the ownership of the certificate, with the most important question being the common name. This should reflect the domain name of the server you are planning to use this certificate for, because most programs, such as web browsers or email clients, will check the domain names to see if they are valid. The result of running this command was the certificate with its embedded public key in file `server.crt`, as well as the corresponding private key for the server called `server.key`.

Next, we created a `.pem` file and provided a `DAYS` parameter to make the certificate valid for five years instead of the default one year when you are running without it. A `pem` file is a container file that contains both parts of the key pair: the private keys and the self-signed certificate (with its embedded public key). This file format is sometimes required by some programs, such as `vsftpd`, to enable SSL encryption instead of providing the key-pair in two separated files. Next, we ran the Makefile target `testcert`, which generates a private key as well as public key, plus the certificate in the correct location, where the Apache web server is expecting them for setting up HTTPS. Please note that, if you need to repeat any Makefile run later, you need to delete the generated output files; for example, for Apache, you need to delete the following files before you can build the output files again:

```
rm /etc/pki/tls/certs/localhost.crt /etc/pki/tls/private/localhost.key
make testcert
```

Finally, we showed you how to generate a CSR file, which will be needed if you plan to purchase an SSL certificate from a trusted certificate authority.

There's more...

We did not cover all the possibilities that the Makefile script has to offer to generate certificates. If you run the command, `make`, without giving any target parameter, the program will print out a usage help text with all possible options.

As we have learned, the public and private keys are generated in pairs, and will encrypt and decrypt each partner's messages. You can verify that your key pairs are valid and belong together by comparing the output of the following (which must be exactly the same):

```
openssl x509 -noout -modulus -in server.crt | openssl md5
openssl rsa -noout -modulus -in server.key | openssl md5
```

Using secure alternatives to FTP

While using FTP is still popular to share data or to transfer files over the network, you must be aware that you are using a very unsecure network protocol that has no protection built into it out-of-the-box. This means that, during network transfer, your data is fully exposed to potential attackers. This is not what you want for transferring sensitive data, such as login credentials, at all. To avoid these potential risks, we will show you in this recipe how to use and set up two alternatives for securing FTP using FTPS (FTP over SSL or FTP/SSL) or SFTPS (SSH-enabled FTP).

Getting ready

To complete this recipe, you will require a minimal installation of the CentOS 7 operating system with root privileges and a console-based text editor of your choice. You should already have installed and configured a basic vsftpd server (see *Chapter 12*, *Providing Web Services* for how to do it). Also, for setting up SFTP, we will need to create some self-signed certificates; if you want to know the details behind it, please read the *Generating self-signed certificates* recipe in this chapter.

How to do it...

You have to choose beforehand if you want to use SFTP or FTPS. These two methods cannot be applied together, so you have to decide which option to choose first. If you switch between those methods, you need to restore the default configuration file state of `vsftpd.conf` or `sshd_config` first.

Securing your vsftpd server with SSL–FTPS

To secure your vsftpd server with SSL-FTPS perform the following steps:

1. Log in as `root` and go to the standard certificate location:

   ```
   cd /etc/pki/tls/certs
   ```

2. Now, let's create a SSL key pair consisting of the certificate and its embedded public key, as well as the private key in one file for our `ftp-server` configuration (remember that the `Common name` value should reflect the domain name of your FTP server):

   ```
   make ftp-server.pem
   ```

3. Change to a more secure file access rule:

   ```
   chmod 400 /etc/pki/tls/certs/ftp-server.pem
   ```

4. Now, before working on it, first make a backup of the `vsftpd.conf` file.

   ```
   cp /etc/vsftpd/vsftpd.conf /etc/vsftpd/vsftpd.conf.BAK
   ```

5. Now, enable SSL and add the key pair file that we just created to our `vsftpd` configuration:

   ```
   echo "rsa_cert_file=/etc/pki/tls/certs/ftp-server.pem
   ssl_enable=YES
   force_local_data_ssl=YES
   force_local_logins_ssl=YES
   pasv_min_port=40000
   pasv_max_port=40100" >> /etc/vsftpd/vsftpd.conf
   ```

6. Next, we need to add a new firewalld service file, so open the following:

```
vi /etc/firewalld/services/ftps.xml
```

7. Put in the following content:

```
<?xml version="1.0" encoding="utf-8"?>
<service>
  <description>enable FTPS ports</description>
  <port protocol="tcp" port="40000-40100"/>
  <port protocol="tcp" port="21"/>
  <module name="nf_conntrack_ftp"/>
</service>
```

8. Finally, reload the firewall, add the `ftps` service, and restart your `vsftpd` server:

```
firewall-cmd --reload; firewall-cmd --permanent --add-service=ftps;
firewall-cmd --reload
```

```
systemctl restart vsftpd
```

Securing your vsftpd server using SSH – SFTP

To secure your vsftpd server using SSL-SFTP perform the following steps:

1. First, create a group for all valid SFTP users:

```
groupadd sshftp
```

2. We will work on the `sshd` main config file, so please make a backup before making any changes:

```
cp /etc/ssh/sshd_config  /etc/ssh/sshd_config.BAK
```

3. Now, open the `sshd_config` file, go to the line containing the `Subsystem` directive, disable it (which means putting a # sign at the beginning of the line), and add the following line to read as shown:

```
#Subsystem        sftp    /usr/libexec/openssh/sftp-server
Subsystem sftp internal-sftp
```

4. Next, add the following lines to the end of the file to enable SFTP:

```
Match Group sshftp
ChrootDirectory /home
ForceCommand internal-sftp
```

5. Finally, restart the `sshd` daemon.

```
systemctl restart sshd
```

How it works...

Here in this recipe, you have learned how to make your file sharing more secure by switching from the standard FTP protocol to using FTP over SSL, or FTP over SSH. Regardless of which option you prefer, SSL is used to encrypt the data during transmitting, which helps you keep your privacy. Which variant you choose is up to you, but remember that SFTP is a bit easier to set up as you do not have to configure additional ports or certificates in your firewall, because everything runs over SSH and this should be enabled by default on most systems.

So, what did we learn from this experience?

We began the recipe by configuring FTPS. We went into a special directory called /etc/pki/ tls/certs, where CentOS stores all its certificates. In it, there is a Makefile, which we used to create a .pem file that contains the public/private key pair and a self-signed certificate that we needed for our FTP server's configuration. Afterwards, we used chmod to ensure that only the root user can read this file. Then, we appended six lines of code to our main vsftpd configuration file (first, we made a backup of the original file); they are pretty self-explanatory: enable the SSL protocol, use the self-signed certificate, disallow any non-SSL communication, and use a static range of passive control ports. Also, we created a new firewall service that will open these passive control ports that are needed for FTPS.

Afterwards, we configured SFTP using a chroot jail. If setting up SFTP without it, every login user can view the root filesystem, which is very unsecure. Configuring SFTP is done completely in the main sshd config file. After making a backup of the original file, we changed the FTP subsystem to internal-sftp, which is a newer FTP server version, has better performance, and runs in the same process. Next, we added three lines to the vsftpd configuration file; only users in the sshftp group are using SFTP and are put into a chroot jail and can only view files up to their home directory. ForceCommand ignores all local settings by the users and enforces these rules here instead. To add new chrooted SFTP users, all you have to do is create a standard Linux user account and add them to the sshftp user group.

There's more...

If you want to test your enabled FTPS server, you need an FTP client that supports "FTP over TLS." You have to find and enable this option in your FTP client's settings. Under Linux, you can install the lftp client to test if you can connect to our FTPS server. First, install the lftp package (for example, yum install lftp). Then, configure the client using TLS:

```
echo "set ftp:ssl-auth TLS
set ftp:ssl-force true
set ftp:ssl-protect-list yes
set ftp:ssl-protect-data yes
set ftp:ssl-protect-fxp yes
set ssl:verify-certificate no" >~/.lftprc
```

Now, you can connect and test your FTPS server using the following:

```
lftp -u username <server name>
```

If you want to test your enabled SFTP server, you need the program called `sftp`:

```
sftp john@<server name or ip address> -p 22
```

 You have to remember that all the changes to `sshd_config` will be reflected in SFTP as well. So, if you disabled root login or ran SSH over a different port than `22`, you have to take it into consideration when you try to log in to SFTP.

7
Building a Network

In this chapter, we will cover the following topics:

- ▸ Printing with CUPS
- ▸ Running a DHCP server
- ▸ Using WebDAV for file sharing
- ▸ Installing and configuring NFS
- ▸ Working with NFS
- ▸ Securely sharing resources with Samba

Introduction

This chapter is a collection of recipes that covers the many facets of today's working environment. From printing and file sharing across different types of office computer systems to keeping your computers online, this chapter provides the necessary details on how quickly you can use CentOS to implement the necessary tools that will maximize efficiencies within your networking environment.

Printing with CUPS

Print servers allow local printing devices to be connected to a network and be shared among several users and departments. There are many advantages using such a system, including the lack of a need to buy dedicated printer hardware for each user, room, or department. The **Common Unix Printing System** (**CUPS**) is the de-facto standard for print servers on Linux, as well as Unix distributions including OS X. It is built with a typical client/server architecture, where clients in the network send print jobs to the centralized print server that schedules these tasks, then delegates and executes the actual printing on a printer that is locally connected to our printer server or sends the print job remotely to the computer that has the physical connection to the requested printer or to a standalone network printer. If you set up your printers within the CUPS system, almost all Linux and OS X printing application on any client in your network will be automatically configured to use them out-of-the box, without the need to install additional drivers. Here, in this recipe, we will show you how to get started with the CUPS printing server system.

Getting ready

To complete this recipe, you will require a working installation of the CentOS 7 operating system with root privileges, a console-based text editor of your choice, and a connection to the Internet in order to download additional packages. In this recipe, we will use the network interface with the IP address, 192.168.1.8, and the corresponding network address of 192.168.1.0/24 to serve the CUPS printer server to our network.

How to do it...

We begin this recipe by installing the CUPS printing server software, which is not available by default on a fresh CentOS 7 minimal system:

1. To do this, log in as `root` and install the following package:

   ```
   yum install cups
   ```

2. Next, create an SSL certificate for the CUPS server, which we will need for secure authentication to the CUPS web application (add a secure password when asked):

   ```
   cd /etc/pki/tls/certs
   make cups-server.key
   ```

3. Now, let's open the CUPS main configuration file to customize the server (backup first):

   ```
   cp /etc/cups/cupsd.conf /etc/cups/cupsd.conf.BAK
   vi /etc/cups/cupsd.conf
   ```

4. First, to make CUPS available on the entire network, find the following line: `Listen localhost:631`, than change it to:

```
Listen 631
```

5. Next, we want to configure access to all normal web pages of the web-based CUPS frontend. Search for the `<Location />` directive (don't confuse this with other directives such as `<Location /admin>`) and change the complete block by adding your network address. After changing, the complete block looks like this:

```
<Location />
 Order allow,deny
 Allow 192.168.1.0/24
</Location>
```

6. Next, set access permissions for the `/admin` and `/admin/conf` `Location` directives, granting access to the local server only:

```
<Location /admin>
    Order allow,deny
    Allow localhost
</Location>
<Location /admin/conf>
    AuthType Default
    Require user @SYSTEM
    Order allow,deny
    Allow localhost
</Location>
```

7. Finally, add our SSL certificate information to the end of the configuration file:

```
ServerCertificate /etc/pki/tls/certs/cups-server.crt
ServerKey /etc/pki/tls/certs/cups-server.key
```

8. Close and save the file, then restart the CUPS server and enable it on boot:

`systemctl restart cups.service systemctl enable cups.service`

9. Now, we have to open the CUPS server ports in firewalld so that other computers in the network can connect to it:

`firewall-cmd --permanent --add-service=ipp firewall-cmd --reload`

10. You can test the accessibility of your CUPS server from another computer in your `192.168.1.0/24` network by browsing to the following location (allow a security exception in the browser when asked):

```
https://<IP address of your CUPS server>:631
```

11. To access the administration area within the CUPS frontend, you need to be on the same server as CUPS is running (on a CentOS 7 minimal installation, please install a window manager and browser), and then use the system user, `root`, with the appropriate password to login.

How it works...

In this recipe, we showed you how easy it is to install and set up a CUPS printing server.

So, what did we learn from this experience?

We began our journey by installing the CUPS server package on our server because it is not available on the CentOS 7 system by default. Afterwards, we generated a SSL key-pair, which we will need later in the process (to learn more, read the *Generating self-signed certificates* recipe in *Chapter 6, Providing Security*). It is used to allow the encrypted submission of your login credentials to the CUPS administration web frontend (over secure HTTPS connections). Next, we opened CUPS's main configuration file, /etc/cups/cupsd.conf, with the text editor of our choice. As you may notice, the configuration format is very similar to the Apache configuration file format. We started changing the Listen address by removing the localhost name, therefore allowing all clients from everywhere in your network (192.168.1.0/24) to access our CUPS server at port 631 instead of allowing only the local interface to connect to the printer server.

> By default, the CUPS server has Browsing On enabled, which will broadcast, every 30 seconds, an updated list of all printers that are being shared in the system to all client computers on the same subnet. If you want to broadcast to other subnets as well, use the BrowseRelay directive.

Next, we configured access to the CUPS web interface. This frontend can be used to conveniently browse all available printers on the network, or even install new printers or configure them if you log in with an administrator account. As there are different tasks in the user interface, there are three different directives that can be used to fine-grain its access. Access to all normal web pages can be set using the <Location /> directive, whereas all administration pages can be managed with <Location /admin> and more specifically to change the configuration within the <Location /admin/conf> tag. In each of these Location tags, we added different Allow directives, thus granting normal CUPS web pages (such as, browsing all available network printers) from your complete network (for example, 192.168.1.0/24) while accessing the special administration pages is restricted to the server that runs the CUPS service (localhost). Remember, if this is too restrictive for your environment, you can always adjust these Allow settings. Also, there are various other Location types available, such as one that is used for activating our service in additional subnets. Please read the CUPS configuration manual using man cupsd.conf. Next, we configured SSL encryption, thus activating secure https:// addresses for the web interface. Then, we started the CUPS server for the first time and enabled it to start automatically when the server boots up. Finally, we added the ipp firewalld service, thus allowing incoming CUPS client connections to the server.

There's more...

Now that we have successfully set up and configured our CUPS server, it's time to add some printers to it and print a test page. Here, we will show you how to add *two different* types of printers to the system using the command line.

 Adding or configuring printers can also be done using the graphical web-based CUPS interface.

First, we will install a true *network* printer that is already available in the same network (in our case, the `192.168.1.0/24` network) as our CUPS server and afterwards a locally connected printer (for example, via USB to our CUPS server or any other computer in the same network).

 Why should you want to install an already connected network printer to our CUPS server? CUPS can do much more than just printing: it is a centralized printer server, thus managing scheduling and queuing of printers and their jobs, serving printers in different subnets, and providing unified printing protocols and standards for convenient access on any Linux or Mac client.

How to add a network printer to the CUPS server

To start adding a network printer to our CUPS server, we will use the command `lpinfo -v` to list all the available printing devices or drivers known to the CUPS server. Normally, the CUPS server will automatically identify all locally (USB, parallel, serial, and so on) and remotely available (network protocols such as `socket`, `http`, `ipp`, `lpd`, and so on) printers from most common printing protocols without any problems. In our example, the following network printer has been successfully identified (the output has been truncated):

```
network dnssd://Photosmart%20C5100%20series%20%5BF8B652%5D._pdl-
datastream._tcp.local/
```

Next, we will install this printer on the CUPS server to put it under its control. First, we need to look for the correct printer driver. As we can see in the last output, it is an HP Photosmart C5100 series printer. So, let's search for the driver in the list of all currently installed drivers on our CUPS server:

```
lpinfo --make-and-model HP -m | grep Photosmart
```

The list does not contain our model C5100, so we have to install an additional HP driver package using:

```
yum install hplip
```

Now, if we issue our command again, we can find the correct driver:

```
lpinfo --make-and-model HP -m | grep Photosmart | grep c5100
```

For other printer models and manufacturers, there are other driver packages available as well, for example, the `gutenprint-cups` RPM package.

The correct driver for this printer will be shown as follows:

```
drv:///hp/hpcups.drv/hp-photosmart_c5100_series.ppd
```

Now, we have everything ready to install the printer using the following syntax:

```
lpadmin -p <printer-name> -v <device-uri> -m <model> -L <location> -E
```

In our example, we installed it using:

```
lpadmin -p hp-photosmart -v "dnssd://Photosmart%20C5100%20series%20
%5BF8B652%5D._pdl-datastream._tcp.local/" -m "drv:///hp/hpcups.drv/hp-
photosmart_c5100_series.ppd" -L room123 -E
```

Now, the printer should be under our CUPS server's control and should immediately be shared and seen in the entire network from any Linux or OS X computer (on a CentOS 7 minimal client, you will first need to install the `cups` package as well and enable incoming `ipp` connections using firewalld's `ipp-client` service before any shared network printer information from our CUPS server will become available).

You can later change the configuration of this printer by opening and changing the file at `/etc/cups/printers.conf`. To actually print a test page, you should now be able to access the printer using its name, `hp-photosmart`, from any client (on a CentOS 7 minimal client, you would need to install the package `cups-client`):

```
echo "Hello printing world" | lpr -P hp-photosmart  -H 192.168.1.8:631
```

How to share a local printer to the CUPS server

If you want to share a local printer physically connected to our CUPS server, just plug in the printer to the system (for example, via USB) and follow the previous recipe, *How to add a network printer to the CUPS server*. In the step `lpinfo -v`, you should see it appear as a `usb://` address, so you need to take this address and follow the rest of the steps.

If you want to connect and share a printer on your centralized CUPS server, which is physically connected to any other computer on your CUPS network, install the `cups` daemon on this other machine (follow all the steps in the main recipe) and then install the printer driver for it as shown here in this section. This will make sure that the local CUPS daemon will make the printer available on the network, as it would be on our centralized CUPS server. Now that it is available on the network, you can easily add it to our main CUPS server to enjoy all the benefits of a centralized printing server.

Here in this recipe, we have only scratched the surface and introduced you to the basics of setting up a CUPS server for your network. There is always more to learn, and you can build very complex CUPS server systems managing hundreds of printers in the corporate environment, which is outside the scope of this recipe.

Running a DHCP server

If a connection to a network needs to be made, every computer needs a correct **Internet Protocol** (**IP**) configuration installed on their system to communicate. Assigning IP client configurations automatically from a *central point* using the **Dynamic Host Control Protocol** (**DHCP**) can make the administrator's life easier and simplify the process of adding new machines to a network in comparison to the tedious work of manually setting up static IP information on each computer system in your network. In small home-based networks, people often use DHCP servers directly installed in silico on their Internet routers, but such devices often lack advanced features and have only a basic set of configuration options available. Most of the time, this is not sufficient for bigger networks or in the corporate environment, where you are more likely to find dedicated DCHP servers for more complex scenarios and better control. In this recipe, we will show you how to install and configure a DHCP server on a CentOS 7 system.

Getting ready

To complete this recipe, you will require a working installation of the CentOS 7 operating system with root privileges, a console-based text editor of your choice, and a connection to the Internet in order to facilitate the download of additional packages. It is expected that your DHCP server will be using a static IP address; if you do not have one, refer to the recipe *Building a static network connection* in *Chapter 2, Configuring the System*. If you plan to send DNS information to the clients through DHCP as well, you should have already applied the recipe *Installing and configuring a simple nameserver* in *Chapter 8, Working with FTP*.

How to do it...

Here in this example, we will configure a DHCP server for a static network interface serving a single network with all its available IP addresses to all the computers connected directly to it (they are all in the same subnet).

1. First, log in as `root` and type the following command in order to install the DHCP server packages:

   ```
   yum install dhcp
   ```

2. In our example, we will use a network interface with the name, `ifcfg-enp5s0f1`, to serve our DHCP requests. Next, we need to collect some very important network information, which we will use later for configuring the DHCP server (change the network interface name to fit your own needs):

```
cat /etc/sysconfig/network-scripts/ifcfg-enp5s0f1
```

3. From this output, we need the following information, so please write it down (most likely, your output will be different):

```
BOOTPROTO="static"

IPADDR="192.168.1.8"

NETMASK="255.255.255.0"

GATEWAY="192.168.1.254"
```

4. We also need the subnet network address, which can be calculated using the following line:

```
ipcalc -n 192.168.1.8/24
```

5. This will print the following output (write it down for later):

```
NETWORK=192.168.1.0
```

6. Now, we will open our main DHCP configuration file, after we make a backup of the original file:

```
cp /etc/dhcp/dhcpd.conf /etc/dhcp/dhcpd.conf.BAK

vi /etc/dhcp/dhcpd.conf
```

7. Append the following lines to the end of the file, taking into account your individual network interface's configuration from the preceding steps (`routers` = `GATEWAY`, `subnet` = `NETWORK`):

```
authoriative;
default-lease-time 28800;
max-lease-time 86400;
shared-network MyNetwork {
    option domain-name              "example.com";
    option domain-name-servers      8.8.8.8, 8.8.4.4;
    option routers                  192.168.1.254;
    subnet 192.168.1.0 netmask 255.255.255.0 {
        range 192.168.1.10 192.168.1.160;
    }
}
```

8. Finally, start and enable the DHCP service:

```
systemctl start dhcpd

systemctl enable dhcpd
```

How it works...

Here in this recipe, we showed you how easy it is to set up a DHCP server for a single network. With this, every time a new machine gets added to the network, the computer gets the correct IP information automatically, which it needs in order to connect to the network without any further human action.

So, what did we learn from this experience?

We started this recipe by installing the DHCP server package because it does not come with CentOS 7 out-of-the-box. Since our DHCP daemon communicates with its clients to assign IP information over a network interface, in the next step we had to choose a network device that would be used for the service. In our example, we selected the device named enp5s0f1. By default, the DHCP server can manage all available IP addresses from the same subnet as the associated network interface. Remember that your primary DHCP server's network interface must be configured to get its own IP information statically and not through (another) DHCP server! Next, we used the cat command to print out all the interesting lines from our enp5s0f1 network interface configuration file, which we will need for configuring the DHCP server. Afterwards, we used the ipcalc tool to calculate the (subnet) network address for our DHCP server's network interface. Then, we opened the main DHCP server configuration, started configuring some *global* settings, and defined a new *shared network*. In the global settings, we first set our DHCP server to be authoritative, which means it is the only and main responsible DHCP server in the network. Next, we defined default-lease-time to 28800 seconds, which is eight hours, and the max-lease-time to 86400, which is 24 hours. The lease time is the amount of time the DHCP server "rents out" an IP address to a client before it has to sign up again on the DHCP server asking for an extension of the IP. If it is not requesting a renewal of an existing lease at that time, the IP address will be released from the client and put into the pool of free IP addresses again, ready to be served to new machines that want to connect to the network. The client can define the amount of time it wants to lease an IP address by itself. If no time frame has been supplied from the client to the DHCP server, the default lease time will be used.

All subnets that share the same physical network interface should be defined within a shared-network declaration, so we defined this area using square brackets. This is also called a scope. In our example, we only have one network, so we only need one shared-network scope. Within it, we first defined a domain-name option, which will be sent and can be used by clients as their base domain name. Next, we added the **domain name servers** (**DNS**) to our configuration. Sending DNS information to the client is not mandatory for the DHCP server but can be useful. The more information a client gets for a given network, the better, because fewer manual configuration steps have to be made.

 You can send out a lot of other useful information to the client (using DHCP) about the network he is connecting to: gateway, time, WINS, and so on.

Here in our example, we used the official Google DNS servers; if you have already set up your own DNS server (see *Chapter 8, Working with FTP*), you could also use these addresses here. Next, we specified a `routers` option, which is another useful piece of information that will be sent out to the clients as well. Afterwards, we specified the most important part of any DHCP server: the `subnet` scope. Here, we defined our network ranges for assigning IP addresses for clients. We need to provide the subnet network address, its submask, and then the starting and ending IP address range that we want to allow to clients. In our example, we allow host IP addresses from `192.168.1.10, 192.168.1.11, 192.168.1.12 ... to 192.168.1.160`. If you have more than one subnet, you can use multiple `subnet` scope directives (called a multihomed DHCP server).

Next, we started the DHCP server and enabled it on boot. Your clients should now be able to get IP addresses dynamically from our new system.

In summary, we have only showed you some very basic DHCP server configuration options to get you started, and there are many more settings available, letting you build very complex DHCP server solutions. To get a better overview of its possibilities, please have a look at the example configuration file provided with the DHCP server documentation at `less /usr/share/doc/dhcp-4*/dhcpd.conf.example`.

There's more...

In the main recipe, we configured our basic DHCP server to be able to send complete IP network information to our clients so that they should be able to join our network. To use this server, you need to enable DHCP addressing on your client's network interfaces. On CentOS clients, please do not forget to use `BOOTPROTO=dhcp` and remove all static entries such as `IPADDR` in the appropriate network-scripts `ifcfg` file (read the recipe, *Building a static network connection* in *Chapter 2, Configuring the System* to get you started on network-scripts files). Then, to make a DHCP request, restart the network using `systemctl restart network` or try to do a reboot of the client system (with the `ONBOOT=yes` option). Confirm with `ip addr list`.

Using WebDAV for file sharing

The **Web-based Distributed Authoring and Versioning (WebDAV)** open standard can be used for sharing files over the network. It is a popular protocol to conveniently access remote data as an *online hard disk*. There are a lot of online storage and e-mail providers who offer online space through WebDAV accounts. Most graphical Linux or Windows systems can access WebDAV servers in their file managers out-of-the-box. For other operating systems, there are also free options available. Another big advantage is that WebDAV is running over normal HTTP or HTTPS ports, so you can be sure that it will work in almost any environment, even behind restricted firewalls.

Here, we will show you how to install and configure WebDAV as an alternative for the FTP protocol for your file sharing needs. We will use HTTPS as our communication protocol for secure connections.

Getting ready

To complete this recipe, you will require a working installation of the CentOS 7 operating system with root privileges and a console-based text editor of your choice. You will need a working Apache web server with SSL encryption enabled and reachable in your network; see *Chapter 11, Providing Mail Services* for how to install the HTTP daemon, and especially the recipe *Setting up HTTPS with SSL*. Also, some experience working with the Apache config file format is advantageous.

How to do it...

1. Create a location for sharing your data and for a WebDAV lock file:

   ```
   mkdir -p /srv/webdav /etc/httpd/var/davlock
   ```

2. Since WebDAV is running as an Apache module over HTTPS, we have to set proper permissions to the standard `httpd` user:

   ```
   chown apache:apache /srv/webdav /etc/httpd/var/davlock
   chmod 770 /srv/webdav
   ```

3. Now, create and open the following Apache WebDAV configuration file:

   ```
   vi /etc/httpd/conf.d/webdav.conf
   ```

4. Put in the following content:

   ```
   DavLockDB "/etc/httpd/var/davlock"
   Alias /webdav /srv/webdav
   <Location /webdav>
        DAV On
        SSLRequireSSL
        Options None
        AuthType Basic
        AuthName webdav
        AuthUserFile /etc/httpd/conf/dav_passwords
        Require valid-user
   </Location>
   ```

5. Save and close the file. Now, to add a new WebDAV user named john (enter a new password for the user as prompted):

   ```
   htpasswd -c /etc/httpd/conf/dav_passwords john
   ```

6. Finally, restart the Apache2 web server:

```
systemctl restart httpd
```

7. To test if we can connect to our WebDAV server, you can use a graphical user interface (most Linux file managers support WebDAV browsing) from any client in your network, or we can mount the drive using the command line.

8. Log in on any client machine as `root` in the same network as our WebDAV server (on CentOS, you need the `davfs2` filesystem driver package to be installed from the EPEL repository, and the usage of file locks must be disabled as the current version is not capable of working with file locks), enter the password for our DAV user account named `john`, and confirm the self-signed certificate when asked:

```
yum install davfs2

echo "use_locks 0" >> /etc/davfs2/davfs2.conf

mkdir /mnt/webdav

mount -t davfs https://<WebDAV Server IP>/webdav /mnt/webdav
```

9. Now, to see if we can write to the new network storage type:

```
touch /mnt/webdav/testfile.txt
```

10. If you've got connection problems, check the firewall settings on your WebDAV server for the services `http` and `https`, as well as on your client.

How it works...

Here in this recipe, we showed you how easy it is to set up a WebDAV server for easy file sharing.

So, what did we learn from this experience?

We started our journey by creating two directories: one, where all the shared files of our WebDAV server will live, and one for creating a lock file database for the WebDAV server process. The latter is needed so that users can *block* access to documents to avoid collisions with others if files are currently modified by them. As WebDAV runs as a native Apache module (`mod_dav`) that is already enabled by default in CentOS 7, all we need to do is create a new Apache virtual host configuration file, where we can set up all our WebDAV settings. First, we have to link our WebDAV host to the full path of the lock database that is used to track user locks. Next, we defined an alias for our WebDAV sharing folder, which we then configured using a `Location` directive. This will be activated if someone is using specific HTTP methods on the `/webdav` path URL. Within this area, we specified that this URL will be a DAV-enabled share, enabled SSL encryption for it, and specified basic user-based password authentication. The user account's passwords will be stored in a user account database called `/etc/httpd/conf/dav_passwords`. To create valid accounts in this database file, we then used the Apache2 `htpasswd` utility on the command line. Finally, we restarted the service to apply our changes.

For testing, we used the davfs filesystem driver, which you need to install on CentOS 7 using the davfs2 package from the EPEL repository. There are many other options available, such as the cadaver WebDAV command-line client (also from the EPEL repository); alternatively, you can access it directly using integrated WebDAV support in a graphical user interface such as GNOME, KDE, or Xfce.

Installing and configuring NFS

The **Network File System** (**NFS**) protocol enables remote access to filesystems over a network connection. It is based on a client-server architecture, allowing a centralized server to share files with other computers. A client can attach those exported shares in their own file system to access it conveniently, as they will be located on a local storage. While Samba and AFP are more common distributed filesystems on Windows and OS X, NFS is now the de-facto standard and a key element of any Linux server system. Here in this recipe, we will show you how easy it is to set up an NFS server for file sharing over the network.

Getting ready

To complete this recipe, you will require a working installation of the CentOS 7 operating system with root privileges, a console-based text editor of your choice, and a connection to the Internet in order to facilitate the download of additional packages. It is expected that your NFS server and all the clients will be able to ping each other and are connected to each other by a static IP address (see the recipe, *Building a static network connection*, in *Chapter 2, Configuring the System*). In our example, the NFS server is running with IP 192.168.1.10 and two clients with the IPs 192.168.1.11 and 192.168.1.12 and the network's domain name example.com.

How to do it...

In this particular section, we are going to learn how to install and configure the NFS server, and create and export a share on a client.

Installing and configuring the NFS server

NFSv4 is not installed by default, and for this reason we will begin by downloading and installing the required packages:

1. To do this, log in as root on the server that you want to run the NFS daemon on and type the following command in order to install the required packages:

```
yum install nfs-utils
```

2. For NFSv4 to work, we need the *same base* domain for all clients and the NFS server. So, let's define sub-domain names for our NFS server and the clients, if you haven't set up a domain name using DNS (see *Chapter 9, Working with Domains*), we will set up a new hostname for our computers in the /etc/hosts file:

```
echo "192.168.1.10 myServer.example.com" >> /etc/hosts
echo "192.168.1.11 myClient1.example.com" >> /etc/hosts
echo "192.168.1.12 myClient2.example.com" >> /etc/hosts
```

3. Now, open the /etc/idmapd.conf file and put in the base domain name (not the full domain name) of your NFS server; search for the line that reads #Domain = local.domain.edu, and replace it with the following:

```
Domain = example.com
```

4. Next, we need to open some firewall ports for the server to have proper NFS access:

```
for s in {nfs,mountd,rpc-bind}; do firewall-cmd --permanent --add-
service $s; done; firewall-cmd --reload
```

5. Finally, let's start the NFS server service and enable it on reboot:

```
systemctl start rpcbind nfs-server systemctl enable rpcbind nfs-
server systemctl status nfs-server
```

Creating an export share

Now that our NFS server is configured and up-and-running, it's time to create some file shares that we can export to our clients:

1. First, let's create a folder for our shares and change its permissions:

```
mkdir /srv/nfs-data
```

2. Create a new group with a specific GID and associate it with the export, and then change permissions:

```
groupadd -g 50000 nfs-share;chown root:nfs-share /srv -R;chmod 775
/srv -R
```

3. Open the following file:

```
vi /etc/exports
```

4. Now, enter the following text, but be very focussed while typing:

```
/srv/nfs-data *(ro) 192.168.1.11(rw) 192.168.1.12(rw) /home
*.example.com(rw)
```

5. Save and close the file, then re-export all entries from /etc/exports using the following:

```
exportfs -ra
```

How it works...

On CentOS 7, you can install version 4 of the NFS, which has some enhancements over former versions, such as more flexible authentication options and being fully backward compatible with older NFS versions. Here, we showed you how easy it is to install and configure the NFS server and create some shared exports for our clients to use.

So, what did we learn from this experience?

We started this recipe by installing the `nfs-utils` package, since the NFS server functionality is not available on CentOS 7 by default. Next, we configured our server's domain name using the `/etc/hosts` file, as in our example, no DNS server of our own has been configured. If you have set up a DNS server, you should follow a similar domain name schema as shown here, because this is very important for NFSv4 to work, as all clients and the server should be in the same base domain. In our example, we specified that they are all sub-domains of `example.com`: `myClient1.example.com`, `myClient2.example.com`, and `myServer.example.com`. This is a means of securing the sharing of data, as the NFS server will only allow access to files from a client to a server if the domain names match (in our example, both server and client are part of the `example.com` domain). Next, we put this base domain in the `idmapd.conf` file, which takes care of mapping user names and group IDs to NFSv4 IDs. Afterwards, we enabled the `nfs`, `mountd`, and `rpc-bind` firewalld services in our firewalld instance, which are all needed for full support and communication between our clients and server. To finish our base configuration, we started the `rpcbind` and NFS servers and enabled them on boot.

After the NFS server was successfully set up, we added some export to it, to actually allow clients to access some shared folders from the server. Therefore, we created a special directory in the filesystem, which will keep all our shared files. We associated this sharing folder, `/srv/nfs-data`, with a new group, `nfs-share`, and gave it read/write/execute permissions. For practical reasons we will control Linux file permissions for our export on a group level. The name is unimportant but its group identifier (GID) has to be set to a static value (for example, `50000`). This new GID must be the same on the server as well as on every client for every user who wants to have write permissions because NFS transfers any access permissions between server and client on a user (UID) or GID level over the network. The whole sharing magic then happens in the `/etc/exports` file. It contains a table; in it you specify all the important information about your shared folders and their access securities for the clients. Every line in this file is equivalent to one shared folder in your system, and a whitespaced list of all the hosts allowed to access them together with their accessing options in brackets. As you can see, there are different possibilities to define your target clients using IP addresses or hostnames. For hostnames, you can use wildcards such as `*` and `?` to keep the file more compact and allow for multiple machines at once, but you can also define export options for each single host name. Explaining all the options is outside the scope of this book; if you need more help, read the exports manual, which can be found using `man exports`.

For example, the line, `/srv/nfs-data *(ro) 192.168.1.11(rw) 192.168.1.12(rw)`, defines that we want to export the content of the folder `/srv/nfs-data` to all hostnames (because of the * symbol); read-only (`ro`) means that every client can read the content of the folder but not write in it. For clients with the IP address `192.168.1`, ending with `11` and `12`, we allow reading and writing (`rw`). The second line defines that we are exporting the `/home` directory to all clients in the subdomain of `*.example.com` with read/write capacity. Whenever you make a change to the `/etc/exports` file, run the `exportfs -r` command to apply your changes to the NFS server.

Finally, we can say that NFSv4 in CentOS 7 is very easy to set up and start. It's the perfect solution for sharing files between Linux systems, or for centralized home directories.

Working with NFS

Before a client computer can use file system exports shared by an NFS server, it has to be configured to correctly access this system. Here in this recipe, we will show you how to set things up and work with NFS on the client machine.

Getting ready

To complete this recipe, you will require a working installation of the CentOS 7 operating system with root privileges, a console-based text editor of your choice, and a connection to the Internet in order to facilitate the download of additional packages. It is expected that you have already followed the *Installing and configuring NFS* recipe and have set up an NFS server, such as in this example. It is expected that all the clients can ping each other and are connected to the NFS server, and will be using a static IP address (see the recipe, *Building a static network connection*, in *Chapter 2, Configuring the System*). In our example, the NFS server is running with the IP `192.168.1.10` and two clients with the IPs `192.168.1.11` and `192.168.1.12`.

How to do it...

On our client systems, we also need the same NFS software package, and a similar configuration to the one on the server, in order to establish a communication between them:

1. To begin, log in on your client as `root`, and apply the exact same steps as in the *Installing and configuring NFS* recipe until the end of step 3. Skip step 4 because no firewalld service must be opened. Then, instead of step 5, use the following commands, which will not start and enable the `nfs-server`, but only the `rpcbind` service instead:

    ```
    systemctl start rpcbind
    systemctl enable rpcbind
    ```

2. Stop there and do not apply anything else from the original recipe. To test the connection to our NFS server, use the following command:

   ```
   showmount -e myServer.example.com
   ```

3. Now, to test if attaching the NFS exports works you can do so manually using a new user, `john`. This needs to be added to the `nfs-share` group first in the following way so that we can write on our share:

   ```
   groupadd -g 50000 nfs-share;useradd john;passwd john;usermod -G
   nfs-share john
   ```

   ```
   mount -t nfs4 myServer.example.com:/srv/nfs-data /mnt
   ```

   ```
   su - john;touch /mnt/testfile.txt
   ```

4. If the creation of the file in the shared directory works, you can put the import in the `fstab` file so that it will be automatically mounted on system boot:

   ```
   vi /etc/fstab
   ```

5. Append the following line:

   ```
   myServer.example.com:/srv/nfs-data   /mnt nfs defaults 0 0
   ```

6. Finally, to remount everything from `fstab`, type the following:

   ```
   mount -a
   ```

How it works...

In this recipe, we showed you how easy it is to use some shared file system exports from an existing NFSv4 server.

So, what did we learn from this experience?

As you have seen, to set up an NFS client, you need a very similar setup to the one on the NFS server itself, with the exception of starting the `rpcbind` service instead of `nfs-server` (which, as the name implies, is only needed for the server side). The `rpcbind` service is a port mapper and is used for **Remote Procedure Calls** (**RPC**), which is a communication standard needed for NFS to work. Another very crucial step in the configuration that you should remember was setting up the domain name in the `/etc/idmapd.conf` file. We will have to use the *same* base domain name as on the server (`example.com`) in order to make the NFSv4 communication between server and client work. After having started and enabled the `rpcbind` service, we could then mount the NFS share to a local directory, either using the `mount` command (with `-t` type `nfs4`) directly, or via the `fstab` file. Remember, that every system user who wants proper read/write/execute permissions to a share needs the *same* permissions on the NFS server; in our example we manage correct permissions on an identical GID level. We used the default options to mount the share; if you need different or advanced options, please refer to `man fstab`. In order to apply changes to the `fstab` file, perform `mount -a` to remount everything from that file.

Securely sharing resources with Samba

Samba is a software package that enables you to share files, printers, and other common resources across a network. It is an invaluable tool for any working environment. One of the most common ways to share file resources across a heterogeneous network (meaning different computer systems such as Windows and Linux) is to install and configure Samba as a standalone file server to provide basic file-sharing services through *user level security* with the use of the system user's home directories. Standalone servers are configured to provide local authentication and access control to all the resources they maintain. All in all, every administrator knows that Samba remains a very popular open source distribution, and it is the purpose of this recipe to show you how to deliver an instant approach to file sharing that provides the seamless integration of any number of users on any type of modern computer across your entire working environment.

Getting ready

To complete this recipe, you will require a working installation of the CentOS 7 operating system with root privileges, a console-based text editor of your choice, and a connection to the Internet in order to facilitate the download of additional packages. It is expected that your server will use a static IP address.

How to do it...

Samba is not installed by default, and for this reason we will begin by downloading and installing the required packages.

1. To do this, log in as `root` and type the following command in order to install the required packages:

   ```
   yum install samba samba-client samba-common
   ```

2. Having done this, the first step is to rename the original configuration file:

   ```
   mv /etc/samba/smb.conf /etc/samba/smb.conf.BAK
   ```

3. Now, create a new configuration file in your preferred text editor by typing the following:

   ```
   vi /etc/samba/smb.conf
   ```

4. Begin building your new configuration by adding the following lines, replacing the values shown with values that better represent your own needs:

   ```
   [global]
   unix charset = UTF-8
   ```

```
dos charset = CP932
workgroup = <WORKGROUP_NAME>
server string = <MY_SERVERS_NAME>
netbios name = <MY_SERVERS_NAME>
dns proxy = no
wins support = no
interfaces = 127.0.0.0/8 XXX.XXX.XXX.XXX/24 <NETWORK_NAME>
bind interfaces only = no
log file = /var/log/samba/log.%m
max log size = 1000
syslog only = no
syslog = 0
panic action = /usr/share/samba/panic-action %d
```

> WORKGROUP_NAME is the name of the Windows workgroup. Use the
> standard Windows name WORKGROUP if you don't have this value.
> MY_SERVERS_NAME refers to the name of your server. In most
> situations, this could be in the form of FILESERVER or SERVER1
> and so on. XXX.XXX.XXX.XXX/XX refers to the primary network
> address that your Samba service is operating at, for example,
> 192.168.1.0/24. NETWORK_NAME refers to the name of your
> Ethernet interface. This could be enp0s8.

5. We will now configure Samba as a standalone server. To do this, simply continue to
   add the following lines to your main configuration file:

```
security = user
encrypt passwords = true
passdb backend = tdbsam
obey pam restrictions = yes
unix password sync = yes
passwd program = /usr/bin/passwd %u
passwd chat = *Enter\snew\s*\spassword:* %n\n *Retype\snew\s*\
spassword:* %n\n *password\supdated\ssuccessfully* .
pam password change = yes
map to guest = bad user
usershare allow guests = no
```

6. For the purpose of this recipe, we do not intend to configure Samba as a domain
   master or master browser. To do this, add the following lines:

```
domain master = no
local master = no
preferred master = no
os level = 8
```

7. We will now add support for home directory sharing by enabling valid users to access their home directories. This feature will support the appropriate read/write permissions and all folders will remain private from other users. To do this, add the following new lines:

```
[homes]
       comment = Home Directories
       browseable = no
       writable = yes
       valid users = %S
       create mask =0755
       directory mask =0755
```

8. Save and close the file. To test the syntax of the Samba configuration file we just created, use the following:

    testparm

9. Now, add an existing system user, john, to the Samba user management system (this is for testing later; change it appropriately to a user name on your system):

    smbpasswd -a john

10. Now, save the file and close it; back on the command line, open the ports in the firewall:

    firewall-cmd --permanent --add-service=samba && firewall-cmd --reload

11. Configure SELinux to use the Samba home directory:

    setsebool -P samba_enable_home_dirs on

12. Now, ensure that the samba and nmb services will start up during the boot process and start them right away:

    systemctl enable smb && systemctl enable nmb systemctl start smb && systemctl start nmb

How it works...

It was the purpose of this recipe to install Samba and configure its file sharing services, thus providing full connectivity across all modern computer systems in your network.

So, what did we learn from this experience?

Having installed the necessary packages, we renamed the originally installed configuration file to have a backup in place if anything broke later, and then we began setting up Samba from scratch, starting with an empty smb.conf configuration file. Having opened this new file, we began with the global configuration options; the first step was to declare compatibility with Unicode-based character sets. You will need to be aware that the values can vary as a result of your circumstances and network. Read more at man smb.conf.

Having done this, we then proceeded to confirm the name of our workgroup and server, disable WINS, establish a Samba log file, and register the network interface. Then, we elected the following standalone options by choosing a user-based security option, password encryption, and a `tdbsam` database backend. The preferred mode of security is user-level security, and using this approach implies that each share can be assigned to a specific user. Therefore, when a user requests a connection for a share, Samba authenticates this request by validating the given username and password with the authorized users in the configuration file and the Samba database. Next, we added the `master` information. In the case of a mixed operating system environment, a known conflict will result when a single client attempts to become the master browser. This situation may not disrupt the file-sharing service as a whole, but it will give rise to a potential issue being recorded by the Samba log files. So by configuring the samba server to not assert itself as the master browser, you will be able to reduce the chance of such issues being reported. So, having completed these steps, the recipe then considered the main task of enabling the `homes` directory file-sharing. Of course, you can experiment with the options shown, but this simple set of instructions not only ensures that valid users will be able to access their home directory with the relevant read/write permissions, but also, by setting the `browseable` flag to `no`, you will be able to hide the home directory from public view and achieve a greater degree of privacy for the user concerned. In our setup, Samba works with your Linux system users, but you should remember that any existing or new user is not added automatically to Samba and must be added manually using `smbpasswd -a`.

So, having saved your new configuration file, we tested its correctness using the `testparm` program and opened the Samba related incoming ports in firewalld using the `samba` service. The next step was to ensure that Samba and its related processes would be made available during the boot process using `systemctl`. Samba requires two primary processes in order to work correctly: `smbd` and `nmbd`. Beginning with `smbd`, it is the role of this service to provide file-sharing, printing services, user authentication, and resource locking to Windows-based clients using the SMB (or CIFS) protocol. At the same time, it is the role of the `nmbd` service to listen, understand, and reply to the NetBIOS name service's requests.

> Samba often includes another service call named `winbindd`, but it has been largely ignored because the intention to provide a **Windows Internet Naming Service** (**WINS**)-based service or Active Directory authentication requires additional consideration, which is beyond the scope of this recipe.

Consequently, our final task was to start both the Samba service (`smb`) and the associated NetBIOS service (`nmb`).

You now know how incredibly simple Samba is to install, configure, and maintain. There is always more to learn, and yet this simple introduction has served to illustrate Samba's relative ease of use and the simplicity of its syntax. It has delivered a solution that has the ability to support a wide variety of different needs and a range of different computer systems, one that will fulfill your file-sharing requirements for many years to come.

There's more...

You can test our Samba server configuration from any client in your network that can ping the server. If it is a windows-based client, open the **Windows Explorer** address bar and use the following syntax: `\\<ip address of the Samba server>\<linux username>`. For example, we use `\\192.168.1.10\john` (on successfully connecting to it, you need to enter your Samba username's password). On any Linux client system, (the package, `samba-client`, needs to be installed on CentOS 7) to list all the available shares of an NFS server, use the following line:

```
smbclient -L <hostname or IP address of NFS server> -U <username>
```

In our example, we would use the following:

```
smbclient -L 192.168.1.10 -U john
```

To test, mount a share (this requires the `cifs-utils` package on CentOS 7) with the following syntax:

```
mount -t cifs  //<ip address of the Samba server>/<linux username> <local
mount point> -o  "username=<linux username>"
```

In our example, we would use the following:

```
mkdir /mnt/samba-share
```

```
mount -t cifs //192.168.1.10/john  /mnt/samba-share -o "username=john"
```

You can also put this import in the `/etc/fstab` file for permanent mounting using the following syntax:

```
//<server>/<share> <mount point> cifs <list of options>  0  0
```

for example:

For example, add the following line to the file:

```
//192.168.1.10/john /mnt/samba-share cifs username=john,password=xyz  0 0
```

If you don't want to use passwords in plaintext in this file, read the section about credentials using `man mount.cifs`, then create a credentials file and protect it with `chmod 600` in your home directory so that no other person can read it.

Here in this chapter, we showed you how to configure Samba as a standalone server and enable home directories, and how to connect to it from a client to get you started. But Samba can do so much more! It can provide printing services or act as a complete domain controller. If you want to learn more, feel free to visit `https://www.packtpub.com/` to learn more about other available material.

8
Working with FTP

In this chapter, we will cover the following topics:

- ▶ Installing and configuring the FTP service
- ▶ Working with virtual FTP users
- ▶ Customizing the FTP service
- ▶ Troubleshooting users and file transfers

Introduction

This chapter is a collection of recipes that provides the steps to unmask one of the most fundamental services in the Linux world and also provides the necessary starting point required to install, configure, and deliver the file transfer protocol without hesitation.

Installing and configuring the FTP service

While there are several modern and very secure network file sharing technologies, the good old **File Transfer Protocol** (**FTP**) remains one of the most widely used and popular protocols to share and transfer files between computers. There are a number of different FTP servers available in the Linux world. In this recipe, you will learn how to install and configure **very secure FTP daemon** (**vsftpd**), which is a well-known FTP server solution that supports a wide range of features and enables you to upload and distribute large files across a local network and the Internet. Here, we will show how to install the vsftpd daemon and provide some basic settings with the main goal being to increase the security of the daemon.

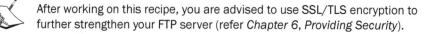

After working on this recipe, you are advised to use SSL/TLS encryption to further strengthen your FTP server (refer *Chapter 6, Providing Security*).

Getting ready

To complete this recipe, you will require a working installation of the CentOS 7 operating system with root privileges, a console-based text editor of your choice, and a connection to the Internet in order to facilitate the downloading of additional packages. It is expected that your server will be using a static IP address and that it maintains one or more system user accounts.

How to do it...

vsftpd is not installed by default. For this reason, we must begin this recipe by installing the relevant packages and associated dependencies:

1. To do this, log in as root and type the following command:

   ```
   yum install vsftpd
   ```

2. After we have created a backup copy of it, open the main configuration file in your favorite text editor as follows:

   ```
   cp /etc/vsftpd/vsftpd.conf /etc/vsftpd/vsftpd.conf.BAK
   vi /etc/vsftpd/vsftpd.conf
   ```

3. To disable anonymous users, scroll down and find the following line: anonymous_enable=YES, and then change this as follows:

   ```
   anonymous_enable=NO
   ```

4. Uncomment (remove # at beginning of the line) the following lines to enable the chroot environment for more security:

   ```
   chroot_local_user=YES
   chroot_list_enable=YES
   ```

5. Next, scroll down to the bottom of the file and add the following line:

   ```
   use_localtime=YES
   ```

6. Finally, add the following line to enable local users to write to their home directories:

   ```
   allow_writeable_chroot=YES
   ```

7. Save and close the file. Then create the following empty file:

   ```
   touch /etc/vsftpd/chroot_list
   ```

8. Next, configure the firewall to allow incoming FTP connections to the server on port 21:

   ```
   firewall-cmd --permanent --add-service=ftp
   firewall-cmd --reload
   ```

9. Now, we allow SELinux to use the FTP home directory feature:

   ```
   setsebool -P ftp_home_dir on
   ```

10. Enable vsftpd at boot:

    ```
    systemctl enable vsftpd
    ```

11. To complete this recipe, type the following command to start the FTP service:

    ```
    systemctl start vsftpd
    ```

12. Now, we can test the connection from any client computer in the same network that our FTP server is in. This computer needs a FTP client installed (if its a CentOS computer, install one using yum install ftp). Log in to this computer with any account and by typing in the following command that replaces <IPADDRESS> with the IP address of the server running your vsftpd service:

    ```
    ftp <IPADDRESS>
    ```

13. On successful connection to the server, the FTP client program will ask you for a username and password. Here, enter a known system user (other than root) from the FTP server. If the login was successful, you will get a 230 login successful message and a ftp> prompt. Now to end our test, type the following FTP command to show all the files in your current ftp directory and check whether you have write-access on the remote server:

    ```
    ls
    mkdir test-dir
    rmdir test-dir
    ```

14. Type the following command to end your FTP session:

    ```
    exit
    ```

How it works...

vsftpd is widely recognized as a fast, lightweight, and reliable FTP server. The purpose of this recipe was to show you how to build a basic FTP service that is optimized to provide excellent performance for any number of valid system users.

So what did we learn from this experience?

We began the recipe by installing the necessary YUM package called `vsftpd`. We then opened the main configuration file located at `/etc/vsftpd/vsftpd.conf`, after we made a backup copy of it. Next, we disabled anonymous FTP access and thereby secured our FTP service against unknown users. We then restricted users to their home directory by enabling a `chroot` jail.

> The `chroot` jail represents an essential security feature; once this is done, all the users will be restricted to access the files in their own home directory only.

We then required `vsftpd` to use local time for our server. Afterwards, we fixed the write permissions for our chrooted FTP users by enabling the `allow_writeable_chroot` option. Having saved our work, we created a new empty `/etc/vsftpd/chroot_list` file, which will hold all the user names that can leave their chroot jails. We have to create this file; otherwise, `vsftpd` will not let us log in to the system. However, you should remember that you must leave it empty all the time because chroot jails are an important protection mechanism for your FTP server.

Next, we added the standard FTP protocol's port 21 to our firewall configuration to allow incoming connections. Then, we reloaded the firewall to apply these changes. After this, we activated our FTP home directories by setting the appropriate SELinux boolean variable `ftp_home_dir` to `true`. This will make the directories valid for SELinux. Please read *Chapter 14, Working with SELinux* to learn more about SELinux. Next, we enabled `vsftpd` on boot and started the service within `systemd`. At this point, `vsftpd` will now be operational and it can be tested with any regular FTP-based desktop software. Users can log in using a valid system username and password by connecting to the server's name, domain, or IP address (depending on the server's configuration).

The purpose of this recipe was to show you that `vsftpd` is not a difficult package to install and configure. There is always more to do but, by following this simple introduction, we have quickly enabled our server to run a standard FTP service.

There's more...

Having installed and configured a basic FTP service, you may wonder how to direct users to a specific folder within their home directory. To do this, open the main configuration file in an editor of your choice using `/etc/vsftpd/vsftpd.conf`.

Scroll down to the bottom of the file and add the following line by replacing the `<users_local_folder_name>` value with something more applicable to your own needs:

```
local_root=<users_local_folder_name>
```

For example, if this FTP server is mainly for accessing and uploading content for an user's private web pages hosted on the same server, you may configure Apache to use the user's home directories in a folder called /home/<username>/public_html. For this reason, you may add the following reference at the bottom of your vsftpd configuration file:

```
local_root=public_html
```

When finished, save and close the configuration file before restarting the vsftpd service. When testing this new feature make sure that the local_root location exists in the home directory of the user you want to login (for example, ~/public_html).

Working with virtual FTP users

In this recipe, you will learn how to implement virtual users in order to break away from the restriction of using local system user accounts. During the lifetime of your server, there may be occasions when you wish to enable FTP authentication for a user that does not have a local system account. You may also want to consider implementing a solution that allows a particular individual to maintain more than one account in order to allow access to different locations on your server. This type of configuration implies a certain degree of flexibility afforded by the use of virtual users. Since you are not using a local system account, it can be argued that this approach gives improved security.

Getting ready

To complete this recipe, you will require a working installation of the CentOS 7 operating system with root privileges and a console-based text editor of your choice. It is expected that your server will be using a static IP address and that vsftpd is already installed with a chroot jail and is currently running. This recipe needs the policycoreutils-python package installed.

How to do it...

1. The first step is to login as root on our vsftpd server and create a plain text file called virtual-users.txt that maintains a list of usernames and passwords of the virtual users. To do this, type the following command:

    ```
    vi /tmp/virtual-users.txt
    ```

2. Now add your usernames and corresponding passwords in the following way:

    ```
    virtual-username1
    password1
    virtual-username2
    password2
    virtual-username3
    password3
    ```

Repeat this process as required for every user you need but, for obvious reasons, maintain a good password policy and do not use the same virtual-username more than once.

3. When you have finished, simply save and close the file in the usual way. Then, proceed to build the database file by typing the following command:

   ```
   db_load -T -t hash -f /tmp/virtual-users.txt /etc/vsftpd/virtual-users.db
   ```

4. Having done this, we will now create the PAM file that will use this database to validate the virtual users. To do this, type the following command:

   ```
   vi /etc/pam.d/vsftpd-virtual
   ```

5. Now add the following lines:

   ```
   auth required pam_userdb.so db=/etc/vsftpd/virtual-users

   account required pam_userdb.so db=/etc/vsftpd/virtual-users
   ```

6. When you have finished, save and close the file in the usual way. Open the main `vsftpd` configuration file in your favorite text editor as follows:

   ```
   vi /etc/vsftpd/vsftpd.conf
   ```

7. Now, in the opened file, search for the line `pam_service_name=vsftpd` and disable it by adding a # sign at the beginning of the line so that it reads as follows:

   ```
   #pam_service_name=vsftpd
   ```

8. Scroll down to the bottom of the file and add the following lines by customizing the value for `local_root` to suit your own specific needs—this will be the base directory in which all your virtual users will *live* in (for example, we will use `/srv/virtualusers/$USER` as shown here):

   ```
   virtual_use_local_privs=YES

   guest_enable=YES

   pam_service_name=vsftpd-virtual

   user_sub_token=$USER

   local_root=/srv/virtualusers/$USER

   hide_ids=YES
   ```

9. Now create a subfolder for each virtual user you defined in a previous step in your `/tmp/virtual-users.txt` file within the directory that you stated with the `local_root` directive. Remember to delegate the ownership of this folder to the FTP user. To keep up with our `/srv/virtualusers` example, we will use the following commands to do this in an automatic way (again, customize the `/srv/virtualusers` directory if needed):

```
for u in `sed -n 1~2p /tmp/virtual-users.txt`;

do

mkdir -p /srv/virtualusers/$u

chown ftp: /srv/virtualusers/$u

done
```

10. Now we need to inform SELinux to allow read/write access to our custom `local_root` directory outside of the typical `/home` directory:

    ```
    setsebool -P allow_ftpd_full_access on

    semanage fcontext -a -t public_content_rw_t "/srv/
    virtualusers(/.*)?"

    restorecon -R -v /srv/virtualusers
    ```

11. Next, restart the FTP service as follows:

    ```
    systemctl restart vsftpd
    ```

12. For security reasons, remove the plain text file now and protect the generated database file with this:

    ```
    rm /tmp/virtual-users.txt

    chmod 600 /etc/vsftpd/virtual-users.db
    ```

How it works...

Having followed the previous recipe, you will be now able to invite an unlimited number of virtual users to access your FTP service. The configuration of this feature was very simple; your overall security has been improved and all access is restricted to a defined `local_root` directory of your choice. Please note that this usage of virtual users will disable your system users' login to the FTP server from the first recipe.

So what did we learn from this experience?

We began this recipe by creating a new temporary text file that will contain all our usernames with the corresponding passwords in plain text. We then added all the required usernames and passwords one after another sequentially separated by newlines. Having done this for each of our virtual users, we then saved and closed the file before proceeding to run the `db_load` command that is installed on CentOS 7 by default. This can be used to generate a BerkeleyDB database out of our text file, which will be used for the FTP user authentication later in this process. Having completed this step, our next task was to create a Pluggable Authentication Modules (PAM) file at `/etc/pam.d/vsftpd-virtual`. This reads the previous database file to provide authentication from it for our `vsftpd` service using a typical PAM configuration file syntax (for more, see `man pam.d`). Then, we opened, modified, and added new configuration directives to the main `vsftpd` configuration file at `/etc/vsftpd/vsftpd.conf` in order to make `vsftpd` aware of our virtual users' authentication via PAM.

The most important setting was the `local_root` directive that defines the base location where all your user directories will be placed for your virtual users. Don't forget to put the `$USER` string at the end of your path. You were then prompted to create the relevant virtual hosting folder for every virtual user you have defined in the text file before.

Since virtual users are not real system users, we had to assign the FTP system user to take full ownership of the files for our new FTP users. We used a bash `for` loop to automate the process for all our users defined in the temporary `/tmp/virtual-users.txt` file. Next, we set the proper SELinux boolean to allow virtual users access to the system and also the right context on our `/srv/virtualusers` directory. Applying all these changes was simply a matter of restarting the `vsftpd` service using the `systemctl` command.

Afterwards, we removed the temporary user text file because it contains our passwords in plain text. We protected the access to the BerkleyDB database file by removing all access other than root. If you update, add, or remove FTP users on a regular basis, it's better to not delete this temporary plain text `/tmp/virtual-users.txt` file but rather put it in a safe place such as the `/root` directory. Then, you should also protect this using `chmod 600`. Then, you can rerun the `db_load` command whenever you make a change to this file to keep your users up-to-date. If you need to add new users at a later point, you have to create new virtual user folders for them as well (Please rerun the commands from step 9). Run the `restorecon -R -v /srv/virtualusers` command afterwards.

You can now test your new virtual user accounts by logging in to the FTP server using your newly created accounts from this recipe.

Customizing the FTP service

In this recipe, you will learn how to customize your `vsftpd` installation. `vsftpd` has a lot of configuration parameters, and here we will show how to create a custom welcome banner, change the server's default-time out, limit user connections, and ban users from the service.

Getting ready

To complete this recipe, you will require a working installation of the CentOS 7 operating system with root privileges and a console-based text editor of your choice. It is expected that your server will be using a static IP address and that `vsftpd` is already installed with a chroot jail and is currently running.

How to do it...

1. To begin with, log in as root and open the main `vsftpd` configuration file:

    ```
    vi /etc/vsftpd/vsftpd.conf
    ```

2. First provide an alternative welcome message, uncomment the following line, and alter the message as required. For example, you could use this:

```
ftpd_banner=Welcome to my new FTP server
```

3. To change the default FTP time-outs, uncomment these lines and substitute the numeric values as required:

```
idle_session_timeout=600

data_connection_timeout=120
```

4. Now, we will limit the connections: the data transfer rate in bytes per second, the number of clients, and the maximum parallel connections per IP address. Add the following lines to the end of the file:

```
local_max_rate=1000000

max_clients=50

max_per_ip=2
```

5. Next, save and close the file. To ban a specific user, you can use the following commands while replacing the username with an appropriate system user value that fits your needs:

```
echo "username" >> /etc/vsftpd/user_list
```

6. Now to apply the changes, restart the FTP service:

```
systemctl restart vsftpd
```

How it works...

In this recipe, we have shown some of the most important vsftpd settings. Covering all the configuration parameters here is outside the scope of this recipe. To learn more about it, read through the entire main vsftpd configuration file at /etc/vsftpd/vsftpd.conf, as it contains a lot of useful comments; alternatively, you can read the man vsftpd.conf manual.

So what did we learn from this experience?

We began by opening the main vsftpd configuration file and then activated and customized the welcome banner using the ftpd_banner directive. On the next successful login, your users should see your new message. Next, when dealing with a large number of users, you may want to consider changing the values for a default timeout and limit the connections in order to improve the efficiency of your FTP service.

First, we changed our server's timeout numbers. An `idle_session_timeout` of `600` seconds will logout the user if he is inactive (not executing FTP commands) for 10 minutes, while a `data_connection_timeout` of `120` seconds will kill the connections when a client data transfer is stalled (not progressing) for 20 minutes. Then we changed the connection limits. A `local_max_rate` of `1000000` bytes per second will limit the data transfer rate of a single user to roughly one megabyte per second. A `max_clients` value of `50` will tell the FTP server to only allow 50 parallel users to the system, while a `max_per_ip` of `2` allows only two connections per IP address.

Then we saved and closed the file. Finally, we showed how to ban users from using our FTP service. If you wanted to ban a specific user from using the FTP service as a whole, the user's name should be added to the `/etc/vsftpd/user_list` file. If you ever need to re-enable the user at any time, simply reverse the previous process by removing the user concerned from `/etc/vsftpd/user_list`.

Troubleshooting users and file transfers

Analyzing log files is the most important technique for troubleshooting all kinds of problems or improving services on Linux. In this recipe, you will learn how to configure and enable vsftpd's extensive logging features in order to help system administrators when problems arise, or simply to monitor usage with this service.

Getting ready

To complete this recipe, you will require a working installation of the CentOS 7 operating system with root privileges and a console-based text editor of your choice. It is expected that your server will be using a static IP address and that `vsftpd` is already installed with a chroot jail and is currently running.

How to do it...

1. To do this, log in as root and type the following command to open the main configuration file in your favorite text editor:

   ```
   vi /etc/vsftpd/vsftpd.conf
   ```

2. Now, add the following lines to the end of the configuration file to enable verbose logging features:

   ```
   dual_log_enable=YES
   log_ftp_protocol=YES
   ```

3. Finally, restart the `vsftpd` daemon to apply the changes:

   ```
   systemctl restart vsftpd
   ```

How it works...

In this recipe, we have shown how to enable two separate logging mechanism: first, the xferlog log file that will log detailed information about user uploads and downloads, then the vsftpd log file that contains every FTP protocol transaction between the client and the server outputting the most detailed logging information possible for vsftpd.

So what did we learn from this experience?

In this recipe, we opened the main vsftpd configuration file and added two directives to the end of the file. First, dual_log_enable will make sure both the xferlog and vsftpd log files will be used for logging. Afterwards, we increased the verbosity of the vsftpd log file by enabling log_ftp_protocol.

After restarting the service, the two log files, /var/log/xferlog and /var/log/vsftdp.log, will be created and filled with useful FTP activity information. Now, before we open the files, let's create some FTP user activity. Log in with any FTP user on the server using the ftp command-line tool and issue the following FTP command at the ftp> prompt to upload a random file from the client to the server:

put ~/.bash_profile bash_profile_test

Now, back on the server, inspect the /var/log/xferlog file to see detailed information about the uploaded file and open /var/log/vsftpd.log for all other user activities (such as login time or other FTP commands that users issued).

Please note that both the log files only keep track of user and FTP activity and are not meant to debug problems with the vsftpd service such as configuration file errors. Use the systemctl status vsftpd -l or journalctl -xn, to debug general problems with the service.

9
Working with Domains

In this chapter, we will cover:

- ▸ Installing and configuring a caching-only nameserver
- ▸ Setting up an authoritative-only nameserver
- ▸ Creating an integrated nameserver solution
- ▸ Populating the domain
- ▸ Building a secondary (slave) DNS server

Introduction

This chapter is a collection of recipes that attempt to demystify a technology that remains the key component in making everything work in the networking world. From e-mail to web pages and remote logins to online chats, this chapter provides the necessary details on how quickly you can use CentOS to deliver a domain name service that will power your working environment.

Installing and configuring a caching-only nameserver

Every network communication between computers can only be made through the use of unique IP addresses to identify the exact endpoints of the communication. For the human brain, numbers are always harder to remember and work with than assigning names to *things*. Therefore, IT pioneers started in the early 70s to invent systems for translating names to physical network addresses using files and later simple databases. In modern computer networks and on the Internet, the relationship between the name of a computer and an IP address is defined in the **Domain Name System** (**DNS**) database. It is a worldwide distributed system and provides domain name to IP address resolution and also the reverse, that is IP address to domain name resolution. DNS is a big subject, and it is the purpose of this recipe to provide the perfect starting point by showing you how to install and setup your own caching-only and forwarding nameserver. Here we will use *Unbound*, which is a highly secure and fast recursive and caching DNS server solution, and therefore our preferred choice. But you need to remember that Unbound cannot be used as a fully authoritative DNS server (which means that it provides its own domain name resolution records) we will use the popular BIND server for this in a later recipe. A caching-only DNS server will serve to forward all the name resolution queries to a remote DNS server. Such a system has the intention of speeding up general access to the Internet by caching the results of any domain resolution request made. When a caching DNS server tracks down the answer to a client's query, it returns the answer to the client. However, it also stores the answer in its cache for a specific period of time. The cache can then be used as a source for subsequent requests in order to speed up the total round-trip time.

Getting ready

To complete this recipe, you will require a working installation of the CentOS 7 operating system with root privileges, a static IP address, and a console-based text editor of your choice. An Internet connection will be required to download additional packages. In this example, our DNS server runs in a private network with the network address `192.168.1.0/24`.

How to do it...

In this recipe, we will first configure a *caching-only* and then a *forwarding only* DNS server.

Configuring a caching-only Unbound DNS server

In this section, we will consider the role of Unbound as a caching-only nameserver, handling recursive DNS requests to the other remote DNS servers and caching the query for a certain time period to improve the response time when the server is asked for the same name resolution again:

1. To begin, log in as root and install the required packages by typing:

    ```
    yum install unbound bind-utils
    ```

2. Now make a copy of the unbound configuration file so we can revert our changes later, and then open it in your favorite text editor:

    ```
    cp /etc/unbound/unbound.conf /etc/unbound/unbound.conf.BAK
    vi /etc/unbound/unbound.conf
    ```

3. Scroll down to find the following line: # interface: 0.0.0.0 Remove the # sign to uncomment it (activate it), so it reads as follows:

    ```
    interface: 0.0.0.0
    ```

4. Next, scroll down to find the line # access-control: 127.0.0.0/8 allow. Uncomment the line to activate it and change the network address to fit your needs:

    ```
    access-control: 192.168.1.0/24 allow
    ```

5. Save and close the file, and then create an RSA keypair with certificates for secure DNSSEC support before you check the correctness of the changed configuration file:

    ```
    unbound-control-setup && unbound-checkconf
    ```

6. Next, open the DNS service in your firewalld configuration on your server because we want to be able to use our new DNS service from other clients in the network for querying as well:

    ```
    firewall-cmd --permanent --add-service dns &&  firewall-cmd
    --reload
    ```

7. Now ensure the service will be available at boot and start it afterwards:

    ```
    systemctl enable unbound && systemctl start unbound
    ```

8. To test if we can reach our Unbound DNS server and make queries, execute the following command from the same server running our Unbound DNS service locally, which should give back the IP address of www.packtpub.com:

    ```
    nslookup www.packtpub.com 127.0.0.1
    ```

9. For a more detailed view of the request you can also run locally on the DNS server:

    ```
    unbound-host -d www.packtpub.com
    ```

10. From any other client in the network (needs `bind-utils` installed), you can query any public domain name using our new DNS server as well. For example, if our DNS server has the IP `192.168.1.7`:

    nslookup www.packtpub.com 192.168.1.7

11. Finally, let us use our new nameserver on the server itself. To do this, open the following file with your favorite text editor after you have made a backup copy:

    cp /etc/resolv.conf /etc/resolv.conf.BAK; vi /etc/resolv.conf

12. Remove all the current nameserver references and replace them with the following:

    nameserver 127.0.0.1

 If you have set some DNS server information in your network-scripts interface (for example, when configuring a static IP address, see *Chapter 2, Configuring the System*), you will want to review the `/etc/sysconfig/network-scripts/ifcfg-XXX` file and modify the current DNS reference to read as `DNS1=127.0.0.1` as well.

Configuring a forwarding only DNS server

Now after we have successfully configured our first caching BIND DNS server, here we will show you how to transform it into a forwarding DNS server which will reduce the total bandwidth for resolving hostnames in comparison to the caching-only solution:

1. Open BIND's main configuration file again:

   vi /etc/unbound/unbound.conf

2. Add the following lines to the end of the file:

   ```
   forward-zone:
         name: "."
         forward-addr: 8.8.8.8
   ```

3. Next, check the correctness of your new configuration file and restart the service:

   unbound-checkconf && systemctl restart unbound

4. Finally, test your new forwarding DNS server using the tests from the preceding caching DNS server section.

How it works...

In this recipe, we have installed a caching-only Unbound DNS server with the basic aim of improving the responsiveness of our overall network by caching the answers to any name-based queries. Using such a process will shorten the waiting time on any subsequent visit to the same location. It is a feature that is particularly useful in saving bandwidth if you happen to be managing a large, busy, or slow network. It does not have its own domain name resolution feature but uses its default root domain's DNS servers in order to perform this task (to learn more about the root domain, see later). Also, as we have seen, you can easily transform your caching nameserver into a pure forwarding system as well. While a caching DNS server makes recursive requests to *several* associated DNS servers and constructs the complete name resolution result from those multiple requests, a forwarding DNS *delegates* the complete recursive DNS search to another resolving DNS server which executes the complete search instead. This saves even more bandwidth for our DNS server because only *single* network requests to communicate with the remote resolving server are made instead of *multiple* when using the caching-only DNS service.

So what did we learn from this experience?

We started this recipe by installing the necessary packages. This included the main DNS server program called Unbound and a reference to bind-utils, a small package that enables you to run many different DNS related network tasks, such as dig, nslookup, and host. The next step was to begin making the necessary configuration changes by editing Unbound's main configuration after we made a simple backup of the original file. Since after installation the default DNS server is completely restricted to doing everything *locally* only, our main purpose was to adjust the server to make connections from the outside possible. We began this process by allowing the DNS server to listen to all the available network interfaces using the interface directive and afterwards defined who on the network was allowed to make requests to our DNS server by setting allow-query to our local network. This means we allowed anyone in our subnetwork to make DNS resolution requests to our server.

At this point we created the RSA keypair with the unbound-control-setup tool, which is needed for the unbound-checkconf command to work. The generated keys and certificate are important if we want to use **Unbound's DNS Security Extensions** (**DNSSEC**) features which help protect DNS data by providing authentication of origin using digital signatures (configuring DNSSEC is outside the scope of this chapter. To learn more, consult the Unbound configuration manual: man unbound.conf). Afterwards, we used the unbound-checkconf command, which was necessary to confirm that Unbound's configuration file was syntactically correct. If the output of the command is empty, there are no errors in the file. We then proceeded by adding the predefined dns firewalld service to our default firewall, thus allowing the other computer systems in our local network to access the DNS server using port 53. Finally, we activated Unbound at boot time and started the service.

Of course, to complete this recipe we then tested if our new DNS server worked as expected in resolving domain names to IP addresses. We ran a simple `nslookup` query locally on the server and also from the other computers in the same network to see if our new DNS service was reachable from the outside. When using `nslookup` without any additional parameters, the program will use the default DNS server resolver known to the system (on CentOS 7 this is defined in `/etc/resolv.conf`) to resolve our host names, so we added another parameter addressing our alternative DNS server we want to query instead (`127.0.0.1`). For successful testing, the output must contain the resolved IP address of the `www.packtpub.com` server. On the DNS server you could also use the `unbound-host -d` command to get a more technical view of the DNS query within the Unbound service.

After we successfully finished these tests, we updated the current nameserver resolver information on our DNS server with our new DNS service running on localhost.

There's more...

Now we want to see how BIND will perform for caching DNS information. To do this, on your DNS server simply select a target website you have not visited before and use the `dig` command. For example:

```
dig www.wikipedia.org
```

Having run this test, you may see a query time that results in something like the following:

```
;; Query time: 223 msec
```

Now repeat this exercise by retesting the same URL. Depending on your networking environment, this may produce the following result:

```
;; Query time: 0 msec
```

Now do it again for another website. On every repeat of the preceding command, you should not only see a reduced query time but also experience a faster response time in delivering the output. This same result will be evident in the browser refresh rate, and as a result we can say that this simple exercise has not only introduced you to Unbound but it will ultimately serve to improve the speed of your local network when surfing the World Wide Web.

Setting up an authoritative-only DNS server

In this recipe, we will learn how to create an *authoritative-only* DNS server, which can give answers to queries about domains under their control themselves instead of redirecting the query to other DNS servers (such as our caching-only DNS server from the previous recipe). We will create a DNS server to resolve all our own hostnames and services in our own private local network.

As said before, while Unbound should be your first choice when needing a caching-only DNS server as it is the most secure DNS server solution available, it has only limited authoritative capabilities which often is not enough for professional DNS server usage. Here, instead of name lookup of our local servers, we will use the popular authoritative BIND DNS server package and configure a new DNS zone to provide highly customizable name resolution. Technically speaking, we will be writing both a *forward* and *reverse zone* file for our domain. Zone files are text files that contain the actual domain name to IP address mappings or the other way around, that is, IP address mappings to domain name mappings. While most queries to any DNS server will be the translation of names to IP addresses, the reverse part is also important to set up if you need the correct domain name for any given IP address. We will configure BIND to be authoritative-only, which means that the server will only answer queries it is authoritative for (has the matching records in its zones), so if the DNS server cannot resolve a requested domain, it will stop the request and not contact other DNS servers using recursive requests to fetch and construct the correct answer.

Getting ready

To complete this recipe, you will require a working installation of the CentOS 7 operating system with root privileges, a static IP address, and a console-based text editor of your choice. An Internet connection will be required to download additional packages. In this example, our DNS server runs in the private network with the network address `192.168.1.0/24`. Our DNS server should manage a local private domain we decide to be `centos7.home` (in the form `domain.toplevel-domain`). The IP address of the new DNS server will be `192.168.1.7` and should get the hostname `ns1`, leading to the Fully Qualified Domain Name (FQDN) `ns1.centos7.home`. (Refer to the *Setting your hostname and resolving the network* recipe in *Chapter 2, Configuring the System* to learn more about FQDNs). Our configured zone will have an administrative e-mail address with the name `admin@centos7.home`, and for simplicity, all the other computers in this network will get hostnames such as `client1`, `client2`, `client3`, and so on. We will also have some mail, web, and FTP servers in our own network, each running on separate dedicated servers. We will be using the port `8053` for our BIND service as we already have Unbound running on the same server using the default DNS port `53`.

How to do it...

For security reasons, we will allow BIND to resolve internal LAN names only (authoritative-only) and only allow localhost to make DNS queries; no other clients in our network can connect to it:

1. To begin with, log in as root on your Unbound DNS server and install the required BIND package and enable the DNS server on boot:

    ```
    yum install bind && systemctl enable named
    ```

2. The actual name of the DNS server in the BIND package is called `named`, so let's open its main configuration file to make some adjustments after creating a backup copy of it first:

   `cp /etc/named.conf /etc/named.conf.BAK; vi /etc/named.conf`

3. First find the line `listen-on port 53 { 127.0.0.1; };` and then change the port number to the custom `port 8053`, so it reads as follows:

   `listen-on port 8053 { 127.0.0.1; };`

4. Next, find the line `listen-on-v6 port 53 { ::1; }` and change it to:

   `listen-on-v6 port 8053 { none; };`

5. Next, since we are configuring an authoritative-only server, we will disable contacting other remote DNS servers, find the line that reads `recursion yes;` and change it to:

   `recursion no;`

6. Save and close the file, and then validate the syntax of our config changes (no output means no errors!):

   `named-checkconf`

7. Now tell SELinux about the changed named DNS port (this needs package `policycoreutils-python`):

   `semanage port -a -t dns_port_t -p tcp 8053`

8. Now type the following command in order to create your forward zone file. Name the file after the domain whose resource records it will contain:

   `vi /var/named/<domain>.<top-level domain>.db`

9. In our example, for our `centos7.home domain`, this will be:

   `vi /var/named/centos7.home.db`

10. Now simply add the following lines (be careful not to forget typing the tailing dots in the domain names). We will start with the **Start of Authority (SOA)** block:

```
$TTL 3h
@ IN SOA ns1.centos7.home. admin.centos7.home. (
 2015082400        ; Serial yyyymmddnn
 3h                ; Refresh After 3 hours
 1h                ; Retry Retry after 1 hour
 1w                ; Expire after 1 week
 1h)               ; Minimum negative caching
```

11. Afterwards, add the rest of the file's content:

```
; add your name servers here for your domain
        IN      NS      ns1.centos7.home.
; add your mail server here for the domain
        IN      MX      10    mailhost.centos7.home.
; now follows the actual domain name to IP
; address mappings:

; first add all referenced hostnames from above
ns1         IN      A       192.168.1.7
mailhost    IN      A       192.168.1.8
; add all accessible domain to ip mappings here
router      IN      A       192.168.1.0
www         IN      A       192.168.1.9
ftp         IN      A       192.168.1.10
; add all the private clients on the Lan here
client1     IN      A       192.168.1.11
client2     IN      A       192.168.1.12
client3     IN      A       192.168.1.13
; finally we can define some aliases for
; existing domain name mappings
webserver   IN      CNAME   www
johnny      IN      CNAME   client2
```

12. When you have finished, simply save and close the file before proceeding to create the reverse zone file for our private subnetwork used by our domain (the C-Class are the first three numbers (octets) which are separated by dots: XXX.XXX.XXX. For example, for the 192.168.1.0/24 subnet the C-Class is 192.168.1:

    vi /var/named/db.<C-Class of our search IP in reverse order>

13. In our example, a reverse zone file resolving our centos7.home's 192.168.1 C-Class subnet will be:

    vi /var/named/db.1.168.192

14. First put in the exact same SOA as in step 10, and then append the following content to the end of the file:

```
;add your name servers for your domain
            IN      NS      ns1.centos7.home.
; here add the actual IP octet to
; subdomain mappings:
7       IN      PTR     ns1.centos7.home.
8       IN      PTR     mailhost.centos7.home.
9       IN      PTR     www.centos7.home.
```

```
10      IN      PTR     ftp.centos7.home.
11      IN      PTR     client1.centos7.home.
12      IN      PTR     client2.centos7.home.
13      IN      PTR     client3.centos7.home.
```

15. Save and close the file, and then add our new zone pair to the named configuration. To do this, open `named.conf` again:

    vi /etc/named.conf

16. Now locate the line including "`/etc/named.rfc1912.zones`";. Immediately following this line, create a space for your work and add the appropriate zone statement to enable your *reverse* zone, as follows (substitute XXX.XXX.XXX with the reversed C-Class of your reverse zone file name, in our example 1.168.192):

    ```
    zone "XXX.XXX.XXX.in-addr.arpa." IN {
      type master;
      file "/var/named/db.XXX.XXX.XXX";
      update-policy local;
    };
    ```

17. Having done this, you can now proceed to add a zone statement for your forward zone right afterwards, as follows (replacing `<domain>.<top-level domain>.db` with your forward zone file name, in our example `centos7.home`):

    ```
    zone "<domain>.<top-level domain>." IN {
      type master;
      file "/var/named/<domain>.<top-level domain>.db";
      update-policy local;
    };
    ```

18. When you have finished, simply save and close the file, and then restart the `bind` service using:

    ```
    named-checkconf && systemctl restart named
    ```

How it works...

All DNS servers are configured to perform caching functions, but where a caching-only server is restricted in its ability to answer queries from remote DNS servers only, an authoritative nameserver is a DNS server that maintains the master zone for a particular record.

So what have we learned from this experience?

The purpose of this recipe was to setup an authoritative-only BIND DNS server and provide a new zone for it. A DNS zone defines all the available resources (hostnames and services) under a single domain. Any DNS zone should always consist of both a forward and reverse zone file. To understand zone configurations, we need to discuss DNS hierarchy first. For example, take a DNS domain from the example in this recipe `client1.centos7.home`. Every computer in our private network has a hostname (for example, `client1` or `www`) and is a member of a domain. A domain consists of the **Second-level Domain** (**SLD**) (for example, `centos7`) and a **Top-level Domain** name (**TLD**) (for example, `home`, `org`, `com`, and so on). On top of that TLD is the root domain (written . dot) which often is neglected when working with other programs or configurations. However, when working or defining FQDN in zone configurations, it is very important to never forget to add this dot . after the TLD. For example, a DNS domain for our `client1` computer would be `client1.centos7.home.`, whereas an FQDN for the `/etc/hosts` file is often written in the format `client1.centos7.home` (technically this is incorrect but most of the time sufficient). The root domain is very important because it contains the root DNS servers which will be queried first if an authoritative DNS server cannot find an existing entry for a requested domain in its own records (zones) or cache. But we have DNS servers in all the other domain hierarchies as well and this is how a DNS server makes its recursive requests. A root DNS server, as any other DNS server, resolves all its subdomains (defined in its zone files) which are the TLDs. These TLDs themselves can resolve all the SLDs (also defined in their zone files). The second-level domains resolve all their hostnames (which are special subdomains as they refer to individual computer or services on your network). So any DNS request traverses through the different DNS server hierarchies from the root DNS over the TLD DNS to the SLD DNS server. The root and the TLD DNS servers cannot fully resolve full domain DNS queries such as `www.centos7.home` and instead will resolve the correct address of the next DNS hierarchy. This system ensures that the root DNS will always find the correct TLD DNS server address and the TLD DNS server will always send the request to the right SLD DNS which has the correct zone file and is finally able to answer the requested DNS query.

So what did we learn from this experience?

As we have learned, a zone file is a simple text file that consists of directives and resource records and can look quite complicated as it contains a lot of two-letter abbreviations. Remember, you need to set up a zone file pair (forward and reverse) on a base domain level (for example, `centos7.home`) for all the hostnames and services running under it (for example, `www`, `host1`, `api`, and so on). After installing the `named` DNS server (which is part of the **Berkeley Internet Name Domain** (**BIND**) package), we made a copy of the original main configuration file and changed the default listening port from 53 to 8053 (as unbound is already listening on port 53) but kept it listening to localhost only, and disabled IPv6 to keep compatibility with the other major DNS servers (as IPv6 support is still limited on the Internet). Also, here we disabled recursion because our BIND DNS server had to be authoritative-only, which means that it is not allowed to forward DNS requests to other remote DNS servers when it could not resolve the query from its own zone records.

Then we began creating and customizing our own forward DNS zone file with the filename convention `/var/named/<domain>.<top-level domain>.db`. This file is opened with the `$TTL` control statement, which stands for **Time to Live** and which provides other nameservers with a time value that determines how long they can cache the records from this zone. This directive, as many others, is defined using seconds as the default time unit, but you can also use other units using BIND specific short forms to indicate minutes (`m`), hours (`h`), days (`d`), and weeks (`w`), as we did in our example (`3h`). Following this, we then provided a **Start of Authority** (**SOA**) record. This record contains specific information about the zone as a whole. This begins with the zone name (`@`), a specification of the zone class (`IN`), the FQDN of this nameserver in the format `hostname.domain.TLD.`, and an e-mail address of the zone administrator. This latter value is typically in the form `hostmaster.hostname.domain.TLD.` and it is formed by replacing the typical `@` symbol with a dot (`.`). Having done this, it was then a matter of opening the brackets to assign the zone's serial number, refresh value, retry value, expire value, and negative caching `time-to-live` value. These directives can be summarized as follows:

- The `serial-number` value is a numeric value, typically taking the form of the date in reverse (`YYYYMMDD`) with an additional value (`VV`), which is incremented every time the zone file is modified or updated, in order to indicate that it is time for the named service to reload the zone. The value `VV` typically starts at `00`, and the next time you modify this file, simply increment it to `01`, `02`, `03`, and so on.

- The `time-to-refresh` value determines how frequently the secondary or slave nameservers will ask the primary nameserver if any changes have been made to the zone.

- The `time-to-retry` value determines how frequently the secondary or slave nameservers should check the primary server after the serial number has failed. If a failure has occurred during the time frame specified by the `time-to-expire` value elapses, the secondary nameservers will stop responding as an authority for requests.

- The `minimum-TTL` value determines how long the other nameservers can cache negative responses.

Having completed this section and having closed the corresponding bracket, we then proceeded to add the authoritative nameserver information (`NS`) with the `IN NS    <FQDN of the nameserver>` definition. Typically speaking, you will have at least two, if not three, nameservers (put each nameserver's FQDN in a new `IN NS` line). However, it is possible to set only one nameserver, which is particularly useful if you are running the server in an office or a home environment and would like to enjoy the benefit of local name resolution, such as `.home`, `.lan`, or `.dev`. The next stage then required us to include a reference for the **Mail eXchanger** (**MX**) records in order for us to specify a mail server for the zone. The format is `IN MX <priority> <FQDN of your mailserver>`. The priority becomes important if you define more than one mail server (each in its separate `IN MX` line)—the lower the number, the higher the priority. In this respect, a secondary mail server should have a higher value.

In the SOA, NS and MX lines we already referenced hostnames which aren't defined as an IP mapping yet (A record). We could do this because the zone file is not processed sequentially. But do not forget to create corresponding A lines for each hostname later.

Depending on your needs, you may also intend to use your name server as your mail server (then you would write instead MX 10 ns1.centos7.home.), although you may have another server dedicated to that role as shown in the example.

Following this, it was then a matter of creating the appropriate A records (A for address) and assigning the appropriate IP address to the values shown. This is the heart of any domain name resolution requests to the server. An A record is used for linking an FQDN to an IP address, but much of the preceding settings will be based on your exact needs. Here you can define all the local host names you want to map in your network. As we have already used and referenced some domain names before in the zone file such as the nameserver or mailserver we would begin with these. Afterwards, we defined all the hostnames to IP address mappings for all public available and afterwards our internal clients. Remember that when using the A records you can have multiple mappings of the same IP address to different hostnames. For example, if you do not have dedicated servers for every service in your network but rather one server running all your DNS, mail, web, and ftp services, you can write the following lines instead:

```
ns1        IN A 192.168.1.7
mailhost   IN A 192.168.1.7
www        IN A 192.168.1.7
ftp        IN A 192.168.1.7
```

You can also use a canonical name (CNAME) record for this task, which is used to assign an alias to an existing A record. Arguably, the CNAME value make your DNS data easier to manage by pointing back to an A record. So if you ever consider the need to change the IP address of the A record, all your CNAME records pointed to that record automatically. However, and as this recipe has tried to show, the alternative solution is to have multiple A records, which implies the need for multiple updates in order to change the IP address.

At this stage of the recipe, we then turned our attention towards the reverse DNS zone. As with the forward zone file, the reverse zone files also have a special naming convention /var/named/db.<C-Class of our search IP in reverse order>. Naming your reverse zone file like db.1.168.192 can look strange first but makes sense when you look at how reverse lookup works. It starts from the highest node (in our example 192, which corresponds to the root domain in the forward zone file) and traverses its way down from it. As you see, the content we put in this file has some similarities between the directives and the resources used in the forward zone file. However, it is important to remember that reverse DNS is wholly separate and distinct from forward DNS.

The reverse DNS zone is designed to assist in the conversion of an IP address to a domain name. This can be done by using the **Pointer Resource Record** (**PTR**) which assigns unique IP addresses to one or more host names. For this reason, you must ensure that a unique PTR record exists for every A record. Every reverse zone file collects IP to hostname translations for a complete Class C address range (the first three dotted numbers, for example, `192.168.1`). The last octets of such an IP range are all the hostnames which can be defined within such a file. Remember, the IP address value for the first column in a PTR record should only show this last octet. For example, the line `9 IN PTR www.centos7.home.` in the reverse zone file `db.1.168.192` will be able to resolve any reverse IP address requests of `192.168.1.9` to the domain value `www.centos7.home`.

Having created our forward and reverse zone files in this recipe, we then completed the configuration of the named service by adding our new zones to our BIND server in order to start our own domain name service resolving local domain names of our network. In these new appended forward and reverse zone definition blocks, we defined that we are the master zone holder and also specified `update-policy local;` because this is needed if we want to use the `nsupdate` command to update our zones dynamically from the localhost (see later). You may add unlimited zone pairs, but remember that each forward or reverse zone definition must be given a single zone entry in curly brackets.

In summary, we can say that forward and reverse zone files are defined on a single base domain name basis, one base domain gets one forward zone file. For reverse zone files, it's a bit different because we are working with IP addresses. We create one zone file based on the Class C address range of the network address of our domain and here the last octet is called the hostname, for which we define our mappings in such a specific file.

BIND is a big subject and there is a lot more to learn as this recipe has only served to introduce you to the subject. In most cases, you may even find that your initial learning period will become known as a process of trial and error, but it will improve. Remember, practice makes perfect and if you do create additional forward zones, always reference them in the reverse zone file.

There's more...

Having created and added your zones to your BIND server, you are now able to test your configuration. To do this, you can use the `host`, `dig` or `nslookup` command to resolve internal hostnames from localhost only. For example, for testing forward DNS resolution we can use the `dig` command by specifying that our DNS server is running on localhost with port `8053`: `dig -p 8053 @127.0.0.1 client2.centos7.home`. This should finish DNS lookup successfully and return the following line (output is truncated):

```
;; ANSWER SECTION:
client2.centos7.home.   10800   IN  A   192.168.1.12
```

For reverse lookup, you will use an IP address instead (in this instance, the IP address used should correspond to a domain for which you have configured reverse DNS): `nslookup -port=8053 192.168.1.12 127.0.0.1`. As we have configured BIND as an authoritative-only DNS server, any DNS request which is outside the local records of our zone should not be able to get fully resolved. To test this use `dig -p 8053 @127.0.0.1 www.google.com` which should return the status `REFUSED` and `WARNING: recursion requested but not available` message.

For security reasons, we restricted our BIND server to localhost only and did not allow it to connect to other DNS servers. Therefore you cannot use it as your only DNS solution for your private network. Instead, in the next recipe, we will learn how to combine Unbound with BIND to create an integrated and very secure all-in-one DNS server solution. But if you don't want to do this and use BIND as your single and full authoritative DNS server solution (which is not recommended on CentOS 7 anymore), you can do this by disabling or uninstalling Unbound, restoring the original `named.conf.BAK` configuration file, and enabling the following directives in the BIND configuration file: `allow-query {localhost;192.168.1.0/24;};` (which enables the complete `192.168.1.0/24` network to make DNS requests), `listen-on port 53 {any;};` (listen for requests on any network), `listen-on-v6 port 8053 { none; };` (for disabling IPv6). If you want BIND to be forwarding everything, which it is not authoritative for, instead of using recursion to find out the answer, add the following directives as well (in this example we use the official Google DNS servers for any forwarding requests, but you can change this to fit your needs): `forwarders { 8.8.8.8;};forward only;`. Then restart the `bind` service.

Creating an integrated nameserver solution

So far in this chapter, we used Unbound as a caching-only DNS server solution because it is very secure and fast, and BIND as our authoritative-only DNS server because its zone management is highly configurable and customizable. BIND has been around for a long time and is the most used DNS software ever. However, a number of critical bugs have been found (and luckily fixed) in the past. Here in this recipe, we will combine Unbound with BIND to get the best of both worlds: Only the very secure Unbound service will be directly exposed to your private network and can take and serve DNS queries from your clients. The BIND service stays bound to localhost only as it was configured in a former recipe and is only allowed to resolve internal hostnames and does not have direct access to the Internet or your clients. If a client connects to your Unbound service and requests to resolve an internal hostname from your private network, Unbound will query the BIND server locally for the DNS resolution and cache the response. On the other hand, if a client requests to resolve an external domain name, Unbound itself will recursively query or forward other remote DNS servers and cache the response. The integration of both DNS server systems makes it the perfect all-round DNS server solution.

Getting ready

To complete this recipe, you will require a working installation of the CentOS 7 operating system and a console-based text editor of your choice. It is expected that a caching-only Unbound server (port 53) and an authoritative-only BIND server (port 8053) have been installed and are already running using recipes found in this chapter.

How to do it...

In this recipe, we will show you how to configure Unbound so it will be able to query our locally running authoritative-only BIND service whenever a client requests an internal hostname. Any other request should go out as a recursive DNS request to a remote root server to construct an answer:

1. Log in as root on our server running the Unbound and BIND service and open Unbound's main configuration file:

   `vi /etc/unbound/unbound.conf`

2. First put the following line somewhere in the `server:` clause:

   `local-zone: "168.192.in-addr.arpa." nodefault`

3. Next, we will have to allow Unbound to connect to localhost which is disabled by default, search for the line that reads: `# do-not-query-localhost: yes`, then activate and set it to no:

   `do-not-query-localhost: no`

4. Next, since our BIND server is not configured using DNSSEC, we need to tell Unbound to use it anyway (Unbound by default refuses to connect to DNS servers not using DNSSEC). Search for the line that starts with `# domain-insecure: "example.com"`, then activate it and change it so it reads as follows:

   `domain-insecure: "centos7.home."`

   `domain-insecure: "168.192.in-addr.arpa."`

5. Next, we need to tell Unbound to forward all the requests for our internal domain `centos7.home.` to the locally running BIND server (on port `8053`). Append the following at the file's end:

   ```
   stub-zone:
           name: "centos7.home."
           stub-addr: 127.0.0.1@8053
   ```

6. Also, we need to tell Unbound to do the same for any reverse lookup to our internal domain using BIND:

```
stub-zone:
        name: "1.168.192.in-addr.arpa."
        stub-addr: 127.0.0.1@8053
```

7. Save and close the file, and then restart the Unbound service:

```
unbound-checkconf && systemctl restart unbound
```

How it works

Congratulations! You now have a full authoritative and very secure DNS server solution using an integrated approach combining all the good parts from Unbound and BIND. In this recipe, we have shown you how to configure the Unbound service using stub-zones to connect to an internally running BIND service for both forward and reverse requests. A stub-zone is a special Unbound feature to configure authoritative data to be used that cannot be accessed using the public Internet servers. Its name field defines the zone name for which Unbound will forward any incoming DNS requests and the stub-addr field configures the location (IP address and a port) of the DNS server to access; in our example, this is the locally running BIND server on port 8053. For Unbound to be able to connect to the localhost, we first had to allow this using the do-not-query-localhost: no directive, had to mark our forward and reverse domain as being insecure, and also had to define a new local-zone, which is necessary that Unbound knows that clients can send queries to a stub-zone authoritative server.

There's more...

In order to test our new Unbound/BIND DNS cluster, make one public and one internal hostname DNS request to the Unbound service from another computer in the same network (you can also run similar tests locally on the DNS server itself). If our Unbound/BIND DNS cluster has the IP 192.168.1.7, you should be able to get correct answers for both dig @192.168.1.7 www.packtpub.com and dig @192.168.1.7 client1.centos7. home from any other computer in your network.

If you have to troubleshoot service problems or need to monitor the DNS queries of your new Unbound/BIND DNS server, you can configure logging parameters. For BIND, in the main configuration file named.conf you can set the verbosity of the logging output (or log level). This parameter is called severity and can be found within the logging directive. It is already set to dynamic; which gives the highest amount of logging messages possible. You can then read your current log using tail -f /var/named/data/named.run. For Unbound, you can set the level of verbosity in its main configuration file unbound.conf using the verbosity directive which is set to the lowest level of 1 but can be increased to 5. To learn more about the different levels, use man unbound.conf. Use journald to read the Unbound logging information using the command journalctl -f -u unbound. service (press *Ctrl+c* key to exit the command).

We can not only log the system and service information but can also enable query logs. For Unbound just use a `verbosity` of 3 or above to record query information. For BIND, in order to activate the query log (query output will go to the log file `named.run`), use the command `rndc querylog on` (to turn it off, use `rndc querylog off`). Remember to turn off any excessive logging information, such as the query log, when configuring your DNS server on a productive system as it can decrease your service's performance. You can also install other third-party tools such as `dnstop` (from the `EPEL` repository) to monitor your DNS activity.

Populating the domain

In this recipe, we will show you how you can quickly add new local domain record entries to your authoritative BIND server which are currently unknown to your nameserver.

Getting ready

To complete this recipe, you will require a working installation of the CentOS 7 operating system and a console-based text editor of your choice. It is expected that Unbound and BIND have both been installed and are already running, and that you have read and applied the zone recipes in this chapter and have prepared the required forward and reverse zone files for resolving hostnames of your private network.

How to do it...

If you want to add new domain names to the IP address mappings to your DNS server, for example for new or unknown hosts in your local network, you have two alternatives. Since we have already created zone files for our local network, we can simply add new `A` (and/or `CNAME`) and corresponding `PTR` entries for every new subdomain within our base domain name into our forward and reverse zone file configuration using our text editor of choice. Alternatively, we can use the `nsupdate` command-line tool to add those records interactively without the need to restart the DNS server. In this section, we will show you how to prepare and work with the `nsupdate` tool. In our example, we will add a new subdomain `client4.centos7.home` for a computer with the IP address `192.168.1.14` to our DNS server's zone:

1. Log in as root on the server running your BIND service. Now first we need to activate `named` to be allowed to write into its zone files by SELinux:

   ```
   setsebool -P named_write_master_zones 1
   ```

2. Next, we need to fix some permission problems with the named configuration directory, otherwise `nsupdate` cannot update our zone files later:

   ```
   chown :named /var/named -R; chmod 775 /var/named -R
   ```

3. Since our BIND server is running on port `8053`, type the following command to start the interactive `nsupdate` session locally:

   nsupdate -p 8053 -d -l

4. At the prompt (`>`), first connect to the local DNS server by typing the following (press *Return* to finish commands):

   local 127.0.0.1

5. To add a new forward domain to IP mapping to your DNS server, type the following:

   update add client4.centos7.home. 115200 A 192.168.1.14

   send

6. Now add the reverse relationship using the following command:

   update add 14.1.168.192.in-addr.arpa. 115200 PTR client4.centos7. home.

   send

   If both the update commands' outputs contained the message NOERROR, press *Ctrl+c* key to exit the interactive `nsupdate` session.

7. Finally, check if both the domain and IP resolution for the new zone entry work (this should also work remotely through the Unbound server):

   dig -p 8053 @127.0.0.1   client4.centos7.home.

   nslookup -port=8053 192.168.1.14 127.0.0.1

How it works...

In this fairly easy recipe, we showed you how easily you can add new domain name resolution records with the `nsupdate` tool dynamically at runtime without needing to restart your BIND DNS server.

So what did we learn from this experience?

In this recipe, we introduced you to the `nsupdate` command-line tool which is a utility for making changes to a running BIND DNS database without the need to edit the zone files or restart the server. If you have already configured the zone files in your DNS server, then this is the preferred way to make changes to the DNS server. It has several options, for example, you can connect to the remote DNS servers but for simplicity and for security reasons we will only use and allow the most simple form and only connect `nsupdate` to our BIND server locally (to connect to a BIND server remotely using `nsupdate`, you need to do more configuration, such as generate secure key-pairs, open the firewall, and so on).

After allowing `named` to write into its own zone files, which otherwise is prohibited by SELinux, and fixing some permission problems on the default named configuration directory, we started the `nsupdate` program with `-1` for local connection, and `-p 8053` to connect to our BIND DNS server on port `8053`. `-d` gives us debug output which can be useful for resolving any problems. We then got prompted by an interactive shell where we could run BIND specific `update` commands. First we set `local 127.0.0.1` which connects to our local server, than we used the commands `update add` to add a new forward A record to our running DNS server. The syntax is similar to defining records in the zone files. Here we used the line `update add <domain-name> <TTL> <type> <IP address>` to add a new A record with a TTL of three days (115200 seconds) for the domain `client4.centos7.home` to resolve to the IP address `192.168.1.14`. The next line was used to config some reverse resolution rules for our new domain and which adds the domain name as a `PTR` entry into our reverse zone. Here it is important to note that you need to define the domain part of the reverse `update add` rule the following way: `<host name for the rule>.<reverse C-class>.in-addr.arpa`. To finally execute our commands and make them permanent in our DNS server's database, without the need to restart the server, we used the `send` command for both the reverse and forward commands separately since they target different zones. Finally, we tested if the new entries into the DNS server's zone files were working by querying the BIND server.

Building a secondary (slave) DNS server

To guarantee high-availability in your network, it can be useful to operate more than one DNS server in your environment to catch up with any server failures. This is particularly true if you run a public DNS server where continuous access to the service is crucial and where it is not uncommon to have five and more DNS servers at once. Since configuring and managing multiple DNS servers can be time consuming, the BIND DNS server uses the feature of transferring zone files between the nodes so that every DNS server has the same domain resolving and configuration information. In order to do this, we need to define one primary and one or more secondary or slave DNS servers. Then we only have to adjust our zone file once on the primary server which will transfer the current version to all our secondary servers, keeping everything consistent and up-to-date. For a client it will then make no difference which DNS server they are connecting to.

Getting ready

To complete this recipe, you will require at least two CentOS 7 servers in the same network which can see and ping each other. An Internet connection will be required to download and install the BIND server software on all the computers we want to include in our DNS server *farm*. In this example, we have two servers, `192.168.1.7` which is already installed and configured as a BIND server, and `192.168.1.15` which will be our second BIND server within the subnet `192.168.1.0/24`. You should also have read and applied the zone file recipe from this chapter and created a forward and reverse zone file because this is what we want to transfer between DNS servers.

How to do it...

We begin this recipe by installing BIND on every CentOS 7 computer we want to include in our BIND DNS server cluster. To do this, follow the recipe *Setting up an authoritative-only DNS server* for all the remaining systems. Before we can start, we need to define which server will be our primary DNS server. For simplicity in our example, we will choose the server with the IP address `192.168.1.7`. Now let's make all our DNS server nodes aware of their role.

Changes to the primary DNS server

1. Let's log in as root on the primary server and open its main configuration:

    ```
    vi /etc/named.conf
    ```

2. Now we define which secondary DNS server(s) will be allowed to receive the zone files at all, write the following command somewhere between the options curly brackets in a new line (we only have one secondary DNS server with the IP address `192.168.1.15`, change accordingly):

    ```
    allow-transfer { 192.168.1.15; };
    notify yes;
    ```

3. Also, we must allow the other nameservers to connect to our primary nameserver. In order to do this, you need to change your `listen-on` directive to include the DNS server's primary network interface (in our example `192.168.1.7`, so change appropriately):

    ```
    listen-on port 8053 { 127.0.0.1;192.168.1.7; };
    ```

4. Save and close the file. Now open the new port `8053` in your server's firewall (or create a firewalld service for it, see *Chapter 6, Providing Security*):

    ```
    firewall-cmd --permanent --zone=public --add-port=8053/tcp --add-
    port=8053/udp;firewall-cmd --reload
    ```

5. Save and close the file. Next, update the zone files we created earlier to include the IP addresses of all the new nameservers we have available in the system. Change both the forward and reverse zone files, `/var/named/centos7.home.db` and `/var/named/db.1.168.192`, to include our new secondary DNS server. In the forward zone file, add the following lines (you can also use the `nsupdate` program to do this) into the appropriate sections:

    ```
    NS   ns2.centos7.home.

    ns2   A    192.168.1.15
    ```

6. In the reverse zone file, add instead into the appropriate sections:

    ```
    NS   ns2.centos7.home.

    15 PTR ns2.centos7.home.
    ```

7. Finally, restart BIND and recheck the configuration file:

```
named-checkconf && systemctl restart named
```

Changes to the secondary DNS server(s)

For simplicity and to demonstrate, just install `named` on any server you want to use as a BIND slave (we only show the important configuration here):

1. Log in to the new server as root, install BIND, and open its main configuration:

```
yum install bind; vi /etc/named.conf
```

2. Now locate the line `include /etc/named.rfc1912.zones;`. Immediately following this line, create a space for your work and add the following zones (replace the zone and file names appropriately):

```
zone "centos7.home" IN {
    type slave;
    masters port 8053 { 192.168.1.7; };
    file "/var/named/centos7.home.db";
};
zone "1.168.192.in-addr.arpa" IN {
    type slave;
    masters port 8053{ 192.168.1.7; };
    file "/var/named/db.1.168.192.db";
};
```

3. Save and close the file. Then fix some incorrect BIND folder permissions and enable `named` to write into its zone file directory before restarting BIND:

```
chown :named /var/named -R; chmod 775 /var/named -R
setsebool -P named_write_master_zones 1
named-checkconf && systemctl restart named
```

4. Now initiate a new zone transfer using:

```
rndc refresh centos7.home.
```

5. After waiting a while, to test if our secondary DNS server is working as expected, check if the master zone files have been transferred:

```
ls /var/named/*.db
```

6. Finally, we can now test if we can query our local domain on the secondary DNS server too:

```
dig @127.0.0.1 client2.centos7.home.
```

How it works...

In this recipe, we showed you how to set up secondary BIND servers in your network which can help in increasing the stability and availability of your DNS server system.

So what did we learn from this experience?

We started our journey by deciding which of our servers should be the primary and which should be the slave DNS servers. Then we opened the BIND main configuration file on the primary server and introduced two lines of code to configure our server to be the head of our DNS cluster. The `allow-transfer` directive defines to which clients we want to transfer our updated zone files while the `notify yes` directive enables automatic transfer when any changes to the zone files happen. If you have got several secondary BIND DNS servers, you can add more than one IP address into the `allow-transfer` directive, separated by semicolons. Then we opened our zone files we created in a former recipe in this chapter and introduced a new line `IN NS <IP address>` which defines the IP address of our secondary DNS servers we need to be aware on every DNS node in our system. If we have got multiple servers, then we introduce multiple `IN NS` lines. Finally, we introduced a small comment to easily check the successful zone file transfer on our secondary servers.

Afterwards, we configured our slave DNS server(s). Here we introduced the same zone file definitions as on the primary server's BIND configuration, with the exceptions that we used type `slave` instead of master to denote we are a secondary DNS server and will get a copy of the zone files from the master node by defining the primary DNS server's IP address using the `masters` directive (please do not forget that our master BIND is listening on the non-default port `8053` in our example).

Since we had not created or copied the zone files ourselves on the slave DNS server, it was then easy to check if the zone file transfer had been successful after restarting the BIND service using the `ls` command. Finally, we verified the transferred zone file content by running test queries using `dig` or `nslookup` to see if we could resolve the same local hostnames on our secondary DNS server. Remember if you later make changes to your master's zone files you have to increase their `serial` number in order that those changes get transferred to all your slaves.

10
Working with Databases

In this chapter, we will cover:

- ► Installing a MariaDB database server
- ► Managing a MariaDB database
- ► Allowing remote access to a MariaDB server
- ► Installing a PostgreSQL server and managing a database
- ► Configuring remote access to a PostgresSQL
- ► Installing phpMyAdmin and phpPgAdmin

Introduction

This chapter is a collection of recipes that deliver the necessary steps to implement and maintain two of the most popular database management systems in the Linux world. The need for data is everywhere and is a *must have service* for almost any server, and this chapter provides the starting point required to deploy these database systems in any environment.

Installing a MariaDB database server

Supporting over 70 collations, more than 30 character sets, multiple storage engines, and deployment in virtualized environment, MySQL is a mission-critical database server that is used by production servers all over the world. It is capable of hosting a vast number of individual databases and it can provide support for various roles across your entire network. MySQL server has become synonymous with the **World Wide Web** (**WWW**), is used by desktop software, extends local services, and is one of the world's most popular relational database systems. The purpose of this recipe is to show you how to download, install, and lockdown MariaDB, which is the default implementation of MySQL in CentOS 7. MariaDB is open source and fully compatible with MySQL and adds several new features; for example, a non-blocking client API library, new storage engines with better performance, enhanced server status variables, and replication.

Getting ready

To complete this recipe, you will require a working installation of the CentOS 7 operating system with root privileges, a console-based text editor of your choice, and a connection to the Internet in order to download additional packages. It is expected that your server will be using a static IP address.

How to do it...

As the MariaDB **Database Management System** (**DBMS**) is not installed by default on CentOS 7, we will start this recipe by installing the required packages.

1. To begin, log in as root and type the following command to install the required packages:

    ```
    yum install mariadb-server mariadb
    ```

2. When complete, ensure the service starts at boot before starting the service:

    ```
    systemctl enable mariadb.service && systemctl start mariadb.service
    ```

3. Finally, begin the secure installation process with the following command:

    ```
    mysql_secure_installation
    ```

4. When you first run the previous command, you will be asked to provide a password but as this value has not been set, press the *Enter* key to represent the value (blank) none.

5. Now you will be asked a number of simple questions which will help you in the process of hardening your MariaDB DBMS system. It is a good advice to choose Yes (Y) to every question for maximum security unless you are already a MariaDB expert and really require a certain feature.

6. Finally, test if you can connect and login to the MariaDB service locally using the MariaDB command-line client called `mysql`. The test passes if the following command outputs all the MariaDB user names together with their associated hosts known to the MariaDB server (enter the administrator root password you set in the last step when prompted):

```
echo "select User,Host from user" | mysql -u root -p mysql
```

How it works...

MariaDB is a fast, efficient, multithreaded, and robust SQL database server. It supports multiple users and provides access to a number of storage engines, and by following a few short steps, you now know how to install, secure, and login to your MariaDB server.

So what did we learn from this experience?

We started the recipe by installing the necessary package for the MariaDB server (`mariadb-server`) and also the client shell interface (`mariadb`) for controlling and querying the server. Having done this, we then proceeded to ensure that the MariaDB daemon (`mariadb.service`) would start during the boot process before we actually started it. At this point we had a working installation, but in order to ensure that our installation was safe we then invoked the secure installation script in order to guide us through a few simple steps to harden our basic installation. As the basic installation process does not enable us to set a default password for the root user, we did it here as a first step in the script, so we could be certain that no one could access the MariaDB root user account without the required authorization. We then discovered that a typical MariaDB installation maintains an anonymous user. The purpose of this is to allow anyone to login to our database server without having to have a valid user account. It is typically used for testing purposes only, and unless you are in unique circumstances that require this facility, it is always advisable to remove this feature. Following this, and to ensure that the root user could not access our MariaDB server installation, we then opted to disallow remote root access before removing the test database and performing a reload of the privilege tables. Finally, we ran a small test to see if we could connect to the database with the root user and query some data from the `user` table (which is part of the standard `mysql` database).

Having completed the steps of the recipe, we have learned that the process of installing and securing the MariaDB server is very simple. Of course, there are always more things that can be done in order to make the installation useful but the purpose of this recipe was to show you that the most important part of installing your new database system was to make it secure. Remember, the act of running `mysql_secure_installation` is recommended for all MariaDB servers and it is advisable regardless of whether you are building a development server or one that is used in a production environment. As a server administrator, security should always remain your top priority.

Managing a MariaDB database

In this recipe, we will learn how to create a new database and database user for the MariaDB server. MariaDB can be used in conjunction with a wide variety of graphical tools (for example, the free MySQL Workbench), but in situations where you simply need to create a database, provide an associated user, and assign the correct permissions, it is often useful to perform this task from the command line. Known as the MariaDB shell, this simple interactive and text based-command line facility supports the full range of SQL commands and affords both local and remote access to your database server. The shell provides you with complete control over your database server, and for this reason it represents the perfect tool for you to start your MariaDB work.

Getting ready

To complete this recipe, you will require a working installation of the CentOS 7 operating system. It is expected that a MariaDB server is already installed and running on your server.

How to do it...

The MariaDB command-line tool supports executing commands in both the batch mode (reading from a file or standard input) and interactively (typing in statements and waiting for the results). We will use the latter in this recipe.

1. To begin, log in on your CentOS 7 server with any system user you like and type the following command in order to access the MariaDB server using the MariaDB shell with the main MariaDB administration user called `root` (use the password created in the previous recipe):

    ```
    mysql -u root -p
    ```

2. On successful login, you will be greeted with the MariaDB command-line interface. This feature is signified by the MariaDB shell prompt:

    ```
    MariaDB [(none)]>
    ```

3. In this first step, we will create a new database. To do this, simply customize the following command by substituting an appropriate value for the new `<database-name>` value using:

    ```
    CREATE DATABASE <database-name> CHARACTER SET utf8 COLLATE utf8_
    general_ci;
    ```

     If this is your first introduction to the MariaDB shell, remember to end each line with a semi-colon (;) and press the *Enter* key after typing each command.

4. Having created our database, we will now create a MariaDB user. Each user will consist of a username and a password that is completely independent of the operating system's user. For reasons of security, we will ensure that access to the database is restricted to localhost only. To proceed, simply customize the following command by changing the values <username>, <password>, and <database-name> to reflect your needs:

```
GRANT ALL ON <database-name>.* TO '<username>'@'localhost'
IDENTIFIED BY '<password>' WITH GRANT OPTION;
```

5. Next, make the MariaDB DBMS aware of your new user:

```
FLUSH PRIVILEGES;
```

6. Now simply type the following command to exit the MariaDB shell:

```
EXIT;
```

7. Finally, you can test the accessibility of your new <username> by accessing the MariaDB shell from the command-line in the following way:

```
mysql -u <username> -p
```

8. Now back at the MariaDB shell (MariaDB [(none)] >), type the following commands:

```
SHOW DATABASES;
```
```
EXIT;
```

How it works...

During the course of this recipe you were shown not only how to create a database, but also how to create a database user.

So what did we learn from this experience?

We started the recipe by accessing the MariaDB shell as the root user with the mysql command. By doing this, we were then able to create a database with a simple SQL function called CREATE DATABASE, providing a custom name for the <database-name> field. We also specified utf8 as the character set of our new database together with a utf8_general_ci collation. A character set is how the characters are encoded in the database and a collation is a set of rules for comparing the characters in a character set. For historic reasons and to keep MariaDB backward-compatible with the older server versions, the default character set is latin1 and latin1_swedish_ci, but for any modern databases you should always prefer to use utf-8 instead as it is the most standard and compatible encoding for international character sets (non-English alphabets). However, this command can be modified to invoke the need to check if a database name is already in use by using: CREATE DATABASE IF NOT EXISTS <database-name>. In this way, you can then drop or remove a database by using the following command:

```
DROP DATABASE IF EXISTS <database-name>;
```

Having done this, it is simply a matter of adding a new database user with the appropriate permissions by running our GRANT ALL command. Here we provided `<username>` with full privileges via a defined `<password>` for localhost. As a specific `<database-name>` was elected, then this level of permission will be restricted to that particular database and using `<database-name>.*` allows us to specify these rules to all the tables (using the asterisks symbol) in this database. The general syntax in order to provide a chosen user with specific permission is:

```
GRANT [type of permission] ON <database name>.<table name> TO
'<username>'@'<hostname>';
```

For security reasons, here in this recipe we limit `<hostname>` to localhost but if you want to grant permissions to remote users you will need to change this value (see later). In our example, we set `[type of permission]` to ALL but you can always decide to minimize the privileges by providing a single or a comma-separated list of privilege-types offered in the following way:

```
GRANT SELECT, INSERT, DELETE ON <database name>.* TO
'<username>'@'localhost';
```

Using the previous technique, here is a summary of the permissions that can be employed:

- ALL: Allows the `<username>` value with all available privilege-types
- CREATE: Allows the `<username>` value to create new tables or databases
- DROP: Allows the `<username>` value to delete tables or databases
- DELETE: Allows the `<username>` value to delete rows from tables
- INSERT: Allows the `<username>` value to insert rows into tables
- SELECT: Allows the `<username>` value to read from tables
- UPDATE: Allows the `<username>` value to update table rows

However, once the privileges were granted, the recipe then showed you that we must FLUSH the system in order to make our new settings available to the system itself. It is important to note that all commands within the MariaDB shell should end in a semicolon (;). Having completed our task, we simply exit the console using the EXIT; statement.

MariaDB is an excellent database system but like all services, it can be abused. So remain vigilant at all times, and by considering the previous advices, you can be confident that your MariaDB installation will remain safe and secure.

There's more...

Creating a restricted user is one way of providing database access but if you have a team of developers who require constant access to a development server, you may wish to consider providing a universal user who maintains superuser privilege. To do this, simply login to the MariaDB shell with your administrator user root, then create a new user in the following way:

```
GRANT ALL ON *.* TO '<username>'@'localhost' IDENTIFIED BY '<password>'
WITH GRANT OPTION;
```

By doing this, you will enable <username> to add, delete, and manage databases across your entire MariaDB server (the asterisks in *.* tell MariaDB to apply the privileges to all the databases and all their associated tables found on the database server), but given the range of administrative features, this new user account will restrict all activities to localhost only. So in simple terms, if you want to provide <username> with access to any database or to any table, always use an asterisk (*) in place of the database name or table name. Finally, every time you update or change a user permission, always be sure to use the FLUSH PRIVILEGES command before exiting the MariaDB shell with the EXIT; command.

Reviewing and revoking permissions or dropping a user

It is never a good idea to keep user accounts active unless they are used, so your first consideration within the MariaDB shell (login with your administrator user root) will be to review their current status by typing:

```
SELECT HOST,USER FROM mysql.user WHERE USER='<username>';
```

Having done this, if you intend to REVOKE permission(s) or remove a user listed here, you can do this with the DROP command. First of all, you should review what privileges the user of interest has by running:

```
SHOW GRANTS FOR '<username>'@'localhost';
```

You now have two options, starting with the ability to revoke the user's privileges as follows:

```
REVOKE ALL PRIVILEGES, GRANT OPTION FROM '<username>'@'localhost';
```

Then you may either reallocate the privilege using the formula provided in the main recipe or alternatively, you can decide to remove the user by typing:

```
DROP USER '<username>'@'localhost';
```

Finally, update all your privileges the usual way using FLUSH PRIVILEGES; before exiting the shell EXIT; command.

Allowing remote access to a MariaDB server

Unless you are running your MariaDB database server to drive some local web applications on the same server hardware, most working environments would be pretty useless if remote access to a database server were forbidden. In many IT surroundings you will find high-available, centralized dedicated database servers optimized in hardware (for example, huge amounts of RAM) and hosting multiple databases allowing hundreds of parallel connections from the outside to the server. Here in this recipe, we will show you how to make remote connections to the server possible.

Getting ready

To complete this recipe, you will require a working installation of the CentOS 7 operating system with root privileges. It is expected that a MariaDB server is already installed and running and you have read and applied the *Managing a MariaDB database* recipe for an understanding of permissions and how to test (local) database connections.

How to do it...

In our example, we want to access a MariaDB database server with the IP address `192.168.1.12` from a client computer in the same network, with the IP address `192.168.1.33`. Please change appropriately to fit your needs:

1. To begin, log in as root on your MariaDB database server and open the firewall for the incoming MariaDB connections:

   ```
   firewall-cmd --permanent --add-service=mysql && firewall-cmd
   --reload
   ```

2. Afterwards, we need to create a user account which can connect to our MariaDB server remotely (as we have prevented `root` from doing this in a further step for security reasons), login your database server using the MariaDB command line interface `mysql` as user `root` and type the following MariaDB statement (replacing the `xxxx` with a password of your choice, also feel free to adjust the username and remote IP of the client who wants to connect to the server—in our case the client has the IP `192.168.1.33`—accordingly):

   ```
   GRANT SELECT ON mysql.user TO 'johndoe'@'192.168.1.33' IDENTIFIED
   BY 'XXXX';
   ```

   ```
   FLUSH PRIVILEGES;EXIT;
   ```

3. Now we can test the connection from our client computer with the IP address of
   `192.168.1.33` in our network. This computer needs the MariaDB shell installed
   (on a CentOS 7 client, install the package `mariadb`) and needs to be able to ping
   the server running the MariaDB service (in our example, the IP `192.168.1.12`).
   You can test connecting to the server by using the following command (on success,
   this will print out the content of the `mysql` user table):

   ```
   echo "select user from mysql.user" | mysql -u johndoe -p mysql -h
   192.168.1.12
   ```

How it works...

We started our journey by opening the standard MariaDB firewall port 3306 using the
firewalld predefined MariaDB service, which is disabled by default on CentOS 7. After this,
we configured which IP addresses were allowed to access our database server, which is
done on a database level using the MariaDB shell. In our example, we used the GRANT
SELECT command to allow the user `johndoe` at the client IP address `192.168.1.33` and
with the password in quotes `'XXXX'` to access the database with the name `mysql` and
the table user to make SELECT queries only. Remember, here you can also apply wildcards
in the `<hostname>` field using the `%` sign (which means any characters). For example, for
defining any possible hostname combination in a Class C network, you can use the `%` sign
like so `192.168.1.%`. Granting access to the `mysql.user` database and table was just for
testing purposes only and you should remove the user `johndoe` from this access permission
whenever you have finished your tests, using: REVOKE ALL PRIVILEGES, GRANT OPTION
FROM `'johndoe'@'192.168.1.33'`;. If you want you can also delete the user DROP USER
`'johndoe'@'192.168.1.33'`; because we don't need it anymore.

Installing a PostgreSQL server and managing a database

In this recipe, we will not only learn how to install the PostgreSQL DBMS on our server, but
we will also discover how to add a new user and create our first database. PostgreSQL is
considered to be the most advanced open source database system in the world. It is known
for being a solid, reliable, and well-engineered system that is fully capable of supporting
high-transaction and mission-critical applications. PostgreSQL is a descendant of the Ingres
database. It is community-driven and maintained by a large collection of contributors from all
over the world. It may not be as flexible or as pervasive as MariaDB, but because PostgreSQL
is a very secure database system that excels in data integrity, it is the purpose of this recipe
to show you how to begin exploring this forgotten friend.

Getting ready

To complete this recipe, you will require a working installation of the CentOS 7 operating system with root privileges, a console-based text editor of your choice, and a connection to the Internet in order to facilitate the download of additional packages. It is expected that your server will be using a static IP address.

How to do it...

PostgreSQL (also known as Postgres) is an object-relational database management system. It supports a large part of the SQL standard and it can be extended by the server administrator in many ways. However, in order to begin, we must start by installing the necessary packages:

1. Start by logging in your server as root and type:

   ```
   yum install postgresql postgresql-server
   ```

2. Having installed the database system, we must now enable the database server at boot by typing:

   ```
   systemctl enable postgresql
   ```

3. When you have finished, initialize the database system as follows:

   ```
   postgresql-setup initdb
   ```

4. Now complete this process by starting the database server:

   ```
   systemctl start postgresql
   ```

5. Now set a new initial password for our `postgres` administrator of your choice. As the default `postgres` user is currently using peer authentication, we need to execute any Postgres-related command with user `postgres`:

   ```
   su - postgres -c "psql --command '\password postgres'"
   ```

6. To get rid of the requirement, that the `postgres` user has to be logged in on a system user basis before he can execute Postgres-related commands such as `psql`, and to allow login with database user accounts in general, we need to change the authentication method for `localhost` from `peer` to `md5` in the Postgres client authentication configuration file. You can do this manually or use the `sed` tool as shown next, after you have made a backup of the file first:

   ```
   cp /var/lib/pgsql/data/pg_hba.conf /var/lib/pgsql/data/pg_hba.conf.BAK
   ```

   ```
   sed -i 's/^\(local.*\)peer$/\1md5/g' /var/lib/pgsql/data/pg_hba.conf
   ```

7. Next, we have to restart the `postgresql` service in order to apply our changes:

   ```
   systemctl restart postgresql
   ```

8. Now you will be able to login to your Postgres server with user `postgres` without the need to login the `postgres` Linux system user first:

   ```
   psql -U postgres
   ```

9. To exit the shell (`postgres=#`), type the following command (followed by the *Return* key):

   ```
   \q
   ```

10. We will now issue a shell command to create a new database user, by substituting `<username>` with a relevant user name to fit your own needs (type in a new password for the user when prompted, repeat it, and afterwards enter the password for the administrator user `postgres` to apply these settings):

    ```
    createuser -U postgres -P <username>
    ```

11. Now, also on the shell create your first database and assign it to our new user by replacing the `<database-name>` and `<username>` values with something more appropriate to your needs (enter the password for the `postgres` user):

    ```
    createdb -U postgres <database-name> -O <username>
    ```

12. Finally, test if you can access the Postgres server with your new user by printing all the database names:

    ```
    psql -U <username> -l
    ```

How it works...

PostgreSQL is an Object-Relational Database Management System and it is available to all CentOS servers. Postgres may not be as common as MariaDB, but its architecture and large array of features do make it an attractive solution for many companies concerned with data integrity.

So what did we learn from this experience?

We began this recipe by installing the necessary server and client `rpm` packages using `yum`. Having done this, we then proceeded to make the Postgres system available at boot before initializing the database system using the `postgresql-setup initdb` command. We completed this process by starting the database service. In the next stage, we were then required to set the password for the Postgres administrator user to harden the system. By default, the `postgresql` package creates a new Linux system user called `postgres` (which is also used as an administrative Postgres user account to access our Postgres DBMS), and by using `su - postgres - c` we were able to execute the `psql` commands as the `postgres` user, which is mandatory upon installation (this is called peer authentication).

Having set the admin password, to have more like a MariaDB shell-type of login procedure where every database user (including the administrator `postgres` user) can log in using the database `psql` client's user `-U` parameter, we changed this `peer` authentication to `md5` database password-based authentication for the localhost in the `pg_hba.conf` file (see the next recipe). After restarting the service, we then used Postgres's `createuser` and `createdb` command line tools to create a new Postgres user and connect it to a new database (we needed to provide the `postgres` user with the `-U` parameter because only he has the privileges for it). Finally, we showed you how to make a test connection to the database with your new user using the `-l` flag (which lists all the available databases). Also, you can use the `-d` parameter to connect to a specific database using the syntax: `psql -d <database-name> -U <username>`.

There's more...

Instead of using the `createuser` or `createdb` Postgres command-line tools, as we have been showing you in this recipe, to create your databases and users, you can also do the same using the Postgres shell. In fact, those command-line tools are actually just wrappers around the Postgres shell commands, and there is no effective difference between the two. `psql` is the primary command-line client tool for entering SQL queries or other commands on a Postgres server, similar to the MariaDB shell shown to you in another recipe in this chapter. Here, we will launch `psql` with a template called `template1`, the boilerplate (or default template) that is used to start building databases. After login (`psql -U postgres template1`), and typing in the administrator password you should be presented with the interactive Postgres prompt (`template1=#`). Now to create a new user in the `psql` shell, type:

```
CREATE USER <username> WITH PASSWORD '<password>';
```

To create a database, type:

```
CREATE DATABASE <database-name>;
```

The option to grant all privileges on the recently created database to the new user is:

```
GRANT ALL ON DATABASE <database-name> to <username>;
```

To exit the interactive shell, use: `\q` followed by pressing the *Return* key.

Having completed this recipe you could say that you not only know how to install PostgreSQL, but this process has served to highlight some simple architectural differences between this database system and MariaDB.

Configuring remote access to PostgreSQL

In this recipe, we will learn how to configure remote access to a Postgres server which is disabled by default. Postgres employs a method called host-based authentication and it is the purpose of this recipe to introduce you to its concepts in order to provide the access rights you need to run a safe and secure database server.

Getting ready

To complete this recipe, you will require a working installation of the CentOS 7 operating system with root privileges and a text editor of your choice. It is expected that PostgreSQL is already installed and running.

How to do it...

In the previous recipe, we have already modified the host-based authentication configuration `pg_hba.conf` file using `sed` to manage our Postgres's client authentication from peer to `md5`. Here we will make changes to it to manage remote access to our Postgres server.

1. To begin, log in as root and first open the firewall to allow any incoming PostgreSQL connections to the server:

   firewall-cmd --permanent --add-service=postgresql;firewall-cmd --reload

2. Now open the host-based authentication configuration file in your favorite text editor by typing:

   vi /var/lib/pgsql/data/pg_hba.conf

3. Scroll down to the end of the file and append the following line, to make these lines read as follows (substitute the XXX.XXX.XXX.XXX/XX value with a network address you want to grant access to. For example, if the IP address of your server was 192.168.1.12 then the network address would be 192.168.1.0/24):

   host   all   all   XXX.XXX.XXX.XXX/XX   md5

4. When you have finished, simply save and close the file in the usual way before opening the main Postgres configuration file by typing:

   vi /var/lib/pgsql/data/postgresql.conf

5. Add the following lines to the end of the file:

   listen_addresses = '*'

   port = 5432

6. When you have finished, save the file in the usual way before restarting the database server by typing the following command:

```
systemctl restart postgresql
```

7. On any other computer which is in the same network (defined by the XXX.XXX.XXX.XXX/XX value set previously), you can now test if the remote connection to your Postgres server is working using the psql shell (if your client computer is CentOS, you need to install it using yum install postgresql) by logging in on the server remotely and printing out some test data. In our example, the Postgres server is running with the IP address 192.168.1.12.

```
psql -h 192.168.1.12 -U <username> -d <database-name>
```

How it works...

PostgreSQL is a safe and secure database system but where we access it (either remotely or locally) can often become a cause of confusion. It was the purpose of this recipe to lift the lid on host-based authentication and provide an easy-to-use solution that will enable you to get your system up-and-running.

So what did we learn from this experience?

We began the recipe by opening the Postgres service's standard ports in firewalld in order to make a connection from any remote computer possible in the first place. Then we opened Postgres's host-based authentication configuration file called pg_hba.conf with our favorite text editor. Remember, we already changed from peer to md5 authentication for all local connections to provide user based authentication in a former recipe. The inserted host record line specifies a connection type, database name, a user name, a client IP address range, and the authentication method. Many of the previous commands may already be understood but it is important to realize that there are several different methods of authentication:

▶ **trust**: Allows the connection unconditionally and enables anyone to connect with the database server without the need for a password.

▶ **reject**: Allows the database server to reject a connection unconditionally, a feature that remains useful when filtering certain IP addresses or certain hosts from a group.

▶ **md5**: Implies that the client needs to supply an MD5-encrypted password for authentication.

▶ **peer and ident**: Access is granted if the client's logged in Linux user name from the operating system can be found as a database user in the system. ident is used for remote connections and peer for local connections.

Having completed this task, we then saved and closed the file before opening the main PostgreSQL configuration file located at `/var/lib/pgsql/data/postgresql.conf`. As you may or may not be aware, remote connections will not be possible unless the server is started with an appropriate value for `listen_addresses`, and where the default setting placed this on a local loopback address it was necessary to allow the database server to listen to all network interfaces (signified by the use of a star symbol or `*`) for incoming Postgres connections on the 5432 port. When finished, we simply saved the file and restarted the database server.

There is always much more to learn, but as a result of completing this recipe, you not only have a better understanding of host-based authentication but you have the ability to access your PostgreSQL database server both locally and remotely.

Installing phpMyAdmin and phpPgAdmin

Working with the MariaDB or Postgres command-line shell is sufficient for performing basic database administration tasks, such as user permission settings or creating simple databases as we have shown you in this chapter. The more complex your schemas and relationships between tables get and the more your data grows, the more you should consider using some graphical database user interfaces for better control and work performance. This is also true for novice database administrators as such tools provide you with syntax highlightning and validation and some tools even have graphical representations of your databases (for example, showing Entity Relationship Models). In this recipe, we will show you how to install two of the most popular graphical open-source database management software for MariaDB and PostgreSQL on the market, namely `phpMyadmin` and `phpPgAdmin,` which are web-based browser applications written in PHP.

Getting ready

To complete this recipe, you will require a working installation of the CentOS 7 operating system with root privileges, a console-based text editor of your choice, and a connection to the Internet in order to facilitate the download of additional packages. It is expected that your MariaDB or PostgreSQL server is already running using the recipes found in this chapter. Also, you will need a running Apache web server with PHP installed, which must be accessible from all the computers in your private network to deploy these applications (refer to *Chapter 12, Providing Web Services* for instructions). In addition, you need to have enabled the EPEL repositories for installing the correct software packages (refer to recipe *Using a third-party repository* in *Chapter 4, Managing Packages with YUM)*. Finally, you will need one computer in your network with a graphical window manager and a modern web-browser to access these web applications.

How to do it...

In this recipe, we will first show you how to install and configure phpMyAdmin for remote access and afterwards how to do the same for phpPgAdmin.

Installing and configuring phpMyAdmin

To install and configure phpMyAdmin, perform the following steps:

1. Type in the following command to install the required package:

    ```
    yum install phpMyAdmin
    ```

2. Now create a copy of the main phpMyadmin configuration file:

    ```
    cp /etc/httpd/conf.d/phpMyAdmin.conf /etc/httpd/conf.d/phpMyAdmin.conf.BAK
    ```

3. Next, open the main phpMyAdmin.conf configuration file and add the line Require ip XXX.XXX.XXX.XXX/XX with your defined subnet's network address you want to grant access to the web application—for example, Require ip 192.168.1.0/24 below the line Require ip 127.0.0.1. You have to do this twice in the file or you can use sed to do this automatically, as shown here. On the command-line define the environment variable NET= accordingly to fit it to your own subnet's network address.

    ```
    NET="192.168.1.0/24"
    ```

4. Then type the following line to apply your changes to the configuration file:

    ```
    sed -i "s,\(Require ip 127.0.0.1\),\1\nRequire ip $NET,g" /etc/httpd/conf.d/phpMyAdmin.conf
    ```

5. Afterwards, reload your Apache server and now you should be able to browse to the phpMyAdmin website from any other computer in your subnet using the server's IP running the web application, for example 192.168.1.12 (log in with your MariaDB administrator user called root or any other database user):

    ```
    http://192.168.1.12/phpMyAdmin
    ```

Installing and configuring phpPgAdmin

Following are the steps to install and configure phpPgAdmin:

1. Type in the following command to install the required package:

    ```
    yum install phpPgAdmin
    ```

2. Before editing the phpPgAdmin main configuration, make a backup of it first:

    ```
    cp /etc/httpd/conf.d/phpPgAdmin.conf /etc/httpd/conf.d/phpPgAdmin.conf.BAK
    ```

3. Allowing remote access to `phpPgAdmin` is very similar to `phpMyAdmin`. Here you can also add a `Require ip XXX.XXX.XXX.XXX/XX` line with your defined subnet's network address below the line `Require local` in the `phpPgAdmin.conf` file, or use the `sed` utility to do this automatically for you:

```
NET="192.168.1.0/24"

sed -i "s,\(Require local\),\1\nRequire ip $NET,g" /etc/httpd/
conf.d/phpPgAdmin.conf
```

4. Restart Apache and browse to the `phpPgAdmin` main page:

```
http://192.168.1.12/phpPgAdmin
```

How it works...

In this fairly simple recipe, we have shown you how to install two of the most popular graphical administration tools for MariaDB and Postgres, running as web applications in your browser (and written in PHP) on the same server where your database service is running, and enabled remote access to them.

So what did we learn from this experience?

Installing `phpMyAdmin` for administering MariaDB databases and `phpPgAdmin` for Postgres databases was as easy as installing the corresponding `rpm` packages using the `yum` package manager. As both the tools are not to be found in the official CentOS 7 repositories, you need to enable the third-party repository EPEL before you can access and install these packages. By default, when installing both the web applications, access is denied to any connection not being made from the server itself (local only). Since we want to have access to it from different computers in our network, having installed a web browser you need to allow remote connections first. For both the web applications, this can be achieved using the Apache `Require ip` directive which is part of the Apache `mod_authz_core` module. In both the configuration files for `phpMyAdmin` and `phpPgAdmin`, we defined a whole subnet, such as `192.168.1.0/24`, to allow connecting to the server, but you can also use a single IP address here which you want to allow access to. The `sed` commands inserted these important `Require` lines into the configuration file, but as said earlier you can also do this manually if you like by editing these files with your text editor of choice. After reloading the Apache configuration, you were then able to browse to the web pages using the two URLs shown in the recipe. On the start page of both the web sites, you can use any database user to log in without the need to enable remote privileges for them; any user with local permissions is sufficient.

In summary, we can say that we only showed you the basic configuration of both administration tools. There is always more to learn; for example, you should consider securing both PHP websites with SSL encryption or configuring your instances to connect to different database servers. Also, if you prefer desktop software for managing your databases, have a look at the open-source MySQL Workbench Community Edition, which can be downloaded from the official MySQL website for all major operating systems (Windows, OS X, Linux).

11

Providing Mail Services

In this chapter, we will cover:

- ▶ Configuring a domain-wide mail service with Postfix
- ▶ Working with Postfix
- ▶ Delivering the mail with Dovecot
- ▶ Using Fetchmail

Introduction

This chapter is a collection of recipes that deliver the necessary steps to implement and maintain one of the oldest and most versatile technologies on the Internet today. Everyone wants to send and receive e-mails and this chapter provides the necessary starting point required to deploy such a service in a timely and efficient manner.

Configuring a domain-wide mail service with Postfix

Postfix is a **Mail Transport Agent** (**MTA**) responsible for the transfer of e-mails between mail servers using the SMTP protocol. Postfix is now the default MTA on CentOS 7. Here, as with most other critical network services, its default configuration allows outgoing but does not accept incoming network connections from any host other than the local one. This makes sense if all you need is a local Linux user mailing system and for sending out mails to other external mail servers from localhost too. But if you want to run your own centralized mail server for your own private network and domain, this is quite restrictive. So the purpose of this recipe is to set up Postfix as a domain-wide mail service to allow e-mails sent from any host in your network and if the recipient is a valid e-mail address within your local domain, deliver them to the correct mailbox on the mail server.

Getting ready

To complete this recipe, you will require a working installation of the CentOS 7 operating system with root privileges, a console-based text editor of your choice, and a connection to the Internet to download additional software packages. You need to set up your local network properly and make sure that all the computers that want to send mails through your single-domain mailserver are in the same network and can ping this server. Also, setting your system time correctly is very important for any mail server. Apply the *Synchronizing the system clock with NTP and the chrony suite* recipe in *Chapter 2, Configuring the System* before beginning your configuration. Finally, you need to set a **Fully Qualified Domain Name** (**FQDN**) for your mail server. Refer to the *Setting your hostname and resolving the network* recipe in *Chapter 2, Configuring the System*. It is expected that your server will be using a static IP address and that it maintains one or more system user accounts. It is also assumed that you are working through this chapter recipe by recipe in the order in which they appear.

How to do it...

Postfix is already installed by default on all CentOS 7 flavors and it should be in a running state. In our example, we want to build a central mail server for our network 192.168.1.0/24 with the local domain name called `centos7.home`.

1. First login as root and test if Postfix is already working locally and can send local mails to your system users. Type the following command to send a mail to a Linux user specified by `<username>`:

   echo "This is a testmail" | sendmail <username>

2. On CentOS 7, Postfix is also already configured to send out mails to external e-mail addresses (but from localhost only) without any changes to the configuration file. For example, you could use right out-of-the-box:

   echo "This is a testmail" | sendmail contact@example.com

    If you don't have a trusted domain and certificate behind your Postfix server, in times of massive spam e-mails most external e-mail servers will reject or put such e-mails directly into the spam folders.

3. To see if the local mail message has been delivered successfully, show the latest mail log (Press *Ctrl+C* to exit the log):

   tail -f /var/log/maillog

4. Next, check if a FQDN for our server is available. This is mandatory, and if not set properly, refer to *Chapter 2, Configuring the System* to set one (in our example, this will output the name `mailserver.centos7.home`):

   hostname --fqdn

5. Now create a backup copy of the main Postfix configuration file before opening this file:

    ```
    cp /etc/postfix/main.cf /etc/postfix/main.cf.BAK && vi /etc/
    postfix/main.cf
    ```

6. First of all, we will want Postfix to listen on all network interfaces instead of only the local one. Activate or uncomment the following line (which means remove the # sign at the beginning of the line) that starts with `inet_interfaces` to read:

    ```
    inet_interfaces = all
    ```

7. Now, some lines below, you will find the line that reads `inet_interfaces = localhost`. Deactivate it or comment it out by putting a # sign at the start of the line:

    ```
    # inet_interfaces = localhost
    ```

8. Next we need to set the local domain-name of the mail server. For example, if our mailserver's FQDN is `mailserver.centos7.home` and this mailserver is responsible for delivering mail for the whole private `centos7.home` domain, the domain name will be (it's best to put it below the line that reads #mydomain = domain.tld):

    ```
    mydomain = centos7.home
    ```

9. With the intention that this server may become a domain-wide mail server, you should now update the following line that starts with `mydestination` to read as follows (for example, in the `mydestination` section, comment out the first `mydestination` line and uncomment the second line):

    ```
    mydestination = $myhostname, localhost.$mydomain, localhost,
    $mydomain
    ```

10. Next, we need to specify the pathname of a mailbox file relative to a user's home directory. To do this, scroll down and locate the line that begins with `home_mailbox` and uncomment the following option (remove the # sign at the line's beginning):

    ```
    home_mailbox = Maildir/
    ```

11. Save and close the file. Now we want to open the correct Postfix server ports in the firewall to allow the incoming SMTP connections to the server:

    ```
    firewall-cmd --permanent --add-service=smtp && firewall-cmd
    --reload
    ```

12. Next, restart the Postfix service as follows:

    ```
    systemctl restart postfix
    ```

13. Afterwards, login to a different computer in the same network and install **Swiss Army Knife SMTP** (**swaks**) to test out our Postfix server connection remotely. On CentOS, type the following (it needs the EPEL repository to be installed in advance):

```
yum install swaks
```

14. Now, to test if you can connect to our new Postfix server using the standard SMTP mail port 25, with our Postfix server running on the IP address `192.168.1.100`, we are sending a mail remotely to a Linux system user `john` which has a system user account on our Postfix server:

```
swaks --server 192.168.1.100 --to john@centos7.home
```

15. Swaks creates output which should give us a hint if the mail transport has been successful. For example (the output has been truncated):

```
-> This is a test mailing
<-  250 2.0.0 Ok: queued as D18EE52B38
 -> QUIT
<-  221 2.0.0 Bye
```

16. You can also test that the last command has been successful by logging in as user `john` on the Postfix server, then checking and reading your local mailbox's inbox, which should contain a file with the test mail sent from the swaks tool (the filename will be different on your computer), as follows:

```
ls ~/Maildir/new
```

```
less ~/Maildir/new/14941584.Vfd02I1M246414.mailserver.centos7.home
```

How it works...

As we have seen, Postfix is installed and running on every CentOS 7 system by default and in its basic configuration the mail server is listening on the localhost address for incoming mails so you can already send out local mails between your server's local Linux system users without the need to contact an external MTA. It is already running because your system is already using it for a number of local services, such as the crond daemon or for sending out warnings about security breaches (for example, running a `sudo` command as a non-sudo user).

Before we can explain how this recipe works, we need to review some more basics about the Postfix MTA system in general. The Postfix MTA service can receive incoming e-mails from mail clients or other remote MTA servers using the SMTP protocol. If an incoming e-mail is destinated for the MTA server's configured final destination domain (for example, a mail sent with the recipient address `john@centos7.home` is incoming to the `centos7.home` configured Postfix MTA server), it will deliver the mail to a local mailbox installed on the server (either in the filesystem or in a database system such as MariaDB). If the incoming mail is not destinated for this server, it will be relayed (forwarded) to another MTA.

Remember that this is all a Postfix server is capable of doing and nothing more: receiving incoming SMTP connections from mail clients or other MTAs, delivering mail to local mailboxes on the server, and forwarding mail to other MTAs using SMTP. Contrary to common belief, Postfix cannot transfer the mails from its local mailboxes to the end users. Here we need another type of MTA called **delivery agent**, which uses different mail protocols, such as IMAP or POP3.

In this recipe, we configured our Postfix server so that the other computers and servers in the same network could also send mails to our Postfix server, which is blocked by default (by default only the server itself can send mails). If an incoming e-mail, sent from another computer in our network, has the same domain name in the recipient's e-mail address as our Postfix server has its FQDN in, then it gets delivered to the appropriate local mailbox defined by the recipient's part of the e-mail; all external e-mail addresses get relayed to an external MTA.

So what did we learn from this experience?

We began our journey by testing if we could send out local mails to system users. Here we logged in as our root user and sent a mail to a valid local system user using the sendmail program, which is included in the Postfix package. For every mail you send using sendmail, you should be able to see some new lines appearing in the `/var/log/maillog` file, which contains status information and other important logging text for the mail. If you sent a message from `root` to the user `john` and the FQDN of your server is `centos7.home`, new output lines appended to the log file should contain amongst other things a `from=<root@centos7.home>`, a `to=<john@centos7.home>` and if delivered successfully, a `status=sent` information. If no such logging information shows up, check the status of the Postfix service.

Afterwards, we displayed the FQDN for our server. It is very important to set this up correctly because this information will be used to authenticate the Postfix server when connecting to other MTAs or mail clients. MTAs check the FQDN which has been announced by their partner and some even refuse to connect if it is not provided or if it differs from the real DNS domain name of the server. After our initial test, we then started editing the main Postfix configuration file after we made a backup copy of it first. As said before, by default only the users sitting on the same server the Postfix service is running on can send mails between them as the server defaults to listening on the loopback device only. So first we enabled Postfix to listen to all the available network interfaces instead, using the `inet_interfaces = all` parameter. This ensured that all our clients in our network could connect to this server. Next, we set the domain name using the `mydomain` parameter we wanted to have for Postfix. In order for Postfix to work in our network, the domain name defined here in this variable must be the exact same value as the domain name for our server's network. Afterwards, we changed the `mydestination` parameter by choosing the line which adds the `$mydomain` parameter to the list of allowed domains. This will define all domains our Postfix mail server considers as the final destination. If a Postfix mail server is configured as the final destination for a domain, it will deliver the messages to the local mailboxes of the recipient users, which can be found in `/var/spool/mail/<username>` (we will change this location in the next step) instead of forwarding the mails to the other MTAs (as we added `$mydomain` to the list of final destinations in our example, we will deliver all mails sent to the `centos7.home` domain).

Here, you also need to remember that, by default, Postfix *trusts* all the other computers (SMTP clients) in the same IP subnetwork as the Postfix server is in to send mails to external e-mail addresses (relay mails to external MTAs) through our centralized server, which could be too relaxed for your network policy. Since e-mail spam is an ongoing problem on the Internet and we don't want to allow any user to abuse our mail server from sending spam (which an open relay mail server does; it this takes anything from any client and sends it to any mail server), we can further increase security by setting `mynetworks_style = host`, which only trusts and allows the localhost to send mails to external MTAs. Another way to reduce the spam risk might be to use the `mynetworks` parameter where you can specify which network or IP address is allowed to connect to our mail server and send e-mails through it; for example, `mynetworks = 127.0.0.0/8, 192.168.1.0/24`. To learn more about all the available Postfix settings, refer to the Postfix configuration parameter manual using the command `man 5 postconf`. Afterwards, we changed where the local mail should be stored. By default, all the incoming mails go to a centralized mailbox space located at `/var/spool/mail/<username>`. In order for local users to receive their mail in their own home directory, we used the `Maildir` parameter for the `home_mailbox` option, which changes this system to deliver all the mails to `/home/<username>/Maildir/` instead. Afterwards, we opened the standard SMTP protocol port in firewalld using the SMPT service, which Postfix uses for communication with the other MTAs or mail clients sending incoming mails through.

Postfix is already configured to start at boot, but to complete this part of the recipe we restarted the Postfix service for it to accept the new configuration settings. At this stage, the process of configuring Postfix was complete, but to test remote access we needed to log into another computer in the same network. Here we installed a small command line-based mail client called `swaks`, which can be used to test local or remote SMTP server connections. We ran our test by sending a mail to our remote Postfix mail server and supplied a recipient user and the IP address of our SMTP server. Having done this, you should have received a test message and as a result you should be happy to know that everything is working correctly. However, if you did happen to encounter any errors, you should refer to the mailserver log file located at `/var/log/maillog`.

There's more...

In this section of the recipe, we will change your e-mail sender address, encrypt SMTP connections, and configure your BIND DNS server to include our new mailserver's information.

Changing an e-mail's appearing domain name

If an MTA sends out an e-mail, Postfix automatically appends the hostname of the sender's e-mail address by default, if not provided explicitly otherwise, which is a great feature to track down which computer in your network sent the e-mail locally (otherwise it would be hard to find the origin of a mail if you got multiple computers sending out mails by a user called **root**). Often when sending messages to a remote MTA, you don't want to have your local hostname appear in the e-mail.

Here it is better to have only the domain name alone. In order to change this, go to the Postfix MTA you want to send mails from, open the Postfix configuration file /etc/postfix/main. cf, and enable this feature by uncommenting (removing the # sign at the beginning of the line) the following line to determine the origin (restart the Postfix service afterwards):

```
myorigin = $mydomain
```

Using TLS- (SSL) encryption for SMTP communication

Even if you are running your own Postfix server in a small or private environment, you should always be aware that normal SMTP traffic will be sent in clear text over the Internet, making it possible that anyone could sniff the communication. TLS will allow us to set up an encrypted SMTP connection between the server and the mail client, meaning that the complete communication will be made enciphered and impossible to be read by a third-party. In order to do this, if you have not already bought an official SSL certificate or generated some self-signed certificates for your domain, start by creating one here (read the *Generating self-signed certificates* recipe in *Chapter 6, Providing Security* to learn more). First login as root on your server and go to the standard certificate location: /etc/pki/tls/certs. Next, create a TLS/SSL keypair consisting of the certificate and its embedded public key as well as the private key (enter your Postfix's FQDN as the Common name, for example, mailserver. centos7.home) to do this type make postfix-server.pem. Afterwards, open the main Postfix configuration file /etc/postfix/main.cf with your favorite text editor and put in the following lines at the end of the file:

```
smtpd_tls_cert_file = /etc/pki/tls/certs/postfix-server.pem
smtpd_tls_key_file = $smtpd_tls_cert_file
smtpd_tls_security_level = may
smtp_tls_security_level = may
smtp_tls_loglevel = 1
smtpd_tls_loglevel = 1
```

Then save and close this file. Note that setting smtpd_tls_security_level to may will activate TLS encryption if available in the mail client program, otherwise it will use an unencrypted connection. You should only set this value to encrypt (which will enforce SSL/TLS encryption in any case) if you are absolutely sure that all your senders to your mail server are supporting this feature. If any sender (external MTA or mail client) does not support this feature, the connection will be refused. This means that e-mails from such sources will not be delivered into your local mailboxes. We also specified TLS encryption for outgoing SMTP connections from our Postfix server to other MTAs where possible using smtp_tls_security_level = may. By setting both the Postfix's client and server mode TLS log level to 1 we get more verbose output so we can check if the TLS connections are working. Some very old mail clients use an ancient port 465 for encrypting SMTP over SSL/TLS instead of the standard SMTP port 25.

In order to activate this feature, open `/etc/postfix/master.cf` and search, then uncomment (remove # at the start of each line) the following lines, so they read:

```
smtps          inet   n      -      n      -      -      smtpd
-o syslog_name=postfix/smtps
-o smtpd_tls_wrappermode=yes
```

Save and close the file, and then restart Postfix. Next, we need to open the SMTPS port in the firewall to allow incoming connections to our server. Since no SMTPS firewalld rule is available in CentOS 7, we will create our own service file first using the `sed` utility:

```
sed 's/25/465/g' /usr/lib/firewalld/services/smtp.xml | sed 's/Mail
(SMTP)/Mail (SMTP) over SSL/g' > /etc/firewalld/services/smtps.xml

firewall-cmd --reload

firewall-cmd --permanent --add-service=smtps; firewall-cmd --reload
```

You should now be able to test if an SMTPS connection can be made by using our `swaks` SMTP command line tool with the `-tls` parameter from a remote computer to our Postfix server running on IP 192.168.1.100, for example `swaks --server 192.168.1.100 --to john@centos7.home -tls`. This command line will test if the SMTP server supports TLS encryption (`STARTTLS`) and exit with an error message if it is not available for any reason. A working output would look as follows (truncated to only show you the most important lines):

```
 -> STARTTLS
<-  220 2.0.0 Ready to start TLS
=== TLS started with cipher TLSv1.2:ECDHE-RSA-AES128-GCM-SHA256:128
 ~> This is a test mailing
<~  250 2.0.0 Ok: queued as E36F652B38
```

You can then also recheck your TLS setup by going to the main mail log file on your Postfix server and watching for the following line corresponding to your swaks test mail from the last step (your output will be different):

```
Anonymous TLS connection established from unknown[192.168.1.22]:
TLSv1.2 with cipher ECDHE-RSA-AES256-GCM-SHA384 (256/256 bits)
```

Configure BIND to use your new mailserver

After our domain-wide Postfix server has been installed and configured, we should now announce this new mail service in our domain using a DNS server. Refer to *Chapter 8, Working with FTP* for details on how to set up and configure a BIND server, and especially read the section about the **Mail eXchanger** (**MX**) record if you haven't already. Then add a new MX entry to your BIND forward and corresponding reverse zone file. In your forward zone file, add the following lines for our Postfix server with the IP 192.168.1.100:

```
IN      MX      10      mailhost.centos7.home.
mailhost                IN      A       192.168.1.100
```

In your reverse zone file, you could add the following lines instead:

```
100                  IN  PTR        mailhost.centos7.local.
```

Working with Postfix

In a previous recipe, we learned how to install and configure Postfix as our domain-wide e-mail server. When it comes to working with e-mails, there are lots of different tools and programs available for Linux and we already showed you how to send e-mails through the `sendmail` program as well as the `swaks` utility. Here in this recipe, we will show you how to work with one of the most commonly used mail utilities in Unix and Linux, called `mailx`, which has some useful features missing in the sendmail package for sending mails or reading your mailbox.

How to do it...

We will begin this recipe by installing the `mailx` package on our server running our domain-wide Postfix service, as it is not available on CentOS 7 by default.

1. Begin by logging in as root and typing the following command:

    yum install mailx

2. The easiest way is to use `mailx` with its standard input mode, as follows:

    echo "this is the mail body." | mail -s "subject" john@centos7.home

3. You can also send mails from a text file. This is useful when calling the `mailx` command from a shell script, using multiple recipients, or attaching some files to the e-mail:

    cat ~/.bashrc | mail -s "Content of roots bashrc file" john
    echo "another mail body" | mail -s "body" john,paul@example.
    com,chris
    echo "this is the email body" | mailx -s "another testmail but
    with attachment" -a "/path/to/file1" -a "/path/to/another/file"
    john@gmail.com

Connecting mailx to a remote MTA

One big advantage over the `sendmail` program is that we can use `mailx` to directly connect to and communicate with remote MTA mail servers. In order to test this feature, log in to another Linux-based computer, which should be in the same network as our Postfix server, install the `mailx` package, and send a mail through our Postfix server's IP address `192.168.1.100` (we have already opened the incoming SMTP firewall port in a previous recipe). In our example, we will send a local mail to the user `john`:

echo "This is the body" | mail -S smtp=192.168.1.100 -s "This is a remote
test" -v john@centos7.home

Reading your local mails from the mailbox

Not only can the `mailx` program send e-mail messages to any SMTP server, it also provides a convenient mail reader interface for your local mailbox when started locally on the Postfix server. If you run the mail program with `-f` specifying a user mailbox, the program will start by showing you all the inbox e-mails. But remember that `mailx` can only read local mailboxes when the program is started on the same server your mailboxes are located at (if you want to use it to access your mailbox remotely you need to install an MTA access agent such as Dovecot—see later—with POP3 or IMAP). For example, login as Linux system user `john` on the Postfix server, and then, to open the mail reader with your user's local mailbox, type: `mailx -f ~/Maildir`.

You will now be presented with a list of all the mail messages in your current inbox. If you want to read a specific mail, you need to type in its number and press the *Return* key. After reading it, you can type *d* followed by *Return* to delete it or *r* followed by *Return* to reply to it. To go back to your current mail message overview screen, type *z* followed by *Return*. If you have more than one screen of mail messages, type *z-* (z minus) followed by *Return* to go back one page. Type *x* followed by *Return* to exit the program. To learn more, refer to the `mailx` manual (`man mailx`).

How it works...

In this recipe, we showed you how to install and use `mailx`, a program to send and read your Internet mail. It is based on an old Unix mail program called Berkely mail and provides the functionality of the POSIX `mailx` command. It should be installed on every serious CentOS 7 server because it has some advantages over the `sendmail` program and understands the protocols IMAP, POP3, and SMTP (If you need an even more user-friendly mail reader and sender, you can check out mutt. Type `yum install mutt` to install it. Then type `man mutt` to read its manual).

So what did we learn from this experience?

We started this recipe by installing the `mailx` package using the YUM package manager on our Postfix server. It includes the `mailx` command line program which can be run either with the command `mail` or `mailx`. Afterwards, we ran the program with the `-s` parameter, which specifies an e-mail subject and; also you need a recipient e-mail address as argument, either an external address or a local Linux system user name or mail. Without anything else, `mailx` suspects it's running on the same server as the mail server is on, so it implicitly sends the mail to the localhost MTA, which is Postfix in our example. Also, in its most simple form, `mailx` starts in interactive mode, which lets you type in the message body fields manually at the command line. This is good for quickly writing a mail for testing, but in most cases you will use `mailx` by piping in content from another source. Here we showed you how to do this by using the `echo` command to write a string to the Standard Input (STDIN) of `mailx,` but you can also `cat` a file content into it.

One often used example is to send some kind of file output or a log file content of a failing command to an administrator user or system reports at a certain scheduled time point using `cron`. Afterwards, we saw that we could also send mails to multiple recipients by comma-separating their e-mail addresses, and showed you how to send attachments along with your mail messages by using the `-a` option. In the next section, we then showed you how to send mails to a remote SMTP mail server using the `-S` option to set internal options (`variable=value`). This is a very useful feature if you haven't specified your standard mail server on your DNS server or for testing a remote mail server. Finally, in the last section we showed you how you could read your local mailbox on your Postfix server using `mailx`. It has a convenient browsing functionality to read, delete, and reply, and do advanced e-mail management for your local mailbox. You do this by typing in commands into the `mailx` interactive sessions followed by pressing the *Return* key. Remember, if you don't like this way of browsing your mails, you can also always read or filter your mails in your user's `~/Maildir` directory using command-line tools, such as `grep`, `less,` and so on. For example, to search all new mails for the case-intensive keyword `PackPub.com`, type `grep -i packtpub ~/Maildir/new`.

Delivering the mail with Dovecot

In a previous recipe, you were shown how to configure Postfix as a domain-wide mail transport agent. As we have learned in the first recipe of this chapter, Postfix only understands the SMTP protocol and does a remarkable job to transport messages from another MTA or mail user client to other remote mail servers or storing mails which are destinated to itself into its local mailboxes. After storing or relaying mails, Postfix jobs end. Postfix can only understand and speak the SMTP protocol and is not capable of sending messages to anything other than MTAs. Any possible recipient user for a mail message who wants to read his mails would now need to log in to the server running the Postfix service using ssh and look into his local mailbox directory, or alternatively use `mailx` locally to view his messages on a regular basis to see if there are any new mails. This is highly inconvenient and nobody would use such a system. Instead, the users choose to access and read their mail from their own workstations other than where our Postfix server is located. Therefore, another group of MTAs has been developed, sometimes are called **access agents** and which have the main functionality to synchronize or transfer those local mailbox messages from the server running the Postfix daemon over to external mailing programs where users can read them. These MTA systems use different protocols than SMTP, namely POP3 or IMAP. One such MTA program is Dovecot. Most professional server administrators would agree that Postfix and Dovecot are perfect partners and it is the purpose of this recipe to learn how to configure Postfix to work with Dovecot in order to provide a basic POP3/IMAP and a POP3/IMAP over SSL (POP3S/IMAPS) service for our mailboxes to provide an industry standard e-mail service for your users across the local network.

Getting ready

To complete this recipe, you will require a working installation of the CentOS 7 operating system with root privileges, a console-based text editor of your choice, and a connection to the Internet in order to download additional packages. It is also assumed that you are working through this chapter recipe by recipe in the order that they appear and for this reason it is expected that Postfix has been configured as a domain-wide MTA.

 This recipe serves as a guide to setting up a basic POP3S/IMAPS service for trusted users on a local network. It is not suitable for general Internet use without applying additional security measures.

How to do it...

Dovecot is not installed by default, and for this reason we must begin by installing the necessary packages by following the given steps:

1. To start, log in as root and type in the following command:

   ```
   yum install dovecot
   ```

2. Once installed, enable the Dovecot service at boot by typing:

   ```
   systemctl enable dovecot
   ```

3. Now open the main Dovecot configuration file in your favorite text editor, after creating a backup copy, by typing:

   ```
   cp /etc/dovecot/dovecot.conf /etc/dovecot/dovecot.conf.BAK
   vi /etc/dovecot/dovecot.conf
   ```

4. Begin by confirming the `protocols` we want to use by activating (removing the # sign at the beginning of the line) and modifying the following line, so it reads:

   ```
   protocols = pop3 imap imaps pop3s
   ```

5. Next, enable Dovecot to listen to all network interfaces instead of only the loopback address. Search for the line `#listen = *, ::`, then modify it so it reads:

   ```
   listen = *
   ```

6. Now save and close the file in the usual way before making a backup of the `10-mail.conf` file and afterwards opening it in your favorite text editor:

   ```
   cp /etc/dovecot/conf.d/10-mail.conf /etc/dovecot/conf.d/10-mail.conf.BAK
   vi /etc/dovecot/conf.d/10-mail.conf
   ```

7. Scroll down and uncomment (remove # character) the following line, so it reads:

   ```
   mail_location = maildir:~/Maildir
   ```

8. Again, save and close the file in the usual way before creating a backup copy and then opening the following file in your favorite text editor:

   ```
   cp /etc/dovecot/conf.d/20-pop3.conf /etc/dovecot/conf.d/20-pop3.conf.BAK

   vi /etc/dovecot/conf.d/20-pop3.conf
   ```

9. Start by uncommenting the following line:

   ```
   pop3_uidl_format = %08Xu%08Xv
   ```

10. Now scroll down and amend the following line:

    ```
    pop3_client_workarounds = outlook-no-nuls oe-ns-eoh
    ```

11. Save and close the file in the usual way. Now we will allow plain text logins. To do this, make a backup before opening the following file:

    ```
    cp /etc/dovecot/conf.d/10-auth.conf /etc/dovecot/conf.d/10-auth.conf.BAK

    vi /etc/dovecot/conf.d/10-auth.conf
    ```

12. Change the line `#disable_plaintext_auth = yes` to state:

    ```
    disable_plaintext_auth = no
    ```

13. Save and close the file. In our final configuration setting, we will tell Dovecot to use our self-signed server certificate. Just use your Postfix certificate from another recipe in this chapter or create a new one (otherwise skip this step):

    ```
    cd /etc/pki/tls/certs; make postfix-server.pem
    ```

14. Open Dovecot's standard SSL config file after making a backup of the file:

    ```
    cp /etc/dovecot/conf.d/10-ssl.conf /etc/dovecot/conf.d/10-ssl.conf.BAK

    vi /etc/dovecot/conf.d/10-ssl.conf
    ```

15. Now change the following line (`ssl = required`) to read:

    ```
    ssl = yes
    ```

16. Now change the following two lines to point to your server's own certificate path:

    ```
    ssl_cert = < /etc/pki/tls/certs/postfix-server.pem
    ssl_key = </etc/pki/tls/certs/postfix-server.pem
    ```

17. Save and close this file. Next, enable IMAP, IMAPS, POP3, and POP3S ports in our firewall to allow incoming connections on the corresponding ports. For POP3 and IMAP, we need to specify our own `firewalld` service files, since they are not available in CentOS 7 by default:

```
sed 's/995/110/g' /usr/lib/firewalld/services/pop3s.xml | sed 's/
over SSL//g' > /etc/firewalld/services/pop3.xml
sed 's/993/143/g' /usr/lib/firewalld/services/imaps.xml | sed 's/
over SSL//g' > /etc/firewalld/services/imap.xml
firewall-cmd --reload
for s in pop3 imap pop3s imaps; do firewall-cmd --permanent --add-
service=$s; done;firewall-cmd --reload
```

18. Now save and close the file before starting the Dovecot service:

```
systemctl start dovecot
```

19. Finally, to test our new POP3/SMTP network service, just login on another computer in the same network and run the following commands to use `mailx` to access the local mailboxes on the remote Postfix server, which is provided by Dovecot with the different access agent protocols. In our example, we want to access the local mailbox of the system user `john` on our Postfix server with the IP `192.168.1.100` (to login to john's account, you need his Linux user password) remotely:

```
mailx -f pop3://john@192.168.1.100
mailx -f imap://john@192.168.1.100
```

20. Next, to test the secure connections, use the following commands and type `yes` to confirm that the certificate is self-signed and not trusted:

```
mailx -v -S nss-config-dir=/etc/pki/nssdb -f pop3s://
john@192.168.1.100
mailx -v -S nss-config-dir=/etc/pki/nssdb -f imaps://
john@192.168.1.100
```

21. For all four commands, you should see the normal `mailx` inbox view of your mailbox with all your mail messages of user `john` as you would run the `mailx` command locally on the Postfix server to read local mails.

How it works...

Having successfully completed this recipe, you have just created a basic POP3/SMTP service, (with or without SSL encryption) for all the valid server users in your network, which will deliver local mails from the Postfix server to the client's e-mail program. Every local system user can directly authenticate and connect to the mail server and fetch their mail remotely. Of course, there is still much more that can be done to enhance the service, but you can now enable all local system account holders to configure their favorite e-mail desktop software to send and receive e-mail messages using your server.

POP3 downloads the mails from the server on a local machine and deletes them afterwards, whereas IMAP synchronizes your mails with your mail server without deleting them.

So what did we learn from this experience?

We started the recipe by installing Dovecot. Having done this, we then enabled Dovecot to run at boot before proceeding to make a few brief changes to a series of configuration files. Starting with the need to determine which protocol will be used in the Dovecot configuration file at `/etc/dovecot/dovecot.cf` here we will use: IMAP, POP3, IMAPS, and POP3S. As with most other essential networking services, after installation they only listen on the loopback device, so we enabled Dovecot to listen to all network interfaces installed in the server. In the `10-mail.conf` file we then confirmed the mailbox directory location for Dovecot (with the `mail_location` directive) as the location Postfix will put them into on receiving mails so Dovecot can find them here and pick them up. Following this, we then opened the POP3 protocol in `20-pop3.conf` by adding a fix relating to various e-mail clients (for example, for the Outlook client) using the `pop3_uidl_format` and `pop3_client_workarounds` directives. Finally, we enabled plain text authorization by making several changes to `/etc/dovecot/conf.d/10-auth.conf`. Remember that using plain text authorization with POP3 or IMAP without SSL encryption is considered insecure but because we were concentrating on a local area network (for a group of trusted server users) we should not necessarily see this as a risk. Afterwards, we enabled POP3 and IMAP over SSL (POP3S and IMAPS) by pointing the `ssl` directives in the `10-ssl.conf` file to some existing self-signed server certificates. Here we changed `ssl = required` to `ssl=yes` to not force the client connecting to the Dovecot service to use SSL encryption, as we do want to give the user the choice to enable encrypted authentication if he likes to but not make it mandatory for older clients. Afterwards, to make our Dovecot service available from the other computers in our network, we had to enable the four ports to allow POP3, IMAP, POP3S, and IMAPS, 993, 995, 110, 143, by using the predefined `firewalld` service files and creating the missing ones for IMAP and POP3 ourselves. Later, we started the Dovecot service and tested our new POP3/IMAP server using the `mailx` command remotely. By supplying an `-f` file parameter, we were able to specify our protocol and location. For using SSL connections, we needed to supply an additional `nss-config-dir` option pointing to our local Network Security Services database where certificates are stored in CentOS 7.

Remember, if you happen to encounter any errors, you should always refer to the log file located at `/var/log/maillog`. Using plain text authorization should not be used in a real corporate environment and POP3/IMAP over SSL should be preferred.

There's more...

In the main recipe, you were shown how to install Dovecot in order to enable trusted local system users with system accounts to send and receive e-mails. These users will be able to use their existing username as the basis of their e-mail address, but by making a few enhancements you can quickly enable aliases, which is a way to define alternative e-mail addresses for existing users.

To start building a list of user aliases, you should begin by opening the following file in your favorite text editor:

```
vi /etc/aliases
```

Now add your new identities to the end of the file, where `<username>` will be the name of the actual system account:

```
#users aliases for mail

newusernamea:     <username>

newusernameb:     <username>
```

For example, if you have a user called `john` who currently (only) accepts e-mails at `john@centos7.home`, but you want to create a new alias for `john` called `johnwayne@centos7.home`, you will write:

```
johnwayne:    john
```

Repeat this action for all the aliases, but when you have finished remember to save and close the file in the usual way before running the following command: `newaliases`.

Setting up e-mail software

There are a vast number of e-mail clients on the market and by now you will want to start setting up your local users to be able to send and receive e-mails. This isn't complicated by any means, but in order to have a good starting point you will want to consider the following principles. The format of the e-mail address will be `system_username@domain-name.home`.

The incoming POP3 settings will be similar to the following:

```
mailserver.centos7.home, Port 110
Username: system_username
Connection Security: None
Authentication: Password/None
```

For POP3S, just change the port to `995` and use `Connection Security: SSL/TLS`. For IMAP, just change the port to `143`, and for IMAPS use port `993` and `Connection Security: SSL/TLS`.

The outgoing SMTP settings will be similar to the following:

```
mailserver.centos7.home, Port 25
Username: system_username
Connection Security: None
Authentication: None
```

Using Fetchmail

So far in this chapter, we have shown you two different forms of MTA. First we introduced you to the Postfix MTA, which is a transport agent used for routing e-mails from a mail client to or between mail servers and delivering them to the local mailboxes on the mail server using the SMTP protocol. Then we showed you another type of MTA which sometimes called an access agent and which the Dovecot program can be used for. This delivers mails from the local Postfix mailboxes to any remote mail client programs using the POP3 or IMAP protocol. Now we will introduce you to a third type of MTA, which can be termed a retrieval agent, and explain what we will use the program Fetchmail for. Nowadays, almost everybody has more than one e-mail account, from one or more different mail providers, which can be hard to maintain if you need to login to all those different webmail sites or use different accounts in your mail program. This is where Fetchmail comes into play. It is a program, running on the same server as your domain-wide Postfix mail server and which can retrieve all your different e-mails from all your different mail providers and pass them into the local user mailboxes of your Postfix MTA. Once they are stored in their appropriate place, users can access all these mails in the usual way provided by the access agent Dovecot over POP3 or IMAP. Here in this recipe we will show you how to install and integrate Fetchmail into your server running the Postfix MTA.

Getting ready

To complete this recipe, you will require a working installation of the CentOS 7 operating system with root privileges, a console-based text editor of your choice, and a connection to the Internet in order to download additional packages. It is assumed that you are working through this chapter recipe by recipe in the order that they appear and for this reason it is expected that Postfix has been configured as a domain-wide MTA and Dovecot has been installed to provide a POP3/IMAP mail access service. In order to test Fetchmail in this recipe, we also need to have registered some external e-mail addresses: you need the name of the external e-mail server address and the port of your e-mail provider, as well as your user login credentials at hand. Often you can find this information from your mail provider's Frequently Asked Questions (FAQ) section on their webpage. Also, for some e-mail addresses you need to first enable POP3 or IMAP in your e-mail settings before you can use Fetchmail.

How to do it...

Fetchmail is not installed by default and for this reason we must begin by installing the necessary packages. Perform the following steps:

1. To begin, log in your mail server running your Postfix server and type:

    `yum install fetchmail`

2. Once installed, we will log into a system's user account for which we want to enable Fetchmail to download external mail from an external mail provider into his local mailbox, in our example it will be the system user `john`: `su - john`. Now let's configure Fetchmail with an external e-mail address. If your e-mail provider is called `mailhost.com` and it runs a POP3 server at `pop.mailhost.com` and IMAP on `imap.mailhost.com` with the username `<user-name>`, here (please substitute your own values) is an example command line to test connecting and fetching mails from this provider:

    `fetchmail pop.mailhost.com -p pop3 -u <user-name> -k -v`

3. If you want to use IMAP with the same provider instead:

    `fetchmail imap.mailhost.com -p IMAP -u <user-name> -v`

4. If the Fetchmail command was successful, all new messages will be downloaded from the server into your local mailbox in your user account.

How it works...

Here in this recipe, we showed you how to install and test Fetchmail, which provides automated mail retrieval capabilities for any user account having a local mailbox on our Postfix server. As a result, for a client connecting to the mail server using POP3 or IMAP, the mails fetched this way look like normal incoming e-mails. Fetchmail is often used to combine and bundle all your different mail accounts into one single account, but you can also use it if your mail provider does not have good virus or spam filter. Here you download the mails from your host's e-mail server, then process the mails using tools such as SpamAssassin or ClamAV before sending mails to your clients.

So what did we learn from this experience?

We began this recipe by installing the YUM package for Fetchmail. As we wanted to set up Fetchmail for a system user's mailbox called `john`, next we logged in as this user, Afterwards, we tested the Fetchmail program by running a simple command line to fetch mail from a single mail provider. As said before, for a successful login to your external mail provider, you need to know the exact login information (server address, port, username, and password, as well as the type of protocol) of the server before you can use Fetchmail.

Remember that, while some e-mail providers let the user decide if he wants to connect securely using SSL or not, some hosters such as gmail.com only allow secure connections. This means that the example command shown here in this recipe is likely to fail on every major e-mail provider if they don't support POP3/IMAP access without SSL connections. Proceed to the next section in order to learn how to use Fetchmail with SSL POP3/IMAP encryption.

You should always prefer SSL encryption if your mail provider offers both. Also, some providers such as gmail.com only let the user use their services via webmail and disable POP3/IMAP service features by default; you need to enable them in your account's settings on your provider's website (see later).

We specified with the -p parameter which mail protocol to use with the fetchmail command. With the -u parameter, we specified the user identification to be used when logging in to the mailserver, which is completely dependent on our e-mail provider. For POP3, we applied the -k flag to ensure that the e-mails only get fetched from the server but never deleted (which is the default when using the POP3 protocol). Finally, we used -v to make the output more verbose and give us more information for our simple test. If your e-mail provider supports SSL, you also need to add a -ssl flag to the Fetchmail command as well as the root certificate of the mail server (see the next section for more information). If you run the previous command, Fetchmail will immediately start asking the mail server for any mail in the inbox on the server and download anything to your user's local mailbox.

There's more...

In this section, we will show you how to configure Fetchmail to download all your e-mails from some real-life mail providers using POP3S, IMAPS, and the POP3 and IMAP protocols to your local mailbox on the Postfix server using a configuration file. Finally, we will show you how to automate the Fetchmail process.

Configuring Fetchmail with gmail.com and outlook.com e-mail accounts

Here we will configure the different external mail accounts which Fetchmail will download from: the popular gmail.com and outlook.com e-mail providers and a hypothetical one at my-email-server.com.

As we learned in the main recipe that Fetchmail processes configuration options on the command line by default, this should not be your preferred way of using Fetchmail to download your mail from different mail accounts automatically. Normally Fetchmail should be running as a service in daemon mode in the background at boot time or with a cron job and polls a list of mail servers defined in a special configuration file at specific time intervals. With this you can conveniently configure multiple mail servers and a long list of other options.

 At the time of writing this book, for gmail.com to work with Fetchmail you need to login to the gmail.com website with your user account and first enable IMAP by going to your accounts settings in **Forwarding and POP/IMAP**. Also, enable **Allow less secure apps** under **Sign-in & security** in **My account**. For outlook.com, login to your mail account on the webpage, then click on **options**, again click on **options**, then click on **Connect devices and apps with POP**, and then click on **enable POP**.

Both outlook.com and gmail.com use secure POP3S and IMAPS protocols, so you need to download and install the root certificates they are signing their SSL certificates with on your Fetchmail server first in order to be able to use their services. Here we can install the Mozilla CA certification bundle, which has been compiled by the Mozilla foundation and includes the most commonly used root server certificates used by all major websites and services, such as those used by our mail providers. For gmail.com we need the Equifax Secure Certificate Authority root certificate and for outlook.com we need the root server certificate from Globalsign. Fetchmail needs these root certificates to verify the validity of any other SSL certificate downloaded from the e-mail server. Login as root on your Postfix server and install the following package:

yum install ca-certificates

Afterwards, login as a Linux system user, for example, john, who we will create a new Fetchmail configuration file for, and who already has a local Postfix mailbox directory on our server located in his home directory under ~/Maildir. Now before configuring any account in the Fetchmail configuration file, you should always first test if the connection and authentication to the specific account are working with the Fetchmail command line, as shown in the previous recipe. For testing our different mail providers' accounts, we need three different command line calls. For testing if your provider is using SSL encryption, you need the -ssl flag; a typical output for a mail provider who is not allowing non-SSL connections could be:

```
Fetchmail: SSL connection failed.
Fetchmail: socket error while fetching from <userid>@<mailserver>
Fetchmail: Query status=2 (SOCKET)
```

If your google and outlook username is johndoe at both mail providers for testing google with the IMAPS protocol try (enter your e-mail user's password when prompted):

```
fetchmail imap.gmail.com -p IMAP --ssl -u johndoe@gmail.com -k -v
```

If the login was successful, the output should be similar to (truncated):

```
Fetchmail: IMAP< A0002 OK johndoe@gmail.com authenticated (Success)
9 messages (2 seen) for johndoe at imap.gmail.com.
Fetchmail: IMAP> A0005 FETCH 1:9 RFC822.SIZE
```

For testing `outlook.com` with **POP3S**, use:

```
fetchmail pop-mail.outlook.com -p POP3 --ssl -u johndoe@outlook.com -k
-v
```

On success, the output should be similar to (it has been truncated):

```
Fetchmail: POP3> USER johndoe@outlook.com
Fetchmail: POP3< +OK password required
Fetchmail: POP3< +OK mailbox has 1 messages
```

For our third hypothetical e-mail account at `my-email-server.com`, we will use **POP3** or **IMAP** without **SSL** so test it using our account:

```
fetchmail pop3.my-email-server.com -p POP3 -u johndoe -k -v
fetchmail imap.my-email-server.com -p IMAP -u johndoe  -v
```

You should also check if all the fetched mails from your external providers have been downloaded correctly. View your system user's local mailbox using the `mailx` command (`mailx -f ~/Maildir`). After we successfully verify that Fetchmail is able to connect to the servers and fetch some mails, we now can proceed to create a local Fetchmail configuration file in our system user's home directory in order to automate this process and configure multiple mail addresses. Start by opening a new empty file using `vi ~/.fetchmailrc`. Remember that all the commands which can be put on the command line can also be used with slightly different names in the configuration file (and much more). Now put in the following content (replace `john` with your actual Linux system user, `johndoe` with your e-mail user account name, and `secretpass` with your actual mail password for this account):

```
set postmaster "john"
set logfile fetchmail.log
poll imap.gmail.com with proto IMAP
user 'johndoe@gmail.com' there with password 'secretpass' is john here
ssl
fetchall
poll pop-mail.outlook.com with proto POP3
user 'johndoe@outlook.com' there with password 'secretpass' is john
here
ssl
fetchall
poll pop3.my-email-server.com with proto POP3
user 'johndoe@my-email-server.com' there with password 'secretpass' is
john here
fetchall
```

Save and close this file. In this file, we used the following important commands:

- ▸ `postmaster`: Defines the local Linux user which will receive all the warning or error mails if Fetchmail runs into problems.

- ▸ `logfile`: Defines a filename for a log file, which can be very helpful for us to supervise and debug Fetchmail output when it's running continuously over a long period of time in the background.

- ▸ `poll` section: Specifies downloading mails from a specific mail provider. For every mail account, you will define one such poll section. As you can see here, the syntax is very similar to the one used on the command line when we tested the single connections. With `proto` we define the `mail` protocol, `user` is the login user for the mail account, `password` is the login password of your account, and with the `is <username> here` parameter you specify which local system user account this mail account is tied to. For SSL connections you need the `ssl` flag, and we specified the `fetchall` parameter to make sure we also download all the e-mail messages flagged as `read` by the e-mail provider as otherwise Fetchmail would not download e-mails that have already been read.

Next change the permissions of the `.fetchmailrc` file because it contains passwords and should therefore not be read by anyone other than our own user:

```
chmod 600 ~/.fetchmailrc
```

Finally, we execute Fetchmail with the settings given in our configuration file. For testing, we will use a very verbose parameter here: `fetchmail -vvvv`. All the new mails from all your different e-mail providers should now be fetched, so afterwards you should go through the output and see if every server was ready and could be polled just as the single tests we did on the command line tests earlier. All the new mails should have been downloaded to the local mailbox, so in order to read your local mails you can use the `mailx` command as usual, like: `mail -f ~/Maildir`.

Automating Fetchmail

As just said, we can now manually start the polling process every time we want by just typing in `fetchmail` on the command line. This will poll and fetch all new mails from the mail servers specified in our new configuration file and then after processing each entry once it will exit the program. Now what's still missing is a mechanism to continuously query our mail servers at a specific interval updating our mailbox whenever new mails can be fetched. Here you can use two approaches. Either run the `fetchmail` command as a cron job or as an alternative you can start Fetchmail in daemon mode (use the parameter `set daemon` in your `.fetchmailrc` config file to activate it.) and put it in the background. This way Fetchmail will run constantly and wake up at a given time point and start the polling until everything finishes processing and then go back to sleep until the next interval has been reached.

As both methods are basically the same, here we will show you how to run Fetchmail as a cron job, which is much easier to set up because we don't have to create some custom systemd service files (currently in CentOS 7 there is no `fetchmail systemd` service available out-of-the box). For every system user (for example, `john`) who has a `fetchmail` configuration file, to start the e-mail server polling process every 10 minutes type in the following command once to register the cron job:

```
crontab -l | { cat; echo "*/10 * * * * /usr/bin/fetchmail &> /dev/null
"; } | crontab -
```

 Do not set the Fetchmail polling cycle shorter than every 5 minutes; otherwise, some mail providers may block or ban you, as it just overloads their systems.

12

Providing Web Services

In this chapter, we will cover the following:

- ► Installing Apache and serving web pages
- ► Enabling system users and building publishing directories
- ► Implementing name-based hosting
- ► Implementing CGI with Perl and Ruby
- ► Installing, configuring, and testing PHP
- ► Securing Apache
- ► Setting up HTTPS with Secure Sockets Layer (SSL)

Introduction

This chapter is a collection of recipes that provides the necessary steps to serve web pages. From installing a web server to delivering a dynamic page through SSL, this chapter provides the starting point required to implement an industry standard hosting solution anywhere and at any time.

Installing Apache and serving web pages

In this recipe, we will learn how to install and configure the Apache web server to enable the serving of static web pages. Apache is one of the world's most popular open source web servers. It runs as the backend for over half of all the Internet's web sites and can be used to serve both static and dynamic web pages. Commonly referred to as `httpd`, it supports an extensive range of features. It is the purpose of this recipe to show you how easily it can be installed using the YUM package manager so that you can maintain your server with the latest security updates. Apache 2.4 is available on CentOS 7.

Getting ready

To complete this recipe, you will require a working installation of the CentOS 7 operating system with root privileges, a console-based text editor of your choice, and a connection to the Internet in order to download additional packages. It is expected that your server will be using a static IP address and a hostname.

How to do it...

Apache is not installed by default and for this reason we will begin by installing the necessary packages using the YUM package manager.

1. To begin, log in as root and type the following command:

   ```
   yum install httpd
   ```

2. Create a home page by typing:

   ```
   vi /var/www/html/index.html
   ```

3. Now add the required HTML. You can use the following code as a starting point but it is expected that you will want to modify it to suit your own needs:

   ```
   <!DOCTYPE html>
   <html lang="en">
   <head><title>Welcome to my new web server</title></head>
   <body><h1>Welcome to my new web server</h1>
   <p>Lorem ipsum dolor sit amet, adipiscing elit.</p></body>
   </html>
   ```

4. You can now remove the Apache 2 test page with the following command:

   ```
   rm -f /etc/httpd/conf.d/welcome.conf
   ```

5. Having completed these steps, we will now consider the need to configure the httpd service for basic usage. To do this, open the httpd configuration file in your favorite text editor by typing (after you have made a backup of the file):

   ```
   cp /etc/httpd/conf/httpd.conf /etc/httpd/conf/httpd.conf.BAK
   ```

   ```
   vi /etc/httpd/conf/httpd.conf
   ```

6. Now scroll down to find the line ServerAdmin root@localhost. The traditional approach to setting this value is based on the use of the webmaster identity, so simply modify the e-mail address to reflect something more relevant to your own needs. For example, if your server's domain name was www.centos7.home then your entry will look similar to this:

   ```
   ServerAdmin webmaster@centos7.home
   ```

7. Now scroll down a few more lines to find the `ServerName` directive as follows: `#ServerName www.example.com:80`. Uncomment this line (which means remove the leading # sign at its beginning) and replace the value `www.example.com` with something more appropriate to your own needs. For example, if your server's domain name was `www.centos7.home` then your entry will look as follows:

`ServerName www.centos7.home:80`

8. Next, we will expand the `DirectoryIndex` directive a bit more. Find the line `DirectoryIndex index.html`, which is part of the `<IfModule dir_module>` block, then change it to:

`DirectoryIndex index.html index.htm`

9. Save and close the file, and then type the following command to test the config file:

`apachectl configtest`

10. Next, let's configure our web server's firewall by allowing incoming `http` connections (this defaults to port 80) to the server:

`firewall-cmd --permanent --add-service http && firewall-cmd --reload`

11. Now proceed to set the `httpd` service to start at boot and start the service:

`systemctl enable httpd && systemctl start httpd`

12. You can now test `httpd` from any computer in the same network as your web server (both systems should be able to see and ping each other), pointing your browser at the following URL by replacing `XXX.XXX.XXX.XXX` with the IP address of your server in order to see our own custom Apache test page we created:

`http://XXX.XXX.XXX.XXX.`

13. Alternatively, if you don't have a web browser, you can check if Apache is up and running using `curl` by fetching our test page on any computer in your network:

`curl http://XXX.XXX.XXX`

How it works...

Apache is a software package that enables you to publish and serve web pages, and is more commonly known as `httpd`, Apache2 or simply Apache. It was the purpose of this recipe to show you how easily CentOS enables you to get started with your very first website.

So what did we learn from this experience?

We began the recipe by installing Apache via the YUM package manager and the package named httpd. Having done this, we learned that on CentOS 7 the default location to serve static HTML is /var/www/html so our first task was to create a suitable home page, which we put in /var/www/html/index.html. Here we used a basic HTML template to get you started and it is expected that you would like to customize the look and feel of this page yourself. Following this, we then removed the default Apache 2 welcome page found in /etc/httpd/conf.d/welcome.conf. Following this, the next stage was to open the httpd.conf configuration file in our favorite text editor after making a backup of it so we could revert our changes if any problems occurred. First we defined the server's e-mail address and the server name, which often appear in the error messages on the server-generated web pages; for this reason it should reflect your domain name. Next, we adjusted the DirectoryIndex directive, which defines which files will be sent first to the browser if a directory is requested. Often people request not a specific web page but a directory instead. For example, if you browse to www.example.com, you request a directory, while www.example.com/welcome.html is a specific web page. By default Apache sends the index.html in the requested directory but we expanded this since a lot of websites use the .htm extension instead. Finally, we saved and closed the httpd configuration file in the usual way before proceeding to check if the Apache configuration file contained any errors by using the apachectl configtest command. This should print out a Syntax OK message so we could enable the httpd service to start at boot time. We had to open the standard HTTP port 80 in our firewalld to allow incoming HTTP requests to the server, and finally we then started the httpd service. Remember, you can also always reload Apache's configuration file if it has been changed without fully restarting the service, by using: systemctl reload httpd. Having completed these steps, it was simply a matter of opening your browser from another computer in the same network and electing a method of viewing our new Apache start page. You can use your server's IP address (for example, http://192.168.1.100), while those with hostname support can type the hostname (for example, http://www.centos7.home) instead. Apache's access and error log files can be found in /var/log/httpd. To get a live view of who is currently accessing your web server, open /var/log/httpd/access_log; to see all the errors, type /var/log/httpd/error_log.

Apache is a big subject and we cannot cover every nuance, but over the coming recipes we will continue to expose additional functionalities that will enable you to build a web server of choice.

Enabling system users and building publishing directories

In this recipe, we will learn how Apache provides you with the option to allow your system users to host web pages within their home directories. This approach has been used by ISPs since the outset of web hosting and in many respects it continues to flourish due to its ability to avoid the more complex method of virtual hosting. In the previous recipe you were shown how to install the Apache web server, and with the desire to provide hosting facilities for system users, it is the purpose of this recipe to show you how this can be achieved in CentOS 7.

Getting ready

To complete this recipe, you will require a working installation of the CentOS 7 operating system with root privileges and a console-based text editor of your choice. It is expected that your server will be using a static IP address that supports a hostname or domain name and that the Apache web server is already installed and currently running. Also, at least one system user account should be available on the server.

How to do it...

To provide the functionality offered by this recipe, no additional packages are required but we will need to make some modifications to the Apache configuration file.

1. To begin, log in as root and open the Apache userdir configuration file in your favorite text editor by typing the following command, after you have created a backup copy of it first:

   ```
   cp /etc/httpd/conf.d/userdir.conf /etc/httpd/conf.d/userdir.conf.BAK
   ```

   ```
   vi /etc/httpd/conf.d/userdir.conf
   ```

2. In the file, locate the directive that reads as `UserDir disabled`. Change it to the following:

   ```
   UserDir public_html
   ```

3. Now scroll down to the `<Directory "/home/*/public_html">` section and replace the existing block with the one here:

   ```
   <Directory /home/*/public_html>
       AllowOverride All
       Options Indexes FollowSymLinks
       Require all granted
   </Directory>
   ```

4. Save and exit the file. Now log in as any system user to work with your publishing web directory (`su - <username>`), and then create a web publishing web folder in your home directory and a new home page for your user:

```
mkdir ~/public_html && vi ~/public_html/index.html
```

5. Now add the required HTML. You can use the following code as a starting point but it is expected that you will modify it to suit your own needs:

```
<!DOCTYPE html>
<html lang="en">
<head><title>Welcome to my web folder's home page</title></head>
<body><h1>Welcome to my personal home page</h1></body>
</html>
```

6. Now modify the permissions of the Linux system user's `<username>` home folders by typing:

```
chmod 711 /home/<username>
```

7. Set the read/write permissions for `public_html` 755 so Apache can execute it later:

```
chmod 755 ~/public_html -R
```

8. Now log in as root again using `su - root` to configure SELinux appropriately for the use of http home directories:

```
setsebool -P httpd_enable_homedirs true
```

9. As root, change the SELinux security context for your user's web public directory (this needs `policycoreutils-python` package to be installed) with the username `<user>`:

```
semanage fcontext -a -t httpd_user_content_t /home/<user>/public_html
```

```
restorecon -Rv /home/<user>/public_html
```

10. To complete this recipe, simply reload the `httpd` service configuration:

```
apachectl configtest && systemctl reload httpd
```

11. You can now test your setup by browsing to (substitute `<username>` appropriately): `http://<SERVER IP ADDRESS>/~<username>` in any browser.

How it works...

In this recipe, we learned how easy it is to host your own peers by enabling user directories on the Apache web server.

So what did we learn from this experience?

We began the recipe by making a few minor configuration changes to Apache's `userdir.conf` in order to set up the user directory support. We activated the user directories by adjusting the `UserDir` directive from disabled to pointing to the name of the HTML web directory within each user's home directory, which will contain all our user's web content, and call this `public_html` (you can change this directory name to anything you like but `public_html` is the de facto standard for naming it). Then we proceeded to modify the `<Directory /home/*/public_html>` tag. This directive applies all its enclosed options to the parts of the filesystem defined in the beginning tag `/home/*/public_html`. In our example, the following options are enabled for this directory: `Indexes` are used whenever a directory does not have `index.html`. This will show the file and folder content of the directory as HTML. As we will see in the recipe *Securing Apache*, this should be avoided for your web root whereas, for serving user directories, this can be a good choice if you just want to make your home folder accessible to your peers so they can quickly share some files (if you have any security concerns, remove this option). The `FollowSymLinks` option allows symbolic links (man `ln`) from this `public_html` directory to any other directory or file in the filesystem. Again, avoid this in your web root folder but for home directories it can be useful if you need to make files or folders accessible within the `public_html` folder without the need to copy them into it (user directories often have disk quotas). Next we configured access control to the `public_html` folder. We did so by setting `Require all granted`, which tells Apache that in this `public_html` folder anyone from everywhere can access the contents through the HTTP protocol. If you want to restrict access to your `public_html` folder then you can replace `all granted` with different options. To allow access based on a hostname use, for example `Require host example.com`. With the `ip` parameter we can restrict the `public_html` folder to an internally available network only, for example `Require ip 192.168.1.0/24`. This is particularly useful if your web server has multiple network interfaces and one IP address is used for connecting to the public Internet and another one for your internal private network. You can add multiple `Require` lines within a `Directory` block. Remember to always set at least `Require local` which allows local access.

Having saved our work, we then began to make various changes to the home directories. First we created the actual `public_html` folder within our user's home directory, which will be the actual personal web publishing folder later. Next, we changed its permissions to `755` which means that our user can do everything in the folder but all the other users and groups can only read and execute its content (and change into this folder). This type of permission is needed because all the files in the `public_html` folder will be accessed by a user named `apache` with the group `apache` if someone requests its content via the Apache web server later. If no read or execute permissions are set for the `other users` flag (man `chmod`), we will get an `Access denied` message in our browser. This will also be the case if we do not change the permissions for the parent `/home/<username>` directory in advance because parent directory permissions can affect its child subfolder permissions. A normal user home directory in CentOS Linux has the permissions `700` which means that the home directory's owner can do anything but everyone else is completely locked out of the home folder and its content.

As written before, the Apache user needs access to the subfolder `public_html` so we have to change the permissions to `711` for the home folder so that everyone else can at least change into the directory (and then access the subfolder `public_html` as well since this is set to be read/write accessible). Next, we set the security context of our new web folder for SELinux. On systems running SELinux, it's mandatory to set all the Apache web publishing folders to the `httpd_user_content_t` SELinux label (along with their contents) in order to make them available to Apache. Also, we made sure to set the correct SELinux Boolean to enable Apache home directories (which is enabled by default): `httpd_enable_homedirs` is `true`. Read *Chapter 14, Working with SELinux* to learn more about SELinux.

You should be aware that the previous process of managing the home directories should be repeated for each user. You will not have to restart Apache every time you enable a new system user but, having completed these steps for the first time, it will be simply a matter of reloading the configuration of the `httpd` service to reflect the initial changes made to the configuration file. From this point on, your local system users can now publish web pages using a unique URL based on their username.

Implementing name-based hosting

Normally, if you install Apache as shown in the previous recipe, you can host exactly one website that is accessible as the server's IP address or the domain name Apache is running on, for example, `http://192.168.1.100` or `http://www.centos7.home`. Such a system is very wasteful for your server resources as you would need individual servers with Apache installed for every single domain you want to host. **Name-based** or **virtual hosting** is used to host multiple domains on the same Apache web server. If a number of different domain names have already been assigned to your Apache web server's IP address using a DNS server or through a local `/etc/hosts` file, virtual hosts can be configured for every available domain name to direct the user to a specific directory on the Apache server containing the site's information. Any modern webspace provider uses this kind of virtual hosting to divide one web server's space into multiple sites. There is no limit to this system and to the number of sites to create from it as long as your web server can handle its traffic. In this recipe, we will learn how to configure name-based virtual hosting on the Apache web server.

Getting ready

To complete this recipe, you will require a working installation of the CentOS 7 operating system with root privileges and a console-based text editor of your choice. It is expected that your server will be using a static IP address and Apache is installed and currently running, and that you have enabled system users publishing directories in an earlier recipe. Virtual host names cannot work without previously setting up one or more domains or subdomains outside Apache.

For testing, you could set up your /etc/hosts (see the *Setting your hostname and resolving the network* recipe in *Chapter 2, Configuring the System*) or configure some A or CNAMES in your BIND DNS server (refer to *Chapter 9, Working with Domains*) to use different domain names or subdomains, such as www.centos7.home, all pointing to your Apache web server's IP address.

> A common misconception is that Apache can create domain names for your Apache web server on its own. This is not true. The different domain names you want to wire to different directories using virtual hosts need to be set up in a DNS server or /etc/hosts file to point to your Apache server's IP address before you can use them with virtual hosts.

How to do it...

For the purpose of this recipe we will be building some local virtual hosts with the following Apache example subdomain names: www.centos7.home, web1.centos7.home, web2.centos7.home and <username>.centos7.home for the corresponding web publishing folders /var/www/html, /var/www/web1, /var/www/web2, and /home/<username>/public_html for the domain's network name centos7.home. These names are interchangeable and it is expected that you will want to customize this recipe based on something more appropriate to your own needs and circumstances.

1. To begin, log in as root on your Apache server and create a new configuration file that will hold all our virtual host definitions:

   ```
   vi /etc/httpd/conf.d/vhost.conf
   ```

2. Now put in the following content, customizing the centos7.home value and the username <username> to fit your own needs:

   ```
   <VirtualHost *:80>
       ServerName centos7.home
       ServerAlias www.centos7.home
       DocumentRoot /var/www/html/
   </VirtualHost>
   <VirtualHost *:80>
       ServerName  web1.centos7.home
       DocumentRoot /var/www/web1/public_html/
   </VirtualHost>
   <VirtualHost *:80>
       ServerName  web2.centos7.home
       DocumentRoot /var/www/web2/public_html/
   </VirtualHost>
   <VirtualHost *:80>
       ServerName  <username>.centos7.home
   ```

```
        DocumentRoot /home/<username>/public_html/
    </VirtualHost>
```

3. Now save and close the file in the usual way before proceeding to create the directories for both virtual hosts that are currently missing:

   mkdir -p /var/www/web1/public_html /var/www/web2/public_html

4. Having done this, we can now create default index pages for the missing subdomains web1 and web2 by using our favorite text editor, as follows:

   echo "<html><head></head><body><p>Welcome to Web1</p></body></ html>" > /var/www/web1/public_html/index.html

   echo "<html><head></head><body><p>Welcome to Web2</p></body></ html>" > /var/www/web2/public_html/index.html

5. Now reload the Apache web server:

   apachectl configtest && systemctl reload httpd

6. Now, for simple testing purposes, we will just configure all our new Apache web server's subdomains in the hosts file of the client computer that wants to access these virtual hosts, but remember that you can also configure these subdomains in a BIND DNS server. Login to this client computer (it needs to be in the same network as our Apache server) as root and add the following lines to the /etc/hosts file, assuming our Apache server has the IP address 192.168.1.100:

   192.168.1.100 www.centos7.home

   192.168.1.100 centos7.home

   192.168.1.100 web1.centos7.home

   192.168.1.100 web2.centos7.home

   192.168.1.100 john.centos7.home

7. Now on this computer, open a browser and test things out by typing the following addresses into the address line (replace <username> with the username you defined for the virtual host): http://www.centos7.home, http://web1. centos7.home, http://web2.centos7.home and http://<username>. centos7.home.

How it works...

The purpose of this recipe was to show you how easy it is to implement name-based virtual hosting. This technique will boost your productivity and using this approach will give you unlimited opportunities to domain-based web hosting.

So what did we learn from this experience?

We began by creating a new Apache configuration file to hold all our virtual host configuration. Remember, all files ending with the .conf extension in the /etc/httpd/conf.d/ directory will be loaded automatically when Apache is started. Following this, we then proceeded to put in the relevant directive blocks, starting with our default server root centos7.home and the alias www.centos7.home. The most important option in any virtual host block is the ServerName directive, which maps an existing domain name for our web server's IP address to a specific directory on the filesystem. Of course, there are many more settings you can include, but the previous solution provides the basic building blocks that will enable you to use it as the perfect starting point. The next step was to then create individual entries for our centos7.home subdomains web1, web2, and <username>. Remember, each virtual host supports the typical Apache directives and can be customized to suit your needs. Refer to the official Apache manual (install the YUM package httpd-manual, then go to the location /usr/share/httpd/manual/vhosts/) to learn more. After we created our virtual host blocks for every subdomain we wanted, we then proceeded to create the directories to hold the actual content and created a basic index.html in each directory. In this example, our web1 and web2 content directories were added to /var/www. This is not to imply that you cannot create these new folders in another place. In fact most production servers generally place these new directories in the home folder, as shown with our /home/<username>/ public_html example. However, if you do intend to take this approach, remember to modify the permissions and ownership, as well as SELinux labels (outside /var/www you need to label Apache directories as httpd_sys_content_t) of these new directories so that they can be used as they were intended. Finally, we reloaded the Apache web service so that our new settings would take immediate effect. We could then directly use the subdomain names in our browser to browse to our virtual hosts when correctly set up in /etc/hosts on the client or on a BIND DNS server.

Implementing CGI with Perl and Ruby

In the previous recipes in this chapter, our Apache service only served static content, which means that everything requested by a web-browser already existed in a constant state on the server, for example as plain HTML text files that don't change. Apache simply sends the content of a specific file from the web server to the browser as a response where it then gets interpreted and rendered. If there were no way to change the contents sent to the client, the Internet would be really boring and not the huge success it is today. Not even the simplest example of dynamic content, such as showing a web page with the web server's current local time would be possible.

Therefore, early in the 1990's, some smart people started inventing mechanisms to make communication possible between a web server and some executable programs installed on the server to generate web pages dynamically. This means that the content of the HTML sent to the user can change in response to different contexts and conditions. Such programs are often written in scripting languages such as Perl or Ruby but can be written in any other computer language as well, such as Python, Java, or PHP (see later). Because Apache is written in pure C and C++, it cannot execute or interpret any other programming language such as Perl directly. Therefore, a bridge between the server and the program is needed to define how some external programs can interact with the server. One of these methods is called the **Common Gateway Interface** (**CGI**) which is a very old way to serve dynamic content. Most Apache web servers use some form of CGI applications and in this recipe we will show you how to install and configure CGI for use with Perl and Ruby to generate our first dynamic content.

 There also exist some special Apache web server modules such as `mod_perl`, `mod_python`, `mod_ruby`, and so on which should be generally preferred as they directly embed the interpreter of the language into the web server process and therefore are a lot faster in comparison to any interface technology such as CGI.

Getting ready

To complete this recipe, you will require a working installation of the CentOS 7 operating system with root privileges, a console-based text editor of your choice, and a connection to the Internet in order to facilitate the download of additional packages.

It is expected that your server will be using a static IP address, Apache is installed and currently running, and that your server supports one or more domains or subdomains.

How to do it...

As both scripting languages Perl as well as Ruby are not installed by default on CentOS 7 Minimal, we will start this recipe by installing all required packages using YUM.

1. To begin, log in as root and type the following command:

    ```
    yum install perl perl-CGI ruby
    ```

2. Next, restart the Apache web server:

    ```
    systemctl restart httpd
    ```

3. Next, we need to configure SELinux appropriately for the use of CGI scripts:

    ```
    setsebool -P httpd_enable_cgi 1
    ```

4. Then we need to change the correct security context for our `cgi-bin` directory for SELinux to work:

```
semanage fcontext -a -t httpd_sys_script_exec_t /var/www/cgi-bin
restorecon -Rv /var/www/cgi-bin
```

Creating your first Perl CGI script

1. Now create the following Perl CGI script file by opening the new file `vi /var/www/cgi-bin/perl-test.cgi` and putting in the following content:

```
#!/usr/bin/perl
use strict;
use warnings;
use CGI qw(:standard);
print header;
my $now = localtime;
print start_html(-title=>'Server time via Perl CGI'),
h1('Time'),
p("The time is $now"),
end_html;
```

2. Next, change the file's permission to 755, so our `apache` user can execute it:

```
chmod 755 /var/www/cgi-bin/perl-test.cgi
```

3. Next, to test and actually see what HTML is being generated from the preceding script, you can execute the `perl` script directly on the command line; just type:

```
/var/www/cgi-bin/perl-test.cgi
```

4. Now open a browser on a computer in your network and run your first Perl CGI script, which will print the local time by using the URL:

```
http://<server name or IP address>/cgi-bin/perl-test.cgi
```

5. If the script is not working, have a look at the log file `/var/log/httpd/error_log`.

Creating your first Ruby CGI script

1. Create the new Ruby CGI script file `vi /var/www/cgi-bin/ruby-test.cgi` and put in the following content:

```
#!/usr/bin/ruby
require "cgi"
cgi = CGI.new("html4")
cgi.out{
    cgi.html{
```

```
        cgi.head{ cgi.title{"Server time via Ruby CGI"} } +
        cgi.body{
            cgi.h1 { "Time" } +
            cgi.p { Time.now}
        }
    }
}
```

2. Now change the file's permission to 755 so our apache user can execute it:

   chmod 755 /var/www/cgi-bin/ruby-test.cgi

3. To actually see what HTML is being generated from the preceding script, you can execute the Ruby script directly on the command line; just type /var/www/cgi-bin/ruby-test.cgi. When the line offline mode: enter name=value pairs on standard input is shown, press *Ctrl+D* to see the actual HTML output.

4. Now open a browser on a computer in your network and run your first Ruby CGI script which will print the local time by using the following URL:

   http://<server name or IP address>/cgi-bin/ruby-test.cgi

5. If it is not working, have a look at the log file /var/log/httpd/error.log.

How it works...

Here in this recipe we showed you how easy it is to create some dynamic web sites using CGI. When a CGI resource is accessed, the Apache server executes that program on the server and sends its output back to the browser. The main advantage of this system is that CGI is not restricted to any programming language but works as long as a program is executable on the Linux command line and generates some form of text output. The big disadvantage of CGI technology is that it is a very old and outdated technology: every user request to a CGI resource starts a new process of the program. For example, every request to a Perl CGI script will start and load a new interpreter instance into memory, which will produce a lot of overhead, therefore making CGI only usable for smaller websites or lower parallel user request numbers. As said before, there are other technologies to deal with this issue, for example FastCGI or Apache modules such as mod_perl.

So what did we learn from this experience?

We began this recipe by logging in as root and installing the perl interpreter and the CGI.pm module for it as it is not included in the Perl standard library (we will use it in our script), as well as by installing the ruby interpreter for the Ruby programming language. Afterwards, to make sure our Apache web server takes notice of our new programming languages installed on the system, we restarted the Apache process.

Next, we made sure that SELinux is enabled to work with CGI scripts and then we provided the standard Apache `cgi-bin` directory `/var/www/cgi-bin` with the proper SELinux context type to allow system-wide execution. To learn more about SELinux, read *Chapter 14, Working with SELinux*. In this directory we then put our Perl and Ruby CGI scripts and made them executable afterwards for the Apache user. In the main Apache configuration file, the `/var/www/cgi-bin` directory has been defined as the standard CGI directory by default, which means that every executable file you put into this directory, with proper access and execution permissions and the `.cgi` extension, is automatically defined as a CGI script and can be accessed and executed from your web browser, no matter which programming or scripting language it has been written in. To test our scripts, we then opened a web browser and went to the URL `http://<server name or IP address>/cgi-bin/` with the name of the `.cgi` script to follow.

There's more...

If you would like to allow execution of CGI scripts in other web directories as well, you need to add the following two lines (`Options` and `AddHandler`) to any virtual host or existing `Directive` directive, or create a new one in the following way (remember that you then also have to set the SELinux `httpd_sys_script_exec_t` label on the new CGI location as well):

```
<Directory "/var/www/html/cgi-new">
    Options +ExecCGI
    AddHandler cgi-script .cgi
</Directory>
```

Installing, configuring, and testing PHP

Hypertext Preprocessor (**PHP**) remains one of the most popular server-side scripting languages designed for web development. It already supports some nice features, such as connecting to relational databases like MariaDB out-of-the-box which can be used to implement modern web applications very fast. While a current trend can be seen for larger enterprises to move away from PHP in favor of some newer technologies such as Node.js (server-side JavaScript), it is still the superior scripting language on the consumer market. Every hosting company in the world provides some kind of LAMP stack (Linux, Apache, MySQL, PHP) to run the PHP code. Also, a lot of very popular web applications are written in PHP, such as WordPress, Joomla, and Drupal, so it's fair enough to say that PHP represents a must-have feature for almost any Apache web server. Here in this recipe, we will show you how to get started with installing and running PHP in your Apache web server with the module `mod_php`.

Getting ready

To complete this recipe, you will require a working installation of the CentOS 7 operating system with root privileges and a console-based text editor of your choice and a Internet connection. It is expected that your server will be using a static IP address and Apache is installed and currently running, and that your server supports one or more domains or subdomains.

How to do it...

We will begin this recipe by installing the PHP Hypertext Processor together with the Apache `mod_php` module, both not installed by default on CentOS 7 minimal.

1. To begin, log in as root and type the following command:

   ```
   yum install mod_php
   ```

2. Now let's open the standard PHP configuration file after we have made a backup of the original file first:

   ```
   cp /etc/php.ini /etc/php.ini.bak && vi /etc/php.ini
   ```

3. Find the line `; date.timezone` = and replace it with your own timezone. A list of all the available PHP time zones can be found at `http://php.net/manual/en/timezones.php`. For example (be sure to remove the leading `;` as this is disabling the interpretation of a command; this is called commenting out) to set the timezone to the city Berlin in Europe use:

   ```
   date.timezone = "Europe/Berlin"
   ```

4. To make sure the new module and settings have been properly loaded, restart the Apache web server:

   ```
   systemctl restart httpd
   ```

5. To be consistent with the CGI examples from the former recipe, here we will create our first dynamic PHP script which will print out the current local server time in the script `vi /var/www/html/php-test.php`, and run the popular PHP function `phpinfo()` that we can use to print out important PHP information:

   ```
   <html><head><title>Server time via Mod PHP</title></head>
   <h1>Time</h1>
   <p>The time is <?php print Date("D M d, Y G:i a");?></p><?php
   phpinfo(); ?></body></html>
   ```

6. To actually see what HTML is being generated from the preceding script, you can execute the PHP script directly on the command line; just type: `php /var/www/html/php-test.php`.

7. Now open a browser on a computer in your network and run your first PHP script which will print the local time by using the following URL: `http://<server name or IP address>/php-test.php`.

How to do it...

In this recipe, we showed you how easy it is to install and incorporate PHP into any Apache web server by using the mod_php module. This module enables an internal PHP interpreter, which directly runs in the Apache process and is much more efficient than using CGI, and should always be your preferred method whenever is available.

So what did we learn from this experience?

We began this recipe by installing the mod_php module using YUM, which will install PHP as a dependency as well as both are not available on any standard CentOS 7 minimal installations. Installing mod_php added the /etc/php.ini configuration file which we then opened after making a backup of the original file first. This file is the main PHP configuration file and should be edited with care because a lot of settings can be security relevant to your web server. If you are just starting out with PHP, leave everything as it is in the file and don't change anything despite the date.timezone variable. We set this to reflect our current time zone and it is necessary for PHP because it is used by a lot of different time and date functions (we will use some date functions in our first PHP script as well, see below). Next, we restarted the Apache web server which automatically reloads the PHP configurations as well. Afterwards, we created our first PHP script and put it in the main web root folder /var/www/html/php-test.php; this prints out the current server time as well as the result of the phpinfo() PHP function. This gives you a well categorized tabular overview of your current PHP installation, helping you diagnose server-related problems or see which modules are available in PHP.

In comparison to CGI, you may ask yourself why we don't have to put the PHP scripts into any special folder such as cgi-bin. By installing mod_php, an Apache configuration file called /etc/httpd/conf.d/php.conf gets deployed into the Apache configuration folder, which exactly answers this question, it specifies that PHP scripts will get executed as valid PHP code whenever they get the extension .php from anywhere in every web directory.

Securing Apache

Even though the Apache HTTP server is one of the most mature and safe server applications included in CentOS 7, there is always room for improvement and a large number of options and techniques are available to harden your web server's security even more. While we cannot show the user every single security feature as it is outside of the scope this book, in this recipe, we will try to teach what is considered to be good practice when it comes to securing your Apache web server for a production system.

Getting ready

To complete this recipe, you will require a working installation of the CentOS 7 operating system with root privileges and a console-based text editor of your choice. It is expected that your server will be using a static IP address and Apache is installed and currently running, and that your server supports one or more domains or subdomains.

How to do it...

Most of the security options and techniques have to be set up in the main Apache configuration file, so we will begin this recipe by opening it in our favorite text editor.

Configuring httpd.conf to provide better security

1. To begin, log in as root and open the main Apache config file:

   `vi /etc/httpd/conf/httpd.conf`

2. Now go to your main document root. To do so, search the directive called:

   `<Directory "/var/www/html">`

3. Within the beginning `<Directory "/var/www/html">` and closing `</Directory>` tags find the line `Options Indexes FollowSymLinks`, then disable (comment out) this line by putting a # in front of it, so it reads:

   `#   Options Indexes FollowSymLinks`

4. Now scroll down to the end of the configuration file and insert the following line one line before the line `# Supplemental configuration`. We do not want our server to leak any detailed information through the header, so we type:

   `ServerTokens Prod`

5. Afterwards, reload the Apache configuration to apply your changes:

   `apachectl configtest && systemctl reload httpd`

Removing unneeded httpd modules

Even the most stable, mature, and well-tested programs can include bugs and cause vulnerabilities, as the latest news about the Heartbleed bug in OpenSSL or Shellshock in Bash have shown, and the Apache web server is no exception. Therefore, it is often beneficial to remove all unneeded software to limit the functionality, and thus the likelihood of security problems in your system. For the Apache web server, we can remove all unneeded modules to increase security (this can also increase performance and memory consumption). Let's start this process by reviewing all the currently installed Apache modules.

1. To show all currently installed and loaded Apache modules, type as user root:

    `httpd -M`

2. All the modules outputted by the preceding command are loaded into the Apache web server by special configuration files in the `/etc/httpd/conf.modules.d` folder where they are grouped together by their primary target into the following files:

    `00-base.conf, 00-dav.conf, 00-lua.conf, 00-mpm.conf, 00-proxy. conf, 00-ssl.conf, 00-systemd.conf, 01-cgi.conf, 10-php.conf`

3. So instead of going through all the modules individually, this file structure in the `conf.modules.d` folder can make our life much easier because we can disable/ enable whole groups of modules. For example, if you know that you will not need any Apache DAV modules because you will not provide any WebDAV server, you can disable all DAV-related modules by renaming the extension of the `00-dav.conf` configuration file since only files with the ending `.conf` are read and loaded automatically by Apache. In order to do so, type:

    `mv /etc/httpd/conf.modules.d/00-dav.conf /etc/httpd/conf. modules.d/00-dav.conf.BAK`

4. Afterwards, reload the Apache configuration to apply your changes to the modules directory:

    `apachectl configtest && systemctl reload httpd`

5. If you need more fine-grained control, you can also enable/disable single modules in all the configuration files in this directory as well. For example, open `00-base.conf` in your favorite text editor and disable a single line by adding a # to the beginning of the line of choice you want to disable. For example:

    `# LoadModule userdir_module modules/mod_userdir.so`

6. If you decide to use some disabled modules files later, just rename the `.BAK` file to the original file name or remove the # in a specific module config file before reloading `httpd` once again.

Protecting your Apache files

Another really simple way to increase the security of your Apache web server is to protect your server-side scripts and configurations. In our scenario, we have one user (root) who alone is responsible and maintains the complete Apache web server, websites (for example, uploading new HTML pages to the server), server-side scripts, and configurations. Therefore, we will give him/her full file permissions (read/write/execute). The apache user still needs proper read and execute permissions to serve and access all Apache related files, thus minimizing the risk that your Apache web server is exposing some potential security risks to other system users or can get compromised through HTTP hacks. Do this in two steps:

1. First we will change or reset the ownership of the complete Apache configuration directory and the standard web root directory to owner root and group apache:

   `chown -R root:apache /var/www/html /etc/httpd/conf*`

2. Afterwards, we will change the file permissions so no one other than our dedicated apache user (and also root) can read those files:

   `chmod 750 -R /var/www/html /etc/httpd/conf*`

How it works...

We began this recipe by opening the main Apache configuration file httpd.conf to change settings for our main Apache root web content directory /var/www/html. Here we disabled the complete Options directive which included the Indexes as well as the FollowSymLinks parameter. As we have learned, if you request a directory instead of a file from the Apache server, index.html or the index.htm file within this directory will be sent automatically. Now the Indexes option configures the Apache web server in such a way that if no such file can be found in the requested directory, Apache will auto-generate a listing of the directory's content, as if you had typed ls (for list directory) in that directory on the command line, and show it to the user as a HTML page. We don't want this feature in general because it can expose secret or private data to unauthorized users and a lot of system administrators will tell you that indexing is considered to be a security threat in general. The FollowSymLinks directive should also not be used in production systems because if you make a mistake with it, it can easily expose parts of the file system, such as the complete root directory. Finally, we add another measurement to increase the server's base security and this is done by disabling the server version banner information. When the Apache web server generates either a web page or an error page, valuable information, for example the Apache server version and the activated modules, is sent automatically to the browser and a possible attacker can gain valuable information about your system. We stopped this from happening by simply setting ServerTokens to Prod. Afterwards, we showed you how to disable Apache modules to reduce the general risk of bugs and exploitations of your system. Finally, we showed how to adjust your Apache file permissions which can also be a good general protection.

There are lots of other things to consider when it comes to hardening your Apache web server but most of these techniques, such as Limiting HTTP request methods, TraceEnable, setting cookies with HttpOnly and secure flags, disabling the HTTP 1.0 protocol or SSL v2, or modifying the HTTP header with useful security-related HTTP or custom headers such as X-XSS-Protection, are much more advanced concepts and can restrict a general purpose Apache web server too much.

Setting up HTTPS with Secure Sockets Layer (SSL)

In this recipe, we will learn how to add a secure connection to the Apache web server by creating a self-signed SSL certificate using OpenSSL. This is often a requirement for web servers if the sites running on them transfer sensitive data such as credit card or login information from the web browser to the server. In a previous recipe you were shown how to install the Apache web server, and with the growing demand for secure connections, it is the purpose of this recipe to show you how to enhance your current server configuration by teaching you how to extend the features of the Apache web server.

Getting ready

To complete this recipe, you will require a working installation of the CentOS 7 operating system with root privileges, a console-based text editor of your choice, and a connection to the Internet in order to facilitate the download of additional packages. It is expected that Apache web server has been installed and that it is currently running. Here we will create a new SSL certificate for Apache. If you want to learn more about it, refer to *Chapter 6, Providing Security* for advice on generating self-signed certificates. As a correct domain name is crucial for SSL to work, we will continue naming our Apache web server's configured domain name centos7.home to make this recipe work (change it to fit your own needs).

How to do it...

Apache does not support SSL encryption by default and for this reason we will begin by installing the necessary package mod_ssl using the YUM package manager.

1. To begin, log in as root and type the following command:

   yum install mod_ssl

2. During installation of the mod_ssl package, a self-signed certificate as well as the key pair for the Apache web server are generated automatically; these lack a proper common name for your web server's domain name. Before we can re-generate our own required SSL files using the `Makefile` in the next steps, we need to delete those files:

```
rm /etc/pki/tls/private/localhost.key /etc/pki/tls/certs/
localhost.crt
```

3. We are now required to create our intended self-signed certificate and server key for our Apache web server. To do this, type the following command:

```
cd /etc/pki/tls/certs
```

4. To create the self-signed Apache SSL keypair, consisting of the certificate and its embedded public key as well as the private key, type:

```
make testcert
```

5. In the process of creating the certificate, first you will be asked to enter a new passphrase and then to verify it. Afterwards, you need to type it in again for the third time. As usual, enter a secure password. You will then be asked a number of questions. Complete all the required details by paying special attention to the common name value. This value should reflect the domain name of your web server or the IP address the SSL certificate is for. For example, you may type:

```
www.centos7.home
```

6. When the process of creating your certificate is complete, we will proceed by opening the main Apache SSL configuration in the following way (after making a backup):

```
cp /etc/httpd/conf.d/ssl.conf /etc/httpd/conf.d/ssl.conf.BAK
```

```
vi /etc/httpd/conf.d/ssl.conf
```

7. Scroll down to the section that begins with `<VirtualHost _default_:443>` and locate the line `# DocumentRoot "/var/www/html"` within this block. Then activate it by removing the # character, so it reads:

```
DocumentRoot "/var/www/html"
```

8. Right below, find the line that reads `#ServerName www.example.com:443`. Activate this line and modify the value shown to match the common name value used during the creation of your certificate, as follows:

```
ServerName www.centos7.home:443
```

9. Save and close the file, next we need to enable the HTTPS port in our firewalld to allow incoming HTTP SSL connections over port `443`:

```
firewall-cmd --permanent --add-service=https && firewall-cmd
--reload
```

10. Now restart the Apache `httpd` service to apply your changes. Note that if prompted you have to enter the SSL passphrase you added when you created the SSL test certificate:

`systemctl restart httpd`

11. Well done! You can now visit your server with a secure connection by replacing all the available HTTP URLs we have defined for the server using HTTPS instead. For example, go to `https://www.centos7.home` instead of `http://www.centos7.home`.

> When you browse to this website, you will get a warning message that the signing certificate authority is not known. This exception is to be expected when using self-signed certificates and can be confirmed.

How it works...

We began the recipe by installing `mod_ssl` using the YUM package manager, which is the default Apache module to enable SSL. The next step was then to go to the standard location where all the system's certificates can be found in CentOS 7, that is, `/etc/pki/tls/certs`. Here we can find a `Makefile`, which is a helper script for conveniently generating self-signed SSL test certificates and which hides away complicated command line parameters for the OpenSSL program from you. Remember that the `Makefile` currently lacks a `clean` option and therefore every time we run it, we need to delete any old versions of the generated files from a former run manually, otherwise it will not start doing anything. After deleting the old Apache SSL files, we used `make` with the `testcert` parameter, which creates self-signed certificates for the Apache web server and puts them in the standard locations, already configured in the `ssl.conf` file (the `SSLCertificateFile` and `SSLCertificateKeyFile` directives), so we didn't have to change anything here. During the process, you were asked to provide a password before completing a series of questions. Complete the questions but pay special attention to the Common name. As was mentioned in the main recipe, this value should reflect either the domain name of your server or your IP address. In the next phase, you were required to open Apache's SSL configuration file in your favorite text editor which can be found at `/etc/httpd/conf.d/ssl.conf`. In it we enabled the `DocumentRoot` directive to put it under SSL control and activated the `ServerName` directive with an expected domain value that must be the same as the one we defined as our common name value. We than saved and closed the configuration file and enabled the HTTPS ports in our firewall, thus allowing incoming connections over the standard HTTPS `443` port. Having completed these steps, you can now enjoy the benefits of a secure connection using a self-signed server certificate. Just type `https://` instead of `http://` for any URL address available on your Apache web browser. However, if you are intending to use an SSL Certificate on a production server for members of the public, then your best option is to purchase an SSL certificate from a trusted Certificate Authority.

There's more...

We learned that since our SSL certificate is protected by a passphrase, so whenever we need to restart our Apache web server, we need to enter the password. This is impractical for server restarts as Apache will refuse to start without a password. To get rid of the password prompt, we will provide the passphrase in a special file and make sure it is only accessible by root.

1. Create a backup of the file that will contain your password:

   ```
   cp /usr/libexec/httpd-ssl-pass-dialog /usr/libexec/httpd-ssl-pass-dialog.BAK
   ```

2. Now overwrite this password file with the following content, replacing XXXX in the following command line with your current SSL passphrase:

   ```
   echo -e '#!/bin/bash\necho "XXXX"' >  /usr/libexec/httpd-ssl-pass-dialog
   ```

3. Finally, change the permissions so that only root can read and execute them:

   ```
   chmod 500 /usr/libexec/httpd-ssl-pass-dialog
   ```

13
Operating System-Level Virtualization

In this chapter, we will cover:

- ▶ Installing and configuring Docker
- ▶ Downloading an image and running a container
- ▶ Creating your own images from Dockerfiles and uploading to Docker Hub
- ▶ Setting up and working with a private Docker registry

Introduction

This chapter is a collection of recipes that provides the essential steps to install, configure, and work with Docker, which is an open platform to build, ship, share, and run distributed applications through operating-system-level virtualization, a technology that has been around for many years in the Linux world and can provide speed and efficiency advantages over traditional virtualization technologies.

Installing and configuring Docker

Traditional virtualization technologies provide *hardware virtualization*, which means they create a complete hardware environment so each **virtual machine** (**VM**) needs a complete operating system to run it. Therefore they have some major drawbacks because they are heavyweight and produce a lot of overhead while running. This is where the open-source Docker containerization engine offers an attractive alternative. It can help you build applications in Linux containers, thus providing application virtualization.

This means that you can bundle any Linux program of choice with all its dependencies and its own environment and then share it or run multiple instances of it, each as a completely isolated and separated process on any modern Linux kernel, thus providing native runtime performance, easy portability, and high scalability. Here, in this recipe, we will show you how to install and configure Docker on your CentOS 7 server.

Getting ready

To complete this recipe, you will require a working installation of the CentOS 7 operating system with root privileges, a console-based text editor of your choice, and a connection to the Internet in order to download additional `rpm` packages and a test Docker image.

How to do it...

While Docker is available as a package in the official CentOS 7 repository, we will use the official Docker repository to install it on our system instead.

1. To begin, log in as root and update your YUM packages before downloading and executing the official Docker Linux installation script using the following command:

   ```
   yum update && curl -sSL https://get.docker.com/ | sh
   ```

2. Next, enable Docker at boot time before starting the Docker daemon (the first time you start, it will take a while):

   ```
   systemctl enable docker && systemctl start docker
   ```

3. Finally, after starting Docker you can verify that it's working by typing:

   ```
   docker run hello-world
   ```

How it works...

When installing any software on CentOS 7, most of the time it is a very good advice to use the packages available in your official CentOS repository instead of downloading and installing from third-party locations. Here by installing Docker using the official Docker repository instead we made an exception. We did this because Docker is a very young project and is evolving fast, and it keeps changing a lot. While you can use Docker for running every Linux application, including critical web servers or programs dealing with confidential data, bugs found or introduced into the Docker program can have severe security consequences. By using the official Docker repository, we make sure we always get the latest updates and patches available as fast as possible right from the developers of this fast-moving project. So anytime you type `yum update` in the future, your package manager will automatically query and check the Docker repos to see if there is a new version of Docker available for you.

So what did we learn from this experience?

We started this recipe by logging into our server as root and updated the YUM package's database. Then we used a command to download and execute the official Docker installation script from `https://get.docker.com/` in one step. What this script does is add the official Docker repository to the YUM package manager as a new package source and then automatically install Docker in the background. Afterwards, we enabled the Docker service at boot-time and started it by using `systemd`. Finally, to test our installation, we issued the command `docker run hello-world`, which downloads a special image from the official Docker registry to test our installation. If everything went fine, you should see the following success message (output truncated):

Hello from Docker

This message shows that your installation appears to be working correctly.

Downloading an image and running a container

A common misconception is that Docker is a system for running containers. Docker is only a build-tool to wrap up any piece of Linux based software with all its dependencies in a complete filesystem that contains everything it needs to run: code, runtime, system tools, and system libraries. The technology to run Linux containers is called operating-system-level virtualization and provides multiple isolated environments built in every modern Linux kernel by default. This guarantees that it will always run the same, regardless of the environment it is deployed in; thus making your application portable. Therefore, when it comes to distributing your Docker applications into Linux containers, two major conceptional terms must be introduced: **Docker images** and **containers**. If you ever wanted to set up and run your own WordPress installation, in this recipe we will show you how to do so the fastest way possible by downloading a pre-made WordPress image from the official Docker hub; we will then run a container from.

Getting ready

To complete this recipe, you will require a working installation of the CentOS 7 operating system with root privileges, a console-based text editor of your choice, and a connection to the Internet in order to facilitate the download of additional Docker images. It is expected that Docker has already been installed and is running.

How to do it...

The official WordPress image from Docker Hub does not contain its own MySQL server. Instead it relies on it externally, so we will start this recipe by installing and running a MySQL docker container from Docker Hub.

1. To begin, log in as root and type the following command by replacing <PASSWORD> in the following command with a strong MySQL database password of your own choice (at the time of writing, the latest WordPress needs MySQL v.5.7; this can change in the future, so check out the official WordPress Docker Hub page):

   ```
   docker run --restart=always --name wordpressdb -e MYSQL_ROOT_
   PASSWORD=<PASSWORD> -e MYSQL_DATABASE=wordpress -d mysql:5.7
   ```

2. Next, install and run the official WordPress image and run an instance of it as a Docker container, connecting it to the MySQL container (providing the same <PASSWORD> string from the previous step):

   ```
   docker run --restart=always -e WORDPRESS_DB_PASSWORD=<password> -d
   --name wordpress --link wordpressdb:mysql -p 8080:80 wordpress
   ```

3. Now the MySQL and WordPress container should already be running. To check the currently running containers, type:

   ```
   docker ps
   ```

4. To get all the Docker WordPress container settings, use:

   ```
   docker inspect wordpress
   ```

5. To check the container's log file for our WordPress container, run the following command:

   ```
   docker logs -f wordpress
   ```

6. Open a browser on a computer in the same network as the server running the Docker daemon and type in the following command to access your Wordpress installation (replace IP address with the one from your Docker server):

   ```
   http://<IP ADDRESS OF DOCKER SERVER>:8080/
   ```

How it works...

A Docker image is a collection of all the files that make up a software application and its functional dependencies, as well as information about any changes as you modify or improve on its content (in the form of a change log). It is a non-runnable, read-only version of your application and can be compared to an ISO file. If you want to run such an image, a Linux container will be created out of it automatically by cloning the image. This is what then actually executes. It's a real scalable system because you can run multiple containers from the same image. As we have seen, Docker is really not only the tools you need to work with images and containers but a complete platform as it also provides tools to access already pre-made images of all kinds of Linux server software. This is really the beauty of the whole Docker system because most of the time you don't have to reinvent the wheel twice trying to create your own docker image from scratch. Just go to the Docker Hub (`https://hub.docker.com`), search for a software you want to run as a container, and when you find it then just use the `docker run` command, providing the Docker Hub name of the image, and you are done. Docker really can be a life-saver when thinking about all the endless hours trying to get the latest trendy programs to work with all the dependencies you need to compile and trying to get it to install.

So what did we learn from this experience?

We started our journey by using the `docker run` command which downloaded two images from the remote Docker Hub repos and put them into a local image store (called `mysql:5.7` and `wordpress`) and then run them (create containers out of them). To get a list of all the images downloaded on our machine, type `docker images`. As we have seen, both `run` command lines provided the `-e` command line parameter, which we need to set some essential environment variables that will then be visible within the container. These include the MySQL database we want to run and the MySQL root password to set and access them. Here we see a very important feature of Docker: containers that can communicate which each other! Often you can just stack your application together from different Docker container pieces and make the whole system very easy to use. Another important parameter was `-p` which is used to create a port mapping from our host port `8080` to the internal HTTP port 80 and opens the firewall to allow incoming traffic on this port as well. `--restart=always` is useful to make the image container restartable, so the containers automatically get restarted on reboot of the host machine. Afterwards, we introduced you to Docker's `ps` command line parameter which prints out all running Docker containers. Here the command should print out two running containers called `wordpressdb` and `wordpress`, together with their `CONTAINER_ID`. This ID is a unique MD5 hash we will use all the time in most of the Docker command line inputs whenever we need to reference a specific container (in this recipe we referenced by container name which is also possible). Afterwards, we showed you how to print out a container's configuration by using the `inspect` parameter. Then, to get the Wordpress container's log file in an open stream, we used the `log -f` parameter. Finally, since the `-p 8080:80` mapping allows incoming access to our server at port 8080, we could then access our Wordpress installation from any computer in the same network using a browser. This will open the Wordpress installation screen.

Note that if you have any connection problems while downloading any containers from Docker at any time, such as `dial tcp: lookup index.docker.io: no such host`, restart the Docker service before trying again.

There's more...

In this section, we will show you how to start and stop a container and how to attach to your container.

Stopping and starting a container

In the main recipe, we used Docker's `run` command which is actually a wrapper for two other Docker commands: `create` and `start`. As the names of these commands suggest, the `create` command creates (clones) a container from an existing image and if it does not exist in the local image cache then it downloads it from a given Docker registry (such as the predefined Docker hub), while the `start` command actually starts it. To get a list of all the containers (running or stopped) on your computer, type: `docker ps -a`. Now identify a stopped or a started container, and find out its specific `CONTAINER_ID`. Then we can start a stopped container or stop a running one by providing the correct `CONTAINER_ID` such as `docker start CONTAINER_ID`. Examples are: `docker start 03b53947d812` or `docker stop a2fe12e61545` (the `CONTAINER_ID` hashes will vary on your computer).

Sometimes you need to remove a container; for example, if you want to completely change its command line parameters when creating from an image. For removing a container, use the `rm` command (but remember that it has to be stopped before): `docker stop b7f720fbfd23; docker rm b7f720fbfd23`

Attaching and interacting with your container

Linux containers are completely isolated processes running in a separated environment on your server and there is no way to log in to it like logging into a normal server using `ssh`. If you need to access your containers BASH shell then you can run the `docker exec` command, which is particularly useful for debugging problems or modifying your container (for example, installing new packages or updating programs or files in it). Note that this only works on running containers and you need to know your container's ID before (type `docker ps` to find out) you run the following command: `docker exec -it CONTAINER_ID /bin/bash`, for example `docker exec -it d22ddf594f0d /bin/bash`. Once successfully attached to the container, you will see a slightly changed command-line prompt with the `CONTAINER_ID` as hostname; for example, `root@d22ddf594f0d:/var/www/html#`. If you need to exit your container, type `exit`.

Creating your own images from Dockerfiles and uploading to Docker Hub

Besides images and containers, Docker has a third very important term called a **Dockerfile**. A Dockerfile is like a recipe on how to create an environment for a specific application, which means that it contains the blueprint and exact description on how to build a specific image file. For example, if we would like to containerize a webserver-based application, we would define all the dependencies for it, such as the base Linux system that provides the system dependencies such as Ubuntu, Debian, CentOS, and so on (this does not mean we *virtualize* the complete operating system but just use the system dependencies), as well as all applications, dynamic libraries, and services such as PHP, Apache, and MySQL in the Dockerfile and also all special configuration options or environment variables. There are two ways to build your own custom images. One, you could download an existing base image as we did in the previous Wordpress recipe and then attach to the container using BASH, install your additional software, make the changes to your configuration files, and then commit the container as a new image to the registry. Alternatively, here in this recipe, we will teach you how to build your own Docker image from a new Dockerfile for an Express.js web application server and upload it to your own Docker Hub account.

Getting ready

To complete this recipe, you will require a working installation of the CentOS 7 operating system with root privileges, a console-based text editor of your choice, and a connection to the Internet in order to communicate with the Docker Hub. It is expected that Docker is already installed and is running. Also, for uploading your new image to the Docker Hub, you need to create a new Docker Hub user account there. Just go to `https://hub.docker.com/` and register there for free. In our example, we will use a fictitious new Docker Hub user ID called `johndoe`.

How to do it...

1. To begin, log in as root and create a new directory structure using your Docker Hub user ID (substitute the `johndoe` directory name appropriately with your own ID), and open an empty Dockerfile where you put in your image's building blueprint:

    ```
    mkdir -p ~/johndoe/centos7-expressjs
    cd $_; vi Dockerfile
    ```

2. Put in the following content into that file:

    ```
    FROM centos:centos7
    RUN yum install -y epel-release;yum install -y npm;
    RUN npm install express --save
    ```

```
COPY . ./src
EXPOSE 8080
CMD ["node", "/src/index.js"]
```

3. Save and close the file. Now create your first Express.js web application, which we will deploy on the new container. Open the following file in the current directory:

```
vi index.js
```

4. Now put in the following JavaScript content:

```
var express = require('express'), app = express();
app.get('/', function (req, res) {res.send('Hello CentOS 7
cookbook!\n');});
app.listen(8080);
```

5. Now to build an image from this Dockerfile, stay in the current directory and use the following command (don't forget the dot at the end of this line and replace johndoe with your own Docker Hub ID):

```
docker build -t johndoe/centos7-expressjs .
```

6. After successfully building the image, let's run it as a container:

```
docker run -p 8081:8080 -d johndoe/centos7-expressjs
```

7. Finally, test if we can make an HTTP request to our new Express.js web application server running in our new container:

```
curl -i localhost:8081
```

8. If the Docker image is successfully running on the Express.js server, the following HTTP response should occur (truncated to the last line):

```
Hello CentOS 7 cookbook!
```

Uploading your image to the Docker Hub

1. After creating a new Docker Hub account ID called johndoe, we will start to login to the site using the following command—stay in the directory where you put your Dockerfile from the last step–for example ~/johndoe/centos7-expressjs (provide the username, the password, and the registration e-mail when asked):

```
docker login
```

2. Now, to push your new image created in this recipe to the Docker Hub (again replace johndoe with your own user ID), use:

```
docker push johndoe/centos7-expressjs
```

3. After uploading, you will be able to find your image on the Docker Hub web page search. Alternatively, you can use the command line:

```
docker search expressjs
```

How it works...

Here in this short recipe, we showed you how to create your first Dockerfile which will create a CentOS 7 container to serve Express.js applications, which is a modern alternative to LAMP stacks where you program JavaScript on the client-and server-side.

So what did we learn from this experience?

As you can see, a Dockerfile is an elegant way to describe all the instructions on how to create an image. The commands are straight-forward to understand and you use special keywords to instruct Docker what to do in order to produce an image out of it. The FROM command tells Docker which base image we should use. Fortunately, someone has already created a base image from the CentOS 7 system dependencies (this will be downloaded from Docker Hub). Next, we used the RUN command, which just executes commands as on a BASH command-line. We use this command to install dependencies on our system in order to run Express.js applications (it's based on the Node.js rpm package which we access by installing the EPEL repository first). The COPY command copies files from our host machine to a specific location on the container. We need this to copy our index.js file which will create all our Express.js web server code in a later step on to the container. EXPOSE, as the name implies, exposes an internal container port to the outside host system. Since by default Express.js is listening on 8080, we need to do this here. While all these commands shown up to this point will only be executed once when creating the image, the next command CMD will be run every time we start the container. The command node /src/index.js will be executed and instructs the system to start the Express.js web server with the index.js file (which we already provided in this directory by copying it from the host machine). We don't want to go into any details about the JavaScript part of the program—it just handles HTTP GET requests and returns the Hello World string. In the second part of this recipe, we showed you how to push our new created image to the Docker Hub. In order to do so, login with your Docker user account. Then we can push our image to the repository.

As this is a very simple Dockerfile, there is much more to learn about this subject. To see a list of all the commands available in the Dockerfile, use man Dockerfile. Also, you should visit the Docker Hub and browse the Dockerfiles (under the section *Source Repository hosted on GitHub*) of some interesting projects to learn how to create some highly sophisticated image files with just a handful of commands on your own.

Setting up and working with a private Docker registry

While we have learned in a former recipe in this chapter how easy it is to upload our own images to the official Docker Hub, everything we put there will be exposed to the public. If you work on a private or closed-source project within a corporate environment or just want to test things out before publishing to everyone, chances are high that you would prefer your own, protected or cooperate-wide private Docker registry. Here in this recipe we will show you how you can set up and work with your own Docker registry that will be available in your own private network and which will be protected by TLS encryption and which will use user authentication so you can control exactly who can use it (push and pull images to and from it).

Getting ready

To complete this recipe, you will require a working installation of the CentOS 7 operating system with root privileges, a console-based text editor of your choice, and a connection to the Internet in order to facilitate the download of additional packages. In our example, we will install the Docker Registry on a server with the IP address `192.168.1.100`. Change the recipe's commands appropriately to fit your needs. You need to have set a FQDN for this server, otherwise the registry will not work. For simplicity, we will use the `/etc/hosts` approach instead of setting up and configuring a DNS server (see *Chapter 9*, *Working with Domains* if you would like to do this instead). Also, you need an Apache web server on your Docker server running which must be accessible from your whole private network.

How to do it...

Complete all the following steps in this recipe with user root on every computer in your network you want to connect to the Docker registry!

1. On each computer you want to access your Docker registry, as well as on our Docker registry server itself, with the IP address `192.168.1.100`, define the domain name of the Docker registry, which in our example will be `dockerserver.home` (replace the `dockerserver.home` part appropriately if you use a different domain name):

    ```
    echo "export DCKREG=dockerserver.home" >> ~/.bash_profile
    source ~/.bash_profile
    ```

2. Now we will define the FQDN of our Docker server registry on each computer in our network we want to use the registry on (as well as on the Docker registry server itself). Log in as root on every machine and type the following command. Skip this step if you have already defined your Docker registry's server's domain name via a BIND DNS server (change the IP address of your Docker service `192.168.1.100` appropriately):

```
echo "192.168.1.100 $DCKREG" >>  /etc/hosts
```

Steps to be done on our Docker registry server (192.168.1.100)

1. First create a TLS certificate for our Docker registry certificate (use the FQDN you defined in DCKREG when asked for a `Common name` (for name; for example your name or your server's hostname) `[] :dockerserver.home`):

```
cd; mkdir -p ~/certs; openssl req -newkey rsa:4096 -nodes -sha256
-keyout certs/domain.key -x509 -days 365 -out certs/domain.crt
```

2. Next, we need to copy the new certificate to the Docker trusted certificate's location as well as to the system's default trusted certificate location and rebuild the certificate index:

```
mkdir -p /etc/docker/certs.d/$DCKREG\:5000
```

```
cp  ~/certs/domain.crt /etc/docker/certs.d/$DCKREG\:5000/ca.crt
```

```
cp ~/certs/domain.crt /etc/pki/ca-trust/source/anchors/docker-
registry.crt
```

```
update-ca-trust
```

3. Also, copy the certificate to our Apache web server so we can easily access it from the Docker clients later:

```
cp ~/certs/domain.crt /var/www/html/docker-registry.crt
```

4. Next, we will finally download, create, and run our Docker registry as a container:

```
mkdir ~/auth; touch ~/auth/htpasswd docker run -d -p 5000:5000
--restart=always --name registry -v /
```

```
root/certs:/certs -v /root/auth:/auth -v /reg:/var/lib/registry -e
REGISTRY_HTTP_TLS_CERTIFICATE=/certs/domain.crt -e
```

```
 REGISTRY_HTTP_TLS_KEY=/certs/domain.key -e "REGISTRY_AUTH_
HTPASSWD_REALM=Registry Realm" -e REGISTRY_AUTH_HTPASSWD_PATH=/
auth/htpasswd -e REGISTRY_AUTH=htpasswd registry:2
```

5. Now check if the registry is running (in the output you should find it listening on `[::]:5000, tls`):

```
docker logs registry
```

6. For setting up user authentication for our registry, use the following command (here we use `johndoe` as the username and `mysecretpassword` as the password for authentication. Change these two values to fit your needs. Repeat this command for every user account you want to have later for your users to login):

```
cd; docker run -it --entrypoint htpasswd -v $PWD/auth:/auth -w /
auth registry:2 -Bbc /auth/htpasswd johndoe mysecretpassword
```

7. Next restart the registry to apply your user account changes:

```
docker restart registry
```

8. Now create a new firewalld service and activate it in our firewall to make incoming connections to our new Docker registry port `5000` possible:

```
sed 's/80/5000/g' /usr/lib/firewalld/services/http.xml | sed
's/WWW (HTTP)/Docker registry/g' | sed 's/<description>.*<\/
description>//g' > /etc/firewalld/services/docker-reg.xml
```

```
firewall-cmd --reload
```

```
firewall-cmd --permanent --add-service=docker-reg; firewall-cmd
--reload
```

Steps to be done on every client needing access to our registry

1. Finally we can test connecting to our own new TLS-enhanced private Docker registry with user authentication by logging in on any computer in the same network as our Docker registry with root.

2. The first step is to install Docker on every client that wants to connect to the Docker registry:

```
yum update && curl -sSL https://get.docker.com/ | sh
```

3. Next, on every client wanting to connect to our new Docker registry, set up the server's certificate on the client first before we are able to connect to it (this step has been tested on CentOS 7 clients only):

```
mkdir -p /etc/docker/certs.d/$DCKREG\:5000
```

```
curl http://$DCKREG/docker-registry.crt -o /tmp/cert.crt
```

```
cp /tmp/cert.crt /etc/docker/certs.d/$DCKREG\:5000/ca.crt
```

```
cp /tmp/cert.crt /etc/pki/ca-trust/source/anchors/docker-registry.
crt
```

```
update-ca-trust
```

4. For testing, we start by pulling a new small test image from the official Docker Hub. Log in to the official Docker Hub by using your Docker Hub account (see a previous recipe in this chapter):

   `docker login`

5. Now pull a small image called `busybox`:

   `docker pull busybox`

6. Afterwards, switch the Docker registry server to use our own that we set up in this recipe (enter the username and password, for example, `johndoe / mysecretpassword`. Leave the e-mail field blank):

   `docker login $DCKREG:5000`

7. Next, to push a Docker image from our client to our new private Docker registry, we need to tag it to be in our registry's domain:

   `docker tag busybox $DCKREG:5000/busybox`

8. Finally, push the image to our own registry:

   `docker push $DCKREG:5000/busybox`

9. Congratulations! You have just pushed your first image to your private Docker repository. You can now pull this image `$DCKREG:5000/busybox` on any other client set up to communicate to our repository. To get a list of all the available images, use (change the account information accordingly):

   `curl https://johndoe:mysecretpassword@$DCKREG:5000/v2/_catalog`

How it works...

In this recipe we showed you how to set up your own Docker registry running in a Docker container on the server. It is very important to understand that you will need to configure a FQDN for your registry server because it is mandatory for the whole system to work.

So what did we learn from this experience?

We began by configuring the Docker registry's FQDN on every computer using the `/etc/hosts` approach. Then we created a new certificate on the Docker registry server which will be used to communicate securely using TLS encryption between clients and registry. Next we installed the new generated certificate on the `httpd` server, so it is accessible to all the clients later; also in a specific Docker directory to make it accessible for Docker as well; and in the default trusted certificate location of the server where we also rebuilt the certificate cache for this server. Afterwards, we used the `docker run` command to download, install, and run our new Docker registry in a docker container itself on this server. We provided a list of parameters to configure TLS encryption and user authentication.

In the next step, we attached to the registry to create new `htpasswd` accounts. You can repeat this step whenever you need new accounts for your registry. Don't forget to restart the registry container afterwards. Next, on every client we want to make communications to our new Docker registry, we need to install the server's certificate also in the same places as on the server itself; thus we downloaded it from the HTTP source implemented previously and copied it to the various locations. To test things out on the client, next we connected to the official Docker Hub to download a random image we wanted to push to our own registry in the next step. We downloaded the `busybox` image to our own image cache and afterwards switched to connecting to our new private Docker registry. Before we could upload the image to the new location, we had to give it a proper tag that fitted the new server name and then we were able to push the image to our new Docker registry. The server is now available at port 5000 in the complete network. Remember that, if you don't want to use your own registry any more on the clients, you can always switch back to the official `docker` repository using `docker login`.

There is so much more to learn about Docker. In the recipes of this chapter we only scratched the surface of the Docker platform. If you want to learn more about it, consider going to `https://www.Packtpub.com` and check out one of the many titles available at this website about it.

14
Working with SELinux

In this chapter, we will cover the following topics:

- ▸ Installing and configuring important SELinux tools
- ▸ Working with SELinux security contexts
- ▸ Working with policies
- ▸ Troubleshooting SELinux

Introduction

This chapter is a collection of recipes that strive to demystify **Security-Enhanced Linux** (**SELinux**), a mature technology for hardening your Linux system using additional security features added to the basic security system. It has been around for many years in the CentOS world but nevertheless is a somewhat little-known and confusing topic for a lot of system administrators.

Installing and configuring important SELinux tools

The most significant security feature of any Linux system is providing access control—often called **Discretionary Access Control** (**DAC**)—which allows the owner of an object (such as a file) to set security attributes for it (for example, deciding who can read or write to a file using the chown and chmod commands). While this old and very simple security system was sufficient in ancient UNIX times, it does not meet all the modern requirements of security, where servers and services are constantly connected to the Internet.

Often, security breaches can be initiated by attackers exploiting buggy or misconfigured applications and the permissions to them. This is why the SELinux has been developed. Its main purpose is to enhance the security of the DAC system in Linux. It does so by adding an additional security layer on top of DAC, which is called **Mandatory Access Control** (**MAC**), and which can provide fine-grain access control to every single component of your system. SELinux has already been enabled on CentOS 7 and is absolutely recommended for any server connected directly to the Internet. Here in this recipe, we will install additional tools and configure them to better manage your SELinux system, and help in the troubleshooting and monitoring process.

Getting ready

To complete this recipe, you will require a working installation of the CentOS 7 operating system with root privileges and a connection to the Internet in order to download additional packages. For the best learning experience, it is also preferred that you work through this chapter recipe by recipe, in the order that they appear, because they build upon each other.

How to do it...

Throughout this book, we already applied programs such as `semanage` from the `rpm policicecoreutils-python` package to manage our SELinux environment. If you missed installing it, we will begin this recipe by doing so (skip step 1 if you have already done this before):

1. Log in as root and install the following basic toolkit to work with SELinux:

    ```
    yum install policycoreutils-python
    ```

2. Now, we need some additional tools that will also be needed later in the course of this chapter:

    ```
    yum install setools setools-console setroubleshoot*
    ```

3. Next, install and configure the SELinux manual pages as they are not available by default on CentOS 7, but are important for getting detailed information about specific policies, security contexts, and SELinux Booleans later. First, we need to install another package:

    ```
    yum install policycoreutils-devel
    ```

4. Afterwards, let's generate all the man pages for all SELinux security context policies currently available on the system, and then update the manual pages database afterwards:

    ```
    sepolicy manpage -a -p /usr/share/man/man8; mandb
    ```

How it works...

By following this recipe, we installed all the tools needed for our daily work with SELinux. Also, we generated all available SELinux manual pages, which will be our primary source of information when working with SELinux, and also for troubleshooting SELinux services later.

SELinux has two primary and fundamental terms that we need to understand before diving into the remaining recipes in this chapter: **labels** (or more technically, security contexts) and **policies**. From SELinux's perspective, a Linux system is divided into a number of different objects. Objects, for example, are all files, processes, users, sockets, and pipes in a system. In a SELinux context, every such object gets a special label. SELinux policies are the rules to control access to these objects using the labels defined on them: On every access attempt to such an object (for example, a file read), all SELinux policies available to the system will be searched if there is a rule for the specific label to make access control decisions (allow or deny the access).

So, what did we learn from this experience?

A lot of system administrators seem to avoid SELinux *like the plague*, and a trend in a lot of instruction manuals and tutorials leans towards disabling it altogether right after the installation of CentOS 7 because people seem to fear it and don't want to mess with it, or are even frustrated if some networking service is not working correctly out-of-the-box. Often, they blame SELinux for any connection problems, so it often looks easier to disable it altogether rather than find out the true reasons by delving into the inner workings of SELinux. If you are disabling it, you are missing out one of the most critical security features of CentOS 7 that can prevent a lot of harm to your system in the event of an attack! In the last few years, the SELinux project has evolved very much and is easier to use than ever. A lot of convenient tools for working with it have emerged, and we get more of a complete set of policies to work with all the major applications and services available. By installing these tools, we are now ready to use SELinux and work with it in the most convenient way possible.

There's more...

There are three different modes when it comes to SELinux. While **Enhanced** is the only true mode that really protects us and enhances our server's security, there are two other modes: **Disabled** and **Permissive**. Disabled means SELinux is turned off, which will never be an option for us in this book and is not discussed any further as it does not make sense to get rid of this fantastic CentOS feature. When disabled, our system is not enhanced by SELinux and the good old DAC system is the only source of protection we have at hand. Permissive mode means SELinux is turned on, the policy rules are loaded, and all objects are labeled with a specific security context, but the system is not enforcing these policies. This is like a dry-run parameter that a lot of Linux based command-line tools have: it simulates the system under SELinux enhanced security protection, and the system logs every SELinux policy violation as it would when running for real. This is a great way to debug the system, or to analyze the consequences that a normal, enforced run would have had on the system.

Often, it is used if you are unsure about the impact of using SELinux. As this mode does not really provide us with any additional security, we will eventually need to switch to **Enforcing** mode if we want enhanced security! Again, this is the only mode that protects us; SELinux is fully running with all the policies loaded and is enforcing these rules on the system. You should always aim for Enforcing mode on any system! To view the current mode, use the command `sestatus`. We can see the current SELinux mode in the `Current mode` line in the output. On CentOS 7, SELinux is in Enforcing mode by default, which again tells us that the system is fully protected by it. To change this mode to permissive mode, use the command `setenforce permissive`. Now, validate your setting using `sestatus` again. To revert your changes back to Enforcing mode, use `setenforce enforcing`. Setting the SELinux mode using `setenforce` is only setting it temporarily, and it will not survive a reboot (take a look at the `Mode from config` file in the `sestatus` output). To change this permanently, open the `/etc/selinux/config` file and change the `SELINUX=` configuration parameter.

Working with SELinux security contexts

As we have learned from the previous recipe in this chapter, SELinux is all about labels and policies. In this recipe, we will show you how to work with these labels, also known as security contexts.

Getting ready

To complete this recipe, you will require a working installation of the CentOS 7 operating system with root privileges. It is assumed that you are working through this chapter recipe by recipe, so by now you should have installed the SELinux tools from the previous recipe and generated all the SELinux man pages for the policies. As you may notice, some of the commands that we will show you in this recipe have already been applied in other recipes in this book. We will explain them here in detail. For using the `netstat` program, install the package, `net-tools`, with the YUM package manager.

How to do it...

As we have learned in a previous recipe, almost every component in a SELinux system is an object (files, directories, processes, users, and so on). We will begin this recipe by showing you how to print out the SELinux labels for all kinds of objects using the `-Z` command-line flag, which a lot of basic Linux commands on a SELinux system support.

1. To begin with, log in as root and type the following commands to explore SELinux security context information from various kinds of objects:

   ```
   id -Z

   ls -Z
   ```

```
ps -auxZ

netstat -tulpenZ
```

2. Next, to list all available security context names for the files and directories on your system, use the following command (which we filtered for `httpd` labels only):

   ```
   semanage fcontext -l | grep httpd
   ```

3. Next, let's create a new empty file that we can work with:

   ```
   touch /tmp/selinux-context-test.txt
   ```

4. Show the current security context of the new file (should contain the type `user_ tmp_t`):

   ```
   ls -Z /tmp/selinux-context-test.txt
   ```

5. Finally, change the `user_tmp_t` type to a random `samba_share_t` label name:

   ```
   semanage fcontext -a -t samba_share_t /tmp/selinux-context-test.txt

   restorecon -v /tmp/selinux-context-test.txt
   ```

6. Perform a test to validate your changes:

   ```
   ls -Z /tmp/selinux-context-test.txt
   ```

How it works...

Here in this recipe, we have shown you how to display labels (security contexts) of various SELinux object types, how to show all available label names, and how to modify or set them on the example of the file object. Working on a SELinux enhanced system on a daily basis, most administrators would confirm that the most important objects we have to manage security contexts for are files, directories, and processes. Also, you need to remember that every SELinux object can have only one security context.

So, what did we learn from this experience?

As we have have seen, we can use the `-Z` parameter on a lot of different standard Linux command-line tools to print out their SELinux security context. Here, we have shown you examples to display labels for users, files and directories, processes, and network connections, which we could query with the `id`, `ls`, `ps`, and `netstat` commands. In the output of these commands, we see that every security context label of every such object consists of three values: user (flagged by `_u`), role (`_r`), and type (`_t`). The type field is used as the main mechanism to do all our access control decisions in the standard SELinux type (which is called targeted), so we often call the whole SELinux access control process **type enforcement** (**TE**).

The other values user and role in an object's label are only necessary for very advanced SELinux configurations not discussed here. In order to show all the available context types for use on our system, use the command-line `seinfo -t`. These SELinux types are a very important concept that we need to understand. For file and directory objects, they are used to *bundle* together groups of objects related to each other, and that should be protected or treated the same so that we can define specific policy rules on them. For example, we can assign each file in the standard mail spool directory, `/var/spool/mail`, of the type `mail_spool_t`, and then create an access rule policy in which we will use this type to allow specific access. In the context of processes, type values are called domains. Here, types are used as a way to isolate and *sandbox* processes: any process that has a specified domain name can only communicate and interact with other processes in the same domain (with some exceptions, such as transitions not discussed here). This *isolating* of processes via domains greatly reduces security risks. When processes get compromised, they can only damage themselves and nothing else.

 SELinux is sometimes called a sandboxing system. Starting from the assumption that software will always have bugs, SELinux provides ways to isolate components of the software such that a breach in one component doesn't compromise another.

If you type in `ps -auxZ`, you will also see that there are processes that run in a domain called `unconfined_t`. Processes running with this label are not protected by SELinux policies, which means that, if an unconfined process is compromised, SELinux does not prevent an attacker from gaining access to other system resources and data. Here, security falls back to standard DAC rules, which will be your only and exclusive protection instead.

After we discussed how to display security contexts, next in the recipe we showed you how you can set and change them. In some older documentation as well as in some SELinux policy man pages, you will encounter examples with a tool called `chcon`, which is used to modify the security context of your objects. The usage of this tool is not the recommended approach any more, and you should always replace such command line examples with the newer `semanage fcontext -a -t` command-line in combination with the `restorecon` program. For `semanage`, you provide the label type name with `-t`, and then provide the filename you want to set it for. Then, with `restorecon`, you provide the filename to which you want to apply the change made by `semanage` earlier. This is needed because security context can be set on two levels. It can be set to the policy and on a filesystem level. The `chcon` command sets the new context directly on the filesystem, while the policy context does not get altered. This can be a problem, for example, if you want to reset or change the security context of your filesystem later (this is called relabeling)—which means that all the security context will be applied from the policy to the filesystem, overwriting all your changes made with `chcon`. So it is better to use `semanage`, which will write to the policy, and then use `restorecon`, which will synchronize the policy labels to the filesystem, keeping everything up-to-date. If you want to set labels for directories instead of single files, you can use regular expressions; to see some examples and further command-line options; type `man semanage-fcontext` and browse to the EXAMPLES section.

Working with policies

At the core of every SELinux system are the policies. These are the exact rules that define the access rights and relationships between all our objects. As we have learned earlier, all our system's objects have labels, and one of them is a type identifier that can then be used to enforce rules laid down by policies. In every SELinux enabled system, by default, all access to any object is prohibited unless a policy rule has been defined otherwise. Here, in this recipe, we will show you how we can query and customize SELinux policies. As you may notice, some of the commands have already been applied in other recipes in this book, such as for the httpd or ftpd daemons. Here, you will find out how policies work.

Getting ready

To complete this recipe, you will require a working installation of the CentOS 7 operating system with root privileges. It is assumed that you are working through this chapter recipe by recipe, so by now you should have installed the SELinux tools from the previous recipe and generated all SELinux man pages for the policies. For our tests here, we will use the Apache web server, so please make sure it is installed and running on your system (Refer to recipe *Installing Apache and serving web pages* in *Chapter 12, Providing Web Services*).

How to do it...

1. To begin, log in as root and type the following command to show all SELinux Boolean policy settings, filtered by the httpd daemon only:

   ```
   semanage boolean -l | grep httpd
   ```

2. To get more information about a specific policy and its contained Booleans, read the corresponding man page; for example, for httpd type the following:

   ```
   man httpd_selinux
   ```

3. Here, within the manual pages for the httpd policy, we will, among others, find detailed information about every httpd policy Boolean available. For example, there is a section about httpd_use_nfso. To toggle single policy features, use the setsebool command together with the policy Boolean name with the on or off parameter, as shown here:

   ```
   setsebool httpd_use_nfs on
   setsebool httpd_use_nfs off
   ```

How it works...

Here in this recipe, we have shown you how to work with SELinux Booleans. Remember that SELinux follows the model of least privilege, which means that SELinux policies enable only the least amount of features to any object; like a system service, they need to perform their task and nothing more. These features of a policy can be controlled (activated or deactivated) using corresponding SELinux Booleans at runtime without the need to understand the inner workings of policy writing. It is a concept to make policies customizable and extremely flexible. In other recipes in this book, we have already worked with enabling SELinux Booleans to add special policy features, such as enabling Apache or FTP home directories, which are all disabled by default.

What did we learn from this experience?

SELinux Booleans are like switches to enable or disable certain functionalities in your SELinux policy. We started this recipe using the `semanage` command to show all Booleans available on the system, and we filtered by `http` to get only those related to this service. As you can see, there are a huge number of Booleans available in your system, and most of them are disabled or off (the model of least privilege); to get more information about a specific policy and its Boolean values, use the SELinux man pages that we installed in a previous recipe. Sometimes, it can be difficult to find a specific man page of interest. Use the following command to search for man page names that are available: `man -k _selinux | grep http`. In our example, `httpd_selinux` is the correct man page to get detailed information about the `httpd` policy. Finally, if we decide to switch a specific SELinux Boolean feature, we will use the `setsebool` command. You should remember that setting Booleans in this way only works until reboot. To make those settings permanent, use the `-p` flag, for example, `setsebool -P httpd_use_nfs on`.

There's more...

With all our knowledge from the previous recipes so far, we are now able to show an example where we put everything together. Here, we will see SELinux security contexts and policies in action for the `httpd` service. If the Apache web server is running, we can get the SELinux domain name of the `httpd` process using the following line:

```
ps auxZ | grep httpd
```

This will show us that the `httpd` domain (type) is called `httpd_t`. To get the SELinux label of our web root directory, type in the following command:

```
ls -alZ /var/www/html
```

This will tell us that the security context type of our Apache web server's web root directory is called httpd_sys_content_t. Now, with this information, we can get the exact rules for the Apache domain from our policy:

sesearch --allow | grep httpd_t

This will print out every httpd policy rule available. If we filter the output for the httpd_sys_content_t context type, the following line comes up for files again:

allow httpd_t httpd_sys_content_t : file { ioctl read getattr lock open }

This shows us which source target context is allowed to access, which destination target context, and with which access rights. In our example for the Apache web server, this specifies that the httpd process that runs as domain httpd_t can access, open, and modify all the files on the filesystem that match the httpd_sys_content_t context type (all files in the /var/www/html directory match this criterion). Now, to validate this rule, create a temporary file and move it to the Apache web root directory: echo "CentOS7 Cookbook" > /tmp/test.txt;mv /tmp/test.txt /var/www/html. Any file inherits the security context of the directory in which it is created. If we had created the file directly in the web root directory, or had copied the file instead of moving it (copying means creating a copy), it would automatically be in the correct httpd_sys_content_t context and fully accessible by Apache. But, as we moved the file from the /tmp directory, it will stay as the user_tmp_t type in the web root directory. If you now try to fetch the URL, for example,, curl http://localhost/test.txt, you should get a 403 forbidden message. This is because the user_tmp_t type is not part of the httpd_t policy rule for file objects, because, as said before, everything that is not defined in a policy rule will be blocked by default. To make the file accessible, we will now change its security context label to the correct type:

semanage fcontext -a -t httpd_sys_content_t /var/www/html/test.txt

restorecon -v /var/www/html/test.txt

Now, again fetch curl http://localhost/test.txt, which should be accessible, and print out the correct text: CentOS7 cookbook.

Remember that, if you copy a file, the security context type is inherited from the targeted parent directory. If you want to preserve the original context when copying, use cp -preserve=context instead.

Troubleshooting SELinux

In this recipe, you will learn how to troubleshoot SELinux policies, which is most often needed when access to some SELinux objects has been denied and you need to find out the reasons for it. In this recipe, we will show you how to work with the `sealert` tool, which will create human-readable and understandable error messages to work with.

Getting ready

To complete this recipe, you will require a working installation of the CentOS 7 operating system with root privileges. It is assumed that you are working through this chapter recipe by recipe, so by now you should have installed the SELinux tools and applied the *Working with policies* recipe in this chapter, as we will produce some SELinux denial events in order to show you how to use the log file tools.

How to do it...

1. To begin, login as root and provoke a SELinux denial event:

   ```
   touch /var/www/html/test2.html
   semanage fcontext -a -t user_tmp_t /var/www/html/test2.html
   restorecon -v /var/www/html/test2.html
   curl http://localhost/test2.html
   ```

2. Now, let's generate an up-to-date human readable log file:

   ```
   sealert -a /var/log/audit/audit.log
   ```

3. In the program's output, you will get a detailed description of any SELinux problem and, at the end of each so called alert, you will even find a suggested solution to fix the problem; in our example, the alert of interest should read (the output is truncated) as shown next:

   ```
   SELinux is preventing /usr/sbin/httpd from open access on the file
   /var/www/html/test2.html.

   /var/www/html/test2.html default label should be httpd_sys_
   content_t
   ```

How it works...

Here in this recipe, we showed you how easily one can troubleshoot SELinux problems using the `sealert` program. We started by provoking a SELinux deny access problem by creating a new file in the web root directory and assigning it a wrong context type of value `user_tmp_t`, which has no access rule defined in the `httpd` policy. Then, we used the `curl` command to try and fetch the website and actually produce the **Access Vector Cache** (**AVC**) denial message in the SELinux logs. Denial messages are logged when SELinux denies access. The primary source where all SELinux logging information is stored is the audit log file, which can be found at `/var/log/audit/audit.log`, and easier-to-read denial messages will also be written to `/var/log/messages`. Here, instead of manually grepping for error messages and combining both log files, we use the `sealert` tool, which is a convenience program that will parse the audit and messages log file and present valuable AVC content in a human-readable format. At the end of each alert message, you will also find a suggested solution to the problem. Please note that those are auto-generated messages and should always be questioned before applying.

15
Monitoring
IT Infrastructure

In this chapter, we will cover the following topics:

- ▶ Installing and configuring Nagios Core
- ▶ Setting up NRPE on remote client hosts
- ▶ Monitoring important remote system metrics

Introduction

This chapter is a collection of recipes that provide the necessary steps to set up the de-facto industry standard, open source network monitoring framework: Nagios Core.

Installing and configuring Nagios Core

In this recipe, we will learn how to install Nagios Core version 4, an open-source network monitoring system that checks whether hosts and services are working and notifies users when problems occur or services become unavailable. Nagios provides solutions to monitor your complete IT infrastructure and is designed with an architecture that is highly extendable and customizable and goes far beyond simple bash scripts to monitor your services. (Refer to the *Monitoring important server infrastructure* recipe in *Chapter 3, Managing the System*.)

Getting ready

To complete this recipe, you will require a working installation of the CentOS 7 operating system with root privileges, a console-based text editor of your choice, and a connection to the Internet in order to facilitate the download of additional packages. Nagios Core 4 is not available in the official sources but from the EPEL repository; make sure to have installed it before (refer to the *Using a third-party repository* recipe in *Chapter 4, Managing Packages with YUM*). For the Nagios web frontend, you need a running Apache2 web server as well as PHP (refer to the recipes from *Chapter 12, Providing Web Services*) installed on your Nagios server. In our example, the Nagios server has the IP address 192.168.1.7, and it will be able to monitor all IT infrastructure in the complete 192.168.1.0/24 subnet.

How to do it...

Nagios Core 4 is not available by default, so let's begin by installing all the required packages:

1. To do so, log in as root and type the following command:

   ```
   yum install nagios nagios-plugins-all nagios-plugins-nrpe nrpe
   ```

2. First, create a new user account called `nagiosadmin`, which is needed for authentication to the web frontend (enter a secure password when prompted), then reload the Apache configuration:

   ```
   htpasswd /etc/nagios/passwd nagiosadmin  && systemctl reload httpd
   ```

3. Now, add an e-mail address for the `nagiosadmin` web user to the Nagios configuration, open the following file, and search and replace the string, `nagios@localhost`, with an appropriate e-mail address you want to use here (it can be a domain-wide or external e-mail address):

   ```
   vi /etc/nagios/objects/contacts.cfg
   ```

4. Now, we need to adjust the main configuration file to activate `/etc/nagios/servers` as our server's definition configuration directory, where we will put all our server config files later, but first, make a backup:

   ```
   cp /etc/nagios/nagios.cfg  /etc/nagios/nagios.cfg.BAK
   sed -i -r 's/^#cfg_dir=(.+)servers$/cfg_dir=\1servers/g'
   /etc/nagios/nagios.cfg
   ```

5. We will have to create the server's config directory that we just defined in the last step:

   ```
   mkdir /etc/nagios/servers
   chown nagios: /etc/nagios/servers;chmod 750 /etc/nagios/servers
   ```

6. Afterwards, to check the correctness of the `nagios.cfg` syntax, run the following:

   ```
   nagios -v /etc/nagios/nagios.cfg
   ```

7. Finally, enable the Nagios daemon on boot and start the service:

```
systemctl enable nagios && systemctl start nagios
```

How it works...

Here in this recipe, we have shown you how to install the Nagios Core v4 server (Core is the open-source version of the Nagios project) on CentOS 7. Besides the main Nagios package, we also required the NRPE package and all the Nagios plugins on our Nagios server. After installing, we created a user account, which is able to log in to the web frontend, and we set the e-mail address for this user in the main Nagios configuration file. Next, we activated the /etc/nagios/servers directory using sed, where all our server definition files will be put in a later recipe in this chapter. Then, we created the directory and changed permissions to the Nagios user. To test the Nagios server installation, open a web browser on a computer in the same subnet 192.168.1.0/24 as your Nagios server, open the following URL (in our example, the Nagios server has the IP 192.168.1.7, so change accordingly), and then log in with your newly created nagiosadmin user account to http://192.168.1.7/nagios.

Setting up NRPE on remote client hosts

The **Nagios Remote Plugin Executor** (**NRPE**) is a system daemon that uses a special client-server protocol and should be installed on all client hosts that you want to monitor via your Nagios server remotely. It allows the central Nagios server to trigger any Nagios checks on these client hosts securely and with low overhead. Here, we will show you how to set up and configure any CentOS 7 client to use NRPE; if you've got more than one computer in your network that you want to monitor, you need to apply this recipe for every instance.

Getting ready

To complete this recipe, you will require a computer other than your Nagios server with an installation of the CentOS 7 operating system and root privileges, which you want to monitor, and which needs a console-based text editor of your choice installed on it, along with a connection to the Internet in order to facilitate the download of additional packages. This computer needs to have access to our Nagios server over the network. In our example, the Nagios server has the IP address 192.168.1.7, and our client system will have the IP address 192.168.1.8.

How to do it...

1. Log in as root on your CentOS 7 client system and install all Nagios plugins as well as NRPE on it:

```
yum install epel-release;yum install nrpe nagios-plugins-all
nagios-plugins-nrpe
```

2. Afterwards, open the main NRPE config file (after making a backup first):

```
cp /etc/nagios/nrpe.cfg /etc/nagios/nrpe.cfg.BAK && vi /etc/
nagios/nrpe.cfg
```

3. Find the line that starts with `allowed_hosts`, and add the IP address of your Nagios server separated by a comma so that we can communicate with it (in our example ,192.168.1.7, so change it accordingly); it should read as follows:

```
allowed_hosts=127.0.0.1,192.168.1.7
```

4. Save and close the file, then enable NRPE at boot and start it:

```
systemctl enable nrpe && systemctl start nrpe
```

5. Then enable the NRPE port in firewalld. To do this, create a new firewalld service file for NRPE:

```
sed 's/80/5666/g' /usr/lib/firewalld/services/http.xml | sed
's/WWW (HTTP)/Nagios NRPE/g' | sed 's/<description>.*<\/
description>//g' > /etc/firewalld/services/nrpe.xml

firewall-cmd --reload

firewall-cmd --permanent --add-service=nrpe; firewall-cmd --reload
```

6. Finally, test the NRPE connection. To do this, log in as root on your Nagios server (for example, at 192.168.1.7) and execute the following command to check NRPE on our client (192.168.1.8):

```
/usr/lib64/nagios/plugins/check_nrpe -H 192.168.1.8 -c check_load
```

7. If the output prints out an `OK - load average` message with some numbers, you have successfully configured NRPE on the client!

How it works...

Here in this recipe, we have shown you how to install NRPE on your CentOS 7 clients that you want to monitor with your Nagios servers. If you want to monitor other Linux systems running other distributions such as Debian or BSD, you should be able to find appropriate packages using their own package managers or compile NRPE from source. Besides the NRPE package, we also installed all the Nagios plugins on this machine since NRPE is only the daemon for running monitoring commands on client computers, but it does not include them. After installation, NRPE is listening only on localhost (127.0.0.1) connections by default, so we then had to change this to also listen to connections from our Nagios server, which runs with the IP 192.168.1.7, using the `allowed_hosts` directive in the main NRPE configuration file. The NRPE port 5666 is needed for incoming connections from the Nagios server, so we also had to open it in the firewall. Since no firewalld rule is available for it by default, we created our own new service file and added it to the current firewalld configuration. Afterwards, we could test our NRPE installation from our Nagios server by running a `check_nrpe` command using the client's IP address and a random check command (`check_load` returns the system's load).

Monitoring important remote system metrics

The Nagios plugin `check_multi` is a convenient tool to execute multiple checks within a single check command that generates an overall returned state and output from it. Here in this recipe, we will show you how to set it up and use it to quickly monitor a list of important system metrics on your clients.

Getting ready

It is assumed that you've gone through this chapter recipe by recipe, therefore by now, you should have a Nagios server running and another client computer that you want to monitor, which can already be accessed via its NRPE service externally by our Nagios server. This client computer that you want to monitor needs an installation of the CentOS 7 operating system with root privileges and a console-based text editor of your choice installed on it, as well as a connection to the Internet in order to facilitate the download of additional packages. The client computer will have the IP address `192.168.1.8`.

How to do it...

The `check_multi` Nagios plugin is available from Github, so we will begin this recipe to install the `git` program by downloading it:

1. Log in as root on your client computer and install Git if not done already:

   ```
   yum install git
   ```

2. Now, download and install the `check_multi` plugin by compiling it from the source:

   ```
   cd /tmp;git clone git://github.com/flackem/check_multi;cd /tmp/
   check_multi
   ```

   ```
   ./configure --with-nagios-name=nagios --with-nagios-user=nagios
   --with-nagios-group=nagios --with-plugin-path=/usr/lib64/nagios/
   plugins --libexecdir=/usr/lib64/nagios/plugins/
   ```

   ```
   make all;make install;make install-config
   ```

3. Next, we install another very useful plugin called `check_mem`, which is not available in the CentOS 7 Nagios plugin `rpms`:

   ```
   cd /tmp;git clone https://github.com/justintime/nagios-plugins.git
   ```

   ```
   cp /tmp/nagios-plugins/check_mem/check_mem.pl  /usr/lib64/nagios/
   plugins/
   ```

4. Next, let's create a `check_multi` command file that will contain all your desired client checks that you want to combine in a single run; open the following file:

   ```
   vi /usr/local/nagios/etc/check_multi/check_multi.cmd
   ```

5. Put in the following content:

```
command[ sys_load::check_load ] = check_load -w 5,4,3 -c 10,8,6
command[ sys_mem::check_mem ] = check_mem.pl -w 10 -c 5 -f -C
command[ sys_users::check_users ] = check_users -w 5 -c 10
command[ sys_disks::check_disk ] = check_disk -w 5% -c 2% -X nfs
command[ sys_procs::check_procs ] = check_procs
```

6. Next, test out the command file that we just created in the last step using the following commandline:

```
/usr/lib64/nagios/plugins/check_multi -f    /usr/local/nagios/etc/
check_multi/check_multi.cmd
```

7. If everything is correct, it should print out the results of your five plugin checks and an overall result, for example, OK - 5 plugins checked. Next, we will install this new command in the NRPE service on our client so that the Nagios server is able to execute it remotely by calling its name. Open the NRPE configuration file:

```
vi /etc/nagios/nrpe.cfg
```

8. Add the following line to the end of the file right below the last # command line to expose a new command called check_multicmd to our Nagios server:

```
command[check_multicmd]=/usr/lib64/nagios/plugins/check_multi -f
/usr/local/nagios/etc/check_multi/check_multi.cmd
```

9. Finally, let's reload NRPE:

```
systemctl restart nrpe
```

10. Now, let's check whether we can execute our new check_multicmd command that we defined in the last step from our Nagios server. Log in as root and type the following command (change the IP address of your client, 192.168.1.8, appropriately):

```
/usr/lib64/nagios/plugins/check_nrpe  -H 192.168.1.8 -c "check_
multicmd"
```

11. If the output is the same as running it locally on the client itself (take a look at the former step), we can successfully execute remote NRPE commands on our client through our server, so let's define the command on our Nagios server system for real so that we can start using it within the Nagios system. Open the following file:

```
vi /etc/nagios/objects/commands.cfg
```

12. Put in the following content at the end of the file to define a new command called check_nrpe_multi, which we can use in any service definition:

```
define command {
  command_name check_nrpe_multi
```

```
  command_line $USER1$/check_nrpe -H $HOSTADDRESS$ -c "check_
multicmd"
}
```

13. Next, we will define a new server definition for the client that we want to monitor on our Nagios server (give the config file an appropriate name, for example, its domain name or IP address):

    ```
    vi /etc/nagios/servers/192.168.1.8.cfg
    ```

14. Put in the following content, which will define a new host with its service, using our new Nagios command that we just created:

    ```
    define host {
            use                   linux-server
            host_name             host1
            address               192.168.1.22
            contact_groups        unix-admins
    }
    define service {
            use generic-service
            host_name host1
            check_command check_nrpe_multi
            normal_check_interval 15
            service_description check_nrpe_multi service
    }
    ```

15. Finally, we need to configure all persons who should get notification e-mails for our new service in case of errors. Open the following file:

    ```
    vi /etc/nagios/objects/contacts.cfg
    ```

16. Put in the following content at the end of the file:

    ```
    define contactgroup{
            contactgroup_name     unix-admins
            alias                 Unix Administrators
    }
    define contact {
            contact_name          pelz
            use                   generic-contact
            alias                 Oliver Pelz
            contactgroups         unix-admins
    ```

email	**oliverpelz@mymailhost.com**

     }

17. Now, restart the Nagios service:

```
systemctl restart nagios
```

How it works...

We started this recipe by installing the `check_multi` and `check_mem` plugins from their author's Github repositories; they are plain command-line tools. Nagios performs checks by running such external commands, and it uses the return code along with output from the command as information on whether the check was successful or not. Nagios has a very flexible architecture that can be easily extended using plugins, add-ons, and extensions. A central place to search for all kinds of extensions is at `https://exchange.nagios.org/`. Next, we added a new command file for `check_multi`, where we put five different system `check_` commands in. These checks act as a starting point for customizing your monitoring needs and will check system load, memory consumption, system users, free space, and processes. All available `check_` commands can be found at `/usr/lib64/nagios/plugins/check_*`. As you can see in our command file, the parameters of those `check_` commands can be very different, and explaining them all is out of the scope of this recipe. Most of them are used to set threshold values to reach a certain state, for example, the `CRITICAL` state. To get more information about a specific command, use the `--help` parameter with the command. For example, to find out what all the parameters in the `check_load -w 5,4,3 -c 10,8,6` command are doing, use run `/usr/lib64/nagios/plugins/check_load --help`. You can easily add any number of new check commands to our command file from existing plugins, or you can download and install any new commands, if you like. There are also a number of command file examples shipped with the `check_multi` plugin, which are very useful for learning, so please have a look at the directory: `/usr/local/nagios/etc/check_multi/*.cmd`.

Afterwards, we checked the correctness of our new command file that we just created by dry-running it as an `-f` parameter from the `check_multi` command locally on the client. In its output, you will find all the single outputs as if you would have run these five commands individually. If one single check fails, the complete `check_multi` will do. Next, we defined a new NRPE command in the NRPE config file called `check_multicmd` that can then be executed from the Nagios server, which we tested in the next step from our Nagios server. For a test to be successful, we expect the same results as we got when calling the command from the client itself. Afterwards, we defined this command in our `commands.cfg` on the Nagios server so that we can reuse it as much as we like in any service definition by referencing the command's name, `check_nrpe_multi`. Next, we created a new server file named as the IP address (you can name it anything you like as long it has the `.cfg` extension in the directory) of the client we want to monitor: `192.168.1.8.cfg`. It contains exactly one host definition and one or multiple service definitions, which are linked by the value of `host_name` of the host with the `host_name` value in your service definitions.

In the host definition, we defined a `contact_groups` contact that links to the `contacts.cfg` file's contact group and contact entry. These will be used to send notification e-mails if the checked service has any errors. The most important value in the service definition is the `check_command check_nrpe_multi` line, which executes the command that we created before as our one and only check. Also, the `normal_check_interval` is important as it defines how often the service will be checked under normal conditions. Here, it gets checked every 15 minutes. You can add as many service definitions to a host as you like.

Now, go to your Nagios web frontend to inspect your new host and service. Here, go to the **Hosts** tab, where you will see the new host, **host1**, that you defined in this recipe, and it should give you information about its status. If you click on the **Services** tab, you will see the **check_nrpe_multi** service. It should show the **Status** as **Pending**, **OK,** or **CRITICAL**, depending on the success of the single checks. If you click on its **check_nrpe_multi** link, you will see details about the checks.

Here in this chapter, we could only show you the very basics of Nagios, and there is always more to learn, so please read the official Nagios Core documentation at `https://www.nagios.org`, or check out the book *Learning Nagios 4, Packt Publishing*, by Wojciech Kocjan.

Module 3

Red Hat Enterprise Linux Server Cookbook

*Over 60 recipes to help you build, configure, and orchestrate RHEL 7 Server
to make your everyday administration experience seamless*

1
Working with KVM Guests

In this chapter, we will cover the following recipes:

- ▸ Installing and configuring a KVM
- ▸ Configuring resources
- ▸ Building VMs
- ▸ Adding CPUs on the fly
- ▸ Adding RAM on the fly
- ▸ Adding disks on the fly
- ▸ Moving disks to another storage
- ▸ Moving VMs
- ▸ Backing up your VM metadata

Introduction

This book will attempt to show you how to deploy RHEL 7 systems without too much of a hassle. As this book is written with automation in mind, I will emphasize on command-line utilities rather than elaborating on its GUI counterparts, which are useless for automation.

This chapter explains how to build and manage KVM guests using the libvirt interface and various tools built around it. It will provide a brief overview on how to set up a KVM on RHEL and manage its resources. The setup provided in this overview is far from the ready enterprise as it doesn't provide any redundancy, which is generally required in enterprises. However, the recipes provided are relevant in enterprise setups as the interface stays the same. Most of the time, you will probably use a management layer (such as RHEV or oVirt), which will make your life easier in managing redundancy.

Libvirt is the API between the user and the various virtualization and container layers that are available, such as KVM, VMware, Hyper-V, and Linux Containers. Check `https://libvirt.org/drivers.html` for a complete list of supported hypervisors and container solutions.

As most tasks performed need to be automated in the end, I tend not to use any graphical interfaces as these do not allow an easy conversion into script. Hence, you will not find any recipes in this chapter involving a graphical interface. These recipes will primarily focus on `virsh`, the libvirt management user interface that is used to manage various aspects of your KVM host and guests. While a lot of people rely on the edit option of `virsh`, it doesn't allow you to edit a guest's configuration in real time. Editing your guest's XML configuration in this way will require you to shut down and boot your guest for the changes to take effect. A reboot of your guest doesn't do the trick as the XML configuration needs to be completely reread by the guest's instance in order for it to apply the changes. Only a fresh boot of the guest will do this.

The `virsh` interface is also a shell, so by launching `virsh` without any commands, you will enter the libvirt management shell. A very interesting command is `help`. This will output all the available commands grouped by keyword. Each command accepts the `--help` argument to show a detailed list of the possible arguments, and their explanation, which you can use.

Installing and configuring a KVM

This recipe covers the installing of virtualization tools and packages on RHEL 7.

By default, a RHEL 7 system doesn't come with a KVM or libvirt preinstalled. This can be installed in three ways:

- Through the graphical setup during the system's setup
- Via a kickstart installation
- Through a manual installation from the command line

For this recipe, you should know how to install packages using yum, and your system should be configured to have access to the default RHEL 7 repository (refer to *Chapter 8, Yum and Repositories*, for more information), which is required for the packages that we will use.

Alternatively, you could install packages from the installation media using `rpm`, but you'll need to figure out the dependencies yourself.

Check the dependencies of an `rpm` using the following command:

```
~]# rpm -qpR <rpm file>
```

This will output a list of binaries, libraries, and files that you need installed prior to installing this package.

Check which package contains these files through this command:

```
~]# rpm -qlp <rpm package>
```

As you can imagine, this is a tedious job and can take quite some time as you need to figure out every dependency for every package that you want to install in this way.

Getting ready

To install a KVM, you will require at least 6 GB of free disk space, 2 GB of RAM, and an additional core or thread per guest.

Check whether your CPU supports a virtualization flag (such as SVM or VMX). Some hardware vendors disable this in the BIOS, so you may want to check your BIOS as well. Run the following command:

```
~]# grep -E 'svm|vmx' /proc/cpuinfo
flags    : ... vmx ...
```

Alternatively, you can run the following command:

```
~]# grep -E 'svm|vmx' /proc/cpuinfo
flags    : ... svm ...
```

Check whether the hardware virtualization modules (such as `kvm_intel` and `kvm`) are loaded in the kernel using the following command:

```
~]# lsmod | grep kvm
kvm_intel            155648  0
kvm                  495616  1 kvm_intel
```

How to do it...

We'll look at the three ways of installing a KVM onto your system.

Manual installation

This way of installing a KVM is generally done once the base system is installed by some other means. You need to perform the following steps:

1. Install the software needed to provide an environment to host virtualized guests with the following command:

    ```
    ~]# yum -y install qemu-kvm qemu-img libvirt
    ```

    The installation of these packages will include quite a lot of dependencies.

2. Install additional utilities required to configure libvirt and install virtual machines by running this command:

    ```
    ~]# yum -y install virt-install libvirt-python python-virthost
    libvirt-client
    ```

3. By default, the libvirt daemon is marked to autostart on each boot. Check whether it is enabled by executing the following command:

    ```
    ~]# systemctl status libvirtd

    libvirtd.service - Virtualization daemon

       Loaded: loaded (/usr/lib/systemd/system/libvirtd.service;
    enabled)

       Active: inactive

         Docs: man:libvirtd(8)

               http://libvirt.org
    ```

4. If for some reason this is not the case, mark it for autostart by executing the following:

    ```
    ~]# systemctl enable libvirtd
    ```

5. To manually stop/start/restart the libvirt daemon, this is what you'll need to execute:

    ```
    ~]# systemctl stop libvirtd

    ~]# systemctl start libvirtd

    ~]# systemctl restart libvirtd
    ```

Kickstart installation

Installing a KVM during kickstart offers you an easy way to automate the installation of KVM instances. Perform the following steps:

1. Add the following package groups to your kickstarted file in the `%packages` section:

   ```
   @virtualization-hypervisor
   @virtualization-client
   @virtualization-platform
   @virtualization-tools
   ```

2. Start the installation of your host with this kickstart file.

Graphical setup during the system's setup

This is probably the least common way of installing a KVM. The only time I used this was during the course of writing this recipe. Here's how you can do this:

1. Boot from the RHEL 7 Installation media.
2. Complete all steps besides the **Software selection** step.

3. Go to **Software Selection** to complete the KVM software selection.

4. Select the **Virtualization host** radio button in **Base Environment,** and check the **Virtualization Platform** checkbox in **Add-Ons for Selected Environment**:

SOFTWARE SELECTION

RED HAT ENTERPRISE LINUX 7.0 INSTALLATION

Done

us

Base Environment

Minimal Install
Basic functionality.

Infrastructure Server
Server for operating network infrastructure services.

File and Print Server
File, print, and storage server for enterprises.

Basic Web Server
Server for serving static and dynamic internet content.

Virtualization Host
Minimal virtualization host.

Server with GUI
Server for operating network infrastructure services, with a GUI.

Add-Ons for Selected Environment

Network File System Client
Enables the system to attach to network storage.

Remote Management for Linux
Remote management interface for Red Hat Enterprise Linux, including OpenLMI and SNMP.

Virtualization Platform
Provides an interface for accessing and controlling virtualized guests and containers.

Compatibility Libraries
Compatibility libraries for applications built on previous versions of Red Hat Enterprise Linux.

Development Tools
A basic development environment.

Smart Card Support
Support for using smart card authentication.

5. Finalize the installation.

6. On the **Installation Summary** screen, complete any other steps and click on **Begin Installation**.

See also

To set up your repositories, check out *Chapter 8, Yum and Repositories*.

To deploy a system using kickstart, refer to *Chapter 2, Deploying RHEL "En Masse"*.

For more in-depth information about using libvirt, go to http://www.libvirt.org/.

RHEL 7 has certain support limits, which are listed at these locations:

https://access.redhat.com/articles/rhel-kvm-limits

https://access.redhat.com/articles/rhel-limits

Configuring resources

Virtual machines require CPUs, memory, storage, and network access, similar to physical machines. This recipe will show you how to set up a basic KVM environment for easy resource management through libvirt.

A storage pool is a virtual container limited by two factors:

- ▸ The maximum size allowed by `qemu-kvm`
- ▸ The size of the disk on the physical machine

Storage pools may not exceed the size of the disk on the host. The maximum sizes are as follows:

- ▸ virtio-blk = 2^63 bytes or 8 exabytes (raw files or disk)
- ▸ EXT4 = ~ 16 TB (using 4 KB block size)
- ▸ XFS = ~8 exabytes

Getting ready

For this recipe, you will need a volume of at least 2 GB mounted on `/vm` and access to an NFS server and export.

We'll use `NetworkManager` to create a bridge, so ensure that you don't disable `NetworkManager` and have `bridge-utils` installed.

How to do it...

Let's have a look into managing storage pools and networks.

Creating storage pools

In order to create storage pools, we need to provide the necessary details to the KVM for it to be able to create it. You can do this as follows:

1. Create a `localfs` storage pool using `virsh` on `/vm`, as follows:

   ```
   ~]# virsh pool-define-as --name localfs-vm --type dir --target /vm
   ```

2. Create the target for the storage pool through the following command:

   ```
   ~# mkdir -p /nfs/vm
   ```

3. Create an NFS storage pool using `virsh` on NFS server:`/export/vm`, as follows:

    ```
    ~]# virsh pool-define-as --name nfs-vm --type network --source-
    host nfsserver --source-path /export/vm -target /nfs/vm
    ```

4. Make the storage pools persistent across reboots through the following commands:

    ```
    ~]# virsh pool-autostart localfs-vm
    ```

    ```
    ~]# virsh pool-autostart nfs-vm
    ```

5. Start the storage pool, as follows:

    ```
    ~]# virsh pool-start localfs-vm
    ```

    ```
    ~]# virsh pool-start nfs-vm
    ```

6. Verify that the storage pools are created, started, and persistent across reboots. Run the following for this:

    ```
    ~]# virsh pool-list
     Name                      State      Autostart
    -------------------------------------------------
     localfs-vm                active     yes
     nfs-vm                    active     yes
    ```

Querying storage pools

At some point in time, you will need to know how much space you have left in your storage pool.

Get the information of the storage pool by executing the following:

```
~]# virsh pool-info --pool <pool name>
Name:           nfs-vm
UUID:           some UUID
State:          running
Persistent:     yes
Autostart:      yes
Capacity:       499.99 GiB
Allocation:     307.33 GiB
Available:      192.66 GiB
```

As you can see, this command easily shows you its disk space allocation and availability.

Be careful though; if you use a filesystem that supports sparse files, these numbers will most likely be incorrect. You will have to manually calculate the sizes yourself!

To detect whether a file is sparse, run `ls -lhs` against the file. The `-s` command will show an additional column (the first), showing the exact space that the file is occupying, as follows:

```
~]# ls -lhs myfile
121M -rw-------. 1 root root  30G Jun 10 10:27 myfile
```

Removing storage pools

Sometimes, storage is phased out. So, it needs to be removed from the host.

You have to ensure that no guest is using volumes on the storage pool before proceeding, and you need to remove all the remaining volumes from the storage pool. Here's how to do this:

1. Remove the storage volume, as follows:

   ```
   ~]# virsh vol-delete --pool <pool name> --vol <volume name>
   ```

2. Stop the storage pool through the following command:

   ```
   ~]# virsh pool-destroy --pool <pool name>
   ```

3. Delete the storage pool using the following command:

   ```
   ~]# virsh pool-delete --pool <pool name>
   ```

Creating a virtual network

Before creating the virtual networks, we need to build a bridge over our existing network interface. For the sake of convenience, this NIC will be called `eth0`. Ensure that you record your current network configuration as we'll destroy it and recreate it on the bridge.

Unlike the storage pool, we need to create an XML configuration file to define the networks. There is no command similar to `pool-create-as` for networks. Perform the following steps:

1. Create a bridge interface on your network's interface, as follows:

   ```
   ~]# nmcli connection add type bridge autoconnect yes con-name
   bridge-eth0 ifname bridge-eth0
   ```

2. Remove your NIC's configuration using the following command:

   ```
   ~]# nmcli connection delete eth0
   ```

3. Configure your bridge, as follows:

```
~]# nmcli connection modify bridge-eth0 ipv4.addresses <ip
address/cidr> ipv4.method manual

~# nmcli connection modify bridge-eth0 ipv4.gateway <gateway ip
address>

~]# nmcli connection modify bridge-eth0 ipv4.dns <dns servers>
```

4. Finally, add your NIC to the bridge by executing the following:

```
~]# nmcli connection add type bridge-slave autoconnect yes con-
name slave-eth0 ifname eth0 master bridge-eth0
```

For starters, we'll take a look at how we can create a NATed network similar to the one that is configured by default and called the default:

1. Create the network XML configuration file, /tmp/net-nat.xml, as follows:

```
<network>
  <name>NATted</name>
  <forward mode='nat'>
    <nat>
      <port start='1024' end='65535'/>
    </nat>
  </forward>
  <bridge name='virbr0' stp='on' delay='0'/>
  <ip address='192.168.0.1' netmask='255.255.255.0'>
    <dhcp>
      <range start='192.168.0.2' end='192.168.0.254'/>
    </dhcp>
  </ip>
</network>
```

2. Define the network in the KVM using the preceding XML configuration file. Execute the following command:

```
~]# virsh net-define /tmp/net-nat.xml
```

Now, let's create a bridged network that can use the network bound to this bridge through the following steps:

1. Create the network XML configuration file, /tmp/net-bridge-eth0.xml, by running the following:

```
<network>
    <name>bridge-eth0</name>
    <forward mode="bridge" />
    <bridge name="bridge-eth0" />
</network>
```

2. Create the network in the KVM using the preceding file, as follows:

```
~]# virsh net-define /tmp/net-bridge-eth0.xml
```

There's one more type of network that is worth mentioning: the isolated network. This network is only accessible to guests defined in this network as there is no connection to the "real" world.

1. Create the network XML configuration file, /tmp/net-local.xml, by using the following code:

```
<network>
  <name>isolated</name>
  <bridge name='virbr1' stp='on' delay='0'/>
  <domain name='isolated'/>
</network>
```

2. Create the network in KVM by using the above file:

```
~]# virsh net-define /tmp/net-local.xml
```

Creating networks in this way will register them with the KVM but will not activate them or make them persistent through reboots. So, this is an additional step that you need to perform for each network. Now, perform the following steps:

1. Make the network persistent across reboots using the following command:

```
~]# virsh net-autostart <network name>
```

2. Activate the network, as follows:

```
~]# virsh net-start <network name>
```

3. Verify the existence of the KVM network by executing the following:

```
~]# virsh net-list --all
```

Name	State	Autostart	Persistent
bridge-eth0	active	yes	yes
default	inactive	no	yes
isolated	active	yes	yes
NATted	active	yes	yes

Removing networks

On some occasions, the networks are phased out; in this case, we need to remove the network from our setup.

Prior to executing this, you need to ensure that no guest is using the network that you want to remove. Perform the following steps to remove the networks:

1. Stop the network with the following command:

   ```
   ~# virsh net-destroy --network <network name>
   ```

2. Then, delete the network using this command:

   ```
   ~]# virsh net-undefine --network <network name>
   ```

How it works...

It's easy to create multiple storage pools using the define-pool-as command, as you can see. Every type of storage pool needs more, or fewer, arguments. In the case of the NFS storage pool, we need to specify the NFS server and export. This is done by specifying--source-host and--source-path respectively.

Creating networks is a bit more complex as it requires you to create a XML configuration file. When you want a network connected transparently to your physical networks, you can only use bridged networks as it is impossible to bind a network straight to your network's interface.

There's more...

The storage backend created in this recipe is not the limit. Libvirt also supports the following backend pools:

Local storage pools

Local storage pools are directly connected to the physical machine. They include local directories, disks, partitions, and LVM volume groups. Local storage pools are not suitable for enterprises as these do not support live migration.

Networked or shared storage pools

Network storage pools include storage shared through standard protocols over a network. This is required when we migrate virtual machines between physical hosts. The supported network storage protocols are Fibre Channel-based LUNs, iSCSI, NFS, GFS2, and SCSI RDMA.

By defining the storage pools and networks in libvirt, you ensure the availability of the resources for your guest. If, for some reason, the resource is unavailable, the KVM will not attempt to start the guests that use these resources.

When checking out the man page for *virsh (1)*, you will find a similar command to `net-define`, `pool-define`: `net-create`, and `pool-create` (and `pool-create-as`). The `net-create` command, similar to `pool-create` and `pool-create-as`, creates transient (or temporary) resources, which will be gone when libvirt is restarted. On the other hand, `net-define` and `pool-define` (as also `pool-define-as`) create persistent (or permanent) resources, which will still be there after you restart libvirt.

See also

You can find out more on libvirt storage backend pools at `https://libvirt.org/storage.html`

More information on libvirt networking can be found at `http://wiki.libvirt.org/page/Networking`

Building guests

After you install and configure a KVM on the host system, you can create guest operating systems. Every guest is defined by a set of resources and parameters stored in the XML format. When you want to create a new guest, creating such an XML file is quite cumbersome. There are two ways to create a guest:

- Using `virt-manager`
- Using `virt-install`

This recipe will employ the latter as it is perfect for scripting, while `virt-manager` is a GUI and not very well suited to automate things.

Getting ready

In this recipe, we will cover a generic approach to create a new virtual machine using the `bridge-eth0` network bridge and create a virtual disk on the `localfs-vm` storage pool, which is formatted as QCOW2. The QCOW2 format is a popular virtual disk format as it allows thin provisioning and snapshotting. We will boot the RHEL 7 installation media located on the `localfs-iso` storage pool (`rhel7-install.iso`) to start installing a new RHEL 7 system.

How to do it...

Let's create some guests and delete them.

Create a guest

Let's first create a disk for the guest and then create the guest on this disk, as follows:

1. Create a 10 GB QCOW2 format disk in the `localfs-vm` pool, as follows:

   ```
   ~]# virsh vol-create-as --pool localfs-vm --name rhel7_guest-vda.
   qcows2 --format qcows2 -capacity 10G
   ```

2. Create the virtual machine and start it through the following command:

   ```
   ~]# virt-install \
   --hvm \
   --name rhel7_guest \
   --memory=2048,maxmemory=4096 \
   --vcpus=2,maxvcpus=4 \
   --os-type linux \
   --os-variant rhel7 \
   --boot hd,cdrom,network,menu=on \
   --controller type=scsi,model=virtio-scsi \
   --disk device=cdrom,vol=localfs-iso/rhel7-install.
   iso,readonly=on,bus=scsi \
   --disk device=disk,vol=localfs-vm/rhel7_guest-vda.
   qcow2,cache=none,bus=scsi \
   --network network=bridge-eth0,model=virtio \
   --graphics vnc \
   --graphics spice \
   --noautoconsole \
   --memballoon virtio
   ```

Deleting a guest

At some point, you'll need to remove the guests. You can do this as follows:

1. First, ensure that the guest is down by running the following:

   ```
   ~]# virsh list -all
    Id     Name                          State
   ---------------------------------------------------
    -      rhel7_guest                   shut off
   ```

   If the state is not `shut off`, you can forcefully shut it down:

   ```
   ~]# virsh destroy --domain <guest name>
   ```

2. List the storage volumes in use by your guest and copy this somewhere:

```
~]# virsh domblklist <guest name>

Type        Device      Target      Source
-------------------------------------------------
file        disk        vda         /vm/rhel7_guest-vda.qcow2
file        cdrom       hda         /iso/rhel7-install.iso
```

3. Delete the guest through the following command:

```
~]# virsh undefine --domain <guest name> --storage vda
```

Adding `--remove-all-storage` to the command will wipe off the data on the storage volumes dedicated to this guest prior to deleting the volume from the pool.

How it works...

The `virt-install` command supports creating storage volumes (disks) by specifying the pool, size, and format. However, if this storage volume already exists, the application will fail. Depending on the speed of your KVM host disks (local or network) and the size of the guest's disks, the process of creating a new disk may take some time to be completed. By specifying an existing disk with `virt-install`, you can reuse the disk should you need to reinstall the guest. It would be possible to only create the disk on the first pass and change your command line appropriately after this. However, the fact remains that using `virsh vol-create-as` gives you more granular control of what you want to do.

We're using the QCOW2 format to contain the guest's disk as it is a popular format when it comes to storing KVM guest disks. This is because it supports thin provisioning and snapshotting.

When creating the guest, we specify both the `maxmemory` option for memory configuration and the `maxvcpus` option for vcpus configuration. This will allow us to add CPUs and RAM to the guest while it is running. If we do not assign these, we'll have to shut down the system before being able to change the XML configuration using the following command:

```
~# virsh edit <hostname>
```

As you can see, we're using the `virtio` driver for any hardware (network, disks, or balloon) that supports it as it is native to the KVM and is included in the RHEL 7 kernel.

> If, for some reason, your guest OS doesn't support `virtio` drivers, you should remove the `--controller` option of the command line and the bus specification from the `--disk` option.
>
> For more information on `virtio` support, go to `http://wiki.libvirt.org/page/Virtio`.

The `--memballoon` option will ensure that we do not run into problems when we overcommit our memory. When specific guests require more memory, the ballooning driver will ensure that the "idle" guests' memory can be evenly redistributed.

The `graphics` option will allow you to connect to the guest through the host using either VNC (which is a popular client to control remote computers) or spice (which is the default client for `virt-manager`). The configuration for both VNC and spice is insecure, though. You can either set this up by specifying a password—by adding `password=<password>` to each graphics stanza—or by editing the `/etc/libvirt/qemu.conf` file on the KVM host, which will be applied to all guests.

There's more...

In this recipe, we used "local" install media in the form of an ISO image to install the system. However, it is also possible to install a guest without a CD, DVD, or an ISO image. The `--location` installation method option allows you to specify a URI that contains your kernel/ initrd pair, which is required to start the installation.

Using `--location` in combination with `--extra-args` will allow you to specify kernel command-line arguments to pass to the installer. This can be used, for instance, to pass on the location of an Anaconda kickstart file for automated installs and/or specifying your IP configuration during the installer.

See also

Check the man page of *virt-install (1)* for more information on how to use it to your advantage.

Adding CPUs on the fly

Imagine an enterprise having to correctly add dimension to all their systems right from the start. In my experience, this is very difficult. You will either underdimension it, and your customers will complain about performance at some point, or you will overdimension it, and then the machine will sit there, idling about, which is not optimal either. This is the reason hardware vendors have come up with `hot-add` resources. This allows a system to have its CPUs, memory, and/or disks to be upgraded/increased without the need for a shutdown. A KVM implements a similar functionality for its guests. It allows you to increase the CPUs, memory, and disks on the fly.

The actual recipe is very simple to execute, but there are some prerequisites to be met.

Getting ready

In order to be able to add CPUs on the fly to a guest, the guest's configuration must support them.

There are two ways to achieve this:

- ▶ It must be created with the max option, as follows:

  ```
  --vcpus 2,maxvcpus=4
  ```

- ▶ You can set the maximum using `virsh` (which will be applied at the next boot) through the following command:

  ```
  ~]# virsh setvcpus --domain <guestname> --count <max cpu count>
  --config --maximum
  ```

- ▶ You can edit the guests' XML files, as follows:

  ```
  ~]# virsh edit <guestname>
  ```

The last two options will require you to shut down and boot (not reboot) your guest as these commands cannot change the "live" configuration.

The guest's XML file must contain the following element with the subsequent attributes:

```
<domain type='kvm'>
...
<vcpu current='2'>4</vcpu>
...
</domain>
```

Here, `current` indicates the number of CPUs in use, and the number within the node indicates the maximum number of vCPUs that can be assigned. This number can be increased but should never exceed the number of cores or threads in your host.

How to do it...

Let's add some CPUs to the guest.

On the KVM host, perform the following steps:

1. Get the maximum number vCPUs that you can assign, as follows:

   ```
   ~]# virsh dumpxml <guestname> |grep vcpu
   <vcpu placement='static' current='4'>8</vcpu>
   ```

2. Now, set the new number of vCPUs through this command:

```
~]# virsh setvcpus --domain <guestname> --count <# of CPUs> --live
```

On the KVM guest, perform the following:

1. Tell your guest OS there are more CPUs available by executing the following command:

```
~]# for i in $(grep -H 0 /sys/devices/system/cpu/cpu*/online | awk
-F: '{print $1}'); do echo 1 > $i; done
```

Adding RAM on the fly

As with CPUs, the possibility to add memory on the fly is an added value in mission-critical environments where downtime can literally cost a company millions of Euros.

The recipe presented here is quite simple, similar to the one on CPUs. Here, your guest needs to be prepared to use this functionality as well.

Getting ready

If you want to be able to add memory on the fly to a guest, it must be configured to support it. As with the CPU, this has to be activated. There are three ways to do this:

- The guest must be created with the maxmem option, as follows:

  ```
  --memory 2G,maxmemory=4G
  ```

- You can set the maximum memory using the virsh command, as follows:

  ```
  ~]# virsh setmaxmem --domain <guestname> --size <max mem> --live
  ```

- You can edit the guests' XML files:

  ```
  ~]# virsh edit <guestname>
  ```

Of course, the latter 2 option requires you to shut down the guest, which is not always possible in production environments.

Ensure that the guests' XML configuration files contain the following elements with the subsequent attributes:

```
<domain type='kvm'>
...
    <memory unit='KiB'>4194304</memory>
    <currentMemory unit='KiB'>2097152</currentMemory>
...
</domain>
```

How to do it...

Let's increase the guest's memory.

On the KVM host, perform the following steps:

1. Get the current and maximum memory allocation for a guest, as follows:

```
~]# virsh dumpxml srv00002 |grep -i memory
  <memory unit='KiB'>4194304</memory>
  <currentMemory unit='KiB'>4194304</currentMemory>
```

2. Set the new amount of memory for the guest by executing the following command:

```
~]# virsh setmem --domain <guestname> --size <memory> --live
```

On the KVM guest, perform the following:

1. Tell your guest OS about the memory increase through this command:

```
~]# for i in $(grep -H offline /sys/devices/system/memory/memory*/
state | awk -F: '{print $1}'); do echo online > $i; done
```

Adding disks on the fly

This recipe includes instructions on how to create different types of storage volumes. Storage volumes are dedicated storage sets aside for use by guests.

Getting ready

There is not a lot of preparation to be done in order to add disks to your guest, which is in contrast to adding CPUs and RAM.

You only need to ensure that the storage pool has enough free disk space to accommodate the new disk.

How to do it...

Similar to the recipe for creating guests, you'll need to create a disk first. This can be done as follows:

1. Let's create a raw disk in the `localfs-vm` pool that is `30` GB big through the following command:

   ```
   ~]# virsh vol-create-as --pool localfs-vm --name rhel7_guest-vdb.
   raw --format raw --capacity 30G
   ```

2. Look up the path of the newly created volume, as follows:

   ```
   ~]# virsh vol-list --pool localfs-vm |awk '$1 ~ /^rhel7_guest-vdb.
   raw$/ {print $2}'
   ```

   This will result in the path of your volume; here's an example:

   ```
   /vm/rhel7_guest-vdb.raw
   ```

3. Attach the disk to the guest, as follows:

   ```
   ~]# virsh attach-disk --domain <guestname> --source <the above
   path> --target vdb --cache none --persistent –live
   ```

How it works...

Creating a disk using `vol-create-as` may take some time depending on the speed of your host's disks and the size of the guest's disks.

We will look up the path of the newly created volume as it is a required argument for the command that attaches the disk to the guest. In most cases, you won't need to do this as you'll know how your host is configured, but when you script this kind of functionality, you will require this step.

Adding a disk in this way will attach a disk using the `virtio` driver, which, as specified earlier, is optimized for use with KVMs.

There's more...

If, for some reason, the original guest doesn't support `virtio` drivers or you do not have the `virtio` controller, you can create this yourself. Store the XML configuration file as `/tmp/controller.xml` with the following contents:

```
<controller type='scsi' model='virtio' />
```

You can find this out by checking the host's XML file for the preceding statement.

Then, import the XML configuration file, as follows:

```
~]# virsh attach-device –domain <guestname> /tmp/controller.xml
```

This will allow you to create disks using `virtio`.

Moving disks to another storage

Moving disks around is part of the life cycle of a guest. Disks in the storage pools (local or network) may fail or fill up due to bad capacity management. Another reason may be the cost or speed of the disks involved. Sooner or later, one of these things will happen, and then you will need to move the storage somewhere else.

Ordinarily, one would have to shut down the guest, copy the storage volume file elsewhere (if it is a file), wait, update the machine's XML configuration, and launch it again. However, in today's mission-critical enterprises, this may not always be possible.

Getting ready

In order to perform this copy, you need the source and destination paths of the disk. You can get the source path by checking the XML configuration file or, even better, by querying the storage volume itself. This does require you to know which storage pool it is located on.

Execute the following command:

```
~]# virsh vol-list --pool <storage pool> |awk '$1 ~ /^<volume name>$/
{print $2}'
```

Ensure that your destination is an existing storage pool; if not, go ahead and create it.

Check out the *Configuring resources* recipe in this chapter to create storage pools.

If you can't remember the path to your pool's location, run the following:

```
~]# virsh pool-dumpxml <poolname> |awk '/<path>.*<\/path>/ {print $1}'
```

How to do it...

Moving disks can take some time, so ensure that you have plenty of time available. Perform the following steps:

1. Dump the inactive XML configuration file for the guest, as follows:

    ```
    ~]# virsh dumpxml --inactive <guestname> > /tmp/<guestname>.xml
    ```

    The `--inactive` file will ensure that it doesn't copy any temporary information that is irrelevant to the guest.

2. Undefine the guest through the following command:

```
~]# virsh undefine <guestname>
```

3. Copy the virtual disk to another location by executing the following:

```
~]# virsh blockcopy --domain <guestname> --path <original path>
--dest <destination path> --wait --verbose --pivot
```

4. Now, edit the guest's XML configuration file and change the path of the disk to the new location.

5. Redefine the guest, as follows:

```
~]# virsh define /tmp/<guestname>.xml
```

6. Remove the source disk after you are happy with the results. Run the following command:

```
~]# virsh vol-delete --pool <poolname> --vol <volname>
```

How it works...

The moving of disks can only be performed on transient domains, which is the reason we execute the `virsh undefine` command. In order to be able to make it persistent again after the transfer, we also need to dump the XML configuration file and modify the storage volume path.

Moving the disk does two things, which are:

- ► Firstly, it copies all the data of the source to the destination
- ► Secondly, when the copying is complete, both source and destination remain mirrored until it is either canceled with `blockjob --abort` or actually switched over to the new target by executing the `blockjob --pivot` command

The preceding `blockcopy` command does everything at the same time. The `--wait` command will not give control back to the user until the command fails or succeeds. It is essentially the same as the following:

```
~]# virsh blockcopy --domain <guestname> --path <source path> --dest
<destination path>
```

Monitor the progress of the copy by executing the following:

```
~]# watch -n10 "virsh blockjob –domain <guestname> --path <source path>
--info"
```

When it's done, execute this:

```
~]# virsh blockjob –domain <guestname> --path <source path> --pivot
```

There's more...

It is also possible to change the disk format on the fly, by specifying the `--format` argument with the format that you want to convert your disk into. If you want to copy it to a block device, specify `--blockdev`.

Moving VMs

Moving disks will mitigate the risk of failing disks. When your CPUs, memory, and other non-disk-related components start failing, you have no other option but to move the guests to other host(s).

The recipe for this task is rather simple, but it's the prerequisites that can make it succeed or fail miserably.

Getting ready

The prerequisites for this recipe are quite extended.

For the host, the following are the requirements:

- ▶ You'll need to have access to shared data. Both the source and destination KVM machine will need to be able to access the same storage—for example, iSCSI, NFS, and so on.
- ▶ Both hosts need the same type of CPU—that is, Intel or AMD (one cannot live migrate a guest from a host with Intel CPUs to a host with AMD CPUs).
- ▶ Both hosts need to be installed with the same version and updates of libvirt.
- ▶ Both hosts need to have the same network ports open.
- ▶ Both hosts must have identical KVM network configurations or at least the same network configurations for the interfaces used by the guest.
- ▶ Both hosts must be accessible through the network.
- ▶ It's a good idea to have a management network set up and connected to the two hosts, which can be used for data transfer. This will cause less network traffic on your "production" network and increase the overall speed.
- ▶ The `No execution` bit must be the same on both hosts.

The requirement for the guest is:

- ▶ The `cache=none` must be specified for all block devices that are opened in write mode.

How to do it...

There are multiple ways to migrate hosts, but we will only highlight the two most common ways.

Live native migration over the default network

This process to migrate a host is luckily very simple and can be summarized in one command.

On the source host, execute the following:

```
~]# virsh migrate --domain <guestname> --live --persistent
--undefinesource --verbose --desturl qemu+ssh://<host 2>/system
```

Live native migration over a dedicated network

It is possible to perform the migration over a dedicated network. By default, this will use the first network it finds that suits it needs. You'll need to specify the listening address (on the host) and the protocol. This requires the same command as before, but we'll need to specify the local listening IP address and protocol, such as TCP.

On the source host, execute the following:

```
~]# virsh migrate --domain <guestname> --live --persistent
--undefinesource --verbose --desturl qemu+ssh://<host 2>/system
tcp://<local ip address on dedicated network>/
```

How it works...

This type of migration is called a "hypervisor native" transport. The biggest advantage of this type of migration is that it incurs the lowest computational cost by minimizing the number of data copies involved.

When we migrate a host, it performs a copy of the memory of the guest to the new host. When the copying is successful, it kills the guest on the source host and starts it on the new host. As the memory is copied, the interruption will be very short-lived.

There's more...

Communication between the two hosts is over SSH, which is already pretty secure. However, it's also possible to tunnel the data over an even more strongly encrypted channel by specifying the `--tunnelled` option. This will impose more traffic on your network as there will be extra data communication between the two hosts.

The `--compress` option can help you out if you wish to reduce the traffic over your network, but this will increase the load on both your hosts as they need to compress/decompress the data, which, in turn, may impact your guests performance. If time is not of the essence but traffic is, this is a good solution.

See also

There's very good and in-depth documentation about this process at `https://libvirt.org/migration.html`.

Backing up your VM metadata

While a KVM stores some of the resources' configuration on the disk in a human readable format, it is a good idea to query libvirt for the configuration of your resources.

How to do it...

In this recipe we'll back up all relevant KVM metadata by performing the following steps:

Here's the network configuration:

```
~]# for i in $(virsh net-list --all | sed -e '1,2d' |awk '{print $1}');
do \
    virsh net-dumpxml --network $i --inactive > /tmp/net-$i.xml; \
done
```

Here's the storage configuration:

```
~]# for i in $(virsh pool-list --all | sed -e '1,2d' |awk '{print $1}');
do \
    for j in $(virsh vol-list --pool $i |sed -e '1,2d') | awk '{print
$1}'; do \
        virsh vol-dumpxml --pool $i --vol $j > /tmp/vol-$j.xml; \
    done \
    virsh pool-dumpxml --pool $i --inactive > /tmp/pool-$i.xml; \
done
```

Here's the guest configuration:

```
~]# for i in $(virsh list --all | sed -e '1,2d' |awk '{print $1}'); do \
    virsh dumpxml --domain $i --inactive > /tmp/domain-$i.xml; \
done
```

How it works...

The `virsh net-dumpxml` command allows you to dump the precise configuration of the specified network. In combination with `virsh net-list`, you can create a loop that enumerates all networks and dumps them on the file. By specifying `--all`, you will export all networks, even those that are not active. If you do not wish to back up the configuration for nonactive networks, substitute `virsh net-list --all` with `virsh net-list`.

Storage pools can be enumerated, similarly to networks, using `virsh net-list`. However, besides the individual storage pool configuration, we are also interested in the configuration of individual storage volumes. Luckily, both implement a `list` and `dumpxml` command! If you're not interested in nonactive pools, you can omit the `--all` option with `virsh pool-list`.

Guests can similarly be enumerated and their XML configuration dumped using `dumpxml`. Again, if you're not interested in nonactive guests, you can omit the `--all` option with `virsh list`.

See also

The man page for *virsh (1)* lists all the possible options for the commands used in the preceding section.

2
Deploying RHEL "En Masse"

In this chapter, the following recipes are provided:

- ▸ Creating a kickstart file
- ▸ Publishing your kickstart file using `httpd`
- ▸ Deploying a system using `pxe`
- ▸ Deploying a system using a custom boot ISO file

Introduction

In this chapter, you will find the answer to deploying multiple systems with the same basic setup. We will first look at creating an answer file, the kickstart file that will drive the unattended installation. Then, we'll take a look at a possible way to make this kickstart file accessible through the Apache web server. Finally, we'll discuss two common ways to install physical and virtual machines.

This chapter assumes that you have a working knowledge of system network configuration components, such as DNS, DNS search, IP addresses, and so on, and yum repositories.

Creating a kickstart file

A kickstart file is essentially a file containing all the necessary answers to questions that are asked during a typical install. It was created by Red Hat in response to the need for automated installs. Using kickstart, an admin can create one file or template containing all the instructions.

There are three ways to create a kickstart file:

- ▸ By hand
- ▸ Using the GUI's `system-config-kickstart` tool
- ▸ Using the standard Red Hat installation program Anaconda

In this recipe, I will cover a combination of the first two.

Getting ready

Before we can get down to the nitty-gritty of generating our base kickstart file or template, we need to install `system-config-kickstart`. Run the following command:

```
~# yum install -y system-config-kickstart
```

How to do it...

First, let's create a base template for our kickstart file(s) through the following steps:

1. First, launch **Kickstart Configurator** from the menu.
2. Select your system's basic configuration from the **Kickstart Configurator** GUI.

   The following screenshot shows the options you can set in the **Basic Configuration** view:

3. Now, select the installation method from the **Kickstart Configurator** GUI.

   The following screenshot shows the options that you can set in the **Installation method** view:

Kickstart Configurator
File Help

   Basic Configuration
   Installation Method
   Boot Loader Options
   Partition Information
   Network Configuration
   Authentication
   Firewall Configuration
   Display Configuration
   Package Selection
   Pre-Installation Script
   Post-Installation Script

   Installation Method
   ● Perform new installation
   ○ Upgrade an existing installation

   Installation source
   ○ CD-ROM
   ○ NFS
   ○ FTP
   ● HTTP
   ○ Hard Drive

   HTTP Server: `repo.critter.be`
   HTTP Directory: `/rhel/7/os/x86_64/`

4. Next, substitute the values for **HTTP Server** and **HTTP Directory** with your own repositories.

5. Ensure that the correct settings are applied for **Boot Loader**.

The following screenshot shows the options that you can set in the **Boot Loader options** view:

6. Configure your disk and partition information. Simply create a /boot partition and be done with it! We'll edit the file manually for better customization.

   The following screenshot shows the options you can set in the **Partition Information** view:

7. Configure your network. You need to know the name of your device if you want to correctly configure your network.

The following screenshot shows the **Network Device** information that you can edit in the **Network Configuration** view:

Kickstart Configurator		
File Help		

Network Configuration

Basic Configuration		
Installation Method		
Boot Loader Options		
Partition Information		
Network Configuration		
Authentication		
Firewall Configuration		
Display Configuration		
Package Selection		
Pre-Installation Script		
Post-Installation Script		

Device	Network Type
eno1	Static IP

Add Network Device

Edit Network Device

Delete Network Device

Network Device Information

Network Device: eno1

Network Type: Static IP

IP Address: 192.168.0.1

Netmask: 255.255.255.0

Gateway: 192.168.0.254

Name Server: 192.168.0.253

Cancel   OK

8. Now, disable **Installing a graphical environment**.

   We want as few packages as possible. The following screenshot shows the options that you can set in the **Display Configuration** view:

Kickstart Configurator		

File   Help

Basic Configuration
Installation Method
Boot Loader Options
Partition Information
Network Configuration
Authentication
Firewall Configuration
Display Configuration
Package Selection
Pre-Installation Script
Post-Installation Script

Display Configuration

☐ Install a graphical environment

On first boot, Setup Agent is: Disabled ⌄

9. Next, perform any preinstallation and/or postinstallation tasks you deem necessary. I always try to make root accessible through SSH and keys.

   The following screenshot shows the options that you can set in the **Post-Installation Script** view:

10. Save the kickstart file.

11. Open the file using your favorite editor and add the following to your partition section:

```
part pv.01 --size=1 --ondisk=sda --grow
volgroup vg1 pv.01
logvol / --vgname=vg1 --size=2048 --name=root
logvol /usr --vgname=vg1 --size=2048 --name=usr
logvol /var --vgname=vg1 --size=2048 --name=var
logvol /var/log --vgname=vg1 --size=1024 --name=var
logvol /home --vgname=vg1 --size=512 --name=home
logvol swap --vgname=vg1 --recommended --name=swap -fstype=swap
```

12. Now, add the following script to your network line:

```
--hostname=rhel7
```

13. Add the following script before %post:

```
%packages –nobase
@core --nodefaults
%end
```

14. Create a password hash for use in the next step, as follows:

~]# openssl passwd -1 "MySuperSecretRootPassword"

1mecIlXKN$6VRdaRkevjw9nngcMtRlO.

15. Save the resulting file. You should have something similar to this:

```
#platform=x86, AMD64, or Intel EM64T
#version=DEVEL
# Install OS instead of upgrade
install
# Keyboard layouts
keyboard 'be-latin1'
# Halt after installation
halt
# Root password
rootpw --iscrypted $1$mecIlXKN$6VRdaRkevjw9nngcMtRlO.
# System timezone
timezone Europe/Brussels
# Use network installation
url –url="http://repo.example.com/rhel/7/os/x86_64/"
# System language
lang en_US
# Firewall configuration
firewall --disabled
# Network information
network  --bootproto=static --device=eno1 --
gateway=192.168.0.254 --ip=192.168.0.1 --nameserver=192.168.0.253
--netmask=255.255.255.0 --hostname=rhel7
# System authorization information
auth  --useshadow  --passalgo=sha512
# Use text mode install
text
# SELinux configuration
selinux --enforcing
# Do not configure the X Window System
skipx
```

```
# System bootloader configuration
bootloader --location=none
# Clear the Master Boot Record
zerombr
# Partition clearing information
clearpart --all --initlabel
# Disk partitioning information
part /boot --fstype="xfs" --ondisk=sda --size=512
part pv.01 --size=1 --ondisk=sda --grow
volgroup vg1 pv.01
logvol / --vgname=vg1 --size=2048 --name=root --fstype=xfs
logvol /usr --vgname=vg1 --size=2048 --name=usr --fstype=xfs
logvol /var --vgname=vg1 --size=2048 --name=var --fstype=xfs
logvol /var/log --vgname=vg1 --size=1024 --name=var --fstype=xfs
logvol /home --vgname=vg1 --size=512 --name=home --fstype=xfs
logvol swap --vgname=vg1 --recommended --name=swap --fstype=swap

%packages --nobase
@core --nodefaults
%end

%post
mkdir -p ~/.ssh
chmod 700 ~/.ssh
# Let's download my authorized keyfile from my key
server...
curl -O ~/.ssh/authrorized_keys
https://keys.example.com/authorized_keys
chmod 600 ~/.ssh/authrorized_keys
%end
```

How it works...

The `system-config-kickstart` is used to generate a minimal install as any addition would be more complex than the tool can handle and we need to be able to add them manually/dynamically afterwards. The fewer the number of packages the better as you'll need to apply bug and security fixes for every package installed.

Although the GUI allows us to configure the brunt of the options we need, I prefer tweaking some portions of them manually as they are not as straightforward through the GUI.

Step 9 adds the necessary information to use the rest of the disk as an LVM physical volume and partitions it so that *big* filesystems can easily be extended if necessary.

The `--recommended` argument for the SWAP partition creates a swap partition as per the swap size recommendations set by Red Hat.

Step 10 adds a hostname for your host. If you do not specify this, the system will attempt to resolve the IP address and use this hostname. If it cannot determine any hostname, it will use `localhost.localdomain` as `fqdn`.

Step 11 ensures that only the core system is installed and nothing more, so you can build from here.

If you want to know exactly which packages are installed in the core group, run the following command on an RHEL 7 system:

```
~# yum groupinfo core
```

There's more...

I didn't cover one option that I mentioned in the *Getting Ready* section as it is automatically generated when you install a system manually. The file can be found after installation at `/root/anaconda-ks.cfg`. Instead of using the `system-config-kickstart` tool to generate a kickstart file, you can use this file to get started.

Starting with RHEL 7, kickstart deployments support add-ons. These add-ons can expand the standard kickstart installation in many ways. To use kickstart add-ons, just add the `%addon addon_name` option followed by `%end`, as with the `%pre` and `%post` sections. Anaconda comes with the `kdump` add-on, which you can use to install and configure `kdump` during the installation by providing the following section in your kickstart file:

```
%addon com_redhat_kdump --enable --reserve-mb=auto
%end
```

See also

For more detailed information about kickstart files, refer to the website `https://github.com/rhinstaller/pykickstart/blob/master/docs/kickstart-docs.rst`.

For the consistent network device naming, refer to `https://access.redhat.com/documentation/en-US/Red_Hat_Enterprise_Linux/7/html/Networking_Guide/ch-Consistent_Network_Device_Naming.html`.

Publishing your kickstart file using httpd

You can save your kickstart file to a USB stick (or any other medium), but this becomes a bit cumbersome if you need to install multiple systems in different locations.

Loading kickstart files over the network from the kernel line during an install only supports NFS, HTTP, and FTP.

In this recipe, I choose HTTP as it is a common technology within companies and easy to secure.

How to do it...

Let's start by installing Apache `httpd`, as follows:

1. Install Apache `httpd` through the following command:

   ```
   ~]# yum install -y httpd
   ```

2. Enable and start the `httpd` daemon, as follows:

   ```
   ~]# systemctl enable httpd
   ln -s '/usr/lib/systemd/system/httpd.service' '/etc/systemd/system/multi-user.target.wants/httpd.service'
   ~]# systemctl start httpd
   ```

3. Create a directory to contain the kickstart file(s) by running the following command:

   ```
   ~]# mkdir -p /var/www/html/kickstart
   ~]# chown apache:apache /var/www/html/kickstart
   ~]# chmod 750 /var/www/html/kickstart
   ```

4. Copy your kickstart file to this new location:

   ```
   ~]# cp kickstart.ks /var/www/html/kickstart/
   ```

5. In a browser, browse to the kickstart directory on your web server, as shown in the following screenshot:

Index of /kickstart – Mozilla Firefox

Index of /kickstart

localhost/kickstart/

Index of /kickstart

Name	Last modified	Size	Description
Parent Directory		-	
kickstart.ks	2015-06-27 11:46	1.5K	

There's more...

In this way, you can create multiple kickstart files, which will be available from anywhere in your network.

Additionally, you could use CGI-BIN, PHP, or any other technology that has an Apache module to dynamically create kickstart files based on the arguments that you specify in the URL.

An alternative to creating your own solution for dynamic kickstart files is Cobbler.

See also

For more info on Cobbler, go to `http://cobbler.github.io/`.

Deploying a system using PXE

PXE, or Preboot eXecution Environment, allows you to instruct computers to boot using network resources. This allows you to control a single source to install servers without the need to physically insert cumbersome DVDs or USB sticks.

Getting ready

For this recipe, you will need a fully working RHEL 7 repository.

How to do it...

With this recipe, we'll install and configure PXE boots from the RHEL 7 installation media, as follows:

1. Install the necessary packages using the following command:

   ```
   ~]# yum install -y dnsmasq syslinux tftp-server
   ```

2. Configure the DNSMASQ server by editing /etc/dnsmasq.conf, as follows:

   ```
   # interfaces to bind to
   interface=eno1,lo
   # the domain for this DNS server
   domain=rhel7.lan
   # DHCP lease range
   dhcp-range= eno1,192.168.0.3,192.168.0.103,255.255.255.0,1h
   # PXE - the address of the PXE server
   dhcp-boot=pxelinux.0,pxeserver,192.168.0.1
   # Gateway
   dhcp-option=3,192.168.0.254
   # DNS servers for DHCP clients(your internal DNS servers,
   and one of Google's DNS servers)
   dhcp-option=6,192.168.1.1, 8.8.8.8
   # DNS server to forward DNS queries to
   server=8.8.4.4
   # Broadcast Address
   dhcp-option=28,192.168.0.255
   pxe-prompt="Press F1 for menu.", 60
   pxe-service=x86_64PC, "Install RHEL 7 from network",
   pxelinux
   enable-tftp
   tftp-root=/var/lib/tftpboot
   ```

3. Enable and start `dnsmasq` using the following:

   ```
   ~]# systemctl enable dnsmasq
   ~]# systemctl start dnsmasq
   ```

4. Now, enable and start the `xinet` daemon by running the following:

   ```
   ~]# systemctl enable xinetd
   ~]# systemctl start xinetd
   ```

5. Enable the `tftp` server's `xinet` daemon, as follows:

   ```
   ~]# sed -i '/disable/ s/yes/no/' /etc/xinetd.d/tftp
   ```

6. Copy the `syslinux` boot loaders to the `tftp` server's boot directory by executing the following command:

   ```
   ~]# cp -r /usr/share/syslinux/* /var/lib/tftpboot
   ```

7. Next, create the PXE configuration directory using this command:

   ```
   ~]# mkdir /var/lib/tftpboot/pxelinux.cfg
   ```

8. Then, create the PXE configuration file, as follows: `/var/lib/tftpboot/pxelinux.cfg/default`.

   ```
   default menu.c32
   prompt 0
   timeout 300
   ONTIMEOUT local
   menu title PXE Boot Menu
   label 1
     menu label ^1 - Install RHEL 7 x64 with Local http Repo
     kernel rhel7/vmlinuz
     append initrd=rhel7/initrd.img method=http://repo.critter.be/
   rhel/7/os/x86_64/
   devfs=nomount ks=http://kickstart.critter.be/kickstart.ks
   label 2
     menu label ^2 - Boot from local media
   ```

9. Copy `initrd` and `kernel` from the RHEL 7 installation media to `/var/lib/tftpboot/rhel7/`, and run the following commands:

   ```
   ~]# mkdir /var/lib/tftpboot/rhel7
   ~]# mount -o loop /dev/cdrom /mnt
   ~]# cp /mnt/images/pxeboot/{initrd.img,vmlinuz} /var/lib/tftpboot/
   rhel7/
   ~]# umount /mnt
   ```

10. Open the firewall on your server using these commands (however, this may not be necessary):

    ```
    ~]# firewall-cmd --add-service=dns --permanent
    ~]# firewall-cmd --add-service=dhcp --permanent
    ~]# firewall-cmd --add-service=tftp --permanent
    ~]# firewall-cmd --reload
    ```

11. Finally, launch your client, configure it to boot from the network, and select the first option shown in the following figure:

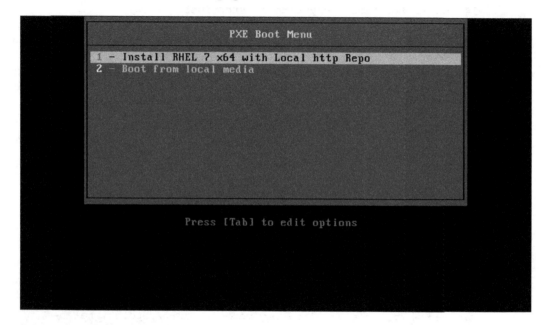

How it works...

DNSMASQ takes care of pointing booting systems to the `tftp` server by providing the `enable-tftp` option in the `dnsmasq` configuration file.

Syslinux is needed to provide the necessary binaries to boot from the network.

The `tftp` server itself provides access to the `syslinux` files, RHEL 7 kernel, and `initrd` for the system to boot from.

The PXE configuration file provides the necessary configuration to boot a system, including a kickstart file that automatically installs your system.

There's more...

This recipe's base premise is that you do not have a DHCP server installed. In most companies, you already have DHCP services available.

If you have an ISC-DHCP server in place, this is what you need to add to the subnet definition(s) you want to allow in PXE:

```
next-server <ip address of TFTP server>;
filename "pxelinux.0";
```

See also

Check out *Chapter 8, Yum and Repositories* to set up an RHEL 7 repository from the installation media.

Deploying a system using a custom boot ISO file

PXE is a widely used way to deploy systems, and so are ISO's. PXE may not always be at hand because of security, hardware availability, and so on.

Many hardware manufacturers provide remote access to their systems without an OS installed. HP has iLO, while Dell has RIB. The advantage of these "remote" control solutions is that they also allow you to mount "virtual" media in the form of an ISO.

How to do it...

Red Hat provides boot media as ISO images, which you can use to boot your systems from. We will create a custom ISO image, which will allow us to boot a system in a similar way.

Let's create an ISO that you can mount as virtual media, write a CD-ROM, or even use dd to write the contents on a USB stick/disk through the following steps:

1. Install the required packages to create ISO9660 images, as follows:

    ```
    ~]# yum install -y genisoimage
    ```

2. Mount the RHEL 7 DVD's ISO image by executing the following command:

    ```
    ~]# mount -o loop /path/to/rhel-server-7.0-x86_64-dvd.iso /mnt
    ```

3. Copy the required files for the custom ISO from the RHEL 7 media via the following commands:

```
~]# mkdir -p /root/iso
~]# cp -r /mnt/isolinux /root/iso
~]# umount /mnt
```

4. Now, unmount the RHEL 7 DVD's ISO image by running the following:

```
~]# umount /mnt
```

5. Next, remove the isolinux.cfg file using the following command:

```
~]# rm -f /root/iso/isolinux/isolinux.cfg
```

6. Create a new isolinux.cfg file, as follows:

```
default vesamenu.c32
timeout 600
display boot.msg
menu clear
menu background splash.png
menu title Red Hat Enterprise Linux 7.0
menu vshift 8
menu rows 18
menu margin 8
menu helpmsgrow 15
menu tabmsgrow 13
menu color sel 0 #ffffffff #00000000 none
menu color title 0 #ffcc000000 #00000000 none
menu color tabmsg 0 #84cc0000 #00000000 none
menu color hotsel 0 #84cc0000 #00000000 none
menu color hotkey 0 #ffffffff #00000000 none
menu color cmdmark 0 #84b8ffff #00000000 none
menu color cmdline 0 #ffffffff #00000000 none
label linux
  menu label ^Install Red Hat Enterprise Linux 7.0
  kernel vmlinuz
  append initrd=initrd.img ks=http://kickstart.critter.be/
kickstart.ks text

label local
  menu label Boot from ^local drive
  localboot 0xffff

menu end
```

7. Now, create the ISO by executing the following command:

    ```
    ~]# cd /root/iso
    ```

    ```
    ~/iso]# mkisofs -o ../boot.iso -b isolinux/isolinux.bin -c
    isolinux/boot.cat -no-emul-boot -boot-load-size 4 -boot-info-table
    -J -r .
    ```

    More information on the options used with the mkisofs command can be found in the man pages for *mkisofs(1)*.

    The following image shows the progress on creating a custom ISO:

    ```
    root@srv00004:~/iso                                          _  □  ✕

    File  Edit  View  Search  Terminal  Help
    ~# cd /root/iso
    ~/iso# mkisofs -o ../boot.iso -b isolinux/isolinux.bin -c isolinux/boot.cat -no-
    emul-boot -boot-load-size 4 -boot-info-table -J -r .
    I: -input-charset not specified, using utf-8 (detected in locale settings)
    Size of boot image is 4 sectors -> No emulation
     13.69% done, estimate finish Sat Jun 27 14:07:07 2015
     27.33% done, estimate finish Sat Jun 27 14:07:07 2015
     41.01% done, estimate finish Sat Jun 27 14:07:07 2015
     54.68% done, estimate finish Sat Jun 27 14:07:07 2015
     68.32% done, estimate finish Sat Jun 27 14:07:07 2015
     82.00% done, estimate finish Sat Jun 27 14:07:07 2015
     95.67% done, estimate finish Sat Jun 27 14:07:08 2015
    Total translation table size: 2048
    Total rockridge attributes bytes: 1362
    Total directory bytes: 2048
    Path table size(bytes): 26
    Max brk space used 0
    36595 extents written (71 MB)
    ~/iso# ▮
    ```

8. Then, use the ISO to install a guest on a KVM server, as shown in the following commands:

    ```
    ~]# virsh vol-create-as --pool localfs-vm --name rhel7_guest-da.
    qcows2 --format qcows2 -capacity 10G
    ```

    ```
    ~]# virt-install \
    --hvm \
    --name rhel7_guest \
    ```

```
--memory 2G,maxmemory=4G \

--vcpus 2,max=4 \

--os-type linux \

--os-variant rhel7 \

--boot hd,cdrom,network,menu=on \

--controller type=scsi,model=virtio-scsi \

--disk device=cdrom,vol=iso/boot.iso,readonly=on,bus=scsi \

--disk device=disk,vol=localfs-vm/rhel7_guest-vda.
qcow2,cache=none,bus=scsi \

--network network=bridge-eth0,model=virtio \

--graphics vnc \

--graphics spice \

--noautoconsole \

--memballoon virtio
```

The following screenshot shows the console when booted with the custom ISO image:

How it works...

Using the RHEL 7 installation media, we created a new boot ISO that allows us to install a new system. The ISO can be used to either burn a CD, with the dd tool to be copied on a USB stick, or to mount as virtual media. The way to mount this ISO as virtual media is different on each hardware platform, so this recipe shows you how to install it using KVM.

3

Configuring Your Network

The recipes we'll be covering in this chapter are as follows:

- ▶ Creating a VLAN interface
- ▶ Creating a teamed interface
- ▶ Creating a bridge
- ▶ Configuring IPv4 settings
- ▶ Configuring your DNS resolvers
- ▶ Configuring static network routes

Introduction

This chapter will attempt to explain how to use `NetworkManager`, which is the default network configuration tool and daemon in RHEL 7. It is a set of tools that makes networking simple and straightforward.

Configuring your network can be hard at times, especially when using the more exotic configuration options in combination with well-known configuration scripts. The `NetworkManager` allows you to easily configure your network without needing to edit the configuration files manually.

You can still edit the network configuration files located in `/etc/sysconfig/network-scripts` using your preferred editor; however, by default, `NetworkManager` does not notice any changes you make. You'll need to execute the following after editing the files located in the preceding location:

`~]# nmcli connection reload`

This is not enough to apply the changes immediately. You'll need to bring down and up the connection or reboot the system.

Alternatively, you can edit `/etc/NetworkManager/NetworkManager.conf` and add `monitor-connection-files=yes` to the `[main]` section. This will cause `NetworkManager` to pick up the changes and apply them immediately.

Within these recipes, you will get an overview on how to configure your network using the `NetworkManager` tools (`nmcli` and `nmtui`) and kickstart files.

Creating a VLAN interface

VLANs are isolated broadcast domains that run over a single physical network. They allow you to segment a local network and also to "stretch" a LAN over multiple physical locations. Most enterprises implement this on their network switching environment, but in some cases, the tagged VLANs reach your server.

Getting ready

In order to configure a VLAN, we need an established network connection on the local network interface.

How to do it...

For the sake of ease, our physical network interface is called `eth0`. The VLAN's ID is 1, and the IPv4 address is `10.0.0.2`, with a subnet mask of `255.0.0.0` and a default gateway of `10.0.0.1`.

Creating the VLAN connection with nmcli

With `nmcli`, we need to first create the connection and then activate it. Perform the following steps:

1. Create a VLAN interface using the following command:

   ~]# nmcli connection add type vlan dev eth0 id 1 ip4 10.0.0.2/8 gw4 10.0.0.1

   Connection 'vlan' (4473572d-26c0-49b8-a1a4-c20b485dad0d) successfully added.

   ~]#

2. Now, via this command, activate the connection:

   ~]# nmcli connection up vlan

   Connection successfully activated (D-Bus active path: /org/freedesktop/NetworkManager/ActiveConnection/7)

   ~]#

3. Check your network connection, as follows:

   ~]# nmcli connection show

   ~]# nmcli device status

   ~]# nmcli device show eth0.1

   Here is an example output of the preceding commands:

```
~]# nmcli connection show
NAME          UUID                                    TYPE            DEVICE
vlan          778fe568-2d9c-469b-99a1-6bba733baa2c    vlan            eth0.1
System eth0   05b32d2d-5298-406a-bc05-86316ed99583    802-3-ethernet  eth0
~]#
~]# nmcli device status
DEVICE   TYPE       STATE        CONNECTION
eth0     ethernet   connected    System eth0
eth0.1   vlan       connected    vlan
lo       loopback   unmanaged    --
~]#
~]# nmcli d show eth0.1
GENERAL.DEVICE:                   eth0.1
GENERAL.TYPE:                     vlan
GENERAL.HWADDR:                   52:54:00:F6:42:F3
GENERAL.MTU:                      1500
GENERAL.STATE:                    100 (connected)
GENERAL.CONNECTION:               vlan
GENERAL.CON-PATH:                 /org/freedesktop/NetworkManager/ActiveConnection/1
IP4.ADDRESS[1]:                   10.0.0.2/8
IP4.GATEWAY:                      10.0.0.1
IP6.ADDRESS[1]:                   fe80::5054:ff:fef6:42f3/64
IP6.GATEWAY:
~]#
```

Creating the VLAN connection with nmtui

The `nmtui` tool is a text user interface to `NetworkManager` and is launched by executing the following in a terminal:

```
~]# nmtui
```

This will bring up the following text-based interface:

Navigation is done using the *Tab* and arrow keys, and the selection is done by pressing the *Enter* key. Now, you need to do the following:

1. Go to **Edit a connection** and select **<OK>**. The following screen will appear:

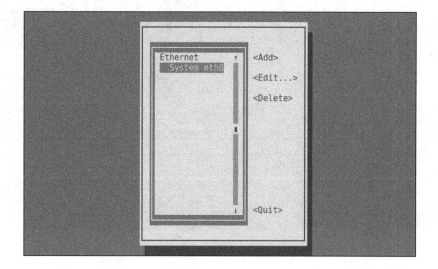

2. Next, select **<Add>** and the **VLAN** option. Confirm by Selecting **<Create>**:

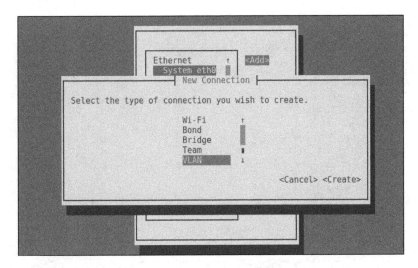

3. Enter the requested information in the following form and commit by selecting **<OK>**:

```
┤ Edit Connection ├
      Profile name VLAN connection 1
            Device eth0.1

  VLAN                                                          <Hide>
            Parent eth0
           VLAN id 1

  Cloned MAC address
               MTU            (default)


  IPv4 CONFIGURATION <Manual>                                   <Hide>
         Addresses 10.0.0.2/8                    <Remove>
                   <Add...>
           Gateway 10.0.0.1
       DNS servers <Add...>
    Search domains <Add...>

           Routing (No custom routes) <Edit...>
  [ ] Never use this network for default route

  [ ] Require IPv4 addressing for this connection

= IPv6 CONFIGURATION <Automatic>                                <Show>

[X] Automatically connect
[X] Available to all users

                                                   <Cancel> <OK>
```

Your new **VLAN** interface will now be listed in the connections list:

Creating the VLAN connection with kickstart

Let's explore what you need to add to your `kickstart` script in order to achieve the same result as in the preceding section:

1. Look for the configuration parameters within your `kickstart` file with the following command:

    ```
    ...
    network --device=eth0
    ...
    ```

2. Replace it with the following configuration parameters:

    ```
    network --device=eth0 --vlanid=1 --bootproto=static --
    ip=10.0.0.2 --netmask=255.0.0.0 --gateway=10.0.0.1
    ```

There's more...

The command line to create a VLAN with `nmcli` is pretty basic as it uses default values for every piece of information that is missing. To make sure that everything is created to your wishes, it is wise to also use `con-name` and `ifname`. These will respectively name your connection and the device you're creating. Take a look at the following command:

```
~]# nmcli connection add type vlan con-name vlan1 ifname eth0.1 dev eth0
id 1 ip4 10.0.0.2/8 gw4 10.0.0.1
```

This will create the `vlan.1` connection with `eth0` as the parent and `eth0.1` as the target device.

As with `nmcli` and `nmtui`, you can name your VLAN connection in `kickstart`; you only need to specify the `--interfacename` option. If you cannot find any previous network configuration in your `kickstart` file, just add the code to your `kickstart` file.

See also

The `nmcli` tool lacks a man page, but execute the following command for for more options to create VLAN connections:

```
~]# nmcli con add help
```

For more `kickstart` information on networks, check the following URL: `https://access.redhat.com/documentation/en-US/Red_Hat_Enterprise_Linux/7/html/Installation_Guide/sect-kickstart-syntax.html`.

Creating a teamed interface

Interface teaming, interface bonding, and link aggregation are all the same. It was already implemented in the kernel by way of the `bonding` driver. The team driver provides a different mechanism (from bonding) to team multiple network interfaces into a single logical one.

Getting ready

To set up a teamed interface, we'll need more than one network interface.

How to do it...

For the sake of ease, our physical network interfaces are called `eth1` and `eth2`. The IPv4 address for the team interface is `10.0.0.2`, with a subnet mask of `255.0.0.0` and a default gateway of `10.0.0.1`.

Creating the teamed interface using nmcli

Using this approach, we'll need to create the team connection and two team slaves and activate the connection, as follows:

1. Use the following command line to create the team connection:

   ```
   ~]# nmcli connection add type team ip4 10.0.0.2/8 gw4 10.0.0.1
   Connection 'team' (cfa46865-deb0-49f2-9156-4ca5461971b4)
   successfully added.
   ~]#
   ```

2. Add `eth1` to the team by executing the following:

   ```
   ~]# nmcli connection add type team-slave ifname eth1 master team
   Connection 'team-slave-eth1' (01880e55-f9a5-477b-b194-
   73278ef3dce5) successfully added.
   ~]#
   ```

3. Now, add `eth2` to the team by running the following command:

   ```
   ~]# nmcli connection add type team-slave ifname eth2 master team
   Connection 'team-slave-eth2' (f9efd19a-905f-4538-939c-
   3ea7516c3567) successfully added.
   ~]#
   ```

4. Bring the team up, as follows:

   ```
   ~]# nmcli connection up team
   Connection successfully activated (master waiting for
   slaves) (D-Bus active path: /org/freedesktop/NetworkManager/
   ActiveConnection/12)
   ~]#
   ```

5. Finally, check your network connections through the following commands:

   ```
   ~]# nmcli connection show
   ~]# nmcli device status
   ~]# nmcli device show nm-team
   ```

   Here's an example output of the preceding commands:

   ```
   ~]# nmcli c s
   NAME              UUID                                     TYPE           DEVICE
   team              fecca686-3d5f-4a61-8fe0-adce4b9a4368     team           nm-team
   System eth0       05b32d2d-5298-406a-bc05-86316ed99583     802-3-ethernet eth0
   team-slave-eth2   23ce3bc3-ab50-4962-9739-f7d2657afd91     802-3-ethernet eth2
   team-slave-eth1   1ef26a49-60c2-4c8c-8772-550c4c3c690b     802-3-ethernet eth1
   ~]#
   ~]# nmcli d s
   DEVICE    TYPE        STATE        CONNECTION
   eth0      ethernet    connected    System eth0
   eth1      ethernet    connected    team-slave-eth1
   eth2      ethernet    connected    team-slave-eth2
   nm-team   team        connected    team
   lo        loopback    unmanaged    --
   ~]#
   ~]# nmcli d show nm-team
   GENERAL.DEVICE:                        nm-team
   GENERAL.TYPE:                          team
   GENERAL.HWADDR:                        52:54:00:F6:42:F4
   GENERAL.MTU:                           1500
   GENERAL.STATE:                         100 (connected)
   GENERAL.CONNECTION:                    team
   GENERAL.CON-PATH:                      /org/freedesktop/NetworkManager/ActiveConnection/6
   IP4.ADDRESS[1]:                        10.0.0.2/8
   IP4.GATEWAY:                           10.0.0.1
   IP6.ADDRESS[1]:                        fe80::5054:ff:fef6:42f4/64
   IP6.GATEWAY:
   ~]#
   ```

Creating the teamed interface using nmtui

Let's fire up `nmtui` and add a connection through the following steps:

1. First, create a team connection by selecting **<Add>**:

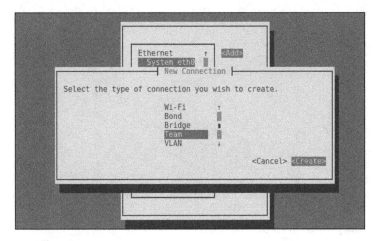

2. Enter the requested information in the following form and click on **<Add>** for every interface to add:

3. Next, select **<Add>** within team slaves to add an interface by filling out the form and selecting **<OK>**. Repeat this for every physical interface:

```
┌──────────────────────────┤ Edit Connection ├──────────────────────────┐
│                                                                        │
│              Profile name Ethernet connection 1                        │
│                    Device eth1                                         │
│                                                                        │
│  ≡ ETHERNET                                                   <Show>   │
│                                                                        │
│  ≡ TEAM PORT                                                  <Show>   │
│  [X] Automatically connect                                             │
│  [X] Available to all users                                            │
│                                                                        │
│                                               <Cancel>  <OK>           │
│                                                                        │
└────────────────────────────────────────────────────────────────────────┘
```

4. Now, select **<OK>** to create the team interface:

```
┌──────────────────────────┤ Edit Connection ├──────────────────────────┐
│                                                                        │
│              Profile name Team connection 1                            │
│                    Device team0                                        │
│                                                                        │
│  ▼ TEAM                                                     <Hide>     │
│    Slaves                                                               │
│                                                                        │
│      ┌──────────────────────────────────────────┐                     │
│      │ Ethernet connection 2                    │↑   <Add>            │
│      │ Ethernet connection 1                    │    <Edit...>         │
│      │                                          │    <Delete>          │
│      │                                          │↓                     │
│      └──────────────────────────────────────────┘                     │
│                                                                        │
│    JSON configuration                                                  │
│                                                                        │
│    <Edit...>                                                           │
│                                                                        │
│  ▼ IPv4 CONFIGURATION <Automatic>                          <Hide>     │
│           Addresses 10.0.0.1                     <Remove>             │
│                     <Add...>                                           │
│             Gateway 10.0.0.2                                          │
│         DNS servers <Add...>                                          │
│      Search domains <Add...>                                          │
│                                                                        │
│              Routing (No custom routes) <Edit...>                     │
│      [ ] Never use this network for default route                     │
│                                                                        │
│      [ ] Require IPv4 addressing for this connection                  │
│                                                                        │
│  ≡ IPv6 CONFIGURATION <Automatic>                          <Show>     │
│                                                                        │
│  [X] Automatically connect                                             │
│  [X] Available to all users                                            │
│                                                                        │
│                                               <Cancel>  <OK>           │
└────────────────────────────────────────────────────────────────────────┘
```

Your new team interface will now be listed in the connections list, as shown in the following screenshot:

Creating the teamed interface with kickstart

Open your `kickstart` file with your favorite editor and perform the following steps:

1. Look for the network configuration parameters within your `kickstart` file by running the following command:

    ```
    ...
    network --device=eth0
    ...
    ```

2. Next, add the following configuration parameters:

    ```
    network --device=team0 --teamslaves="eth1,eth2" --
    bootproto=static --ip=10.0.0.2 --netmask=255.0.0.0 --
    gateway=10.0.0.1
    ```

There's more...

Teaming comes with runners—a way of load-sharing backup methods that you can assign to your team:

*   **active-backup**: In this, one physical interface is used, while the others are kept as backup
*   **broadcast**: In this, data is transmitted over all physical interfaces' selectors

> ▸ **LACP:** This implements `802.3ad` Link Aggregation Control Protocol
> ▸ **loadbalance**: This performs active Tx load balancing and uses a BPF-based Tx port
> ▸ **round-robin**: The data is transmitted over all physical interfaces in turn

These can also be defined upon creation using either of the presented options here:

nmcli

Add `team.config "{\"runner\":{\"name\": \"activebackup\"}}"` to your command to create your team interface, and substitute `activebackup` with the runner that you wish to use.

nmtui

Fill out the JSON configuration field for the team interface with `{"runner": {"name": "activebackup"}}`, and substitute `activebackup` with the runner that you wish to use.

kickstart

Add `--teamconfig="{\"runner\":{\"name\": \"activebackup\"}}"` to your team device line, and substitute `activebackup` with the runner that you wish to use.

The options provided to create the team interface are bare bones using `nmcli`. If you wish to add a connection and interface name, use `con-name` and `ifname`, respectively, in this way:

```
~]# nmcli connection add type team con-name team0 ifname team0 ip4
10.0.0.2/8 gw4 10.0.0.1
Connection 'team0' (e1856313-ecd4-420e-96d5-c76bc00794aa) successfully
added.
~]#
```

The same is true for adding the team slaves, except for `ifname`, which is required to specify the correct interface:

```
~# nmcli connection add type team-slave con-name team0-slave0 ifname eth1
master team0
Connection 'team0-slave0' (3cb2f603-1f73-41a0-b476-7a356d4b6274)
successfully added.
~# nmcli connection add type team-slave con-name team0-slave1 ifname eth2
master team0
Connection 'team0-slave1' (074e4dd3-8a3a-4997-b444-a781114c58c9)
successfully added.
~#
```

See also

For more information on the networking team daemon and "runners", refer to the following URL:

```
https://access.redhat.com/documentation/en-US/Red_Hat_Enterprise_
Linux/7/html/Networking_Guide/sec-Understanding_the_Network_Teaming_
Daemon_and_the_Runners.html
```

For more information on using `nmcli` to create team interfaces, take a look at the following link:

```
https://access.redhat.com/documentation/en-US/Red_Hat_Enterprise_
Linux/7/html/Networking_Guide/sec-Configure_a_Network_Team_Using-the_
Command_Line.html
```

For more information on using `nmtui` to create team interfaces, follow this link:

```
https://access.redhat.com/documentation/en-US/Red_Hat_Enterprise_
Linux/7/html/Networking_Guide/sec-Configure_a_Network_Team_Using_the_
Text_User_Interface_nmtui.html
```

For more information on creating team interfaces in kickstart scripts, the following link will be useful:

```
https://access.redhat.com/documentation/en-US/Red_Hat_Enterprise_
Linux/7/html/Installation_Guide/sect-kickstart-syntax.html
```

Creating a bridge

A network bridge is a logical device that forwards traffic between connected physical interfaces based on MAC addresses. This kind of bridge can be used to emulate a hardware bridge in virtualization applications, such as KVM, to share the NIC with multiple virtual NICs.

Getting ready

To bridge two physical networks, we need two network interfaces. Your physical interfaces should never be configured with any address as the bridge will be configured with the IP address(es).

How to do it...

For the sake of ease, the physical network interfaces we will bridge are `eth1` and `eth2`. The IPv4 address will be `10.0.0.2` with a subnet mask of `255.0.0.0` and a default gateway of `10.0.0.1`.

Creating a bridge using nmcli

Make sure that you activate the bridge after configuring the bridge and interfaces! Here are the steps that you need to perform for this:

1. First, create the bridge connection via the following command:

    ```
    ~]# nmcli connection add type bridge ip4 10.0.0.2/8 gw4 10.0.0.1
    Connection 'bridge' (36e40910-cf6a-4a6c-ae28-c0d6fb90954d)
    successfully added.
    ~]#
    ```

2. Add `eth1` to the bridge, as follows:

   ```
   ~]# nmcli connection add type bridge-slave ifname eth1 master
   bridge
   ```

   ```
   Connection 'bridge-slave-eth1' (6821a067-f25c-46f6-89d4-
   a318fc4db683) successfully added.
   ```

   `~]#`

3. Next, add `eth2` to the bridge using the following command:

   ```
   ~]# nmcli connection add type bridge-slave ifname eth2 master
   bridge
   ```

   ```
   Connection 'bridge-slave-eth2' (f20d0a7b-da03-4338-8060-
   07a3775772f4) successfully added.
   ```

   `~]#`

4. Activate the bridge by executing the following:

   `~# nmcli connection up bridge`

   ```
   Connection successfully activated (master waiting for
   slaves) (D-Bus active path: /org/freedesktop/NetworkManager/
   ActiveConnection/30)
   ```

   `~]#`

5. Now, check your network connection by running the following commands:

   `~]# nmcli connection show`

   `~]# nmcli device status`

   `~]# nmcli device show bridge`

   Here is an example output of the preceding commands:

   ```
   ~]# nmcli connection show
   NAME              UUID                                  TYPE            DEVICE
   System eth0       05b32d2d-5298-406a-bc05-86316ed99583  802-3-ethernet  eth0
   bridge-slave-eth2 96203d35-1d55-4366-8110-b7b4c0becc2b  802-3-ethernet  eth2
   bridge-slave-eth1 e49b4127-cc2a-4710-86bc-a12220fa85ca  802-3-ethernet  eth1
   bridge            4cef8132-1f93-4936-af45-ea2f01c95246  bridge          nm-bridge
   ~]#
   ~]# nmcli device status
   DEVICE    TYPE      STATE      CONNECTION
   nm-bridge bridge    connected  bridge
   eth0      ethernet  connected  System eth0
   eth1      ethernet  connected  bridge-slave-eth1
   eth2      ethernet  connected  bridge-slave-eth2
   lo        loopback  unmanaged  --
   ~]#
   ~]# nmcli device show nm-bridge
   GENERAL.DEVICE:               nm-bridge
   GENERAL.TYPE:                 bridge
   GENERAL.HWADDR:               52:54:00:F6:42:F4
   GENERAL.MTU:                  1500
   GENERAL.STATE:                100 (connected)
   GENERAL.CONNECTION:           bridge
   GENERAL.CON-PATH:             /org/freedesktop/NetworkManager/ActiveConnection/12
   IP4.ADDRESS[1]:               10.0.0.2/8
   IP4.GATEWAY:                  10.0.0.1
   IP6.ADDRESS[1]:               fe80::5054:ff:fef6:42f4/64
   IP6.GATEWAY:
   ~]#
   ```

Creating a bridge using nmtui

Launch `nmtui` and select **Edit a connection**. After this, follow these steps to create a bridge using `nmtui`:

1. Create a bridge connection by selecting **<Add>** and **Bridge** from the connection list and then click on **<Create>**:

2. Fill out the presented form with the required information:

3. Next, add the two network interfaces by selecting **\<Add\>** and providing the requested information for each interface:

```
┌──────────────────────────┤ Edit Connection ├──────────────────────────┐
│                                                                      1 │
│         Profile name Ethernet connection 1                             │
│                Device eth1                                             │
│  = ETHERNET                                                    <Show>  │
│                                                                        │
│  ┬ BRIDGE PORT                                                 <Hide>  │
│  │          Priority 32                                                │
│  │         Path cost 100                                               │
│  [ ] Hairpin mode                                                      │
│                                                                        │
│  [X] Automatically connect                                             │
│  [X] Available to all users                                            │
│                                                                        │
│                                                   <Cancel> <OK>        │
│                                                                        │
│                                                                        │
└────────────────────────────────────────────────────────────────────────┘
```

4. Finally, select **\<OK\>** to create the bridge:

```
┌──────────────────────────┤ Edit Connection ├──────────────────────────┐
│                                                                      ↑ │
│         Profile name Bridge connection 1                             │ │
│                Device bridge0                                          │
│  ┬ BRIDGE                                                      <Hide>  │
│   Slaves                                                               │
│    ┌──────────────────────────────────────┐                           │
│    │ Ethernet connection 2              ↑ │  <Add>                     │
│    │ Ethernet connection 1                │                           │
│    │                                      │  <Edit...>                 │
│    │                                    ▮ │                           │
│    │                                    ↓ │  <Delete>                  │
│    └──────────────────────────────────────┘                           │
│                                                                        │
│          Aging time 300       seconds                                  │
│   [X] Enable STP (Spanning Tree Protocol)                              │
│            Priority 32768                                              │
│       Forward delay 15        seconds                                  │
│          Hello time 2         seconds                                  │
│                                                                        │
│  ┬ IPv4 CONFIGURATION <Manual>                                <Hide>   │
│          Addresses 10.0.0.2/8                  <Remove>                │
│                    <Add...>                                            │
│            Gateway 10.0.0.1                                            │
│        DNS servers <Add...>                                           │
│      Search domains <Add...>                                          │
│                                                                        │
│             Routing (No custom routes) <Edit...>                      │
│    [ ] Never use this network for default route                       │
│                                                                        │
│    [ ] Require IPv4 addressing for this connection                    │
│                                                                        │
│  = IPv6 CONFIGURATION <Automatic>                             <Show>   │
│                                                                        │
│  [X] Automatically connect                                            │
│  [X] Available to all users                                           │
│                                                   <Cancel> <OK>       │
│                                                                      ↓ │
└────────────────────────────────────────────────────────────────────────┘
```

Your new bridge will now be listed in the connections list:

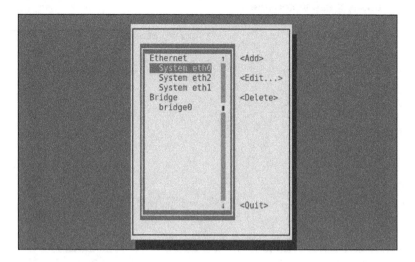

Creating a bridge with kickstart

Edit your `kickstart` file with your favorite editor through the following steps:

1. Look for the configuration parameters within your `kickstart` file using this command line:

   ```
   . . .
   network --device=eth0
   . . .
   ```

2. Now, add the following configuration parameters:

   ```
   network --device=bridge0 --bridgeslaves="eth1,eth2" --
   bootproto=static --ip=10.0.0.2 --netmask=255.0.0.0 --
   gateway=10.0.0.1
   ```

There's more...

The options provided to create the bridge are bare bones using `nmcli`. If you wish to add a connection and interface name, use `con-name` and `ifname`, respectively, in this way:

```
~# nmcli connection add type bridge con-name bridge0 ifname bridge0 ip4
10.0.0.2/8 gw4 10.0.0.1
Connection 'bridge0' (d04180be-3e80-4bd4-a0fe-b26d79d71c7d) successfully
added.
~#
```

The same is true for adding the bridge slaves, except for `ifname`, which is required to specify the correct interface:

```
~]# nmcli connection add type bridge-slave con-name bridge0-slave0 ifname
eth1 master bridge0
Connection 'bridge0-slave0' (3a885ca5-6ffb-42a3-9044-83c6142f1967)
successfully added.
~]# nmcli connection add type team-slave con-name team0-slave1 ifname
eth2 master team0
Connection 'bridge0-slave1' (f79716f1-7b7f-4462-87d9-6801eee1952f)
successfully added.
~]#
```

See also

For more information on creating network bridges using `nmcli`, go to the following URL:

```
https://access.redhat.com/documentation/en-US/Red_Hat_Enterprise_
Linux/7/html/Networking_Guide/sec-Network_Bridging_Using_the_
NetworkManager_Command_Line_Tool_nmcli.html
```

For more information on creating network bridges using `nmtui`, go to this website:

```
https://access.redhat.com/documentation/en-US/Red_Hat_Enterprise_
Linux/7/html/Networking_Guide/ch-Configure_Network_Bridging.html
```

For more information on kickstart and bridging, go to the following website:

```
https://access.redhat.com/documentation/en-US/Red_Hat_Enterprise_
Linux/7/html/Installation_Guide/sect-kickstart-syntax.html
```

Configuring IPv4 settings

Changing your IP addresses is pretty straightforward in the old `ifcfg`-style files, and it's actually pretty simple using `NetworkManager` tools as well.

As kickstart is only used to set up a system, it is not relevant to go in depth into this matter in this recipe.

How to do it...

Let's change our current IPv4 address and gateway for `eth1` to `10.0.0.3/8`, with `10.0.0.2` as the default gateway.

Setting your IPv4 configuration using nmcli

Perform the following steps:

1. Set the ipv4 information by executing the following command line:

   ~]# `nmcli connection modify eth0 ipv4.addresses 10.0.0.3/8 ipv4.gateway 10.0.0.2`

2. Now, run the following to verify the information:

   ~]# `nmcli connection show eth0`

   Here is an example output of the preceding commands:

```
~]# nmcli connection show eth0
connection.id:                          eth0
connection.uuid:                        05b32d2d-5298-406a-bc05-86316ed99583
connection.interface-name:              eth0
connection.type:                        802-3-ethernet
connection.autoconnect:                 yes
connection.autoconnect-priority:        0
connection.timestamp:                   1446820183
connection.read-only:                   no
connection.permissions:
connection.zone:                        --
connection.master:                      --
connection.slave-type:                  --
connection.secondaries:
connection.gateway-ping-timeout:        0
802-3-ethernet.port:                    --
802-3-ethernet.speed:                   0
802-3-ethernet.duplex:                  --
802-3-ethernet.auto-negotiate:          yes
802-3-ethernet.mac-address:             52:54:00:F6:42:F3
802-3-ethernet.cloned-mac-address:      --
802-3-ethernet.mac-address-blacklist:
802-3-ethernet.mtu:                     auto
802-3-ethernet.s390-subchannels:
802-3-ethernet.s390-nettype:            --
802-3-ethernet.s390-options:
ipv4.method:                            manual
ipv4.dns:
ipv4.dns-search:                        example.com
ipv4.addresses:                         10.0.0.3/8
ipv4.gateway:                           10.0.0.2
ipv4.routes:
ipv4.route-metric:                      -1
ipv4.ignore-auto-routes:                no
ipv4.ignore-auto-dns:                   no
ipv4.dhcp-client-id:                    --
ipv4.dhcp-send-hostname:                yes
ipv4.dhcp-hostname:                     --
ipv4.never-default:                     no
ipv4.may-fail:                          yes
ipv6.method:                            auto
ipv6.dns:
ipv6.dns-search:
ipv6.addresses:
ipv6.gateway:                           --
ipv6.routes:
ipv6.route-metric:                      -1
ipv6.ignore-auto-routes:                no
ipv6.ignore-auto-dns:                   no
ipv6.never-default:                     no
ipv6.may-fail:                          yes
ipv6.ip6-privacy:                       -1 (unknown)
ipv6.dhcp-send-hostname:                yes
ipv6.dhcp-hostname:                     --
GENERAL.NAME:                           eth0
GENERAL.UUID:                           05b32d2d-5298-406a-bc05-86316ed99583
GENERAL.DEVICES:                        eth0
GENERAL.STATE:                          activated
GENERAL.DEFAULT:                        yes
GENERAL.DEFAULT6:                       no
GENERAL.VPN:                            no
GENERAL.ZONE:
GENERAL.DBUS-PATH:                      /org/freedesktop/NetworkManager/ActiveConnection/0
GENERAL.CON-PATH:                       /org/freedesktop/NetworkManager/Settings/1
GENERAL.SPEC-OBJECT:                    /
GENERAL.MASTER-PATH:                    --
IP4.ADDRESS[1]:                         10.0.0.3/8
IP4.GATEWAY:                            10.0.0.2
IP6.ADDRESS[1]:                         fe80::5054:ff:fef6:42f3/64
IP6.GATEWAY:
~]#
```

Setting your IPv4 configuration using nmtui

The `nmtui` tool takes a bit more work, but the end result remains the same. Perform the following steps:

1. Start `nmtui`, select the interface that you wish to modify, and click on **<Edit...>**:

2. Now, modify the IPv4 configuration to your liking and click on **<OK>**.

There's more...

Managing IPv6 ip addresses is as straightforward as configuring your IPv4 counterparts.

The options you need to use in kickstart to set your ip address and gateway are:

- ► `--ip`: This is used to set the system's IPv4 address
- ► `--netmask`: This is used for the subnet mask
- ► `--gateway`: This is used to set the IPv4 gateway

Configuring your DNS resolvers

DNS servers are stored in `/etc/resolv.conf`. You can also manage this file using `NetworkManager`.

As with the previous recipe, and for the same reasons, this recipe won't go into the `kickstart` options.

How to do it...

Let's set the DNS resolvers for `eth1` to point to Google's public DNS servers: `8.8.8.8` and `8.8.4.4`.

Setting your DNS resolvers using nmcli

Perform the following steps:

1. Set the DNS servers via the following command:

    ```
    ~]# nmcli connection modify System\ eth1 ipv4.dns
    "8.8.8.8,8.8.4.4"
    ```

2. Now, use the following command to check your configuration:

    ```
    ~]# nmcli connection show System\ eth1
    ```

Here is an example output of the preceding commands:

```
~]# nmcli c s System\ eth0
connection.id:                              System eth0
connection.uuid:                            05b32d2d-5298-406a-bc05-86316ed99583
connection.interface-name:                  eth0
connection.type:                            802-3-ethernet
connection.autoconnect:                     yes
connection.autoconnect-priority:            0
connection.timestamp:                       1446820783
connection.read-only:                       no
connection.permissions:
connection.zone:                            --
connection.master:                          --
connection.slave-type:                      --
connection.secondaries:
connection.gateway-ping-timeout:            0
802-3-ethernet.port:                        --
802-3-ethernet.speed:                       0
802-3-ethernet.duplex:                      --
802-3-ethernet.auto-negotiate:              yes
802-3-ethernet.mac-address:                 52:54:00:F6:42:F3
802-3-ethernet.cloned-mac-address:          --
802-3-ethernet.mac-address-blacklist:
802-3-ethernet.mtu:                         auto
802-3-ethernet.s390-subchannels:
802-3-ethernet.s390-nettype:                --
802-3-ethernet.s390-options:
ipv4.method:                                manual
ipv4.dns:                                   8.8.8.8,8.8.4.4
ipv4.dns-search:                            example.com
ipv4.addresses:                             10.0.0.3/8
ipv4.gateway:                               10.0.0.2
ipv4.routes:
ipv4.route-metric:                          -1
ipv4.ignore-auto-routes:                    no
ipv4.ignore-auto-dns:                       no
ipv4.dhcp-client-id:                        --
ipv4.dhcp-send-hostname:                    yes
ipv4.dhcp-hostname:                         --
ipv4.never-default:                         no
ipv4.may-fail:                              yes
ipv6.method:                                auto
ipv6.dns:
ipv6.dns-search:
ipv6.addresses:
ipv6.gateway:                               --
ipv6.routes:
ipv6.route-metric:                          -1
ipv6.ignore-auto-routes:                    no
ipv6.ignore-auto-dns:                       no
ipv6.never-default:                         no
ipv6.may-fail:                              yes
ipv6.ip6-privacy:                           -1 (unknown)
ipv6.dhcp-send-hostname:                    yes
ipv6.dhcp-hostname:                         --
GENERAL.NAME:                               System eth0
GENERAL.UUID:                               05b32d2d-5298-406a-bc05-86316ed99583
GENERAL.DEVICES:                            eth0
GENERAL.STATE:                              activated
GENERAL.DEFAULT:                            yes
GENERAL.DEFAULT6:                           no
GENERAL.VPN:                                no
GENERAL.ZONE:                               --
GENERAL.DBUS-PATH:                          /org/freedesktop/NetworkManager/ActiveConnection/0
GENERAL.CON-PATH:                           /org/freedesktop/NetworkManager/Settings/1
GENERAL.SPEC-OBJECT:                        /
GENERAL.MASTER-PATH:                        --
IP4.ADDRESS[1]:                             10.0.0.3/8
IP4.GATEWAY:                                10.0.0.2
IP6.ADDRESS[1]:                             fe80::5054:ff:fef6:42f3/64
IP6.GATEWAY:
~]#
```

Setting your DNS resolvers using nmtui

The nmtui tool requires a bit more work to set the DNS resolvers, as follows:

1. Start nmtui, select the interface that you wish to modify, and click on **<Edit...>**:

```
┌─────────────────┤ Edit Connection ├─────────────────┐

         Profile name System eth1
               Device eth1 (52:54:00:73:0C:17)

  ═ ETHERNET                                            <Show>

  ═ IPv4 CONFIGURATION <Manual>                         <Hide>
            Addresses 10.0.0.2/8              <Remove>
                      <Add...>
              Gateway 10.0.0.1
          DNS servers 8.8.8.8                 <Remove>
                      8.8.4.4                 <Remove>
                      <Add...>
       Search domains <Add...>

              Routing (No custom routes) <Edit...>
       [ ] Never use this network for default route

       [ ] Require IPv4 addressing for this connection

  ═ IPv6 CONFIGURATION <Ignore>                         <Show>

  [ ] Automatically connect
  [X] Available to all users

                                           <Cancel> <OK>
```

There's more...

The nmcli tool supports adding multiple DNS servers by separating them with a semicolon. Using a blank value (" ") will remove all the DNS servers for this connection.

Similarly, you can set the DNS search domains for your environment. When using nmcli, you'll need to specify the ipv4.dns-search property.

Kickstart will allow you to specify the DNS servers using the `--nameserver` option for each DNS server. If you do not wish to specify any DNS servers, use `--nodns`. Unfortunately, there is no native way to set the DNS domain search using `kickstart`. You will have to use `nmcli`, for example, in the `%post` section of your `kickstart` script.

> Be careful when setting DNS configurations for multiple network interfaces. `NetworkManager` adds all your nameservers to your `resolv.conf` file, but libc may not support more than six nameservers.

Configuring static network routes

In some cases, it is required to set static routes on your system. As static routes are not natively supported in `kickstart`, this is not covered in this recipe.

How to do it...

Add static routes to both the `192.168.0.0/24` and `192.168.1.0/24` networks via `10.0.0.1`.

Configuring static network routes using nmcli

Here's what you need to do:

1. Set the route using the following command:

   ```
   ~]# nmcli connection modify eth0 ipv4.routes "192.168.0.0/24
   10.0.0.1,192.168.1.0/24 10.0.0.1"
   ```

2. Now, execute the following command line to verify the configuration:

   ```
   ~]# nmcli connection show eth0
   ```

Here is an example output of the preceding commands:

```
~]# nmcli connection show eth0
connection.id:                        eth0
connection.uuid:                      05b32d2d-5298-406a-bc05-86316ed99583
connection.interface-name:            eth0
connection.type:                      802-3-ethernet
connection.autoconnect:               yes
connection.autoconnect-priority:      0
connection.timestamp:                 1446821383
connection.read-only:                 no
connection.permissions:
connection.zone:                      --
connection.master:                    --
connection.slave-type:                --
connection.secondaries:
connection.gateway-ping-timeout:      0
802-3-ethernet.port:                  --
802-3-ethernet.speed:                 0
802-3-ethernet.duplex:                --
802-3-ethernet.auto-negotiate:        yes
802-3-ethernet.mac-address:           52:54:00:F6:42:F3
802-3-ethernet.cloned-mac-address:    --
802-3-ethernet.mac-address-blacklist:
802-3-ethernet.mtu:                   auto
802-3-ethernet.s390-subchannels:
802-3-ethernet.s390-nettype:          --
802-3-ethernet.s390-options:
ipv4.method:                          manual
ipv4.dns:                             8.8.8.8,8.8.4.4
ipv4.dns-search:                      example.com
ipv4.addresses:                       10.0.0.3/8
ipv4.gateway:                         10.0.0.2
ipv4.routes:                          { ip = 192.168.0.0/24, nh = 10.0.0.1 }; { ip = 192.168.1.0/24, nh = 10.0
.0.1 }
ipv4.route-metric:                    -1
ipv4.ignore-auto-routes:              no
ipv4.ignore-auto-dns:                 no
ipv4.dhcp-client-id:                  --
ipv4.dhcp-send-hostname:              yes
ipv4.dhcp-hostname:                   --
ipv4.never-default:                   no
ipv4.may-fail:                        yes
ipv6.method:                          auto
ipv6.dns:
ipv6.dns-search:
ipv6.addresses:
ipv6.gateway:                         --
ipv6.routes:
ipv6.route-metric:                    -1
ipv6.ignore-auto-routes:              no
ipv6.ignore-auto-dns:                 no
ipv6.never-default:                   no
ipv6.may-fail:                        yes
ipv6.ip6-privacy:                     -1 (unknown)
ipv6.dhcp-send-hostname:              yes
ipv6.dhcp-hostname:                   --
GENERAL.NAME:                         eth0
GENERAL.UUID:                         05b32d2d-5298-406a-bc05-86316ed99583
GENERAL.DEVICES:                      eth0
GENERAL.STATE:                        activated
GENERAL.DEFAULT:                      yes
GENERAL.DEFAULT6:                     no
GENERAL.VPN:                          no
GENERAL.ZONE:                         --
GENERAL.DBUS-PATH:                    /org/freedesktop/NetworkManager/ActiveConnection/0
GENERAL.CON-PATH:                     /org/freedesktop/NetworkManager/Settings/1
GENERAL.SPEC-OBJECT:                  /
GENERAL.MASTER-PATH:                  --
IP4.ADDRESS[1]:                       10.0.0.3/8
IP4.GATEWAY:                          10.0.0.2
IP6.ADDRESS[1]:                       fe80::5054:ff:fef6:42f3/64
IP6.GATEWAY:
~]#
```

Configuring network routes using nmtui

Here are the steps for this recipe:

1. Launch `nmtui`, select the interface that you wish to modify the static routes for, and click on **<Edit...>**:

2. Now, select **<Edit...>** next to the **IPv4 Configuration – Routing** entry and enter your routes. Select **<OK>** to confirm:

3. Finally, click on **<OK>** to confirm the changes and save them.

4
Configuring Your New System

Here's an overview of the recipes that we'll be covering in this chapter:

- ▶ The `systemd` service and setting runlevels
- ▶ Starting and stopping `systemd` services
- ▶ Configuring the `systemd` journal for persistence
- ▶ Monitoring services using `journalctl`
- ▶ Configuring `logrotate`
- ▶ Managing time
- ▶ Configuring your boot environment
- ▶ Configuring `smtp`

Introduction

Once your system is installed and the network is configured, it's time to start configuring everything else.

RHEL 7 comes with the `systemd init` daemon, which takes care of your daemon or service housekeeping and more, replacing the old SysV (UNIX System V) init system.

Its main advantages are automatic dependency handling, parallel startup of services, and the monitoring of started services with the ability to restart crashed services.

For a good read on `systemd` and its inner workings, head over to `https://n0where.net/understanding-systemd`.

The systemd service and setting runlevels

The `systemd` service doesn't use runlevels as SysV or Upstart do. The alternatives for `systemd` are called targets. Their purpose is to group a set of `systemd` units (not only services, but also sockets, devices, and so on) through a chain of dependencies.

How to do it...

Managing targets with `systemd` is pretty simple, as shown through the following steps:

1. List all target units, as follows:

```
~]# systemctl list-unit-files --type target
UNIT FILE                 STATE

anaconda.target           static

basic.target              static

bluetooth.target          static

cryptsetup.target         static

ctrl-alt-del.target       disabled

default.target            enabled

...


sysinit.target            static

system-update.target      static

time-sync.target          static

timers.target             static

umount.target             static


58 unit files listed.
~]#
```

This list shows all target units available followed by information regarding whether the target is enabled or not.

2. Now, show the currently loaded target units.

The `systemd` targets can be chained unlike SysV runlevels, so you'll not only see one target but a whole bunch of them, as follows:

```
~]# systemctl list-units --type target
UNIT                  LOAD   ACTIVE SUB    DESCRIPTION
basic.target          loaded active active Basic System
```

```
cryptsetup.target        loaded active active Encrypted Volumes
getty.target             loaded active active Login Prompts
local-fs-pre.target      loaded active active Local File Systems
(Pre)
local-fs.target          loaded active active Local File Systems
multi-user.target        loaded active active Multi-User System
network-online.target loaded active active Network is Online
network.target           loaded active active Network
nfs-client.target        loaded active active NFS client services
paths.target             loaded active active Paths
remote-fs-pre.target     loaded active active Remote File Systems
(Pre)
remote-fs.target         loaded active active Remote File Systems
slices.target            loaded active active Slices
sockets.target           loaded active active Sockets
swap.target              loaded active active Swap
sysinit.target           loaded active active System Initialization
time-sync.target         loaded active active System Time
Synchronized
timers.target            loaded active active Timers


LOAD   = Reflects whether the unit definition was properly loaded.
ACTIVE = The high-level unit activation state, i.e. generalization
of SUB.
SUB    = The low-level unit activation state, values depend on
unit type.


18 loaded units listed. Pass --all to see loaded but inactive
units, too.
To show all installed unit files use 'systemctl list-unit-files'.
~]#
```

3. Next, change the default systemd target by running the following commands:

```
~]# systemctl set-default graphical.target
rm '/etc/systemd/system/default.target'
ln -s '/usr/lib/systemd/system/graphical.target' '/etc/systemd/
system/default.target'
~]#
```

There's more...

Sometimes, you want to change targets on the fly as you would in the past with runlevel or telinit. With `systemd`, this is accomplished in the following way:

```
~]# systemctl isolate <target name>
```

Here's an example:

```
~]# systemctl isolate graphical.target
```

Let's take an overview of the former runlevels versus the `systemd` targets in the following table:

Runlevel	Target units	Description
0	`runlevel0.target` or `poweroff.target`	This is used to shut down and power off the system
1	`runlevel1.target` or `rescue.target`	This is used to enter a rescue shell
2	`runlevel2.target` or `multi-user.target`	This is used to set up a command-line multiuser system
3	`runlevel3.target` or `multi-user.target`	This is used to set up a command-line multiuser system
4	`runlevel4.target` or `multi-user.target`	This is used to set up a command-line multiuser system
5	`runlevel5.target` or `graphical.target`	This is used to set up a graphical multiuser system
6	`runlevel6.target` or `reboot.target`	This is used to reboot the system

See also

For more in-depth information about RHEL 7 and `systemd` targets, refer to the following link: `https://access.redhat.com/documentation/en-US/Red_Hat_Enterprise_Linux/7/html/System_Administrators_Guide/sect-Managing_Services_with_systemd-Targets.html`

Starting and stopping systemd services

Although this recipe uses services by their base name, they can also be addressed by their full filename. For example, `sshd` can be substituted by `sshd.service`.

How to do it...

The following steps need to be performed to successfully start or stop `systemd` services:

1. List all available `systemd` services, as follows:

```
~]# systemctl list-unit-files --type service
UNIT FILE                                STATE
atd.service                              enabled
auditd.service                           enabled
auth-rpcgss-module.service               static
autovt@.service                          disabled
avahi-daemon.service                     disabled
blk-availability.service                 disabled
brandbot.service                         static


...


systemd-udev-trigger.service             static
systemd-udevd.service                    static
systemd-update-utmp-runlevel.service     static
systemd-update-utmp.service              static
systemd-user-sessions.service            static
systemd-vconsole-setup.service           static
tcsd.service                             disabled
teamd@.service                           static
tuned.service                            enabled
wpa_supplicant.service                   disabled
xinetd.service                           enabled


161 unit files listed.
```

This shows all service units available followed by information regarding whether the service is enabled or not.

2. Now, list all the loaded `systemd` services and their status, as follows:

```
~]# systemctl list-units --type service --all
UNIT                     LOAD    ACTIVE    SUB      DESCRIPTION
```

```
atd.service              loaded active    running Job spooling
tools
auditd.service           loaded active    running Security
Auditing Service
auth-rpcgss-module.service loaded inactive dead    Kernel Module
supporting RPC
brandbot.service         loaded inactive dead    Flexible
Branding Service
cpupower.service         loaded inactive dead    Configure CPU
power related
crond.service            loaded active    running Command
Scheduler
cups.service             loaded inactive dead    CUPS Printing
Service
dbus.service             loaded active    running D-Bus System
Message Bus
...


systemd-...es-setup.service loaded active    exited  Create
Volatile Files and Di
systemd-...-trigger.service loaded active    exited  udev Coldplug
all Devices
systemd-udevd.service    loaded active    running udev Kernel
Device Manager
systemd-update-utmp.service loaded active    exited  Update UTMP
about System Reb
systemd-...sessions.service loaded active    exited  Permit User
Sessions
systemd-...le-setup.service loaded active    exited  Setup Virtual
Console
tuned.service            loaded active    running Dynamic System
Tuning Daemon
xinetd.service           loaded active    running Xinetd A
Powerful Replacemen
LOAD   = Reflects whether the unit definition was properly loaded.
ACTIVE = The high-level unit activation state, i.e. generalization
of SUB.
SUB    = The low-level unit activation state, values depend on
unit type.


103 loaded units listed.
```

```
To show all installed unit files use 'systemctl list-unit-files'.
~]#
```

3. Next, get the status of a service.

   To get the status of a particular service, execute the following, substituting `<service>` with the name of the service:

   ```
   ~]# systemctl status <service>
   ```

   Here's an example:

   ```
   ~]# systemctl status sshd
   sshd.service - OpenSSH server daemon
       Loaded: loaded (/usr/lib/systemd/system/sshd.service; enabled)
       Active: active (running) since Fri 2015-07-17 09:13:55 CEST; 1
   weeks 0 days ago
    Main PID: 11880 (sshd)
      CGroup: /system.slice/sshd.service
              └─11880 /usr/sbin/sshd -D


   Jul 22 12:07:31 rhel7.mydomain.lan sshd[10340]: Accepted publickey
   for root...
   Jul 22 12:12:29 rhel7.mydomain.lan sshd[10459]: Accepted publickey
   for root...
   Jul 22 12:13:33 rhel7.mydomain.lan sshd[10473]: Accepted publickey
   for root...
   Jul 24 21:27:24 rhel7.mydomain.lan sshd[28089]: Accepted publickey
   for root...
   Hint: Some lines were ellipsized, use -l to show in full.
   ~]#
   ```

4. Now, start and stop the `systemd` services.

   To stop a `systemd` service, execute the following, substituting `<service>` with the name of the service:

   ```
   ~]# systemctl stop <service>
   ```

   Here's an example:

   ```
   ~]# systemctl stop sshd
   ```

   To start a `systemd` service, execute the following, substituting `<service>` with the name of the service:

   ```
   ~]# systemctl start <service>
   ```

Here's an example:

```
~]# systemctl start sshd
```

5. Next, enable and disable the `systemd` services.

   To enable a `systemd` service, execute the following, substituting `<service>` with the name of the service:

   ```
   ~]# systemctl enable <service>
   ```

   Here's an example:

   ```
   ~]# systemctl enable sshd
   ln -s '/usr/lib/systemd/system/sshd.service' '/etc/systemd/system/
   multi-user.target.wants/sshd.service'
   ~]#
   ```

   To disable a `systemd` service, execute the following, substituting `<service>` with the name of the service:

   ```
   ~]# systemctl disable <service>
   ```

   Here's an example:

   ```
   ~]# systemctl disable sshd
   rm '/etc/systemd/system/multi-user.target.wants/sshd.service'
   ~]#
   ```

6. Now, configure a service to restart when crashed.

   Let's make the `ntpd` service restart if it crashes after 1 minute.

   1. First, create the directory, as follows: `/etc/systemd/system/ntpd.service.d`.

      ```
      ~]# mkdir -p /etc/systemd/system/ntpd.service.d
      ```

   2. Create a new file in that directory named `restart.conf` and add the following to it:

      ```
      [Service]
      Restart=on-failure
      RestartSec=60s
      ```

   3. Next, reload the unit files and recreate the dependency tree using the following command:

      ```
      ~]# systemctl daemon-reload
      ```

   4. Finally, restart the `ntpd` service by executing the following command:

      ```
      ~]# systemctl restart ntpd
      ```

There's more...

When requesting the status of a service, the most recent log entries are also shown when executed as `root`.

The service status information can be seen in the following table:

Field	Description
Loaded	This provides information on whether the service is loaded and enabled. It also includes the absolute path to the service file.
Active	This provides information on whether the service is running, followed by the time it started.
Main PID	This provides PID of the corresponding service, followed by its name.
Status	This provides information about the corresponding service.
Process	This provides information about the related process.
Cgroup	This provides information about related control groups.

In some (rare) cases, you want to prevent a service from being started, either manually or by another service; there is an option to mask the service, which is as follows:

```
~]# systemctl mask <service>
```

To unmask, execute the following:

```
~]# systemctl unmask <service>
```

When modifying service unit files (and this is not limited to services only), it is best practice to copy the original service file, which is located at `/lib/systemd/system` to `/etc/systemd/service`. Alternatively, you can create a directory in `/etc/systemd/service` appended with `.d`, in which you will create `conf` files containing only the directives that you wish to add or change, as in the previous recipe. The advantage of the latter is that you don't need to keep up with changes in the original service file as it will be "updated" with whatever is located in the `service.d` directory.

See also

For more information about managing `systemd` services, go to `https://access.redhat.com/documentation/en-US/Red_Hat_Enterprise_Linux/7/html/System_Administrators_Guide/sect-Managing_Services_with_systemd-Services.html`.

Configuring the systemd journal for persistence

By default, the journal doesn't store log files on disk, only in memory or the `/run/log/journal` directory. This is sufficient for the recent log history (with the journal) but not for long-term log retention should you decide to go with journal only and not with any other `syslog` solution.

How to do it...

Configuring `journald` to keep more logs than memory allows is fairly simple, as follows:

1. Open `/etc/systemd/journald.conf` with your favorite text editor with root permissions by executing the following command:

   ```
   ~]# vim /etc/systemd/journald.conf
   ```

2. Ensure that the line containing `Storage` is either remarked or set to `auto` or `persistent` and save it, as follows:

   ```
   Storage=auto
   ```

3. If you select `auto`, the journal directory needs to be manually created. The following command would be useful for this:

   ```
   ~]# mkdir -p /var/log/journal
   ```

4. Now, restart the journal service by executing the following command:

   ```
   ~]# systemctl restart systemd-journald
   ```

There's more...

There are many other options that can be set for the journal daemon.

By default, all the data stored by `journald` is compressed, but you could disable this using `Compress=no`.

It is recommended to limit the size of the journal files by either specifying a maximum retention age (`MaxRetentionSec`), a global maximum size usage (`SystemMaxUse`), or a maximum size usage per file (`SystemMaxFileSize`).

See also

For more information about using the journal with RHEL 7, go to `https://access.redhat.com/documentation/en-US/Red_Hat_Enterprise_Linux/7/html/System_Administrators_Guide/s1-Using_the_Journal.html`.

Take a look at the man page for *journald (5)* for more information on what can be configured.

Monitoring services using journalctl

Systemd's journal has the added advantage that its controls allow you to easily narrow down on messages generated by specific services.

How to do it...

Here are the steps you need to perform for this recipe:

1. First, display all the messages generated by your system.

   This will show all the messages generated on the system; run the following commands:

   ```
   ~]# journalctl
   -- Logs begin at Fri 2015-06-26 23:37:30 CEST, end at Sat 2015-07-
   25 00:30:01 CEST. --
   Jun 26 23:37:30 rhel7.mydomain.lan systemd-journal[106]: Runtime
   journal is using 8.0M (max 396.0M, leaving 594.0M of free 3.8G,
   current limit 396.0M).
   Jun 26 23:37:30 rhel7.mydomain.lan systemd-journal[106]: Runtime
   journal is using 8.0M (max 396.0M, leaving 594.0M of free 3.8G,
   current limit 396.0M).
   Jun 26 23:37:30 rhel7.mydomain.lan kernel: Initializing cgroup
   subsys cpuset
   ...
   ~]#
   ```

2. Now, display all system-related messages.

   This command shows all the messages related to the system and not its users:

   ```
   ~]# journalctl --system
   -- Logs begin at Fri 2015-06-26 23:37:30 CEST, end at Sat 2015-07-
   25 00:30:01 CEST. --
   Jun 26 23:37:30 rhel7.mydomain.lan systemd-journal[106]: Runtime
   journal is using 8.0M (max 396.0M, leaving 594.0M of free 3.8G,
   current limit 396.0M).
   Jun 26 23:37:30 rhel7.mydomain.lan systemd-journal[106]: Runtime
   journal is using 8.0M (max 396.0M, leaving 594.0M of free 3.8G,
   current limit 396.0M).
   Jun 26 23:37:30 rhel7.mydomain.lan kernel: Initializing cgroup
   subsys cpuset
   ...
   ~]#
   ```

3. Display all the current user messages.

   This command shows all messages related to the user that you are logged on with:

   ```
   ~]# journalctl --user
   No journal files were found.
   ~]#
   ```

4. Next, display all messages generated by a particular service using the following command line:

   ```
   ~]# journalctl --unit=<service>
   ```

   Here's an example:

   ```
   ~]# journalctl --unit=sshd
   -- Logs begin at Fri 2015-06-26 23:37:30 CEST, end at Sat 2015-07-
   25 00:45:01 CEST. --
   Jun 26 23:40:18 rhel7.mydomain.lan systemd[1]: Starting OpenSSH
   server daemon...
   Jun 26 23:40:18 rhel7.mydomain.lan systemd[1]: Started OpenSSH
   server daemon.
   Jun 26 23:40:20 rhel7.mydomain.lan sshd[817]: Server listening on
   0.0.0.0 port 22.
   Jun 26 23:40:20 rhel7.mydomain.lan sshd[817]: Server listening on
   :: port 22.
   Jun 27 11:30:08 rhel7.mydomain.lan sshd[4495]: Accepted publickey
   for root from 10.0.0.2 port 42748 ssh2: RSA cf:8a:a0:b4:4c:3d:d7:4
   d:93:c6:e0:fe:c0:66:e4
   ...
   ~]#
   ```

5. Now, display messages by priority.

   Priorities can be specified by a keyword or number, such as debug (7), info (6), notice (5), warning (4), err (3), crit (2), alert (1), and emerg (0). When specifying a priority, this includes all the lower priorities as well. For example, err implies that crit, alert, and emerg are also shown. Take a look at the following command line:

   ```
   ~]# journalctl -p <priority>
   ```

   Here's an example:

   ```
   ~]# journalctl -p err
   -- Logs begin at Fri 2015-06-26 23:37:30 CEST, end at Fri 2015-07-
   24 22:30:01 CEST. --
   Jun 26 23:37:30 rhel7.mydomain.lan kernel: ioremap error for
   0xdffff000-0xe0000000, requested 0x10, got 0x0
   ```

```
Jun 26 23:38:49 rhel7.mydomain.lan systemd[1]: Failed unmounting /
usr.
...
~]#
```

6. Next, display messages by time.

   You can show all messages from the current boot through the following commands:

   ```
   ~]# journalctl -b
   -- Logs begin at Fri 2015-06-26 23:37:30 CEST, end at Sat 2015-07-
   25 00:45:01 CEST. --
   Jun 26 23:37:30 rhel7.mydomain.lan systemd-journal[106]: Runtime
   journal is using 8.0M (max 396.0M, leaving 594.0M of free 3.8G,
   current limit 396.0M).
   Jun 26 23:37:30 rhel7.mydomain.lan systemd-journal[106]: Runtime
   journal is using 8.0M (max 396.0M, leaving 594.0M of free 3.8G,
   current limit 396.0M).
   Jun 26 23:37:30 rhel7.mydomain.lan kernel: Initializing cgroup
   subsys cpuset
   Jun 26 23:37:30 rhel7.mydomain.lan kernel: Initializing cgroup
   subsys cpu
   Jun 26 23:37:30 rhel7.mydomain.lan kernel: Initializing cgroup
   subsys cpuacct
   Jun 26 23:37:30 rhel7.mydomain.lan kernel: Linux version 3.10.0-
   229.4.2.el7.x86_64 (gcc version 4.8.2 20140120 (Red Hat 4.8.2-
   Jun 26 23:37:30 rhel7.mydomain.lan kernel: Command line: BOOT_
   IMAGE=/vmlinuz-3.10.0-229.4.2.el7.x86_64 root=/dev/mapper/rhel7_
   system-root ro vconsole.keymap=
   Jun 26 23:37:30 rhel7.mydomain.lan kernel: e820: BIOS-provided
   physical RAM map:
   ~]#
   ```

   You can even show all the messages within a specific time range by running the following:

   ```
   ~]# journalctl --since="2015-07-24 08:00:00" --until="2015-07-24
   09:00:00"
   -- Logs begin at Fri 2015-06-26 23:37:30 CEST, end at Sat 2015-07-
   25 00:45:01 CEST. --
   Jul 24 08:00:01 rhel7.mydomain.lan systemd[1]: Created slice user-
   48.slice.
   Jul 24 08:00:01 rhel7.mydomain.lan systemd[1]: Starting Session
   3331 of user apache.
   J
   ```

```
. . .
Jul 24 08:45:01 rhel7.mydomain.lan systemd[1]: Starting Session
3335 of user apache.
Jul 24 08:45:01 rhel7.mydomain.lan systemd[1]: Started Session
3335 of user apache.
Jul 24 08:45:01 rhel7.mydomain.lan CROND[22909]: (apache) CMD (php
-f /var/lib/owncloud/cron.php)
~]#
```

There's more...

The examples presented in this recipe can all be combined. For instance, if you want to show all the error messages between 8:00 and 9:00 on 2015-07-24, your command would be the following:

```
~]# journalctl -p err --since="2015-07-24 08:00:00" --until="2015-07-24
09:00:00"
```

A lot of people tend to "follow" log files to determine what is happening, hoping to figure out any issues. The `journalctl` binary is an executable one, so it is impossible to use the traditional "following" techniques such as `tail -f` or using `less` and pressing *CTRL + F*. The good folks that coded `systemd` and `systemctl` have provided a solution to this: simply add `-f` or `--follow` as an argument to the `journalctl` command.

Although most environments are used to create `syslog` messages to troubleshoot, the journal does provide the added value of being able to create simple filters that allow you to monitor their messages live.

See also

For more information about using the journal with RHEL 7, go to `https://access.redhat.com/documentation/en-US/Red_Hat_Enterprise_Linux/7/html/System_Administrators_Guide/s1-Using_the_Journal.html`.

Take a look at the man page of *journalctl (1)* for more information on what can be configured.

Configuring logrotate

The `logrotate` tool allows you to rotate the logs that are generated by applications and scripts

It keeps your log directories clutter-free and minimizes disk usage when correctly configured.

How to do it...

The `logrotate` tool is installed by default, but I will include the installation instructions here for completeness. This recipe will show you how to rotate logs for `rsyslog`. We will rotate the logs everyday, add an extension based on the date, compress them with a one-day delay, and keep them for 365 days. Perform the following steps:

1. First, to install `logrotate`, perform the following command:

   ```
   ~]# yum install -y logrotate
   ```

2. Ensure that it's enabled through the following:

   ```
   ~]# systemctl restart crond
   ```

3. Open `/etc/logrotate.d/syslog` with your favorite editor. The contents of this file are the following, by default:

   ```
   /var/log/cron
   /var/log/maillog
   /var/log/messages
   /var/log/secure
   /var/log/spooler
   {
       sharedscripts
       postrotate
           /bin/kill -HUP `cat /var/run/syslogd.pid 2>
   /dev/null` 2> /dev/null || true
       endscript
   }
   ```

4. Now, replace this with the following code:

   ```
   /var/log/cron
   /var/log/maillog
   /var/log/messages
   /var/log/secure
   /var/log/spooler
   {
       compress
       daily
       delaycompress
       dateext
       missingok
       rotate 365
       sharedscripts
       postrotate
   ```

```
              /bin/kill -HUP `cat /var/run/syslogd.pid 2>
    /dev/null` 2> /dev/null || true
        endscript
    }
```

5. Finally, save the file.

How it works...

The `logrotate` tool is a script that is launched by cron everyday.

The directives added to the default `logrotate` definition are `compress`, `daily`, `delaycompress`, `dateext`, `missingok`, and `rotate`.

The `compress` directive compresses old versions of the log files with gzip. This behavior is somewhat changed by specifying `delaycompress`. This causes us to always have the most recently rotated log file available uncompressed.

The `daily` directive makes `logrotate` execute the definition every day. The `rotate` directive only keeps x rotated log files before deleting the oldest. In this case, we have specified this to be 365, which means that while rotating daily, the logs are kept for 365 days.

The `missingok` directive makes it alright for `syslog` to not create a file, which, however unlikely, is possible.

The `dateext` directive appends a date to the rotated file in the form of `yyyymmdd` instead of a number, which is the default.

There's more...

The `/etc/logrotate.conf` file contains the defaults directives for all definitions. If you don't specifically use a directive within a definition for a file, the values in this file will be used if specified.

It would make sense to change the settings in this file so that all the definitions are affected, but this is not practical; not all log files are made equal. The `syslog` service generates a lot of messages, and it would probably clutter up your system before long. However, yum, for instance, doesn't generate a lot of messages, and it keeps this log file readable for much longer than your `syslog` files. This, by the way, is reflected in the definition for yum.

If you want to debug your new configuration, this can be achieved by executing the following to test just one configuration:

```
~# /usr/sbin/logrotate -v /etc/logrotate.d/<config file>
```

Alternatively, you can use the following to test everything:

```
~]# /usr/sbin/logrotate -v /etc/logrotate.conf
```

Here's an example:

```
~]# /usr/sbin/logrotate -v /etc/logrotate.d/syslog
reading config file /etc/logrotate.d/syslog

Handling 1 logs

rotating pattern: /var/log/cron
/var/log/maillog
/var/log/messages
/var/log/secure
/var/log/spooler
 1048576 bytes (no old logs will be kept)
empty log files are rotated, old logs are removed
considering log /var/log/cron
  log does not need rotating
considering log /var/log/maillog
  log does not need rotating
considering log /var/log/messages
  log does not need rotating
considering log /var/log/secure
  log does not need rotating
considering log /var/log/spooler
  log does not need rotating
not running postrotate script, since no logs were rotated
~]#
```

See also

Take a look at the man page of *logrotate (8)* for more information on configuring logrotate.

Managing time

RHEL 7 comes preinstalled with Chrony. While everybody knows Ntpd, Chrony is a newcomer to the game of timekeeping.

Chrony is a set of programs that maintains the time on your computer using different time sources, such as NTP servers, your system's clock, and even custom-made scripts/programs. It also calculates the rate at which the computer loses or gains time to compensate while no external reference is present—for example, if your NTP server(s) is(are) down.

Chrony is a good solution for systems which are intermittently disconnected and reconnected to a network.

Ntpd should be considered for systems that are normally kept on permanently.

How to do it...

When talking about managing time in RHEL, it can be done through:

- Chrony
- Ntpd

We'll take a look at each of the methods separately.

Managing time through chrony

Ensure that `chrony` is installed and enabled, and perform the following steps:

1. First, install `chrony` through the following command:

   ```
   ~]# yum install -y chrony
   ```

2. Enable `chrony`, as follows:

   ```
   ~]# systemctl enable chrony
   ~]# systemctl start chrony
   ```

3. Now, open `/etc/chrony.conf` with your favorite editor and look for lines starting with the `server` directive using the following commands:

   ```
   server 0.rhel.pool.ntp.org iburst
   server 1.rhel.pool.ntp.org iburst
   server 2.rhel.pool.ntp.org iburst
   server 3.rhel.pool.ntp.org iburst
   ```

4. Next, replace these lines with NTP servers that are near you and save the file:

```
server 0.pool.ntp.mydomain.lan iburst
server 1.pool.ntp.mydomain.lan iburst
```

The `iburst` option causes NTP to send a burst of eight packets at the next poll instead of just one if the time master is unavailable, causing the NTP daemon to speed up time synchronization.

5. Finally, restart `chrony` by executing the following command:

```
~]# systemctl restart chrony
```

Managing time through ntpd

Ensure that `ntpd` is installed and enabled, and perform the following steps:

1. First, install `ntpd` by running the following:

```
~]# yum install -y ntpd
```

2. Enable `ntpd` through this command:

```
~]# systemctl enable ntpd
```

3. Open `/etc/ntp.conf` with your favorite editor and look for the lines starting with the `server` directive. Run the following:

```
server 0.rhel.pool.ntp.org iburst
server 1.rhel.pool.ntp.org iburst
server 2.rhel.pool.ntp.org iburst
server 3.rhel.pool.ntp.org iburst
```

4. Replace these lines with the NTP servers near you and save the file:

```
server 0.pool.ntp.mydomain.lan iburst
server 1.pool.ntp.mydomain.lan iburst
```

5. Replace the contents of `/etc/ntp/step-tickers` with all your NTP servers, one per line:

```
0.pool.ntp.mydomain.lan
1.pool.ntp.mydomain.lan
```

6. Now, restart `ntpd` by executing the following:

```
~]# systemctl restart ntpd
```

There's more...

While `ntpd` is the obvious choice for time synchronization, it doesn't fare well in environments where time masters are intermittently accessible (for whatever reason). In these environments, `chronyd` thrives. Also, `ntpd` can be quite complex to configure correctly, whereas `chronyd` is a little bit simpler.

The reason for modifying `/etc/ntp/step-tickers` when using the `ntpd` file is for the startup of the service. It uses `ntpdate` to synchronize time in one step before actually starting the NTP daemon itself, which is a lot slower in synchronizing time.

To figure out whether your system is synchronized, use the following command:

- For `chrony`, use the following command:

  ```
  ~]# chronyc sources
  ```

- For `ntpd`, run the following:

  ```
  ~]# ntpq -p
  ```

Your output will be similar to:

```
remote          refid       st t when poll reach   delay   offset  jitter
==========================================================================
 LOCAL(0)       .LOCL.       5 1  60m   64    0     0.000   0.000   0.000
*master.exam 178.32.44.208   3 u   35  128  377     0.214  -0.651  14.285
```

The asterisk (*) in front of an entry means that your system is synchronized to this remote system's clock.

See also

For more information on configuring `chrony` for RHEL 7, go to `https://access.redhat.com/documentation/en-US/Red_Hat_Enterprise_Linux/7/html/System_Administrators_Guide/ch-Configuring_NTP_Using_the_chrony_Suite.html`.

For more information on configuring `ntpd` for RHEL 7, go to `https://access.redhat.com/documentation/en-US/Red_Hat_Enterprise_Linux/7/html/System_Administrators_Guide/ch-Configuring_NTP_Using_ntpd.html`.

Configuring your boot environment

GRUB2 is the default boot loader for RHEL 7. By default, it doesn't use any fancy configuration options, but it is wise to at least secure your grub boot loader.

How to do it...

There are many advantages to having your grub and boot environment output to serial console in an enterprise environment. Many vendors integrate virtual serial ports in their remote control systems, as does KVM. This allows you to connect to the serial port and easily grab whatever is displayed in a text editor.

Setting a password on the GRUB2 boot loader mitigates possible hacking attempts on your system when you have physical access to the server or console. Perform the following steps for this recipe:

1. First, edit /etc/sysconfig/grub with your favorite editor.

2. Now, modify the GRUB_TERMINAL_OUTPUT line to include both console and serial access by executing the following command line:

    ```
    GRUB_TERMINAL_OUTPUT="console serial"
    ```

3. Add the GRUB_SERIAL_COMMAND entry, as follows:

    ```
    GRUB_SERIAL_COMMAND="serial --speed=9600 --unit=0 --word=8
    --parity=no -stop=1"
    ```

4. Now, save the file.

5. Create the /etc/grub.d/01_users file with the following contents:

    ```
    cat << EOF
    set superusers="root"
    password root SuperSecretPassword
    EOF
    ```

6. Next, update your grub configuration by running the following commands:

    ```
    ~]# grub2-mkconfig -o /boot/grub2/grub.cfg
    Generating grub configuration file ...
    Found linux image: /boot/vmlinuz-3.10.0-229.4.2.el7.x86_64
    Found initrd image: /boot/initramfs-3.10.0-229.4.2.el7.x86_64.img
    Found linux image: /boot/vmlinuz-3.10.0-229.1.2.el7.x86_64
    Found initrd image: /boot/initramfs-3.10.0-229.1.2.el7.x86_64.img
    Found linux image: /boot/vmlinuz-0-rescue-fe045089e49942cb97db6758
    92395bc8
    Found initrd image: /boot/initramfs-0-rescue-fe045089e49942cb97db6
    75892395bc8.img
    done
    ~]#
    ```

How it works...

The behavior of `grub2-mkconfig` is defined by the directives of the files in `/etc/grub.d`. These files, based on the configuration in `/etc/sysconfig/grub`, autogenerate all the menu entries in the `grub.cfg` file. You can modify its behavior by adding files with bash code in this directory.

For instance, you could add a script that would add a menu entry to boot from the CD/DVD ROM drive.

The user root, which is added to `/etc/grub.d/01_users`, is the only one allowed to edit menu entries from the console, mitigating the weakness in GRUB to force rescue mode by adding `1` or `rescue` at the end of the `kernel` line.

There's more...

The `grub2-mkconfig` command is specific for BIOS-based systems. In order to do the same on UEFI systems, modify the command as follows:

```
~]# grub2-mkconfig -o /boot/efi/EFI/redhat/grub.cfg
```

In order to access the GRUB terminal over the same serial connection, you need to specify an additional kernel option: `console=ttyS0,9600n8`.

You can either modify the kernel lines in `/boot/grub2/grub.cfg` (or `/boot/efi/EFI/redhat/grub.cfg` manually, but you do risk losing the change when your kernel is updated), or manually regenerate the file using `grub2-mkconfig`.

It's best to add it to the `GRUB_CMDLINE_LINUX` directive in `/etc/sysconfig/grub` and regenerate your `grub.cfg` file.

Passwords for GRUB users can be encrypted using the `grub2-mkpasswd-pbkdf2` command, as follows:

```
~]# grub2-mkpasswd-pbkdf2

Enter password:

Reenter password:

PBKDF2 hash of your password is grub.pbkdf2.sha512.10000.C208DD5E318B1D64
77C4E51035649C197411259C214D0B83E3E83753AD58F7676B62CDF48E31AF0E739844A5
CF9A95F76AF5008AF340336DB50ECA23906ECC13.9D20A66F0CADA12AA617B293B5BBF7
AAD44423ECA513F302FEBF5CB92A0DC54436E16D7CD6E09685323084A27462C2A981054
D52F452F5C2F71FBACD2C31AEFA

~]#
```

Then, you can substitute the clear text password in `/etc/grub.d/01_users` with the generated hash. Here's an example:

```
password root
grub.pbkdf2.sha512.10000.C208DD5E318B1D6477C4E51035649C197411259C2
14D0B83E3E83753AD58F7676B62CDF48E31AF0E739844A5CF9A95F76AF5008AF34
0336DB50ECA23906ECC13.9D20A66F0CADA12AA617B293B5BBF7AAD44423ECA513
F302FEBF5CB92A0DC54436E16D7CD6E09685323084A27462C2A981054D52F452F5
C2F71FBACD2C31AEFA
```

All the entries that are automatically generated are bootable but not editable from the console, unless you know the user and password. If you have custom menu entries and want to protect them in a similar way, add `--unrestricted` to the menu entry definition before the accolades. Here's an example:

```
menuentry 'My custom grub boot entry' <options> --unrestricted {
```

See also

For more information about working with the GRUB2 boot loader, go to `https://access.redhat.com/documentation/en-US/Red_Hat_Enterprise_Linux/7/html/System_Administrators_Guide/ch-Working_with_the_GRUB_2_Boot_Loader.html`.

Configuring smtp

Many programs use (or can be configured to use) SMTP to send messages about their status and so on. By default, postfix is configured to deliver all messages locally and not respond to incoming mails. If you have an environment of multiple servers, this can become quite tedious to log on to each server to check for new mail. This recipe will show you how to relay messages to a central mail relay or message store that also uses SMTP.

Postfix is installed by default on RHEL 7.

How to do it...

In this recipe, we'll combine several options:

- We'll allow the server to accept incoming mails
- We'll only allow the server to relay messages from recipients in the `mydomain.lan` domain
- We'll forward all mails to the `mailhost.mydomain.lan` mailserver

To complete this recipe, perform the following steps:

1. Edit `/etc/postfix/main.cf` with your favorite editor.

2. Modify `inet_interface` to accept mails on any interface through the following command:

   ```
   inet_interface = all
   ```

3. Add the `smtpd_recipient_restrictions` directive to only allow incoming mails from the `mydomain.lan` domain, as follows:

   ```
   smtpd_recipient_restrictions =
       check_sender_access hash:/etc/postfix/sender_access,
       reject
   ```

   As you can see, the last two lines are indented. The `postfix` considers this block as one line instead of three separate lines.

4. Add the `relayhost` directive to point to `mailhost.mydomain.lan`, as follows:

   ```
   relayhost = mailhost.mydomain.lan
   ```

5. Now, save the `postfix` file.

6. Create `/etc/postfix/sender_access` with the following contents:

   ```
   mydomain.lan OK
   ```

7. Next, hash the `/etc/postfix/access` file using the following command:

   ```
   ~]# postmap /etc/postfix/access
   ```

8. Finally, restart `postfix`, as follows:

   ```
   ~]# systemctl restart postfix
   ```

There's more...

To monitor your mail queue on the system, execute the following:

```
~]# postqueue -p
```

Whenever your mail relay cannot forward mails, it stores them locally and tries to resend them at a later time. When you restore the mailflow, you can flush the queue and attempt delivery by executing the following:

```
~]# postqueue -f
```

The kind of setup presented in this recipe is quite simple and assumes that you don't have malicious users on your network. There are software that allow you to mitigate spam and viruses. Popular solutions for this are `spamassassin` and `amavis`.

See also

For more information on using postfix with RHEL 7, go to `https://access.redhat.com/documentation/en-US/Red_Hat_Enterprise_Linux/7/html/System_Administrators_Guide/s1-email-mta.html#s2-email-mta-postfix`.

For more information on postfix, check out the postfix rpm (`rpm -ql postfix`) or go to `http://www.postfix.org/`. This site provides good documentation and *how to*'s for a large number of scenarios.

5
Using SELinux

Here is an overview of the recipes presented in this chapter:

- ► Changing file contexts
- ► Configuring SELinux booleans
- ► Configuring SELinux port definitions
- ► Troubleshooting SELinux
- ► Creating SELinux policies
- ► Applying SELinux policies

Introduction

SELinux is a Linux kernel module that allows supporting **mandatory access control** (MAC) security policies. The Red Hat implementation of SELinux combines **role-based access control** (**RBAC**) with **type enforcement** (**TE**). Optionally, **multilevel security** (**MLS**) is also available but isn't widely used as it implements fewer policies than the default Red Hat SELinux policies.

SELinux is enabled by default in RHEL 7 and supported for all software packaged by Red Hat.

The recipes presented in this chapter will not only provide you with a solid base to troubleshoot SELinux issues and fix them, but also a peek into how to create your own SELinux policies.

Changing file contexts

Files and processes are labeled with a SELinux context, which contains additional information about a SELinux user, role type, and level. This information is provided by the SELinux kernel module to make access control decisions.

The SELinux user, a unique identity known by the SELinux policy, is authorized for a number of roles.

SELinux roles, as we already alluded to before, are attributes of SELinux users and part of the RBAC SELinux policy. SELinux roles are authorized for SELinux domains.

SELinux types define the type for files and domain for processes. SELinux policies define access between types and other files and processes. By default, if there is no specific rule in the SELinux policy, access is denied.

The SELinux level is only used when the SELinux type is set to MLS and should be avoided altogether on anything other than servers. This set of policies doesn't cover the same domains as defined by the default Red Hat SELinux policy. The SELinux level is an attribute of MLS and **multi-category security (MCS)**.

Getting ready

All files and processes on a system are labeled to represent security-relevant information. This information is called the SELinux context. To view the contexts of files (and directories), execute the following:

```
~# ls -Z
-rw-r--r--. root root unconfined_u:object_r:admin_home_t:s0 file
~#
```

How to do it...

You can temporarily change the context of a file (or files) or permanently change their context. The first option allows easy troubleshooting if you need to figure out whether changing the context solves your problem. Persistent changes are mostly used when your applications refer to data that is not in the standard location—for example, if your web server serves data from /srv/www.

Temporary context changes

Temporary SELinux context changes remain until the file, or the filesystem that the file resides on, is relabeled.

To change the SELinux user of a file, execute the following:

```
~# chcon --user <SELinux user> <filename>
```

To change the SELinux role of a file, execute the following:

```
~# chcon --role <SELinux role> <filename>
```

To change the SELinux type of a file, execute the following:

```
~# chcon --type <SELinux typs> <filename>
```

Persistent file context changes

Changing the application data location doesn't automatically modify SELinux contexts to allow your application to access this data.

To permanently relabel files or directories, perform the following:

1. Change the SELinux user for your files or directories via this command:

   ```
   ~# semanage fcontext -a --seuser <SELinux user> <filename|dirname>
   ```

2. Change the SELinux type of your files or directories by running the following:

   ```
   ~# semanage fcontext -a --type <SELinux type> <filename|dirname>
   ```

3. Finish with this command line by applying the directive to the `files/directories`:

   ```
   ~# restorecon <filename|dirname>
   ```

There's more...

To show all the available SELinux users, execute the following:

~# **semanage user -l**

```
~]# semanage user -l

                Labeling   MLS/       MLS/
SELinux User    Prefix     MCS Level  MCS Range              SELinux Roles

guest_u         user       s0         s0                     guest_r
root            user       s0         s0-s0:c0.c1023         staff_r sysadm_r system_r unconfined_r
staff_u         user       s0         s0-s0:c0.c1023         staff_r sysadm_r system_r unconfined_r
sysadm_u        user       s0         s0-s0:c0.c1023         sysadm_r
system_u        user       s0         s0-s0:c0.c1023         system_r unconfined_r
unconfined_u    user       s0         s0-s0:c0.c1023         system_r unconfined_r
user_u          user       s0         s0                     user_r
xguest_u        user       s0         s0                     xguest_r
~]# []
```

Alternatively, you can install the `setools-console` package and run the following:

~# **seinfo -u**

```
~]# seinfo -u

Users: 8
   sysadm_u
   system_u
   xguest_u
   root
   guest_u
   staff_u
   user_u
   unconfined_u
~]# 
```

To show all the available SELinux types, install the `setools-console` package and run the following:

```
~# seinfo -t
```

```
~]# seinfo -t

Types: 4624
   bluetooth_conf_t
   cmirrord_exec_t
   colord_exec_t
   foghorn_exec_t
   jacorb_port_t
   pki_ra_exec_t
   pki_ra_lock_t
   sosreport_t
   squid_script_exec_t
   etc_runtime_t
   fenced_tmp_t
   git_session_t
   glance_port_t
   osad_log_t
   presence_port_t
   samba_secrets_t
   snort_exec_t
   sshd_sandbox_t
   audisp_var_run_t
   auditd_var_run_t
   blktap_var_run_t
   cfengine_execd_t
   cinder_var_lib_t
   cinder_var_run_t
   colord_var_lib_t
   comsat_var_run_t
   condor_var_lib_t
   condor_var_run_t
   conman_var_run_t
```

To show the available SELinux roles, install the `setools-console` package and run the following:

```
~# seinfo -r
```

```
~]# seinfo -r

Roles: 14
   auditadm_r
   dbadm_r
   guest_r
   staff_r
   user_r
   logadm_r
   object_r
   secadm_r
   sysadm_r
   system_r
   webadm_r
   xguest_r
   nx_server_r
   unconfined_r
~]# 
```

The `semanage` tool doesn't have an option to include all files recursively, but there is a solution to this. The filename or dirname you specify is actually a regular expression filter. So, for example, if you want to recursively include all the files in /srv/www, you could specify "/srv/www(/.*)?".

> For now, there's no way to change the SELinux role using `semanage`. A way to get around this is to change the SELinux user or type using `semanage` and then edit it, as follows: /etc/selinux/targeted/contexts/files/file_contexts.local.

Here's a wrong SELinux context example of an AVC denial report found in the `audit.log` file:

```
type=AVC msg=audit(1438884962.645:86): avc:  denied  { open } for
pid=1283 comm="httpd" path="/var/www/html/index.html" dev="dm-5"
ino=1089 scontext=system_u:system_r:httpd_t:s0
tcontext=system_u:object_r:user_home_t:s0 tclass=file
```

This command can be explained as follows:

Commands	Description
`type=AVC`	This is the log type
`msg=audit(1438884962.645:86)`	This is the log entry timestamp
`avc`	This is a repetition of the log type
`denied`	This states whether enforcing is enabled
`{ open }`	This is a permission that causes AVC denial
`for  pid=1283`	This is the process ID
`comm="httpd"`	This is the process command
`path="/var/www/html/index.html"`	This is the path that is accessed
`dev="dm-5"`	This blocks the device that the preceding file is located on
`ino=1089`	This is the inode of the preceding file
`scontext=system_u:system_r:httpd_t:s0`	This is the source SELinux context
`tcontext=system_u:object_r:user_home_t:s0`	This is the target SELinux context
`tclass=file`	This is the target SELinux class

See also

Refer to the man page for *chcon (1)* and *semanage-fcontext (8)* for more information.

Configuring SELinux booleans

SELinux booleans allow you to change the SELinux policy at runtime without the need to write additional policies. This allows you to change the policy without the need for recompilation, such as allowing services to access NFS volumes.

How to do it...

This is the way to temporarily or permanently change SELinux booleans.

Listing SELinux booleans

For a list of all booleans and an explanation of what they do, execute the following:

```
~# semanage boolean -l
```

```
~]# semanage boolean -l
SELinux boolean                         State  Default Description

ftp_home_dir                            (off  ,  off)  Allow ftp to home dir
smartmon_3ware                          (off  ,  off)  Allow smartmon to 3ware
mpd_enable_homedirs                     (off  ,  off)  Allow mpd to enable homedirs
xdm_sysadm_login                        (off  ,  off)  Allow xdm to sysadm login
xen_use_nfs                             (off  ,  off)  Allow xen to use nfs
mozilla_read_content                    (off  ,  off)  Allow mozilla to read content
ssh_chroot_rw_homedirs                  (off  ,  off)  Allow ssh to chroot rw homedirs
mount_anyfile                           (on   ,  on)   Allow mount to anyfile
cron_userdomain_transition              (on   ,  on)   Allow cron to userdomain transition
icecast_use_any_tcp_ports               (off  ,  off)  Allow icecast to use any tcp ports
openvpn_can_network_connect             (on   ,  on)   Allow openvpn to can network connect
zoneminder_anon_write                   (off  ,  off)  Allow zoneminder to anon write
minidlna_read_generic_user_content (off  ,  off)  Allow minidlna to read generic user content
spamassassin_can_network                (off  ,  off)  Allow spamassassin to can network
gluster_anon_write                      (off  ,  off)  Allow gluster to anon write
deny_ptrace                             (off  ,  off)  Allow deny to ptrace
selinuxuser_execmod                     (on   ,  on)   Allow selinuxuser to execmod
httpd_can_network_relay                 (off  ,  off)  Allow httpd to can network relay
openvpn_enable_homedirs                 (on   ,  on)   Allow openvpn to enable homedirs
glance_use_execmem                      (off  ,  off)  Allow glance to use execmem
telepathy_tcp_connect_generic_network_ports (on  ,  on)  Allow telepathy to tcp connect generic network ports
httpd_can_connect_mythtv                (off  ,  off)  Allow httpd to can connect mythtv
unconfined_mozilla_plugin_transition (on  ,  on)  Allow unconfined to mozilla plugin transition
saslauthd_read_shadow                   (off  ,  off)  Allow saslauthd to read shadow
tor_bind_all_unreserved_ports           (off  ,  off)  Allow tor to bind all unreserved ports
httpd_can_network_connect_db            (off  ,  off)  Allow httpd to can network connect db
use_ecryptfs_home_dirs                  (off  ,  off)  Allow use to ecryptfs home dirs
postgresql_can_rsync                    (off  ,  off)  Allow postgresql to can rsync
```

Now, let's try to get the value of a particular SELinux boolean. It is possible to get the value of a single SELinux boolean without the use of additional utilities, such as **grep** and/or **awk**. Simply execute the following:

```
~# getsebool <SELinux boolean>
```

This shows you whether or not the boolean is set. Here's an example:

```
~# getsebool virt_use_nfs
virt_use_nfs --> off
~#
```

Changing SELinux booleans

To set a boolean value to a particular one, use the following command:

```
~# setsebool <SELinux boolean> <on|off>
```

Here's an example command:

```
~# setsebool virt_use_nfs on
```

This command allows you to change the value of the boolean, but it is not persistent across reboots. To allow persistence, add the `-P` option to the command line, as follows:

```
~# setsebool -P virt_use_nfs on
```

There's more...

If you would like a list of all the bare bones of SELinux booleans and their values, `getsebool -a` is an alternative, as follows:

```
~# getsebool -a
```

```
~]# getsebool -a | head -n32
abrt_anon_write --> off
abrt_handle_event --> off
abrt_upload_watch_anon_write --> on
antivirus_can_scan_system --> off
antivirus_use_jit --> off
auditadm_exec_content --> on
authlogin_nsswitch_use_ldap --> off
authlogin_radius --> off
authlogin_yubikey --> off
awstats_purge_apache_log_files --> off
boinc_execmem --> on
cdrecord_read_content --> off
cluster_can_network_connect --> off
cluster_manage_all_files --> off
cluster_use_execmem --> off
cobbler_anon_write --> off
cobbler_can_network_connect --> off
cobbler_use_cifs --> off
cobbler_use_nfs --> off
collectd_tcp_network_connect --> off
condor_tcp_network_connect --> off
conman_can_network --> off
cron_can_relabel --> off
cron_system_cronjob_use_shares --> off
cron_userdomain_transition --> on
cups_execmem --> off
cvs_read_shadow --> off
daemons_dump_core --> off
daemons_enable_cluster_mode --> off
daemons_use_tcp_wrapper --> off
daemons_use_tty --> off
```

Managing SELinux booleans can be rather complex as there are a lot of booleans, and their names are not always simple to remember. For this reason, the setsebool, getsebool, and semanage tools come with tab completion. So, whenever you type any boolean name, you can use the tab key to complete or display the possible options.

Here's an example of an AVC denial report found in the audit.log file that can be solved by enabling a boolean:

```
type=AVC msg=audit(1438884483.053:48): avc:  denied  { open } for
pid=1270 comm="httpd" path="/nfs/www/html/index.html" dev="0:38"
ino=2717909250 scontext=system_u:system_r:httpd_t:s0
tcontext=system_u:object_r:nfs_t:s0 tclass=file
```

This is an example of a service (httpd in this case) accessing a file located on an NFS share, which is disabled by default.

This can be allowed by setting the httpd_use_nfs boolean to "on".

Configuring SELinux port definitions

SELinux also controls access to your TCP/IP ports. If your application is confined by SELinux, it will also deny access to your ports when starting up the application.

This recipe will show you how to detect which ports are used by a particular SELinux type and change it.

How to do it...

Let's allow the HTTP daemon to listen on the nonstandard port 82 through the following steps:

1. First, look for the ports that are accessed by HTTP via these commands:

    ```
    ~# semanage port -l |grep http
    http_cache_port_t              tcp       8080, 8118, 8123, 10001-
    10010
    http_cache_port_t              udp       3130
    http_port_t                    tcp       80, 81, 443, 488, 8008,
    8009, 8443, 9000
    pegasus_http_port_t            tcp       5988
    pegasus_https_port_t           tcp       5989
    ~#
    ```

    The SELinux port assignment we're looking for is http_port_t. As you can see, only the displayed ports (80, 81, 443, 488, 8008, 8009, 8443, and 9000) are allowed to be used to listen on by any process that is allowed to use the http_port_t type.

2. Add port `82` to the list of allowed ports, as follows:

```
~# semanage port -a -t http_port_t -p tcp 82
~#
```

3. Next, verify the port assignment, as follows:

```
~# semanage port -l |grep ^http_port_t
http_port_t                        tcp        82, 80, 81, 443, 488,
8008, 8009, 8443, 9000
~#
```

There's more...

In this example, there is reference to the HTTP daemon as the SELinux policy governing HTTP daemons is implemented not only for the Apache web server, but also for Nginx. So, as long as you use the packages provided by Red Hat, the SELinux policies will be used correctly.

Take a look at the following example of an AVC denial report found in the `audit.log` file that is caused because the domain is not allowed to access a certain port:

```
type=AVC msg=audit(1225948455.061:294): avc: denied { name_bind }
for pid=4997 comm="httpd" src=82
scontext=unconfined_u:system_r:httpd_t:s0
tcontext=system_u:object_r:port_t:s0 tclass=tcp_socket
```

This AVC denial shows that the `httpd` daemon attempted to listen (`name_bind`) on port `82` but was prohibited by SELinux.

Troubleshooting SELinux

Troubleshooting SELinux is not as straightforward as it may seem as at the time of writing this book, there is no integration with SELinux to return SELinux-related events back to the applications. Usually, you will find that access is denied with no further description of it in log files.

Getting ready

Make sure that `setroubleshoot-server` and `setools-console` are installed by executing the following command:

```
~# yum install -y setroubleshoot-server setools-console
```

If you have X server installed on your system, you can also install the GUI, as follows:

```
~# yum install -y setroubleshoot
```

Make sure that `auditd`, `rsyslog`, and `setroubleshootd` are installed and running before reproducing the issue.

How to do it...

There are several ways to detect SELinux issues.

This is a classic issue where the SELinux context of a file is incorrect, causing the application trying to access the file to fail.

In this case, the context of `/var/www/html/index.html` is set to `system_u:object_r:user_home_t:s0` instead of `system_u:object_r:httpd_sys_content_t:s0`, causing `httpd` to throw a `404`. Take a look at the following command:

```
# ls -Z /var/www/html/index.html

-rw-r--r--. apache apache system_u:object_r:user_home_t:s0 /var/www/html/
index.html

~#
```

audit.log

Use the following command to look for denied or failed entries in the audit log:

```
~# egrep 'avc.*denied' /var/log/audit/audit.log

ype=AVC msg=audit(1438884962.645:86): avc:  denied  { open } for
pid=1283 comm="httpd" path="/var/www/html/index.html" dev="dm-5" ino=1089
scontext=system_u:system_r:httpd_t:s0 tcontext=system_u:object_r:user_
home_t:s0 tclass=file

~#
```

syslog

You can look for SELinux messages in `/var/log/messages` via the following command:

```
~# grep 'SELinux is preventing' /var/log/messages

Aug  6 20:16:03 localhost setroubleshoot: SELinux is preventing /usr/
sbin/httpd from read access on the file index.html. For complete SELinux
messages., run sealert -l dc544bde-2d7e-4f3f-8826-224d9b0c71f6

Aug 6 20:16:03 localhost python: SELinux is preventing /usr/sbin/httpd
from read access on the file index.html.

~#
```

ausearch

Use the audit search tool to find SELinux errors, as follows:

```
~# ausearch -m avc

time->Thu Aug  6 20:16:02 2015

type=SYSCALL msg=audit(1438884962.645:86): arch=c000003e syscall=2
success=yes exit=25 a0=7f1bcfb65670 a1=80000 a2=0 a3=0 items=0 ppid=1186
pid=1283 auid=4294967295 uid=48 gid=48 euid=48 suid=48 fsuid=48 egid=48
sgid=48 fsgid=48 tty=(none) ses=4294967295 comm="httpd" exe="/usr/sbin/
httpd" subj=system_u:system_r:httpd_t:s0 key=(null)

type=AVC msg=audit(1438884962.645:86): avc:  denied  { open } for
pid=1283 comm="httpd" path="/var/www/html/index.html" dev="dm-5" ino=1089
scontext=system_u:system_r:httpd_t:s0 tcontext=system_u:object_r:user_
home_t:s0 tclass=file

type=AVC msg=audit(1438884962.645:86): avc:  denied  { read } for
pid=1283 comm="httpd" name="index.html" dev="dm-5" ino=1089 scontext=s
ystem_u:system_r:httpd_t:s0 tcontext=system_u:object_r:user_home_t:s0
tclass=file

~#
```

Once we restore the context of `/var/www/html/index.html` to its original, the file is accessible again. Take a look at the following commands:

```
~# restorecon /var/www/html/index.html

~# ls -Z /var/www/html/index.html

-rw-r--r--. apache apache system_u:object_r:httpd_sys_content_t:s0 /var/
www/html/index.html

~#
```

There's more...

It's not always easy to determine whether a file has the correct context. To view the actual SELinux context and compare it to what it should be without modifying anything, execute this command:

```
~# matchpathcon -V index.html

index.html has context system_u:object_r:user_home_t:s0, should be
system_u:object_r:httpd_sys_content_t:s0

~#
```

This tells you what the current context is and what it should be.

As you can see in the preceding syslog example, the output comes with the following command:

```
... run sealert -l dc544bde-2d7e-4f3f-8826-224d9b0c71f6
```

This command provides you with a richer description of the problem:

```
~# sealert -l dc544bde-2d7e-4f3f-8826-224d9b0c71f6
SELinux is preventing /usr/sbin/httpd from read access on the file index.
html.


***** Plugin catchall_boolean (89.3 confidence) suggests
******************


If you want to allow httpd to read user content
Then you must tell SELinux about this by enabling the 'httpd_read_user_
content' boolean.
You can read 'None' man page for more details.
Do
setsebool -P httpd_read_user_content 1


***** Plugin catchall (11.6 confidence) suggests
**************************


If you believe that httpd should be allowed read access on the index.html
file by default.
Then you should report this as a bug.
You can generate a local policy module to allow this access.
Do
allow this access for now by executing:
# grep httpd /var/log/audit/audit.log | audit2allow -M mypol
# semodule -i mypol.pp



Additional Information:
Source Context              system_u:system_r:httpd_t:s0
Target Context              system_u:object_r:user_home_t:s0
Target Objects              index.html [ file ]
Source                      httpd
```

Source Path	/usr/sbin/httpd
Port	<Unknown>
Host	localhost.localdomain
Source RPM Packages	httpd-2.4.6-31.el7.rhel.x86_64
Target RPM Packages	
Policy RPM	selinux-policy-3.13.1-23.el7_1.7.noarch
Selinux Enabled	True
Policy Type	targeted
Enforcing Mode	Permissive
Host Name	localhost.localdomain
Platform	Linux localhost.localdomain
	3.10.0-229.4.2.el7.x86_64 #1 SMP Wed May 13
	10:06:09 UTC 2015 x86_64 x86_64
Alert Count	1
First Seen	2015-08-06 20:16:02 CEST
Last Seen	2015-08-06 20:16:02 CEST
Local ID	dc544bde-2d7e-4f3f-8826-224d9b0c71f6

Raw Audit Messages

```
type=AVC msg=audit(1438884962.645:86): avc:  denied  { read } for
pid=1283 comm="httpd" name="index.html" dev="dm-5" ino=1089 scontext=s
ystem_u:system_r:httpd_t:s0 tcontext=system_u:object_r:user_home_t:s0
tclass=file
```

```
type=AVC msg=audit(1438884962.645:86): avc:  denied  { open } for
pid=1283 comm="httpd" path="/var/www/html/index.html" dev="dm-5" ino=1089
scontext=system_u:system_r:httpd_t:s0 tcontext=system_u:object_r:user_
home_t:s0 tclass=file
```

```
type=SYSCALL msg=audit(1438884962.645:86): arch=x86_64 syscall=open
success=yes exit=ENOTTY a0=7f1bcfb65670 a1=80000 a2=0 a3=0 items=0
ppid=1186 pid=1283 auid=4294967295 uid=48 gid=48 euid=48 suid=48 fsuid=48
egid=48 sgid=48 fsgid=48 tty=(none) ses=4294967295 comm=httpd exe=/usr/
sbin/httpd subj=system_u:system_r:httpd_t:s0 key=(null)
```

```
Hash: httpd,httpd_t,user_home_t,file,read
~#
```

This will actually give you more details about the problem at hand, and it will also make a couple of suggestions. Of course, in this case, the real solution is to restore the SELinux context of the file.

If you have installed a graphical desktop environment, you will get a notification each time your system encounters an "AVC denied" alert:

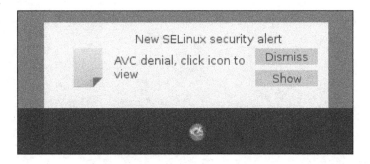

Clicking on the icon will present you with the following dialog:

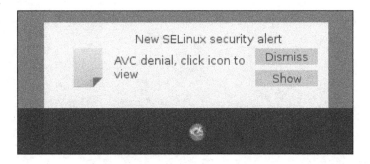

Clicking on the **Troubleshoot** button will provide you with additional information and a (or multiple) possible solution(s) for your problem, as shown in the following screenshot:

In this case, the first option (the one marked with a green line) is the correct solution.

Some AVC denial messages may not be logged when SELinux denies access. Applications and libraries regularly probe for more access than is actually required to perform their tasks. In order to not flood the audit logs with these kinds of messages, the policy can silence the AVC denials that are without permissions using `dontaudit` rules. The downside of this is that it may make troubleshooting SELinux denials more difficult.

To disable the `dontaudit` rules, execute the following command:

```
~# semanage dontaudit off
```

This will disable the `dontaudit` rules and rebuild the SELinux policy.

It is advisable to reenable the `dontaudit` rules when you're done troubleshooting as this may flood your disks. You can do this by executing the following command:

```
~# semanage dontaudit on
```

To get a full list of `dontaudit` rules, run the following:

```
~# sesearch --dontaudit
Found 8361 semantic av rules:
```

```
    dontaudit user_ssh_agent_t user_ssh_agent_t : udp_socket listen ;
    dontaudit openshift_user_domain sshd_t : key view ;
    dontaudit user_seunshare_t user_seunshare_t : process setfscreate ;
    dontaudit ftpd_t selinux_config_t : dir { getattr search open } ;
    dontaudit user_seunshare_t user_seunshare_t : capability sys_module ;
    dontaudit xguest_dbusd_t xguest_dbusd_t : udp_socket listen ;
    dontaudit tuned_t tuned_t : process setfscreate ;
...
~#
```

If you know the domain that you wish to check for `dontaudit` rules, add the `-s` argument followed by the domain, as shown here:

```
~# sesearch --dontaudit -s httpd_t
Found 182 semantic av rules:
    dontaudit httpd_t snmpd_var_lib_t : file { ioctl read write getattr
lock open } ;
    dontaudit domain rpm_var_lib_t : file { ioctl read write getattr lock
append } ;
    dontaudit httpd_t snmpd_var_lib_t : dir { ioctl read getattr lock
search open } ;
    dontaudit domain rpm_var_lib_t : dir getattr ;
    dontaudit httpd_t snmpd_var_lib_t : lnk_file { read getattr } ;
...
~#
```

See also

Take a look at the man page for *ausearch (8)*, *matchpathcon (8)*, and *sealert (8)* for more information.

Creating SELinux policies

In some cases, you'll need to create a new SELinux policy—for instance, when installing a piece of software from source. Although I do not recommend installing software from source on enterprise systems, this is sometimes your only option for company-developed software.

It is then time to create your own SELinux policy.

Getting ready

For this recipe, you need to have `policycoreutils-python` installed.

How to do it...

We'll use the `denied` entries in the `audit.log` log file to build our SELinux policy with `audit2allow`.

In this recipe, we'll use the same example as in the previous recipe: the SELinux context of `/var/www/html/index.html` that is changed to `system_u:object_r:user_home_t:s0`. Perform the following steps:

1. First, create a human readable policy for verification via the following command:

   ```
   ~# egrep 'avc.*denied' /var/log/audit/audit.log |audit2allow -m
   example_policy

   module example_policy 1.0;

   require {
           type httpd_t;
           type user_home_t;
           class file { read open };
   }

   #============= httpd_t ==============

   #!!!! This avc can be allowed using the boolean 'httpd_read_user_
   content'
   allow httpd_t user_home_t:file { read open };
   ~#
   ```

2. When this policy is validated, you can create a compiled SELinux policy file, as follows:

   ```
   egrep 'avc.*denied' /var/log/audit/audit.log |audit2allow -M
   example_policy
   ******************** IMPORTANT ***********************
   To make this policy package active, execute:

   semodule -i example_policy.pp
   ~#
   ```

How it works...

When you generate a module package, two files are created: a type enforcement file (`.te`) and a policy package file (`.pp`) file. The `te` file is the human readable policy as generated using `audit2allow -m`.

The `pp` file is the SELinux policy module package, which will later be used to enable the new policy.

There's more...

If you believe you have discovered a bug in an existing SELinux policy, you'll need to produce a type enforcing and policy package file to report with Red Hat Bugzilla.

It's important to make sure that you only parse the correct `AVC denial` entries with `audit2allow` as it may result in more access than required. It's a good idea to pipe the `AVC denial` entries to a temporary file and remove what is not needed before you parse the file with `audit2allow`.

If the policy you generate in this way is not exactly what you need, you can always edit the generated `te` policy file, and when you're done, compile a new policy file using the `te` policy file. You can do this as follows:

1. Build a binary policy module out of the policy file through this command:

    ```
    ~# checkmodule -M -m -o example_policy.mod example_policy.te
    checkmodule:  loading policy configuration from example_policy.te
    checkmodule:  policy configuration loaded
    checkmodule:  writing binary representation (version 17) to
    example_policy.mod
    ~#
    ```

2. Create the SELinux policy module package by executing the following:

    ```
    ~# semodule_package -o example_policy.pp -m example_policy.mod
    ~#
    ```

See also

Take a look at the man page for *audit2allow(1)* for more options on creating a policy

To report bugs, go to `https://bugzilla.redhat.com/`.

Applying SELinux policies

We've learned how to create SELinux policies in the previous recipe. This recipe will show you how to apply your newly created SELinux policies.

Getting ready

In order to apply a policy, we need a policy package file (`pp`). This can be obtained by parsing AVC denials to `audit2allow` or compiling your own policy package file, as explained in the *Create SELinux policies* recipe.

How to do it...

Follow these steps:

1. Activate the policy (this can take quite a while, depending on the number of policies applied to your system) by running the following command:

    ```
    ~# semodule -i example_policy.pp
    ~#
    ```

2. Next, verify that the policy is actually activated via these commands:

    ```
    ~# semodule -l |grep example_policy
    example_policy  1.0
    ~#
    ```

How it works...

When executing the `semodule` command, the policy file is copied to `/etc/selinux/targeted/modules/active/modules/`, and the complete SELinux policy is recompiled and applied.

> [Be careful when applying custom-made policies as these may allow more access than required!]

There's more...

To remove policies, execute the following command:

```
~# semodule -r example_policy
~#
```

This is particularly practical when you want to test the effect with and without the policy.

There's also a way to upgrade the module without removing it first, which is as follows:

```
~# semodule -u example_policy
~#
```

See also

Refer to the man page for *semodule (8)* for more information.

6

Orchestrating with Ansible

In this chapter, the following recipes will be addressed:

- ▶ Installing Ansible
- ▶ Configuring the Ansible inventory
- ▶ Creating the template for a kickstart file
- ▶ Creating a playbook to deploy a new VM with kickstart
- ▶ Creating a playbook to perform system configuration tasks
- ▶ Troubleshooting Ansible

Introduction

Ansible is an easy-to-use agentless system configuration management tool. It allows us to deploy complex configurations without the hassle of a complex interface or language.

Ansible uses playbooks, which are collections of tasks to deploy configurations and applications to multiple nodes over SSH in a controlled way. However, it doesn't stop there.

Ansible's modules, which are used to execute tasks, are all built to be idempotent in their execution.

The definition of Idempotence, according to Wikipedia, is as follows:

> *Idempotence (/ˌaɪdɪmˈpoʊtəns/ eye-dəm-poh-təns [citation needed]) is the property of certain operations in mathematics and computer science that can be applied multiple times without changing the result beyond the initial application.*

In short, any module will detect the changes to be applied and perform them. If it doesn't need to change anything, it will not reapply the requested changes or interfere with file metadata.

The Ansible company also provides Tower, a paid subscription with extra features, as an add-on to Ansible. Tower provides a graphical interface to control your Ansible orchestration tool. However, this is out of the scope of this chapter.

Install Ansible

Ansible is not in the default RHEL 7 repositories, but in this recipe, I will show you how to install it in several ways.

Getting ready

Ansible needs the following packages installed:

- ▶ Python v2.7 (Ansible doesn't support v3 yet)
- ▶ `python-httplib2`
- ▶ `python-jinja2`
- ▶ `python-paramiko`
- ▶ `python-setuptools`
- ▶ `PyYAML`

So, in order to achieve this, execute the following command:

```
~]# yum install -y python-httplib2 python-jinja2 python-keyczar python-
paramiko python-setuptools PyYAML
```

As RHEL 7 and some other major distributions come preinstalled with Python (yum requires it, as do most of the Red Hat tools), we don't have to include it in the preceding command.

How to do it...

In this recipe, I will cover the three most used methods of installing Ansible.

Installing the latest tarball

This method is quite simple as you just download the tarball and extract it in a location of your choosing. Perform the following steps:

1. Grab the latest tarball located at `http://releases.ansible.com/ansible/` via the following command:

    ```
    ~]$ curl -o /tmp/ansible-latest.tar.gz http://releases.ansible.
    com/ansible/ansible-latest.tar.gz
    ```

```
  % Total    % Received % Xferd  Average Speed   Time    Time
Time   Current

                                  Dload  Upload   Total   Spent
Left   Speed
100  905k  100  905k    0     0   870k      0  0:00:01  0:00:01
--:--:--   870k
~]$
```

2. Extract the tarball to /opt, as follows:

```
~]# tar zxf /tmp/ansible-latest.tar.gz -C /opt/
```

3. Now, create a symbolic link for easy access using this command:

```
~]# ln -s /opt/ansible-1.9.2 /opt/ansible
```

4. Add the Ansible binaries and man pages to your environment's path by executing the following:

```
~]# cat << EOF > /etc/profile.d/ansible.sh
# Ansible-related stuff
export ANSIBLE_HOME=/opt/ansible
export PATH=\${PATH-""}:${ANSIBLE_HOME}/bin
export MANPATH=\${MANPATH-""}:${ANSIBLE_HOME}/docs/man
export PYTHONPATH=\${PYTHONPATH-""}:${ ANSIBLE_HOME}/lib
EOF
~]#
```

5. Next, source the Ansible PATH and MANPATH by running this command line:

```
~]# . /etc/profile.d/ansible.sh
```

6. Finally, use the following command to regenerate the man pages:

```
~]# /etc/cron.daily/man-db.cron
```

Installing cutting edge from Git

Git makes keeping your local copy of Ansible up to date quite simple.

It automatically updates/removes files where needed. Perform the following steps:

1. Make sure git is installed using this command:

```
~]# yum install -y git
```

2. Clone the Ansible `git` repository to `/opt`, as follows:

   ~]# **cd /opt**

   ~]# **git clone git://github.com/ansible/ansible.git --recursive**

3. Add the Ansible binaries and man pages to your environment's path, through the following command:

   ~]# **cat << EOF > /etc/profile.d/ansible.sh**

   # Ansible-related stuff

   export ANSIBLE_HOME=/opt/ansible

   export PATH=\\${PATH-""}:${ANSIBLE_HOME}/bin

   export MANPATH=\\${MANPATH-""}:${ANSIBLE_HOME}/docs/man

   export PYTHONPATH=\\${PYTHONPATH-""}:${ ANSIBLE_HOME}/lib

   EOF

   ~]#

4. Now, source the Ansible PATH and MANPATH via this command:

   ~]# **. /etc/profile.d/ansible.sh**

5. Finally, using the following line, regenerate the man pages:

   ~]# **/etc/cron.daily/man-db.cron**

Installing Ansible from the EPEL repository

Installing from a repository has the advantage that you can keep your version of Ansible up to date along with your system. Here are the steps you need to perform:

1. Install the extra packages for the **Enterprise Linux** (**EPEL**) repository from `https://fedoraproject.org/wiki/EPEL` via this command:

   ```
   ~]# yum install -y https://dl.fedoraproject.org/pub/epel/epel-release-latest-7.noarch.rpm
   ```

2. Now, install Ansible using yum, as follows:

   ```
   ~]# yum install -y ansible
   ```

There's more...

If you want to keep your Git clone up to date, remember that the sources tree also contains two subtrees. You'll have to execute the following:

```
~]# git pull --release
~]# git submodule update --init --recursive
```

Configuring the Ansible inventory

The Ansible inventory is the heart of the product as it provides a lot of variables about your environment to the deployment mechanism. These variables are known as `facts` and serve Ansible to make decisions, template text-based files, and so on.

How to do it...

There are several ways of adding information about your environment to your inventory.

The static inventory file

The static inventory is basically a mini-formatted file containing the definitions for hosts and groups. Here's what you need to do:

1. Create `/etc/ansible/hosts` with the following contents:

   ```
   ~]# cat << EOF >> /etc/ansible/hosts
   localhost          ansible_connection=local
   srv1.domain.tld    ansible_connection=ssh ansible_ssh_user=root

   [mail]
   ```

```
mail[01..50].domain.tld


[mail:vars]
dns_servers=[ '8.8.8.8', '8.8.4.4' ]
mail_port=25
EOF
~]#
```

The dynamic inventory file

The dynamic inventory file has to be an executable file, generating a JSON string containing information about your hosts and groups. Follow these steps::

1. Create an ~/inventory.py script with the following contents:

```
-]# cat << EOF >> ~/inventory.py
#!/usr/bin/python -tt
# -*- coding: utf-8 -*-
# vim: tabstop=8 expandtab shiftwidth=4 softtabstop=4
import json


def main():
    inventory = {
        '_meta': {
            'hostvars': {
                'localhost': {
                    'ansible_connection': 'local' },
                'srv1.domain.tld': {
                    'ansible_connection': 'ssh',
                    'ansible_ssh_user': 'root' },
                }
            },
        'all': {
            'hosts': [
                'localhost',
                'srv1.domain.tld' ] },
        'mail': {
            'hosts': [],
            'vars': {
```

```
                        'dns_servers': [ '8.8.8.8', '8.8.4.4' ],
                        'mail_port': 25} }
            }


            for x in range(1,50):
                hostname = 'mail' + ('00%d' % x)[-2:] + '.domain.tld'
                inventory['_meta']['hostvars'].update({ hostname: {} })
                inventory['mail']['hosts'].append(hostname)




            print json.dumps(inventory, sort_keys=True, indent=4,
        separators=(',',': '))


        if __name__ == '__main__':
            main()
        ~]#
```

2. Now, make the script executable, as follows:

```
~]# chmod +x ~/inventory.py
```

host_vars files

A host_vars file is a yml-formatted one containing extra facts, which will only be applied to the host with the same name as the file. Simply do the following:

1. Create a host_vars file for srv1.domain.tld through this command:

```
~]# cat << EOF >> ~/host_vars/srv1.domain.tld.yml
ansible_connection: ssh
ansible_ssh_user: root
EOF
~]#
```

group_vars files

Like `host_vars`, `group_vars` files are `yml`-formatted ones containing extra facts. These will be applied to the group with the same name as the file. Perform the following:

1. Create a `group_vars` file for mail via the following command:

```
~]# cat << EOF >> ~/group_vars/mail.yml
dns_servers: [ '8.8.8.8', '8.8.4.4' ]
mail_port: 25
EOF
~]#
```

How it works...

The inventory file location is set in the Ansible configuration file—look for the line starting with `hostfile` within the `defaults` section. This file is either a static file, or a script returning a JSON-formatted list of hosts and groups, as shown in the preceding recipe. Ansible automatically detects whether a file is a script and treats it this way to import information.

There is one caveat, however: the script needs to show the JSON-formatted information by specifying `--list`.

Ansible can automatically combine the inventory with the `host_vars` and `group_vars` files if the latter two directories are in the same directory as the inventory file / script. Take a look at the following:

```
/etc/ansible/hosts
/etc/ansible/host_vars
/etc/ansible/host_vars/srv1.domain.tld.yml
/etc/ansible/host_vars/...
/etc/ansible/group_vars
/etc/ansible/group_vars/mail.yml
/etc/ansible/group_vars/...
```

The same can be achieved by putting the `host_vars` and `group_vars` directories in the same directory as the playbook you are executing.

> The facts in `host_vars` and `group_vars` take priority over the variables returned through the inventory.

There's more...

Ansible already seeds the inventory with the facts that it retrieves from the host itself. You can easily find out which facts Ansible prepares for your use by executing the following command:

```
~]# ansible -m setup <hostname>
```

This will produce a lengthy JSON-formatted output with all the facts Ansible knows about your destination host.

If you want even more information, on RHEL systems, you can install `redhat-lsb-core` to have access to LSB-specific facts.

Enterprises tend to have databases containing information regarding all their systems for change management. This is an excellent source for the inventory script to get its information.

See also

If you want more detailed information about the Ansible inventory, go to `http://docs.ansible.com/ansible/intro_inventory.html`.

Shameless self-promotion for a personal project and a tool to automate the inventory calls for a mention of `https://github.com/bushvin/inventoryd/`.

Creating a template for a kickstart file

A `template` is one of the core modules of Ansible. It is used to easily generate files (for example, configuration files) based on a common set of facts. It uses the Jinja2 template engine to interpret template files.

For this recipe, we'll use a simple `kickstart` script that is generic enough to deploy any host. Refer to *Chapter 2, Deploying RHEL "En Masse"*, to find out about `kickstart` files.

Getting ready

The facts that we need for this host are `repo_url`, `root_password_hash`, `ntp_servers`, `timezone`, `ipv4_address`, `ipv4_netmask`, `ipv4_gateway`, and `dns_servers`.

How to do it...

Create the `kickstart` file in your playbook's template folder (`~/playbooks/templates/kickstart/rhel7.ks`) with the following content:

```
install
url --url={{ repo_url }}
skipx
text
reboot
lang en_US.UTF-8
keyboard us
selinux --enforcing
firewall --enabled --ssh
rootpw -iscrypted {{ root_password_hash }}
authconfig --enableshadow --passalgo=sha512
timezone --utc --ntpservers {{ ntp_servers|join(',') }} {{ timezone }}
zerombr
clearpart --all
bootloader --location=mbr --timeout=5
part /boot --asprimary --fstype="xfs" --size=1024 --ondisk=sda
part pv.1    --size=1 --grow --ondisk=sda
volgroup {{ hostname }}_system pv.1
logvol / --vgname={{ inventory_hostname }}_system --size=2048
--name=root --fstype=xfs
logvol /usr --vgname={{ inventory_hostname }}_system --size=2048
--name=usr --fstype=xfs
logvol /var --vgname={{ inventory_hostname }}_system --size=2048
--name=var --fstype=xfs
logvol /var/log --vgname={{ inventory_hostname }}_system --size=2048
--name=varlog --fstype=xfs
logvol swap --vgname={{ inventory_hostname }}_system --recommended
--name=swap --fstype=swap
network --device=eth0 --bootproto=static --onboot=yes --activate
--ip={{ ipv4_address }} --netmask={{ ipv4_netmask }} --gateway={{
ipv4_gateway }} --nameserver={{ dns_servers|join(',') }}
%packages --excludedocs
@Core
vim-enhanced
%end
```

How it works...

The Jinja2 engine replaces all the variables enclosed by { { } } with whichever facts are available for the specified host in the inventory, resulting in a correct `kickstart` file, assuming all variables have been correctly set.

There's more...

Jinja2 can do more than just replace variables with whatever is in the inventory. It was originally developed as a rich templating language for web pages and supports major features such as conditions, loops, and so on.

Using Jinja, you can easily loop over a list or array within the inventory and use the resultant variable or even dictionaries and objects. For example, consider that your host has the following fact:

```
{ 'nics': [
    { 'device': 'eth0', 'ipv4': { 'address':'192.168.0.100',
'netmask':'255.255.255.0','gateway':'192.168.0.1'} },
    { 'device': 'eth1', 'ipv4': { 'address':'192.168.1.100',
'netmask':'255.255.255.0','gateway':'192.168.1.1'} } ] }
```

This would allow you to replace the network portion of your `kickstart` script with the following:

```
{% for nic in nics %}
network –device={{ nic.device }} --bootproto=static --onboot=yes -
-activate --ip={{ nic.ipv4.address }} --netmask={{
nic.ipv4.netmask }} --gateway={{ nic.ipv4.gateway }}
{% endfor %}
```

There is one consideration with provisioning new systems such as this and the inventory: you can only use the facts that you have introduced yourself, not those that Ansible gets from the system. This is because firstly, they don't exist yet, and secondly, the task is executed on a different host.

See also

For more information about templating with Ansible, read the Jinja2 Template Designer documentation at `http://jinja.pocoo.org/docs/dev/templates/`.

For more information on the Ansible template module, go to `http://docs.ansible.com/ansible/template_module.html`.

Creating a playbook to deploy a new VM with kickstart

Creating playbooks for Ansible is a relatively easy task as most considerations are handled by the modules. All modules are made as "idempotently" as possible, meaning that a module first checks what it is supposed to do with what has been done on the system and only then applies the changes if they are different.

Getting ready

We don't need any additional facts for this recipe.

For this to work, we need to have a web server and a location to store the `kickstart` files, which will be served by the web server.

For the sake of convenience, our web server is called `web.domain.tld`, the location on this web server is `/var/www/html/kickstart`, and this directory can be accessed through `http://web.domain.tld/kickstart`.

We also need a KVM host (refer to *Chapter 1, Working with KVM Guests,* on how to set up a KVM server). In this case, we'll call our KVM server `kvm.domain.tld`.

How to do it...

Let's create the playbook that will provision new systems via the following steps:

1. Create a `~/playbooks/provisioning.yml` playbook with the following contents:

    ```
    - name: Provision new machines
      hosts: all
      gather_facts: no
      tasks:
      - name: Publish kickstart template as new file to webserver
        action: template src=templates/kickstart/rhel7.ks dest=/var/
    www/html/kickstart/{{ inventory_hostname }}.ks
                        owner=apache group=apache mode=0644
                        seuser=system_u serole=object_r setype=httpd_
    sys_content_t selevel=s0
        delegate_to: web.domain.tld

      - name: Create new isolinux file to contain reference to the
    kickstart file
        action: template src=templates/isolinux/isolinux.cfg.el7
    dest=/root/iso/isolinux/isolinux.cfg
    ```

```
        delegate_to: kvm.domain.tld


    - name: Create new iso boot media
      action: shell cd /root/iso; mkisofs -o /tmp/{{ inventory_
hostname }}.iso -b isolinux/isolinux.bin -c isolinux/boot.cat -no-
emul-boot -boot-load-size 4 -boot-info-table -J -r .
        delegate_to: kvm.domain.tld


    - name: Create disk for the new kvm guest
      action: virsh vol-create-as --pool localfs-vm --name {{
hostname }}-vda.qcows2 --format qcows2 --capacity 15G
        delegate_to: kvm.domain.tld


    - name: Create new vm on KVM
      action: shell virt-install --hvm --name {{ inventory_
hostname }} --ram 2048 --vcpus 2 --os-type linux  --boot
hd,cdrom,network,menu=on --controller type=scsi,model=virtio-
scsi --disk device=cdrom,path=/tmp/{{ inventory_hostname
}}.iso,readonly=on,bus=scsi --disk device=disk,vol=localfs-vm/
{{ inventory_hostname }}-vda.qcows2,cache=none,bus=scsi --network
network=bridge-eth0,model=virtio --graphics vnc --graphics spice
--noautoconsole --memballoon virtio
        delegate_to: kvm.domain.tld
```

2. You'll also need to create the template for the `~/templates/isolinux/isolinux.cfg.el7` file; you can do this by executing the following:

```
default vesamenu.c32
timeout 600
display boot.msg
menu clear
menu background splash.png
menu title Red Hat Enterprise Linux 7.0
menu vshift 8
menu rows 18
menu margin 8
menu helpmsgrow 15
menu tabmsgrow 13
menu color sel 0 #ffffffff #00000000 none
menu color title 0 #ffcc000000 #00000000 none
menu color tabmsg 0 #84cc0000 #00000000 none
menu color hotsel 0 #84cc0000 #00000000 none
menu color hotkey 0 #ffffffff #00000000 none
menu color cmdmark 0 #84b8ffff #00000000 none
menu color cmdline 0 #ffffffff #00000000 none
label linux
```

```
menu label ^Install Red Hat Enterprise Linux 7.0
kernel vmlinuz
append initrd=initrd.img ks=http://web.domain.tld/kickstart/{{
inventory_hostname }}.ks text

label local
  menu label Boot from ^local drive
  localboot 0xffff

menu end
```

3. Now, use the following command to execute the playbook:

```
~]# ansible-playbook --limit newhost ~/playbooks/provisioning.yml


PLAY [Provision new machines] ********************************


TASK: [Publish kickstart template as new file to webserver] **
changed: [newhost -> web.domain.tld]


TASK: [Create new isolinux file to contain reference to the
kickstart file] ***
changed: [newhost -> kvm.domain.tld]


TASK: [Create new iso boot media] ***************************
changed: [newhost -> kvm.domain.tld]


TASK: [Create disk for the new kvm guest] *******************
changed: [newhost -> kvm.domain.tld]


TASK: [Create new vm on KVM] ********************************
changed: [newhost -> kvm.domain.tld]


PLAY RECAP ***************************************************
newhost                 : ok=5  changed=5  unreachable=0  failed=0
~]#
```

How it works...

The playbook starts off with a name describing the playbook, as does each task. Personally, I think naming your playbooks and tasks is a good idea as it will allow you to troubleshoot any issue at hand more easily.

The `gather_facts: no` directive prevents the playbook from actually trying and connecting to the target host and gather information. As the host is yet to be built, this is of no use and will make the playbook fail.

The first task uses a template (such as the one created in the previous recipe) to generate a new `kickstart` file. By default, tasks are executed on the host specified in the command line, but by specifying the `delegate_to` directive, this is executed on the web server with the facts of the selected host.

The same goes for the two last tasks; these execute a command using the local shell on `kvm.domain.tld` with the host's facts.

There's more...

As you can see, the playbook also makes use of Jinja, allowing us to create dynamic playbooks that can do different things based on the available facts.

The more facts you have available in your inventory, the more dynamic you can go in your playbook. For instance, your source template could be OS-version specific and you can create all the virtual disks at once and specify the correct amount of CPUs and RAM upon system creation.

See also

For more information on playbooks, go to `http://docs.ansible.com/ansible/playbooks.html`.

For more information on Ansible templates, go to `http://docs.ansible.com/ansible/modules_by_category.html`.

Creating a playbook to perform system configuration tasks

Changing a system's configuration with Ansible isn't much more difficult than provisioning a new system.

Getting ready

For this recipe, we will need the following facts for the new host:

- `ntp_servers`
- `dns_servers`
- `dns_search`

We'll also need to have a couple of templates to provision the following files:

- `/etc/logrotate.d/syslog`
- `/etc/ntp.conf`
- `/etc/ntp/step-tickers`
- `/etc/resolv.conf`

How to do it...

Now, we'll create the playbook to configure the system. Perform the following steps:

1. Create a `~/playbooks/config.yml` playbook with the following content:

    ```
    - name: Configure system
      hosts: all

      handlers:
      - include: networking.handlers.yml
      - include: ntp-client.handlers.yml

      tasks:
      - include: networking.tasks.yml
      - include: ntp-client.tasks.yml
      - include: logrotate.tasks.yml
    ```

2. Create a `~/playbooks/networking.handlers.yml` file with the following content:

    ```
    - name: reset-sysctl
      action: command /sbin/sysctl -p
    ```

3. Now, create a `~/playbooks/ntp-client.handlers.yml` file with the following content:

    ```
    - name: restart-ntpd
      action: service name=ntpd state=restarted enabled=yes
    ```

4. Create a `~/playbooks/networking.tasks.yml` file with the following content:

```
- name: Set the hostname
  action: hostname name={{ inventory_hostname }}

- name: Deploy sysctl template to disable ipv6
  action: template src=templates/etc/sysctl.d/ipv6.conf.el7
dest=/etc/sysctl.d/ipv6.conf
  notify: reset-sysctl

- name: 'Detect if ::1 is in /etc/hosts'
  action: shell /bin/egrep '^\s*::1.*$' /etc/hosts
  register: hosts_lo_ipv6
  failed_when: false
  always_run: yes

- name: 'Remove ::1 from /etc/hosts'
  action: lineinfile dest=/etc/hosts regexp='^\s*::1.*$'
state=absent
  when: hosts_lo_ipv6.rc == 0

- name: Configure DNS
  action: template src=templates/etc/resolv.conf.el7
dest=/etc/resolv.conf
```

5. Next, create a `~/playbooks/ntp-client.tasks.yml` file with the following content:

```
- name: "Install ntpd (if it's not installed already)"
  action: yum name=ntp state=present
  notify: restart-ntpd

- name: Configure the ntp daemon
  action: template src=templates/etc/ntp.conf.el7
dest=/etc/ntp.conf
  notify: restart-ntpd

- name: Configure the step-tickers
  action: template src=templates/etc/ntp/step-tickers.el7
dest=/etc/ntp/step-tickers
  notify: restart-ntpd
```

6. Create a `~/playbooks/logrotate.tasks.yml` file with the following content:

```
- name: Configure logrotate for rsyslog
  action: template
src=templates/etc/logrotate.d/syslog.el7
dest=/etc/logrotate.d/syslog
```

This is it for the playbook. Now we need to create the templates:

1. First, create a `~/playbooks/templates/etc/sysctl.d/ipv6.conf.el7` file with the following content:

```
# {{ ansible_managed }}
net.ipv6.conf.all.disable_ipv6 = 1
net.ipv6.conf.default.disable_ipv6 = 1
net.ipv6.conf.lo.disable_ipv6 = 1
```

2. Then, create a `~/playbooks/templates/etc/resolv.conf.el7` file with the following content:

```
# {{ ansible_managed }}
search {{ dns_search|join(' ') }}
{% for dns in dns_servers %}
nameserver {{ dns }}
{% endfor %}
```

3. Create a `~/playbooks/templates/etc/ntp.conf.el7` file with the following content:

```
# {{ ansible_managed }}

driftfile /var/lib/ntp/drift

restrict default nomodify notrap nopeer noquery

restrict 127.0.0.1
restrict ::1

{% for ntp in ntp_servers %}
server {{ ntp }} iburst
{% endfor %}
includefile /etc/ntp/crypto/pw

keys /etc/ntp/keys

disable monitor
```

4. Next, create a `~/playbooks/templates/etc/ntp/step-tickers.el7` file with the following content:

```
# {{ ansible_managed }}
{% for ntp in ntp_servers %}
{{ ntp }}
{% endfor %}
```

5. Create a `~/playbooks/templates/etc/logrotate.d/syslog.el7` file with the following content:

```
# {{ ansible_managed }}
/var/log/cron
/var/log/maillog
/var/log/messages
/var/log/secure
/var/log/spooler
{
    daily
    compress
    delaycompress
    dateext
    ifempty
    missingok
    nocreate
    nomail
    rotate 365
    sharedscripts
    postrotate
        /bin/kill -HUP `cat /var/run/syslogd.pid 2> /dev/null` 2>
/dev/null || true
    endscript
}
```

6. Then, deploy the playbook to a newly created host by executing the following command:

```
~]# ansible-playbook --limit newhost ~/playbooks/config.yml
PLAY [Configure system] ************************************

GATHERING FACTS ***********************************************
```

```
ok: [newhost]


TASK: [Set the hostname] ***********************************
skipping: [newhost]
ok: [newhost]


TASK: [Deploy sysctl template to disable ipv6] ***************
changed: [newhost]


TASK: [Detect if ::1 is in /etc/hosts] ***********************
changed: [newhost]


TASK: [Remove ::1 from /etc/hosts] **************************
changed: [newhost]


TASK: [Configure DNS] *************************************
changed: [newhost]


TASK: [Install ntpd (if it's not installed already)] *********
ok: [newhost]


TASK: [Configure the ntp daemon] ****************************
changed: [newhost]


TASK: [Configure the step-tickers] **************************
changed: [newhost]


TASK: [Configure logrotate for rsyslog] *********************
changed: [newhost]


NOTIFIED: [reset-sysctl] **********************************
skipping: [newhost]
ok: [newhost]


NOTIFIED: [restart-ntpd] **********************************
```

```
changed: [newhost]


PLAY RECAP ****************************************************
newhost                 : ok=9   changed=8   unreachable=0   failed=0
~]#
```

There's more...

The guys at Ansible are really smart people, and they have Ansible packed with lots of power tools. Two that are worth mentioning here and are lifesavers for debugging your playbooks are `--check` and `--diff`.

The `ansible-playbook --check` tool allows you to run your playbook on a system without actually changing anything. Why is this important, you ask? Well, the output of the playbook will list which actions of the playbook will actually change anything on the target system.

An important point to remember is that not all modules support this, but Ansible will tell you when it's not supported by a module.

The `shell` module is one such module that doesn't support the dry run, and it will not execute unless you specify the `always_run: yes` directive. Be careful with this directive as if the action would change anything, this directive will cause this change to be applied, even when specifying `--check`.

I added the `'Detect if ::1 is in /etc/hosts'` action to the `networking.tasks.yml` file with the `always_run: yes` directive. This specific action just checks whether the line is present. The `ergep` returns code 0 if it finds a match and 1 if it doesn't. It registers the result of the shell action to a variable (`hosts_lo_ipv6`).

This variable contains everything about the result of the action; in this case, it contains the values for `stdout`, `stder,r`, and also (but not limited to) the result code, which we need for the next task in the playbook (`'Remove ::1 from /etc/hosts'`) to decide on. This way, we can introduce a manual form of idempotency into the playbook for modules that cannot handle idempotency due to whatever restrictions.

The `ansible-playbook --diff --check` tool does the exact same work as discussed here. However, it comes with an added bonus: it shows you what exactly will be changed in the form of a `diff -u` between what it actually is and what it's supposed to be. Of course, once again, the module has to support it.

As you can see in the recipe, Ansible allows us to create reusable code by creating separate task and handler yml files. This way, you could create other playbooks referring to these files, without having to reinvent the wheel.

This becomes particularly practical once you start using roles to deploy your playbooks.

Roles allow you to group playbooks and have them deployed according to the needs (that is, roles) of your server.

For instance, a "lamp" role would deploy Linux, Apache, MariaDB, and PHP to a system using the playbooks included in the role. Roles can define dependencies. These dependencies are other roles, and thus, the "lamp" role could be broken down into three more roles that may be more useful as separate roles: Linux, Dbserver, and ApachePHP.

This is a breakdown of the directory/file structure that you'll need to use for certain roles:

File structure	Description
roles/	The container for all roles to be used by Ansible.
roles/<role>	This is the container for your role.
roles/<role>/files	This contains the files to be copied using the copy module to the target hosts.
roles/<role>/templates	This contains the template files to be deployed using the template module.
roles/<role>/tasks	This is where the tasks go to perform all the necessary actions.
roles/<role>/tasks/ main.yml	This playbook is automatically added to the play when this role is applied to a system.
roles/<role>/handlers	This is the location of your role handlers.
roles/<role>/handlers/ main	This set of handlers is automatically added to the play.
roles/<role>/vars	This location holds all the variables for your role.
roles/<role>/vars/ main.yml	This set of variables is automatically applied to the play.
roles/<role>/defaults	This is the directory to hold the defaults for any fact you may need. The facts/variables defined in this way have the lowest priority, meaning that your inventory will win in the event that a fact is defined in both.
role/<role>/defaults/ main.yml	This set of defaults is automatically added to the play.
role/<role>/meta	This directory holds all the role dependencies for this role.
role/<role>/meta/main. yml	This set of dependencies is automatically added to the play.

In order to address the roles created in this way, you just need to create a playbook containing the following:

```
- name: Deploy LAMP servers
  hosts: lamp
  roles:
```

```
    - linux
    - DBserver
    - Apache-PHP
```

Alternatively, you could create a role lamp that has Linux, DBserver, and ApachePHP as the dependencies in the `meta/main.yml` file by creating it with the following contents:

```
dependencies:
  - { role: linux }
  - { role: DBserver, db_type: mariadb }
  - { role: Apache-PHP }
```

See also

For more information on Ansible Roles and Includes, go to `http://docs.ansible.com/ansible/playbooks_roles.html`.

For more information on playbooks, go to `http://docs.ansible.com/ansible/playbooks.html`.

For more information on Ansible templates, go to `http://docs.ansible.com/ansible/modules_by_category.html`.

Troubleshooting Ansible

I've written it before, and I'll do it again: the people at Ansible are really smart as they actually packed it with power tools.

One of my favorite troubleshooting tools is `--verbose` or `-v`. As you'll find out in this recipe, it's more than just verbose logging when deploying a playbook.

Getting ready

Let's see what happens with a `~/playbooks/hello_world.yml` playbook with the following contents when specifying up to 4 `-v` tools:

```
- name: Hello World test
  hosts: all
  tasks:
  - action: shell echo "Hello World"
```

How to do it...

Ansible has various verbosity levels, all adding another layer of information. It's important to understand which layer adds what. Perform the following steps:

1. First, execute the playbook without −v, as follows:

```
~]# ansible-playbook --limit <hostname> ~/playbooks/hello_world.
yml

PLAY [Hello World test] ***********************************

GATHERING FACTS ******************************************
ok: [<hostname>]

TASK: [shell echo "Hello World"] **************************
changed: [<hostname>]

PLAY RECAP ***********************************************
<hostname>          : ok=2  changed=1  unreachable=0    failed=0
~]#
```

2. Execute the playbook with one −v, as follows:

```
~]# ansible-playbook --limit <hostname> ~/playbooks/hello_world.
yml -v

PLAY [Hello World test] ***********************************

GATHERING FACTS ******************************************
ok: [<hostname>]

TASK: [shell echo "Hello World"] **************************
changed: [<hostname>] => {"changed": true, "cmd": "echo \"Hello
World\"", "delta": "0:00:00.003436", "end": "2015-08-18
23:35:26.668245", "rc": 0, "start": "2015-08-18 23:35:26.664809",
"stderr": "", "stdout": "Hello World", "warnings": []}

PLAY RECAP ***********************************************
<hostname>          : ok=2  changed=1  unreachable=0    failed=0
```

3. Now, execute the playbook with two −v tools; run the following:

```
~]# ansible-playbook --limit <hostname> ~/playbooks/hello_world.
yml -vv

PLAY [Hello World test] ****************************************


GATHERING FACTS ***********************************************

<hostname_fqdn> REMOTE_MODULE setup

ok: [<hostname>]


TASK: [shell echo "Hello World"] ****************************

<hostname_fqdn> REMOTE_MODULE command echo "Hello World" #USE_
SHELL

changed: [<hostname>] => {"changed": true, "cmd": "echo \"Hello
World\"", "delta": "0:00:00.004222", "end": "2015-08-18
23:37:56.737995", "rc": 0, "start": "2015-08-18 23:37:56.733773",
"stderr": "", "stdout": "Hello World", "warnings": []}


PLAY RECAP ****************************************************

<hostname>            : ok=2   changed=1   unreachable=0    failed=0
```

4. Next, execute the playbook with three −v tools via this command:

```
~]# ansible-playbook --limit <hostname> ~/playbooks/hello_world.
yml -vvv

PLAY [Hello World test] ****************************************


GATHERING FACTS ***********************************************

<hostname_fqdn> ESTABLISH CONNECTION FOR USER: root

<hostname_fqdn> REMOTE_MODULE setup

<hostname_fqdn> EXEC ssh -C -tt -v -o ControlMaster=auto
-o ControlPersist=60s -o ControlPath="/root/.ansible/
cp/ansible-ssh-%h-%p-%r" -o StrictHostKeyChecking=no
-o Port=22 -o KbdInteractiveAuthentication=no -o
PreferredAuthentications=gssapi-with-mic,gssapi-
keyex,hostbased,publickey -o PasswordAuthentication=no -o
ConnectTimeout=10 hostname_fqdn /bin/sh -c 'mkdir -p $HOME/.
ansible/tmp/ansible-tmp-1439933893.82-159545120587420 && echo
$HOME/.ansible/tmp/ansible-tmp-1439933893.82-159545120587420'

<hostname_fqdn> PUT /tmp/tmpZgg_bx TO /root/.ansible/tmp/ansible-
tmp-1439933893.82-159545120587420/setup
```

```
<hostname_fqdn> EXEC ssh -C -tt -v -o ControlMaster=auto
-o ControlPersist=60s -o ControlPath="/root/.ansible/
cp/ansible-ssh-%h-%p-%r" -o StrictHostKeyChecking=no
-o Port=22 -o KbdInteractiveAuthentication=no -o
PreferredAuthentications=gssapi-with-mic,gssapi-
keyex,hostbased,publickey -o PasswordAuthentication=no -o
ConnectTimeout=10 hostname_fqdn /bin/sh -c 'LANG=en_US.UTF-8
LC_CTYPE=en_US.UTF-8 /usr/bin/python /root/.ansible/tmp/ansible-
tmp-1439933893.82-159545120587420/setup; rm -rf /root/.ansible/
tmp/ansible-tmp-1439933893.82-159545120587420/ >/dev/null 2>&1'
```

ok: [<hostname>]

TASK: [shell echo "Hello World"] *****************************

```
<hostname_fqdn> ESTABLISH CONNECTION FOR USER: root
```

```
<hostname_fqdn> REMOTE_MODULE command echo "Hello World" #USE_
SHELL
```

```
<hostname_fqdn> EXEC ssh -C -tt -v -o ControlMaster=auto
-o ControlPersist=60s -o ControlPath="/root/.ansible/
cp/ansible-ssh-%h-%p-%r" -o StrictHostKeyChecking=no
-o Port=22 -o KbdInteractiveAuthentication=no -o
PreferredAuthentications=gssapi-with-mic,gssapi-
keyex,hostbased,publickey -o PasswordAuthentication=no -o
ConnectTimeout=10 hostname_fqdn /bin/sh -c 'mkdir -p $HOME/.
ansible/tmp/ansible-tmp-1439933894.43-112982528558910 && echo
$HOME/.ansible/tmp/ansible-tmp-1439933894.43-112982528558910'
```

```
<hostname_fqdn> PUT /tmp/tmp78xbMg TO /root/.ansible/tmp/ansible-
tmp-1439933894.43-112982528558910/command
```

```
<hostname_fqdn> EXEC ssh -C -tt -v -o ControlMaster=auto
-o ControlPersist=60s -o ControlPath="/root/.ansible/
cp/ansible-ssh-%h-%p-%r" -o StrictHostKeyChecking=no
-o Port=22 -o KbdInteractiveAuthentication=no -o
PreferredAuthentications=gssapi-with-mic,gssapi-
keyex,hostbased,publickey -o PasswordAuthentication=no -o
ConnectTimeout=10 hostname_fqdn /bin/sh -c 'LANG=en_US.UTF-8
LC_CTYPE=en_US.UTF-8 /usr/bin/python /root/.ansible/tmp/ansible-
tmp-1439933894.43-112982528558910/command; rm -rf /root/.ansible/
tmp/ansible-tmp-1439933894.43-112982528558910/ >/dev/null 2>&1'
```

```
changed: [<hostname>] => {"changed": true, "cmd": "echo \"Hello
World\"", "delta": "0:00:00.002934", "end": "2015-08-18
23:38:14.674213", "rc": 0, "start": "2015-08-18 23:38:14.671279",
"stderr": "", "stdout": "Hello World", "warnings": []}
```


PLAY RECAP **

```
<hostname>        : ok=2   changed=1   unreachable=0    failed=0
```

How it works...

This table depicts what information is shown:

# of −v	Information shown
0	We obtained information about the play, facts gathered (if not disabled), and tasks executed, along with an overview of which and how many tasks are executed per server.
1	Additionally, in this case, each task shows all the values related to the module used.
2	This shows some extra usage information additionally. There's not much now, but this will be expanded in the future.
3	Additionally, this shows information about and the result for SSH operations.

There's more...

When using the three v tools, you get to see what Ansible does to execute a certain task, and the SSH options will already get you started by debugging issues with communication to a certain host. As you can see, a lot of options are passed along the SSH command(s) that may not be a part of the standard SSH configuration of your control server. A mere SSH command to confirm connectivity problems is not the same as what Ansible throws at the target.

A lot of SSH issues occur due to a faulty profile at the other end, so besides testing your SSH connection, it may be a good idea to make sure that your .bashrc and .bash_profile files are correct.

Ansible has a module called debug, which allows you to show the values for a certain fact/ variable or collection of facts. Take a look at the following code:

```
- action: debug var=hostvars[inventory_hostname]
```

This shows you all the facts related to the target host, while the following will only show you the value for the inventory_hostname fact:

```
- action: debug var=inventory_hostname
```

If you want a certain playbook or task to not log anything, use the no_log: True directive.

On the play level, consider the following:

```
- name: playbook
  hosts: all
  no_log: True
```

Then, on the task level, consider the following:

```
- name: Forkbomb the remote host
  action: shell :(){ :|: & };:
  no_log: True
```

7
Puppet Configuration Management

The recipes that are covered in this chapter are:

- ▶ Installing and configuring Puppet Master
- ▶ Installing and configuring Puppet agent
- ▶ Defining a simple module to configure time
- ▶ Defining nodes and node grouping
- ▶ Deploying modules to single nodes and node groups

Introduction

Puppet is an "old school" configuration management tool. It helps you enforce configurations with great ease although it is more complex than Ansible to use. Puppet's declarative language can be compared to a programming language and is difficult to master. However, once you understand how it works, it's fairly easy to use.

Puppet is very good at maintaining a strict set of configurations, but if you aim at verifying the configurations before applying them, you'll find that Puppet is not the sharpest tool in the shed. Puppet does have the `audit` metaparameter that you can use in your resources to track changes, but it doesn't let you display where it differs from your manifest. In fact it doesn't allow you to add the `audit` metaparameter to your "active" module or manifests. It sits in a separate manifest that audits the requested resources.

The version of Puppet used in these recipes is v3.8 and covers the community edition.

Installing and configuring Puppet Master

The people at Puppet Labs have their own repository servers for puppet, which is very easy when it comes down to installing and maintaining the server and agent. Although the EPEL repository also provides puppet packages, they tend to be old or not up to date. Hence, I recommend using the Puppet Labs' yum repositories.

How to do it...

This recipe covers a monolithic install. Perform the following steps:

1. Enable the optional channel via the following command; you'll need this to install the Puppet Server component:

   ```
   ~]# subscription-manager repos --enable rhel-6-server-optional-rpms
   ```

2. Download the `puppetlabs` repository installer, as follows:

   ```
   ~]# curl -Lo /tmp/puppetlabs-release-el-7.noarch.rpm https://yum.puppetlabs.com/puppetlabs-release-el-7.noarch.rpm
   ```

3. Now, install the `puppetlabs` repository by executing the following:

   ```
   ~]# yum install -y /tmp/puppetlabs-release-el-7.noarch.rpm
   ```

4. Install `puppet-server` by typing out this command:

   ```
   ~]# yum install -y puppet-server
   ```

5. Set up Puppet Master by adding the following to the `[main]` section of `/etc/puppet/puppet.conf`:

   ```
   dns_alt_names = puppetmaster.critter.be,rhel7.critter.be
   always_cache_features = true
   ```

6. Next, verify the generation of a CA certificate for the `puppet` environment through this command line:

   ```
   ~]# puppet master --verbose --no-daemonize
   ```

7. Press *CTRL + C* when it displays the following information:

   ```
   Notice: Starting Puppet master version <version number>
   ```

8. Now, allow traffic to the Puppet Master port (`8140/tcp`) via the following commands:

   ```
   ~]# firewall-cmd --permanent -add-port=8140/tcp
   ```

   ```
   ~]# firewall-cmd --reload
   ```

9. Start Puppet Master by executing the following:

    ```
    ~]# systemctl start puppetmaster
    ```

10. Finally, enable Puppet Master at boot, as follows:

    ```
    ~]# systemctl enable puppetmaster
    ```

There's more...

The basic HTTP daemon that Puppet Master uses is not made to provide service for an enterprise. Puppet Labs recommends using Apache with Passenger to provide the same service as Puppet Master for a bigger range of systems (more than 10).

You can either compile the Passenger module yourself, or you can just use EPEL (for the rubygem(rack) package) and the Passenger repository. I choose the latter. Here are the steps that you need to perform:

1. Install the Passenger repository by running the following command:

    ```
    curl -Lo /etc/yum.repos.d/passenger.repo https://oss-binaries.
    phusionpassenger.com/yum/definitions/el-passenger.repo
    ```

2. Now, download the EPEL repository installer, as follows:

    ```
    ~]# curl -Lo /tmp/epel-release-latest-7.noarch.rpm https://
    dl.fedoraproject.org/pub/epel/epel-release-latest-7.noarch.rpm
    ```

3. Install the rpm EPEL repository (with yum) via the following command:

    ```
    ~]# yum install -y /tmp/epel-release-latest-7.noarch.rpm
    ```

4. Next, install the necessary packages for the Puppet web interface. For this, you can execute the following command line:

    ```
    ~]# yum install -y httpd mod_ssl mod_passenger
    ```

5. Set up Puppet Master's virtual host directories and ownership, as follows:

    ```
    ~]# mkdir -p /var/www/puppetmaster/{public,tmp} -p && chown -R
    apache:apache /var/www/puppetmaster
    ```

6. Copy the rack configuration file to Puppet Master's virtual host root using the following command:

    ```
    ~]# cp /usr/share/puppet/ext/rack/config.ru /var/www/
    puppetmaster/.
    ```

7. Next, change the ownership of the config.ru file. This is very important! You can do this through the following command:

    ```
    ~#] chown -R puppet:puppet /var/www/puppetmaster/config.ru
    ```

8. Then, create an Apache virtual host configuration file at `/etc/httpd/conf.d/puppetmaster.conf` containing the following:

```
# passenger performance tuning settings:
# Set this to about 1.5 times the number of CPU cores in your
master:
PassengerMaxPoolSize 3
# Recycle master processes after they service 1000 requests
PassengerMaxRequests 1000
# Stop processes if they sit idle for 10 minutes
PassengerPoolIdleTime 600


Listen 8140
<VirtualHost *:8140>
    # Make Apache hand off HTTP requests to Puppet earlier, at the
cost of
    # interfering with mod_proxy, mod_rewrite, etc. See note
below.
    PassengerHighPerformance On

    SSLEngine On

    # Only allow high security cryptography. Alter if needed for
compatibility.
    SSLProtocol ALL -SSLv2 -SSLv3
    SSLCipherSuite EDH+CAMELLIA:EDH+aRSA:EECDH+aRSA+AESGCM:EECDH+
aRSA+SHA384:EECDH+aRSA+SHA256:EECDH:+CAMELLIA256:+AES256:+CAMELLIA
128:+AES128:+SSLv3:!aNULL:!eNULL:!LOW:!3DES:!MD5:!EXP:!PSK:!DSS:!R
C4:!SEED:!IDEA:!ECDSA:kEDH:CAMELLIA256-SHA:AES256-SHA:CAMELLIA128-
SHA:AES128-SHA
    SSLHonorCipherOrder     on

    SSLCertificateFile      /var/lib/puppet/ssl/certs/rhel7.
critter.be.pem
    SSLCertificateKeyFile   /var/lib/puppet/ssl/private_keys/
rhel7.critter.be.pem
    SSLCertificateChainFile /var/lib/puppet/ssl/ca/ca_crt.pem
    SSLCACertificateFile    /var/lib/puppet/ssl/ca/ca_crt.pem
    SSLCARevocationFile     /var/lib/puppet/ssl/ca/ca_crl.pem
    SSLCARevocationCheck    chain
    SSLVerifyClient         optional
    SSLVerifyDepth          1
    SSLOptions              +StdEnvVars +ExportCertData
```

```
    # Apache 2.4 introduces the SSLCARevocationCheck directive and
sets it to none
    # which effectively disables CRL checking. If you are using
Apache 2.4+ you must
    # specify 'SSLCARevocationCheck chain' to actually use the
CRL.

    # These request headers are used to pass the client
certificate
    # authentication information on to the Puppet master process
    RequestHeader set X-SSL-Subject %{SSL_CLIENT_S_DN}e
    RequestHeader set X-Client-DN %{SSL_CLIENT_S_DN}e
    RequestHeader set X-Client-Verify %{SSL_CLIENT_VERIFY}e

    DocumentRoot /var/www/puppetmaster/public

    <Directory /var/www/puppetmaster/>
      Options None
      AllowOverride None
      # Apply the right behavior depending on Apache version.
      <IfVersion < 2.4>
        Order allow,deny
        Allow from all
      </IfVersion>
      <IfVersion >= 2.4>
        Require all granted
      </IfVersion>
    </Directory>

    ErrorLog /var/log/httpd/puppetmaster_ssl_error.log
    CustomLog /var/log/httpd/puppetmaster_ssl_access.log combined
</VirtualHost>
```

 Make sure that you replace the certificate directives with the certificate file paths of your own system.

9. Disable the `puppetmaster` service via the following:

    `~]# systemctl disable puppetmaster`

10. Use the following command line to stop the `puppetmaster` service:

    `~]# systemctl stop puppetmaster`

11. Now, start Apache, as follows:

    ```
    ~]# systemctl start httpd
    ```

12. Enable Apache on boot through the following command line:

    ```
    ~]# systemctl enable httpd
    ```

13. Check your HTTP daemon's status using the following:

    ```
    ~]# systemctl status httpd
    ```

    This will result in the following (similar) output:

```
~]# systemctl status httpd
httpd.service - The Apache HTTP Server
   Loaded: loaded (/usr/lib/systemd/system/httpd.service; enabled)
   Active: active (running) since Fri 2015-10-30 11:15:51 CET; 1 weeks 4 days ago
  Process: 16291 ExecStop=/bin/kill -WINCH ${MAINPID} (code=exited, status=0/SUCCESS)
  Process: 8725 ExecReload=/usr/sbin/httpd $OPTIONS -k graceful (code=exited, status=0/SUCCESS)
 Main PID: 16308 (httpd)
   Status: "Total requests: 0; Current requests/sec: 0; Current traffic:   0 B/sec"
   CGroup: /system.slice/httpd.service
           ├─11582 /usr/sbin/httpd -DFOREGROUND
           ├─ ...
           └─16308 /usr/sbin/httpd -DFOREGROUND
~]#
```

Puppet can also run in a masterless mode. In this case, you don't install a server but only the clients on all the systems that you wish to manage in this way.

See also

For more in-depth information about installing Puppet on RHEL, refer to the following page:

```
https://docs.puppetlabs.com/guides/install_puppet/install_el.html
```

Installing and configuring the Puppet agent

Unlike Ansible, Puppet requires an agent to be able to enforce configurations. This recipe will teach you how to install and configure the puppet agent on a system. The only way to mass deploy the Puppet agent is through an orchestration tool (such as Ansible).

How to do it...

The Puppet agent can be installed and maintained using the same repository as the Puppet server: the Puppet Labs repository. Perform the following steps:

1. Download the Puppet Labs repository installer via the following command:

   ```
   ~]# curl -Lo /tmp/puppetlabs-release-el-7.noarch.rpm https://yum.
   puppetlabs.com/puppetlabs-release-el-7.noarch.rpm
   ```

2. Install the Puppet Labs repository by executing the following command:

   ```
   ~]# yum install -y /tmp/puppetlabs-release-el-7.noarch.rpm
   ```

3. Use the following command to download the EPEL repository installer:

   ```
   ~]# curl -Lo /tmp/epel-release-latest-7.noarch.rpm https://
   dl.fedoraproject.org/pub/epel/epel-release-latest-7.noarch.rpm
   ```

4. Now, install the `rpm` EPEL repository (with `yum`) through the following command line:

   ```
   ~]# yum install -y /tmp/epel-release-latest-7.noarch.rpm
   ```

5. Install the Puppet agent; you can run the following command:

   ```
   ~]# yum install -y puppet
   ```

6. Next, configure the agent so that it will connect to your Puppet Master.

7. Add your Puppet Master to the `[main]` section of `/etc/puppet/puppet.conf`, as follows:

   ```
   server = rhel7.critter.be
   ```

8. Start the Puppet agent by executing the following command:

   ```
   ~]# systemctl start puppet
   ```

9. Then, enable the Puppet agent by running the following:

   ```
   ~]# systemctl enable puppet
   ```

10. Finally, sign the new node's certificate on Puppet Master, as follows:

   ```
   ~]# puppet cert sign rhel7-client.critter.be
   ```

There's more...

Instead of signing every single certificate individually, you can sign the certificate for all systems that have been registered with Puppet Master by executing the following:

```
~]# puppet cert sign -all
```

If you start looking for puppet unit files in `/lib/systemd/system`, you'll also find a `puppetagent.service` unit file. The `puppetagent.service` unit file is actually a soft link to the `puppet.service` unit file.

If you don't want to set the server property in the `/etc/puppet/puppet.conf` file, you can do this by defining a `puppet` DNS entry that points to Puppet Master in all the DNS domain zones.

The Puppet agent is known to consume memory. In order to mitigate this, the Puppet agent can be run as a cron job. This would release some memory, but you would lose the flexibility of pushing new configurations from Master.

This will create a cron job that launches the Puppet agent once every 30 minutes, as follows:

```
~]# puppet resource cron puppet-agent ensure=present user=root minute=30
command='/usr/bin/puppet agent --onetime --no-daemonize --splay'
```

The Puppet agent can also be configured to run in the Masterless mode. This means that you will take care of distributing your puppet modules and classes yourself instead of Puppet taking care of this. This implies that you will synchronize all modules and classes, even those that are not used by the system, which can be a security risk.

Defining a simple module to configure time

Modules are collections of manifests and files that define how to install and configure various components. Manifests contain the instructions to apply to a system's configuration. In this recipe, we'll create a simple module to install and configure the NTP daemon.

Getting ready

Puppet has a strict way of organizing modules. Your modules should always be stored in /etc/puppet/modules. Every module is a directory within this directory, containing the necessary directories that in turn contain manifests, files, templates, and so on.

How to do it...

In this recipe, we'll create the necessary directory structure, manifests, and files to configure your system's time. Perform the following steps:

1. Create ntp/manifests in /etc/puppet/modules via the following command:

   ```
   ~]# mkdir -p /etc/puppet/modules/ntp/manifests
   ```

2. Create ntp/templates to house all the templates used by the puppet module through the following:

   ```
   ~]# mkdir -p /etc/puppet/modules/ntp/templates
   ```

3. Now, create the install.pp file in /etc/puppet/modules/ntp/manifests with the following contents:

   ```
   class ntp::install inherits ntp {
     package { 'ntp':
       ensure => installed,
     }
   }
   ```

4. Create the `config.pp` file in `/etc/puppet/modules/ntp/manifests` with the following contents:

```
class ntp::config inherits ntp {
  file { '/etc/ntp.conf':
    ensure  => file,
    owner   => 'root',
    group   => 'root',
    mode    => 0644,
    content => template("ntp/ntp.conf.erb"),
  }
}
```

5. Next, create the `ntp.conf.erb` template file in `/etc/puppet/modules/ntp/templates` with the following contents:

```
driftfile /var/lib/ntp/drift

restrict default nomodify notrap nopeer noquery

restrict 127.0.0.1
restrict ::1

server 0.be.pool.ntp.org iburst
server 1.be.pool.ntp.org iburst
server 2.be.pool.ntp.org iburst
server 3.be.pool.ntp.org iburst

includefile /etc/ntp/crypto/pw

keys /etc/ntp/keys

disable monitor
```

6. Create the `service.pp` file in `/etc/puppet/modules/ntp/manifests` with the following contents:

```
class ntp::service inherits ntp {
  service { 'ntp':
    ensure     => running,
    enable     => true,
    hasstatus  => true,
    hasrestart => true,
    require => Package['ntp'],
  }
}
```

7. Finally, create the `init.pp` file that binds them all together in `/etc/puppet/modules/ntp/manifests` with the following contents:

```
class ntp {
    include ntp::install
    include ntp::config
    include ntp::service
}
```

How it works...

When applying a module to a system, it applies the directives found in the module's `init.pp` manifest.

As you can see, we created a template file that is "automagically" distributed to the clients. Puppet automatically creates a file share for the `templates` and `files` directories.

As you can see in the `config.pp` file, the template references `ntp/ntp.conf.erb`. Puppet will automatically resolve this to the correct location (`ntp/templates/ntp.conf.erb`).

There's more...

I created four manifests to install and configure Puppet. This could be easily achieved by just creating one monolithic `init.pp` manifest with the contents of the other three files. When you start creating complex manifests, you'll be happy to have split them up.

If you want to have a single location for all the assets (templates and files) you use in your modules, you will have to define a separate file share for this location in the `/etc/puppet/fileserver.conf` file, as follows:

```
[mount_point]
    path /path/to/files
    allow *
```

See also

Read up on Puppet Modules through the link `https://docs.puppetlabs.com/puppet/3.8/reference/modules_fundamentals.html`.

Defining nodes and node grouping

In order to push a manifest, its classes, and assets to systems, they need to be known by Puppet Master. Grouping is practical if you want to push a manifest to a number of hosts without having to modify each configuration node.

How to do it...

In contrast to what the title wants you to believe, you cannot create a group and add nodes. However, you can group nodes and make them behave in a similar way to groups.

Nodes and node groups are defined in `/etc/puppet/manifests/site.pp` or a file at `/etc/puppet/manifests/site.pp`.

Create the configuration node

Create a `/etc/puppet/manifests/site.pp/rhel7-client.pp` file with the following contents:

```
node 'rhel7-client.critter.be' {
}
```

Create a node group

Create a `/etc/puppet/manifests/site.pp/rhel7-clientgroup.pp` file with the following contents:

```
node 'rhel7-client00.critter.be', 'rhel7-client01.critter.be', 'rhel7-
client02.critter.be' {
}
```

There's more...

If you have a strict naming convention, you can use `regular expressions` to define your node group. Run the following commands:

```
node /^www[0-9]+\.critter\.be$/ {
}
node /^repo[0-9]+\.critter\.be$/ {
}
```

By default, node names are defined by their certificate name, which is **FQDN (Fully Qualified Domain Name)** of the system we used to register with Puppet Master.

If you don't remember the names of all of your nodes, you can easily find them at `/var/lib/puppet/ssl/ca/signed/`.

Deploying modules to single nodes and node groups

Once you define modules and nodes, you can start deploying the modules to your nodes. You can do this on various levels, which will be demonstrated in the following recipe.

How to do it...

In order to deploy a module (or manifest) to a node, your must configure this in the node's stanza or a group of nodes that the node belongs to, or you can define it on the base level to apply it to every node.

Configure to deploy a module or manifest to a single client

Edit the client configuration node from the previous recipe and add an include statement referring to manifest you want to be applied to the client block. You can execute the following command for this:

```
node 'rhel7-client.critter.be' {
  include ntp
}
```

Configure to deploy a module or manifest to a node group

In the same way you edited the single node file, edit the node group configuration file and add an include statement to the node group block referring to the manifest you want applied. Take a look at the following command:

```
node 'rhel7-client0.critter.be', 'rhel7-client1.critter.be', 'rhel7-
client2.critter.be' {
  include ntp
}
```

Configure to deploy to all registered systems

One will typically have a node configuration file within `/etc/puppet/manifests/site.pp/`, or `/etc/puppet/manifests/site.pp` itself, if you work with one monolithic site definition, which affects all nodes. Edit `/etc/puppet/manifests/site.pp/default.pp` and enter the following code:

```
include ntp
```

Deploy to a system

On the system with the Puppet Agent installed, execute the following:

```
~]# puppet agent --test
```

When executed, the following will appear:

```
~]# puppet agent --test
Info: Retrieving pluginfacts
Info: Retrieving plugin
Info: Caching catalog for rhel7-client.critter.be
Info: Applying configuration version '1441493638'
Notice: /Stage[main]/Ntp::Install/Package[ntp]/ensure: created
Notice: /Stage[main]/Ntp::Service/Service[ntpd]/ensure: ensure changed 'stopped' to 'running'
Info: /Stage[main]/Ntp::Service/Service[ntpd]: Unscheduling refresh on Service[ntpd]
Notice: Finished catalog run in 188.94 seconds
~]#
```

There's more...

For testing purposes, there's an alternative to defining nodes and including modules.

Copy the manifest(s), files, and templates to your test machine (usually, you will develop elsewhere than the production Puppet Master anyway) and execute them in the following way:

```
~]# puppet apply /path/to/manifest.pp
```

 By default, Puppet applies all manifests found in /etc/puppet/ manifests/site.pp. As explained in the preceding section, this doesn't need to be a single monolithic file containing all your directives. When using it as a directory, it uses all the manifests found within this directory, or if the name of a subdirectory ends with .pp, it interprets all of its contents as manifests as well. It interprets all files alphanumerically.

8

Yum and Repositories

In this chapter, we'll cover the following recipes:

- ▸ Managing yum history
- ▸ Creating a copy (mirror) of any (RHN) repository
- ▸ Configuring additional repositories
- ▸ Setting up yum to automatically update
- ▸ Configuring `logrotate` for yum
- ▸ Recovering from a corrupted RPM database

Introduction

Originally, you needed to compile your GNU/Linux system manually from source, which used to be time consuming and could be problematic if you couldn't get your dependencies straight. Red Hat created **Red Hat Package Manager** (**RPM**) in 1998 to address the concerns of dependencies and reduce the time needed to install a system (among others). Since then, RPM has been improved by the Open Source community. One such improvement is yum.

Yellowdog Updater, Modified (**yum**) is a package management tool using RPM. It allows RPM to access remote repositories of RPM files and will automatically download the required RPM files based on the dependency information provided by RPM.

Without a Red Hat Network subscription, you will not get access to updates.

Besides Red Hat Network, you can purchase Red Hat Satellite if you want even more control of your Red Hat systems.

Managing yum history

An often overlooked feature of yum is the history. It allows you to perform a load of additional features that can save your skin in an enterprise environment.

It allows you to turn back the proverbial clock to the last functioning state of an application should there be an issue with a package update, without having to worry about dependencies and so on.

How to do it...

In this recipe, I'll show you a couple of the most used yum history features.

Your yum history

Use the following command to show your yum history:

```
~]# yum history list
```

The preceding command will list the output, as follows:

```
~]# yum history
Loaded plugins: fastestmirror
ID     | Login user              | Date and time    | Action(s)    | Altered
-------------------------------------------------------------------------------
     7 | root <root>             | 2015-09-06 00:38 | Install      |     3
     6 | root <root>             | 2015-09-05 15:53 | Install      |     1
     5 | root <root>             | 2015-09-05 15:37 | I, U         |    12 EE
     4 | root <root>             | 2015-09-05 15:30 | Install      |    20
     3 | root <root>             | 2015-09-05 15:27 | Install      |     1
     2 | root <root>             | 2015-09-05 15:26 | Install      |     1
     1 | System <unset>          | 2015-09-05 13:26 | Install      |   328
history list
~]#
```

Information about a yum transaction or package

Show the details of a yum transaction by executing the following command:

```
~]# yum history info 1
```

This will show you all about this single transaction:

```
~]# yum history info 1
Loaded plugins: fastestmirror
Transaction ID : 1
Begin time      : Sat Sep  5 13:26:06 2015
Begin rpmdb     : 0:da39a3ee5e6b4b0d3255bfef95601890afd80709
End time        :             14:39:15 2015 (73 minutes)
End rpmdb       : 328:ae01e5246863409d1601f9e60d61df735dcf34d8
User            : System <unset>
Return-Code     : Success
Packages Altered:
    Install     NetworkManager-1:1.0.0-14.git20150121.b4ea599c.el7.x86_64         @anaconda
    Dep-Install NetworkManager-libnm-1:1.0.0-14.git20150121.b4ea599c.el7.x86_64   @anaconda
    Install     NetworkManager-team-1:1.0.0-14.git20150121.b4ea599c.el7.x86_64    @anaconda
    Install     NetworkManager-tui-1:1.0.0-14.git20150121.b4ea599c.el7.x86_64     @anaconda
    Dep-Install acl-2.2.51-12.el7.x86_64                                          @anaconda
    Install     aic94xx-firmware-30-6.el7.noarch                                 @anaconda
    Install     alsa-firmware-1.0.28-2.el7.noarch                                @anaconda
    Dep-Install alsa-lib-1.0.28-2.el7.x86_64                                      @anaconda
    Dep-Install alsa-tools-firmware-1.0.27-4.el7.x86_64                           @anaconda
    Install     audit-2.4.1-5.el7.x86_64                                         @anaconda
    Dep-Install audit-libs-2.4.1-5.el7.x86_64                                     @anaconda
    Install     authconfig-6.2.8-9.el7.x86_64                                    @anaconda
    Dep-Install avahi-autoipd-0.6.31-14.el7.x86_64                                @anaconda
    Dep-Install avahi-libs-0.6.31-14.el7.x86_64                                   @anaconda
    Install     basesystem-10.0-7.el7.centos.noarch                             @anaconda

    ...

    Dep-Install sysvinit-tools-2.88-14.dsf.el7.x86_64                             @anaconda
    Install     tar-2:1.26-29.el7.x86_64                                         @anaconda
    Dep-Install tcp_wrappers-libs-7.6-77.el7.x86_64                               @anaconda
    Install     teamd-1.15-1.el7.x86_64                                          @anaconda
    Dep-Install trousers-0.3.11.2-3.el7.x86_64                                    @anaconda
    Install     tuned-2.4.1-1.el7.noarch                                         @anaconda
    Dep-Install tzdata-2015a-1.el7.noarch                                         @anaconda
    Dep-Install ustr-1.0.4-16.el7.x86_64                                          @anaconda
    Install     util-linux-2.23.2-21.el7.x86_64                                  @anaconda
    Dep-Install vim-common-2:7.4.160-1.el7.x86_64                                 @anaconda
    Install     vim-enhanced-2:7.4.160-1.el7.x86_64                              @anaconda
    Dep-Install vim-filesystem-2:7.4.160-1.el7.x86_64                             @anaconda
    Install     vim-minimal-2:7.4.160-1.el7.x86_64                               @anaconda
    Dep-Install virt-what-1.13-5.el7.x86_64                                       @anaconda
    Dep-Install which-2.20-7.el7.x86_64                                           @anaconda
    Dep-Install wpa_supplicant-1:2.0-13.el7_0.x86_64                              @anaconda
    Install     xfsprogs-3.2.1-6.el7.x86_64                                      @anaconda
    Dep-Install xz-5.1.2-9alpha.el7.x86_64                                        @anaconda
    Dep-Install xz-libs-5.1.2-9alpha.el7.x86_64                                   @anaconda
    Install     yum-3.4.3-125.el7.centos.noarch                                 @anaconda
    Dep-Install yum-metadata-parser-1.1.4-10.el7.x86_64                           @anaconda
    Dep-Install yum-plugin-fastestmirror-1.1.31-29.el7.noarch                     @anaconda
    Dep-Install zlib-1.2.7-13.el7.x86_64                                          @anaconda
history info
~]# []
```

Show the details of a package installed with yum through the following:

```
~]# yum history info ntp
```

This will show information about all the transactions that have modified the `ntp` package in some way (installed/updated/removed):

```
~]# yum history info ntp
Loaded plugins: fastestmirror
Transaction ID : 7
Begin time      : Sun Sep  6 00:38:46 2015
Begin rpmdb     : 361:b754cc21c60ca660eec9eb15121f919e59721f8b
End time        :             00:42:35 2015 (229 seconds)
End rpmdb       : 364:1e0b6904ff288549efaadd97c131bcc3314a58c2
User            : root <root>
Return-Code     : Success
Command Line    : install ntp
Transaction performed with:
    Installed     rpm-4.11.1-25.el7.x86_64                        @anaconda
    Installed     yum-3.4.3-125.el7.centos.noarch                 @anaconda
    Installed     yum-metadata-parser-1.1.4-10.el7.x86_64         @anaconda
    Installed     yum-plugin-fastestmirror-1.1.31-29.el7.noarch @anaconda
Packages Altered:
    Dep-Install autogen-libopts-5.18-5.el7.x86_64        @base
    Install     ntp-4.2.6p5-19.el7.centos.1.x86_64       @updates
    Dep-Install ntpdate-4.2.6p5-19.el7.centos.1.x86_64 @updates
history info
~]# 
```

Undoing/redoing certain yum transactions

Undo a specific transaction through the following command:

```
~]# yum history undo 7
```

This command undoes a specific transaction (defined by the ID), as shown in the following screenshot:

```
~]# yum history undo 7
Loaded plugins: fastestmirror
Undoing transaction 7, from Sun Sep  6 00:38:46 2015
    Dep-Install autogen-libopts-5.18-5.el7.x86_64        @base
    Install     ntp-4.2.6p5-19.el7.centos.1.x86_64       @updates
    Dep-Install ntpdate-4.2.6p5-19.el7.centos.1.x86_64 @updates
Resolving Dependencies
--> Running transaction check
---> Package autogen-libopts.x86_64 0:5.18-5.el7 will be erased
---> Package ntp.x86_64 0:4.2.6p5-19.el7.centos.1 will be erased
---> Package ntpdate.x86_64 0:4.2.6p5-19.el7.centos.1 will be erased
--> Finished Dependency Resolution

Dependencies Resolved

================================================================================
 Package          Arch          Version              Repository       Size
================================================================================
Removing:
 autogen-libopts  x86_64        5.18-5.el7           @base            142 k
 ntp              x86_64        4.2.6p5-19.el .centos.1   @updates     1.4 M
 ntpdate          x86_64        4.2.6p5-19.el .centos.1   @updates      121 k

Transaction Summary
================================================================================
Remove  3 Packages

Installed size: 1.6 M
Is this ok [y/N]: y
Downloading packages:
Running transaction check
Running transaction test
Transaction test succeeded
Running transaction
  Erasing    : ntp-4.2.6p5-19.el7.centos.1.x86_64                       1/3
  Erasing    : autogen-libopts-5.18-5.el7.x86_64                        2/3
  Erasing    : ntpdate-4.2.6p5-19.el7.centos.1.x86_64                   3/3
  Verifying  : ntp-4.2.6p5-19.el7.centos.1.x86_64                       1/3
  Verifying  : autogen-libopts-5.18-5.el7.x86_64                        2/3
  Verifying  : ntpdate-4.2.6p5-19.el7.centos.1.x86_64                   3/3

Removed:
  autogen-libopts.x86_64 0:5.18-5.el7           ntp.x86_64 0:4.2.6p5-19.el7.centos.1
  ntpdate.x86_64 0:4.2.6p5-19.el7.centos.1

Complete!
~]#
```

Now, you can redo a specific transaction using the following:

```
~]# yum history redo 7
```

This command will reperform a specific transaction (as defined by the transaction ID), as follows:

```
~]# yum history redo 7
Loaded plugins: fastestmirror
Repeating transaction 7, from Sun Sep  6 00:38:46 2015
    Dep-Install autogen-libopts-5.18-5.el7.x86_64       @base
    Install       ntp-4.2.6p5-19.el7.centos.1.x86_64    @updates
    Dep-Install ntpdate-4.2.6p5-19.el7.centos.1.x86_64 @updates
Loading mirror speeds from cached hostfile
 * base: ftp.belnet.be
 * epel: epel.mirror.nucleus.be
 * extras: ftp.belnet.be
 * updates: ftp.belnet.be
Resolving Dependencies
--> Running transaction check
---> Package ntp.x86_64 0:4.2.6p5-19.el7.centos.1 will be installed
--> Processing Dependency: ntpdate = 4.2.6p5-19.el7.centos.1 for package: ntp-4.2.6p5-19.el7.centos.1.
x86_64
--> Processing Dependency: libopts.so.25()(64bit) for package: ntp-4.2.6p5-19.el7.centos.1.x86_64
--> Running transaction check
---> Package autogen-libopts.x86_64 0:5.18-5.el7 will be installed
---> Package ntpdate.x86_64 0:4.2.6p5-19.el7.centos.1 will be installed
--> Finished Dependency Resolution

Dependencies Resolved

================================================================================
 Package             Arch         Version                    Repository     Size
================================================================================
Installing:
 ntp                 x86_64       4.2.6p5-19.el7.centos.1     updates       540 k
Installing for dependencies:
 autogen-libopts     x86_64       5.18-5.el7                  base           66 k
 ntpdate             x86_64       4.2.6p5-19.el7.centos.1     updates        82 k

Transaction Summary
================================================================================
Install  1 Package (+2 Dependent packages)

Total download size: 689 k
Installed size: 1.6 M
Is this ok [y/d/N]: y
Downloading packages:
(1/3): autogen-libopts-5.18-5.el7.x86_64.rpm                |  66 kB  00:00:00
(2/3): ntpdate-4.2.6p5-19.el7.centos.1.x86_64.rpm           |  82 kB  00:00:00
(3/3): ntp-4.2.6p5-19.el7.centos.1.x86_64.rpm               | 540 kB  00:00:00
--------------------------------------------------------------------------------
Total                                          540 kB/s | 689 kB  00:00:01
Running transaction check
Running transaction test
Transaction test succeeded
Running transaction
  Installing : autogen-libopts-5.18-5.el7.x86_64                         1/3
  Installing : ntpdate-4.2.6p5-19.el7.centos.1.x86_64                    2/3
  Installing : ntp-4.2.6p5-19.el7.centos.1.x86_64                        3/3
  Verifying  : ntp-4.2.6p5-19.el7.centos.1.x86_64                        1/3
  Verifying  : ntpdate-4.2.6p5-19.el7.centos.1.x86_64                    2/3
  Verifying  : autogen-libopts-5.18-5.el7.x86_64                         3/3

Installed:
  ntp.x86_64 0:4.2.6p5-19.el7.centos.1

Dependency Installed:
  autogen-libopts.x86_64 0:5.18-5.el7            ntpdate.x86_64 0:4.2.6p5-19.el7.centos.1

Complete!
~]# 
```

Roll back to a certain point in your transaction history

This allows you to undo all transactions up until the transaction ID that you specify. Run the following command:

~]# **yum history rollback 6**

Here, the transaction ID up to which you roll back is 6. You will get the following output:

```
~]# yum history rollback 6
Loaded plugins: fastestmirror
Rollback to transaction 6, from Sat Sep  5 15:53:49 2015
  Undoing the following transactions: 7, 8, 9
    Dep-Install autogen-libopts-5.18-5.el7.x86_64        @base
    Install     ntp-4.2.6p5-19.el7.centos.1.x86_64       @updates
    Dep-Install ntpdate-4.2.6p5-19.el7.centos.1.x86_64 @updates
Resolving Dependencies
--> Running transaction check
---> Package autogen-libopts.x86_64 0:5.18-5.el7 will be erased
---> Package ntp.x86_64 0:4.2.6p5-19.el7.centos.1 will be erased
---> Package ntpdate.x86_64 0:4.2.6p5-19.el7.centos.1 will be erased
--> Finished Dependency Resolution

Dependencies Resolved

================================================================================
 Package          Arch        Version                    Repository      Size
================================================================================
Removing:
 autogen-libopts  x86_64      5.18-5.el7                 @base          142 k
 ntp              x86_64      4.2.6p5-19.el7.centos.1    @updates       1.4 M
 ntpdate          x86_64      4.2.6p5-19.el7.centos.1    @updates       121 k

Transaction Summary
================================================================================
Remove  3 Packages

Installed size: 1.6 M
Is this ok [y/N]: y
Downloading packages:
Running transaction check
Running transaction test
Transaction test succeeded
Running transaction
  Erasing    : ntp-4.2.6p5-19.el7.centos.1.x86_64                        1/3
warning: file /etc/ntp.conf: remove failed: No such file or directory
  Erasing    : autogen-libopts-5.18-5.el7.x86_64                         2/3
  Erasing    : ntpdate-4.2.6p5-19.el7.centos.1.x86_64                    3/3
  Verifying  : ntp-4.2.6p5-19.el7.centos.1.x86_64                        1/3
  Verifying  : autogen-libopts-5.18-5.el7.x86_64                         2/3
  Verifying  : ntpdate-4.2.6p5-19.el7.centos.1.x86_64                    3/3

Removed:
  autogen-libopts.x86_64 0:5.18-5.el7             ntp.x86_64 0:4.2.6p5-19.el7.centos.1
  ntpdate.x86_64 0:4.2.6p5-19.el7.centos.1

Complete!
~]#
```

There's more...

You have to be careful when you use history options such as undo and rollback. Yum does its best to comply, but it cannot restore configurations, and it will not restore previous versions of your configuration files if you have edited them. This is not a fail-safe option if you don't have any backups. Although both options are very useful, I recommend that you do not use them too often. When you do use them, try to keep the impact of the transactions as small as possible. The smaller the delta, the more chance of succeeding in undoing or rolling back!

See also

Refer to the *yum(8)* man pages for more information about yum history options.

Creating a copy of an RHN repository

In this recipe, I'll show you how you can set up a yum repository for Red Hat Network-based and "plain" yum repositories.

Getting ready

Before you create a copy of an RHN repository, you need to ensure that you have a valid subscription to the repository that you want to duplicate. When this prerequisite is met, you can perform this recipe from the machine that uses the subscription.

How to do it...

Before being able to create yum repositories, we need to install a couple of tools by performing the following steps:

1. Install the `createrepo` and `yum-utils` packages using the following command:

    ```
    ~]# yum install -y yum-utils createrepo
    ```

2. Now, install the Apache web server, as follows:

    ```
    ~]# yum install -y httpd
    ```

Syncing RHN repositories

You can only sync RHN subscriptions that you have access to. Perform the following steps:

1. Create a directory to hold the RHN `rhel7` repository, as follows:

    ```
    ~]# mkdir /var/www/html/repo/rhel/rhel-x86_64-server-7/packages
    ```

2. Now, create `/mnt/iso` by executing the following command:

   ```
   ~]# mkdir -p /mnt/iso
   ```

3. Mount the RHEL 7 Server DVD through the following:

   ```
   ~]# mount -o loop,ro /tmp/rhel-server-7.0-x86_64-dvd.iso /mnt/iso
   ```

4. Now, copy the `*-comps-Server.x86_64.xml` file from the RHEL Server DVD to your `repo` directory. The following command will help in this:

   ```
   ~]# cp /mnt/iso/repodata/*-comps-Server.x86_64.xml /var/www/html/repo/rhel/comps-Server.x86_64.xml
   ```

5. Unmount the RHEL Server DVD, as follows:

   ```
   ~]# umount /mnt/iso
   ```

6. Synchronize the RHEL 7 OS repository by running the following command: (This may take a while... I suggest you kill time drinking a cup of freshly ground Arabica coffee!)

   ```
   ~]# reposync --repoid=rhel-7-server-rpms --norepopath –download_path=/var/www/html/repo/rhel/rhel-x86_64-server-7/packages
   ```

7. Next, create the local repository (depending on your hardware, this may take a long time), as follows:

   ```
   ~]# cd /var/www/html/repo/rhel/rhel-x86_64-server-7/
   ```

   ```
   ~]# createrepo --groupfile=/var/www/html/repo/rhel/comps-Server.x86_64.xml .
   ```

8. Finally, test your repository through the following:

   ```
   ~]# curl http://localhost/repo/rhel/rhel-x86_64-server-7/repodata/repomd.xml
   ```

Let's create a copy of the EPEL repository through the following steps:

1. First, install the EPEL repository, as follows:

   ```
   ~]# yum install -y epel-release
   ```

2. Create a directory to hold the EPEL repository by executing the following command:

   ```
   ~]# mkdir -p /var/www/html/repo/epel/7/x86_64
   ```

3. Now, download the `*-comps-epel7.xml` file to `/repo` as `comps-epel7.xml`, as follows:

   ```
   ~]# curl -o /var/www/html/repo/epel/comps-epel7.xml http://mirror.kinamo.be/epel/7/x86_64/repodata/xxxxxxxxxxxxxxxxxxxx-comps-epel7.xml
   ```

You will need to replace the multiple x's with the correct MD5 hash, as found in the `repodata` folder.

1. Next, synchronize the EPEL repository by executing the following (this may take a very long time, depending on your hardware and internet speed):

    ```
    ~]# reposync --repoid=epel --norepopath -download_path=/var/www/
    html/repo/epel/7/x86_64
    ```

2. Create the local repository (again, depending on your hardware, this may take a long time), as follows:

    ```
    ~]# cd /var/www/html/repo/epel/7/x86_64
    ```

    ```
    ~]# createrepo --groupfile=/var/www/html/repo/epel/comps-epel7.xml
    .
    ```

3. Finally, test your repository by executing the following command:

    ```
    ~]# curl http://localhost/repo/epel/7/x86_64/repodata/repomd.xml
    ```

There's more...

When synchronizing RHEL 7 repositories, you will only be able to sync those you have entitlement to. To find out what entitlements you have on a given system connected to RHN, execute the following:

```
~]# cd /etc/yum/pluginconf.d/ && echo *.conf | sed "s/rhnplugin.
conf//"|sed 's/\([0-9a-zA-Z\-]*\).conf/--disableplugin=\1/g'|xargs yum
repolist && cd - >/dev/null
```

Whenever you synchronize a repository, try to keep the same directory structure as the original. I have found that it makes life easier when you want to rewrite your /etc/yum. repos.d files.

In an enterprise, it is useful to have a point in time when you "freeze" your yum repositories to ensure that all your systems are at the same RPM level. By default, any repository is "live" and gets updated whenever a new package is added. The advantage of this is that you always have the latest version of all packages available; the downside is that your environment is not uniform and you can end up troubleshooting for different versions of the same package.

The easiest way to achieve a "frozen" repository is to create a central location that holds all the RPMs as you would a normal yum mirror or copy.

Every x time, which you predefine, create a new directory with a timestamp, in which you hard link all the RPMs you mirror. Then finally, create a hard link to the directory, which you will later use in your repo configuration.

Here's an example:

Directories	Description
`/rhel7/x86_64.all`	This directory contains a mirror which is synced nightly. RPMs are added, never deleted.
`/rhel7/x86_64.20150701`	This directory contains hard links to the RPMs in `/rhel7/x86_64`, all of which were synced on 01/07/2015, along with monthly iterations of the `/rhel6/x86_64.20150701` directory.
`/rhel7/x86_64`	This directory contains a hard link to the monthly iteration, which is deemed in production.

Of course, you need to ensure that you create a repository for each new sync!

See also

Refer to the *createrepo(8)* man pages for more information about creating a repository.

Also, refer to the *reposync(1)* man pages for more information on keeping your repository up-to-date.

Configuring additional repositories

Whether you create your own mirror repository or organizations provide software for you in repositories, setting up additional repositories on your RHEL system is quite simple. This recipe will show you how to set them up. Many repositories have their own repo files or even an RPM that automatically installs the repository. When these are available, don't hesitate to use them!

Getting ready

For this to work, you will need to have a repository set up, which can be accessed through the following URL: `http://repo.example.com/myrepo/7/x86_64`.

How to do it...

In order to create an additional repository, create a file in `/etc/yum.repos.d` called `myrepo.repo`, which contains the following information:

```
[myrepo]
name=My Personal Repository
baseurl=http://repo.example.com/myrepo/$releasever/$basearch
gpgcheck=0
enabled=1
```

There's more...

The `gpgcheck=1` option only functions if you or the provider of a repo has signed all the RPMs in the repo. This is generally a good practice and provides extra security to your repositories.

The `$releasever` and `$basearch` variables allow you to create a single repository file that can work on multiple systems as long as you have a repository for the URLs. The `$releasever` variable expands to the major version of the OS (7 in our case), and the `$basearch` will expands to x86_64. On an i386 system (RHEL 7 only comes in the x86_64 architecture), `$basearch` expands to i386.

You can find many repositories on the Internet, such as `epel` and `elrepo`, but it may not always be a good idea to use them. Any software provided by the Red Hat standard repositories are also supported by Red Hat, and they will no longer support you if you start using the same software provided through another repository. So, you better ensure that you don't care about support or have another party that is willing to support you.

See also

Although I do not condone the use of these in production without taking the appropriate support actions, here is a list of some popular repositories that you can use:

The ELRepo repository can be found at:

`http://elrepo.org/tiki/tiki-index.php`

The EPEL repository is at:

`https://fedoraproject.org/wiki/EPEL`

The Puppetlabs repositories can be found at:

`https://docs.puppetlabs.com/guides/puppetlabs_package_repositories.html`

The Zabbix repositories are at the following link:

`https://www.zabbix.com/documentation/2.0/manual/installation/install_from_packages`

For the RepoForge repositories, refer to the following website:

`http://repoforge.org/use/`

Remi's repositories can be found at:

`http://rpms.famillecollet.com/`

The Webtatic repositories are at:

`https://webtatic.com/projects/yum-repository/`

Setting up yum to automatically update

In enterprises, automating the systematic updating of your RHEL systems is very important. You want to stay ahead of hackers or, in general, people trying to hurt you by exploiting the weaknesses in your environment.

Although I do not recommend applying this recipe to all systems in an enterprise, this is quite useful to ensure that certain systems are kept up to date as the patches and bugfixes are applied to the RPMs in Red Hat's (and other) repositories.

Getting ready

In order for this recipe to work, you'll need to be sure that the repositories you are using are set up correctly and you have valid mail setup (using Postfix or Sendmail, for example).

How to do it...

We'll set up yum to autoupdate your system once a week (at 03:00) and reboot if necessary through the following steps:

1. Install the yum cron plugin, as follows:

   ```
   ~]# yum install -y yum-cron
   ```

2. Then, disable the hourly and daily yum cron jobs through the following commands:

   ```
   ~]# echo > /etc/cron.dhourly/0yum-hourly.cron
   ~]# echo > /etc/cron.daily/0yum-daily.cron
   ```

3. Create the configuration file for the weekly yum update cron job via the following:

   ```
   ~]# cp /etc/yum/yum-cron.conf /etc/yum/yum-cron-weekly.conf
   ```

4. Modify the created configuration file to apply updates and send a notification through e-mail by setting the following values:

   ```
   apply_updates = yes
   emit_via = email
   email_to = <your email address>
   ```

5. Next, create a weekly cron job by adding the following contents to `/etc/cron.weekly/yum-weekly.cron`:

```bash
#!/bin/bash


# Only run if this flag is set. The flag is created by the yum-cron init
# script when the service is started -- this allows one to use chkconfig and
# the standard "service stop|start" commands to enable or disable yum-cron.
if [[ ! -f /var/lock/subsys/yum-cron ]]; then
   exit 0
fi


# Action!
exec /usr/sbin/yum-cron /etc/yum/yum-cron-weekly.conf
if test "$(yum history info |egrep '\skernel'|wc -1)" != "0"; then
    /sbin/shutdown --reboot +5 "Kernel has been upgraded, rebooting the server in 5 minutes. Please save your work."
fi
```

6. Finally, make the cron job executable by executing the following command:

```
~]# chmod +x /etc/cron.weekly/yum-weekly.cron
```

How it works...

By default, `yum-cron` sets up a cron job that is run every hour (`/etc/cron.dhourly/0yum-hourly.cron`) and every day (`/etc/cron.daily/0yum-daily.cron`).

There's more...

This recipe will upgrade all your packages when there's an update available. If you just want to apply security fixes, modify the `update_cmd` value of your yum cron configuration file in the following way:

```
update_cmd = security
```

Alternatively, you can even use the following configuration if you only want critical fixes:

```
update_cmd = security-severity:Critical
```

See also

Check the *yum cron(8)* man page or the default `yum-cron.conf` file located at `/etc/yum/yum-cron.conf` for more information.

Configuring logrotate for yum

Every time you use yum to install and/or update packages, it logs to `/var/log/yum.log`. A lot of people don't want to rotate the file a lot as they believe (incorrectly) that it is their only source to the history of their yum tasks. They may even believe that it provides a way to restore your rpm database if it gets corrupted - it does not.

I do recommend keeping your complete yum history as it doesn't grow a lot, unless you reinstall packages a lot.

For a rich interface to your yum history, I suggest you use yum history.

By default, your yum log file is rotated yearly, and even then, it only rotates if the size of your log file exceeds 30 KB, and your logs are only kept for 4 years. Usually, this is enough in the physical world as physical servers tend to be replaced every 3-4 years. However, virtual servers have the potential to stay "alive" beyond these 3-4 years.

How to do it...

Modify `/etc/logrotate.d/yum` to the following:

```
/var/log/yum.log {
    missingok
    notifempty
    size 30k
    rotate 1000
    yearly
    create 0600 root root
}
```

How it works...

This configuration will only rotate the yum log when it exceeds 30 KB in size on a yearly basis, and it will keep 1000 rotated logs, which is basically log files for 1000 years!

For more information on how to use and configure logrotate, refer to the *logrotate(8)* man page.

Recovering from a corrupted RPM database

Although everything is done to ensure that your RPM databases are intact, your RPM database may become corrupt and unuseable. This happens mainly if the filesystem on which the `rpm db` resides is suddenly inaccessible (full, read-only, reboot, or so on).

This recipe will show you the two ways in which you can attempt to restore your RPM database.

Getting ready

Verify that your system is backed up in some way.

How to do it...

We'll start with the easiest option and the one with the highest success rate in these steps:

1. Start by creating a backup of your corrupt `rpm db`, as follows:

   ```
   ~]# cd; tar zcvf rpm-db.tar.gz /var/lib/rpm/*
   ```

2. Remove stale lock files if they exist through the following command:

   ```
   ~]# rm -f /var/lib/rpm/__db*
   ```

3. Now, verify the integrity of the `Packages` database via the following:

   ```
   ~]# /usr/lib/rpm/rpmdb_verify /var/lib/rpm/Packages; echo $?
   ```

   If the previous step prints 0, proceed to Step 7.

4. Rename the `Packages` file (don't delete it, we'll need it!), as follows:

   ```
   ~]# mv /var/lib/rpm/Packages  /var/lib/rpm/Packages.org
   ```

5. Now, dump the `Packages db` from the original `Packages db` by executing the following command:

   ```
   ~]# cd /usr/lib/rpm/rpmdb_dump Packages.org | /usr/lib/rpm/rpmdb_
   load Packages
   ```

6. Verify the integrity of the newly created `Packages` database. Run the following:

   ```
   ~]# /usr/lib/rpm/rpmdb_verify /var/lib/rpm/Packages; echo $?
   ```

   If the exit code is not 0, you will need to restore the database from backup.

7. Rebuild the `rpm` indexes, as follows:

   `~]# rpm -vv --rebuilddb`

8. Next, use the following command to check the `rpm db` with yum for any other issues (this may take a long time):

   `~]# yum check`

9. Restore the SELinux context of the `rpm` database through the following command:

   `~]# restorecon -R -v /var/lib/rpm`

```
~]# tar zcvf rpm-db.tar.gz /var/lib/rpm/*
tar: Removing leading '/' from member names
/var/lib/rpm/Basenames
/var/lib/rpm/Conflictname
/var/lib/rpm/Dirnames
/var/lib/rpm/Group
/var/lib/rpm/Installtid
/var/lib/rpm/Name
/var/lib/rpm/Obsoletename
/var/lib/rpm/Packages
/var/lib/rpm/Providename
/var/lib/rpm/Requirename
/var/lib/rpm/Shalheader
/var/lib/rpm/Sigmd5
/var/lib/rpm/Triggername
~]# rm -f /var/lib/rpm/__db*
~]# /usr/lib/rpm/rpmdb_verify /var/lib/rpm/Packages; echo $?
BDB5105 Verification of /var/lib/rpm/Packages succeeded.
0
~]# rpm -vv --rebuilddb
D: rebuilding database /var/lib/rpm into /var/lib/rpmrebuilddb.13427
D: opening  db environment /var/lib/rpm private:0x401
D: opening  db index       /var/lib/rpm/Packages 0x400 mode=0x0
D: locked   db index       /var/lib/rpm/Packages
D: opening  db environment /var/lib/rpmrebuilddb.13427 private:0x401
D: opening  db index       /var/lib/rpmrebuilddb.13427/Packages (none) mode=0x42
D: opening  db index       /var/lib/rpmrebuilddb.13427/Packages 0x1 mode=0x42

...

D: adding 1 entries to Installtid index.
D: adding 1 entries to Sigmd5 index.
D: adding "22f5db5a1d2a3be92a0457d47020c1fb0baa22b0" to Shalheader index.
D: closed    db index       /var/lib/rpm/Packages
D: closed    db environment /var/lib/rpm
D: closed    db index       /var/lib/rpmrebuilddb.13427/Shalheader
D: closed    db index       /var/lib/rpmrebuilddb.13427/Sigmd5
D: closed    db index       /var/lib/rpmrebuilddb.13427/Installtid
D: closed    db index       /var/lib/rpmrebuilddb.13427/Dirnames
D: closed    db index       /var/lib/rpmrebuilddb.13427/Triggername
D: closed    db index       /var/lib/rpmrebuilddb.13427/Obsoletename
D: closed    db index       /var/lib/rpmrebuilddb.13427/Conflictname
D: closed    db index       /var/lib/rpmrebuilddb.13427/Providename
D: closed    db index       /var/lib/rpmrebuilddb.13427/Requirename
D: closed    db index       /var/lib/rpmrebuilddb.13427/Group
D: closed    db index       /var/lib/rpmrebuilddb.13427/Basenames
D: closed    db index       /var/lib/rpmrebuilddb.13427/Name
D: closed    db index       /var/lib/rpmrebuilddb.13427/Packages
D: closed    db environment /var/lib/rpmrebuilddb.13427
~]#
```

There's more...

If, for some reason, you are unable to recover your RPM database, there is one final option left. Enterprises tend to have standardized builds, and many servers are installed with the same packages, so copy the healthy `/var/lib/rpm` directory from another server with the exact same package set to the corrupted one, and perform the preceding recipe's steps to ensure that everything is okay.

Although you'll find additional tools that can save your skin (such as RPM cron), it's usually more practical to have a decent backup.

9
Securing RHEL 7

In this chapter, you will learn all about:

- ▶ Installing and configuring IPA
- ▶ Securing the system login
- ▶ Configuring privilege escalation with sudo
- ▶ Securing the network with `firewalld`
- ▶ Using kdump and SysRq
- ▶ Using ABRT
- ▶ Auditing the system

Introduction

Security is an important aspect of your environment. The recipes provided in this chapter are not a definitive set of how-tos; rather, they are a start to addressing security in an environment as every environment is different. This chapter is meant to give you an idea of what you can do with a simple set of tools included in Red Hat Enterprise Server 7.

In this chapter, I will not attempt explaining where the system stores syslog messages and what they mean as this can be quite an exhaustive topic. The most important security-related syslog messages can be found in `/var/log/secure` and `/var/log/audit/audit.log`.

Installing and configuring IPA

The **IPA** (**Identity Policy Audit**) server allows you to manage your kerberos, DNS, hosts, users, sudo rules, password policies, and automounts in a central location. IPA is a combination of packages, including—but not limited to—bind, ldap, pam, and so on. It combines all of these to provide identity management for your environment.

Getting ready

In this recipe, I will opt for an integrated DNS setup, although it is possible to use your existing DNS infrastructure.

How to do it...

First, we'll install the server component, followed by what needs to be done on an IPA client.

Installing the IPA server

Follow these instructions to install an IPA server:

1. Install the necessary packages via the following command:

   ```
   ~]# yum install -y ipa-server bind bind-dyndb-ldap
   ```

2. When the packages are installed, invoke the ipa installer, as follows:

   ```
   ~]# ipa-server-install
   ```

At this stage, you will be asked a couple of questions on how to set up your IPA server.

1. Configure integrated DNS as follows:

   ```
   Do you want to configure integrated DNS (BIND)? [no]: yes
   ```

2. Overwrite existing /etc/resolv.conf as follows:

   ```
   Existing BIND configuration detected, overwrite? [no]: yes
   ```

3. Provide the IPA server's hostname, as follows:

   ```
   Server host name [localhost.localdomain]: master.example.com
   ```

4. Now, confirm the DNS domain name for the IPA server as follows:

   ```
   Please confirm the domain name [example.com]:
   ```

5. Provide an IP address for the IPA server as follows:

   Please provide the IP address to be used for this host name: 192.168.0.1

6. Next, provide a Kerberos `realm` name, as follows:

   Please provide a realm name [EXAMPLE.COM]:

7. Create the directory manager's password and confirm it as follows:

   Directory Manager password:

8. Create the IPA manager's password and confirm it as follows:

   IPA admin password:

9. Now, configure the DNS forwarders as follows:

   Do you want to configure DNS forwarders? [yes]: no

10. Finally, configure the reverse DNS zones as follows:

    Do you want to configure the reverse zone? [yes]:

    Please specify the reverse zone name [0.168.192.in-addr.arpa.]:

    The installer will now provide an overview similar to the following:

    The IPA Master Server will be configured with:

    Hostname: master.example.com

    IP address: 192.168.0.1

    Domain name: example.com

    Realm name: EXAMPLE.COM

    BIND DNS server will be configured to serve IPA domain with:

    Forwarders: No forwarders

    Reverse zone: 0.168.192.in-addr.arpa.

11. Now, confirm the information by typing "yes", as follows:

    Continue to configure the system with these values? [no]: yes

At this point, you will see a lot of information scrolling on your screen, indicating what the installer is doing: installing or configuring NTP, LDAP, BIND, Kerberos, HTTP, the certificate server, and IPA-related modifications to the preceding examples.

The installation and configuration process can take a while, so be patient.

Installing the IPA client

Perform these steps to install and configure the IPA client on your system:

 Ensure that the hostname of your system is different from `localhost.localdomain`. If it is not, the client configuration will fail.

1. Install the necessary packages via the following command:

    ```
    ~]# yum install -y ipa-client
    ```

2. Ensure that the IPA server is used as a DNS server through the following:

    ```
    ~]# cat /etc/resolv.conf
    search example.com
    nameserver 192.168.0.1
    ```

3. Invoke the IPA client configuration by running this command line:

    ```
    ~]# ipa-client-install --enable-dns-updates
    ```

The installer will now show an overview of the detected IPA server and ask for a user (the IPA manager) and password to register your system, as shown in the following screenshot:

```
~]# ipa-client-install --enable-dns-updates
Discovery was successful!
Hostname: guest.example.com
Realm: EXAMPLE.COM
DNS Domain: example.com
IPA Server: master.example.com
BaseDN: dc=example,dc=com

Continue to configure the system with these values? [no]: yes
User authorized to enroll computers: admin
Synchronizing time with KDC...
Password for admin@EXAMPLE.COM:
Successfully retrieved CA cert
    Subject:    CN=Certificate Authority,O=EXAMPLE.COM
    Issuer:     CN=Certificate Authority,O=EXAMPLE.COM
    Valid From:  Fri Oct 30 13:40:04 2015 UTC
    Valid Until: Tue Oct 30 13:40:04 2035 UTC

Enrolled in IPA realm EXAMPLE.COM
Created /etc/ipa/default.conf
New SSSD config will be created
Configured /etc/sssd/sssd.conf
Configured /etc/krb5.conf for IPA realm EXAMPLE.COM
trying https://master.example.com/ipa/xml
Forwarding 'ping' to server 'https://master.example.com/ipa/xml'
Forwarding 'env' to server 'https://master.example.com/ipa/xml'
Hostname (guest.example.com) not found in DNS
DNS server record set to: guest.example.com -> 192.168.0.2
Adding SSH public key from /etc/ssh/ssh_host_rsa_key.pub
Adding SSH public key from /etc/ssh/ssh_host_ecdsa_key.pub
Forwarding 'host_mod' to server 'https://master.example.com/ipa/xml'
SSSD enabled
Configured /etc/openldap/ldap.conf
NTP enabled
Configured /etc/ssh/ssh_config
Configured /etc/ssh/sshd_config
Client configuration complete.
~]# 
```

There's more...

Once installed, you can manage your IPA environment using the command line tool IPA or the web interface, which can be accessed by pointing your browser to your IPA master server over HTTPS. In this case, the URL is `https://master.example.com`.

By default, the IPA client doesn't create `homedirs` for new users at first login. If you want to enable this, use the `--mkhomedir` argument with `ipa-client-install`. If you happen to have forgotten about this, there's no need to reinstall the IPA client. You can just reconfigure this by executing the following command:

```
~]# authconfig --enablemkhomedir --update
```

See also

For more in-depth information about installing and configuring your IPA server, go to `https://access.redhat.com/documentation/en-US/Red_Hat_Enterprise_Linux/7/html/Linux_Domain_Identity_Authentication_and_Policy_Guide/installing-ipa.html`.

For more information about managing your IPA environment through the command line, read the *ipa (1)* man pages.

Securing the system login

The default settings applied to system login are based on what Red Hat deems basic security. If, for some reason, you want to change this, this recipe will show you a couple of examples. Authconfig has two tools that you can use to configure authentication: `authconfig` and `authconfig-tui`.

These two tools configure `pam` for you in such a way that the changes are consistent throughout rpm updates.

The `authconfig-tui` tool is not as feature-rich as the plan `authconfig` tool, which I personally recommend you to use as it allows you to do more.

You can manually edit the files located in `/etc/pam.d` if and when you know what you're doing, but this is not recommended.

How to do it...

Perform the following steps:

First, change the hash encryption of the passwords stored in /etc/shadow to sha512, as follows:

```
~]# authconfig --passalgo=sha512 --update
```

Enable NIS authentication through the following command:

```
~]# authconfig --enablenis –nisdomain=NISDOMAIN --nisserver=nisserver.
example.com --update
```

Now, set the minimum length requirement for passwords to 16 via the following:

```
~]# authconfig --passminlen=16 --update
```

The user requires at least one lowercase letter in the password; you can set this requirement by running the following:

```
~]# authconfig --enablereqlower --update
```

Also, the user requires at least one uppercase letter in the password, for which you can run the following:

```
~]# authconfig --enablerequpper --update
```

Now, the user requires at least one number in the password. Execute the following command for this:

```
~]# authconfig --enablereqdigit --update
```

Finally, the user requires at least one nonalphanumeric character in the password, which you can set using the following command:

```
~]# authconfig --enablereqother --update
```

How it works...

authconfig and authconfig-tui are wrapper scripts that modify a variety of files, including, but not limited to, /etc/nsswitch.conf, /etc/pam.d/*, /etc/sssd.conf, /etc/openldap/ldap.conf, and /etc/sysconfig/network.

The advantage of the tool is that it uses the correct syntax, which can sometimes be a little tricky, especially for the files in /etc/pam.d.

There's more...

One of the interesting features of this tool is the backup and restore functions. In case you do not use any centralized identification and authentication infrastructure, such as IPA, you can use this to make a backup of a correctly configured machine and distribute this through whichever means you wish to use.

To back up your `authconf` configuration, execute the following:

```
~]# authconfig --savebackup=/tmp/auth.conf
```

This will create a `/tmp/auth.conf` directory, which contains all the files modified by `authconfig`.

Copy this directory over to another server and restore the configuration by executing the following:

```
~]# authconfig --restorebackup=/tmp/auth.conf
```

All of the security changes you apply through `authconfig` can also be managed through IPA.

See also

For information about and more configuration options, take a look at the *authconfig (8)* man pages.

You can also find more information on Red Hat's page on authentication at `https://access.redhat.com/documentation/en-US/Red_Hat_Enterprise_Linux/7/html/System-Level_Authentication_Guide/Configuring_Authentication.html`.

Configuring privilege escalation with sudo

Sudo allows users to run applications and scripts with the security privileges of another user.

Getting ready

Before allowing someone to elevate their security context for a specific application or script, you need to figure out which user or group you wish to elevate from and to, which applications/scripts you use, and on which systems to run them.

The default syntax for a sudo entry is the following:

```
who where = (as_whom) what
```

How to do it...

These simple five steps will guide you through setting up privilege escalation:

1. Create a new `sudoers` definition file in `/etc/sudoers.d/` called clustering through the following command:

    ```
    ~]# visudo -f /etc/sudoers.d/clustering
    ```

2. Create a command alias for the most-used clustering tools called CLUSTERING by executing the following:

    ```
    Cmnd_Alias CLUSTERING = /sbin/ccs, /sbin/clustat, /sbin/clusvcadm
    ```

3. Now, create a host alias group for all the clusters called CLUSTERS, as follows:

    ```
    Host_Alias CLUSTERS = cluster1, cluster2
    ```

4. Next, create a user alias for all cluster admins called CLUSTERADMINS by executing the following:

    ```
    User_Alias CLUSTERADMINS = spalpatine, dvader, okenobi, qjinn
    ```

5. Now, let's create a sudo rule that allows the users from CLUSTERADMINS to execute commands from CLUSTERING on all servers within the CLUSTERS group, as follows:

    ```
    CLUSTERADMINS CLUSTERS = (root) CLUSTERING
    ```

There's more...

To edit the `sudoers` file, you can either use a text editor and edit `/etc/sudoers`, the `visudo` tool, which automatically checks your syntax when exiting.

It's always a good idea to leave the original `/etc/sudoers` file alone and modify the files located in `/etc/sudoers.d/`. This allows the sudo rpm to update the `sudoers` file should it be necessary.

See also

For more information about sudo, take a look at the *sudoers (5)* man page.

Secure the network with firewalld

firewalld is a set of scripts and a daemon that manage netfilter on your RHEL system. It aims at creating a simple command-line interface to manage the firewall on your systems.

How to do it...

By default, firewalld is included in the "core" rpm group, but it may not be installed for some reason (that you left it out of your kickstart would be one!). Perform the following steps:

1. Install firewalld via the following command line:

    ~]# **yum install -y firewalld**

2. Now, enable firewalld through the following:

    ~]# **systemctl enable firewalld**

3. Finally, ensure that firewalld is started by executing the following command line:

    ~]# **systemctl restart firewalld**

Showing the currently allowed services and ports on your system

List all the allowed services using the following command:

~]# **firewall-cmd –list-services**

You can see the output as follows, where all the allowed services are listed:

```
~]# firewall-cmd --list-services
dhcpv6-client http https ssh
~]#
```

Now, show the tcp/udp ports that are allowed by your firewall using the following command:

~]# **firewall-cmd --list-ports**

Here's what the output should look like:

Allowing incoming requests for NFS (v4)

Perform the following steps to allow NFSv4 traffic on your system:

1. First, allow `nfs` traffic via this command:

   ```
   ~]# firewall-cmd --add-service nfs --permanent
   success
   ~]#
   ```

2. Then, reload the configuration as follows:

   ```
   ~]# firewall-cmd --reload
   success
   ~]#
   ```

3. Now, check the newly applied rule by executing the following command line:

   ```
   ~]# firewall-cmd --list-services
   nfs
   ~]#
   ```

Allowing incoming requests on an arbitrary port

Perform the following steps to allow incoming traffic on port `1234` over both `tcp` and `udp`:

1. First, allow traffic on port `1234` over `tcp` and `udp` by running the following:

   ```
   ~]# firewall-cmd --add-port 1234/tcp --permanent
   success
   ~]# firewall-cmd --add-port 1234/udp --permanent
   success
   ~]#
   ```

2. Reload the configuration by executing the following command:

```
~]# firewall-cmd --reload
success
~]#
```

3. Check the newly applied rule via the following:

```
~]# firewall-cmd --list-ports
1234/tcp 1234/udp
~]#
```

There's more...

`firewalld` comes with a set of predefined port configurations, such as HTTP and HTTPS. You can find all such definitions in `/lib/firewalld/services`. When creating your own port definitions or modifying the existing ones, you should create new port definition files in `/etc/firewalld/services`.

When creating new "rules" by adding ports, services, and so on, you need to add the `--permanent` option, or your changes would be lost upon the rebooting of the system or the reloading of the `firewalld` policy.

See also

For more information on configuring your firewall, check the man pages for *firewall-cmd(1)*.

Using kdump and SysRq

The kdump mechanism is a Linux kernel feature, which allows you to create dumps if your kernel crashes. It produces an exact copy of the memory, which can be analyzed for the root cause of the crash.

SysRq is a feature supported by the Linux kernel, which allows you to send key combinations to it even when your system becomes unresponsive.

How to do it...

First, we'll set up kdump and SysRq, and afterwards, I'll show you how to use it to debug a dump.

Installing and configuring kdump and SysRq

Let's take a look at how this is installed and configured:

1. Install the necessary packages for kdump by executing the following command:

    ```
    ~]# yum install -y kexec-tools
    ```

2. Ensure that crashkernel=auto is present in the GRUB_CMDLINE_LINUX variable declaration in the /etc/sysconfig/grub file using this command:

    ```
    GRUB_CMDLINE_LINUX="rd.lvm.lv=system/usr
    rd.lvm.lv=system/swap vconsole.keymap=us
    rd.lvm.lv=system/root vconsole.font=latarcyrheb-sun16
    crashkernel=auto"
    ```

3. Start kdump by running the following:

    ```
    ~]# systemctl start kdump
    ```

4. Now, enable kdump to start at boot, as follows:

    ```
    ~]# sysctl enable kdump
    ```

5. Configure SysRq to accept all commands via the following commands:

    ```
    ~]# echo "kernel.sysrq = 1" >> /etc/sysctl.d/sysrq.conf
    ```

    ```
    ~]# systemctl -q -p /etc/sysctl.d/sysrq.conf
    ```

6. Regenerate your **intramfs** (**initial RAM file system**) to contain the necessary information for kdump by executing the following command:

    ```
    ~]# dracut --force
    ```

7. Finally, reboot through the following command:

    ```
    ~]# reboot
    ```

Using kdump tools to analyze the dump

Although you'll find most of the information you're looking for in the vmcode-dmesg.txt file, it can be useful sometimes to look into the bits and bytes of the vmcore dump, even if it is just to know what the people at Red Hat do when they ask you to send you a vmcore dump. Perform the following steps:

1. Install the necessary tools to debug the vmcore dump via the following command:

    ```
    ~]# yum install -y --enablerepo=\*debuginfo crash kernel-debuginfo
    ```

2. Locate your vmcore by executing the following:

    ```
    ~]# find /var/crash -name 'vmcore'
    ```

    ```
    /var/crash/127.0.0.1-2015.10.31-12:03:06/vmcore
    ```

If you don't have a core dump, you can trigger this yourself by executing the following:

```
~]# echo c > /proc/sysrq-trigger
```

3. Use `crash` to analyze the contents, as follows:

```
~]# crash /var/crash/127.0.0.1-2015.10.31-12:03:06/vmcore /usr/
lib/debug/lib/modules/<kernel>/vmlinux
```

Here, `<kernel>` must be the same kernel as the one that the dump was created for:

```
crash 7.0.2-6.el7
Copyright (C) 2002-2013  Red Hat, Inc.
Copyright (C) 2004, 2005, 2006, 2010  IBM Corporation
Copyright (C) 1999-2006  Hewlett-Packard Co
Copyright (C) 2005, 2006, 2011, 2012  Fujitsu Limited
Copyright (C) 2006, 2007  VA Linux Systems Japan K.K.
Copyright (C) 2005, 2011  NEC Corporation
Copyright (C) 1999, 2002, 2007  Silicon Graphics, Inc.
Copyright (C) 1999, 2000, 2001, 2002  Mission Critical Linux, Inc.
This program is free software, covered by the GNU General Public License,
and you are welcome to change it and/or distribute copies of it under
certain conditions.  Enter "help copying" to see the conditions.
This program has absolutely no warranty.  Enter "help warranty" for details.

GNU gdb (GDB) 7.6
Copyright (C) 2013 Free Software Foundation, Inc.
License GPLv3+: GNU GPL version 3 or later <http://gnu.org/licenses/gpl.html>
This is free software: you are free to change and redistribute it.
There is NO WARRANTY, to the extent permitted by law.  Type "show copying"
and "show warranty" for details.
This GDB was configured as "x86_64-unknown-linux-gnu".

      KERNEL: /usr/lib/debug/lib/modules/3.10.0-123.el7.x86_64/vmlinux
    DUMPFILE: /var/crash/127.0.0.1-2015.10.31-12:03:06/vmcore  [PARTIAL DUMP]
        CPUS: 2
        DATE: Sat Oct 31 12:03:06 2015
      UPTIME: 02:04:36
LOAD AVERAGE: 0.00, 0.01, 0.00
       TASKS: 122
    NODENAME: guest.example.com
     RELEASE: 3.10.0-123.el7.x86_64
     VERSION: #1 SMP Mon May 5 11:16:57 EDT 2014
     MACHINE: x86_64
      MEMORY: 2 GB
       PANIC: "Oops: 0002 [#1] SMP " (check log for details)
         PID: 4389
     COMMAND: "bash"
        TASK: f196d560  [THREAD_INFO: ef4da000]
         CPU: 2
       STATE: TASK_RUNNING (PANIC)

crash>
```

4. Display the kernel message buffer (this can also be found in the `vmcore-dmesg.txt` dump file) by running the following command:

```
crash> log
```

Here's what the output should look like:

```
crash> log
...
EIP: 0060:[<c068124f>] EFLAGS: 00010096 CPU: 2
EIP is at sysrq_handle_crash+0xf/0x20
EAX: 00000063 EBX: 00000063 ECX: c09e1c8c EDX: 00000000
ESI: c0a09ca0 EDI: 00000286 EBP: 00000000 ESP: ef4dbf24
 DS: 007b ES: 007b FS: 00d8 GS: 00e0 SS: 0068
Process bash (pid: 5591, ti=ef4da000 task=f196d560 task.ti=ef4da000)
Stack:
 c068146b c0960891 c0968653 00000003 00000000 00000002 efade5c0 c06814d0
<0> fffffffb c068150f b7776000 f2600c40 c0569ec4 ef4dbf9c 00000002 b7776000
<0> efade5c0 00000002 b7776000 c0569e60 c051de50 ef4dbf9c f196d560 ef4dbfb4
Call Trace:
 [<c068146b>] ? __handle_sysrq+0xfb/0x160
 [<c06814d0>] ? write_sysrq_trigger+0x0/0x50
 [<c068150f>] ? write_sysrq_trigger+0x3f/0x50
 [<c0569ec4>] ? proc_reg_write+0x64/0xa0
 [<c0569e60>] ? proc_reg_write+0x0/0xa0
 [<c051de50>] ? vfs_write+0xa0/0x190
 [<c051e8d1>] ? sys_write+0x41/0x70
 [<c0409adc>] ? syscall_call+0x7/0xb
Code: a0 c0 01 0f b6 41 03 19 d2 f7 d2 83 e2 03 83 e0 cf c1 e2 04 09 d0 88 41 03 f3 c3 90 c7 05 c8 1b 9e c0 01 00 00 00
0f ae f8 89 f6 <c6> 05 00 00 00 00 01 c3 89 f6 8d bc 27 00 00 00 00 8d 50 d0 83
EIP: [<c068124f>] sysrq_handle_crash+0xf/0x20 SS:ESP 0068:ef4dbf24
CR2: 0000000000000000
crash>
```

5. Display the kernel stack trace through the following:

   `crash> bt`

   Here's what the output should look like:

```
crash> bt
PID: 4389   TASK: f196d560 CPU: 2   COMMAND: "bash"
 #0 [ef4dbdcc] crash_kexec at c0494922
 #1 [ef4dbe20] oops_end at c080e402
 #2 [ef4dbe34] no_context at c043099d
 #3 [ef4dbe58] bad_area at c0430b26
 #4 [ef4dbe6c] do_page_fault at c080fb9b
 #5 [ef4dbee4] error_code (via page_fault) at c080d809
    EAX: 00000063 EBX: 00000063 ECX: c09e1c8c EDX: 00000000 EBP: 00000000
    DS:  007b    ESI: c0a09ca0 ES:  007b    EDI: 00000286 GS:  00e0
    CS:  0060    EIP: c068124f ERR: ffffffff EFLAGS: 00010096
 #6 [ef4dbf18] sysrq_handle_crash at c068124f
 #7 [ef4dbf24] __handle_sysrq at c0681469
 #8 [ef4dbf48] write_sysrq_trigger at c068150a
 #9 [ef4dbf54] proc_reg_write at c0569ec2
#10 [ef4dbf74] vfs_write at c051de4e
#11 [ef4dbf94] sys_write at c051e8cc
#12 [ef4dbfb0] system_call at c0409ad5
    EAX: ffffffda EBX: 00000001 ECX: b7776000 EDX: 00000002
    DS:  007b    ESI: 00000002 ES:  007b    EDI: b7776000
    SS:  007b    ESP: bfcb2088 EBP: bfcb20b4 GS:  0033
    CS:  0073    EIP: 00edc416 ERR: 00000004 EFLAGS: 00000246
crash>
```

6. Now, show the processes at the time of the core dump, as follows:

   `crash> ps`

Here's what the output should look like:

```
crash> ps
   PID    PPID  CPU    TASK   ST  %MEM    VSZ    RSS  COMM
>    0       0    0  c09dc560  RU  0.0      0      0  [swapper]
>    0       0    1  f7072030  RU  0.0      0      0  [swapper]
     0       0    2  f70a3a90  RU  0.0      0      0  [swapper]
>    0       0    3  f70ac560  RU  0.0      0      0  [swapper]
     1       0    1  f705ba90  IN  0.0   2828   1424  init
...
  4221       1    1  f2592560  IN  0.0  12876    784  auditd
  4222       1    2  ef427560  IN  0.0  12876    784  auditd
  4387    4362    0  f196d030  IN  0.0  11064   3184  sshd
>  4389    4387    2  f196d560  RU  0.0   5084   1648  bash
crash>
```

There's more...

The default kdump configuration uses /var/crash to dump its memory on. This MUST be on the root filesystem. Some systems are configured with a separate filesystem for /var, so you need to change the location in /etc/kdump.conf or use a different target type, such as raw, nfs, and so on. If your crash directory is located on a nonroot filesystem, the kdump service will fail!

Although the crash utility can provide a lot of details about the crash, usually you're set with the contents of the vmcore-dmesg.txt file, which resides in the same directory as the vmcore file. So, I suggest that you parse this file before digging into the bits and bytes of the memory dump.

SysRq, as stated before, allows you to control your system even if it is in a state that doesn't allow you to do anything at all. However, it does require you to have access to the system's console.

By default, kdump creates a dump and reboots your system. In the event that this doesn't happen and you don't want to push the power button on your (virtual) system, SysRq allows you to send commands through the console to your kernel.

The key combination needed to send the information differs a little from architecture to architecture. Take a look at the following table for reference:

Architecture	Key combination
x86	`<Alt><SysRq><command key>`
Sparc	`<Alt><Stop><command key>`
Serial console (PC style only)	This sends a BREAK and, within 5 seconds, the command key. Sending BREAK twice is interpreted as a normal BREAK.
PowerPC	`<Alt><Print Screen>`(or `<F13>`)`<command key>`

So, on an x86 system, you would attempt to sync your disks before rebooting it by executing the following commands:

`<Alt><SysRq><s>`

`<Alt><SysRq><b>`

Alternatively, if you still have access to your terminal, you can do the same by sending characters to `/proc/sysrq-trigger`, as follows:

```
~]# echo s > /proc/sysrq-trigger
~]# echo b > /proc/sysrq-trigger
```

The following key commands are available:

Command key	Function
b	This immediately reboots your system. It does not sync or unmount disks. This can result in data corruption!
c	This performs a system crash by a NULL pointer dereference. A crashdump is taken if kdump is configured.
d	This shows all the locks held.
e	This sends a SIGTERM signal to all your processes, except for init.
f	This calls oom_kill to kill any process hogging the memory.
g	This is used by the **kernel debugger** (**kgdb**).
h	This shows help. (Memorize this option!)
i	This sends a SIGKILL signal to all your processes, except for init.
j	This freezes your filesystems with the FIFREEZE ioctl.
k	This kills all the programs on the current virtual console. It enables a secure login from the console as this kills all malware attempting to grab your keyboard input, for example.
l	This shows a stack trace for all active CPUs.
m	This dumps the current memory info to your console.
n	You can use this to make real-time tasks niceable.
o	This shuts down your system and turns it off (if configured and supported).
p	This dumps the current registers and flags to your console
q	This will dump a list of all armed hrtimers (except for timer_list timers) per CPU together with detailed information about all clockevent devices.
r	This turns off your keyboard's raw mode and sets it to XLATE.
s	This attempts to sync all your mounted filesystems, committing unwritten data to them.

Command key	Function
t	This dumps a list of current tasks and their information to your console.
u	This attempts to remount all your filesystems as read-only volumes.
v	This causes the ETM buffer to dump (this is ARM-specific).
w	This dumps all the tasks that are in an uninterruptable (blocked) state.
x	This is used by xmon on ppc/powerpc platforms. This shows the global PMU registers on SPARC64.
y	This shows global CPU registers (this is SPARC64-specific).
z	This dumps the ftrace buffer.
0 - 9	This sets the console's log level, controlling which messages will be printed. The higher the number, the more the output.

See also...

For more information about SysRq and systemd, refer to the following page: `https://github.com/systemdaemon/systemd/blob/master/src/linux/Documentation/sysrq.txt`

Red Hat has a complete crash dump guide at `https://access.redhat.com/documentation/en-US/Red_Hat_Enterprise_Linux/7/html/Kernel_Crash_Dump_Guide/index.html`.

Using ABRT

ABRT (**Automatic Bug Reporting Tool**), is a set of tools that help users detect and analyze application crashes.

How to do it...

First, we'll install the necessary packages and then take a look at how to use these tools.

Installing and configuring abrtd

Let's install `abrt` and get it running:

1. Install the `abrt` daemon and tools via the following command line:

```
~]# yum install -y abrt-cli
```

2. Now, enable and start the `abrt` daemon through these commands:

```
~]# systemctl enable abrtd
~]# systemctl restart abrtdThere's more...
```

Using abrt-cli

List all detected segmentation faults by executing the following command:

```
~]# abtr-cli list
```

Here's what the output should look like:

The displayed location contains all the information about the segmentation fault. You can use this to analyze what went wrong, and if you need help from Red Hat, you can use `abrt-cli report` to report to Red Hat Support.

There's more...

When your RHEL 7 system is registered with a satellite, all bugs will automatically be reported to the satellite system.

You can install additional plugins to automatically report bugs in the following ways:

▸ to Bugzilla (`libreport-plugin-bugzilla`)

▸ via ftp upload (`libreport-plugin-reportuploader`)

▸ to Red Hat Support (`libreport-plugin-rhtsupport`)

▸ to an `abrt` server (`libreport-plugin-ureport`)

Besides the basic bug reporting, you can also create automatic bug reports for Java by installing the `abrt-java-connector` package.

See also

For more information on how to use the abrt tool, refer to `https://access.redhat.com/documentation/en-US/Red_Hat_Enterprise_Linux/7/html/System_Administrators_Guide/ch-abrt.html`.

Auditing the system

The Linux audit system allows you to track security-related information about your systems. It allows you to watch security events, filesystem access, network access, commands run by users, and system calls.

How to do it...

By default, audit is installed as part of the core packages. So, there's no need to install this.

Configuring a centralized syslog server to accept audit logs

Perform these steps to set up the `syslog` server:

1. On the `syslog` server, create a `/etc/rsyslog.d/audit_server.conf` file containing the following:

```
# Receive syslog audit messages via TCP over port 65514
$ModLoad imtcp
$InputTCPServerRun 65514
$AllowedSender TCP, 127.0.0.1, 192.168.1.0/24
$template HostAudit, "/var/log/audit/%$YEAR%%$MONTH%%$DAY%-%HOSTNAME%/audit.log"
$template auditFormat, "%msg%\n" local6.*
?HostAudit;auditFormat
```

2. On the `syslog` server, restart `rsyslog`, as follows:

```
~]# systemctl restart rsyslog
```

3. On the client, create a `/etc/rsyslog.d/audit_client.conf` file containing the following:

```
$ModLoad imfile
$InputFileName /var/log/audit/audit.log
$InputFileTag tag_audit_log:
$InputFileStateFile audit_log
$InputFileFacility local6
$InputFileSeverity info
$InputRunFileMonitor local6.* @@logserver.example.com:65514
```

4. Next, on the client, restart `rsyslog`, as follows:

```
~]# systemctl restart syslog
```

Some audit rules

You can use the following command to log activity on `/etc/resolv.conf`:

```
~]# auditctl -w /etc/resolv.conf -p w -k resolv_changes
```

You can execute the following commands to log all the commands executed by root:

```
~]# echo "session    required pam_tty_audit.so disable=* enable=root" >> /
etc/pam.d/system-auth-ac
```

```
~]# echo "session    required pam_tty_audit.so disable=* enable=root" >> /
etc/pam.d/password-auth-ac
```

Showing audit logs for the preceding rules

You can search for the audit events that have changed `/etc/resolv.conf` using the preceding rule by executing the following command:

```
~]# ausearch -k resolv_changes
```

Here's what the output should look like:

```
~]# ausearch -k resolv_changes
----
time->Sat Oct 31 15:29:20 2015
type=CONFIG_CHANGE msg=audit(1446301760.079:404): auid=0 ses=1 subj=unconfined_u:unconfined_r:unconfined_t:s0-s0:
c0.c1023 op="add rule" key="resolv_changes" list=4 res=1
----
time->Sat Oct 31 15:46:06 2015
type=CONFIG_CHANGE msg=audit(1446302766.693:430): auid=0 ses=5 op="updated rules" path="/etc/resolv.conf" key="re
solv_changes" list=4 res=1
----
time->Sat Oct 31 15:46:06 2015
type=PATH msg=audit(1446302766.693:431): item=3 name="/etc/resolv.conf~" inode=6303581 dev=fd:02 mode=0100644 oui
d=0 ogid=0 rdev=00:00 obj=system_u:object_r:net_conf_t:s0 objtype=CREATE
type=PATH msg=audit(1446302766.693:431): item=2 name="/etc/resolv.conf" inode=6303581 dev=fd:02 mode=0100644 ouid
=0 ogid=0 rdev=00:00 obj=system_u:object_r:net_conf_t:s0 objtype=DELETE
type=PATH msg=audit(1446302766.693:431): item=1 name="/etc/" inode=6291585 dev=fd:02 mode=040755 ouid=0 ogid=0 rd
ev=00:00 obj=system_u:object_r:etc_t:s0 objtype=PARENT
type=PATH msg=audit(1446302766.693:431): item=0 name="/etc/" inode=6291585 dev=fd:02 mode=040755 ouid=0 ogid=0 rd
ev=00:00 obj=system_u:object_r:etc_t:s0 objtype=PARENT
type=CWD msg=audit(1446302766.693:431):  cwd="/root"
type=SYSCALL msg=audit(1446302766.693:431): arch=c000003e syscall=82 success=yes exit=0 a0=219e270 a1=21c40c0 a2=
ffffffffffffffea0 a3=7fff14c2bbc0 items=4 ppid=12455 pid=12474 auid=0 uid=0 gid=0 euid=0 suid=0 fsuid=0 egid=0 sgi
d=0 fsgid=0 tty=pts0 ses=5 comm="vim" exe="/usr/bin/vim" subj=unconfined_u:unconfined_r:unconfined_t:s0-s0:c0.c10
23 key="resolv_changes"
----
time->Sat Oct 31 15:46:06 2015
type=CONFIG_CHANGE msg=audit(1446302766.693:432): auid=0 ses=5 op="updated rules" path="/etc/resolv.conf" key="re
solv_changes" list=4 res=1
----
time->Sat Oct 31 15:46:06 2015
type=PATH msg=audit(1446302766.693:433): item=1 name="/etc/resolv.conf" inode=6303580 dev=fd:02 mode=0100644 ouid
=0 ogid=0 rdev=00:00 obj=unconfined_u:object_r:net_conf_t:s0 objtype=CREATE
type=PATH msg=audit(1446302766.693:433): item=0 name="/etc/" inode=6291585 dev=fd:02 mode=040755 ouid=0 ogid=0 rd
ev=00:00 obj=system_u:object_r:etc_t:s0 objtype=PARENT
type=CWD msg=audit(1446302766.693:433):  cwd="/root"
type=SYSCALL msg=audit(1446302766.693:433): arch=c000003e syscall=2 success=yes exit=3 a0=219e270 a1=241 a2=1a4 a
3=0 items=2 ppid=12455 pid=12474 auid=0 uid=0 gid=0 euid=0 suid=0 fsuid=0 egid=0 sgid=0 fsgid=0 tty=pts0 ses=5 co
mm="vim" exe="/usr/bin/vim" subj=unconfined_u:unconfined_r:unconfined_t:s0-s0:c0.c1023 key="resolv_changes"
~]# 
```

To check all the commands executed by root today, you can run the following:

`~]# aureport --tty -ts today`

Here's what the output should look like:

```
~]# aureport --tty -ts today
TTY Report
===============================================
# date time event auid term sess comm data
===============================================
1. 10/31/2015 15:57:27 484 0 ? 7 bash "less /var",<backspace>,<backspace>,<backspace>,<backspace>,<backspace>,<ba
ckspace>,<backspace>,<backspace>,<backspace>,<backspace>,<backspace>,<backspace>,<backspace>,<backspace>,"aurepor
t --tty -ts today",<ret>
2. 10/31/2015 15:57:40 488 0 ? 7 bash <up>,<up>,<ret>
3. 10/31/2015 15:57:39 486 0 ? 7 bash "ls",<ret>
4. 10/31/2015 15:58:57 490 0 ? 7 bash "cat /etc/pass",<tab>,<backspace>,<backspace>,<backspace>,<backspace>,"m/pa
ss",<tab>,<tab>,<tab>,<backspace>,<backspace>,<backspace>,<backspace>,<backspace>,<tab>,"pass",<tab>,<tab>,<tab>,
"o",<tab>,<tab>,"-",<tab>,<up>,<down>,<up>,<ret>
5. 10/31/2015 15:59:13 492 0 ? 7 bash <up>,<ret>
6. 10/31/2015 15:59:15 494 0 ? 7 bash <up>,<ret>
7. 10/31/2015 15:59:54 496 0 ? 7 bash <up>," >> au",<tab>,<backspace>,<backspace>,<backspace>,<backspace>,<backsp
ace>,<backspace>,<backspace>,<backspace>,<backspace>,<backspace>,<backspace>,"root.txt",<ret>
~]#
```

See also

For more in-depth information about audit, refer to `https://access.redhat.com/ documentation/en-US/Red_Hat_Enterprise_Linux/7/html/Security_Guide/ chap-system_auditing.html`.

10
Monitoring and Performance Tuning

In this chapter, I'll explore the following topics:

- ▸ Tuning your system's performance
- ▸ Setting up PCP – Performance Co-Pilot
- ▸ Monitoring basic system performance
- ▸ Monitoring CPU performance
- ▸ Monitoring RAM performance
- ▸ Monitoring storage performance
- ▸ Monitoring network performance

Introduction

Monitoring your infrastructure is an important aspect of your environment as it teaches you much about its behavior. It will tell you where your bottlenecks are and where room for improvement is. In this chapter, we will monitor performance and not create triggers when certain metrics exceed specific values.

Tuning your system's performance

Companies buy the best hardware their money can get, and they want to use everything optimally. However, it's not just the hardware that makes your applications run faster. Your OS will also behave differently under specific circumstances.

Tuned is a set of tools and a daemon that tunes your system's settings automatically depending on its usage. It periodically collects data from its components through plugins, which it uses to change system settings according to the current usage.

How to do it...

In this recipe, we'll ask tuned which profile to use and apply it through the following steps:

1. First, run the following command to install the required packages:

    ```
    ~]# yum install -y tuned
    ```

2. Enable and start tuned by executing the following commands:

    ```
    ~]# systemctl enable tuned
    ~]# systemctl restart tuned
    ```

3. Have tuned guess the profile to be used via the following:

    ```
    ~]# tuned-adm recommend
    virtual-guest
    ```

4. Finally, apply the recommended profile to tuned, as follows:

    ```
    ~]# tuned-adm profile virtual-guest
    ```

There's more...

You can find the system's tuned profiles used in /lib/tuned/. When you create your own, create them in /etc/tuned in the same way as they are organized in /lib/tuned. I do not recommend creating new profiles in /etc/tuned with the same name as in /lib/tuned, but if you do, the one in the /etc/tuned directory will be used. It is better to create a new one with a different name, including the one you want to modify, and then make the necessary changes in your new profile.

Every profile has a directory, which contains a set of files controlling the behavior of your system. If you explore the `tuned.conf` files in these directories, you will see that these files define the exact settings that other tools (such as **cpufreq**) need to be configured on and that some profiles include other profiles. For instance, if you create a profile for, say, a laptop that is a little better on the battery by applying the `powersave` CPU governor, you could create a new file located at `/etc/tuned/laptop/tuned.conf` containing the following:

```
#
# laptop tuned configuration
#

[main]
include=desktop

[cpu]
replace=1
governor=powersave
```

When you know the bottlenecks of your systems, you can find out how to mitigate them by configuring your system in a specific way. Tuned can come in handy to create and apply profiles based on the performance monitoring of your components.

See also

For more information about tuning your system, refer to the Red Hat Performance Tuning guide at `https://access.redhat.com/documentation/en-US/Red_Hat_Enterprise_Linux/7/html/Performance_Tuning_Guide/index.html`.

Check out the man pages of *tuned (8)*, *tuned-adm (8)*, *tuned-main.conf (5)*, and *tuned.conf (5)* for more information.

Setting up PCP – Performance Co-Pilot

Over the years, a lot of tools have been created to troubleshoot performance issues on your systems, such as `top`, `sar`, `iotop`, `iostat`, `iftop`, `vmstat`, `dstat`, and others. However, none of these integrate with each other, some are extensions to others, and so on.

PCP seems to have a couple of things right: it monitors just about every aspect of your system, it allows the centralized storage of (important) performance data, and it allows you to use not only live data, but also saved data among others.

How to do it...

In this recipe, we'll look at both the "default" setup and "collector" configuration, which allows you to pull in all the performance data you want.

The default installation

This is the basic setup of PCP:

1. Let's install the necessary packages; run the following command:

   ```
   ~]# yum install -y pcp
   ```

2. Now, enable and start the necessary daemons, as follows:

   ```
   ~]# systemctl enable pmcd
   ~]# systemctl enable pmlogger
   ~]# systemctl start pmcd
   ~]# systemctl start pmlogger
   ```

3. If you want to have the system monitored by a central collector, execute the following:

   ```
   ~]# firewall-cmd --add-service pmcd --permanent
   ```

The central collector

Each host that is to act as a collector requires additional configuration. Here's how you can do this:

1. Add a line per system to collect data from `/etc/pcp/pmlogger/control`, as follows:

   ```
   <hostname> n n PCP_LOG_DIR/pmlogger/<hostname> -r -T24h10m -c
   config.<hostname>
   ```

   Here, `<hostname>` is the FDQN to this host. Take a look at the following example:

   ```
   guest.example.com n n PCP_LOG_DIR/pmlogger/guest.example.com -r
   -T24h10m -c config.guest.example.com
   ```

2. After adding a host in this way, you need to restart the `pmlogger` daemon. Execute the following command line:

   ```
   ~]# systemctl restart pmlogger
   ```

There's more...

By default, PCP logs information every 60 seconds. If you want to increase this and want to gather performance statistics every 30 seconds, you need to change the line starting with LOCALHOSTNAME and add -t 30s at the end.

Modifying the statistics you gather is a bit more difficult. You can find the configuration for pmlogger in /var/lib/pcp/config/pmlogconf/. Every file in this directory contains information about which pointers to gather. The syntax is not very hard to understand, but it is complex to explain. The *pmlogconf (1)* man page contains everything you need to know.

If you want to visualize the data on a host, you need to install pcp-gui, as follows:

```
~]# yum install -y pcp-gui dejavu-sans-fonts
```

This package comes with a tool called pmchart, which allows you to create graphics with the data collected by PCP. The fonts are needed to properly display the characters.

See also

For more information about PCP and its components, refer to their online manuals, which you can find at http://www.pcp.io/documentation.html.

Monitoring basic system performance

We need to keep an eye out on global system values. The ones that are particularly of interest are the following:

- kernel.all.pswitch
- kernel.all.nprocs
- kernel.all.load

How to do it...

I'll show you a way to display both text-based and graphical output. Here are the steps:

1. Display live data for the metrics with a 1-second interval for the guest.example. com host by executing the following command:

```
~]# pmdumptext -H -t 1 -i -l kernel.all.pswitch kernel.all.nprocs
kernel.all.load -h guest.example.com
```

```
~]# pmdumptext -H -t 1 -i -l kernel.all.pswitch kernel.all.nprocs kernel.all.load -h guest.exampl
e.com
              Source      guest.  guest.  guest.  guest.  guest.
              Metric      switch  nprocs    load    load    load
                Inst         n/a     n/a  1 minu  5 minu  15 min
              Normal        0.00    0.00    0.00    0.00    0.00
               Units         c/s    none    none    none    none
Sun Nov  1 21:34:37            ?   0.16K    0.00    0.01    0.05
Sun Nov  1 21:34:38        55.12   0.16K    0.00    0.01    0.05
Sun Nov  1 21:34:39        64.99   0.16K    0.00    0.01    0.05
Sun Nov  1 21:34:40        54.00   0.16K    0.00    0.01    0.05
Sun Nov  1 21:34:41        69.00   0.16K    0.00    0.01    0.05
Sun Nov  1 21:34:42        53.00   0.16K    0.00    0.01    0.05
Sun Nov  1 21:34:43        67.01   0.16K    0.00    0.01    0.05
Sun Nov  1 21:34:44        53.00   0.16K    0.00    0.01    0.05
Sun Nov  1 21:34:45        75.99   0.16K    0.00    0.01    0.05
Sun Nov  1 21:34:46        61.00   0.16K    0.00    0.01    0.05
```

2. Create a configuration file for `pmchart` to display live data called `system.conf` with the following contents:

    ```
    #kmchart
    version 1

    chart style plot antialiasing off
            plot color #ffff00 metric kernel.all.pswitch
    chart style plot antialiasing off
            plot color #ffff00 metric kernel.all.nprocs
    chart style plot antialiasing off
            plot color #ffff00 metric kernel.all.load instance "1
    minute"
            plot color #ff924a metric kernel.all.load instance "5
    minute"
            plot color #ff0000 metric kernel.all.load instance "15
    minute"
    ```

3. Next, use `pmchart` to plot a live chart for `guest.example.com` via the following command:

`~]# pmchart -h guest.example.com -c system.conf`

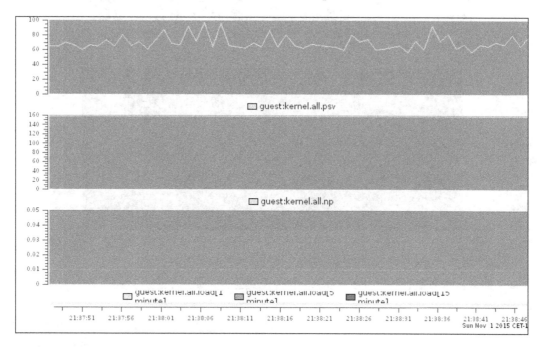

There's more...

The preceding examples are based on "live" data; however, you're not limited to live data. You could increase the interval of `pmlogger` in order to get more data about a troublesome system and then take a look at the generated data afterwards. With other tools, you'd have to use additional tools through cronjob and so on, while PCP allows you to do both.

Here's how you can do this:

1. Show the the data of `guest.example.com` for November 1, 2015 between `15:30` and `16:30` with a 5-minute interval via the following command:

   ```
   ~]# pmdumptext -H -t 5m -i -l -S @15:30 -T @16:30 kernel.all.
   pswitch kernel.all.nprocs kernel.all.load -a /var/log/pcp/
   pmlogger/guest.example.com/20151101
   ```

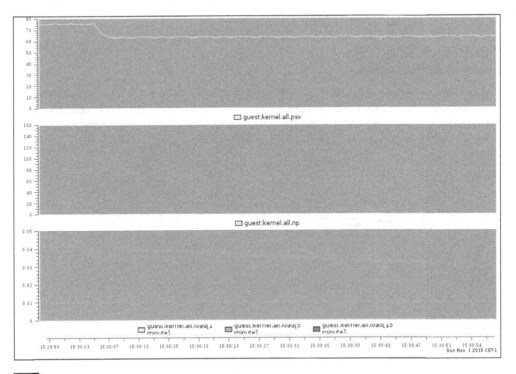

2. You can do the same with `pmchart`, as follows:

   ```
   ~]# pmchart -a /var/log/pcp/pmlogger/guest.example.com/20151101 -c
   system.conf -S @15:30 -T @16:30 -W -o output.png
   ```

Monitoring CPU performance

This recipe will show you how to visualize using `pmchart` and command-line tools to monitor your CPU's performance. We will have a look at the following metrics:

- `kernel.all.cpu.wait.total`
- `kernel.all.cpu.irq.hard`
- `kernel.all.cpu.irq.soft`
- `kernel.all.cpu.steal`
- `kernel.all.cpu.sys`
- `kernel.all.cpu.user`
- `kernel.all.cpu.nice`
- `kernel.all.cpu.idle`

How to do it...

This will show you how to create the text and graphical representation of performance data. Perform the following steps:

1. Display live data for the preceding metrics with a 1-second interval for the host, `localhost`. Execute the following command:

   ```
   ~]# pmdumptext -H -t 1 -i -l kernel.all.cpu.wait.total kernel.all.
   cpu.irq.hard kernel.all.cpu.irq.soft kernel.all.cpu.steal kernel.
   all.cpu.sys kernel.all.cpu.user kernel.all.cpu.nice kernel.all.
   cpu.idle -h localhost
   ```

```
~]# pmdumptext -H -t 1 -i -l kernel.all.cpu.wait.total kernel.all.cpu.irq.hard kernel.all.cpu.irq
.soft kernel.all.cpu.steal kernel.all.cpu.sys kernel.all.cpu.user kernel.all.cpu.nice kernel.all.
cpu.idle -h localhost
                  Source    localh   localh   localh   localh   localh   localh   localh   localh
                  Metric     total     hard     soft    steal      sys     user     nice     idle
                  Normal      0.00     0.00     0.00     0.00     0.00     0.00     0.00     0.00
                  Units       util     util     util     util     util     util     util     util
Sun Nov  1 21:45:55             ?        ?        ?        ?        ?        ?        ?        ?
Sun Nov  1 21:45:56          0.00     0.00     0.00     0.00     0.07     0.20     0.00     3.69
Sun Nov  1 21:45:57          0.00     0.00     0.00     0.00     0.04     0.16     0.00     3.78
Sun Nov  1 21:45:58          0.00     0.00     0.00     0.00     0.05     0.21     0.00     3.71
Sun Nov  1 21:45:59          0.00     0.00     0.00     0.00     0.05     0.18     0.00     3.73
Sun Nov  1 21:46:00          0.00     0.00     0.00     0.00     0.04     0.12     0.01     3.79
Sun Nov  1 21:46:01          0.00     0.00     0.00     0.00     0.04     0.13     0.00     3.81
Sun Nov  1 21:46:02          0.00     0.00     0.00     0.00     0.03     0.13     0.00     3.81
Sun Nov  1 21:46:03          0.00     0.00     0.01     0.00     0.04     0.15     0.00     3.79
Sun Nov  1 21:46:04          0.00     0.00     0.00     0.00     0.04     0.13     0.01     3.78
Sun Nov  1 21:46:05          0.00     0.00     0.00     0.00     0.05     0.17     0.00     3.75
Sun Nov  1 21:46:06          0.00     0.00     0.00     0.00     0.05     0.16     0.03     3.61
Sun Nov  1 21:46:07          0.00     0.00     0.00     0.00     0.09     0.16     0.00     3.62
Sun Nov  1 21:46:08          0.01     0.00     0.00     0.00     0.05     0.16     0.00     3.74
Sun Nov  1 21:46:09          0.00     0.00     0.00     0.00     0.06     0.14     0.00     3.62
Sun Nov  1 21:46:10          0.00     0.00     0.00     0.00     0.07     0.13     0.00     3.72
^C
~]#
```

2. Create a configuration file for `pmchart` to display live data called `cpu_stack.conf` with the following contents:

```
#kmchart
version 1

chart style stacking antialiasing off
        plot color #aaaa7f metric kernel.all.cpu.wait.total
        plot color #008000 metric kernel.all.cpu.irq.hard
        plot color #ee82ee metric kernel.all.cpu.irq.soft
        plot color #666666 metric kernel.all.cpu.steal
        plot color #aa00ff metric kernel.all.cpu.user
        plot color #aaff00 metric kernel.all.cpu.sys
        plot color #aa5500 metric kernel.all.cpu.nice
        plot color #0000ff metric kernel.all.cpu.idle
```

You will notice that I don't use all the metrics in the graph as some of the metrics are combined with one another.

3. Use `pmchart` to plot a live chart for `guest.example.com`, as follows:

```
~]# pmchart -h guest.example.com -c cpu_stack.conf
```

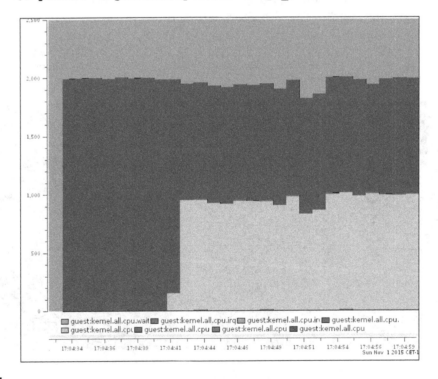

Monitoring RAM performance

To monitor RAM performance, I am only interested in a couple of metrics, not all the memory-related ones. Take a look at this list:

- ▶ `mem.util.used`
- ▶ `mem.util.free`
- ▶ `mem.util.bufmem`
- ▶ `mem.util.cached`
- ▶ `swap.free`
- ▶ `swap.used`
- ▶ `swap.pagesin`
- ▶ `swap.pagesout`

How to do it...

This recipe will explain you how to create text-based and graphical outputs:

1. First, display live data for the preceding metrics through this command:

   ~]# **pmdumptext -H -t 1 -i -l mem.util.used mem.util.free mem.util. bufmem mem.util.cached swap.free swap.used swap.pagesin swap. pagesout -h guest.example.com**

```
~]# pmdumptext -H -t 1 -i -l mem.util.used mem.util.free mem.util.bufmem mem.util.cached swap.free swap.used swa
p.pagesin swap.pagesout -h guest.example.com
                Source   guest.   guest.   guest.   guest.   guest.   guest.   guest.   guest.
                Metric     used     free   bufmem   cached     free     used   agesin   gesout
                Normal     0.00     0.00     0.00     0.00     0.00     0.00     0.00     0.00
                 Units        b        b        b        b        b        b      c/s      c/s
Sun Nov  1 17:35:10       0.38G    1.55G    8.19K    0.17G    1.61G     0.00        ?        ?
Sun Nov  1 17:35:11       0.38G    1.55G    8.19K    0.17G    1.61G     0.00     0.00     0.00
Sun Nov  1 17:35:12       0.38G    1.55G    8.19K    0.17G    1.61G     0.00     0.00     0.00
Sun Nov  1 17:35:13       0.38G    1.55G    8.19K    0.17G    1.61G     0.00     0.00     0.00
Sun Nov  1 17:35:14       0.38G    1.55G    8.19K    0.17G    1.61G     0.00     0.00     0.00
Sun Nov  1 17:35:15       0.38G    1.55G    8.19K    0.17G    1.61G     0.00     0.00     0.00
Sun Nov  1 17:35:16       0.38G    1.55G    8.19K    0.17G    1.61G     0.00     0.00     0.00
Sun Nov  1 17:35:17       0.38G    1.55G    8.19K    0.17G    1.61G     0.00     0.00     0.00
Sun Nov  1 17:35:18       0.38G    1.55G    8.19K    0.17G    1.61G     0.00     0.00     0.00
Sun Nov  1 17:35:19       0.38G    1.55G    8.19K    0.17G    1.61G     0.00     0.00     0.00
Sun Nov  1 17:35:20       0.38G    1.55G    8.19K    0.17G    1.61G     0.00     0.00     0.00
Sun Nov  1 17:35:21       0.38G    1.55G    8.19K    0.17G    1.61G     0.00     0.00     0.00
Sun Nov  1 17:35:22       0.38G    1.55G    8.19K    0.17G    1.61G     0.00     0.00     0.00
Sun Nov  1 17:35:23       0.38G    1.55G    8.19K    0.17G    1.61G     0.00     0.00     0.00
Sun Nov  1 17:35:24       0.38G    1.55G    8.19K    0.17G    1.61G     0.00     0.00     0.00
Sun Nov  1 17:35:25       0.38G    1.55G    8.19K    0.17G    1.61G     0.00     0.00     0.00
Sun Nov  1 17:35:26       0.38G    1.55G    8.19K    0.17G    1.61G     0.00     0.00     0.00
```

2. Create a configuration file for `pmchart` to display live data called `memory.conf` with the following contents:

```
#kmchart
version 1

chart style stacking
        plot color #ffff00 metric mem.util.used
        plot color #ee82ee metric mem.util.free
chart style stacking
        plot color #ffff00 metric swap.used
        plot color #0000ff metric swap.free
chart style plot antialiasing off
        plot color #19ff00 metric swap.pagesin
        plot color #ff0004 metric swap.pagesout
```

3. Now, use `pmchart` to plot a live chart for `guest.example.com` by executing the following command line:

```
~]# pmchart -h guest.example.com -c memory.conf
```

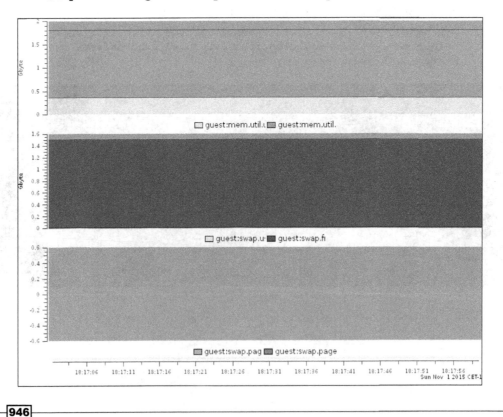

I haven't included the buffer and cached memory in this graph as it's part of the memory-used metric.

Monitoring storage performance

In this recipe, we'll look at the following metrics:

- `disk.all.read`
- `disk.all.write`
- `disk.all.read_bytes`
- `disk.all.write_bytes`

How to do it...

Let's create a text and graphical representation of the performance data through the following steps:

1. Display live data for the preceding metrics; you can use the following command for this:

   `~]# pmdumptext -H -t 1 -i -l disk.all.read disk.all.write disk.all.read_bytes disk.all.write_bytes -h guest.example.com`

```
~]# pmdumptext -H -t 1 -i -l disk.all.read disk.all.write disk.all.read_bytes disk.all.write_bytes -h guest.exam
ple.com
                Source    guest.   guest.   guest.   guest.
                Metric     read    write   _bytes   _bytes
                Normal     0.00     0.00     0.00     0.00
                Units      c/s      c/s      b/s      b/s
Sun Nov  1 19:57:13          ?        ?        ?        ?
Sun Nov  1 19:57:14        0.00     0.00     0.00     0.00
Sun Nov  1 19:57:15        0.00     0.00     0.00     0.00
Sun Nov  1 19:57:16        0.00     0.00     0.00     0.00
Sun Nov  1 19:57:17        0.00     0.00     0.00     0.00
Sun Nov  1 19:57:18        0.00     1.81     0.00     0.93K
Sun Nov  1 19:57:19        0.00     0.00     0.00     0.00
Sun Nov  1 19:57:20        0.00     0.00     0.00     0.00
Sun Nov  1 19:57:21        0.00     0.00     0.00     0.00
Sun Nov  1 19:57:22        0.00     0.00     0.00     0.00
Sun Nov  1 19:57:23        0.00     0.00     0.00     0.00
Sun Nov  1 19:57:24        0.00     0.00     0.00     0.00
Sun Nov  1 19:57:25        0.00     0.00     0.00     0.00
Sun Nov  1 19:57:26        0.00     0.00     0.00     0.00
Sun Nov  1 19:57:27        0.00     0.00     0.00     0.00
Sun Nov  1 19:57:28        0.00    29.00     0.00    14.97M
Sun Nov  1 19:57:29        0.00    76.91     0.00    39.52M
Sun Nov  1 19:57:30        0.00     0.00     0.00     0.00
Sun Nov  1 19:57:31        0.00     1.99     0.00    20.40K
Sun Nov  1 19:57:32        0.00     0.16K    0.00    79.95M
Sun Nov  1 19:57:33        0.00     2.00     0.00     0.32M
Sun Nov  1 19:57:34        0.00     0.00     0.00     0.00
Sun Nov  1 19:57:35        0.00     0.00     0.00     0.00
Sun Nov  1 19:57:36        0.00     0.00     0.00     0.00
Sun Nov  1 19:57:37        0.00     0.00     0.00     0.00
Sun Nov  1 19:57:38        0.00     0.00     0.00     0.00
Sun Nov  1 19:57:39        0.00     0.00     0.00     0.00
Sun Nov  1 19:57:40        0.00     0.00     0.00     0.00
Sun Nov  1 19:57:41        0.00     0.00     0.00     0.00
Sun Nov  1 19:57:42        0.00     0.00     0.00     0.00
Sun Nov  1 19:57:43        0.00     0.00     0.00     0.00
Sun Nov  1 19:57:44        0.00     0.00     0.00     0.00
^C
~]#
```

2. Next, create a configuration file for `pmchart` to display live data called `disk.conf` with the following contents:

```
#kmchart
version 1

chart style stacking
        plot color #ffff00 metric mem.util.used
        plot color #ee82ee metric mem.util.free
chart style stacking
        plot color #ffff00 metric swap.used
        plot color #0000ff metric swap.free
chart style plot antialiasing off
        plot color #19ff00 metric swap.pagesin
        plot color #ff0004 metric swap.pagesout
```

3. Now, use `pmchart` to plot a live chart for `guest.example.com`, as follows:

```
~]# pmchart -h guest.example.com -c memory.conf
```

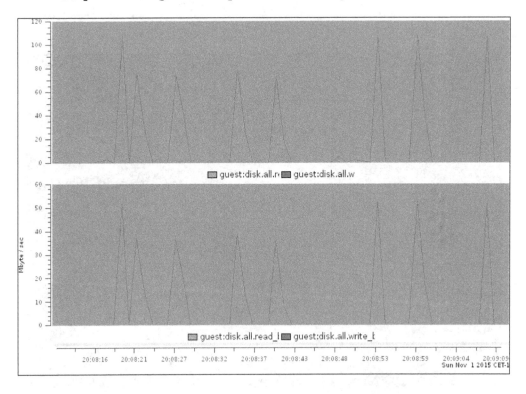

Monitoring network performance

In this recipe, we'll look at the following network metrics:

- `network.interface.collisions`
- `network.interface.in.bytes`
- `network.interface.in.packets`
- `network.interface.in.errors`
- `network.interface.in.drops`
- `network.interface.out.bytes`
- `network.interface.out.packets`
- `network.interface.out.errors`
- `network.interface.out.drops`

How to do it...

Now, one last time, we'll look at how we can create a text and graphical representation of data. Perform the following steps:

1. Display live data for the preceding metrics; run the following command:

   ```
   ~]# pmdumptext -H -t 1 -i -l network.interface.collisions network.
   interface.in.bytes network.interface.in.packets network.interface.
   in.errors network.interface.in.drops network.interface.out.
   bytes network.interface.out.packets network.interface.out.errors
   network.interface.out.drops -h guest.example.com
   ```

2. Create a configuration file for `pmchart` to display live data called `network.conf` with the following contents:

```
#kmchart
version 1

chart style plot antialiasing off
        plot color #ff0000 metric network.interface.collisions
instance "eth0"
chart style plot antialiasing off
        plot color #00ff00 metric network.interface.in.bytes
instance "eth0"
        plot color #ff0000 metric network.interface.out.bytes
instance "eth0"
chart style plot antialiasing off
        plot color #00ff00 metric network.interface.in.packets
instance "eth0"
        plot color #ff0000 metric network.interface.out.packets
instance "eth0"
chart style plot antialiasing off
        plot color #00ff00 metric network.interface.in.errors
instance "eth0"
        plot color #ff0000 metric network.interface.out.errors
instance "eth0"
chart style plot antialiasing off
        plot color #00ff00 metric network.interface.in.drops
instance "eth0"
        plot color #ff0000 metric network.interface.out.drops
instance "eth0"
```

3. Next, use pmchart to plot a live chart for guest.example.com via this command line:

```
~]# pmchart -h guest.example.com -c network.conf
```

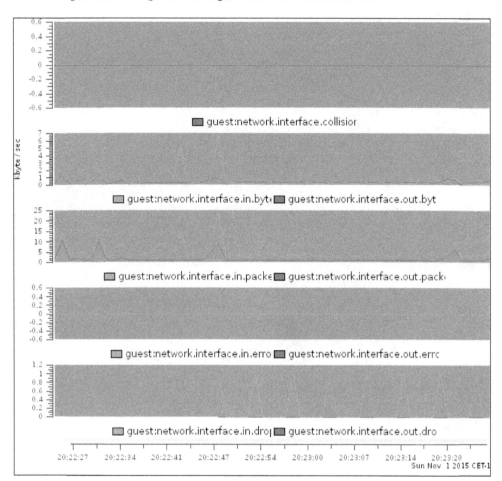

Bibliography

This course is a blend of different projects and texts all packaged up keeping your journey in mind. It includes the content from the following Packt products:

- *Ubuntu Server Cookbook by Uday R. Sawant*

- *CentOS 7 Linux Server Cookbook- Second Edition by Oliver Pelz and Jonathan Hobson*

- *Red Hat Enterprise Linux Server Cookbook by William Leemans*

Index

A

abrt
reference 931
abrt-cli
using 930
abrtd
configuring 929
installing 929
access agents 653
access rights
assigning 154, 155
Access Vector Cache (AVC) 715
Active Directory (AD) support 184
additional repositories
configuring 905, 906
references 906
Ampache
reference 289
used, for streaming music 296
Ampache Server
installing 283-289
Ansible
about 853
file structure 874
installing 854
installing, from Enterprise Linux (EPEL)
    repository 857
installing, from GIT 855, 856
latest tarball, installing 854, 855
reference 854
troubleshooting 875-879
Ansible inventory
configuring 857-861
dynamic inventory file 858
group_vars file 860

host_vars file 859
reference 861
static inventory file 857
Ansible template module
reference 863
Apache
about 80
benchmarking 115, 116
installing 667-670
performance tuning 115, 116
securing 683, 684
Apache Bench (ab) 115
Apache files
protecting 686
Apache web server
about 84
configuring 82, 83
HTTP version 2 support 85
installing 81
working 84
API access
enabling, for remote streaming 294-296
arbitrary port
incoming requests, allowing on 922
audit
reference 933
audit.log file
commands 836
denied or failed entries, searching 841
audit logs
displaying, for preceding rules 932, 933
audit rules 932
ausearch tool
using 842
authconfig tool 917, 918
authconfig-tui tool 917, 918

authentication methods
  md5 638
  peer and ident 638
  reject 638
  trust 638
authentication page, RedHat
  reference 919
authoritative-only DNS server
  about 606
  setting up 607-610
  working 611-615
Automatic Bug Reporting Tool (ABRT)
  using 929
automatic installation, of CentOS 7
  performing, kickstart file used 441-444

B

background services
  knowing 478-481
  managing 478-481
  troubleshooting 482, 483
backups
  setting up 160, 161
bare repository 334
batch mode
  user account, creating 8, 9
Bazaar
  reference 333
benchmarking, with Sysbench
  reference 411
Berkeley Internet Name Domain
      (BIND) 611
Bidirectional-streams Over Synchronous
      HTTP (BOSH) 316
binary large object (blob) 338
block device 527
boot environment
  configuring 825-827
bridge
  creating 790
  creating, kickstart used 794
  creating, nmcli used 790, 791
  creating, nmtui used 792-794
brute force attacks
  reference 74
  securing against 71-74

btrfs 528
Bugzilla
  reference 849
bulk data
  exporting 152, 153
  importing 152, 153

C

C10k problem 80
caching-only nameserver
  configuring 602
  installing 602
caching-only Unbound DNS server
  configuring 603, 604
cadaver WebDAV command-line client 579
cAdvisor 278
Candy
  reference 324
catalog
  creating 290-292
CentOS
  downloading 432-434
  references 432, 520
CentOS 7 installation
  language settings, changing 455-458
CentOS boot loader
  re-installing 449
CentOS installation
  preparing, graphical installer used 437-439
centralized syslog server
  configuring, to accept audit logs 931, 932
centralized version control systems
      (CVCS) 330
Certificate Signing Request (CSR) 559
  generating 98, 99
certification authority (CA) 560
chat server
  with Node.js 324-326
checksum
  confirming, on OS X 432-434
  confirming, on Windows 432-434
chrony
  reference 824
  used, for managing time 822
chrony suite
  used, for synchronizing system

clock 459-462
Cloud 9 IDE
reference 371
Cobbler
reference 767
command line interface (CLI) 348
commands, for network connectivity
dig 61
ethtool 61
ifdown 61
ifup 61
ip addr 61
ip link 61
ip route 61
iptables 61
Lsmod 61
lspci 61
netstat 61
Nmap 61
route 61
telnet 61
tracepath/traceroute 61
Common Gateway Interface (CGI)
implementing, with Perl 677, 678
implementing, with Ruby 677, 678
Common Internet File System (CIFS)
    protocol 182
common tasks
automating, with Git hooks 354-357
Common Unix Printing System (CUPS)
about 568
printing with 568-571
configuration node
creating 891
container
about 236
attaching 696
deploying, with LXD 240-244
interacting with 696
running 693-695
starting 696
stopping 696
containerd 259
container networking model (CNM) 275
contents
uploading 290-292
Coordinated Universal Time (UTC) 462

corrupted RPM database
recovering 910-912
CPU
adding, on fly to guest 744, 745
adding, on KVM guest 746
adding, on KVM host 745
monitoring 384-390
references 390
cpufreq 937
CPU performance
monitoring 943, 944
CPU utilization
defining 388
crash dump guide, Red Hat
reference 929
cron
used, for scheduling tasks 489-491
CUPS server
local printer, adding to 572
network printer, adding to 571, 572
custom boot ISO
used, for system deployment 771-775

D

data
retrieving, MongoDB used 176-180
retrieving, MySQL used 149-152
storing, MongoDB used 176-180
storing, MySQL used 149-152
data backups
maintaining 494, 495
database
managing 633-636
Database Management System (DBMS) 626
Data Definition Language (DDL) 152
Data Manipulation Language (DML) 152
dd
reference 435
debootstrap 269
delivery agent 647
DHCP server
installing 34, 35
IP reservation 36
manual allocation 36
running 573-576
Diffie Hellman parameters 63

Directory Information Tree (DIT) 413
Discretionary Access Control (DAC) 705
disk quotas
  group quotas, enabling 533
  limiting system, setting up 532
  project (directory) quotas, enabling 533-535
  user quotas, enabling 533
  using 532
  working 535-537
disks
  adding, on fly 747, 748
  moving, to another storage 749, 750
DNS configuration guide, on Ubuntu server
    guide
  reference 43
DNS resolvers
  configuring 798
  setting up, nmcli used 798
  setting up, nmtui used 800
DNS server
  authoritative-only DNS server,
    configuring 606-615
  caching-only Unbound DNS server,
    configuring 603, 604
  forwarding only DNS server,
    configuring 604-606
  installing 36-43
  primary DNS server changes, making 621
  secondary DNS server changes,
    making 622, 623
  secondary (slave) DNS server, building 620
Docker
  configuring 691-693
  Hackpad, using with 370
  installing 256-693
  reference 693
Docker containers
  managing 260-264
  monitoring 277, 278
  securing 279-281
  starting 260-264
Dockerfile
  about 265
  images, creating with 265-269, 697, 698
Docker Hub
  images, uploading to 697-699
  reference 695, 697

Docker network
  used, for deploying WordPress 273-275
Docker registry server
  setting up 701, 702
Docker volumes 270-272
domain
  about 601
  populating 618-620
domain name servers (DNS) 575
Domain Name System (DNS) 462
domain-wide mail service
  BIND, configuring for new mailserver 650
  configuring, with Postfix 643-648
  e-mail's appearing domain name,
    modifying 648
  TLS- (SSL) encryption, used for SMTP com-
    munication 649, 650
Dovecot
  e-mail software, setting up 658, 659
  reference 131
  used, for delivering mail 653-658
  used, for enabling IMAP and POP3 129-131
dump
  analyzing, kdump tools used 924-927
dynamic contents
  serving, with PHP 86-88
  support, for scripting languages 89
Dynamic Host Control Protocol (DHCP)
  about 34, 573
  dynamic allocation 34
  manual allocation 34
dynamic inventory file 858

E

Ejabberd
  about 299
  installing 300-303
  references 303, 315
Ejabberd docs, LDAP section
  reference 428
Ejabberd installation
  configuring 310-314
Ejabberd users
  authenticating, with LDAP 425-428
ELRepo
  about 517

reference 517
e-mails
  accounts, adding 132-134
  sending, Postfix used 125-129
Enterprise Linux (EPEL) repository
  Ansible, installing 857
  reference 857
Etherpad
  reference 371
event driven approach 80
existing firewalld service (ssh)
  changing 556
Ext4 528
Extensible Messaging and Presence Protocol (XMPP) 299
extensions
  reference 724

F

fail2ban
  configuring 549, 551
  installing 549, 551
Fetchmail
  about 659
  automating 664, 665
  configuring, with Gmail account 661-664
  configuring, with Outlook account 661-664
  using 659-661
file amount (inodes) 535
file contexts
  modifying 832
  modifying, permanently 833
  modifying, temporarily 833
file permissions
  managing 13-16
file revisions
  storing, with Git commit 335-338
files
  navigating, with less controls 454
  synchronizing 492, 493
  synchronizing, Rsync used 191-195
file sharing
  WebDAV, using for 576-579
file size (blocks) 535
filesystem
  accessing 448

capacity, extending 539-543
  formatting 528-531
  maintaining 537-539
  mounting 528-531
filesystems formatting 528
File Transfer Protocol (FTP) server 189
file transfers
  troubleshooting 598, 599
firewall
  about 551
  working with 552-555
firewalld
  about 921
  network, securing with 921
  working 923
firewalld service
  creating 556-558
firewalld service definitions
  creating 555
ForceCommand 564
forwarding only DNS server
  configuring 604-606
forward proxy 44
FQDN (Fully Qualified Domain Name) 891
free hosting
  reference 342
FTP
  securing, with FTPS 561
  securing, with SFTPS 561
FTP service
  configuring 589-593
  customizing 596-598
  installing 589-593
full JID 317
Fully Qualified Domain Name (FQDN) 463, 644

G

GID (group ID) 6
Git
  Ansible, installing from 855, 856
  installing 330-332
  reference 333
  used, for versioning of config files 497-500
Git CLI
  local repository, creating with 333, 334

Git clone
  reference 335
Git commit
  file revisions, storing with 335-338
Git hooks
  references 358
GitHub 333
Git init
  reference 335
GitLab
  installing 348-350
  repository, creating with 352, 353
GitLab server
  users, adding to 350-352
Git merge
  reference 346
Git pull
  reference 346
  updates, receiving with 343-346
Gmail account
  reference 661, 662
  used, for configuring Fetchmail 661-664
graphical installer
  used, for preparing CentOS
    installation 437-439
Graphical User Interfaces (GUI) 456
graphing tools
  references 410
group
  creating 9, 10
  managing 487-489
  members, adding 10, 11
group chat
  enabling 320-323
group_vars file 860
GRUB2
  about 445, 824
  reference 827
GRUB2 boot loader
  customizing 445, 446
guests
  building 741-744
  creating 742
  deleting 742

H

H2load 117
Hackpad
  installing 365-370
  repo, URL 371
  using, with Docker 370
  using with Docker, URL 371
HAProxy
  about 108
  load balancing algorithms 52
  load balancing, with 50-52
help command 730
hostname
  setting 462-465
host_vars file 859
HTTP
  about 94
  netinstall, running over 439-441
httpd
  used, for publishing kickstart file 766, 767
httpd.conf
  configuring 684
Httperf 117
HTTPS
  about 94
  setting up, with Secure Sockets
    Layer (SSL) 687-690
  web traffic, securing with 94-98
HTTPs communication
  enabling, on Nginx 112, 114

I

Idempotence 853
Identity Policy Audit (IPA)
  configuring 914
  installing 914
images
  creating, from Dockerfiles 697, 698
  creating, with Dockerfile 264-269
  downloading 693-695
  uploading, to Docker Hub 697-699
IMAP, and POP3
  enabling, Dovecot used 129-131
incoming requests
  allowing, for NFS (v4) 922
  allowing, on arbitrary port 922
InnoDB storage engine

reference 165
InnoDB table compression
reference 169
installation
caching-only nameserver 602
fail2ban 549-551
MariaDB database server 626, 627
Nagios Core 717
phpMyAdmin 639, 640
phpPgAdmin 639-641
PostgreSQL server 633-636
integrated nameserver solution
about 615, 616
creating 615-618
internal hostname 617
Internet Protocol (IP) 573
intramfs (initial RAM file system) 924
IPA client
installing 916
IPA server
installing 914, 915
reference link 917
IPv4 configuration
setting, nmcli used 796
setting, nmtui used 797
IPv4 settings
configuring 795
ISC-DHCP 35

J

Jinja2 Template Designer
reference 863
journalctl
reference 818
used, for monitoring services 815-818
journald
configuring 486, 487
used, for tracking system resources 484-486

K

kdump
configuring 924
installing 924
using 923
kdump tools
used, for analyzing dump 924-927

kernel debugger (kgdb) 928
kernel parameters
reference 56
kickstart
about 789
reference 783
used, for creating bridge 794
used, for creating teamed interface 787
VLAN connection, creating with 782
kickstart file
about 755
creating 755-765
playbook, creating for VM 864-867
publishing, httpd used 766, 767
references 765, 864
template, creating 861, 863
used, for automatic installation of
CentOS 7 441-444
kickstart, team interfaces
reference 790
KVM
configuring 730, 731
graphical setup 733, 734
installing 730, 731
kickstart installation 733
manual installation 732

L

labels 707
LAMP stack
installing 89
language settings, CentOS 7 installation
changing 455-458
Launchpad
reference 333
Layer two tunneling protocol (L2TP) 62
LDAP
Ejabberd users, authenticating
with 425-428
Ubuntu server logins, defining
with 422-424
LDAP client authentication
reference 425
less controls
used, for navigating through file 454
libcontainer 257

libstrophe 316
libvirt
    about 730
    networking, URL 741
    storage backend pools, URL 741
    references 730, 734
Lightweight Directory access Protocol
        (LDAP) 413
limits.conf
    used, for setting resource limits 19, 20
Linux Container Daemon (LXD)
    about 237
    installing 237-240
    networking with 252-256
Linux home server Samba guide
    reference 189
Linux kernel
    priming 473, 474
Linux performance analysis
    reference 411
load balancing
    with HAProxy 50-52
    with Nginx 108-111
load balancing algorithms
    leastconn 52
    Round-robin 52
    source 52
load sharing backup methods, for teams
    active-backup 787
    broadcast 787
    LACP 788
    loadbalance 788
    round-robin 788
local printer
    sharing, to CUPS server 572
local repository
    creating, with Git CLI 333, 334
logical volume (lv) 542
Logical Volume Manager (LVM) 239, 539
logrotate
    configuring 818-821
    configuring, for yum 909
loop device 527
LXC 237
LXD containers
    advance options 247
    dealing 247, 248

managing 244-246
resource limits, setting 248-251
LXD GUI
    reference 246

M

mail
    delivering, with Dovecot 653-657
mailbox formats
    reference 129
Mail eXchanger (MX) 612, 650
mail filtering
    with spam-assassin 135-137
mail server
    troubleshooting 137, 139
Mail Transport Agent (MTA) 643
Mandatory Access Control (MAC) 706
manifest
    deploying, to node group 892
    deploying, to single client 892
MariaDB database server
    installing 626, 627
    managing 628-631
    permission, reviewing 631
    permission, revoking 631
    remote access, allowing 632, 633
    user, dropping 631
Mattermost
    features, URL 376
    installing 371-376
    references 371, 372
    Source Code on Github, URL 376
    web-hooks, URL 376
Mattermost Dockerfile
    reference 376
md5sum.exe
    reference 433
memory
    monitoring 390-395
messages
    customizing 471, 472
minimal install
    enhancing 450, 451
Mnesia 313
module
    deploying, to node group 892

deploying, to registered systems 892
deploying, to single client 892
deploying, to system 893
modules
deploying, to node groups 892
deploying, to single nodes 892
MongoDB
installing 175
installing, URL 176
used, for retrieving data 176-179
used, for storing data 176-179
MongoDB query documents
reference 180
mounting formatting 528
msdos 527
multilevel security (MLS) 831
multiple websites
hosting, with virtual domain 90-93
multi-processing modules (MPM) 80
Multi User Chat (MUC) 320
music
streaming, Ampache used 296
MySQL
about 146
installation, securing 149
performance, optimizing 161-164
performance tuning 166-168
sharding 165
table compression 168
troubleshooting 173, 174
used, for installing relational
database 146-148
used, for retrieving data 149-152
used, for storing data 149-152
web access, installing 156-159
MySQL backup methods
reference 161
MySQL binary log
reference 161
MySQL docs
reference 168
MySQL load data infile syntax
reference 153
MySQL optimization guide
reference 165
MySQL query execution plan
reference 165

MySQL replicas
creating, for high availability 169-173
creating, for scaling 169-172
MySQL select-into syntax
reference 153
MySQL test database
reference 166
MySQL tuner script
reference 168
Mysql user account management
reference 156

N

Nagios Core
configuring 717-719
installing 717-719
reference 725
Nagios Remote Plugin Executor (NRPE)
setting up, on remote client hosts 719
name based hosting
implementing 674-677
NamedVirtualHost 92
netfilter 67, 551
netinstall
running, over HTTP 439-441
network
connecting, with static IP 30-32
IPv6 configuration 33
monitoring 396-401
resolving 462-465
securing, with firewalld 921
securing, with uncomplicated
firewall 67-70
temporary IP assignment 32, 33
Network Address Translation (NAT) 252
network bridges, kickstart
reference 795
network bridges, nmcli
reference 795
network bridges, nmtui
reference 795
**network configuration, at Ubuntu server
guide**
reference 33
network connectivity
troubleshooting 56-60

Network File System (NFS)
about 201
installing 201-203
networking 30
networking team daemon
reference link 789
network performance
monitoring 949, 951
network printer
adding, to CUPS server 571, 572
Network Time Protocol (NTP)
about 47, 459
reference 460
used, for synchronizing system
clock 459-462
NFS
configuring 579
installing 579
reference 204
working with 582, 583
NFS exports options
reference 204
NFS server
configuring 579
export share, creating 580-582
installing 579
NFS (v4)
incoming requests, allowing for 922
Nginx
HTTPs, setting 112, 114
installing, with PHP_FPM 99-103
load balancing with 108-111
setting, as reverse proxy 104-108
nmcli
about 788
used, for configuring static network
routes 801
used, for creating bridge 790, 791
used, for creating teamed interface 783, 784
used, for setting IPv4 configuration 796
used, for setting up DNS resolvers 798
VLAN connection, creating with 779
nmcli, team interfaces
reference 789
nmtui
about 788
used, for configuring static network

routes 803
used, for creating bridge 792-794
used, for creating teamed interface 785-787
used, for setting IPv4 configuration 797
used, for setting up DNS resolvers 800
VLAN connection, creating with 780-782
nmtui, team interfaces
reference 790
node grouping
defining 891
node groups
creating 891
modules, deploying to 892
Node.js
chat server, defining with 324-326
references 327
nodes
defining 891
NoSQL 146
Not Found error 378
ntpd
reference 824
used, for managing time 823
ntpdate 47

O

on-the-fly transcoding
setting 292, 293
OpenLDAP
installing 414-417
references 418
OpenLDAP admin guide
reference 414
OpenVPN
remote access, securing with 62-65
VPN client, configuring 65, 66
Organizational Unit (OU) 424
OS X
checksum, confirming on 432-434
USB installation media, creating on 434-436
Outlook account
references 661, 662
used, for configuring Fetchmail 661-664
OwnCloud
admin manual, URL 381
installing 377-380

repositories, URL 381

P

package management 503
packages
  installing, YUM used 507, 508
  removing, YUM used 509, 510
  searching, YUM used 505, 506
Parallel NFS
  reference 204
partition table 527
password authentication 25
password less sudo
  setting 18
Percona
  configuration wizard 168
Percona XtraBackup
  reference 161
Perfkit 117
performance benchmarks
  graphing tools 410
  setting 406-409
Performance Co-Pilot (PCP)
  central collector 938
  installation 938
  reference 939
  setting up 937
performance tuning
  Samba server 195, 196
Perl
  CGI, implementing with 677, 678
Perl CGI script
  creating 679
personal file sharing
  tools 184
PHP
  configuring 681-683
  dynamic contents, serving with 86-88
  installing 681-683
  settings 88
  testing 681-683
  upgrading, under Ubuntu 14 89, 90
PHP_FPM
  Nginx, installing with 99-103
phpLDAPadmin
  installing 418-422

references 418, 422
phpMyAdmin
  installing 639
  reference 159
phpPgAdmin
  configuring 640, 641
  installing 639-641
physical volume (pv) 542
playbook
  creating, for deploying VM with
    kickstart 864-867
  creating, for system configuration
    tasks 867-875
  reference 867, 875
Pluggable Authentication Modules
    (PAM) 595
Pointer Resource Record (PTR) 614
Point-to-Point Tunneling Protocol
    (PPTP) 62
policies
  about 707
  working with 711-713
port definitions
  configuring, with SELinux 839, 840
ports
  displaying, on system 921
Postfix
  local mails, reading from mailbox 652
  lookup table types, URL 135
  mailx, connecting to remote MTA 651
  reference 135
  used, for configuring domain-wide mail
    service 643-648
  used, for sending e-mails 125-129
  working with 651, 652
PostgreSQL server
  installing 633-636
  remote access, configuring 637-639
Preboot eXecution Environment (PXE)
  used, for system deployment 768-771
print server 568
private Docker registry
  setting up 700, 701
  working with 700, 701
privilege escalation
  configuring, with sudo 919, 920
process ID (pid) 389

proxy **44**
public hostname **617**
public key authentication
 setting up 21, 22
public key cryptography (PKI) **560**
publishing directories
 building 671-674
Puppet agent
 configuring 886-888
 installing 886-888
Puppet installation, on RHEL
 reference link 886
Puppet Master
 configuring 882-886
 installing 882-886
Puppet Modules
 reference 890

R

RAM
 adding, on fly 746, 747
RAM performance
 monitoring 945-947
Red Hat
 performance tuning, URL 937
Red Hat Package Manager (RPM) **505, 895**
relational database
 installing, MySQL used 146-148
remote access
 locking 546-548
 securing, with OpenVPN 62-65
 to MariaDB server, allowing 632, 633
 to PostgreSQL, configuring 637-639
remote client hosts
 Nagios Remote Plugin Executor (NRPE),
  setting up 719, 720
remote server
 repository, synchronizing with 339-342
remote servers
 images 242
 Ubuntu 242
 Ubuntu-daily 242
remote streaming
 API access, enabling 294-296
remote system metrics
 monitoring 721-725

repository
 creating, with GitLab 352, 353
 GitHub pages 342
 synchronizing, with remote server 339-342
repository clones
 creating 346, 347
requirements, for GitLab installation
 reference 350
rescue mode
 reaching 447
 system, troubleshooting in 446, 447
resource limits
 setting, limits.conf used 19, 20
resources
 configuring 735-740
 networks, removing 739
 sharing, with Samba 584-588
 virtual network, creating 737-739
reverse proxy **44**
RHEL 7
 support limits, URL 734
RHN repository
 copy, creating 902
 syncing 902-905
role-based access control (RBAC) **831**
root **648**
root privileges
 getting, sudo used 17, 18
RPM package manager
 working with 521-524
rsync
 used, for synchronizing files 191-194
 using 492, 493
Ruby
 CGI, implementing with 677, 678
Ruby CGI script
 creating 679-681
runc **259**
runlevels
 setting 806-808
 versus systemd targets 808
runners
 reference 789

S

SAAS (Software as a Service) product **359**

Samba
  about 584
  reference 188
  resources, sharing with 584-588
Samba, and LDAP integration
  reference 188
Samba server
  installing 182-184
  network connectivity, checking 197, 198
  performance tuning 195, 196
  Samba configuration, checking 200
  Samba logs, checking 199
  Samba service, checking 198
  troubleshooting 197
  users, adding 185-187
Sarg
  about 46
  used, for analyzing squid logs 46
sar (System Activity Reporter) 386
secondary (slave) DNS server
  building 621
  primary DNS server changes,
      making 621, 622
  working 623
second-level domain (SLD) 611
secure FTP server
  installing 189-191
Secure Shell (SSH) 546
Secure Sockets Layer (SSL) 558
  HTTPS, setting up with 687-690
security 913
Security-Enhanced Linux (SELinux)
  about 705, 831
  audit log, troubleshooting 841
  port definitions, configuring 839, 840
  roles, displaying 835, 836
  troubleshooting 714, 715, 840-847
  troubleshooting, with ausearch tool 842
  troubleshooting, with syslog command 841
  types, displaying 835
  users, displaying 834
self-signed certificates
  generating 558-561
SELinux booleans
  about 837
  configuring 837
  listing 837-839

  modifying 838
SELinux policy
  applying 850
  creating 847-849
  removing 850
SELinux security contexts
  working with 708-710
SELinux tools
  configuring 705-708
  installing 705-707
ServerAlias 92
server infrastructure
  monitoring 496, 497
Server Message Block (SMB) 182
ServerName 92
services
  displaying, on system 921
  monitoring, journalctl used 815-818
service status
  Active 813
  Cgroup 813
  Loaded 813
  Main PID 813
  Process 813
  Status 813
SFTP 66
simple module
  defining, for configuring time 888-890
single nodes
  modules, deploying to 892
smtp
  configuring 827, 828
snapshots
  capturing 494, 495
spam-assassin
  used, for mail filtering 135-137
squid
  about 44
  access control list 46
  cache refresh rules, setting 46
  used, for hiding behind proxy 44, 45
squid guard 46
squid logs
  analyzing, with Sarg 46
SSH
  group access, limiting 549
  hardening 546-548

server port number, changing 548
user access, limiting 549
SSH authentication
about 24
SSH connections, troubleshooting 23
SSH tools, for Windows platform 24
working 23
SSH connections
troubleshooting 23
SSH keys
reference 342
SSH - SFTP
used, for securing FTP 561
used, for securing vsftpd server 563, 564
SSH tools
for Windows platform 24
SSL-FTPS
used, for securing FTP 561
used, for securing vsftpd server 562
standalone time server
setting up, for internal network 47, 49
Standard Input (STDIN) 652
Start of Authority (SOA) 608, 612
static inventory file 857
static IP
for connecting to network 30-32
static network connection
building 466, 467, 468
static network routes
configuring 801
configuring, nmcli used 801
configuring, nmtui used 803
storage
monitoring 402-405
storage performance
monitoring 947, 948
storage pools
about 735
creating 735, 736
local storage pools 740
network storage pools 740
querying 736
removing 737
shared storage pools 740
stratum 47
Strophe.js
references 320

web client, creating with 315-319
Strophe.js MUC plugin
reference 324
Strophe.js site
reference 316
Structured Query Language (SQL) 149
subversion
used, for versioning of config files 497-500
sudo
password less sudo, setting 18
privilege escalation, configuring
with 919, 920
used, for getting root privileges 17, 18
uses 19
sudo (superuser do) command
about 468
testing 469, 470
supermin 269
supervisord 276
su (substitute user) command 470
Swap
monitoring 390-395
Swiss Army Knife SMTP (swaks) 646
Sysbench 406
Sysbench documentation
reference 411
Sysbench GitHub repo
reference 411
Sysbench logs
reference 410
Sysbench tests
reference 411
Sysdig 279
syslog command
using 841
SysRq
configuring 924
installing 924
reference link 929
using 923
system
auditing 931
ports, displaying on 921
services, displaying on 921
troubleshooting, in rescue mode 446, 447
updating 450, 451
updating, YUM used 503-505

system banners
customizing 471, 472
system clock
synchronizing, with chrony suite 459-462
synchronizing, with NTP 459-462
system configuration tasks
performing, with playbook 867-875
systemd
references 805, 929
system deployment
with custom boot ISO 771-775
with Preboot eXecution Environment (PXE) 768-771
systemd journal
configuring, for persistence 814
reference link 814
systemd service
about 806-808
reference link 813
starting 808-813
stopping 808-813
systemd targets
reference link 808
versus runlevels 808
system login
securing 917, 918
system performance
monitoring 939-942
tuning 936, 937
system resources
tracking, with journald 484-486
system users
enabling 671-673

T

table maintenance statements
reference 166
tasks
scheduling, with cron 489-491
TCP stack
tuning 53-56
teamed interface
creating 783
creating, kickstart used 787
creating, nmcli used 783, 784
creating, nmtui used 785-787

template
creating 861, 863
third-party repository
using 515-517
time
managing 822
managing, through chrony 822
managing, through ntpd 823
top-level domain name (TLD) 611
Transmission Control Protocol and Internet Protocol (TCP/IP) 53
Transport Layer Security (TLS) protocol 94
troubleshooting, web server
about 121
access denied 124
Apache downloads .php files 124
forbidden errors 124
virtual host not accessible 122, 124
web server not accessible 121, 122
type enforcement (TE) 709 831

U

Ubuntu
installation, URL 376
Ubuntu security best practices 75-77
Ubuntu server guide
references 149, 185
UFW community page
reference 71
UID (user ID) 6
unbound 605
Unbound DNS Security Extensions (DNSSEC) 605
Uncomplicated Firewall (UFW) 67
unneeded httpd modules
removing 685
USB installation media
creating, on OS X 434-436
creating, on Windows 434-436
user account
connecting, with XMPP client 303-310
creating 4-7, 303-310
creating, in batch mode 8, 9
deleting 11, 12
securing 24, 25
user accounts

removing 156
resource limits, setting 156
useradd command 7
usermod command
reference 7
users
adding 154, 155
adding, to GitLab server 350-352
adding, to Samba server 185-188
managing 487-489
troubleshooting 598, 599

V

Varnish 108
very secure FTP daemon (vsftpd) 589
Vim
about 454
working with 455
Vimbadmin package 135
virsh interface 730
virt-install command 743
virtio support
reference 743
virtual block device
creating 526, 527
virtual domain
multiple websites, hosting with 90-92
virtual FTP users
about 593
working with 593-596
Virtual Host file 83
virtual machine (VM)
about 691
guest migration, URL 753
live native migration, over dedicated
network 752
live native migration, over default
network 752
moving 751, 752
playbook, creating 864-867
VLAN connection
creating, with kickstart 782
creating, with nmcli 779
creating, with nmtui 780-782
VLAN interface
creating 778

VM metadata
backing up 753, 754
VNC
on Stack Overflow, URL 365
VNC Server
installing 360-364
VNC (Virtual Network Computing) 360-364
volume group (vg) 542
vsftpd server
securing, with SSH - SFTP 563
securing, with SSL-FTPS 562

W

web access
installing, MySQL used 156-159
Web-based Distributed Authoring and
Versioning. *See* **WebDAV**
web client
creating, with Strophe.js 315-319
Web console
for virtual mailbox administration 135
WebDAV
using, for file sharing 576-579
web pages
serving 667-670
web server
about 79, 80
securing 117-120
troubleshooting 121
web traffic
securing, with HTTPS 94-98
Windows
checksum, confirming on 432-434
USB installation media, creating on 434-436
Windows Internetworking Name Server
(WINS) 587
WinSCP 66
WordPress
deploying, Docker network used 273-276
WordPress blog 257
World Wide Web (WWW) 626 506
Wrk 117

X

XFS 528
XML files

reference 153
XMPP client tools
reference 310
XMPP extensions
reference 315

Y

yum
about 895
logrotate, configuring 909
optimizing 510-512
updating, automatically 907, 908
used, for installing packages 507, 508
used, for removing packages 509, 510
used, for searching packages 505, 506
used, for updating system 503-505
yum history
displaying 896
managing 896
rolling back 901, 902
yum transaction, obtaining 897, 898
yum transaction, redoing 899
yum transaction, undoing 898

Z

Zimbra collaboration server
installing 140-144

About Packt Publishing

Packt, pronounced 'packed', published its first book, *Mastering phpMyAdmin for Effective MySQL Management*, in April 2004, and subsequently continued to specialize in publishing highly focused books on specific technologies and solutions.

Our books and publications share the experiences of your fellow IT professionals in adapting and customizing today's systems, applications, and frameworks. Our solution-based books give you the knowledge and power to customize the software and technologies you're using to get the job done. Packt books are more specific and less general than the IT books you have seen in the past. Our unique business model allows us to bring you more focused information, giving you more of what you need to know, and less of what you don't.

Packt is a modern yet unique publishing company that focuses on producing quality, cutting-edge books for communities of developers, administrators, and newbies alike. For more information, please visit our website at www.packtpub.com.

Writing for Packt

We welcome all inquiries from people who are interested in authoring. Book proposals should be sent to author@packtpub.com. If your book idea is still at an early stage and you would like to discuss it first before writing a formal book proposal, then please contact us; one of our commissioning editors will get in touch with you.

We're not just looking for published authors; if you have strong technical skills but no writing experience, our experienced editors can help you develop a writing career, or simply get some additional reward for your expertise.